REFORMED
ETHICS

※ VOLUME ONE ※

REFORMED
ETHICS

CREATED, FALLEN,
AND CONVERTED HUMANITY

HERMAN BAVINCK
EDITED BY JOHN BOLT

WITH JESSICA JOUSTRA,
NELSON D. KLOOSTERMAN,
ANTOINE THERON, DIRK VAN KEULEN

Ⓑ
Baker Academic
a division of Baker Publishing Group
Grand Rapids, Michigan

Published by Baker Academic
a division of Baker Publishing Group
PO Box 6287, Grand Rapids, MI 49516-6287
www.bakeracademic.com

Printed in the United States of America

Library of Congress Cataloging-in-Publication Data
Names: Bavinck, Herman, 1854–1921, author. | Bolt, John, 1947– editor.
Title: Reformed ethics / Herman Bavinck ; edited by John Bolt.
Other titles: Gereformeerde ethiek. English
Description: Grand Rapids : Baker Publishing Group, 2019– | Includes bibliographical references and indexes. Contents: Volume 1. Created, fallen, and converted humanity.
Identifiers: LCCN 2018036415 | ISBN 9780801098024 (volume 1 : cloth : alk. paper)
Subjects: LCSH: Christian ethics—Reformed authors. | Reformed Church—Doctrines. | Theology, Doctrinal
Classification: LCC BJ1251 .B3613 2019 | DDC 241/.0442—dc23
LC record available at https://lccn.loc.gov/2018036415

19 20 21 22 23 24 25   7 6 5 4 3 2

For Rimmer and †Ruth De Vries
in gratitude for your kingdom-minded generosity

Contents

Editor's Preface

The book you hold in your hands took a long journey to get there, an unlikely, unplanned, and uncharted journey. It is the first volume of a projected three-volume set that gives readers access to Herman Bavinck's lectures on Reformed ethics, delivered to his students at the Theological School in Kampen, from 1883/84 through the fall of 1902. Though the work is methodologically identical to Bavinck's *Reformed Dogmatics*, and there are hints that Bavinck may have intended eventually to publish it, he did not, leaving behind only a 1,100-page handwritten manuscript. After Bavinck's death in 1921, the manuscript languished in the Bavinck Archives at the Historical Documentation Center for Dutch Protestantism (1800 to present) at the Vrije Universiteit, Amsterdam, until it was discovered by Dirk van Keulen in 2008.[1] Readers of this volume are, therefore, among the privileged first group to gain access to Bavinck's systematic reflection on theological ethics since his own students who heard the lectures in the last two decades of the nineteenth century.

History buffs love playing "What if?" parlor games, and the temptation is hard to resist when reflecting on the pilgrimage of this material from Bavinck's own hand to this published translation. The word that comes to mind for me, with intentional bilingual wordplay, is "wonder." In the Dutch language (German *Wunder*) the word means "miracle." I want to be careful not to devalue the word "miracle" with overuse, but it is accurate to say that I and the editorial team that worked on this project are filled with wonder and awe at God's gracious, providential care and guidance as we make this work available for the worldwide church. Not only were we richly supplied by generous

---

1. For the story in greater detail, see Dirk van Keulen and John Bolt, "Introduction to Herman Bavinck's *Reformed Ethics*," the next section of this volume.

benefactors with ample provisions for a long and demanding journey, but so many unconnected events had to fall into place at just the right time for the project even to get started, much less brought to successful completion. All this feels like the inverse of the well-known proverb, "For want of a nail . . . the kingdom was lost,"[2] a series of connected events that positively and constructively accumulated to help publish this work. In remarkable ways, today has proved to be just the "right time" for this project.

This project is unimaginable without the preparatory project of translating and publishing the English version of Bavinck's four-volume *Reformed Dogmatics*, completed in 2008. To commemorate this occasion, along with the centenary of Bavinck's Princeton Stone Lectures, "The Philosophy of Revelation,"[3] in September 2008 Calvin Theological Seminary hosted a conference, "A Pearl and a Leaven: Herman Bavinck for the 21st Century." In preparation for this conference, while researching Bavinck material for a paper on the imitation of Christ, Dr. Dirk van Keulen "stumbled on" the *Reformed Ethics* manuscript (along with others) in the Bavinck archives. After he presented his paper, reporting the discovery of his find, an international group of Bavinck scholars conferred and agreed that the manuscript needed to be translated and published. They also indicated the value of creating a network of scholars and students interested in staying informed about each other's research and scholarship. The Bavinck Institute at Calvin Theological Seminary, the Bavinck Society, and the annual electronic journal, *The Bavinck Review*, were the result.[4] To sum this up: the *Reformed Dogmatics* project paved the way for these *Reformed Ethics* volumes by bringing together people (including a supportive publisher) who had demonstrated the competent ability to complete it; and the positive reception of the *Reformed Dogmatics* also created a large audience of students, pastors, and scholars eager to see this work on ethics become available.

In addition, to be able to speak of a "group" of Bavinck scholars in 2008 was itself quite remarkable. When I completed my dissertation on Bavinck in 1982, sixty years after Bavinck's death, mine was only the fifth doctoral dissertation devoted to Bavinck's theology;[5] there was no "community" of

2. Usually, but mistakenly, taken as a reference to the death of King Richard III of England at the Battle of Bosworth Field in 1485.

3. Bavinck, *Philosophy of Revelation*.

4. For more information see the Bavinck Institute website at https://bavinckinstitute.org/.

5. They are, in chronological order, Hoekema, "Bavinck's Doctrine of the Covenant"; Heideman, *Relation of Revelation and Reason*; Bremmer, *Bavinck als Dogmaticus*; Veenhof, *Revelatie en inspiratie*; and Bolt, *Theological Analysis*. However, scholarly attention at the highest (doctoral) level to Bavinck's philosophy and psychology of education, his pedagogy, began shortly after his death; for details see note 4 in our "Introduction to Herman Bavinck's *Reformed Ethics*."

Bavinck scholars. However, since that time another nine doctoral dissertations have been defended, either focused entirely on Bavinck or making significant contributions to Bavinck scholarship by analyzing his theology and comparing it with others.[6] In addition, an international congress on Bavinck's theology at the 150th anniversary of his birth was held in Kampen, the Netherlands, on October 28–30, 2004, and a collection of twenty lectures given there was published under the conference's theme, "Encounters with Bavinck."[7] And finally, a full-length biography of Bavinck in the English language has also appeared.[8]

All this is to say that conditions were ripe for generating interest and support for translating and publishing Bavinck's *Reformed Ethics* in English. But that is not all; we have to go back to the earlier and equally unlikely project of translating and publishing his *Reformed Dogmatics*. Bavinck's *Gereformeerde Dogmatiek* was well known and appreciated in North America, and an early attempt was made to translate it into English.[9] William Hendrickson had competed the translation of the first part of volume 2 (*The Doctrine of God*) by July 1930, but had to wait until 1951 to see it published.[10] No additional volumes were translated, perhaps because during this same time the basic outline of Bavinck's *Reformed Dogmatics* was being introduced to North American Reformed students of theology through the writings of Louis Berkhof, professor at Calvin Theological Seminary from 1906 to 1944.[11] Berkhof published his own *Reformed Dogmatics* in two volumes in 1932, followed by an accompanying *Introduction to Reformed Theology* as a separate volume that same year.[12] However, in the preface to his *Introduction to Reformed Theology*, "Berkhof acknowledged that the general plan of his work was based on the first volume of Bavinck's *Gereformeerde Dogmatiek* and that in a few

6. Hielema, "Bavinck's Eschatological Understanding of Redemption"; Gleason, "Centrality of the *unio mystica*"; van Keulen, *Bijbel en dogmatiek*; van den Belt, *Authority of Scripture in Reformed Theology*; Burger, *Being in Christ*; de Wit, *On the Way to the Loving God*; Mattson, *Restored to Our Destiny*; Eglinton, *Trinity and Organism*; Huttinga, *Participation and Communicability*.

7. Harinck and Neven, *Ontmoetingen met Bavinck*.

8. Gleason, *Herman Bavinck*.

9. See Bolt, "Bavinck Speaks English," 120–22.

10. Published in Grand Rapids by Eerdmans; reprint, Grand Rapids: Baker, 1977.

11. For more on Louis Berkhof, including the relationship of his own *Systematic Theology* to Bavinck's *Gereformeerde Dogmatiek*, see Zwaanstra, "Louis Berkhof."

12. Published in Grand Rapids by Eerdmans. The multivolume edition, minus the *Introduction (Prolegomena)*, was brought into a single volume and repackaged under the title *Systematic Theology* in 1938; it went through numerous printings, and a new edition that incorporated the *Introduction* was published in 1996. In part or whole it has been translated into Chinese, French, Korean, Japanese, Portuguese, and Spanish. For more on the history of Berkhof's *Systematic Theology*, in particular the prolegomena, *Introduction to Reformed Theology*, see Richard Muller's preface to the 1996 combined edition of Berkhof's *Systematic Theology*.

chapters he followed Bavinck's argumentation as well."[13] Henry Zwaanstra concludes that "Berkhof's theology was essentially the theology of Herman Bavinck."[14] It was through Berkhof's *Systematic Theology* that I was *indirectly* introduced to Herman Bavinck during my student days at Calvin Seminary.[15]

With this popularity of Berkhof's *Systematic Theology* in view, who could have contemplated the possibility of translating Bavinck's four-volume *Gereformeerde Dogmatiek* into English? Why would a publisher take on this major project of bringing a late nineteenth-century Dutch theology, and a competitor to Berkhof, into print? By the 1990s the memory of Herman Bavinck had practically vanished from the Dutch immigrant community of Reformed people, restricted for the most part to the Christian Reformed Church of North America, a relatively small denomination. Where would the market be for such a venture? Who was interested? To be truthful, while I was still in the dissertation-writing stage of my PhD program, a Canadian publisher, knowing that I was working on Bavinck, passed on to me a translation of one section and asked for advice about publishing it. For a variety of reasons, I strongly recommended against it. When I began teaching at Calvin Seminary in the fall semester of 1989, the very notion of translating this work was farthest from my mind. If the efforts in the 1930s had floundered, among other reasons undoubtedly because of the worldwide Depression, who today would be willing to front the required cost, now substantially increased? The prospect for this project was remote and its possible success highly unlikely. And then . . .

Shortly after I began teaching at Calvin Seminary, I was approached by a number of graduate students from Korea who wanted to study Bavinck's theology. They arranged for John Vriend to translate, on an ad hoc basis, key sections of the *Reformed Dogmatics*. When the demand grew, he raised the possibility of a more systematic approach to translating the entire work, indicating his willingness to serve as translator. The then-president of Calvin Seminary, James De Jong, convened a group of pastors and seminary teachers from West Michigan, along with Rich Baker, president of Baker Publishing Group, at a lunch meeting to discuss forming a translation society for this purpose. From this gathering the ecumenical Dutch Reformed Translation Society was formed in January 1994. We started by doing two sections as trial

13. Zwaanstra, "Louis Berkhof," 166.
14. Zwaanstra, "Louis Berkhof," 167.
15. In addition, one of my systematic theology professors, Anthony Hoekema, who was deeply indebted to Bavinck, frequently referred to him in class and even passed out to us his own translations of a few key passages from the *Gereformeerde Dogmatiek*, notably "The Wideness of God's Mercy," one of the last sections of Bavinck's eschatology (*RD*, 4:724–27).

balloons; the second half of volume 4 (eschatology) was published in 1996 as *The Last Things: Hope for This World and the Next*, and the second half of volume 2 (creation) in 1999 as *In the Beginning: Foundations of Creation Theology*. Thanks to the positive response to these two volumes, the board of the DRTS, with the encouragement of Baker Publishing, committed to completing all four volumes. Volumes 1 through 4 appeared, in successive order, in 2003, 2005, 2006, and 2008. We therefore completed our work roughly one hundred years after Bavinck ended his work on the second, revised, and definitive edition of his *Gereformeerde Dogmatiek*.

During the same time we began work on our project, Calvin Theological Seminary inaugurated its new doctoral program. Under the leadership of my colleague and friend Richard Muller, CTS over time developed a reputation for being a place to study Reformed theology and especially the Protestant orthodoxy of the sixteenth through eighteenth centuries. Bavinck's late nineteenth-century appropriation of this tradition and bringing it into engagement with modern theology and philosophy served as a perfect complement to this; CTS graduate students provided much-needed informed assistance for work on the *Reformed Dogmatics* and now continue to provide help on the *Reformed Ethics*.

As translators and editors of the *Reformed Ethics*, we faced numerous new challenges not encountered in the earlier project. Rather than a text carefully edited and prepared for publication, we were working from a digitally transcribed 1,100-page handwritten manuscript that Bavinck used for his lectures to his students. In many places the text consists of series of phrases and key words in Hebrew, Greek, or Latin that required significant additional narrative sinew and tissue on Bavinck's skeleton to create a readable, understandable work. After experimenting with rigorous scrupulosity and placing all editorial completions, insertions, and transitions in the conventional square brackets [ ], we have decided to forgo the practice for the most part, although instances of substantial construction and reconstruction will be indicated in the footnotes. We also wanted to keep the text clean from the excessive clutter of parentheses or brackets and foreign-language original words, phrases, or titles that are significant from a scholarly point of view. All of these will generally be provided in footnotes, using the following abbreviations: DO = Dutch-language original; FO = French-language original; GO = German-language original; GrO = Greek-language original; HO = Hebrew-language original; LO = Latin-language original. (Occasionally, Bavinck creates an interesting term or phrase by combining a non-Dutch term with a specific Dutch word; e.g., the combination of Dutch and German in *in zichzelf begründen*. We mark these as DO/GO.) Exceptions to this practice of putting foreign terms in footnotes can be found in sections where Bavinck engages in significant word-study analysis of important biblical terms, and it was necessary to highlight them in the text.[16] Paralleling the *Reformed Dogmatics*, a précis prepared by the editor is provided for each chapter. The length and complexity of Bavinck's chapters are a challenge for even the best-informed and attentive reader, and the précis serve as narrative outline guides. All this is to say that you will be reading a work that has been significantly reconstructed and amplified for clarity and utility. However, we have not altered its message; you are hearing the genuine voice of Herman Bavinck, including prejudices we might not share and claims with which we might disagree. Furthermore, those who are eager to have full access to the original for scholarly, historical purposes will be able to consult the Dutch critical edition being prepared simultaneously by Dirk van Keulen and to be published by Boekencentrum, Zoetermeer, the Netherlands.

An important part of the "wonder" we experienced with the publication of this volume comes from the gratitude we feel to God for the many people who have contributed to the project. This is our "Thank you!" For more than twenty years now, from the beginning of my work as editor of the *Reformed Dogmatics* and now continuing with the *Reformed Ethics*, Baker Academic has been a wonderful partner, everything one could wish for in a publisher. Executive vice president Jim Kinney has served with distinction for many years on the board of the Dutch Reformed Translation Society, has been an enthusiastic supporter of the *Reformed Ethics* project, has demonstrated flexibility and encouragement when the project morphed from an initial one-volume work to its current three volumes, and has been a good friend and wise counselor. Wells Turner, who headed Baker's editorial team on the *Reformed Dogmatics*, was the initial point person for the *Reformed Ethics* and provided helpful counsel and competent service as we struggled with the numerous editorial decisions involved with a translated and unedited text. Tim West, who has assumed the leadership of editing this volume and the two that remain, has also been a patient, understanding, and constructive partner. Thank you to both.

The board of the Dutch Reformed Translation Society has been a source of encouragement, good advice, and financial backing from the beginning. For that reason, thanks are also due to the many who have supported the DRTS with their gifts over the past twenty years. The Heritage Fund of Calvin Theological Seminary provided funds to make possible our weeklong editorial team sessions in the summers of 2015, 2016, and 2017. Dr. Rimmer and

16. Notably in chap. 2, §8, where Bavinck explores biblical imagery and terminology for humanity in the state and condition of sin.

Mrs. Ruth De Vries[17] have been generous contributors to the greater project of bringing the work of Dutch neo-Calvinism to the attention and utility of the non-Dutch-speaking world through, among other things, the work of the Kuyper Center at Princeton Theological Seminary and the Kuyper Translation Project headquartered at the Acton Institute in Grand Rapids, Michigan. They also stepped in at critical moments when we needed funds to keep the work going on Bavinck's *Reformed Ethics*. For all that and more, Rimmer and Ruth, thank you! This book is for you.

We would not have been able to continue our work without the support of a number of other friends of good Reformed theology: Sid and Cate Jansma, Doug and Kathy Kool, Ray and Linda Mulder, Henk and Sharon Ottens, John and Candy Steen, Harry and Joan Van Tol, the estate of Hubert and Aletta Slegers, and the 110+ members of the Bavinck Society. Your kindness and generosity are also one of the important "wonders" that come to mind in my reflections about our work.

For a number of reasons already mentioned, Calvin Theological Seminary was the right place for this project. Herewith my thanks to the administration and board of CTS for several sabbatical leaves and a publication leave. The following CTS students provided essential assistance in researching obscure references, chasing down internet resources and links, creating bibliographies, and copyediting and proofreading: Ashley Stam-Bonnes, Thiago da Silva, Laura De Jong, Gayle Doornbos-Kloostra, Jessica Joustra, Philip Djung, Philip Kim, Antoine Theron, and Erin Zoutendam.[18] The high quality of that assistance may be inferred from the fact that two members of that list are also included in the list of editorial team members who not only met for an intensive weeklong session in the summer of 2015 but also were willing to repeat the experience in 2016 and 2017. In addition, they continued to work on the material, translating and editing, during the time between our summer sessions. To Jessica Joustra, Nelson D. Kloosterman, Antoine Theron, and Dirk van Keulen: working with you on this wonderful manuscript has been a joy, intellectually and spiritually. Our friendship, shared deep appreciation for Herman Bavinck, and our common bond in Christ are the greatest "wonder" of this project.

And finally, I want to thank those whose translating (and editing) skills were an essential part of this production: Raymond Blacketer, Harry Boonstra, Anthony and Femke Elenbaas, Gerrit Sheeres, and Harry Van Dyke. Your work was not easy. Working from a manuscript that was compact and even

---

17. Ruth De Vries went to be with her Lord and Savior on August 29, 2018, while this volume was in its final stages of production. We miss her.

18. It is also worth mentioning that this is an international group with representatives from Brazil, Canada, Indonesia, South Africa, and South Korea as well as the United States.

fragmentary and that included Hebrew, Greek, Latin, French, and German words, phrases, and works presented challenges that you met and conquered. Translating can be a lonely work, but we trust that seeing the final product and knowing that you played an important role in bringing it forth may provide its own rewards. Well done and thank you! There were times when I as editor reached the limit of my linguistic ability. The following helped me too many times to keep track of the number: Ken Bratt for Latin, Barbara Carville for German, Dean Deppe and Jeff Weima for Greek, Herman De Vries for Dutch and German, Arie Leder and Carl Bosma for Hebrew (and Dutch), and Richard Muller for all of the above and more. Both Dirk van Keulen and I are also indebted to Dr. J. P. de Vries, who transcribed Herman Bavinck's handwritten manuscript into an electronic format for our great benefit. Thank you all!

John Bolt

NOTE TO THE READER

The English Standard Version has been our default Bible translation; to be true to Bavinck we wanted a translation that was more "literal" and less "dynamically equivalent" in its approach to the biblical text. Other translations used will be clearly marked in the text.

The World Wide Web has been another of the "wonders" for those of us working on this project. Not only does it make the task of tracking bibliographic items much easier (e.g., via WorldCat); the several projects dedicated to digitizing the books of ages present and past has been a real gift. My appreciation for Google Books, Internet Archive, and the Hathi Trust Digital Library, in particular, is unbounded. We discovered that most of the sources Bavinck cites are available online. Adding all these links to our footnotes would have added a significant number of pages to this volume and made it more expensive as well as cumbersome and unattractive. Instead, as part of our editorial work on this volume, we have created files for each chapter (and the bibliography) consisting only of the footnotes and hyperlinks to what we judge to be the best of these sources online. This will be a major time-saver for students and scholars who want to explore any of the subjects covered in this volume, and has the added bonus of increasing one's bibliographic "repertoire" of contemporary ethics, adding important works from the history of Christian ethical reflection that researchers should but usually do not know. Information on how to access these files will be available on the website of The Bavinck Institute at Calvin Theological Seminary at https://bavinckinstitute.org/.

Abbreviations

ACW	Ancient Christian Writers
ANF	*The Ante-Nicene Fathers*. Edited by Alexander Roberts and James Donaldson. 10 vols. New York: Christian Literature Co., 1885–96. Reprint, Grand Rapids: Eerdmans, 1950–51.
art.	article
ASV	American Standard Version
Bavinck Archives	Archive no. 346 of the Historical Documentation Centre, Free University, Amsterdam.
BLGNP	*Biographisch Lexicon voor de Geschiedenis van het Nederlandse Protestantisme*. 6 vols. Kampen: Kok, 1978–2006.
ca.	*circa*, about
CEV	Contemporary English Version
chap(s).	chapter(s)
Christ. Encycl.¹	*Christelijke Encyclopaedie voor het Nederlands Volk*. Edited by F. W. Grosheide, et al. 6 vols. Kampen: Kok, n.d. [1925?–1931].
Christ. Encycl.²	*Christelijke Encyclopedie*. Edited by F. W. Grosheide and G. P. van Itterzon. 2nd rev. ed. 6 vols. Kampen: Kok, 1956–61.
CSEL	Corpus Scriptorum Ecclesiasticorum Latinorum
CTJ	*Calvin Theological Journal*
d.	died
Denzinger	Denzinger, Henry. *The Sources of Catholic Dogma*. Translated by Roy J. Deferrari. Fitzwilliam, NH: Loreto, 2002.
DO	Dutch original
ed. note	editor's note
ESV	English Standard Version

ET	English translation
FC	Fathers of the Church
FO	French original
GE-De Jong	de Jong, J. M. "Gereformeerde ethiek van Profess. Dr. H. Bavinck." Bavinck Archives, no. 197.
GE-Lindeboom	Lindeboom, Cornelis [?]. "Gereformeerde ethiek—Dictaat van Prof. Bavinck." Library of the Protestant Theological University at Kampen.
GE-Van der Veen	Veen, Reinder Jan van der. "Gereformeerde ethiek. Acroam. van: Prof. Dr. H. Bavinck." Library of the Protestant Theological University at Kampen.
GO	German original
GrO	Greek original
HO	Hebrew original
Institutes	John Calvin, *Institutes of the Christian Religion*
ISV	International Standard Version
KJV	King James Version
LCL	Loeb Classical Library
lit.	literally
LO	Latin original
LSJ	Liddell, Henry George, Robert Scott, Henry Stuart Jones. *A Greek-English Lexicon*. 9th ed. with revised supplement. Oxford: Clarendon, 1996.
NIV	New International Version
NLT	New Living Translation
no(s).	number(s)
NPNF[1]	*A Select Library of Nicene and Post-Nicene Fathers of the Christian Church*. Edited by Philip Schaff. 1st series. 14 vols. New York: Christian Literature Co., 1887–1900. Reprint, Grand Rapids: Eerdmans, 1956.
NPNF[2]	*A Select Library of Nicene and Post-Nicene Fathers of the Christian Church*. Edited by Philip Schaff and Henry Wace. 2nd series. 14 vols. New York: Christian Literature Co., 1890–1900. Reprint, Grand Rapids: Eerdmans, 1952.
NRSV	New Revised Standard Version
p(p).	page(s)
PG	*Patrologiae cursus completus: Series graeca*. 161 vols. Edited by J.-P. Migne. Paris: Migne, 1857–66.
PL	*Patrologiae cursus completus: Series latina*. Edited by J.-P. Migne. 221 vols. Paris: Migne, 1844–65.
PRE[1]	*Realencyklopädie für protestantische Theologie und Kirche*. Edited by J. J. Herzog. 1st ed. 22 vols. Hamburg: R. Besser, 1854–68.

PRE^2	*Realencyklopädie für protestantische Theologie und Kirche.* Edited by J. J. Herzog and G. L. Plitt. 2nd rev. ed. 18 vols. Leipzig: J. C. Hinrichs, 1877–88.
PRE^3	*Realencyklopädie für protestantische Theologie und Kirche.* Edited by Albert Hauck. 3rd rev. ed. 24 vols. Leipzig: J. C. Hinrichs, 1896–1913.
RD	Bavinck, Herman. *Reformed Dogmatics.* Edited by John Bolt. Translated by John Vriend. 4 vols. Grand Rapids: Baker, 2003–8.
RE	Bavinck, Herman. *Reformed Ethics.* The present translation of "Gereformeerde Ethiek." Bavinck Archives, no. 56. Historical Documentation Centre, Free University, Amsterdam.
RSV	Revised Standard Version
Schaff-Herzog	*The New Schaff-Herzog Encyclopedia of Religious Knowledge.* 13 vols. Edited by Samuel Macauley Jackson. London and New York: Funk and Wagnalls, 1906–14.
ST	Thomas Aquinas, *Summa theologiae*
TBR	*The Bavinck Review*

Introduction to Herman Bavinck's
Reformed Ethics

DIRK VAN KEULEN AND JOHN BOLT

THE PROFESSOR AND HIS MANUSCRIPTS

On August 24, 1882, the synod of the Dutch Christian Reformed Church[1] appointed Herman Bavinck to be a professor at its Theological School in Kampen. He began his duties with an inaugural address on January 10, 1883, "The Science of Sacred Theology."[2] His primary teaching responsibility was dogmatics or systematic theology and culminated in his four-volume magnum opus, the *Reformed Dogmatics*.[3] This is the work for which he is best known and his major theological legacy.[4]

This introduction is the fruit of Dirk van Keulen's research and was originally presented at the "A Pearl and a Leaven: Herman Bavinck for the 21st Century" conference in Grand Rapids, Michigan, in September 2008 and published as "Herman Bavinck's Reformed Ethics: Some Remarks about Unpublished Manuscripts in the Libraries of Amsterdam and Kampen," *TBR* 1 (2010): 25–56. It has been adapted and revised for this volume by John Bolt with Dirk van Keulen's concurrence and approval. The first-person judgments toward the end of this essay are originally those of van Keulen and based on his research but are shared by Bolt.

    1. The Christelijke Gereformeerde Kerk.

    2. Bavinck, *De wetenschap der heilige godgeleerdheid*.

    3. *Gereformeerde Dogmatiek*. The volumes of the first edition (Kampen: Bos) appeared 1895–1901; a second, revised and enlarged edition (Kampen: Kok) was published 1906–11.

    4. The emphasis on *theological* is deliberate. Although scholarly work on Bavinck the theologian did not begin until some thirty years after his death in 1921, significant attention, both in Europe and in North America, was paid to his educational philosophy and writings on pedagogy in the two decades immediately following his death: Rombouts, *Bavinck, gids bij de*

However, it is not well known that during the years of his professorate at Kampen, Bavinck also taught ethics. Several documents which Bavinck used for his lectures in ethics are stored in the Bavinck archives.[5] For example, the archives contain a small lecture notebook which likely dates from the beginning of Bavinck's career at Kampen (or even earlier).[6] In this notebook, Bavinck arranges his ethics course into ten sections: (1) "Sin," (2) "Human Beings as Moral Creatures," (3) "Election (The Foundation of the Christian Life)," (4) "Faith (The Source and Organizing Principle of the Christian Life)," (5) "Penance (The Origin of the Christian Life)," (6) "Law (The Rule of the Christian Life)," (7) "Freedom (The Privilege of the Christian Life)," (8) "The Altruistic Character of Christian Life," (9) "The Relation between Christian and Civic Life," and (10) "The Christian Life in Community."[7]

In addition to this small notebook, the archives contain an extensive manuscript of some 1,100 pages with the title *Reformed Ethics*.[8] The numerous notebooks in which Bavinck wrote the manuscript have been severely damaged; many pages have been torn from each other, and the paper is crumbling. Furthermore, the manuscript is incomplete. It breaks off in the middle of a discussion about the Christian family. In the margins of the text, Bavinck has added notes and references to literature studied or published after he wrote the initial draft and repeated his series of lectures. It is this manuscript that serves as the basis for this volume and the two that will follow.

It is difficult to date the document. Because of its length and elaborate references to Holy Scripture as well as to Protestant theologians from the sixteenth through nineteenth centuries, Bavinck must have worked on it for years. Though incomplete and in rough form, there is sufficient material in this manuscript for a multivolume work on Reformed ethics. Although it is not possible to date the

---

studie van zijn paedagogische werken; Brederveld, *Hoofdlijnen der paedagogiek van Dr. Herman Bavinck*; van der Zweep, *De paedagogiek van Bavinck*; Jaarsma, *Educational Philosophy of Herman Bavinck*; and van Klinken, *Bavinck's paedagogische beginselen*.

5. Archive no. 346 of the Historical Documentation Centre, Free University, Amsterdam (hereafter abbreviated as "Bavinck Archives"). Note: the numbers for the Bavinck Archives are revised from van Keulen, "Bavinck's Reformed Ethics," because of a recataloguing at the Historical Documentation Center.

6. This notebook may hark back to Bavinck's days as a student in Leiden; the sections overlap perfectly with the ten chapters of his dissertation, *De ethiek van Ulrich Zwingli*.

7. Bavinck Archives, no. 184. DO: §1. *De zonde*; §2. *De mens als zedelijk wezen*; §3. *De verkiezing (grondslag van het christelijk leven)*; §4. *Het geloof (bron en principe van het christelijk leven)*; §5. *De boete (ontstaan van het christelijk leven)*; §6. *De wet (regel van het christelijk leven)*; §7. *De vrijheid (voorrecht van het christelijk leven)*; §8. *Het altruïstisch karakter van het christelijk leven*; §9. *De verhouding van het christelijk tot het burgerlijk leven*; §10. *Het christelijk leven in de gemeenschap*.

8. Bavinck Archives, no. 56. DO: *Gereformeerde ethiek*.

origin of the *Reformed Ethics* based on the data in the manuscript itself, there is correlative evidence which suggests that Bavinck used his *Reformed Ethics* manuscript during the academic years 1884–86 and 1894–95. This evidence is found in two other unpublished, handwritten manuscripts.

The first manuscript, "Reformed Ethics. Class Notes of Prof. Dr. H. Bavinck," was written by Reinder Jan van der Veen (1863–1942), who studied theology at Kampen from September 1878 until July 1886 and whose signature is on the manuscript's title page.[9] Van der Veen's manuscript of 327 pages originally consisted of two volumes, but unfortunately the first volume has been lost. On several pages in the second volume, van der Veen dates his class notes, providing evidence that these notes refer to Bavinck's lectures in ethics of the years 1884–85 and 1885–86. The lost first volume likely contained notes on Bavinck's lectures of the year 1883–84, the first year of Bavinck's professorate at Kampen!

The second manuscript, "Reformed Ethics—Class Notes from Prof. Bavinck," is a 406-page manuscript, registered at the Library archives of the Protestant Theological University at Kampen in 1983.[10] Unfortunately, there is no information available about the manuscript's author or origin. It is possible that the library obtained the manuscript in 1983 and failed to note its origin. But it is also possible that the manuscript was present in the library for many years and was not catalogued until 1983. Whatever the case may be, comparison with other manuscripts in Kampen's library suggests that that the author may have been Cornelis Lindeboom (1872–1938), who studied theology at Kampen in the years 1889–95.[11] The manuscript can, therefore, be dated tentatively to the year 1895.[12]

9. DO: "Gereformeerde ethiek. Acroam. van: Prof. Dr. H. Bavinck," Library of the Protestant Theological University at Kampen, shelf mark 101A20 (hereafter abbreviated as *GE-Van der Veen*); biographical information from van Gelderen and Rozemond, *Gegevens betreffende de Theologische Universiteit Kampen, 1854–1994*, 110.

10. DO: "Gereformeerde ethiek—Dictaat van Prof. Bavinck," Library of the Protestant Theological University at Kampen, shelf mark E2 (hereafter abbreviated as *GE-Lindeboom*).

11. Cornelis Lindeboom (1872–1938), the only son of Kampen's New Testament professor Lucas Lindeboom (1845–1933), studied theology at Kampen from September 1889 until July 1895 (van Gelderen and Rozemond, *Gegevens betreffende de Theologische Universiteit Kampen, 1854–1994*, 116). After one year of study at Lausanne he worked as a minister in Sprang (1896), Bolnes (1900), Apeldoorn (1905), Gorinchem (1908), and Amsterdam (1914–37). See Lindeboom and Lindeboom, *In uwe voorhoven*; Wielenga, "Ds. C. Lindeboom"; and Mulder, "Lindeboom, Cornelis."

12. The manuscript refers once to volume 1 of the first edition of Bavinck's *Gereformeerde Dogmatiek* (*GE-Lindeboom*, 38). Because this volume was published in 1895, the manuscript must be dated to this year or later. If it is true that Cornelis Lindeboom is the author of the manuscript, the date can be narrowed more precisely to 1895 because Lindeboom ended his studies at Kampen in the summer of that year. This date would also explain why the manuscript

Both manuscripts offer a fine impression of Bavinck's lectures on ethics. The text of the manuscripts is written down very carefully. Every sentence is completely written out and grammatically correct. The style is typically Bavinck's. When, for instance, biblical references to a theme are listed, this is done exactly as biblical references are listed in Bavinck's *Reformed Dogmatics*. The style of the manuscripts, therefore, gives the impression that Bavinck verbally dictated the text.[10]

Moreover, it is striking that the structure of van der Veen's and Lindeboom's class notes is almost identical to the composition of Bavinck's *Reformed Ethics* manuscript. This similarity makes it likely that Bavinck gave these lectures on ethics in the school years 1884–86 and then again in 1894–95. If this inference is correct, the manuscript can be dated going back to the first years of Bavinck's professorate at Kampen.

At the same time, there is evidence of some distance between Bavinck's lectures and the texts from his students' notebooks. This is suggested by passages that indicate either in-class or after-class engagement and even disagreement by students with their professor's judgment. On page 150 of Lindeboom's text there is a reference to John 6:29: "Faith is the work of God." An accompanying observation follows: "This scripture passage was perhaps chosen wrongly by the professor; 'of God' is here an objective genitive."[13] A comment like this is most likely the sort that is added by a student after class. The student notes provide us with a clear impression of Bavinck's lectures in 1895.

Lindeboom's comment about John 6:29 is also a reminder that Bavinck repeatedly referred to Scripture and engaged in exegesis of biblical texts, along with his many references to Protestant theologians (Reformed and Lutheran) from the era of Protestant Orthodoxy in the sixteenth and seventeenth centuries, as well as more recent eighteenth- and nineteenth-century theologians. Since these are unlikely to have been added after class by students, it is reasonable to claim that the structure—the main lines as well as the details—must be attributed to Bavinck himself.

THE STRUCTURE OF BAVINCK'S *REFORMED ETHICS*

As mentioned earlier, it appears that Bavinck worked on the manuscript of *Reformed Ethics* for years. This was the period in which he was also working

---

is incomplete. The notes break off in the middle of a discussion of the Ten Commandments. Bavinck probably continued this discussion after the summer of 1895, when Lindeboom no longer attended Bavinck's classes.

13. DO: *Deze tekst is wellicht foutief gekozen door den Prof: "Gods" is Gen. Obj. hier.*

on his *Reformed Dogmatics*. The four volumes of the latter were published successively in the years 1895, 1897, 1898, and 1901. It is not surprising, therefore, that Bavinck's *Reformed Ethics* resembles his *Reformed Dogmatics* in several ways.

A good example of this resemblance is the similar structure of the two works. Bavinck begins the *Reformed Dogmatics* with an introduction to the science of dogmatic theology and its method and organization.[14] He follows this with a chapter on the history and literature of dogmatics.[15] The *Reformed Ethics* manuscript has a similar introduction, although Bavinck reverses the order by beginning with an outline of the history of Reformed ethics and its literature.[16] He follows this with sections on terminology, organization, and methodology.[17]

Bavinck prefers the term "ethics" to "morality."[18] The task of ethics is to describe the birth, development, and manifestation of spiritual life in reborn humanity.[19] In other words, "ethics is the scientific description of the grace of Jesus Christ in operation, i.e., his divine life-content in the Form of a person's life."[20]

Bavinck considers ethics and dogmatics to be closely related but also insists that they be distinguished. He put it this way in the *Reformed Dogmatics*:

Dogmatics describes the deeds of God done for, to, and in human beings; ethics describes what renewed human beings now do on the basis of and in the strength of those divine deeds. In dogmatics human beings are passive; they

14. *RD*, 1:25–112.
15. *RD*, 1:115–204.
16. *RE*, §1.
17. *RE*, §§2–4.
18. *RE*, §2: "We choose 'ethics' [*ethiek*] because the word does not yet carry the negative associations [*kwade reuk* = "evil smell"] that 'morality' [*moraal*] has, at least as understood in terms of moral preaching [*zedepreek*]. In addition, a distinction is usually made between 'morality' understood as practical morality, rules for living, inductively describing what is externally *done*, and 'ethics' as the more strictly scientific and deductive expression of what *is*. Practical morality is the cluster of rules by which people live and is thus an inductive description of what people outwardly *do*. Ethics is thus deeper and normative." Cf. *GE-Lindeboom*, 10.
19. *GE-Lindeboom*, 14; cf. *RE*, §2: "Ethics must concern itself with (a) how human beings as rational, responsible beings appropriate and use the gifts and powers of the first creation and accept the gospel of grace; (b) how humans are regenerated and how that life remains subject to sickness, temptation, and struggle; and (c) how, in ethical lives, human acts (of understanding, will, etc.) are directed toward God's law, which is to be manifested in all circumstances of their lives. In other words, ethics is concerned with the preparation, birth, development, and outward manifestation of the spiritual person."
20. *RE*, §2; cf. *GE-Lindeboom*, 14: "Ethics is the scientific description of the realization [*verwerkelijking*] of Christ's grace in our personal human life; in other words, it describes the realization of God's salvation [*heil*] in us."

receive and believe; in ethics they are themselves active agents. In dogmatics, the articles of faith are treated; in ethics, the precepts of the decalogue. In the former, that which concerns faith is dealt with; in the latter, that which concerns love, obedience, and good works. Dogmatics sets forth what God is and does for human beings and causes them to know God as their Creator, Redeemer, and Sanctifier; ethics sets forth what human beings are and do for God now; how, with everything they are and have, with intellect and will and all their strength, they devote themselves to God out of gratitude and love. Dogmatics is the system of the knowledge of God; ethics is that of the service of God.[21]

In his *Reformed Ethics* manuscript Bavinck describes the difference in identical terms:

> In dogmatics we are concerned with what God does for us and in us. In dogmatics God is everything. Dogmatics is a word from God to us, coming from outside of us, from above us; we are passive, listening, and opening ourselves to being directed by God. In ethics, we are interested in the question of what it is that God now expects of us when he does his work in us. What do we do for him? Here we are active, precisely because of and on the grounds of God's deeds in us; we sing psalms in thanks and praise to God. In dogmatics, God descends to us; in ethics, we ascend to God. In dogmatics, he is ours; in ethics, we are his. In dogmatics, we know we shall see his face; in ethics, his name will be written on our foreheads [Rev. 22:4]. Dogmatics proceeds from God; ethics returns to God. In dogmatics, God loves us; in ethics, therefore, we love him.[22]

The method of ethics, Bavinck argues, is the same as in dogmatics. The point of departure is God's revelation; Holy Scripture is the principle of knowledge and the norm for ethics.[23] Accordingly, three methodological steps must be distinguished: (1) collecting and systematizing biblical data, (2) describing how these data have been adopted in the church, and (3) developing these data normatively or thetically with a view to our own time.[24] This threefold method in his *Reformed Ethics* manuscript follows exactly the way Bavinck proceeds in the *Reformed Dogmatics*.

With respect to the composition of his ethical theory, Bavinck first discusses the ethical frameworks of several other Protestant theologians, including Antonius Driessen, Willem Teellinck, Campegius Vitringa, Benedictus Pictetus,

---

21. *RD*, 1:58.
22. Translated from *GE-Lindeboom*, 14–15; cf. *RE*, §2.
23. DO: *kenbron, norma*; *RE*, §4; cf. *GE-Lindeboom*, 21.
24. *RE*, §4; cf. *GE-Lindeboom*, 22.

Petrus van Mastricht, August Friedrich Christian Vilmar, Hans Lassen Martensen, Heinrich Heppe, and Adolf von Harless. After observing that these theologians follow roughly the same general structure, Bavinck chooses a similar, traditional, tripartite structure himself:

I. Humanity before conversion, in the condition of sin, conscience, morality; this is the realm of natural ethics.

II. Converted humanity: the new life in its preparation, origin, aspects, circumstances, aids, blessing, marks, sickness and death, fulfillment; this is the realm of practical theology.

III. Regenerated humanity in the family, vocation, society, state, and church.

Bavinck indicates that he intends to end his ethics on an eschatological note with some reflections on the kingdom of God "in its origin, development, and completion."[25] Later in the manuscript Bavinck expands his structure by dividing the second part into two: Converted Humanity (Humanity *in* Conversion) and Humanity *after* Conversion.[26] He then adds a fourth part: "The Life-Spheres in Which the Moral Life Is to Be Manifested." In our edition, these four parts will be designated as Books I–IV.[27]

A BRIEF OVERVIEW OF BOOK I

In the remainder of this introduction we will provide a general overview of the main themes and topics of *Reformed Ethics*. The tripartite structure described above clearly demonstrates the thoroughly dogmatic character of the work. Dogmatics precedes ethics, and ethics is completely dependent on dogmatics. This interrelationship is confirmed when we read the first part of Bavinck's *Reformed Ethics*: "Humanity before Conversion." This part is divided into three chapters and twelve sections. In the table below, the left-hand columns are the titles used in this volume; to their right are Bavinck's original Dutch titles.[28] The table also reveals that while we retained Bavinck's basic fourfold division of the material, we divided the chapters differently, primarily to even out the length of each chapter as much as possible. In this section, Bavinck's three chapters became our six.

25. *RE*, §3; cf. *GE-Lindeboom*, 18.
26. Cf. *GE-Lindeboom*, 23, 137, 256.
27. In our edition, volume 1 will contain Books I–II, volume 2 will contain Book III, and volume 3 will contain Book IV.
28. The divisions and titles are almost identical in the *GE-Lindeboom* manuscript.

Book I: Humanity before Conversion	Deel 1: De Mensch voor de Bekering
CHAPTER 1: ESSENTIAL HUMAN NATURE	HOOFDSTUK 1: DE MENSCHELIJKE NATUUR, OP ZICHZELF BESCHOUWD
(The Essence of Humanity)	Het Wezen van de Mensch
§5 Human Beings, Created in God's Image	De Mensch, Geschapen naar Gods Beeld
§6 The Content of Human Nature	De Inhoud der Menschelijke Natuur
§7 Human Relationships	De Levensvertrouwingen/Betrekkingen van den Mensch
CHAPTER 2: HUMANITY UNDER THE POWER OF SIN	HOOFDSTUK 2: DE MENSCH IN DE TOESTAND DER ZONDE
§8 The Devastation of the Image of God in Humanity	De Oude/Natuurlijke Mensch
§9 The Organizing Principle and Classification of Sins	Beginsel en Verdeeling der Zonden
CHAPTER 3: THE SELF AGAINST THE NEIGHBOR AND GOD	(continuation of Hoofdstuk 2)
§10 Sins of Egoism in the Narrow Sense	Zelfzuchtige Zonden in Engeren Zin
§11 Sins against the Neighbor	Zonden tegen den Naaste
§12 Sins against God	Zonden tegen God
CHAPTER 4: THE FALLEN IMAGE OF GOD	HOOFDSTUK 3: DE ZEDELIJKE NATUUR DES MENSCHEN IN DEN TOESTAND DER ZONDE
§13 The Image of God in Fallen Human Beings	Het Beeld Gods in den Gevallen Mensch
CHAPTER 5: HUMAN CONSCIENCE	(continuation of Hoofdstuk 3)
§14 The Conscience	Het Geweten
CHAPTER 6: THE SINNER AND THE LAW	(continuation of Hoofdstuk 3)
§15 The Law	De Wet
§16 Natural Morality	De Justitia Civilis

In his first chapter, on "human nature considered on its own," Bavinck begins with the crucial starting point for ethics: human creation in the image of God. He derives three basic principles from human creation in God's image: (1) originally human beings were good; (2) it is impossible to understand human morality apart from God; and (3) human nature was corrupted by sin. Bavinck defends these basic principles against Fichte, Hegel, Rothe, and Darwin.[29]

29. *RE*, §5; cf. *GE-Lindeboom*, 25–30; cf. *RD*, 2:530–62 (chap. 12: "Human Nature"); Bavinck begins this chapter with these words: "The essence of human nature is its being [created in] the image of God."

Bavinck devotes the second chapter of Book I to the doctrine of sin, distinguishing those topics that properly belong in dogmatics from those that should nonetheless be discussed in ethics. He assumes and does not examine the dogmatic understanding of "the origin, essence, and nature of sin," as well as "the changed relation to God brought about by sin, namely guilt and punishment of sin."[30] At the same time, theologians like Johann Franz Buddeus (1667–1729), Friedrich Adolph Lampe (1683–1729), August Friedrich Christian Vilmar (1800–68), and others, taught him that the doctrine of sin did need to be dealt with in theological ethics as well.[31] In an extensive examination of biblical terminology for sin, Bavinck explores the many dimensions and varieties of sins. This is the proper task of ethics. Specifically, ethics considers the "appearances, forms, manifestations of the one sin," and Bavinck asks, "Is it possible to construct a system from that variety and number, and is there a connection between them all? In other words, is there an organizing principle from which all sins can be objectively and substantively derived?"[32]

Bavinck, therefore, proceeds to develop a typology of sin. He agrees with writers who posit *egocentricity* or self-centeredness to be the "organizing principle" of sin, with the two important qualifications that this be understood "in a very broad sense and include the problems of haughtiness and unbelief," and that "it is not understood as though all sins *logically* flow from this foundation."[33] Bavinck distinguishes three basic types of sins: (1) sins against oneself, (2) sins against one's neighbor, and (3) sins against God. Each of these three types can be further divided into *sensual* sins and *spiritual* sins.[34] Thus, sins against one's neighbor are sins in which the neighbor or what belongs to the neighbor is used for oneself. These sins can be sensual in character: sins against the neighbor's decency, property, or life. They also can be spiritual in character: sins against the neighbor's good reputation or authority.[35] Bavinck's ethical doctrine of sin, therefore, is clearly a supplement to the doctrine of sin offered in his *Reformed Dogmatics*.

In his third chapter, on "the moral condition of humanity in the state of sin," Bavinck describes the consequences of sin for human nature, for soul and body, and for reason, will, and feelings, and he concludes that the natural person lacks all capacity for doing good.[36] God preserves humanity, however,

---

30. *RE*, §8; Bavinck discussues these topics in *RD*, 3:25–190.
31. *RE*, §8; cf. *GE-Lindeboom*, 49; Buddeus, *Institutiones Theologiae Moralis*; Lampe, *Schets der dadelyke Godt-geleertheid*; Vilmar, *Theologische Moral*.
32. *RE*, §9.
33. *RE*, §9.
34. *RE*, §§10–12; cf. *GE-Lindeboom*, 70–80.
35. *RE*, §11; cf. *GE-Lindeboom*, 75–79.
36. *RE*, §13; cf. *GE-Lindeboom*, 86.

by his general grace, which curbs the human inclination to do evil. Even fallen
human beings retain a reasonable, moral nature which manifests itself in their
consciences.[37] The conscience is bound to God's law, and Bavinck, therefore,
follows his section on conscience with one on law (natural and moral) and
another on the way in which law takes shape in individuals, society, and the
state.[38]

A BRIEF OVERVIEW OF BOOK II

Book II, "Converted Humanity," offers a comprehensive analysis of the spiritual life of the Christian. Bavinck organized the material into a single chapter
with ten sections.[39] Here is a table with the divisions used in this volume on
the left and those of the Dutch original to the right.[40]

Book II: Converted Humanity	Deel 2: De Mensch in de Bekering
CHAPTER 7: LIFE IN THE SPIRIT	HOOFDSTUK I
§17 The Nature of the Spiritual Life	De Natuur van het Geestelijk Leven
§18 The Origin of the Spiritual Life	Oorsprongen van het Geestelijk Leven
§19 The First and Basic Activity of the Spiritual Life	De (Eerste, Grond) Werkzaamheid van het Geestelijk Leven
CHAPTER 8: LIFE IN THE SPIRIT IN THE CHURCH'S HISTORY	(continuation of Hoofdstuk 1)
§20 Mysticism, Pietism, and Methodism	Mysticisme, Pietisme, en Methodisme

37. *RE*, §§13–15; cf. *GE-Lindeboom*, 81–91, 124; *RD*, 3:32. We see here a prime example of
Bavinck's distinction between dogmatics and ethics. Bavinck pays little attention to the human
conscience in *Reformed Dogmatics*, apart from this comment in 3:173 about Adam and Eve's
transgression in Gen. 3:

> Immediately after the fall, the eyes of Adam and Eve were opened, and they discovered
> that they were naked. Implied here is that they knew and recognized that they had done
> wrong. Shame is the fear of disgrace, an unpleasant and painful sense of being involved
> in something wrong or improper. Added to the shame was fear before God and the
> consequent desire to hide from him—that is to say, the human conscience was aroused.
> Before the fall, strictly speaking, there was no conscience in humans. There was no gap
> between what they were and what they knew they had to be. Being and self-consciousness
> were in harmony. But the fall produced separation. By the grace of God, humans still
> retain the consciousness that they ought to be different, that in all respects they must
> conform to God's law. But reality witnesses otherwise; they are not who they ought to
> be. And this witness is the conscience.

In addition to his extensive treatment of the subject in §14 (chap. 5 below), Bavinck published
an article on conscience already in 1881: "Het geweten" (ET: Bavinck, "Conscience").
   38. *RE*, §§15–16; cf. *GE-Lindeboom*, 124–36.
   39. *RE*, §§17–26; we have divided the material into six chapters in this volume.
   40. This outline is virtually identical to that of *GE-Lindeboom*.

Book II: Converted Humanity	Deel 2: De Mensch in de Bekering
CHAPTER 9: THE SHAPE AND MATURATION OF THE CHRISTIAN LIFE	(continuation of Hoofdstuk 1)
§21 The Shape of the Christian Life: The Imitation of Christ	De Vorm van het Geestelijk Leven (De Navolging van Christus)
§22 The Growth of the Spiritual Life	De Ontwikkeling van het Geestelijk Leven
CHAPTER 10: PERSEVERING IN THE CHRISTIAN LIFE	(continuation of Hoofdstuk 1)
§23 Security and Sealing	De Verzekering (en Verzegeling)
CHAPTER 11: PATHOLOGIES OF THE CHRISTIAN LIFE	(continuation of Hoofdstuk 1)
§24 Diseases of the Spiritual Life and Their Roots	De Krankheden van het Geestelijk Leven en Hare Oorzaken
CHAPTER 12: RESTORATION AND CONSUMMATION OF THE CHRISTIAN LIFE	(continuation of Hoofdstuk 1)
§25 Means of Restoration	Middelen tot Herstel
§26 Consummation of the Spiritual Life; Meditation on Death	Volmaking van 't Geestelijk Leven; Meditatio Mortis

For Bavinck, the basic principle of ethics is loving God, a love that is accomplished by the Holy Spirit.[41] Thus, regeneration is the origin of the spiritual life (§18), and faith is its fundamental activity (§19). Before setting forth his own constructive view of the spiritual life, Bavinck devotes a lengthy historical section to what he considers aberrations to a healthy Christian life in the history of Christian mysticism and pietism (§20). The heart of such a spiritual life is to be found in the imitation of Christ, a topic that intrigued and captivated Bavinck throughout his life.[42] Christ is not only a king, a priest, and a prophet, he argues, but also a model, an example, and an ideal. This implies that we must follow Christ.[43] The imitation of Christ does not mean that we are to duplicate his way of living literally or physically, not even his poverty, chastity, and obedience, as was taught in Roman Catholic monasteries.[44] Nor does imitating Christ involve any kind of mysticism or a rationalistic obedience to Christ's commandments.[45] For Bavinck, rather,

41. *RE*, §17; cf. *GE-Van der Veen*, 5; *GE-Lindeboom*, 139.
42. See Bolt, *Theological Analysis*; Bolt, "Christ and the Law." Bavinck published two essays on the imitation of Christ, one at the beginning of his academic career, 1885–86, and the other in 1918; both are published in English translation in Bolt, *Theological Analysis*, 372–440.
43. *RE*, §21; cf. *GE-Van der Veen*, 41–42; *GE-Lindeboom*, 174.
44. *RE*, §21; cf. *GE-Van der Veen*, 56–58; *GE-Lindeboom*, 184–85.
45. *RE*, §21; cf. *GE-Van der Veen*, 57–58; *GE-Lindeboom*, 185; the outline here is practically identical to that used by Bavinck in his 1885–86 "Imitation of Christ" article, more evidence of the manuscript's date. The essay appeared in the journal *De Vrije Kerk* (The Free Church), a

imitating Christ consists in "the recognition of Christ as a Mediator." Christ must take shape in us inwardly, while outwardly our lives must be shaped in conformity with the life of Christ. The imitation of Christ becomes manifest in virtues like righteousness, sanctity, love, and patience.[46]

Bavinck continues this chapter with sections on the growth of the spiritual life, the assurance of faith, pathologies of the spiritual life (i.e., the struggle between flesh and spirit, temptations, and spiritual abandonment), remedies to restore spiritual life (prayer, meditation, reading God's Word, singing, solitude, fasting, vigils, and vows), and finally the consummation of spiritual life after death.[47]

The very long section on assurance of faith[48] is especially striking since one could well ask whether this theme is appropriate for ethics. After a long historical survey of the topic Bavinck pays special attention to the doctrine of the marks[49] of a genuine believer, such as grief over sin, love of God's Word, and serving God. This section undoubtedly reflects the situation of the Dutch Christian Reformed Church[50] in Bavinck's day, including Bavinck's own responsibility as a seminary professor for this church. In the tradition of the Secession,[51] the doctrine of the marks of grace was a difficult theme, one which directly influenced the spirituality of the local churches. Moreover, discussions about this doctrine could be linked to heated disputes over Abraham Kuyper's theory of presumptive regeneration.[52] It is telling, therefore, that we find in van der Veen's and Lindeboom's class notes on this section a reference to Bavinck's own years as a minister in the congregation of the Christian Reformed Church at Franeker! The report is of a woman "in his former congregation who was sealed by Isaiah 27:1."[53] There are no other

---

monthly periodical "of Christian Reformed voices" that sought to bring the church out of its isolation in order to engage the cultural and scientific challenges of the day. One of its stated goals was "to oppose a superficial and unhealthy mysticism with a more biblical spirituality." Bavinck served as its editor from 1881 to 1883 (Bolt, *Theological Analysis*, 80–81).

46. *RE*, §21; cf. *GE-Van der Veen*, 58–60; *GE-Lindeboom*, 185–87.

47. *RE*, §§22–26; cf. *GE-Van der Veen*, 60–160; *GE-Lindeboom*, 187–255.

48. *RE*, §23, "Security and Sealing" (chap. 10).

49. DO: *kentekenen*.

50. DO: Christelijke Gereformeerde Kerk.

51. The Secession of 1834 from the national Dutch Reformed Church (Nederlandse Hervormde Kerk), which led to the formation of the Christian Reformed Church (Christelijke Gereformeerde Kerk). This church established its own theological school in Kampen in 1854.

52. See Veenhof, "History of Theology and Spirituality in the Dutch Reformed Churches"; Veenhof, "Discussie over het zelfonderzoek."

53. *GE-Van der Veen*, 89: "Prof. B. vertelde, dat een vrouw uit zijn vroegere gem. verzegeld was geworden door Jesaja 27:1!"; *GE-Lindeboom*, 208: "Ja zelfs heb ik in mijne Gemeente te Franeker—aldus verhaalde Prof. Bavinck—eene vrouw gekend, die verzegeld was met Jes. 27:1." The reference to Franeker is missing in *RE*, and provides a rare instance of a Bavinck

references to Bavinck's pastorate in Franeker in either the van der Veen or Lindeboom texts.

It is also interesting that Bavinck twice criticizes Abraham Kuyper in this section, a critique also noted in both van der Veen's and Lindeboom's class notes.[54] Kuyper's views on so-called presumptive regeneration were highly controversial in his Christian Reformed denomination.[55] Notwithstanding his important position as a leading teacher in that church, Bavinck was very careful to avoid *public* criticism of Kuyper.[56] That he was willing to do so in the more private setting of a classroom indicates the vital importance Bavinck attributed to the doctrine of assurance and the marks of grace.

A Brief Overview of Book III

Since the translation of Books III and IV will be published in future volumes, our treatment here will be even briefer than it was for Books I and II. Book III has the title "Humanity after Conversion" and is composed of four chapters: (1) "Sanctification in General" (§§27–31);[57] (2) "Duties toward God" (§§32–35); (3) "Duties toward the Self" (§§36–42); and (4) "Duties toward the Neighbor" (§§43–49). The operative term in this book is "duty." After a general discussion on the relationship between the Christian and the law,[58] Bavinck indicates why he rejects the Roman Catholic distinction between *precepts* and *counsels of perfection*,[59] discusses the so-called *adiaphora*, or acts that are morally indifferent,[60] and, finally, discusses the clash of moral duties.[61] These topics are

---

classroom pastoral ad lib. The exclamation mark in the van der Veen manuscript is telling; Isa. 27:1 is an extraordinary text by which one is sealed by the Holy Spirit: "In that day the Lord with his hard and great and strong sword will punish Leviathan the fleeing serpent, Leviathan the twisting serpent, and he will slay the dragon that is in the sea."

54. *RE*, §22; see *GE-Van der Veen*, 101–3, 113; *GE-Lindeboom*, 217, 226. We do not find Kuyper's name elsewhere in the *GE-Van der Veen* and *GE-Lindeboom* manuscripts.

55. For an excellent introduction to this controversy and Bavinck's own perspective on it, see Bavinck, *Saved by Grace*; the editor's introduction is a superb overview of the historical and theological issues in the controversy.

56. The emphasis on "public" is deliberate; he did privately indicate such disagreement to his students, notably in his differences with Kuyper on the matter of theological encyclopedia and the nature of theology. In a letter to Kuyper (October 29, 1894) he expressed his reservations directly but then added this: "I am reluctant to discuss all this in public. The manner in which some discuss your work and judge it on the basis of isolated statements offends me. I do not wish to support such a critique in any way" (cited by Bremmer, *Bavinck als Dogmaticus*, 24).

57. Bavinck also discusses the topic of sanctification in *RD*, 4:230–72.

58. *RE*, §27; cf. *GE-Van der Veen*, 161–80; *GE-Lindeboom*, 256–66.

59. LO: *praecepta, consilia*; *RE*, §28.

60. *RE*, §29.

61. LO: *collisio*; *RE*, §30.

mentioned briefly in the *Reformed Dogmatics*,[62] but their broad elaboration in the *Reformed Ethics* shows that Bavinck intentionally distinguished topics in dogmatics from those in ethics and also that he regarded his *Reformed Ethics* as a complementary companion to the *Reformed Dogmatics*.

In Book III, chapters 2–4, Bavinck connects the doctrine of duty to the Ten Commandments. In the second chapter, he analyzes the first four commands as duties toward God, including a lengthy section on the Fourth Commandment and the Sabbath.[63] In the third chapter, duties toward ourselves, he discusses this duty in general (self-preservation, self-love, self-denial, §36), then toward our bodily life in general (§37), including food and drink (§38), clothing (§39), and life itself (§40). Bavinck then considers duties toward bodily life that flow from the Seventh, Eighth, and Ninth Commandments (§41). Our final duty to ourselves is the duty we have toward our soul (§42). Finally, in the fourth chapter Bavinck discusses Christian charity and links this duty to the Sixth through Tenth Commandments (§§43–49).

A BRIEF OVERVIEW OF BOOK IV

In the fourth part of *Reformed Ethics* Bavinck planned to discuss how the Christian life should manifest itself in various spheres. The only extant chapter (§§50–58) is devoted to the family. Bavinck explains in detail the obligation to marry, impediments to marriage, degrees of consanguinity, engagement, the celebration of marriage, the nature of marriage, divorce, and the relationship between husband and wife.[64] Then the document breaks off. Bavinck would likely have added sections on topics such as raising children, brothers and sisters, friendship, vocation, society, nation, and church. This much may be inferred from the introduction of the manuscript and from another unpublished document in the Bavinck Archives, which was likely used by Bavinck in his lectures on ethics and which most likely dates from the 1880s or possibly from the 1890s.[65] As we shall see, these multiple manuscripts also provide

---

62. *RD*, 4:239, 260.

63. *RE*, §§32–35; cf. *GE-Van der Veen*, 268–327; *GE-Lindeboom*, 325–85.

64. Here are the topics of the nine sections: §50, the family in history; §51, marriage as an obligation; §52, impediments to marriage; §53, degrees of consanguinity; §54, engagement/ betrothal; §55, consummation of marriage; §56, the nature/essence of marriage; §57, divorce; §58, husband and wife.

65. The document has the title *Ethiek* and can be found in the Bavinck Archives, no. 197. After an introductory section covering terminology, the "Ethics" document contains sections about philosophical ethics in general, principal schools of philosophical ethics, a brief history of philosophical ethics, and contemporary views of philosophical ethics. These sections are followed by a short sketch of Reformed ethics comprising three main sections: (1) an introduction (with

a clue to the intriguing question: Why did Bavinck never publish a finished monograph on *Reformed Ethics*?

INTERMEZZO: THE QUESTION OF PUBLICATION

As we have already noted, Bavinck must have worked on his *Reformed Dogmatics* and his *Reformed Ethics* at the same time for many years, and his clear demarcation between the subject matter of dogmatics and that of ethics suggests that his *Reformed Ethics* was intended as a companion to his *Reformed Dogmatics*. So, then, why did Bavinck not finish and publish his *Reformed Ethics*? This question is even more compelling when we realize that around 1900 there was an urgent need in the Dutch Reformed Churches for a Reformed ethics. In 1897, Wilhelm Geesink, professor of ethics at the Vrije Universiteit, delivered a rectorial address, "Ethics in Reformed Theology," in which he complained about "the dearth of specifically Reformed ethical studies in our time."[66] Bavinck himself was fully aware of this need. In the preface to his 1902 published lecture, *Morality Today*, he wrote the following: "Our circles lack good literature that discusses and elucidates moral principles and applies them to the questions of the day. We suffer from a lamentable shortfall that will hopefully be overcome soon through the cooperative work of many."[67]

With this "dearth" (Geesink) and "lamentable shortfall" (Bavinck),[68] why did Bavinck not publish his *Reformed Ethics*? Possibly because he was reluctant to give an impression of upstaging his Vrije Universiteit colleague Geesink, who was responsible for teaching ethics in the faculty Bavinck had just joined. If so, Bavinck's situation would have been comparable to the position in which Abraham Kuyper found himself with respect to dogmatics. Kuyper gave up on a plan to write a Reformed dogmatics after he completed his three-volume *Encyclopedia of Sacred Theology* in 1894 when he heard

---

subsections on terminology, the history of Reformed ethics, and the foundations of Reformed ethics); (2) the untitled first part, divided into (a) doctrine of sin, (b) the origin of spiritual life, (c) its development, (d) its consummation, (e) its resources, (f) its blessing, and (g) its norm; and (3) the second part, entitled "Revelation of That [Spiritual] Life in the World" and divided into (a) in the family (here Bavinck plans to speak of marriage; monogamy; the single state; second marriage; adultery; celibacy; divorce; the duties, aim, and blessing of marriage; parents and children; upbringing; education; brothers and sisters; shaping of character; servants; family friends; and friendship), (b) in vocation, (c) in society, (d) in the state, (e) in the church, and finally (f) a section on the kingdom of God.

66. Geesink, *De ethiek in de gereformeerde theologie*, 6: "Deze armoede van onzen tijd aan specifiek Gereformeerde ethische studie."

67. Bavinck, *Hedendaagsche moraal*, 7.

68. DO: *armoede, jammerlijk tekort.*

that Bavinck was working on such a project.[69] Geesink did in fact write a Reformed ethics, but it was prepared for publication by Valentijn Hepp and published posthumously in 1931.[70] Or did Bavinck have another reason for not publishing his *Reformed Ethics*?

Perhaps another manuscript gives a clue here.

THE DE JONG MANUSCRIPT ON REFORMED ETHICS

The Bavinck Archives also contain another handwritten manuscript with the title "Reformed Ethics of Prof. Bavinck."[71] Like the van der Veen and Lindeboom manuscripts, the de Jong manuscript is composed of lecture notes. The manuscript's author is Jelle Michiels de Jong (1874–1927), who began studying theology at Kampen in September 1901. In 1903 de Jong followed Bavinck to Amsterdam to continue his studies at the Free University.[72] Subsequently, he worked as a minister in the small Frisian villages of Foudgum (1906), Wons (1913), and Duurswoude (1918–24).[73] De Jong signed the title page of the manuscript and dated it "November 1902"—a few weeks before Bavinck moved from Kampen to the Free University on December 16, 1902.[74] De Jong's date explains why the manuscript is incomplete: Bavinck no longer gave lectures in ethics at Kampen after November 1902. Just like the van der Veen and Lindeboom manuscripts, the de Jong manuscript often gives the impression that the text comes from Bavinck himself. We even find a sentence with the verb in the first person singular.[75]

The de Jong manuscript, of 331 pages, begins with a general introduction about terminology, definitions of key terms like "habit," "usage," "custom,"

69. Kuyper, *Encyclopaedie der heilige godgeleerdheid*; see Stellingwerff, "Over de bibliotheek en de boeken van dr. A. Kuyper." Kuyper's lectures on dogmatics to his Vrije Universiteit students between 1880 and 1902 did get *unofficially* published in a number of five-volume editions as *Dictaten dogmatiek*.

70. Geesink, *Gereformeerde ethiek*.

71. De Jong, "Gereformeerde ethiek van Profess. Dr. H. Bavinck," hereafter abbreviated as *GE-De Jong*. The Library of the Protestant Theological University at Kampen preserves a handwritten duplicate of the *GE-De Jong* manuscript (shelf mark 187D15). This anonymous duplicate once belonged to G. C. Berkouwer, longtime professor of dogmatics at the Vrije Universiteit. He received the manuscript as a gift on the occasion of his inaugural address on October 11, 1940.

72. Van Gelderen and Rozemond, *Gegevens betreffende de Theologische Universiteit Kampen*, 122.

73. *Gemeenten en predikanten*, 316; see also van der Meulen, "Ds J. M. de Jong."

74. Van Gelderen and Rozemond, *Gegevens betreffende de Theologische Universiteit Kampen*, 32.

75. *GE-De Jong*, 26.

and "morality," along with key differences between them.[76] As in the other manuscripts, Bavinck prefers to use the term "ethics" to describe this discipline rather than "morality" or the German *Sittenlehre*.[77] The task of ethics is "to let us see and know the principle and the system of morality."[78] After this general introduction the manuscript is divided into two parts: philosophical ethics (pp. 18–139) and theological ethics (pp. 139–331). This order is something of a surprise considering what we noted earlier about Bavinck's understanding of the relation between ethics and dogmatics along with his comments about the method of both disciplines. Bavinck stated the relation thus:

> In dogmatics we are concerned with what God does for us and in us. In dogmatics God is everything. Dogmatics is a word from God to us, coming from outside of us, from above us; we are passive, listening, and opening ourselves to being directed by God. In ethics, we are interested in the question of what it is that God now expects of us when he does his work in us. What do we do for him? Here we are active, precisely because of and on the grounds of God's deeds in us; we sing psalms in thanks and praise to God.[79]

The key point here is that the *method* of both disciplines must be identical. The point of departure is God's revelation; Holy Scripture is the principle of knowledge and the norm for ethics.[80] But now, Bavinck turns to philosophy!

Bavinck begins by raising the classic questions: "What is good?" and "Why is it good?"[81] In Bavinck's view ethics is grounded in philosophy; thus, "someone's philosophical ethics," he writes, "will be in accordance with the principles of his philosophy."[82] Bavinck proceeds as usual with an outline of the history of philosophical ethics, opting for a systematic approach.[83] He describes and analyzes six philosophical systems that seek the principle and the norm for ethics in humanity itself.[84] This survey is followed by an analysis of nine

76. DO: *gewoonte, gebruik, zede, zedelijkheid*; GE-De Jong, 1–12; cf. 153.

77. GE-De Jong, 12–17.

78. DO: "Ethiek heeft dus tot taak om ons te doen zien en kennen: Het Principe in de eerste plaats en het systeem van het zedelijke in de tweede plaats" (*GE-De Jong*, 17).

79. RE, §2; cf. GE-Lindeboom, 14–15.

80. DO: *kenbron, norma*. This results, as we have seen, in a threefold methodology: (1) collecting and systematizing biblical data, (2) describing how these data have been adopted in the church, and (3) developing these data normatively or thetically with a view to our own time (*RE*, §4).

81. GE-De Jong, 24.

82. GE-De Jong, 23, 142.

83. GE-De Jong, 25–26.

84. They are (1) the rational ethics of classical Greek philosophy; (2) the ethics of a special moral faculty, a *semen virtutis* or moral sense (Ralph Cudworth, Henry More, Shaftesbury, Francis Hutcheson); (3) the ethics of moral sentiment (Adam Smith); (4) the ethics of aesthetic

philosophical systems which seek the principle and the norm for ethics outside of humanity.[85] Finally, Bavinck discusses what he terms "the despair of
all morality or pessimism" (Eduard von Hartmann, Arthur Schopenhauer).[86]

For the most part these descriptions are stated in a neutral and instruc-
tional style, and Bavinck withholds his own judgments, making comments
only a few times. At the end of the section on classical Greek philosophy,
for instance, Bavinck observes that many Scholastic theologians adopted
Aristotelian thought in their ethics. According to Bavinck, "in itself there
is no great objection to this."[87] "We can profit," continues Bavinck, "from
Aristotelian thought, and without doubt, in its essentials, Aristotle's *Ethics* is the best philosophical ethics available" because of its "agreement
with Christian ethics that human morality involves developing all the gifts
and powers given to us in harmonious agreement with our moral nature."
Aristotle's "only error was to think that human beings could achieve this
ideal in their own strength."[88] Bavinck is very critical of the ethics of evolutionism and severely opposes the theories of Darwin repeatedly.[89] Present-
day readers will find it striking that Bavinck hardly pays any attention to
Nietzsche. Bavinck occasionally mentions his name,[90] but compared with
other philosophers the treatment of Nietzsche seems inadequate. This is
understandable, however, when we realize that around 1900 Nietzsche was
not well-known in the Netherlands.[91]

---

formalism (Johann Friedrich Herbart); (5) the ethics of practical reason (Immanuel Kant); and
(6) the ethics of intuitive cognition (Thomas Reid); *GE-De Jong*, 26–64.

85. They are (1) in God; (2) in nature (Heraclitus, the Stoa, Tolstoy); (3) in the government
(Thomas Hobbes); (4) hedonism (Aristippus); (5) eudaemonism (Democritus, Epicurus, Lu-
cretius); (6) the ethics of self-improvement (*zelfvolmaking*, Spinoza); (7) utilitarianism (Jeremy
Bentham, John Stuart Mill); (8) the ethics of evolutionism (Charles Darwin, Herbert Spencer);
and (9) positivism (Auguste Comte); *GE-De Jong*, 64–128.

86. *GE-De Jong*, 129–38.

87. DO: "Op zichzelf is hiertegen niet zoo groot bezwaar" (*GE-De Jong*, 36).

88. DO: "Ook met de gedachten van Aristoteles kunnen we onze winst doen en zonder
twijfel is de Ethiek van Aristoteles de beste philosophische ethiek in hoodzaak; Want wat is het
schone er in? Dat hij met de Christenen hierin overeenstemt dat de mensch in het zedelijke al
de hem geschonken gaven en krachten harmonisch ontwikkelen moet in overeenstemming met
zijne zedelijke natuur. Hij dwaalt alleen daarin dat dat ideaal voor den mensch in eigen kracht
bereikbaar zou zijn"; *GE-De Jong*, 36.

89. See, for example, *GE-De Jong*, 18, 161, 166, 174, 205, 281, 291–92. In his other writings Bavinck sharply and frequently criticizes Darwin: see *RD*, 2:83, 511–20, 525–26, 535–37;
Bavinck, "Evolution"; cf. de Wit, "Beeld van gorilla."

90. See *GE-De Jong*, 24, 136–38, 176, 251, 267; there is also a paucity of references to
Nietzsche in the *Reformed Dogmatics*: *RD*, 1:118; 2:44, 89, 210, 526; 3:59, 238, 531; 4:258, 647.

91. To the best of our knowledge, Abraham Kuyper introduced Nietzsche's philosophy in
the Netherlands in his 1892 rectorial address entitled *De verflauwing der grenzen*; ET: "Blurring of the Boundaries."

The second part of the de Jong manuscript is devoted to theological ethics. Two sections can be distinguished. On pages 139–60 we find a short outline of Bavinck's theological ethics. It is possible that Bavinck began his 1901–2 lectures on ethics in September 1901 with philosophical ethics.[92] Producing these lectures took so much time that Bavinck could not offer his students an elaborated theological ethics before the summer of 1902. For that reason, he confined himself to an outline.

Bavinck begins his outline with an introduction to the following topics: related terminology; the inadequacy of philosophical ethics (i.e., theoretically speaking philosophical ethics cannot find a norm for morality, and practically speaking it cannot overcome human selfishness); the relationship between dogmatics and ethics; and the history and organization of theological ethics.[93] After the introduction Bavinck divides his theological ethics into three chapters: (1) "The Doctrine of the Moral Subject," which is then divided into twelve sections;[94] (2) "The Doctrine of the Law," which has four sections covering broad topics related to law that are followed by ten sections, one devoted to each of the Ten Commandments;[95] and (3) "The Purpose of Morality," with nine sections.[96]

92. Other evidence, however, suggests that Bavinck taught theological ethics during the academic year 1901–2 and again in 1902–3; see *Handelingen der twee-en-zestigste vergadering*, 26, and cf. *Almanak van het studentencorps 1903*, 37. During the year 1900–1901 Bavinck would have taught "Survey of the History of Ethics" ("Overzicht van de geschiedenis der ethiek"), which could be interpreted as philosophical ethics; see *Handelingen der een-en-zestigste vergadering*, 35, and cf. *Almanak van het studentencorps 1902*, 33. Perhaps de Jong attended Bavinck's lectures in ethics one year before he officially started his theological studies.

93. GE-*De Jong*, 139–45.

94. DO: "Deel A: Leer van het zedelijk subject." The sections are §1: humanity as image of God ("De mensch als beeld Gods"); §2: disruption of the image of God by humans ("Verstoring van het beeld Gods door de mensch"); §3: humans as moral creatures in the situation of sin ("De mensch als zedelijk wezen in de toestand der zonde"); §4: the content of human morality ("De inhoud van het zedelijke in de mensch"); §5: human moral qualities (doctrine of virtue) ("De zedelijke kwaliteiten van de mensch [leer van de deugd]"); §6: human moral activity ("De zedelijke handelingen van de mensch"); §7: inadequacy of natural morality ("Ongenoegzaamheid der natuurlijke moraal"); §8: special grace ("Bijzondere genade"); §9: the spiritual life ("'t Geestelijk leven"); §10: growth in the spiritual life ("Ontwikkeling van het geestelijk leven"); §11: connecting spiritual life and moral life ("Geestelijk leven in verband met het zedelijk leven"); and §12: special gifts ("Bijzondere gaven"); GE-*De Jong*, 145.

95. DO: "Deel B: Leer van de wet." The four general sections are §13: the law as a rule of gratitude ("De wet als regel der dankbaarheid"); §14: the nature of the (moral) law ("De natuur der [zede]wet"); §15: division of the law ("Verdeeling der wet"); and §16: breaking the law ("Overtreding der wet"). Sections 17–26 comprise the ten sections on the Commandments.

96. DO: "Deel C: Het doel van het zedelijke." The nine sections are §27: the purpose of morality ("Doel der zedelijkheid"); §28: the glory of God ("De eere Gods"); §29: the purpose of the moral good for individual persons ("Doel van het zedelijk goede van den enkelen mensch"); §30: the moral good of families ("'t Zedelijk goede van de familiën"); §31: the moral good in

From this we can discern both similarities and differences between the de Jong manuscript and Bavinck's *Reformed Ethics* manuscript. Both manuscripts begin with humanity created in the image of God and conclude with the kingdom of God. Furthermore, themes and contents of many sections are duplicated. But there are also noteworthy differences.

In the first place, the titles of the main parts differ. In the *Reformed Ethics* manuscript we have the dogmatic- and schematic-sounding "Humanity before Conversion," "Converted Humanity," and "Humanity after Conversion." In the de Jong manuscript, we find the more philosophical-sounding "The Doctrine of the Moral Subject," "The Doctrine of Law," and "The Purpose of Morality." In the second place, the first and the second parts of the *Reformed Ethics* manuscript have been fused together into the first chapter of the de Jong manuscript. In the third place, the third and the fourth parts of the *Reformed Ethics* manuscript have become the second and the third chapters of the de Jong manuscript. As a result, the composition of the de Jong manuscript corresponds roughly with the composition Bavinck sketched in the introduction of his *Reformed Ethics* manuscript. Finally, the doctrine of sin in the first part of the *Reformed Ethics* manuscript has been moved to the second chapter of the de Jong manuscript. Page 161 of the de Jong manuscript restarts its numbering at chapter 1, section 1: "Humanity as the Image of God."[97] Detailed sections follow on human vocation, fallen humanity, the organizing principle and classification of sins, stages and development of sin, and the image of God in fallen humanity. All of these are recognizable from Bavinck's *Reformed Ethics* and from the student notes of those lectures. From this it seems safe to conclude that Bavinck had decided to deliver his lectures on theological ethics once more after the summer of 1902.[98] Thus, the placement of the doctrine of sin in chapter 2 of the de Jong manuscript is striking, for Bavinck discusses sin again in the first part of his *Reformed*

society ("'t Zedelijk goede in de maatschappij"); §32: the moral good in the sphere of social interaction ("'t Zedelijk goede in den kring van het gezellig leven"); §33: the state ("De staat"); §34: the church from a moral perspective ("De kerk uit zedelijk standpunt"); and §35: the kingdom of God ("Het rijk Gods"). In §32, the Dutch word *gezellig* is notoriously difficult to translate; it suggests settings and social interactions that are "enjoyable," "pleasant," "convivial," "entertaining," and, applied to homes, "cozy." In view is the informal social life of human beings rather than formal or "official" interactions.

97. *GE-De Jong*, 161–80.

98. This conclusion is also warranted by information provided in the minutes of the Directors of the Theological School in Kampen concerning a course to be taught by Bavinck: "In the school year 1902/03, DV, Prof. Dr. H. Bavinck will cover [among others] Ethics: the doctrine of humanity's moral nature in the situation of sin" ("Door Prof. Dr. H. Bavinck [zal D.V. in den cursus 1902/03 behandeld worden]: [. . .] Ethiek: De leer van de zedelijke natuur des menschen in den toestand der zonde"); see *Handelingen der twee-en-zestigste vergadering*, 26.

Ethics. This repetition may be explained as Bavinck—realizing that his forth-coming transfer to Amsterdam was taking more time than he liked—reusing his *Reformed Ethics* manuscript in the autumn of the year 1902.

HERMAN BAVINCK, REFORMED ETHICS, AND PHILOSOPHICAL ETHICS

During his long career, Herman Bavinck was interested not only in dogmatics but also in ethics.[99] This is evident from Bavinck's other writings. Bavinck obtained his doctorate in 1880 at the University of Leiden with a dissertation on the ethics of Ulrich Zwingli.[100] One year later he published two articles on the human conscience.[101] In 1885–86 Bavinck wrote a series of three articles on the imitation of Christ.[102] He revisited this topic in 1918 and published it as *The Imitation of Christ and Life in the Modern World*.[103] We have already referred to his 1902 lecture/booklet *Morality Today*. We could also note Bavinck's speech "Ethics and Politics," which he delivered at a meeting of the Dutch Royal Academy of Science in 1915.[104] And finally, we need to mention his writing on the question of war during World War I.[105]

We have also shown that Bavinck lectured extensively and repeatedly on ethics during his professorate at Kampen and that the parallels in method and contrasts in content of the *Reformed Dogmatics* and the *Reformed Ethics* indicate that Bavinck was working simultaneously on both projects and that he intended the latter to be a companion to the former. Comparison of the *Reformed Ethics* manuscript with the van der Veen and Lindeboom manuscripts shows that Bavinck, at least in 1884–86 and 1894–95, delivered his lectures on ethics from his *Reformed Ethics* manuscript. And, it is important to note, comparison of the *Reformed Ethics* manuscript with the de Jong manuscript reveals that Bavinck struggled with the composition of his ethics. In the introduction of *Reformed Ethics* he opts for a traditional composition in three parts. The subsequent, detailed elaboration, however, consists of four parts. The de Jong manuscript shows how Bavinck returned to a composition in three parts but bade farewell to the scheme "Humanity before Conversion," "Converted Humanity," and "Humanity after Conversion." Perhaps he became dissatisfied with its dogmatic simplicity. The biggest

99. Cf. Bolt, "Christ and the Law."
100. Bavinck, *De ethiek van Ulrich Zwingli*.
101. Bavinck, "Het geweten."
102. Bavinck, "De navolging van Christus."
103. Bavinck, *De navolging van Christus en het moderne leven*.
104. Bavinck, "Religion and Politics."
105. See van Keulen, "Bavinck and the War Question."

xlii	Introduction to Herman Bavinck's Reformed Ethics

difference between Bavinck's *Reformed Ethics* manuscript and the de Jong manuscript is the place of philosophical ethics. In *Reformed Ethics* (and in the van der Veen and Lindeboom manuscripts) Bavinck pays hardly any attention to philosophical ethics. In the de Jong manuscript, however, the whole first part is devoted to it.

We should not conclude from this difference that Bavinck taught philosophical ethics for the first time in the academic year 1901–2. In an earlier section of this essay ("A Brief Overview of Book IV") we referred to another unpublished manuscript, *Ethiek*, which probably dates from the 1880s (or possibly from the 1890s).[106] In this document Bavinck discusses philosophical ethics in general, gives a brief outline of its history, and surveys contemporary views of it.[107] Compared with the de Jong manuscript, the outline in "Ethics" is somewhat simplified, although Bavinck voices critiques more explicitly. The "Ethics" manuscript also shows that Bavinck paid attention to philosophical ethics in his lectures on ethics earlier than the academic year 1901–2. Possibly he taught ethics in a biennial program in which philosophical ethics alternated with theological ethics.

In the Bavinck Archives we find another manuscript, though a relatively small one, that probably dates back to Bavinck's last years at Kampen.[108] After an introduction the manuscript is divided into two parts: (1) philosophical ethics and (2) Reformed ethics. The first philosophical sections are briefly worked out. Compared with the de Jong manuscript, almost all the section titles are the same. The only changes in the philosophical part are two added sections, one on "Buddhism" and another on "Anarchism." It is likely that Bavinck delivered his 1901–2 lectures in ethics with this smaller manuscript in front of him.

When we compare all these manuscripts, it becomes evident that Bavinck's interest in philosophy increased during his years at Kampen.[109] At minimum we must conclude that by 1902, philosophy had become a serious discussion partner for Bavinck. It seems that Bavinck had become convinced that Reformed ethics could no longer afford to neglect philosophy. We see this in his 1902 lecture/booklet *Morality Today* and in his 1915 speech "Ethics and Politics."

106. Bavinck, *Ethiek*, Bavinck Archives, no. 197.
107. The brief outline of the history of philosophical ethics is divided into three sections: (1) Greek philosophy; (2) newer times (Descartes, Hobbes, Spinoza); and (3) newest philosophy: criticism and speculation (Kant, Fichte, Hegel, Schleiermacher). Furthermore, Bavinck discusses five "contemporary views of philosophical ethics"—namely, independent morality, positivism, utilitarianism, evolution theory, and pessimism.
108. Bavinck, "Gereformeerde Ethiek," Bavinck Archives, no. 61.
109. For an overview of Bavinck's attitude toward philosophy, see Veenhof, "De God van de filosofen."

Philosophical engagement has an important place in both publications. At the same time we see a diminishing number of references to the writings of sixteenth- through eighteenth-century Protestant theologians. Frequent references to Protestant "fathers" in the *Reformed Ethics* manuscript (and in the van der Veen and Lindeboom manuscripts) have become rare in the de Jong manuscript. These differences between the *Reformed Ethics* and the de Jong manuscript may also explain why Bavinck did not publish the former: he was no longer satisfied with it. Its composition had to be changed, with likely more philosophical input. This is of course conjecture; we do not know beyond any reasonable doubt. Nonetheless, we believe it is a reasonable conjecture.

A final word concerning a conventional portrait in Bavinck scholarship about the last decade of his life at the Vrije Universiteit. It has frequently been alleged that during his years at Amsterdam, after the second edition of his *Reformed Dogmatics* had been published (1911), Bavinck lost interest in dogmatics and instead turned to questions in culture, philosophy, psychology, and pedagogy. While there is indeed a shift in Bavinck's published work during these years along the general lines just sketched, the claim is vastly overstated and was corrected some years ago by George Harinck, Kees van der Kooi, and Jasper Vree when they published Bavinck's notes on an ecclesiastical conflict in the Gereformeerde Kerken Nederland (GKN) surrounding the controversial views of a certain Rev. J. B. Netelenbos.[110] The notes show that Bavinck did not lose his interest in dogmatics but was actively engaged in important questions before the synod of the GKN. And, on the other side of the coin, the ethical manuscripts in the Bavinck Archives that we have examined in this essay clearly show that Bavinck was already interested in philosophy and culture during his time at Kampen. We agree, therefore, with Jan Veenhof's proposition that we should not exaggerate the distance between Bavinck's first (Kampen) and second (Amsterdam) periods and that we should not interpret the differences between the two periods as a disjunction, creating "two Bavincks."[111]

---

110. Harinck et al., *"Als Bavinck nu maar eens kleur bekende."*
111. Veenhof, *Revelatie en inspiratie*, 101; cf. Harinck, "Eén uur lang is het hier brandend en licht geweest."

Introduction

We will develop our concept or idea of Christian ethics from the ground up, from the actual history of the church's practice and reflection. Christianity entered the Greco-Roman world, where philosophers of various schools provided answers to questions about individual morality and common life in society. Christians became known for their high moral conduct and wrote about such ethical matters as patience, prayer, penance, chastity, celibacy, and marriage. When the church became more established in the world, the world also entered the church and brought forth an ascetic and monastic response. The church developed its moral teachings as part of its practice of discipline and penance. Moralism and legalism were real dangers.

Through the work of Peter Lombard, Albert the Great, and especially Thomas Aquinas, medieval theology produced an impressive virtue ethics, including the three theological virtues of faith, hope, and love and the four cardinal virtues of prudence, justice, fortitude, and temperance. Bonaventure is the foremost representative of a more contemplative and spiritual approach to the Christian life, but this gave way to the speculative mysticism developed by Meister Eckhardt, Johannes Tauler, Jan van Ruysbroeck, Thomas à Kempis, and the Theologia Germanica.

The Reformation separated Christian or theological ethics from philosophical ethics, using the law of the Ten Commandments as the basis for the former, and often structuring the latter with the help of Aristotle's Nicomachean Ethics. Calvin integrated a biblical ethics into his dogmatics, and many Reformed thinkers followed suit. Some sought to give guidance for the spiritual lives of Christians by developing casuistry—judging and deciding moral matters in specific instances or cases. Reformed thinkers, however, were more inclined to writing works of "practical theology" or "spiritual theology," along with works in "ascetic theology" that spell out *required duties and practices. In particular, ascetic theology directs us to the means by which piety is exercised, especially prayer, fasting, vigil, and so forth.*

Since 1750 the discipline of ethics can be characterized by the equivalent terms of eudaemonistic, utilitarian, and rationalistic. In various ways the moral life became a matter of self-determination, with the spirit of human subjects in one way or another overcoming the limitations of nature and matter. The distinction between religion and morality, the church and the world, disappears.

The term "ethics" comes from Greek words that signify accustomed places, habits, and manners. The word "morality" has Latin roots and points to the customary manner of people's lives in community. Since a normative understanding of the Christian life must be more than custom or the perceived practice of a society, we understand "ethics" to be the more scientific and normative designation of what is and what ought to be. Ethics probes deeply and reaches high to the idea of the Good, the essence of what is truly human. Morality must be free and not coerced and lead to the flourishing of what is essentially and truly human.

Ethics is "the art of fruitful, godly living and dying well, to God's glory." Our moral life must not be identified with our religious life of fellowship with God, but it must also never be separated from it. Each must become manifest in the other: what we do must give evidence of who we are. Ethics concerns itself with how we use our natural, created gifts, how we receive the gospel of grace and are regenerated, and how our lives, remaining subject to sickness, temptation, and struggle, can be directed to God's law.

Our ethics proceeds from God and is through God and for God. It is this relation to and dependence upon Holy Scripture that distinguishes theological ethics from philosophical ethics. The method of theological ethics is identical to that of dogmatic theology: we gather material from Scripture and arrange what it says about sins, regeneration, sanctification, and the like; we examine carefully the way the Christian church in its history has handled this material; we develop this further and apply it to our own day. Because ethics deals with the course of the Christian life, its content can be divided into the human condition before conversion (natural ethics), regenerated humanity (practical theology), and the life of regenerated humanity in a variety of social spheres.

§1. HISTORICAL OVERVIEW OF CHRISTIAN ETHICS[1]

We begin with the history of Christian ethics so that we will be able to see the idea of ethics arising and growing in the Christian church, and then,

1. Ed. note: Bavinck originally wrote "*naam en begrip*" (lit., "name and idea"; i.e., "terminology") but struck this through so as to start with "Historical Overview of Christian Ethics." He

on the basis of history, establish our concept of Christian ethics. The idea of ethics arose among the Greeks, who divided philosophy into dialectics (principles of thought, logic), physics (principles about the being of things), and ethics (principles about the actualizing of laws of reason and morality, concerning what is good in human conduct). Socrates was the father of ethics and sought its foundation in reason and knowledge. Plato deepened this and called virtue the harmony or health of the soul. Aristotle provided a practically useful, measured morality that was satisfying in practice and found its basis in the will. The Stoics placed the foundation of ethics in disposition, the Epicureans in desire, and the followers of Plotinus in contemplation. Morality deepened and strengthened to the degree that life became worse. These philosophical ethics were characterized by intellectualism. Among the common folk, ethics was joined with politics. Ethics was always political, civil justice[2] or moral customs that became law. Piety is temperance, moderation, and sound judgment;[3] morality is righteousness or justice,[4] a matter of acknowledging the rights of others, giving to each person what is due to them.[5]

Antiquity

Christianity arose in the world of a thoroughly depraved antiquity.[6] In its earliest days, people noted the distinctive lives of Christians and described their conduct and their motives for obeying characteristic Christian commandments and admonitions. Christians lived as their Lord had while hoping for the future return of Christ.[7]

---

thus intentionally reversed the order he used in the *Gereformeerde Dogmatiek*, where *"naam en begrip"* comes first (*RD*, 1, chap. 1) and is followed by the history of dogma (chaps. 3–6).

2. LO: *justitia civilis*.

3. GrO: σωφροσύνη.

4. GrO: δικαιοσύνη.

5. LO: *suum cuique*. Ed. note: The term comes from Aristotle; see *Rhetoric* 1366B: "Justice is the virtue through which everybody enjoys his own possessions in accordance with the law; its opposite is injustice, through which men enjoy the possessions of others in defiance of the law" (Aristotle, *Rhetoric* [trans. Roberts and Bywater]).

6. Ed. note: For literature about the history of Christian ethics, see the historical sections of works of the following authors in the bibliography: W. M. L. de Wette, F. Schleiermacher, A. Wuttke, A. Neander, H. J. Bestmann (part 1, pagan and biblical ethics), E. von Hartmann (*Phänomenologie des sittlichen Bewusstseins*), W. Gass, C. E. Luthardt ("Die christliche Ethik," in Zöckler, *Handbuch der theologischen Wissenschaften*), J. T. Beck (*Vorlesungen*, 1:1–75), F. J. Winter (*Die Ethik des Clemens von Alexandrien*), J. G. Walch, and the literature that follows in the notes. The order in the preceding list is Bavinck's.

7. Ed. note: Bavinck develops his own understanding of the heart of Christian ethics from the early church's emphasis on the imitation of Christ; see chap. 9, §21.

The first Christian ethicist was Clement of Alexandria, followed by Origen, who became ascetically spiritualistic. The West remained more practical and reserved as its morality became more tied to the church. In particular, Tertullian wrote about ethical subjects such as patience, prayer, penance, chastity, and monogamy.[8] For him ethics is above all teaching about virtues. With Constantine the world pushed into the church, and monasticism along with asceticism rose in opposition. Representatives of this ascetic spirit include Athanasius, Basil the Great's *Ascetica*,[9] Gregory of Nyssa, and others. Monks were considered the true "philosophers." "Desensualization became morality."[10]

The Western church was more practical, but morality became more legalistic. Lists of good works such as prayer, fasting, almsgiving, and pilgrimages arose, and a distinction was made between mortal and venial sins. The kingdom of God was identified with the church, while the earthly realm was not acknowledged and valued in its own right. This was true even for Augustine, whose influential ethical works include *On the Morals of the Catholic Church*,[11] *Concerning the Nature of Good*,[12] and *Enchiridion*.[13]

Ecclesiastical morality amounted to this: evil is forbidden, the good is commanded, that which is "in-between"[14] is free, and the perfect is recommended. Precepts were distinguished from counsels, and lower virtues from higher virtues. This distinction was paired with the doctrine of penance: the church forgives and imposes penance. This gave rise to "penitential books" (Theodore,[15] Bede,[16] etc.): lists of tariffs for sins. Casuistry, developed first

8. Ed. note: Tertullian, *Of Patience* (ANF 3:707–14); *On Prayer* (ANF 3:681–92); *On Repentance* (ANF 3:657–79); *On Exhortation to Chastity* (ANF 4:50–58); *On Monogamy* (ANF 4:59–73).

9. Ed. note: Bavinck simply inserted the Greek term ἠθικά in the text. According to Quasten (*Patrologia*, 3:211), "*Ascetica* is the title of a group of thirteen writings attributed to Basil." The best-known of these is *Moralia* (Τὰ ἠθικά), "a collection of eighty rules or moral instructions (*regulae*), each of them supported by quotations from the New Testament."

10. GO: "Entsinnlichung werd Sittlichkeit." Ed. note: Bavinck does not provide a reference for this phrase, but he may have obtained it from Luthardt, *Geschichte der christlichen Ethik*, 1:6, 16–18.

11. *De moribus ecclesiae et catholicae* (ET: *On the Morals of the Catholic Church*; NPNF¹ 4:41–63). Bavinck mentions only *De moribus ecclesiae* here, though this work is usually accompanied by another written in the same year (AD 388), *De moribus Manichaeorum* (*On the Morals of the Manichaeans*; NPNF¹ 4:69–89).

12. *De natura boni* (ET: *Concerning the Nature of Good, Against the Manichaeans*; NPNF¹ 4:351–65).

13. *Enchiridion de fide, spe et caritate* (ET: *The Enchiridion*; NPNF¹ 3:237–66).

14. GrO: διάφορος.

15. Ed. note: This is a reference to Theodore of Tarsus (602–90), archbishop of Canterbury from 668 to 690. See Charles-Edwards and Lapidge, *Penitential of Theodore*.

16. Ed. note: This is a reference to the English monk the Venerable Bede (672–735), best known for his *Ecclesiastical History of the English People*. Though a penitential book was

by Raymund in the thirteenth century,[17] was a pragmatic way to investigate whether or not something was a sin, the extent of the sin, and the price of the penance. In this way the boundary between good and evil was blurred; casuistry led to probabilism,[18] which was perfected by the Jesuits and opposed by Pascal in his *Provincial Letters*. The collections of the moral teachings of the church fathers[19] by the Venerable Bede, Isidore of Seville, and John of Damascus, along with Alcuin's *Of Virtues and Vices*,[20] provided a bridge to Scholasticism.[21]

Middle Ages

In the prior era, a systematic treatment of ethics was still lacking. People started with a collation of moral proverbs after the example of the pagan philosophers; gospel became law. The Scholastics, however, began a systematic treatment of ethical ideas. Peter Lombard (d. 1164) provided the example by starting with the virtues, then sins, followed by the theological virtues (faith, hope, and love), then the cardinal virtues (justice, courage, prudence, and temperance), and finally the seven gifts of the Holy Spirit (according to the Vulgate of Isa. 11:2–3): wisdom, understanding, counsel, power, knowledge, fear of the Lord, and delight in the fear of the Lord. This structure was essentially retained by Alexander of Hales (ca. 1186–1245), Albert the Great (d. 1280), and by the greatest ethicist of them all, Thomas Aquinas (1225–74). Thomas considers ethics in the First and Second Parts

attributed to him, many historians since Bavinck dispute this. See Laistner, "Was Bede the Author of a Penitential?"; cf. Frantzen, "Englishness of Bede."

17. Ed. note: This is a reference to Raymund of Penyafort (1175–1275), a Catalan Dominican friar who compiled the Decretals of Gregory IX, a major component of Roman Catholic Canon Law. Bavinck cites as his source Zöckler, *Handbuch der theologischen Wissenschaften*, 3:484. Zöckler is likely also the source of Bavinck's references to Theodore and Bede.

18. Ed. note: "Probabilism" is a term used in moral philosophy to refer to the view that when a matter of conscience is difficult, one only has to satisfy the criterion that a choice is probable even if the opposite is more probable. The doctrine was defended by sixteenth- and seventeenth-century Jesuits such as Luis Molina (1528–81) and severely criticized by Blaise Pascal, in his *Provincial Letters*, as promoting moral laxity.

19. *Scintillae patrum.*

20. *De virtutibus et vitiis liber ad Widonem Comitem* (PL 101:613–38D).

21. Ed. note: Bavinck listed the Venerable Bede (672/673–735) only as the author of a *Scintillae patrum* and linked Alcuin (ca. 740–804) with Isidore of Seville (ca. 560–636) and John of Damascus (ca. 650–ca. 750). Koch brings this group together in his *Handbook of Moral Theology*, 1:51: "The ecclesiastical writers of the early Middle Ages contented themselves with gathering up the moral teachings of the Fathers, expounding and adapting them to practical use by means of encyclopedic collections known as *Libri Sententiarum*, *Scintillae Patrum*, or *Sacra Parallela*. It is sufficient to mention St. Isidore of Seville, St. John of Damascus, St. Bede, St. Peter Damian, and Alcuin."

of the Second Part of his *Summa theologiae*. In the First Part he discusses the virtues in general (Ia IIae qq. 49–89), the affections and passions (qq. 21–48), freedom (qq. 8–18), law (qq. 90–108), and grace (qq. 109–13).[22] In the Second Part he deals with the specific[23] three theological virtues of faith, hope, and love (IIa IIae qq. 1–46), followed by the four cardinal virtues of prudence, justice, fortitude, and temperance (qq. 47–170). This is in substance a virtue ethic.

Mysticism reacted against the scholastic method. Its representatives included Bernard of Clairvaux (1090–1153), Richard of St. Victor (d. 1173), and Bonaventure (ca. 1217–74), all of whom combined contemplative and ascetic elements in the direction they took mysticism, especially in the speculative mysticism developed by Meister Eckhardt (ca. 1260–ca. 1328). Other important figures include Johannes Tauler (d. 1361), Jan van Ruysbroeck (1293–1381), Thomas à Kempis (ca. 1380–1471), and the *German Theology*.[24]

The Reformation

The Reformation introduced another basis for morality. Works were separated from grace, faith became the principle of virtue, and Scripture was considered the only source of moral knowledge. As a result, philosophical ethics was taken to be essentially different from Christian ethics, which acquired its own basis, content, and purpose.

The Reformers did not treat ethics as a separate discipline, but they did set forth ethical principles.[25] Melanchthon treated ethics in his *Commonplaces*,[26] where he gives an exposition of the Ten Commandments and also covers ethical subjects such as natural law, good works, penance, and prayer. For a considerable time this structure governed the foundation of theological ethics. Melanchthon also composed philosophical ethics in his commentary on

22. Ed. note: It is clear from the order of the list in this sentence and in the next that Bavinck is providing a topical summary rather than an analytic summary of *ST* Ia IIae and IIa IIae; the specific references in the parentheses have been added by the editor.

23. LO: *in specie*.

24. Ed. note: Bavinck adds "German theology" ("Duitsche Theologie") as the concluding item after a list of three names. The context, however, suggests that this may be a reference to the anonymous medieval German spiritual treatise published by Martin Luther in 1516 and 1518 and given the simple title *Deutsch Theologia*. Or it could simply be a general reference to the German tradition of spirituality. For a contemporary English translation see Luther, *Theologia Germanica*.

25. On Luther, see Luthardt, *Die Ethik Luthers*; on Calvin, see Lobstein, *Die Ethik Calvins*; on Zwingli, see Bavinck, *De ethiek van Ulrich Zwingli*.

26. *Loci Communes*.

Aristotle's *Nicomachean Ethics*[27] and his 1538 *Book of Moral Philosophy*.[28] As a result, philosophical and theological ethics were not clearly distinguished from each other. Georg Calixt (1586–1656) was the first to properly separate them in his 1634 *Abridgement of Moral Theology*.[29] Johann Conrad Dürr (1625–77), in his *Handbook of Moral Theology*,[30] constructed the first ethical system in the Lutheran Church. Other Lutheran ethicists include Johann Adam Osiander (1657–1724), Gebhardt Theodor Meier (1633–93), Johann Wilhelm Baier (1647–95), and Johann Franz Buddeus (1667–1729).[31] Casuistry was treated by Balduin,[32] Olearius, Dannhauer, König, and Dedekenn.[33] Siegmund Jakob Baumgarten (1706–57) was influenced by the philosophy of Christian Wolff.[34] Johann Lorenz von Mosheim (1693–1755)[35] took ethics in a eudaemonistic direction, as did Michaelis[36] and Bahrdt.[37] A supranaturalist ethic was provided by Franz Volkmar Reinhard (1753–1812).[38]

27. Melanchthon, *Enarratio*. Ed. note: According to Sinnema, "Discipline of Ethics," 11, "Melanchthon lectured on Aristotle's *Ethics* at least eight times, beginning in 1527–28, and from this teaching came his 1529 commentary."
28. Melanchthon, *Philosophiae Moralis*. Ed. note: The numerous authors and titles that follow in the text and in the notes have been checked with or provided by the online Post-Reformation Digital Library, http://www.prdl.org.
29. Calixt, *Epitome Theologiae Moralis*.
30. Dürr, *Enchiridion Theologiae Moralis*.
31. Osiander, *Theologia Moralis*; Meier and Holste, *Disputationes Theologicae*; Baier, *Compendium Theologiae Moralis*; Buddeus, *Institutiones Theologiae Moralis*.
32. Ed. note: In the margin Bavinck clarifies his manuscript's simple reference to "Balduinus" with a reference to Johann Georg Walch's *Bibliotheca Theologia Selecta*, 2:1127 (VI, § xiii). Walch refers to Friedrich Balduin's *Tractatus de Casibus Conscientiae* (1628), which is undoubtedly the work Bavinck had in mind and is part of a larger work, Balduin's *Tractatus Luculentus*. Balduin (1575–1627) was a Lutheran professor of theology at Wittenberg (1607–27).
33. Ed. note: Bavinck mentions no first name or title for the last four men named in this sentence but is most likely referring to Lutheran theologian Johannes Olearius (1639–1713), professor of Greek and later of theology at Leipzig, and his *Doctrina Theologiae Moralis*; Lutheran theologian Johann Conrad Dannhauer (1603–66) and possibly his *Collegium Exercitationum Ethico-Politicarum*; Georg König (1590–1654), Lutheran professor of theology at Altdorf and author of *Casus Conscientiae*; and Georg Dedekenn (1564–1628), a Lutheran theologian and author of *Trewhertzige Warnung*.
34. Baumgarten, *Unterricht von rechtmäßigen Verhalten eines Christen*. Ed. note: Christian Wolff (1679–1754) was the preeminent German philosopher between Leibniz and Kant, noted for his high claims for autonomous human reason.
35. Mosheim, *Sitten-Lehre der Heiligen Schrift*. Ed. note: Eudaemonism is a theory of ethics that identifies moral value with what produces human happiness.
36. Ed. note: Bavinck gives no first name or title; he likely had in mind Lutheran theologian Daniel Michaelis (1621–52), author of *De Primo Hominis Primi Peccato Exercitatio*.
37. Ed. note: Bavinck gives no first name or title; he likely had in mind Lutheran theologian Carl (or Karl) Friedrich Bahrdt (1741–92), author of *Christliches Sittenbuch fürs Gesinde* and *System der moralischen Religion*.
38. Reinhard, *System der Christlichen Moral*. Ed. note: For Bavinck's assessment of "supranaturalism," see *RD*, 1:355–62; 2:539–48. At this point Bavinck adds a separate line in the

Reformed Churches

The ethical literature in the Reformed Churches is much richer and more edifying.[39] Dogmatics and ethics are still united in Zwingli. Above all, he sought ethical reformation, a renewal of life and morality in accordance with Holy Scripture. His fundamental error was in his understanding of the relation between civil and divine justice, between nature and grace.[40] Calvin did not treat ethics separately but throughout his *Institutes*, especially in book III, chapters 6–10, where, in order, he deals sequentially with regeneration (*poenitentia*),[41] self-denial, cross-bearing, meditation on the future life, and the proper use of this life. Other important ethical themes included Christian liberty (III.xix), prayer (III. xx), and the exposition of the moral law (II.viii). Calvin developed ethics from a purely Christian foundation and distinguishes it clearly from philosophical ethics. Many Reformed thinkers continued to include ethical material in their dogmatics: Wolfgang Musculus (1497–1563),[42] Georg Sohn (1552–89),[43] and the *Leiden Synopsis*.[44] Others treated it in a second volume (teaching on faith and teaching on love). This was done by Polanus;[45] Heidegger (locus 14);[46] Hoornbeeck;[47] van Mastricht, who wrote a theology emphasizing morals and duties;[48]

---

manuscript, "Roman Catholic Ethicists," and refers to Walch, *Bibliotheca Theologica Selecta*, 2:1113–25 (VI, §§ xi–xii). Walch's list of some forty names and treatises includes the important Jesuit casuists Tomàs Sanchez (1550–1610), Francisco Suárez (1548–1617), Gabriel Vásquez (1549–1604), and Leonard Lessius (1554–1623).

39. Cf. Schweizer, "Die Entwicklung des Moralsystems"; Lobstein, "Zum evangelischen Lebensideal."

40. Ed. note: Cf. Bavinck, *De ethiek van Ulrich Zwingli*, esp. chap. 9, "Christian Life and Civic Life."

41. Ed. note: Unlike the later Protestant orthodox theologians who developed highly differentiated orders of salvation (*ordines salutis*) in which "regeneration" became a technical term for the new-birth initiation of salvation, Calvin uses *poenitentia* more broadly for the new life, especially repentance; see *Institutes*, III.iii, esp. III.iii.9.

42. Musculus, *Common Places of Christian Religion*.

43. Sohn, *Methodus Theologiae*, in *Operum*, 1:154–82. Ed. note: Sohn treats ethics under God's postlapsarian work of providence, where it is one of three aspects of God's civil rule (the other two are economics and politics).

44. Polyander et al., *Synopsis Purioris Theologiae*. Ed. note: Bavinck edited the sixth edition of this work, which was published in 1881.

45. Polanus von Polansdorf, *Syntagma Theologiae Christianae*, books VIII–X.

46. Heidegger, *Corpus Theologiae Christianae*. Ed. note: Locus XIV is titled "De decalogo."

47. Hoornbeeck, *Theologia Practica*.

48. Ed. note: Bavinck is referring to Petrus van Mastricht (1630–1706), *Theoretico-Practica Theologia*. This work is divided into two parts. "Mastricht himself argues that the 'art of living to God' consists of two aspects: how one is made spiritually alive and, being alive, how one lives to God (*Deo vivere*)." After the eight books of the first part, which "could be described as systematic theology," the second major section "presents an outline of moral theology (*idea theologiae moralis*) and *theologia ascetica*." Moral theology, in turn, "is divided into three sections: (1) Christian obedience in general, (2) religion, i.e., obedience in relationship

Wollebius (book II);[49] Ames (book II);[50] Brakel (book II);[51] Marcus Friedrich Wendelin;[52] and others.

The following separated ethics from dogmatics: Lambert Daneau, who divided the material into three parts (anthropological foundation, law, and virtues);[53] Bartholomew Keckermann, in his *Systema Ethices*;[54] Antony Walaeus, whose "Compendium of Aristotelian Ethics Called Back to the Norm of Christian Truth"[55] is also divided into three parts: (a) "Concerning the highest good," (b) "Concerning the natural virtues in general," and (c) "Concerning the particular virtues";[56] Daniel Puerari in his *Logical and Ethical Theses*;[57] Amyraut of Saumur, who worked historically in his six-volume *Christian Morality*;[58] and Antonius Driessen, *Evangelical Ethics*.[59] The order of sins first, followed by duties to God, neighbor, and self, was followed by

---

to God, and (3) justice, i.e., obedience in relationship to one's neighbor" (Neele, *Petrus van Mastricht*, 67–70).

Ed. note: Bavinck usually cites the Dutch translation of van Mastricht's work, *Beschouwende en praktikale godgeleerdheit*, which is being translated into English for the first time and will be published under the auspices of the Dutch Reformed Translation Society. To facilitate access in all versions, references will be given by part (I, II, III), book (i, ii, iii, iv, etc.), chapter (1, 2, 3, 4, 5, etc.), and paragraph number (§). Each reference will thus have this format: I.ii.2 §3. The three parts of *Theoretico-Practica Theologia* are (in Latin/Dutch): I. *Theologia/Godgeleerdheid*; II. *Idea Theologia Moralis / Zedelyke godgeleerdheid*; III. *Hypotyposis Theologiae Asceticae, de exercitia pietatis / Plichtvermanende godgeleerdheid*. This more complete information clarifies Bavinck's own references, which are usually given simply in terms of the Dutch volume number (I–IV) and the page. Cross-references to the 1749–53 Dutch edition used by Bavinck appear in square brackets indicating the volume and page numbers (e.g., [4:357]).

49. Ed. note: Bavinck is referring to Johannes Wollebius (1589–1629), author of *Theologiae Epitomen*, "First Book: Concerning the Knowledge of God"; "Second Book: Concerning the Worship of God" deals with virtues and works as explained by the Decalogue.

50. Ed. note: Bavinck is referring to Ames, *Marrow of Theology*. Ames divides theology into two parts and his work into two books: "Faith in God" and "Observance to God" (p. 79).

51. Ed. note: Bavinck is referring to W. à Brakel (1635–1711), *Christian's Reasonable Service*. Book II of the Dutch version is contained in vols. 3 and 4 of the English translation and covers the Christian life of sanctification, the Ten Commandments, the Lord's Prayer, and the practice of Christian discipline.

52. Wendelin, *Philosophia Moralis*.

53. Daneau, *Ethices Christianae*.

54. Keckermann, *Systema Ethicae Tribus Libris*.

55. Walaeus, *Compendium Ethicae Aristotelicae*.

56. Walaeus, *Compendium Ethicae Aristotelicae*. LO: (a) *de summo bono*; (b) *de virtutis natura in genere*; (c) *de virtutibus singularibus*.

57. Puerari, *Theses Logicae atque Ethicae*. Bavinck's manuscript mistakenly indicates Johannes Polyander (1568–1646), professor of theology at Leiden (1611–46) and one of the contributors to the Leiden *Synopsis Purioris Theologiae* (Polyander et al.), as the author of *Theses Logicae atque Ethicae*, which is properly attributed to Daniel Puerari (1621–92), professor of philosophy at Geneva.

58. Amyraut, *La morale chrestienne*.

59. Driessen, *Evangelische zedekunde*.

Bénédict Pictet in his *Christian Ethics*.[60] In his "First Elements of Christian Ethics," J. H. Heidegger does not tie himself strictly to the Decalogue, but utilizes more of Aristotle and divides the subject into love toward God and love toward neighbor.[61] J. F. Ostervald of Neuenberg wrote "A Compendium of Christian Ethics."[62] Other writers include Werenfels[63] and J. A. Turretin.[64] J. G. Altmann of Bern first considers the natural state of humanity,[65] then the civil order, etc., and abandons the Decalogue, distinguishing between natural and revealed ethics.[66] J. F. Stapfer of Bern adopted the philosophy of Christian Wolff; the Dutch edition of his ethics appeared in 1760.[67] Daniel Wyttenbach of Marburg was another Wolffian,[68] while J. C. Beck concentrated on the Decalogue.[69] With Samuel Endemann's *Institutes of Moral Theology*[70] a distinctive Reformed ethics comes to a close; Endemann utilizes numerous Lutheran theologians.

All of these works, from Daneau to Endemann, are to a greater or lesser degree under the influence of philosophical ethics, initially from Aristotle, and then from Wolff. The division between Christian ethics and philosophical ethics had not yet been completely developed. In fact, Peter Martyr Vermigli used Aristotle's *Ethics* as a foundation for his lectures on ethics;[71] using a pagan morality held back the formation of his own ethics. The following are significant:[72]

60. Pictet (1655–1724), *De christelyke zedekunst*.

61. Heidegger (1633–98), *Ethicae Christianae Prima Elementa*.

62. Ostervald, *Ethicae Christianae Compendium*.

63. Ed. note: Bavinck does not identify this author more precisely or provide a title. The two possibilities are Peter Werenfels (1627–1703), professor of New Testament at Basel and author of *Dissertatio Theologica de Sabbathi Moralitate* and the ten-volume *Dissertationis Theologicae de Velamine Iudaeorum*, and Samuel Werenfels (1657–1740), professor of theology at Basel and author of *Philosophiae Moralis*.

64. J. A. Turretin, *Dilucidationes*.

65. LO: *status hominum naturalis*.

66. J. G. Altmann (1697–1758), professor of philosophy at Bern (1734–57) and author of *Delineatio Oratoriae Sacrae Brevibus Praeceptis Exhibita*.

67. Stapfer, *Sittenlehre* (Dutch: *De zeden-leer*). Ed. note: On Christian Wolff, see n. 34 above.

68. Wyttenbach (1706–79), *Compendium Theologiae Dogmaticae et Moralis*. Ed. note: Daniel Wyttenbach (1706–79) was a Reformed theologian who served as professor of theology at the University of Marburg from 1756 until his death. He is not to be confused with Daniel Albert Wittenbach/Wyttenbach (1746–1820), who was an Arminian-Remonstrant philosopher.

69. J. C. Beck (1711–85), *Synopsis Institutionum*. Ed. note: The last section of this work is titled "Practical Theology" (*Theologiae Practicae*); the Ten Commandments are covered in the first eleven chapters and followed by additional sections on the summary of the divine law, the Lord's Prayer, and the sacred ministry.

70. Endemann, *Institutiones Theologiae Moralis*.

71. Hoedemaker, *De verhouding der ethiek tot de dogmatiek*, 35.

72. Ed. note: For the most part, Bavinck takes the following summary list of names (and works) from de Wette, *Lehrbuch der christlichen Sittenlehre*, 174–76.

Jean La Placette, [73] Samuel Basnage, John Forbes of Corse, Daniel Whitby, Simon Oomius, Petrus Wittewrongel, and Jacques Saurin.[74]

The Spiritual Life: Casuistry and Ascetic Theology

In addition to these works on ethics—each of which has the moral life as its object—*casuistry* had its own development. Casuistry stands in relation to ethics as jurisprudence (case law) does to the philosophy of law.[75] In general, judging and deciding specific cases coincided with the treatment of the moral law: What must I do in this specific instance? However, casuistry became its own theological science and pushed real ethics to the side. Examples of casuistry in Scripture include Matthew 22:15–22 (Is it lawful to pay taxes to Caesar?); Luke 14:3 (Is it lawful to heal on the Sabbath?); and 1 Corinthians 7:8, 10 (Paul's instruction to the married and the unmarried). Casuistry was developed further by Tertullian, by Augustine, and then with great subtlety in the Middle Ages by Thomas Aquinas in his *Summa theologiae*.[76] All possible situations were considered, and the door was opened to all sorts of arbitrariness. The freedom of the individual was taken away, the conscience was confused, and the result was skepticism and probabilism. The last-mentioned strategy enabled someone to be free from a command if one could appeal to some spiritual authority who *could* have given permission.[77]

The Reformers did not have their own distinctive ethics or casuistry. However, they faced situations in which they had to make judgments about marriage, usury, tribute and taxes, obedience to civil authority, and so forth. In and of itself, casuistry is a good thing; we all need it. Therefore, it also developed among the Reformed, but definitely not in the manner that earlier Scholasticism had done it—in fact, particularly in opposition to it. A form of casuistry was developed by William Perkins, professor at Cambridge, who wrote an "Anatomy of the Human Conscience"[78] along with a casebook of the conscience.[79] Perkins first provides a general doctrine of good and evil and a categorization of sin and then asks a series of questions: First, how

---

73. La Placette (1629–1718), *La morale chrétienne* and various pamphlets; see Walch, *Bibliotheca Theologica Selecta*, 2:1109–10 (VI, § x).

74. De Flottemanville, *Morale théologique et politique*; Forbes, *Opera Omnia*; Whitby, *Ethices Compendium*; Oomius, *Dissertatie van de onderwijsingen in de practycke der godgeleerdheid*; Wittewrongel, *Oeconomia Christiana*; Saurin, *Abregé de la théologie et de la morale chrétienne*.

75. DO: *rechtsphilosofie*.

76. Ed. note: *ST* IIa IIae qq. 1–170.

77. LO: *sententia probabilis*.

78. Ed. note: Perkins, *Anatomia Sacra Humanae Conscientiae*; as we will see in chap. 5, §14, Bavinck uses a Dutch translation, Perkins, *Eene Verhandeling van de Gevallen der Conscientie*.

79. Perkins, *Whole Treatise of the Cases of Conscience*.

can one come into God's favor and be assured and comforted? Second, how does one stand in relation to God? How is one to serve him and beseech him? How must one use the Word, the sacraments, and oaths? And finally, how do we stand in relation to our neighbor? How we must conduct ourselves? and so forth. Perkins's student William Ames also wrote a book on casuistry[80] that sets forth the duties of humans in a practical manner, through questions and answers. A third casuist is Johannes Alsted, whose *Theology of Cases*[81] was designed to comfort the conscience in the face of various trials.[82]

Casuistry has a right to exist; there are difficult instances that need adjudication. But as long as one does not multiply the instances with excess subtlety, the medieval casuistry, avoided by the Jesuits, is actually a special section of ethics. Except for the three just-mentioned, casuistry was no longer practiced in the Reformed churches. Maresius wanted nothing to do with it.[83] A few continued with it—Joseph Hall,[84] Jeremy Taylor,[85] Robert Sanderson[86]—but the practice died out. It did, however, continue in the Lutheran Church for a long time. The following topics were included in it:[87] 1. laws; 2. human activities: [which include] (a) games of chance, (b) dances, (c) theater; 3. duties toward God; 4. duties to self, including discussions of self-denial and warnings against impurity, drunkenness, and suicide; 5. duties to others, including discussions

80. Ames, *Conscience with the Power and Cases Thereof.*
81. Alsted, *Theologia Casuum.*
82. Ed. note: At this point, Bavinck inserts in square brackets: "In the Lutheran Church: Balduinus †1627, Finck 1631, Dunte 1636, König 1654, Kessler 1658, Dannhauer, Osiander, Olearius, Bechmann, etc." He also adds a marginal reference to Walch, *Bibliotheca Theologica Selecta*, 2:1127 (VI, § xvi). The entire bracket is footnoted: "See E. Schwarz, 'Casuistik,' *PRE*[1] 2:608–19." In addition to Schwarz's article, Bavinck also gathers his information from de Wette, *Lehrbuch der christlichen Sittenlehre*, 173–74.
83. Ed. note: Bavinck is referring to Samuel Maresius (1599–1673), author of *Collegium Theologicum* and *Systema Theologicum.* Chap. 8 of the latter deals with the law (*De Lege*).
84. Ed. note: Joseph Hall (1574–1656) was an Anglican, Reformed theologian and author of *Resolutions and Decisions of Divers Practical Cases of Conscience.* Hall deals with "Cases of Profit and Traffick," "Cases of Life and Liberty," "Cases of Piety and Religion," and "Cases Matrimonial." Bavinck also refers to the German translation of this work, *Gewissens Rath.*
85. Taylor, *Ductor Dubitantium.*
86. Sanderson, *De Obligatione Conscientiae.* Ed. note: Bavinck refers to Rivetus, *Praelectiones*, in the note and adds in the margin Lodensteyn, *Weegschaal*; Maccovius, *Casus Conscientiae.*
87. Walch, *Bibliotheca Theologica Selecta*, 2:1141–60 (VI, § xvi). Ed. note: The Latin titles of Walch's topics, with the pages on which they are treated, are 1. *de legibus* (1140–41); 2. *de actionibus humanis* (1141–45); 2a. *ludi fortunae* (1141–42); 2b. *saltationes* (1141–44); 2c. *ludi theatreales* (1144–45); 3. *de officias erga deum* (1145–46); 4. *de officiis erga se ipsos* (1145–49); 5. *de officiis erga alios* (1149–50); 6. *de officiis coniugum* (1150–59); 7. *de officiis parentum* (1159–60); 8. *de officiis dominorum et servorum* (1160); and 9. *de officiis imperantium et subditorum* (1160).

of kindness, almsgiving,[88] and giving offense;[89] 6. duties of spouses, including discussions of polygamy, adultery, and divorce; 7. duties of parents, including discussion of nurture/education in (a) the Christian faith and (b) life at all age levels, for boys and girls; 8. masters and servants; and 9. magistrates and subjects.

In addition, included in the field of ethics are all those activities in which the life of the spirit is the object, activities that are ordinarily spoken of as "practical theology" or the "spiritual life."[90] Works in this vein include Hoornbeeck's *Practical Theology* and C. Vitringa's *Types of Practical Theology or the Spiritual Life*.[91] H. Witsius, in *Practical Divinity*,[92] divides the material into duties toward God, duties to self, and duties to our neighbor. Lampe's *Sketch of Practical Theology*[93] joins together practical, moral, casuistic, and ascetic theology. Other works include Antonius Driessen, *The Old and New Man, Brought to a Collection of Practical Theology*; J. H. Hottinger, *Types of the Christian Life*; and Simon Oomius, *Institutes of Practical Theology*.[94] Edifying reading material from the writings of W. Teellinck can be found in F. Ridderus, *The Man of God*.[95]

To all of this, we need to add *ascetic theology*, theology that is concerned with required dutes and practices.[96] Ascetic theology directs us to the means by which piety is exercised, especially prayer, fasting, vigil, and so forth, and thus has its right to exist. After all, the purpose of ethics is that we grow in grace and not stay at the level of theory. The term has a bad odor thanks to the monastic ascetic practices of the Middle Ages. But there is a genuine, biblical, Reformed ascetic theology, summed up in 1 Timothy 4:7 (cf. Acts 24:16): "Train yourself in godliness."[97] Properly, it is not a discipline on its own, though it was practiced in the early church; for example, Basil the Great penned his *Ascetica*.[98] In the Reformed Church, others followed suit, especially in England: Lewis Bayly, *The Practice of Piety* (1672);[99] Jeremy Taylor, *The Rule and Exercises of Holy Living*

---

88. GrO: ἐλεημοσύνη.
89. LO: *de scandalis.*
90. LO: *theologia practica; vita spirituali.*
91. Hoornbeeck, *Theologiae Practicae*; Vitringa, *Typus Theologiae Practicae.*
92. Witsius, *Prakticale godgeleertheid.*
93. Lampe, *Schets der dadelyke Godt-geleertheid.*
94. Driessen, *Oude en nieuwe mensch*; Hottinger, *Typus Vitae Christianae*; Oomius, *Institutiones Theologiae Practicae.*
95. *De mensche Godts.*
96. Walch, *Bibliotheca Theologica Selecta*, 2:1171–83 (VI, § xviii).
97. GrO: γύμναζε δὲ σεαυτὸν πρὸς εὐσέβειαν.
98. Ed. note: See n. 9 above.
99. Ed. note: Bavinck wrote "Bayle," but is most likely referring to Bayly (ca. 1575–1631), *Practice of Piety*. A Dutch translation edited by Gisbert Voetius was published in 1642: *De practycke ofte oeffeninge der godsaligheydt*. There is also a German edition: *Praxis Pietatis.*

(1688);[100] R. Baxter, *A Christian Directory, or, A Summ of Practical Theology* (1678);[101] H. Hammond, *A Practical Catechism* (1644);[102] Willem Teellinck, "The Most Important Christian Practices";[103] G. Voetius, *The Exercise of Piety;*[104] P. van Mastricht, the third part of *Theoretico-Practica Theologia (Ascetica);*[105] Pierre Roques, *The True Pietism;*[106] R. Allestree, *The Whole Duty of Man;*[107] Ewald Kist, *Ascetica.*[108] To these we can add various and sundry writings on prudence, the attributes of the pastor:[109] Fr. Junius, *Ecclesiasticus;*[110] Vedelius, *The Wisdom of the Ancient Church;*[111] and so forth.

Ethics in the Nineteenth Century

Since 1750 the discipline of ethics can be characterized as eudaemonistic, utilitarian, and rationalistic. (The terms are equivalent.)[112] A new era commenced with Kant, who opposed utilitarianism, acknowledged the majesty of duty, and banned all heteronomy. Kant provided only an abstract and legalistic morality. Schleiermacher published his *Outlines of a Critique of Previous Ethical Theory* in 1803, and after 1812/13 lectured on virtues and duties, the highest good, the permissible, and the distinction between natural law and moral law.[113] This was followed by *Sketch of a Moral System,* produced by

100. Taylor, *Rule and Exercises of Holy Living.* Ed. note: Between the lines, Bavinck added: "also in German" (*Die Richtschnur und Ubung eines Heiligen Wandels*). Bavinck's information comes from Walch, *Bibliotheca Theologica Selecta,* 2:1107 (VI, § x).
101. Baxter, *Christian Directory.*
102. Hammond, *Practicall Catechisme.*
103. Ed. note: Most likely Bavinck has in view here Whately, *Corte verhandelinge van de voornaemste christelicke oeffeninghen,* which was *translated* by Teellinck. The English original of this work was apparently never published.
104. Voetius, *De praktijk der godzaligheid.*
105. Van Mastricht, *Theoretico-Practica Theologia,* III.i–iv [4:669–840].
106. Roques, *Le vray pietisme ou traité.*
107. Allestree, *Whole Duty of Man.* Ed. note: Bavinck indicates that the author is unknown; this work has also been attributed to Lady Dorothy Coventry Pakington, Richard Sterne, John Fell, and Humphrey Henchman.
108. Ed. note: Most likely Bavinck is referring to Kist, *Beöeffeningsleer.* An English translation, with the translator identified in the preface simply as V., was published in 1852.
109. Walch, *Bibliotheca Theologica Selecta,* 2:1162–71 (VI, § xvii).
110. Junius, *Ecclesiastici.* Ed. note: Junius's book I provides a theology of the church ("*de ecclesiae*"); book II deals with offices of the church: pastors, elders, deacons, teachers (doctors), and all believers ("*de ecclesiae administrationibus*"); book III with qualifications for office in the church and the duties of those offices ("*de formis*").
111. Vedelius, *De Prudentia Veteris Ecclesiae, Libri Tres.*
112. Ed. note: Bavinck noted this equivalence with equal signs: "eudaemonistic = utilitarian = rationalistic."
113. Schleiermacher, *Grundlinien einer Kritik der bisherigen Sittenlehre.* Ed. note: Bavinck had "1819" in his text, but Schleiermacher lectured on the doctrine of goods, virtues, and

Alexander Schweizer (1835),[114] and subsequently published by Twesten under a different title, *An Outline of Philosophical Ethics*,[115] in 1841. Yet another version was produced by Ludwig Jonas in 1843 under the title *The Christian Ethic*.[116]

Schleiermacher's theological ethics is rooted in his philosophy. It is to his credit that he deals with the ethical material systematically; there is a unity in it. The good, according to Schleiermacher, is the existence of rationality in nature. Ethics is concerned about activity in this sense: the church, the ecclesiastical common spirit (which is the Holy Spirit)[117] must become realized in the individual, just as philosophical ethics studies the reason that is realized in nature. However, the church is surely not the norm for morality? And if it were, which church? There are no objective norms in Schleiermacher, no adequate designations of good and evil. Evil is mere denial.

Richard Rothe's *Theological Ethics*[118] is filled with beautiful, rich, deep insights but suffers from three foundational errors. First, Rothe understands ethics as a discipline within speculative theology and constructs it entirely on the basis or source of Christian consciousness. The foundation is therefore subjectivist, with the subject standing above the Christian faith, although Rothe still considers Christianity to be the absolute truth. Second, Rothe has an erroneous understanding of ethics itself. Everything personal is moral; everything that occurs through the power of human self-determination is ethical. The ethical process involves freeing ourselves from what is natural, material, and self-seeking, and becoming personal spirits. Sin is a necessity and thus not really sin. Finally, for Rothe, what is religious is attached to the ethical; the religious is merely the form, while the ethical is the content. The ethical devours the religious life; the latter has no independent existence, and the church must morph into the state.

In addition, the following are the foremost ethicists of the ninetenth century: (a) Gottlieb Chr. A. von Harless, *Christian Ethics* (1842).[119] The title is "Christian" but the content is Lutheran (for example, with respect to regeneration). The volume is not constructed and executed well and is difficult to

---

duties from 1812/13 through 1817; see Schleiermacher, *Lectures on Philosophical Ethics*, v. The *Lectures* volume includes an extensive historical overview of Schleiermacher's lectures and writings on ethics, pp. vii–xxx.

114. Schleiermacher, *Entwurf eines systems der Sittenlehre*.

115. Schleiermacher, *Grundriß der philosophischen Ethik*.

116. Ed. note: Schleiermacher, *Die christliche Sitte nach den Grundsätzen der evangelischen Kirche im Zusammenhange dargestellt*.

117. GO: "Gemeingeist = heilige Geist."

118. Rothe, *Theologische Ethik*.

119. Von Harless, *Christliche Ethik*.

read. He does understand the Christian life properly as a life out of and in Christ, but he fails to do justice to many themes—law, duties, sanctification—because of the way he divides the material into the blessing of salvation, the possession of salvation, and the preservation of salvation.[120] (b) Christian Friedrich Schmid, *Christian Ethics* (1861);[121] a fine, foundational, philosophically sharp work. (c) A. Wuttke, *Manual of Christian Ethics* (1861),[122] contains a great deal of historical material but is less *in* the Scriptures than above and beyond them. It also lacks a systematic order and method. (d) Ph. Th. Culmann, *Christian Ethics* (1864–66),[123] has depth in spite of being built on a mystical foundation; however, it is excessive and theosophical. (e) Martensen's three-volume *Christian Ethics* (1871–78)[124] is clear and expansive but lacks precise delineation of the distinctively Christian and substitutes general ideas for specific issues. His viewpoint is existential-ethical[125] and, occasionally, modernist. (f) A. F. C. Vilmar's *Theologische Moral* (1871)[126] is morally serious and definitely Christian but also occasionally displays a strained rigorism and fanciful exegesis.[127]

120. GO: *das Heilsgut, der Heilsbesitz, die Heilsbewahrung.*

121. C. F. Schmid, *Christliche Sittenlehre.*

122. Wuttke, *Handbuch der Christlichen Sittenlehre.*

123. Culmann, *Die christliche Ethik.*

124. Ed. note: It is a challenge to track the publication history of Martensen's *Christian Ethics*; some dates in WorldCat (https://www.worldcat.org) entries are uncertain, and many entries fail to specify the edition. As best as can be determined, the original Danish work, *Den christelige Ethik*, was published from 1871 to 1878 in Copenhagen by Gyldendal. It consisted of two parts, published in three volumes: "General Part" (vol. 1), "Special Part I: Individual Ethics" (vol. 2), and "Special Part II: Social Ethics" (vol. 3). An English version of vol. 1 was translated from the Danish by C. Spence and published in 1871 by T&T Clark. A German edition of vol. 1, *Die christliche Ethik*, was published in 1871 by R. Besser. Vols. 2 and 3 in German, *Die individuelle Ethik* and *Die sociale Ethik*, were published in 1878 by the same publisher. Vol. 2 was translated into English from the German by W. Affleck and published in 1881 by T&T Clark. Vol. 3 was translated from the German by Sophia Taylor and published in 1882 by the same publisher. There is also a volume that combines two of the authors in this paragraph: Martensen and Harless, *Christian Ethics*.

125. Ed. note: Bavinck succinctly describes Martensen as "ethisch," which we have translated with the double term "existential-ethical." The term is mistranslated as simply "ethical" because it refers to a specific school of Dutch theology in the late nineteenth century whose leaders were Daniel Chantepie de la Saussaye (1818–74) and J. H. Gunning (1829–1905). Both emphasized the personal, relational, existential, and Christocentric character of the Christian faith. Truth is an "ethical" or relational reality. For a brief summary of this "ethical theology" in the Dutch Reformed Church, see Blei, *Netherlands Reformed Church*, 80–81. Also see Bavinck, *De theologie van Prof. Dr. Daniel Chantepie de la Saussaye.*

126. Vilmar, *Theologische Moral.*

127. On the literature of ethics, see Runze, *Ethik*, 1:1–16 ("Einleitung"); Schulze, "Zur Geschichte der christlichen Ethik." Ed. note: Bavinck failed to note that the previous volume of the journal containing Schulze's two-part article, *Theologisches Literaturblatt*, also contained a survey of philosophical ethics; see Rabus, "Eine Moralphilosophie aus dem Kreise der neuen

§2. Terminology[128]

The term "ethics" comes from the Greek ἦθος, which is "a lengthened form of ἔθος" and in the first place signifies "*an accustomed place:* in plural *the haunts* or *abodes* of animals.*" With respect to humans it signifies both temper, character, and disposition, on the one hand, and habit, custom, and manner, on the other. The plural indicates manners (Latin *mores*).[129] The term is found in the New Testament at 1 Corinthians 15:33: "Do not be deceived: bad company corrupts good *character*";[130] at Acts 16:21: "by advocating *customs* unlawful for us as Romans to accept or practice";[131] and at Acts 26:3: "You are familiar with all the *customs* and controversies of the Jews.*"[132] Originally ἦθος meant "dwelling," "stay," "action," "manner of acting." It is not identical in meaning to morality (*mores*), but is a certain kind of morality (Quintilian).[133] It is often used as a synonym for τρόπος (= manner, way, kind, character).

The Latin *mos* refers to the manner of people's lives as it flows forth from the disposition, character, and life of nations; that is to say, it equals custom, morals, and manners.[134] According to Vilmar, *mos* is "more 'internal' than ἦθος.*"[135] However, Dorner argues the exact opposite.[136] With respect to their etymological work, whether we translate *mos* as "morality" or "ethics" is a matter of indifference. We choose "ethics" because the word does not yet carry the negative associations that "morality" has, at least as understood in

Scholastik." Bavinck also refers to *Philosophisches Jahrbuch*, *Theologisches Jahresbericht*, and other journals.

The first 35 volumes of *Philosophisches Jahrbuch* are available at https://catalog.hathitrust .org/Record/008883008, and a useful index for vols. 1–20 (1888–1907) is at https://archive.org /details/philosophischesj1a20gruoft.

128. Ed. note: The Dutch title is "*Naam en Begrip*" ("Name and Idea").

129. Ed. note: Liddell, *Intermediate Greek-English Lexicon*, s.v. "ἦθος." These first two sentences are a constructed elaboration, based on Liddell and Scott, of Bavinck's cryptic text. Bavinck's point is that the ἔθος/ἦθος semantic field has the double signification of behaviors, habits, customs, manners, and rituals on the one hand and the personal moral disposition, character, and temper of people on the other. Furthermore, ἔθος has the former primarily in view while ἦθος points to the latter, fuller meaning.

130. GrO: μὴ πλανᾶσθε Φθείρουσιν ἤθη χρηστὰ ὁμιλίαι κακαί.

131. GrO: καὶ καταγγέλλουσιν ἔθη ἃ οὐκ ἔξεστιν ἡμῖν παραδέχεσθαι οὐδὲ ποιεῖν Ῥωμαίοις οὖσιν.

132. GrO: μάλιστα γνώστην ὄντα σε πάντων τῶν κατὰ Ἰουδαίους ἐθῶν τε.

133. Ed. note: Bavinck's text has "niet = *mores, maar morum quaedam proprietas* (Quintil- iaan)." Bavinck has taken this straight from Vilmar, *Theologische Moral*, 1:3; Vilmar identifies Quintillian's *Institutes* 6.2 as the source.

134. Ed. note: Bavinck uses the single term *zede* here.

135. GO: *mehr etwas Inneres*. Ed. note: Vilmar, *Theologische Moral*, 1:3–4; in the margin Bavinck added: *Heraut* 487, a reference to Abraham Kuyper's commentary on Lord's Day 8 of the Heidelberg Catechism (Q&A 6), republished in Kuyper, *E Voto Dordraceno*, 1:176–82.

136. Ed. note: I. A. Dorner, "*Ethik*."

terms of moral preaching. In addition, a distinction is usually made between *morality* understood as practical morality and *ethics* as the more purely scientific and deductive expression of what *is*. Practical morality is the cluster of rules by which people live and is thus an inductive description of what people outwardly *do*. Ethics is thus deeper and normative.[137] This parallels the distinction between ethics and moral philosophy.[138]

The Dutch word *zede*, the German *Sitte*, and Sanskrit *sat* all refer to "living, dwelling";[139] a similar word in the Gothic language is *sidus*, which is used in the Gothic version in 1 Corinthians 15:33 and 2 Timothy 3:10.[140] Nomads do not have moral customs;[141] customs and morals develop when people "sit," when they settle down and dwell in a place.[142]

For our scientific purposes this etymology is insufficient; it provides only the normative principle that we are concerned about life in society. All societies have already existing and firm customs, rules, social behaviors, and morals from which one may not deviate. One's nation, family, and circle determine an individual's conduct. Morality consists of what is in agreement with the dominant customs. Scripture does not speak of morality but of righteousness, holiness, and godliness, because it *always* views human beings in terms of their relationship to God, who rules their conduct. According to etymological explanations of morality, a moral life is a life that is normatively governed by and in agreement with the customs of the people.

But gradually this moral life was viewed in a more profound way. A rational person cannot, upon reflection, locate the highest norm for living within customs, which can serve only as a standardized norm.[143] There has to be another, higher, absolute standard. People looked for the essence of morality—what is moral in its own right, independent of society's judgment and valid for all

137. Ed. note: Bavinck's terms are "inwendig, principieel, deductief." The term *principieel* is characteristic of Kuyperian neo-Calvinism, and although North American neo-Calvinists use "principial," *principieel* is best translated as "normative."

138. DO: *zedenleer, zedenkunde*.

139. DO: *wonen*.

140. Ed. note: Variants of *sidus* in the passages Bavinck cites are found in the Gothic Bible of Ulfila (ca. 311–83), the missionary and Bible translator to the Goths. Bavinck's source for this is Vilmar, *Theologische Moral*, 1:4. Bavinck's reference to the Gothic Bible illustrates the fluidity of the terms for ethics/morality in Scripture. According to Vilmar, the Gothic *sidus* appears once in the New Testament as a translation of ἤθη (1 Cor. 15:33; "morals"); it was also inserted in the text of 2 Tim. 3:10 to explain the two terms τῇ ἀγωγῇ ("conduct") and τῇ προθέσει ("purpose"). Modern translations capture this by translating τῇ ἀγωγῇ as "my conduct" (ESV, NRSV) or "my way of life" (NIV).

141. DO: *zeden*.

142. Cf. von Jhering, *Der Zweck im Recht*, 2:15–20; for the opposing view see Freybe, "Die Bedeutung der Sitte."

143. LO: *norma normata*.

people at all times. There has to be a foundation for ethics, a supreme basis, a comprehensive and all-regulating principle that governs all conduct always. Morality, in other words, cannot be custom, but must be an idea, something that does not just exist but *must be*; something that needs to be concretized in real life. This is the idea of the Good, the ethical ideal, the idea of the truly human or humane. Morality is thus considered more deeply than what is customarily human; it is normed by the *essence of the human.*

Consequently, there are two crucial dimensions in morality. First, it involves free acts of human personality and not those that are necessary or arbitrary. Second, the norm for morality is what is essentially human, or humane.

This is a purely formal understanding, and materially, we see great differences of opinion on how to conceive of these dimensions. No one is in full agreement with another about what constitutes "normal humanity." It is the task of philosophical ethics to search after this and to provide definitions of the normally human and to indicate the foundations and maxims of morality. On the face of it, this exploration cannot be in conflict with Christian ethics, any more than the truly human in itself is in conflict with the genuinely Christian. However, in reality, these often conflict. At this time, we are not entering into the questions of philosophical ethics, but only with specifically Christian ethics. Today, when one considers the etymology of the word "ethics," the designation "Christian ethics" seems like a contradiction in terms. "Christian" suggests a different norm than the word "ethics," understood as the genuinely human or humane. That raises the question: Is a Christian and Reformed ethic possible?[144] In other words, can one speak of a moral life among Reformed Christians? Most definitely! For these reasons:

1. The moral life is not degraded by conversion; our moral life provides the form, first for our natural life and then for our spiritual life. Our life as a member of a family, in vocation, in society, in church, in the state, in art and science, remain the same. That has to be considered in ethics.
2. Faith, regeneration, and sanctification are effected in us by God in a human manner, in accord with our nature, character, etc.; that is to say, in an ethical manner. Our thinking, feeling, willing, acting, our whole being and our whole life, can and must be viewed from a moral perspective.

There is, therefore, such a thing as Christian ethics because (a) the life of Christ is implanted in us in a moral way and is developed, and (b) the life

---

144. Ed. note: In the preceding sentences, where he speaks of "Christian ethics," Bavinck originally wrote "Christian Reformed" ("*Christ. Geref.*"), but crossed out "*Geref.*"

of Christ manifests itself outwardly. Presupposed here is the existence of a moral life with its own basis, content, and goal; a moral life by which human beings can be or become what they should be. To accept in part or whole the possiblity that such a moral life does not exist is anti-Christian and is to stand in the broken covenant of works. The content of such a so-called moral life is either natural, Adamic, and sinful, or it is spiritual, a regenerated life, the life of Christ.

This spiritual life can also be considered in its own right as a life from God and in saving fellowship with him. We are able to investigate that life in its origin, its maladies, its conflict, and its development. Thus we describe the life history of the person in Christ. Reformed theologians did so under the rubric of practical theology (e.g., Driessen[145] and Witsius[146]), the "old" and "new" person (Costerus[147]), the person in Christ (van den Honert[148]), and active theology (Lampe[149]). This is a necessary task. We need to know the nature, character, and fruit of the spiritual life, because we need to unmask hypocrites, lift up the downtrodden, comfort the sorrowful, heal the sick, and guide the strong. Diagnosis of the spiritual life is necessary especially for a pastor. Soul care is exceedingly important. A person's salvation sometimes hangs on a single word, a hint, or advice.

Now we face the difficult question: Are ethics and this practical theology two distinct disciplines, or can they be handled together? It seems that they are two distinct things because ethics is concerned with morality, and practical theology with religion; religion and morality must not be confused or mixed together. At the same time, there is much to be said for considering them together. (It remains good and necessary, nonetheless, for one to write about the spiritual life as something distinct; this does not, however, mean that they are two distinct disciplines.) Here are some reasons for keeping them together:

1. If ethics is separated from practical theology, the human factor is treated too lightly and ethics is set free from dogmatics, leading to Pelagianism.

2. As we have seen, the only content or the matter of the moral life is the spiritual life of fellowship with God—that is, religion. Considering the

---

145. Driessen, *Oude en nieuwe mensch*.
146. Witsius, *Prakticale godgeleertheid*.
147. Ed. note: Bavinck's reference to "Costerus" is not entirely clear. *Old and New Man* is the title of Antonius Driessen's work (above). Bavinck may have had in mind Florentius Costerus (1635–1703), author of *De geestelike mensch, in sijn begin, voort-gang, en uyt-eynde, voorgestelt in verscheyden predicatien*, 2nd rev. ed. (Hoorn: Stoffel Iansz., 1695).
148. Van den Honert, *De mensch in Christus*.
149. Lampe, *Schets der dadelyke Godt-geleertheid*.

spiritual life and moral life together guards us against seeing the moral life as a life unto itself; it protects us from establishing a covenant of works.

3. Even though religion and morality are two distinct things, they are nonetheless intrinsically bound together. One must manifest itself in the other. What we do must give evidence of who we are. Treating practical theology and ethics together furthers the mutuality of religion and morality; protects us from letting the spiritual life drift into feeling, quietiesm, or Pietism; and helps it [the spiritual life] to become evident in deeds, in action, in walking according to God's Word. Keeping them together also expresses the conviction that a normal and true life of faith must reveal itself through a strong moral life.

We can now specify what ethics is.

There is much to be said against the idea of treating ethics, as we have described it, as a separate discipline. One should link it either to dogmatics or to practical theology. We choose the latter because ethics that is linked with dogmatics does not properly come into its own; far too much is left undiscussed and ignored. History teaches that ethics is most closely bound with practical theology, but a pure, complete division of the two is impossible.

Ethics must concern itself with (a) how human beings as rational, responsible beings appropriate and use the gifts and powers of the first creation and accept the gospel of grace; (b) how humans are regenerated and how that life remains subject to sickness, temptation, and struggle; and (c) how, in ethical lives, human acts (of understanding, will, etc.) are directed toward God's law, which is to be manifested in all circumstances of their lives. In other words, ethics is concerned with the preparation, birth, development, and outward manifestation of the spiritual person. Ethics is the "developmental history of people redeemed by God,"[150] the "scientific description of the grace of Jesus Christ in operation, i.e., his divine life-content in the form of a human

150. Ed. note: Bavinck's quotation, "Entwicklungsgeschichte des von Gott erlösten Menschen," is his own reconstruction of two phrases in Harless, *Christliche Ethik*, 2: "geschichtlicher Entwicklungsprozess im Leben der von Christo gewonnenen Seelen" and "Entwicklungsgeschichte der von ihm erlöseten Menschen." Bavinck is quoting from Harless's first edition; the revised and expanded sixth edition, as well as the English translation based on the sixth edition, does not have these passages. Instead, Harless indicates his concurrence with a definition of ethics given in Jäger, *Die Grundbegriffe der Christlichen Sittenlehre*, 9. Jäger distinguishes ethics from dogmatics, with the latter describing the "creating, revealing, and saving deeds of God," while ethics reflects on the way in which those deeds "take shape in individual persons as free beings in their life activities."

person's life."[151] Ethics describes the concretizing of the kingdom of God in humanity; the origin, growth, and completion of Christ's body;[152] in other words, how, from beginning to end, on the foundation of and by means of God's acts for us and in us, the regenerated community comes into being. Ethics is the truth about our internal and external sanctification (Daneau),[153] the art of living unto God (van Mastricht),[154] the art of fruitful, godly living and dying well (Pictet).[155]

The distinction between dogmatics and ethics has become clear.[156] The difference does not lie in the fact that the former deals with the understanding and knowledge, while the latter is concerned with the will and conduct.[157] This would boil down to a division of human beings into two parts, of which one half is purely intellectual and the other purely ethical. No. In dogmatics[158] we are concerned with what God does for us and in us. In dogmatics God is everything. Dogmatics is a word from God to us, coming from outside us and above us; we are passive, listening, and opening ourselves to being directed by God. In ethics, we are interested in the question of what it is that God now expects of us when he does his work in us. What do we do for him? Here we are active, precisely because of and on the grounds of God's deeds in us; we sing psalms in thanks and praise to God. In dogmatics, God descends to us; in ethics, we ascend to God. In dogmatics, he is ours; in ethics, we are his. In dogmatics, we know we shall see his face; in ethics, his name will be written on our foreheads (Rev. 22:4). Dogmatics proceeds from God; ethics returns to God. In dogmatics, God loves us; in ethics, therefore, we love him.

The difference, therefore, does not consist in our weakening the doctrine of election in our examination of ethics, or that we become semi-Pelagian by allowing the human person finally "to come into his own" to achieve his rightful place. All Pelagianism must be rooted out; it is simply anti-ethical. It is precisely because God is everything that humans are truly great. There is no division of labor here where God does his part and we do ours. Not at all! We establish our calling precisely because God works all in all. This is a

---

151. Beck, *Vorlesungen über Christliche Ethik*, 1:84.

152. Ed. note: The source is unknown. Bavinck inserted a question mark in the text.

153. Daneau, *Ethices Christianae*.

154. Van Mastricht, *Theoretico-Practica Theologia*, II."Prologue" [4:521]: "The art of living for God . . . consists of two parts: (a) knowing how we who are spiritually dead can be made alive, and (b) having been made alive how we can live for God. The first is found in *faith* [*in fide*]; the second in the *obedience of faith* [*in obedientia fidei*]."

155. Pictet, *De christelyke zedekunst*.

156. Ed. note: Cf. *RD*, 1:56–58.

157. Which was the way the Reformed theologian Voetius distinguished dogmatics from ethics.

158. Ethics is also concerned with how the understanding must be regenerated, sanctified, etc.

mystery: just because God is everything, we can be great. A mystery, yes, but far better this mystery than a Pelagian, Remonstrant slice of the Gordian knot that divides God and humanity so that God cannot be God and human beings cannot be genuinely human.

§3. DIVISION AND ORGANIZATION OF ETHICS

In earlier centuries, ethics was frequently little more than instruction in virtues[159] and duties,[160] listed one after another in an unsystematic manner. This changed with Schleiermacher, who, in his philosophical ethics, insisted that the moral life can and must be considered from three perspectives that complement each other. As a *duty* the good stands over against human beings as *commandment*, a "must"; as *virtue* it is the *power* to do the good; as *goal* it is the *ideal* that duty pursues in harmony with virtue.[161] From these we get instruction in duties, in virtues, and in moral goods.[162] According to Schleiermacher, up to that point each one of these has been emphasized with a resulting ethic of law (Kant), an ethic of virtues (a "flat morality"), or a eudaemonistic, utilitarian ethics (the highest good). Instead, Schleiermacher claimed that the ethical is first of all brought forth in all three of these notions, that any two always produce the third, that duty cannot be fulfilled without virtue, virtue cannot exist without being normed by duty, and the highest good can only be realized by virtue that is identical with duty.

This order, followed by Rothe,[163] may be fine for philosophical ethics, but it cannot be used in theological ethics, however insightful it may be. It is an abstract scheme, and the material of theological ethics cannot be incorporated into it. It is an extrinsic division that defies the maxim that a proper ordering of the material must arise from the content itself. The good is not law (but grace); it is not goal or human striving (but gift!).

In some sense, the division is not difficult. Ethics is the description of the Christian life, and its course is therefore given to us. For all intents and purposes the divisions of the Protestant orthodox are virtually the same. Driessen's "Practical Divinity"[164] is divided into two parts: the old person

---

159. Pictet, *De christelyke zedekunst.*
160. Frequently also expansion of the Decalogue.
161. Cf. Chr. D. F. Palmer, "Die christliche Lehre vom höchsten Gut"; Heman, "Schleiermachers Idee."
162. GO: *Pflichtenlehre, Tugendlehre, Güterlehre.*
163. Rothe, *Theologische Ethik.* Ed. note: See Bavinck's discussion of Rothe toward the end of §2 above.
164. DO: *Practikale godgeleertheid.*

and the new. Teellinck's "The Man of God"[165] into three parts: humanity in sin, regenerated, flourishing/blessed.[166] Vitringa deals only with the spiritual life: its nature, origin, states, and perfection.[167] Pictet considers the disordered human condition, virtues in general, and then virtues particularly with a view to God, the neighbor, and ourselves;[168] van Mastricht considers only the virtues with respect to God and our neighbor;[169] Vilmar divides the material into sin, regeneration, etc., and sanctification.[170] Other divisions are found in Martensen: life before conversion, in imitation of Christ, in the spheres of family, state, etc.;[171] in Heppe: humanity before possessing salvation, in possession of salvation, and in confirmation of salvation's possession;[172] and in Harless: "the content of salvation" (humanity, law, gospel), the acquiring of salvation (regeneration, conversion), the preservation of salvation (piety, virtues in vocations, spheres).[173]

We thus obtain a threefold division:

165. DO: *De mensche Godts*.
166. Ed. note: Bavinck here alludes to a work of W. Teellinck, *De mensche Godts*, which consists of a description of human beings in eight "states": (1) corrupt nature (*verdorven natuure*), (2) regeneration and conversion (*der wedergeboorte en bekeeringe*), (3) the good life (*des wel levens*), (4) government (*der regeringe*), (5) offenses (*der struyckelingen*), (6) miseries (*der ellenden*), (7) reformation ("*der reformatie*"), and (8) blessedness (*der geluck-saligheyd*). *De mensche Godts* was prepared for publication by Franciscus Ridderus and also published under his name: *De mensche Godts: Uyt de geschriften en tractaten van Willem Teellingh* (1658).
167. Vitringa, *Korte schets*.
168. Ed. note: Here Bavinck paints in broad summary strokes the sequence of chapters in Pictet, *De christelyke zedekunst*.
169. Ed. note: Bavinck is referring to *Theoretico-Practica Theologia*, II.ii.1–15 and iii.1–8 (*Theologia Moralis*; *Zedelyke godgeleertheid*); the two chapters have the titles "Concerning Religion" (*De Religione*; *Van den godsdienst*) and "Concerning Righteousness and Injuries against the Neighbor" (*De Justitia et Injuria versus Proximum / Van de rechtvaardigheit en onrechtvaardigheit, of verongelykinge omtrent den naasten*) [4:564–668].
170. Ed. note: Bavinck is referring to Vilmar, *Theologische Moral*. The first volume includes, after the introduction, part I, "Doctrine of Sin" (*Lehre von der Sünde*) or "History of Illness" (*Krankheitsgeschichte*). The second volume includes part II, "The Doctrine of Regeneration and Conversion" (*Lehre von der Wiedergeburt und Bekehrung*) or "History of Cures" (*Heilungsgeschichte*), and part III, "The Doctrine of Sanctification" (*Die Lehre von der Heiligung*) or "History of Healing" (*Genesungsgeschichte*).
171. Martensen, *Christian Ethics*, 1:53.
172. Heppe, *Christliche Sittenlehre*. Ed. note: Heppe's "System of Ethics" consists of three parts, successively titled "The Human Person and the Saving Good in Itself" (*Der Mensch und das Heilsgut desselben*), "The Possession of Salvation" (*Der Heilsbesitz*), and "The Preservation of Salvation's Possession in the Essential Ordinances and Relationships of Human Life" (*Die Bewährung des Heilsbesitzes in den wesentlichen Ordnungen und Beziehungen des menschlichen Lebens*).
173. Ed. note: Harless's *System of Christian Ethics* is subdivided into three parts: "The Blessing of Salvation" (*Das Heilsgut*), "The Possession of Salvation" (*Der Heilsbesitz*), and "The Preservation of Salvation" (*Die Heilsbewahrung*).

1. Humanity before conversion, in the condition of sin, conscience, morality; this is the realm of natural ethics.

2. Converted humanity: the new life in its preparation, origin, aspects, circumstances, aids, blessing, marks, sickness and death, fulfillment;[174] this is the realm of practical theology.

3. Converted humanity in the family, vocation, society, state, and church.[175]

Those three sections will be treated in what follows and concluded in a summary, which will incorporate the result of ethical actions: the kingdom of God in its origin, development, and completion.[176]

§4. Foundation and Method of Ethics

Up to this point we have not yet clearly defined the theological character of ethics. Rothe[177] and Vilmar[178] both call their work "theological ethics," which is appropriate but insufficient, as can be seen from the significant differences between them. The question therefore is: "What is theological about the work?" According to Rothe, speculation that proceeds from self-consciousness is *philosophical*, whereas speculation that proceeds from the fact of God-consciousness—that is, from self-consciousness determined by God—is *theological*. Theology proceeds from God; philosophy comes to God from the outside. In Rothe's view, God is really nothing more than an idea of God that he develops dialectically and from which he deduces all moral concepts. Vilmar considers the theological character of ethics to be found in the real and objective saving deeds of God. This is correct. Theological ethics does not proceed from a nature in humanity, in a principle embedded in

---

174. Ed. note: Bavinck inserts a parenthetical reference here to Vitringa and Beets. The former is clearly Vitringa, *Korte schets*. The latter may be the Dutch Reformed poet, pastor, and Leiden University professor Nikolaas Beets (1814–1903).

175. Ed. note: The original manuscript contains the following lines, crossed out by Bavinck: "Each of these three sections is preceded with a special introduction or foundation that is anthropological and includes the following general presuppositions: humanity created originally in the image of God, with a moral nature, freedom, religion, and morality."

176. Ed. note: Book IV of Bavinck's manuscript, "The Life-Spheres in Which the Moral Life Must Be Manifested," has only three sections, all under the chapter title "The Family, Marriage, Divorce" (§§50–58). But Bavinck's notes indicate that four additional chapters were planned: "Society," "Art and Science," "The State," and "The Church, Humanity, and the Kingdom of God." A brief overview of this material may be found in an appendix in vol. 3 of *Reformed Ethics*.

177. Rothe, *Theologische Ethik*.

178. Vilmar, *Theologische Moral*.

creation, but from a revealed principle that comes from God and his deeds, his words for and to us, deeds and words that lead us back to God and find in him their goal.

One could object here that in ethics we consider the regenerated human person as the subject and that we consider the regenerate from the perspective of who they are and what they do on the basis of God's acts. Does this then not set aside the theological character of ethics? Not in any way, and for the following reasons:

1. We are considering the *regenerated* or converted person[179] who has been "born of God" in a supernatural manner; in other words, not the "natural" but the "theological" human person.
2. We are considering regenerated persons not from the human side but *as God views them* and desires that we consider them. This is something we are not naturally capable of doing; we can truly do it insofar as it is *revealed* to us.

Our ethics is therefore theological because truth in ethics, to the extent that it can be said to be true, is revealed to us; it is supernatural. Our ethics proceeds from God, is through God, and is for God. Also, in our ethics it is God who reveals to us the truth about sin, regeneration, sanctification, how we are to live in the state, and so forth.

The foundation of ethics now becomes clear to us. We understand this foundation differently from that of philosophical ethics, where the basic principle can be taken, for example, as intuitive or utilitarian morality. Rather, we take it in the sense of a source of knowledge, in parallel with dogmatics.[180] Since we are speaking of *theological* ethics, there can be only one source of knowledge that discloses to us God's viewpoint. And then, having abandoned natural theology, we have only Holy Scripture as the source. Scripture is the rule for teaching/doctrine and *life*. Our *Confession of Faith* says simply that Scripture is "for the regulating . . . of our faith."[181] Ethics is as closely related to and fully dependent on Holy Scripture as is dogmatics. On this point Vilmar is correct.[182] But, for the rest, matters are up for grabs. One person defines "Christian" in terms of the current beliefs and practices of the Christian community, another by what is consistent

---

179. Ed. note: Between the lines Bavinck wrote, "Consider *church* history, also a theological discipline."

180. LO: *principium cognoscendi*. Ed. note: *RD*, 1:207–33.

181. Belgic Confession, art. 5.

182. Vilmar, *Theologische Moral*, 1:15.

with the spirit of Jesus.[183] Rothe claims that Holy Scripture is the norm
of speculative theology, but very little comes of it in practice.[184] From the
fact that Reformed people, without noting it every time, derive their entire
teaching on virtues and duties from the Ten Commandments and the Lord's
Prayer, it is clear that they also consider Scripture as the source and norm
of ethics. This is what the Heidelberg Catechism does.[185] Daneau is correct
in claiming that philosophical ethics and Christian ethics proceed from different sources; the former is derived from nature, the latter from Scripture.[186]
According to Samuel Endemann, "Revealed moral theology is taken from
the whole of Scripture in the Old and New Testaments."[187]

There are differences over the use of the Old Testament. Even Lessius[188]
claimed that the Old Testament had no place in ethics.[189] This is incorrect;
the Old Testament has as much value and authority for ethics as it does for
dogmatics.[190] The moral law in the Old and New Testaments is identical;
Christ set forth no new moral laws. Nonetheless, we must not lose sight of
the differences between the Old and New Testaments. This is a difficult question because the Old Testament is, on the one hand, absolutely the word of
God and, on the other, also historical. In general, this is the rule to follow:
whatever in the Old and New Testaments is not of temporal, passing, historical significance, but of significance for the church of all ages, is authoritative
both in dogmatics and ethics.

Its derivation from Scripture is what gives ethics its Christian, theological
character. But our concern is also with a Reformed ethics. Ever since roughly
1750 there has been an aversion to distinguishing ethics along confessional,
ecclesiastical lines. According to Endemann,[191] there is no difference between
Reformed and Lutheran ethics (not so for Roman Catholic ethics); our
differences in theology "truly do not change our practice of the truth."[192]
(Unfortunately! Doctrine with no influence on life.) It was believed, and
this conviction grew stronger and stronger, that the moral realm was a free

---

183. Ed. note: Bavinck provides no specifics here, but the former sounds a great deal like
Schleiermacher and the latter like Ritschl.

184. Rothe, *Theologische Ethik*, §10.

185. Heidelberg Catechism, Lord's Days 34–52.

186. Ed. note: See Daneau, *Ethices Christianae*, 3:3–8 (book I, chap. 2).

187. Endemann, *Institutiones Theologiae Moralis*, 1:11 (§3). The Latin reads: "*theologia
moralis revelata ex tota sacra scriptura Veteris et Novi Testamenti est desumenda.*"

188. Ed. note: Leonardus Lessius, SJ (1554–1623), was professor of theology at Leuven.

189. According to Endemann, *Institutiones Theologiae Moralis*, 1:12 (§3).

190. Contra J. T. Beck, *Vorlesungen über christliche Ethik*, 1:103.

191. Endemann, *Institutiones Theologiae Moralis*, 1:12 (§3).

192. LO: "*Veritatis practicas plane non mutat*"; Endemann, *Institutiones Theologiae Moralis*,
1:11 (the opening sentence of §3).

territory where everyone could agree; while differences existed in theology, the moral law was the same for everyone. This was the illusion by which people sought to find unity in the church, in the school, and in the state, an illusion that still lives on. But it is an illusion; the history of our age has proved that. It is true, nonetheless, that confessional differences do not become apparent in ethics as quickly as in theology. There are two reasons for this:

1. because it takes a long time before life gets turned around and governed by new doctrine: we tend to remain inconsistent for some time, sticking with the tradition;
2. because the differences in ethics are often internal: externally, for example, we stay the same while the motives and intentions of our actions are different; it is these that really determine what is ethical.

At the present time, there is general agreement, albeit rather reluctantly by some (after all, it was a grand illusion), that ethics too is an ecclesiastical matter.[193] Doedes[194] denies any distinction: Jesus presents us with only one vision of the Christian life, not a Reformed or Lutheran or Roman Catholic one; it is the task of ethics simply to find that one presentation. What superficial chitter-chatter! Whether one likes it or not, there are differences. Harless calls his work *Christliche Ethik*, Beck the same, Rothe uses *Theologische Ethik* and Vilmar *Theologische Moral*—but it is clear again and again, on every page, whether an author holds to a Lutheran or Reformed or Roman Catholic theology or another. Since this is factually so, let us acknowledge it. According to Doedes, however, this is a failure: we must strive for a Christian ethic alone. Undoubtedly, but we will achieve this by searching not behind or above ecclesiastical differences but precisely through them. A Christian ethic lies before us. The general "catholic" Christian church subsists *in* the diversity of church communions. In addition, it is fortunate that there is a variety of ethical presentations; it is evidence that doctrine does daily influence life (let us not restrict this influence even more) and has the advantage that the Christian life is seen as even more rich when it is viewed from a variety of perspectives.

We offer here, therefore, a Reformed ethics, which is quite a different type of Christian living than the Roman Catholic, the Lutheran, the Anabaptist, the Methodist, the Moravian, the Darbyist, and so forth. How is

193. Hagenbach, *Encyklopädie und Methodologie*, 362–63 (§92).
194. J. I. Doedes, *Encyclopedie der christelijke theologie*, 196–97n3.

this Reformed ethic derived? Do we include in our sources the confessions, writers, and church historians? In that case we would have two sources: Scripture and Reformed documents. This is not permitted; it would be quite un-Reformed. Holy Scripture is the only source of our knowledge and stands by itself alone; neither a confession nor any other writing stands beside it.[195] How, then? After all, we do need to use these Reformed documents; we may not isolate ourselves from them and withdraw to our solitary rooms to read and explain Scripture. What, then, is our relationship to them? In the same way that the words "Christian" and "Reformed" are joined together in the name "Christian Reformed Church." This does not mean half Christian and half Reformed, or one-quarter Christian and three-quarters Reformed Church. There is no division here, no composition, no conglomeration. Instead, it means "Christian, in the sense of being 'Reformed,'" "Christian as it is most purely and clearly understood and confessed in the Reformed Church." "Christian Reformed Ethics" thus says the same thing as "Christian ethics, as it is most purely confessed and derived from Holy Scripture in the Reformed Church." "Christian" and "Reformed," therefore, do not represent a contrast, a composition, or a juxtaposition but a synthesis, a unity. It is Christian and, precisely for that reason, Reformed. That which is Christian comes to us through Reformed lenses; it shines most purely through the Reformed prism.

The method thus becomes clear; it is identical to that of dogmatic theology.

1. We need to gather together the material from Holy Scripture and arrange what it teaches about sins, regeneration, sanctification, the relationship between parents and children, and so forth.
2. We need to examine carefully the way in which the Christian church has handled this material, particularly the Reformed churches, taking note of:
   a. the way in which thinkers took ethical dogma very seriously; all the "older writers" [oude schrijvers] have to be considered here.
   b. the articulation of this "ethical dogma" in the confessions; the harvest is not rich here, although there is something; for example, in the Heidelberg Catechism, Lord's Days 34–52 are completely ethical.

195. Ed. note: Bavinck inserted an additional page between pp. 24 and 25 of the manuscript, on which the following was written: "Scripture and confession are not two sources. Because a confession is not a source, nothing wells up from it. A source, no matter how small, brings something forth. 'Reformed' adds nothing to 'Christian': a confession calls attention to Scripture. Reformed people say: 'Behold the pure water; others have also brought forth water, but with a polluted pail.'"

      c. in what manner and to what extent this "ethical dogma" comes to expression in the lives of Christians, particularly in the Reformed Church; a great deal of attention must be paid to this.

3. Finally, we need to develop this further in a normative way and apply it to our own day, in particular pointing the way by which we can complete ethical dogma (ascetics, not distinct from but shining through each topic).

BOOK I

HUMANITY
BEFORE CONVERSION

1

Essential Human Nature

How we must live is determined by our answers to the fundamental questions of our origin, purpose, and destiny.[1] *Scripture teaches us that the image of God belongs to the very essence of our humanity, created good, fallen, and redeemable in Christ. For Christians the moral good is not a purpose or ideal to be achieved through striving and exertion; it is a gift, a condition of being, a state. We must be good in order to do good. Adam was created good, and, after his fall, the Second Adam provides the gift of new righteousness and holiness.*

This confession directly contradicts the contemporary dogma that we become good through the conflict between our ego, which strives for autonomy, and the external world of nature and matter, which restricts us; the end goal is to overcome nature by reason and spirit. This is part of a pantheistic worldview in which God himself becomes a person only after a process of overcoming. This movement from below to above, from the material to the spiritual, from the earthly to the heavenly, from humanity to God, from the visible to the invisible, from the temporal to the eternal, directly contradicts Christian belief in revelation. It is a system from the abyss.

We believe that the image of God belongs to the essence of our humanity; humanity apart from God, therefore, is unimaginable; all human beings always and everywhere stand in some relation to God. To be fully and truly human we must image God. As

---

1. Ed. note: Bavinck's title for this chapter was "Human Nature Considered on Its Own" (*De menschelijke natuur op zichzelve beschouwd*). He inserted as an interlinear new title "The Essence of Humanity" (*Het wezen van de mensch*). Our title, "Essential Human Nature," is intended to capture both ideas.

image-bearers of God, we consist of body and soul, which exist together in a reciprocal interaction of spirit and matter that is complex and mysterious. This must not be understood dualistically, although while the body cannot live without the soul, the soul can exist apart from the body. Persons are unities of body and soul; we are persons because we can say "I." Our consciousness of this "I" develops gradually and is a wonder, inexplicable and simply to be accepted. Its two movements are theoretical (thinking and knowing) and practical (willing and doing), and both are mediated by feeling. These three abilities are distinct, have their own laws, and are free acts of the one person.

Human beings find themselves in three relations to what is external to them: to God (religion), to other persons (morality), and to nature. People cannot be viewed atomistically as mere individuals: we are members of a human race in a relationship to God that is an office or post of obedience and service to him. This is true religion and rests upon and arises from knowledge of God; its essence is piety. The word "religion" is derived from a Latin root that means "regathered" and reminds us that repetition of God's commands and ordinances is necessary for their observance. This is objective religion—walking in the ways of the Lord—which must be matched by subjective religion—that is, faith or believing. The objective is not the product of the subjective but a gift of the Holy Spirit. Religion should not be defined as "communion with God" because it makes subjective religion all-important and devalues objective religion. Instead, it is the distinctive relationship or position of human beings to God, expressing itself in all of life and based on the distinctive relation of God to human beings.

Our relation to other persons begins before birth and starts in the family, which is the type of all other relations in society and the state. Our life in all these relationships constitutes our moral life and must be guided by a standard that is external to us. For Christians that standard is the Word of God. Our moral lives have always been connected to our religious lives, but they are properly distinct, with the latter governing the former. Though the two tables of the law come from one Lawgiver and constitute a single law, it is important to distinguish religion (our love toward God) from morality (our love toward our neighbor). The Bible itself keeps them close and connected but still distinct. The two sinful misconstruals of the relation between religion and morality—absolute separation and identification—both lead to false religion and poor morality. Either morality is divorced from God and true virtue becomes impossible, or God is identified with the world and religion is completely absorbed by ethics and eventually disappears. The Sabbath can and should penetrate the other days of the week, but the fullness of this Sabbath penetration will not be realized in this dispensation and awaits the next.

§5. HUMAN BEINGS, CREATED IN GOD'S IMAGE

Questions about what human beings are, where they are headed, and the end and purpose of their existence depend on the answer to a prior question: Where did human beings come from? Origin determines direction and purpose. There is a big difference between saying that human beings are the image and offspring of the chimpanzee and orangutan and saying they are the image and offspring of God, between saying human beings are from below and saying they are from above. That governs the entire discipline of ethics. Without the Bible, it is impossible to answer the question of where human beings are from, and thus no answer can be given to the questions of what they are or where they are headed: one can only surmise, suspect, presuppose, and philosophize. The Greeks regarded human beings as autochthonous, as having originated from the earth, by chance, of their own accord. And contemporary thought, under the influence of materialistic pantheism,[2] which erases all boundaries, levels all things and makes all things uniform, sees human beings as originating from a primate ancestry through a series of missing links and extinct mediating forms (species) influenced by natural selection and the struggle for survival over the course of many millennia. No one has furnished proof of this; it is not a conclusion reached by science or even a hypothesis that is occasionally borne out. No, it is simply a philosophical idea which people assume because they will not recognize a Creator God. This was openly stated by Professor du Bois-Reymond in Berlin.[3]

By proceeding from a wholly different presupposition we reach a different ethic. Ethics in the true sense of the word does not exist within a Darwinian framework.[4] Every view of human beings starts from an axiom, a point of departure, a proposition of faith or hypothesis. This is the case with Darwin as well: his proposition of faith is that a human being is an evolved animal. For us, on the other hand, by faith, we understand that human beings are created in the image of God and are God's offspring (Acts 17:28). This has to be a

---

2. Ed. note: Bavinck regarded pantheism as one of the great threats of his day to a Christian worldview. See, inter alia, *RD*, 1:80; 2:408–15, 426–38; 3:42, 236, 299, 529; 4:60, 75, 92, 108, 161, 250, 576, 691, 699, 711.

3. Ed. note: Bavinck refers here to an essay by Emil du Bois-Reymond, "Naturwissenschaft und Philosophie von Nathusius," in *Zeitfragen des christlichen Volkslebens*; it was not possible to verify this reference. See https://en.wikipedia.org/wiki/Emil_du_Bois-Reymond. The reference to Nathusius is most likely to Martin Friedrich von Nathusius (1843–1906), author of *Naturwissenschaft und Philosophie: Zur beleuchtung der neuesten materialistchen Kundgebungen du Bois-Reymond u.a.* (Heilbronn: Henninger, 1883). Bavinck deals with du Bois-Reymond's views at greater length in his essay "Christianity and Natural Science," 85–87, 101–2.

4. Ed. note: Bavinck's note here reads "See last year's lecture" ("Zie dictaat vorig jaar"), an indication that he used these notes over and over again.

fixed and controlling principle when we examine humankind, a presupposition that governs all further reflection. To call human beings God's image is to say that the human person is God's likeness, his portrait in miniature, his imprint, effigy, or ectype.[5] The image of God is the human similarity to God whereby we display, in our own creaturely way, the highest perfection of God.[6] We are God's image with respect to all of our existence, in the soul with all its capabilities (thinking, feeling, willing) and also in the body.[7]

The image of God, therefore, exists

1. in the essence of our humanity: with soul and body as substrate;
2. in the capacities and abilities of that essence: knowing, feeling, willing, and acting;
3. in the properties and gifts of that essence and their capabilities: holiness, knowledge, righteousness.[8]

But the question now arises: What is the relation between the human essence and those properties of the image of God? In other words, is the image of God the essence, the nature of a human being, or something added to its nature? The Flacians say the image of God (thus also its properties, including original righteousness)[9] belongs to the *essence*, the nature of human beings.[10] This cannot be correct, because then humanity, on losing its original righteousness, would have lost and changed its essence. The Roman Catholics say that human beings were created with an unblemished nature[11]—hence neither righteous nor unrighteous by nature—and that original righteousness was added as a "superadded gift" to curb the naturally existing disharmony between flesh and spirit.[12] But

5. Ed. note: See *RD*, 2:531–33.

6. Van Mastricht, *Theoretico-Practica Theologia*, I.iii.9, §30 [2:99]. Ed. note: For an explanation of the format we are using to cite this work, see the extended note in the introduction, §1, in the section "Reformed Churches" (pp. 8–9n48). The volume and page numbers come from the 1749–53 Dutch edition used by Bavinck.

7. Van Mastricht, *Theoretico-Practica Theologia*, I.iii.9, §31 [2:99].

8. Van Mastricht, *Theoretico-Practica Theologia*, I.iii.9, §30–33 [2:99].

9. LO: *justitia originalis*.

10. Ed. note: Matthias Flacius Illyricus (1520–75) was a Lutheran reformer from present-day Croatia who held the view that the human fall into sin substantially transformed human nature into something evil.

11. LO: *in puris naturalibus*.

12. LO: *donum superadditum*. Ed. note: Bavinck's critique of Roman Catholic thought on this point can be found in *RD*, 2:539–48. However, Bavinck's treatment of Roman Catholic thought needs to be nuanced and corrected in places, particularly through a closer examination of Thomas Aquinas; see Bolt, *Theological Analysis*, 172n24, 180n29, 189n50. Cf. Vos, *Aquinas, Calvin, and Contemporary Protestant Thought*. An affinity between Bavinck and Thomas has

this also cannot be correct because then the struggle between flesh and spirit would be natural and good, coming directly from God, who would then be the cause of sin. The Reformed say that the image of God is neither the sum and total of human essence nor a "superadded gift." Rather, Reformed theology understands the image of God in a broad sense to include the essence and capabilities of a human being, while a narrower sense of the image involves true knowledge, righteousness, and holiness.[13] As original righteousness it belongs *naturally* to a human being, so that human essence or nature can no longer be complete and right without it. The image of God, therefore, belongs to the essence of human beings, although not in the Flacian sense.[14]

This statement is of paramount importance for ethics. *First*, because it implies that humans were good by nature, that the image of God by nature properly belonged to them, that they did not need to *become* good, holy, and righteous but *were* so already. Human beings by nature possessed goodness. This directly contradicts contemporary teachings. J. G. Fichte (1762–1814) taught with impressive intellectual power that morality only comes into existence out of conflict. The intelligent *ego* strives after freedom, self-sufficiency, and independence and wants to be absolutely autonomous but finds itself restricted by the *non-ego*. The *non-ego* has to be conquered and pushed back; the *ego* has to dominate the *non-ego*; reason has to rule over nature, and spirit over matter. Morality, thus, is the result of conflict, struggle, and wrestling; it lies at the end of the road, it is not a point of departure but an end goal. The *ego* is born as restricted by the *non-ego* (which is sinful, because for Fichte sin is restriction).

Similarly, for Hegel, humanity is at first only natural and evil by nature; it needs to free itself from the power of nature and, as spirit, needs to break free from nature and oppose it. For Schleiermacher, too, the goal of ethos is that nature becomes reason and spirit. The position of Rothe in his *Theologische Ethik* is similar; for him the personhood of God is itself the result of a process because the Spirit cannot be made but must bring himself forth, be his own effect and cause.[15] This is also the case with human beings.[16] God can create spirits only mediately; that is, he creates material creatures, which then raise themselves up out of materiality toward spirituality.[17] The *ego* is its own act and action only; the human being thus destines itself to be *ego*, a person. And

---

been clearly demonstrated recently by two younger scholars: Sytsma, "Bavinck's Thomistic Epistemology"; and Van Raalte, "Unleavened Morality."

13. Ed. note: These three terms that summarize the original image of God in Reformed orthodoxy are conflated from Eph. 4:24 and Col. 3:10.

14. Van Mastricht, *Theoretico-Practica Theologia*, I.iii.9, §44 [2:110–11].

15. LO: *sui ipsius effectus, causa sui*; Rothe, *Theologische Ethik*, §§31, 34.

16. Rothe, *Theologische Ethik*, §47.

17. Rothe, *Theologische Ethik*, §73.

morality exists in the fact that personhood becomes spirit.[18] The personal
creature has to treat itself as an end in itself[19] and has to create itself. Rothe
writes, "Morality is what is caused, what becomes by means of creaturely
self-determination, more specifically through the personal creature's own
self-determination in the human's earthly created sphere."[20] Rothe sketches
the moral process[21] as one in which human beings determine themselves absolutely to become persons, and this task is twofold: (a) it is *moral* with
respect to our material nature, which has to be appropriated and be made
our instrument;[22] and (b) it is *religious*, religion being the process by which
we become spirits, through our own causality.[23] Thus, we *become* immortal,
and so forth, through our own action.[24]

Overall, therefore, morality is a goal, the result of a process, an ideal which
human beings finally reach through their own efforts and self-determination.
This ethics, constructed on pantheism, a philosophy of process, and the theory
of evolution, shares with pantheism an extraordinary number of core ideas.
Everywhere in the physical, ethical, religious, civil, social, and political domains, the higher development is seen as having evolved from the lower. From
below to above, from the material to the spiritual, from the earthly to the
heavenly, from humanity to God, from the visible to the invisible, from the
temporal to the eternal. This is directly the opposite of what we confess as
Christians because it is directly contrary to God's revelation. It is a system
from the abyss. It has influenced a good deal of the ethics of our day, and
yet many believers do not perceive its terrifying nature but unconsciously accept its thoughts and perspectives, which only fit in that anti-biblical system.
Thus Harless speaks of a purpose which is given to the Christian in Christ,
and Martensen considers morality as an idea, an end goal, a final task for the
will.[25] Vilmar, however, understood this better.[26]

Directly opposing these pantheistic theories[27] is the view of human beings
as created in God's image. The moral and the good is not an ideal hovering

---

18. Rothe, *Theologische Ethik*, §83.
19. GO: *Selbstzweck*.
20. GO: *Selbstbestimmung*; Rothe, *Theologische Ethik*, §87. Ed. note: Bavinck adds two
German words after the quotation: *kausirte* = "caused"; *gewordene* = "become."
21. Rothe, *Theologische Ethik*, §§93–126.
22. Rothe, *Theologische Ethik*, §§97–113.
23. LO: *causa sui*.
24. Rothe, *Theologische Ethik*, §§109–10.
25. Harless, *System of Christian Ethics*, 5 (§2); Martensen, *Christian Ethics*, 1:4, 10–13 (§§1, 4).
26. Vilmar, *Theologische Moral*, 1:23–37.
27. Ed. note: What Bavinck calls "pantheism" here is better described as "panentheism."
On panentheism see Cooper, *Panentheism*; on Schleiermacher, see pp. 80–89, and on Schelling
and Hegel, see pp. 90–119.

far off in the distance from humanity and which we need to reach. The good
is not the end goal of life, a destination for humans, but the foundation on
which we stand and the environment within which we stand. The good is not
before us but above us and behind us; we stand in it with both feet and are
upheld by it. Adam did not have to *become* good, he *was* good and had to
ensure that he *remained* good. This is not striving and chasing after something,
but remaining and resting in that which he was and had. He came from the
hand of God holy, righteous, and wise. It is utterly false to say that holiness
could not be inborn and cocreated but must be the result of a process of free
self-determination, of one's own action. Holiness is a gift; otherwise we shall
never have it. But we receive it now, at once, through justifying faith in Christ.
For this reason, moral virtue (holiness, the image of God) is *one*, a seamless
garment, which cannot be reached and obtained in piecemeal fashion. Whoever
has moral virtue has it wholly; whoever lacks it in part lacks it completely. The
Stoics already recognized this. From evil to good is not a walkway or bridge;
we reach it only by a leap (a leap of life rather than the proverbial fatal leap,
to change the expression). It is precisely the fundamental error of pantheism
that it wipes out all boundaries, relativizes all oppositions, and reduces the
distinction between sin and holiness, God and devil, to a difference of degree
only.[28] For Christians, therefore, Adam *was* holy and had to *remain* such.
The fall into sin was not a step forward, but undoubtedly a *fall*, a downfall.
The moral good, therefore, is not a purpose or ideal to be obtained through
striving and exertion; it is a gift, a condition of being, a state. It remains true
forever that a tree has to *be good* if it is to bear good fruit.[29] Pantheism also
obliterates the distinction between human beings and animals and views us
as developing from an animalistic (unthinking, etc.) state into our humanity.

Now it is true that Reformed Christians, in distinction from Lutherans,
can also speak of a goal in the case of Adam: we acknowledge that Adam had
not yet reached the end; he did not yet have eternal life; he did not yet have
the ability not to sin.[30] In that sense we can also speak of a goal in the case of
Adam. But there is also a significant difference. We do not consider this "end"
so much a *goal* as a *result*. Adam did not have to strenuously exert himself
to obtain it but had merely to do what his own nature recommended—that

28. Ed. note: See Kuyper, "Blurring of the Boundaries."
29. Ed. note: Matt. 7:17.
30. LO: *non posse peccare*. Ed. note: This phrase comes from Augustine and describes the
fourth and final state in outline of redemptive history. In order, the four states of humanity are
(1) innocence: able to sin or not to sin (*posse peccare aut non peccare*); (2) fall: not able not to
sin (*non posse non peccare*); (3) grace: able to sin or not to sin (*posse peccare aut non peccare*);
and (4) glory: not able to sin (*non posse peccare*). See Augustine, *Enchiridion* 118 (NPNF[1] 3:275).

is, to remain what he was. The command not to eat was a *prohibition*.[31] By remaining what he was, he would obtain what he was not.

That we cannot understand or imagine humanity without God and that all human beings always and everywhere stand in some relation to God is the *second* implication of the claim that the image of God belongs to the essence of our humanity. God is the archetype, the exemplar, the original. We are only truly human to the extent that we display God, also in our daily lives. The human person, therefore, has to be viewed theologically, and also in ethics. Morality, too, finds its principle and standard in the relation in which a human being stands to God. This principle is also strongly contested in our time. It is Fichte who dominates our present age: he sees the essence of morality involving the *ego* governing the *non-ego* and reason governing nature; the world is the material content of our moral obligation. This is also the case with Hegel: spirit has to realize its rational content, to mentally permeate nature. According to Schleiermacher the subject matter of ethics is reason acting on nature, and Rothe's position is similar.[32] Humanity stands in relation to nature and to God. The first relation is *moral*, the second *religious*. The moral task of human beings is to condition nature as an organ, an instrument, to make nature our property, a natural organism. Here morality is not only a result but the result of a process, the unity of two (relative) opposites, the product of conflict and struggle. But it is also wrong to think that the good and the moral only become possible by and after struggle, for then good, in order to exist now and to come in the future, needs evil; light needs darkness, and God needs the devil. Evil is then inevitable and actually no longer evil but a necessary intermediate stop, a barrier, a limitation, a transition phase, the condition and sine qua non for the good. And this means that the good is no longer good, since it is not free, independent, and eternal.

As Christians we believe and teach the contrary. The first human was God's image at once, good and holy; the struggle we now experience only came because of our falling away; it is a struggle with sin, in sin, and after sin. The good, as we see it, is victory, rest, salvation, peace, love; not "storm and stress"[33] but calmness. It is eternal, independent, free, in need of nothing, existing in and through itself and by itself, because God himself is the good

---

31. DO: *verbod*.

32. Rothe, *Theologische Ethik*, §96–113.

33. GO: *Sturm und Drang*. Ed. note: The term is connected with the early Romantic movement in German music and literature in the late eighteenth and early nineteenth centuries. It stressed individual subjectivity, action, and intense emotional freedom producing turbulence and turmoil in reaction to the constraints of Enlightenment rationalism. The term was popularized by the title of a work by German dramatist and poet Friedrich von Klinger (from https://en.wikipedia.org/wiki/Sturm_und_Drang).

and no goodness exists apart from him. Martensen also acknowledges the fact that morality cannot presuppose a struggle, etc., but thinks that, among other things, morality is the unity of opposites.[34] This is completely wrong.

Men like Fichte have to search for such binary structures because they view morality as a unity of opposites, as the result of struggle. Various names are used to describe these opposites. Autonomous philosophical ethics looks for them in the empirical and the ideal (reasonable) will; in the individual and in humanity, egoism and altruism (like Darwin and those following his thought); or in personality and in nature.[35] The first opposition, between the empirical and ideal will, does not work. It is an abstraction: human beings have but *one* will, and the (empirical) will is evil, sinful, inclined to hate God and the neighbor.[36] What some call the ideal or reasonable will is not a *will*—that is to say, *power*—but (since human beings are powerless) only an idea, an ideal, given to us by our conscience. In the battle between the empirical will and the idea of the good, the empirical will always triumphs. The second opposition, between the individual and humanity, does not work either. It is completely socialist and sacrifices the individual for the sake of the majority, allowing a majority of one-half plus one to determine what is good and evil.

The third binary opposition, morality as the product of the conflict between personality and nature or reason and nature (Fichte, Schleiermacher, Rothe), is also not a viable option. This was essentially the view of the Greeks, a view that is once again being proposed by some of our anthropological philosophers in a somewhat more profound manner. Spirit and matter, personality and nature, are not inherently opposed (at least not originally; now, thanks to sin, they are); personality is by no means dissolved in its relations with nature.[37] But there is some truth in these oppositions: human beings stand in relation to themselves (with duties toward themselves), to their neighbors, and to nature, but all of this is only part of a whole, and to reduce our entire duty to any one of these would be wrong. Regarding nature, Genesis 1:28 teaches us to be fruitful, multiply, fill the earth and subdue it, and have dominion over the fish of the sea and so forth. There exists, therefore, also a relation between humans and animals. But that is by no means the only

34. Martensen, *Christian Ethics*, 1:10–13 (§4).

35. Ed. note: In the margin Bavinck added, "We cannot do away with God if we want to define the good; neither in the case of Kant nor by the socialists."

36. Ed. note: Bavinck alludes here to Heidelberg Catechism, Q&A 5: "Can you live up to all this [God's Law] perfectly?" Answer: "No. I have a natural tendency to hate God and my neighbor."

37. Cf. Martensen, *Christian Ethics*, 1:10–13 (§4), but use with discretion.

calling of humanity; it is only one of the entailments and consequences of being created in God's image (Gen. 1:27). And one must read carefully: to have dominion over the earth was not an end goal for human striving through considerable conflict. It was not a distant ideal, a destination at the end of a path of exertion. No! It was a part but not the sole content and consequence of being made in God's image. Adam did not have to *become* lord and master of the earth, conquer it, and exercise dominion over it. Instead, he *was* the lord and master and sovereign and had to *demonstrate* this fact and continue to exercise lordship.

Martensen also argues against this contrast but replaces it with another: morality is produced by conflict, but not between personality and nature but between two personalities, me and you, will and will, specifically human will and God's will. Thus he says that morality consists of the free unity of the human and the divine wills.[38] These are notes that sound orthodox,[39] embroidered with pantheistic philosophical patterns. But Martensen does not start with correct principles. He should have rejected the root idea that morality (being moral and good) is the result of struggle and a unity of opposites. That is a false notion. For us, the moral good is not something in process of *becoming* but something that *is*. It is not a *product* but a *producer*; it is not a *result* but a *point of departure*. Furthermore, the foundational idea of the moral good is not derived from our relation to ourselves, to our neighbor, or to nature, but from the central, all-governing relation of human beings to God. Martensen gets this right. But one has to understand this properly. It does not mean that somebody who stands in the right relation to God (for example, one who is converted) is by virtue of this already moral and can be described as moral. This would blur the difference between religion and morality; more will be said about relation between them later. But it does mean that the relation to God is the central relation controlling everything. Humans are to be viewed as image-bearers of God in our relations to ourselves, our neighbors, and nature. This reality must be seen in and through everything we do or leave undone and in everything effected with us, in us, or through us.

In other words, that which is considered to be *normally* human cannot truly serve as the standard of ethics. It is not enough to be a person exercising dominion over nature. We can only be truly *good* at home, in the public square, and everywhere else, when we are the image of God. After all, we

---

38. Cf. Martensen, *Christian Ethics*, 1:10–13 (§4). Ed. note: In the opening sentence of §5 (p. 13) Martensen speaks of "union with God . . . as the final aim of human effort."

39. Ed. note: Bavinck originally wrote "shining" (*schijnende*) but changed it to "sounding" (*klinkende*).

cannot know proper dominion over nature apart from God and his revelation. In an etymological sense, ethics has its roots in religion. The notion of ethics therefore cannot fully satisfy us; it is too narrow. Etymologically, the word points to humanity as the standard, but our standard is humanity as God's image and thus, in the final analysis, God himself.

Third, the notion of humanity as God's image entails the essence of human beings having been corrupted through sin. After all, the image of God is part of the essence of humanness, not a *donum superadditum*, not an added trimming. According to Rome, humankind is not corrupt and corrupted but is still what it was supposed to be; but it lost this accessory, this bridle, and because it is no longer controlled and restrained, concupiscence (which humans had before the fall as well) now reigns.

We would say that by the loss of the image of God people's very essence became corrupted, deteriorated and twisted,[40] deformed, misshaped, and wrong. More about this, however, in chapter 2. Sin did not remove something and leave all the rest the same, as Rome would say. Neither did sin become the substance or essence of human beings. The human being remained a human being, not a machine, not a wooden thing or block, not a devil, but a human being. But the human became abnormal; though still human, its humanity is cankered and rotten.

The ethical meaning of the covenant of works is relevant here.[41] The covenant of works assumes that humanity is the image of God. Humankind *is* good, but still has a task: good works. The covenant therefore involves not carefree idleness or quiet rest, as Rome and Luther described, but work, task, goal, thus exertion, zeal, and development of all powers and gifts. It involves becoming the image of God more and more through procreation, worship, and culture. From humanity's creation in the image of God it follows that humans are moral beings and have to develop as such. In this regard the *moral law* must also be mentioned. The moral law is one of many sorts of law,[42] and its basic principle is love for God and one's neighbor. At this point law must be mentioned because the very notion of sin presupposes *law* (see question 3 of the Heidelberg Catechism).[43]

---

40. DO: *verwrongen*.

41. Ed. note: On the covenant of works, see *RD*, 2:567–79, 585–88. This classic Reformed doctrine is defined in the Westminster Confession of Faith (7.2) as follows: "The first covenant made with man was a covenant of works, wherein life was promised to Adam; and in him to his posterity, upon condition of perfect and personal obedience."

42. Ed. note: Bavinck inserts here a general reference to his *Hedendaagsche moraal*, a translation of which appears as an appendix in the third volume of *Reformed Ethics*.

43. Ed. note: Heidelberg Catechism, Q&A 3: "From where do you come to know your sins and misery? The Law of God teaches me."

§6. The Content of Human Nature

That human beings are the image of God has to be central; it is the assumption and standard of all true anthropology. But other questions then follow: What does it mean to be human? Wherein does our humanity consist? What are the constituent parts of that humanity? Furthermore, is likeness of God the formal or the material essence of a human being? The usual answer to this question is to say that we consist of a soul and a body. In this answer it is helpful to conceive of human persons as having at once a spiritual and material, supernatural and natural, supersensory and sensory, heavenly and earthly, eternal and temporal side.

We do not fully understand the *relation between body and soul*.[44] We are sensory, reasonable beings; we have plantlike/vegetative life, animalistic life, and a thinking life.[45] Alternatively one could say that a human being has a body, a soul, and a spirit (or, as Hegel put it, life, consciousness, and self-consciousness). In this case, "soul" then has a broader meaning and refers to that which humans share with animals. In a narrower sense, contrary to what all materialists claim, the soul is the thinking, mental life of human beings and is not only different in degree but essentially distinct from vegetative and animal life. Materialism denies this fact, but matter as such is without consciousness, and even supposing that matter could rise to a level of consciousness, such a consciousness would always remain the consciousness of something material.[46] But the soul is not only conscious, it is also conscious that it is not material; and it can imagine the total absence of matter in which its consciousness would remain. Moreover, while matter can only have a composite unity, the unity by which the soul is conscious of itself is of a simple, single, and noncomposite kind. For this reason du Bois-Reymond admits that self-consciousness cannot be physically explained. The soul, then, is essentially different from the body. It is not a property or quality of matter, but something on its own, yet related to the body. The soul depends on the body, as we see in sleep, sickness, and old age. It depends on the senses, through which the soul mainly receives content from outside. It also reveals itself to the outside world through language, voice, and organs of speech. Its character and temperament is formed by outside influences; climate, diet, nationality, gender have a great influence on human beings.

44. Cf. Lindner, *Lehrbuch der empirischen Psychologie*, 11–25 (§§7–12); Lichtenfels, *Lehrbuch zur Einleitung in die Philosophie*, 21–52.

45. GrO: θρεπτικόν, αἰσθητικόν and νοητικόν, λογικόν.

46. Bruch, *Theorie des Bewußtseins*, 84–125.

Conversely the body depends on the soul, as we see in sickness, in weeping, and in laughter. Similarly, the soul forms or shapes the body (hence the existence of physiognomy).[47] There is therefore a reciprocal influence of body and soul. This is also why a distinction is made between *sensory* nerves, by which something is brought from the outside to the inside, and a "sensation" is caused, and *motor* nerves, by which something is brought from inside to the outside, and a movement is caused. The nerves are the organ of interaction between body and soul. And there are various explanations of this interaction. Descartes, Geulinx, and Malebranche maintained that body and soul are completely heterogenous and that the one cannot operate upon the other. This is why they invented Occasionalism, according to which God is the mediator who repeatedly orders the sensible world (the body) according to our ideas, and orders the ideas (soul) according to the sensible world. This is a thoroughly mechanical system which does not really explain anything, because if the spiritual cannot produce effects on the material, how can God produce effects on bodies and in nature? It also tends toward pantheism (Spinoza) and attributes sin to God. Spinoza only recognized one substance of which spirit and matter were modes, and he saw no further need for explanation because both spirit and matter were ultimately suspended and subsumed in a single substance. Leibniz attempted to explain the interaction through what he called preestablished harmony,[48] the eternal predetermination by God of the objective agreement of all things with one another. Kant did not offer an explanation because he wondered whether the duality of body and soul might merely be an assumption; over time it might appear that the two were not so dissimilar after all. Schelling and Hegel handle subject and object, spirit and matter, just as Spinoza did.[49]

It appears therefore that the reciprocal interaction of spirit and matter is a most complicated question which remains unresolved. All the attempted explanations basically suggest analogies between what is psychical and what is physical. And one should take into account that cause and effect do not have to be simultaneous: movement may only eventually produce heat, for

---

47. Ed. note: Physiognomy (from Greek φύσις = nature, natural characteristics + γνώμων = judge, interpreter) is "the assessment of a person's character or personality from his or her outer appearance, especially the face." Though it goes back to antiquity and possesses an extensive literature, "as understood in the past [it] meets the contemporary definition of a pseudoscience." However, "recent studies have suggested that facial appearances do 'contain a kernel of truth' about a person's personality" (https://en.wikipedia.org/wiki/Physiognomy). The "recent study" cited here is Highfield, Wiseman, and Jenkins, "How Your Looks Betray Your Personality."

48. LO: *harmonia praestabilita*.

49. Bruch, *Theorie des Bewußtseins*, 123.

example. And it is also the case that there are other interactions that cannot be explained, such as the effect of atoms upon one another, for example how sulphur reacts upon mercury to produce cinnabar.[50]

To the extent that it involves a dualism, it is an error to define human beings simply as consisting of a body and a soul. While we do not accept materialism or spiritualism, we also do not accept the dualism of, for example, Plato, the Manichaeans, or the Ascetics. This is because Genesis 2:7 informs us that God formed Adam out of the dust[51] and breathed into him the breath of life,[52] so that he became a living soul.[53] The joining of dust and breath does not cause the two to exist dualistically next to each other but produces something new, a living unity, a living soul. We therefore subscribe to the position of Harmonism—namely, that matter does not continue its own existence and life next to the spiritual as one with equal rights, but that matter is subservient to and serves as instrument for the spiritual. The body cannot exist without the soul, but the soul can exist apart from the body. There is not a unity, identity, and sameness of matter and spirit, but a harmonious joining in which matter is subject to spirit. Briefly summarized, the body is an organism of the soul which inspirits, spiritualizes, eternalizes, and governs it.

The unity of the human being lies in his or her *I*. That is the root, the center, the kernel, the core of every person. Everything else lies around it and is near to it and attaches to it: I *have* intellect, feelings, a will, a body, hand, foot, etc., but I *am* . . . *I*. Holy Scripture calls this the heart, out of which are the issues of life (Prov. 4:23). We are persons because we can say "I." This *I* is what forms our humanity in us, what is actually human. This *I* always and under all circumstances remains the same and identical with itself. The *I* is a wonder, inexplicable, and simply to be accepted. This consciousness or *I* develops gradually. It starts with a sense of existence, which is usually initially painful. When a child first enters the world, she cries when air suddenly enters her lungs,[54] and senses a unity with the body (and senses pain in the foot but not, for example, in the table). But the child does not yet reliably distinguish herself from surrounding objects. She plays with her foot like she plays with a toy. Little by little she begins

50. Lindner, *Lehrbuch der empirischen Psychologie*, 18; cf. Stahl, *Fundamente einer christlichen Philosophie*, 48–50. Ed. note: Cinnabar is a bright red toxic mercury sulfide mineral with the chemical formula HgS; it was used as a pigment for jewelry and ornaments (http://geology.com/minerals/cinnabar.shtml).
51. HO: עָפָר.
52. HO: נִשְׁמַת חַיִּים.
53. HO: נֶפֶשׁ חַיָּה.
54. Bruch, *Bewußtseins*, 29.

to sense that this hand or this foot is hers, and she distinguishes it from objects, and contrasts it with objects, and thus begins to sense her own individual existence.[55] Yet she still stands across from herself, and sees herself as an object, and refers to herself in the third person. But gradually[56] the consciousness awakes that that object is I myself, gradually one comprehends oneself more fully, *knows* oneself (no longer *feels* oneself) and says, "*I.*" This is the sunrise in the inner life: the human person is no longer a stranger to himself, he has come to himself, all others stand outside, across from him. This *I*-consciousness then develops more and more, and understands itself more and more clearly, and distinguishes itself more definitely from what it has rather than is. What it is, is only the *I*.[57] That *I* has a real existence, it is no idea or representation,[58] but a being, or rather *the* being in us (all the others are but revelations of the *I*). It forms a complete unity, it always remains the same, it is simple and noncomposite, it is always the one, *whole I* that reveals itself.[59] It is nonspatial: although empirically united with a body, it has no length and breadth but is ubiquitous in the body, and where it is, the whole soul is. The soul does not really have a seat in the body; although it works mainly through the brain, it remains permanently identical, and the elderly know that their *I* is the same as it was during their childhood.[60] The soul is thus timeless, and therefore transcendant and supernatural.

This one, indivisible human *I* moves in two ways:

1. theoretical: thinking, knowing, receiving, and the ability of attraction whereby things are taken up in our spirit in a spiritualized form, and
2. practical: willing or doing, spontaneity and the ability of repulsion through which we realize the thoughts of our spirit outside of us.[61]

Both the theoretical and practical abilities of the soul are mediated by *feeling*. A thought works through *feeling* to have an effect upon the will and vice versa.[62] There are consequently three abilities of the *I*. These are not three parts, they are not three potencies separated from the *I*. In all three it is the same single, undivided, and entire *I* revealing itself. It is the same single and

55. Bruch, *Bewußtseins*, 38.
56. Bruch, *Bewußtseins*, 40.
57. Bruch, *Bewußtseins*, 47.
58. Bruch, *Bewußtseins*, 53.
59. Bruch, *Bewußtseins*, 55–56.
60. Bruch, *Bewußtseins*, 57, 58; Lichtenfels, *Lehrbuch zur Einleitung in die Philosophie*, 48.
61. Bruch, *Bewußtseins*, 133.
62. Bruch, *Bewußtseins*, 135, 136.

entire *I* which thinks, wills, and feels. It is not one part of the *I* which thinks and another part which wills, but it is the same *I*[63] which, when it works, reveals three sides of itself. All three abilities presume the *I*, the self-consciousness, the foundation on which the edifice stands.

These three abilities have their own life, character, laws, and conditions. The laws of thought are different from those of the will.[64] The domain of the first ability, thinking, is perceiving through the senses, forming representations, keeping these representations in memory and reproducing it in unchanged form through remembering or in changed form through the power of imagination. It is also about thinking,[65] abstracting, forming concepts without representation, judging, deciding, and revealing all of these activities through language. The laws of thought are revealed through and in the activity of thinking. Logicians have derived the discipline of logic from the activity of thinking and according to the activity of thinking. The laws of thought are therefore a priori in our thinking soul. By thinking, we spiritually absorb the external world into ourselves.

The second ability, feeling, is passive and receptive. The soul and the body do not actively express themselves in the feelings, but are affected by the representations which each receives, whether pleasant or unpleasant.[66] The existence and life of the spirit are thereby hindered or promoted. All feelings can be one of two kinds: like or dislike, inclination or disinclination. These feelings are distinguished depending on the objects which affect us. The number of feelings is innumerable. They are often roughly divided into *lower* and *higher* feelings. Lower feelings include sensations of life, of energy and of exertion and their opposites; and all the sensual perceptions of taste, sight (such as colors), hearing (shrill tones, for example). Higher feelings are intellectual, aesthetic, moral, religious, self-esteem, and compassion. The domain of the second ability, feeling, is therefore the residence of our rich human life of feeling, all the variety of affections of admiration, anger, courage, ecstasy, fear, shame, remorse, despair, and the like.

The third ability, willing, can be either sensual or spiritual according to its content. Sensual willing is called a drive, desire, or urge, and is originally simply an instinct. It is really the urge for life and self-preservation, comprising the desires for food, movement, freedom, and sex. There are also urges for social interaction, for honor, possession, rule, etc. These drives can become inclinations, tendencies, or passions (the desire for self-indulgence,

---

63. Bruch, *Bewußtseins*, 134n.
64. Bruch, *Bewußtseins*, 138.
65. An animal has representations, but no comprehension.
66. Bruch, *Bewußtseins*, 136.

lust, addiction to play, etc.). Spiritually this ability is primarily the willing of something. And to will is, properly speaking, the ability to do something for a reason, after preceding consideration; yet willing does not consist of an independent indifference and arbitrariness. The human will is free, but not unmotivated. It is free of compulsion whether by God or by the world. The will is a spontaneous ability of free self-determination according to the insight, and so on, which the *I* currently enjoys. Bruch says that freedom is an attribute not only of the ability of the will but of all three abilities; the *I* itself is free in its thinking, feeling, and willing.[67]

§7. HUMAN RELATIONSHIPS[68]

Having investigated how we should view human beings (as the image of God) and what is involved in being human, we must now consider the relations humans have to what is external to them. People cannot be viewed loosely as mere individuals; human beings are not atoms or numbers. This atomistic view was the error of the French philosophers like Rousseau and is the fundamental error of revolutionary thought. The term "individual" belonged to the revolution and expressed its all-consuming character. Our fathers did not know the word "individualism" because for them there were no mere individuals; to be human was always to be the image of God, a member of the human race. For the revolution, humanity is an aggregate mass of individuals who can be arbitrarily combined, like the random collision of Epicurus's atoms, into state, society, etc.[69] Today, individualism is still the basis of our politics. This result is inevitable, because once God is taken out of the picture and his

67. Bruch, *Bewußtseins*, 139–43.

68. Ed. note: Bavinck's heading was "The Life-Relations of Humans" (*De levensverhoudingen van den mensch*), and he inserted between the lines a different Dutch term, *levensbetrekkingen* (life's posts/positions/jobs/offices); for the most part we will be translating *betrekkingen* as "relationships," with the understanding that these relationships are not loose and undefined but stable, defined positions or offices.

69. Ed. note: Bavinck is reflecting the nineteenth-century Dutch historian and statesman Guillaume Groen van Prinsterer's signature work *Lectures on Unbelief and Revolution*, lecture 9. Groen van Prinsterer insists that "the common foundation of all rights and duties lies in the sovereignty of God." When this sovereignty is denied, it is true that "all men are, in a revolutionary sense, free and equal." But then, he adds, "state and society disintegrate, dissolving into a collection of isolated human beings, of *individuals*—a term of the Revolution's naively expressive of its all-destructive character" (p. 203). The Dutch original, *Ongeloof en revolutie*, 189, refers explicitly to Epicurus: "like the world according to the familiar system of Epicurus—'from the chance concurrence of atoms'" (*ex concursu fortuito atomorum*), which Bavinck cites. Epicurus (341–270 BC) was a Greek philosopher known for his emphasis on sophisticated hedonism.

providence denied, there is no conceivable reason why there should be social hierarchies, why one person should be richer than another, why one should rule and others be subjects. Instead, everything has to be made equal, smoothed out, leveled. (And the guillotine is the instrument to accomplish this.) This requires everything to be trimmed and cut away until what remains is equal in all respects. This effort has to reach far back and deep into history. In reality, however, nothing remains.[70] The revolutionary view is false. We have to be understood in the relations in which we stand, naturally and historically. We all stand in a threefold set of relations: to God, to other human beings, and to nature.

1. Our Relation to God

As humans we are God's image and have an innate idea of God.[71] Never and nowhere are we independent of God but always dependent on the highest power. Yet this is not the relation of which we are speaking here. Animals and plants are also dependent on God. All creatures live and move and have their being in God (Acts 17:28). Animals and plants also stand in relation to God. But in the case of humanity, that relation is a *relationship* and a *post* or *office*.[72] An animal exists before God in a state of bondage, a human person in a state of dependence. This peculiar human relation to God we call "religion." What is religion?[73] We are born to obey, know, and follow God. "By this bond of piety, we are bound and obligated to God, and this is whence it received the name 'religion' itself, not, as Cicero thought, from the word 'reread.'"[74]

---

70. Cf. Groen van Prinsterer, *Ongeloof en revolutie*, 189; *Lectures on Unbelief and Revolution*, 203; Fabius, *De Fransche revolutie*, 72–85.

71. Ed. note: For more on Bavinck's understanding of an "innate" or "implanted" knowledge of God, see *RD*, 1:302; 2:54, 59–68, 71–72.

72. DO: *verhouding [is] eene betrekking*; van der Hoeven, *De godsdienst het wezen van den mensch*, 28. Ed. note: See n. 68 above.

73. Ed. note: Bavinck refers here to the fuller treatment of religion in *RD*, 1:235–382, esp. 236–37. Bavinck also added two marginal notes at this point:

　　1. Vilmar, *Dogmatik*, 9. Ed. note: Bavinck points to Vilmar's *Dogmatik* because in a footnote Vilmar explained the possible etymology of the word *religio* as either *religare* (= to bind together, from Lactantius) or *religere* (= to reread, do over, observe with care, from Cicero). See further the discussion on this issue later in the chapter.

　　2. Religion in the subjective sense (*religio subjectiva*) includes three things: (a) religious representation; (b) inclination, affection for the object of this religious representation; and (c) will or disposition to worship this object of religious representation. Religion thus includes the mind (recognition [*cognitio*]), inclination (affection [*amor*]), and will (intentional worship [*cultus*]).

74. LO: "*Hoc vinculo pietatis obstricti Deo et religati sumus, unde ipsa religio nomen accepit, non, ut Cicero interetatus est, a relegendo,*" cited by Hagenbach, *Lehrbuch der*

"Religion ordains a person to live solely for God," according to Augustine, Ambrose, and Jerome. Thomas wrote that religion "exists in giving God the service and honor which he is due."[75] Thomas also distinguished between *immediate* acts of religion (prayer, offering) and *mediate* acts of religion elicited by sympathy, such as visiting widows.[76]

According to Thomas, *religion* and *piety* are different things; one can also be pious toward one's parents. Calvin defines religion as the sense of God's excellencies, the sense that God is the one who sustains everything and is the source of all good. This feeling is "for us a fit teacher of piety, from which religion is born." Piety is then described by Calvin as "that reverence joined with love of God which the knowledge of his benefits induces."[77] "The seed of religion," according to Calvin, "is implanted in all."[78] Therefore, to know the excellencies of God nurtures piety, *pietas*, reverence and love for God, and this brings forth religion.

Zwingli says, "I take 'religion' in that sense which embraces the whole piety of Christians: namely, faith, life, laws, worship, sacraments." Religion "involves two factors": (a) the one to whom religion is directed (God) and (b) those who reach out to God by means of religion.[79] Zwingli deals first with the subject of God and humanity. Religion began when God sought Adam and called, "Adam, where are you?"[80] God's loyal devotion to his own children "springs from God even to our day, but for our benefit . . . pious devotion is complete only when we turn to the one who calls us away from ourselves and our designs." When we have turned to him, our lives become a "clinging to God, therefore, with an unshakable trust in Him as the only good, as the only one who has the knowledge and the power to relieve all our troubles and to turn away all evils or to turn them to His own glory and the benefit of His people, and with filial dependence on Him as a father—this is piety, is religion."[81] And somewhat later he writes, "True religion is that

---

Dogmengeschichte, §116; ET *History of Christian Doctrines*, 2:2 (§116). Ed. note: At issue here is whether Cicero's link of religion with *relegere* ("to reread") is etymologically correct. Bavinck here cites Lactantius, who contested this and posited *religare* ("to tie, bind") as the source. As we shall see, Bavinck agrees with Cicero; he cites Lactantius at this point to underscore "the bond of piety, [by which] we are bound and obligated to God," and not to indicate agreement with his etymology.

75. *ST* IIa IIae q. 81 art. 1; cf. *RD*, 1:239–40.
76. *ST* IIa IIae q. 101 art. 4.
77. *Institutes*, I.ii.1.
78. *Institutes*, I.iv.1.
79. Zwingli, *Commentary on True and False Religion*, 57–58.
80. Zwingli, *Commentary on True and False Religion*, 89–90.
81. LO: "*Ea adhaesio, qua (homo) deo utpote summo bono, inconcusse fidit, eoque parentis loco utitur, pietas est, religio est*"; Zwingli, *Commentary on True and False Religion*, 90–91.

which clings to the one and only God." And then: "Religion is the marriage of the soul and God."[82]

According to Polanus, religion does not consist of "certain external ceremonies," but of "faith joined with an earnest fear of God, which . . . involves reverence and leads to the proper worship of God, in accordance with God's law."[83] Strictly speaking, "religion" is different from the "worship of God, as cause is different from effect. Religion or piety is the internal cause of the worship of God."[84] And, according to Georg Sohn, the worship of God takes place when due honor is presented to the Triune God; "the efficient and impelling cause of divine worship is the knowledge of God."[85] According to Heidegger, "religion is the proper method of giving glory to God."[86] Elsewhere he writes, "Religion is reason rightly knowing and honoring the true God."[87] Wyttenbach's definition is similar.[88]

The following, then, are some features of the Reformed and Lutheran views:[89]

1. In establishing what religion is, they start from true religion and on that basis determine what false religion is. This is especially the case with Zwingli.

2. The Reformed definition always makes it apparent that religion rests upon and arises from knowledge of God. The views of Calvin and Sohn serve as examples.

---

82. LO: "*vera religio est, quae uni solique deo haeret; est animae deique connubium*"; Zwingli, *Commentarhy on True and False Religion*, 92, 99.

83. Polanus von Polansdorf, *Syntagma Theologiae Christianae*, 575 (IX.i.A).

84. Polanus von Polansdorf, *Syntagma Theologiae Christianae*, 580 (IX.vi.A).

85. LO: "*cultus Dei est, cum Deo uni et trino . . . debitus honor exhibetur; [causa] efficiens et impulsiva cultus divini est cognitio Dei*"; Sohn, *Operum*, 1:110. Ed. note: The two Latin passages given by Bavinck are not direct quotations from Sohn. The first clause adequately summarizes the specific passage cited in Sohn; the second clause seems to have little connection to the specific reference, although see 1:164, where Sohn says this about honor: "*ut & obedientiam eis praesient & reverentia debita eos profequantur*"; on 1:203 Sohn uses phrasing similar to the second clause: "*Ergo causa efficiens atque impulsiva hujus jejunii . . .*"

86. LO: "*religio est recta ratio deum glorificandi*"; Heidegger, *Medulla Theologiae Christianae*, 2 (I.iv), according to Schweizer, *Die Glaubenslehre*, 1:145. Ed. note: Bavinck captures the idea but not the exact words from Heidegger, who wrote, "The knowledge and worship of God comes under the name of *Religion*, which is the right way of rightly knowing and dutifully worshiping the true God" ("*Notitia & cultus Dei* Religionis *nomine venit. quae Recta verum Deum rite cognoscendi, & piè colendi ratio est*"). In the margin Bavinck added a reference to Hoornbeeck, *Summa Controversianum Religionis*, 7–11.

87. Heidegger, *Medulla Theologiae Christianae*, 2 (I.v); cf. Schweizer, *Die Glaubenslehre*, 1:146.

88. Ed. note: See n. 68 in Bavinck's introduction (p. 10). Wyttenbach's definition of religion as "that which is rightly to be known about God and worshiped" ("*quod sit rectas Deum cognoscendi eumque colendi*") is found in his *Tentamen Theologiae Dogmatica Methodo Scientifica Pertractate*, 1:11 (no. 19); cf. Schweizer, *Die Glaubenslehre*, 1:147.

89. Cf. Köstlin, "Religion."

3. The Reformed maintain that the essence of religion is not abstract knowledge, but knowledge and activity (trusting, believing, willing faith).[90]

Rationalists tear apart *knowing* from *doing* and simply place the one alongside the other in disjointed fashion, as they also do with systematic theology and ethics. According to Kant, religion is the knowledge of all our duties as divine commandments—here religion is subjected to ethics. According to Fichte, the moral world order, whose reign we have to advance ethically, is itself God. According to Hegel, religion is the self-consciousness of the Absolute Spirit in the finite spirit. In this case, religion is only a matter of *knowing*. According to Schleiermacher, piety is neither *knowing* nor *doing*, but a certainty of *feeling* or of *immediate self-consciousness*.[91] Schleiermacher, then, understood feeling not in our ordinary sense as a passive capacity, but as immediate self-consciousness. Religious worship is then a particular state, a change of self-consciousness, the highest, most powerful, full self-consciousness.[92] Most scholars (e.g., Twesten, Nitzsch, de Wette, von Hase, Wegscheider, and Hagenbach)[93] followed Schleiermacher. Others placed greater emphasis on the conscience or made it the organ of religion (Schenkel, cf. Lange, Ebrard, and J. T. Beck).[94] Still others placed greater emphasis on the intellect, such as Stendel and Philippi; the latter defines religion as human "communion with God."[95]

Religion always rests upon the communion of God with humans as they are restored in Christ, established by God's revelation in word and deed. This is objective religion.[96] We subjectively appropriate the revelation of God and enter that objectively established fellowship by faith. This faith is an act of the entire person, and it resides in the innermost center, in the heart. It is an immediate, original act, an act of the knowing and willing human person. Faith is not one or the other, orthodoxy *or* mysticism, but *both*. Feeling

90. Heidelberg Catechism, Q&A 21.

91. Schleiermacher, *Christian Faith*, §3.

92. Van der Hoeven, *De godsdienst het wezen van den mensch*, 16.

93. Twesten, *Vorlesungen über die Dogmatik*; Nitzsch, *System of Christian Doctrine*; de Wette, *Lehrbuch der christlichen Sittenlehre*; von Hase, *Evangelische Dogmatik*; Wegscheider, *Institutiones Theologiae Christianae Dogmaticae*; Hagenbach, *Encyklopädie und Methodologie*.

94. Ed. note: Bavinck is likely referring to Schenkel, *Die christliche Dogmatik*; Lange, *Christliche Dogmatik*, 1:185–96 (§36); Ebrard, *Christliche Dogmatik*, 1:11; Bavinck provides no reference for J. T. Beck but may have had in mind Beck's *Outlines of Biblical Psychology*, 142–48 (§27: "Relation of Heart to Revelation").

95. GO: "Gemeinschaft des Menschen mit Gott"; Philippi, *Kirchliche Glaubenslehre*, 1:46; Stendel, *Kritik der Religion*.

96. LO: *religio objectiva*.

comes after faith; it is not faith's root but its fruit. Conversion, however, starts
with illumination of the mind.[97] According to des Amorie van der Hoeven Jr.,
religion is the essence of our humanity; religion is a fixed feature not of self-
consciousness but of the "self," of the *being* of persons. Human beings are
human to the extent that they are religious.[98]

In Holy Scripture there is no name for what we call religion.[99] After all, we
understand religion to encompass all human relations to God in their entirety
and in all their connections.[100] Piety, love, trust, adoration, hoping on God, all
taken together, are therefore what we describe as religion. Holy Scripture always deals with some concrete element of religion. Thus Scripture uses various
names because it is not furnishing scientific theology even though it provides
the elements for such a science. In the Old Testament a common expression is
to "walk with God" (Gen. 5:22 and 6:9) or to "walk before God" (Gen. 17:1).
Especially common is "the fear of the LORD" (Prov. 1:7). The usual terms are to
walk in his ways, laws, etc. (Ps. 119) or to *know* him (Hosea 6:6). In the New
Testament the most common words are πίστις (faith) and its cognate πιστεύειν
(believe). Also important are the words εὐσέβεια ("godliness" or "holy reverence
for God," as Cremer translates it) and θεοσέβεια ("godliness" or "the fear of
the Lord").[101] A more objective term, which can also have a negative meaning (as seen in Col. 2:18), is a word usually translated as "religious worship,"
"religious practice," or "rite."[102] The religious way of life in an objective sense
is also called the "way" or "road" (Acts 19:9; 22:4).[103] In a subjective sense it
is usually called "faith," which is undoubtedly a matter of the "heart" (Josh.
24:23; 1 Sam. 7:3; Ezek. 11:19; Prov. 23:26; Matt. 5:8; Rom. 10:10; Eph. 3:17;
Phil. 4:7; Col. 3:15; Heb. 13:9) but also involves an intellectual element (Christ
is the "truth" [John 1:14; 14:6; 17:3]). The heart is also the seat of the mind
(Eph. 1:18).[104] The apostle Paul speaks of "the eye of the heart" (Eph. 1:18;
cf. 4:23; Rom. 7:25; 12:2). In the Old and the New Testament, *knowing* as a
theoretical-practical matter is greatly emphasized (Isa. 11:9; Jer. 31:34; Hosea
6:6; John 17:3 [cf. 6:29]; Col. 1:9–10; 2 Thess. 1:8; 1 Tim. 2:4). On the other
hand, faith is the source of love for God and the neighbor and of good works.

According to Cicero, "religion" is derived from *relegere* (to go through or
over again in reading, speech, or thought) and points to devout and observant

---

97. Philippi, *Kirchliche Glaubenslehre*, 1:57–119.
98. Ed. note: Van der Hoeven, *De godsdienst het wezen van den mensch*.
99. Ed. note: Cf. *RD*, 1:237–38.
100. Hagenbach, *Encyklopädie und Methodologie*, 18.
101. θεοσέβεια = Hebrew *jirath Elohim*; Cremer, *Biblico-Theological Lexicon*, s.v. εὐσέβεια.
102. GrO: θρησκεία.
103. GrO: ὁδός.
104. GrO: νοῦς.

religious people "who carefully reviewed and so to speak retraced all the lore of ritual."[105] Further, the word "religious" was a term of approval and contrasted with "superstitious," a term of censure.[106] Lactantius, however, disputed this and sought the etymology for "religion" in *religare* (to bind together).[107] Arguments in favor of Cicero's view include appeals to passages in Cicero that link religion with the notion of obligation[108] and the fact that words ending in "-io" are derived from third-conjugation verbs (cf. *optio* from *opere*). Lactantius's view, however, is defended by Fleck, Hahn, and Lange.[109]

It is peculiar that the Germans, including the early Reformed, always spoke of Lutheran or Reformed "religion." Schleiermacher uses the term "piety" (*Frömmigkeit*), from the word *vrum*, which, according to J. G. Müller, was the Gothic word for *primus* or "first," and also meant "virtuous, useful, alert, valiant [in the liturgical form for baptism]."[110] It was related to the word *vram*, which meant "onward." The word expresses only subjective religiosity; the Pharisees were also pious. Terms like "godliness," "devotion," or "piety" are too ethical, too practical, too specific to embrace everything which we include in the term "religion."[111] The word "faith," which is related to the terms "believe," "promise," "vow," "betroth," "allow," and "love," is also too specific for this purpose.[112] The root of "faith" expresses a loving surrender and dedication to someone. By contrast, "religion" is too external and the word "service" is too harsh,[113] insufficiently tender and affectionate. Des Amorie van der Hoeven Jr. suggests the expression: "Godward life."[114]

---

105. Cicero, *De natura deorum* II.28 (trans. Rackham, p. 193). Ed. note: For the sake of clarity, Bavinck's original has been reconstructed and amplified by the editor.

106. Cicero, *De natura deorum* II.28 (trans. Rackham, p. 193).

107. Ed. note: The Lactantius reference is to *Institutiones divinae* IV.28. Etymological battles over the word "religion" go back to the early days of the Christian church, among Greek and Roman writers as well as Christian thinkers. For a helpful, brief survey of this discussion, see Hoyt, "Etymology of Religion." Hoyt's conclusion (128): "If all points are carefully considered, Cicero's view would seem to be preferable, so that religion is not derived from *religare*, but from *relegere*."

108. Ed. note: Hoyt, "Etymology of Religion," 128; the passages are *Oratio de domo* 105, 106, 124. The idea here is that religion involves conscientious observance and keeping of God's commands and ordinances. That is why they need to be reread and reread; in other words, liturgies are important.

109. Ed. note: Bavinck does not specify here but is likely referring to Fleck, *System der christlichen Dogmatiek*; Hahn, *Lehrbuch des christlichen Glaubens*, 39; Lange, *Christliche Dogmatik*, 1:189 (according to Philippi, *Kirchliche Glaubenslehre*, 1:6–7); Köstlin, "Religion," 641–50.

110. J. G. Müller, "Über Bildung und Gebrauch"; Köstlin, "Religion," 649.

111. Ed. note: The first three terms translate two virtually synonymous Dutch words: *godsvrucht* and *godzaligheid*; "religion" translates *godsdienst*.

112. Ed. note: The etymological link between the words, which may not be evident in English translation, is clear in Dutch: *geloof, gelooven, belofte, gelofte, verloven, veroorloven*, and *lieven*.

113. DO: *godsdienst, dienst*.

114. DO: *gode-leven*; van der Hoeven, *De godsdienst het wezen van den mensch*, 5–6.

So, then, what is religion?[115] It is of formost importance that we acknowledge Christianity as the only source for determining the essence of religion. To want to determine the essence of religion by trying to find what all religions have in common yields only an abstraction without substance. What is true and good in other religions can be determined and measured only by the true Christian religion.[116] One also has to distinguish between religion in an objective sense and in a subjective sense. Once we understand both, we may be able to grasp what they have in common.

1. What is objective religion? God himself shows us in the first table of the Decalogue. It consists of the service of God,[117] which is described for us in Holy Scripture: worshiping God alone, going to church, observing the Sabbath, using the sacraments, and communal prayer. Holy Scripture very fittingly describes it as walking in the Lord's laws, duties, statutes, and ways. Objective religion thus corresponds with what God has revealed concerning himself and how he expects us to serve him; it corresponds with the Torah and with the Holy Scripture itself. Francken therefore says that religion is the content of Holy Scripture.[118] Philippi describes objective religion as the Christ-effected restoration of the communion of God with humanity.[119] This raises the question whether religion is communion with God, which will be addressed presently.[120]

2. What is subjective religion? The New Testament usually indicates subjective religion by the words "faith" or "believing."[121] This faith resides in the heart (Rom. 10:10). It is with the heart that one believes unto righteousness; it is the center, the core, the innermost point of our being, our *I*. And because faith resides in the *I*, it is an act of the whole human person, of mind, will, soul, and strength (Deut. 6:4–5; Matt. 22:37; Mark 12:30; Luke 10:27). How is this faith worked in us? The Holy Spirit works it in us, but does so through the preaching of the Word, which aims at the mind and the will. It is thus mediated through mind and will: these are the two portals, points of entry to our innermost being, to our *I*, by which the Holy Spirit carries the seed of the Word into us and there causes faith to arise (Rom. 10:14–15). And just as faith, subjective religion, is mediated by the mind and the will, it proceeds from the *I* to again work on the mind and the will. The Reformed therefore

---

115. DO: *godsdienst*.
116. Philippi, *Kirchliche Glaubenslehre*, 1:2–3.
117. LO: *cultus Dei*.
118. Francken, *Stellige God-geleertheyd*, 1:56.
119. Philippi, *Kirchliche Glaubenslehre*, 1:47.
120. DO: *gemeenschap met God*. Ed. note: "Religion" in the preceding paragraph translated the Dutch word *godsdienst*.
121. GrO: πίστις; πιστεύειν.

did not make a mistake when they placed *knowing* and *worshiping* next to each other in the definition of religion.[122] Religion is mediated by both and manifests itself in both. Faith truly is knowing and trusting, and does not exist without both. And the Reformed definition is far better than Schleiermacher's. Feeling is passive and receptive. Faith is reflected in feeling, and one who believes will experience, to some extent, feelings of contentedness and bliss. But faith is not identical to feeling. Rather, feeling is a fruit and reflection of faith. To be sure, Schleiermacher explained feeling as immediate self-consciousness. This is impossible, however; it cannot be both at once, it has to be either feeling or self-consciousness. The one can absolutely not include the other.[123] Faith, then, is the unity of knowing and being able, of knowledge and deed.[124] Its only object is God; it knows God, engages and deals with God.

   3. What is the relation between objective religion and subjective religion? Polanus wrote, "Religion or piety is the internal cause of the worship of God, the former is the cause, the latter the effect."[125] To some extent this is true. Subjective religion impels us and enables us to serve God according to his will. But objective religion is not the product, effect, and creation of subjective religion. Self-imagined or self-made objective religion is not service of God, but idolatry or self-willed worship[126] (see, e.g., Matt. 15:9; Mark 7:7; Col. 2:23). No, objective religion is already there, contained and described in Holy Scripture. Only God can decide what objective religion is and how he wants us to serve him. Subjective religion begins by abandoning all self-willed religion and ceasing to be active, instead becoming passive and entering into the service of God according to his will. This is why Holy Scripture speaks of walking in the ways and laws of the Lord, and not walking according to our imagination. This is not compulsion, because subjective religion makes us willing to walk in the Lord's ways. And objective religion, too, is no forced system, no pressing or constricting mold for subjective religion. Quite the contrary; while objective religion is the pure and true and adequate form of the subjective, subjective religion is the perfectly fitting content of objective religion. Both are intended to permeate each other with increasing intimacy. To some extent it is still the case that objective religion stands over us like

122. LO: *cognoscere, colere*; DO: *godsdienst*.
123. Philippi, *Kirchliche Glaubenslehre*, 1:52–71; Lange, *Christliche Dogmatik*, 1:133.
124. Ed. note: The first of the pairings involves a Dutch-language pun: *kennen* and *kunnen*. The second pair is *kennis* and *daad*.
125. LO: "*religio (pietas) est causa interna cultus Dei*"; Polanus von Polansdorf, *Syntagma Theologiae Christianae*, 580A.
126. GrO: ἐθελοθρησκία.

a law; it had to be objectively revealed as a rule for our lives to protect us from straying. But as subjective religion increases in us and as faith becomes stronger and more spontaneous, objective religion increasingly becomes our own being. The two may for the moment remain partially in conflict, but they are directed to each other and inclined toward each other. One day they will fully correspond. In heaven they will be *one*.

To conclude: religion should not be defined as communion with God.[127] This is currently a common definition, for example, of Oosterzee.[128] However, notice the following: (a) Communion is reciprocal.[129] There is communion between husband and wife but not between father and child, between whom an intimate relationship of piety exists. If there were religious communion between God and us, God, too, would have religion. This is not the case: religion is something human, the most human thing about our humanity,[130] and therefore to speak of "human religion" is really a pleonasm, a redundancy. (b) The definition "religion is communion between God and human beings" excludes all objective religion and makes it seem as if objective religion is a matter of indifference and inferior. But such a notion is contradicted by Holy Scripture, which in the Second Commandment identifies the sin of idolatry and specifies that it should be punished with death in the land of Israel. This idea, however, is reflected in the subjectivism of Schleiermacher and of the entire present age. (c) Because of the reasons listed in (a) and (b), the definition "religion is communion between God and human beings" is incomplete and inaccurate. Religion is not the reciprocal rapport between God and a human being, and even less is it an activity or consciousness in us.[131] It is not the relation itself or the communion between God and humans as such but the "certainty of human subjects that they exist and live in this relation and communication," a way of life for humans by virtue of and through the peculiar relationship between them and God.[132] Human beings stand in a special and unique relationship to God, essentially distinct from that of angels and animals and every creature, and are thus distinguished from all other creatures. Because of the unique relationship to God in which we stand (come to stand by faith), this relationship is distinctively expressed in all of human

---

127. DO: *gemeenschap met God.*

128. Ed. note: Johannes Jacob van Oosterzee (1817–82) was a professor of biblical and practical theology at the University of Utrecht. Though Bavinck does not refer to a specific title, he may have in mind *Christelijke dogmatiek.*

129. DO: *wederkerig.*

130. Van der Hoeven, *De godsdienst het wezen van den mensch,* 5–6.

131. GO: *Wechselrapport, Thätigkeit;* DO: *bewustzijn.*

132. Köstlin, "Religion," 641–42.

life. And because God places himself in a relationship to human beings in a special way, they too place themselves in a unique relationship[133] to him.

Thus we obtain the following definition: Formally, religion[134] is the distinctive relationship or position of human beings to God, expressing itself in all of life, and based on the distinctive relation of God to human beings.[135] Materially, religion is the childlike relationship to God that arises in a human being, based on the reconciled relation in which God, in Christ and through the Holy Spirit, places himself to the believer. This makes God the object of believers' knowledge and action and leads them to walk in the ways of the Lord, according to his will and for his glory. Religion is serving God in childlike fear, in faith, with all powers in the entirety of life according to his will and for his glory. Piety and religion are therefore not identical.[136] As Calvin correctly distinguishes, religion arises from piety. Religion is thus our human way of life with respect to God, determined by piety (our childlike relation to God). Religion is not communion with God and the spiritual life as such, but the piety that directs the mind, will, feeling, all powers, and all actions and the daily walk. Religion is decidedly a matter of the mind, of the will, of all the powers, flowing from a heart in right relationship to God. Religion is thus the relationship[137] of the *whole* person with heart, soul, etc. to God, governed by the standard of God's will.

Incidentally it can be asked whether human beings also stand in a relationship with angels and whether we have duties to them. Without a doubt the angels serve humans (Pss. 34:7; 91:11; Isa. 37:36; Dan. 10:13; Matt. 4:6; 18:10; Luke 15:10; 16:22; Acts 12:15; Heb. 1:14). Contrary to Scripture, Roman Catholics say that we should bring them religious honor (Col. 2:18; Rev. 19:10; 22:8–9; Judg. 13:15–16). The Reformed say that religious honor is due unto God alone (Deut. 6:13; 10:20; Matt. 4:10). But civil honor is different (1 Cor. 11:10; 1 Tim. 5:21; Heb. 1:4). As the church we certainly live in relationship to them (see Eph. 3:10), and we also owe them duties of reverence and respect. At the same time, according to all of Holy Scripture, the evil angels also have influence on us, and we have to guard against them (Matt. 8:29; 10:1; 15:22;

133. DO: *verhouding*.
134. Ed. note: Here and in the remainder of this paragraph, "religion" translates the Dutch *godsdienst*.
135. Ed. note: Bavinck uses the Dutch word *verhouding* ("relation") to describe the relational direction from God to humanity, and the Dutch word *betrekking* ("post, position, job, office") to describe the opposite direction from humanity to God.
136. Ed. note: Here and in the remainder of this paragraph, "religion" translates the Latin *religio*, and "piety" translates the Latin *pietas* or the Dutch *godsdienst*.
137. DO: *betrekking*.

17:21; 2 Tim. 2:25–26; 1 Pet. 5:8). This issue will also be addressed when we discuss temptation and other matters.[138]

2. Our Relation to Other People

A person is the product of a community and does not exist alone but has been in relation to others since even before birth. Without the mutual relationship between others we would not have existed. We are born *out of*, *in*, *with*, and *toward* various relationships. This *one* relationship of family is germinal and is the type of all the others. From the household family and its relationships stem all the others in variegated complexity. The case is entirely different with the angels. Among them such a manifold, rich, and full set of relationships is absent: they are all equal, because all were created that way. There is only a hierarchy that by its manifold diversity may perhaps somewhat compensate them for what we possess. Birth or physical descent is therefore the foundation and germ of all human relationships. Yet this does not say enough. After all, this is also true of animals, because there too each variety descends from its single pair. This is something, therefore, that people and animals have in common.

But there is a distinction between animals and people in this matter, because with animals the physical relationship is the only one. The physical relationship becomes weaker and passes away as soon as the animal can function on its own, and then the animal lives by itself alongside its parents, brothers, and sisters. Kinship falls silent, the sensual is transitory and disappears. Animals form no family, society, or state. The mutual physical relationship is a passing one. For people, the physical, natural relation is also the first, and also passes away; but *ethical* relationships develop out of and on the basis of the physical. Although the natural relationship is first, the moral and spiritual relationships follow. People remain in relationship to each other until the end of their lives and beyond. Those ethical ties are many and manifold.

1. Relationships that center on the *family*. Such relationships are first of all physical but increasingly assume ethical dimensions. In the family these are rich and several: First, between husband and wife; second, between parents and children; third, between siblings; fourth, between all of these and domestic staff; fifth, between these and all who lodge with the family such as uncles, aunts, and grandparents. All relationships, even in such a small circle, are endlessly nuanced and varied and advance the richness of life and of human personality.

138. Ed. note: In chap. 11.

2. Relationships that exist in *society* and by virtue of society. When various sorts of people live together, relationships come into existence through all attempts to elevate and sustain life, especially through trade and industry. These relationships give rise to a number of others: offices, trades, occupations, associations, partners, employers and employees, the rich and the poor, and the first, second, third, and presently even the fourth estates.[139] These relationships become more numerous and complex depending on the size of the household.

3. Relationships of, in, and for the sake of the *state*. The society becomes a state. A group of people are a folk, a nation. Here we can identify the rights and duties of the citizen, civil liberties, justice for all, patriotism, the duty to serve the fatherland, war, government officials, and government and subjects.

4. Relationships of and for the sake of *humanity*. Just like every family and every nation, humanity in its successive generations is a unity, an organism to which we are related. We stand on the shoulders of our ancestors and have inherited their financial, moral, spiritual, and intellectual legacy, which makes our progress possible. What we think, feel, and enjoy we owe to those who went before us. Their science and skill are now ours. And these, in turn, create relationships of learned and unlearned, of teachers and students, and of schools and universities.

The relationships that people have cannot be numbered, and all, without exception, have a *moral* character. Life in these relationships is called the *moral* life. Morality is thus to live in appropriate relationships to people according to some requirement. (For us, this requirement is God's law.) No actual moral life exists, however, where people can live according to this requirement in their own strength. We are by nature inclined also to hate our neighbor.[140] In the ordinary sense of the word, people are moral when they live according to the human standard—or, somewhat more profoundly, according to the notion of humanity—in all these relations. In our view, the moral person is one who also in this respect meets God's standard, his law, and his demand, made known to us in his Word, also for the sake of these human relationships.

3. Our Relation to Nature

Our bodies were formed from the dust of the earth (Gen. 2:7). The constitutive parts of the earth (lime, iron, minerals, phosphorus, sulphur, magnesium,

139. Ed. note: Classically there were three estates: clergy, nobility, and common people; the growing prominence and power of the press in the nineteenth century led to its being referred to as the "fourth estate."
140. Ed. note: Heidelberg Catechism, Q&A 5.

etc.) are also those of our bodies. What veins are for our bodies, rivers are for the earth. Our bodily frame is related to that of the animals. We have a vegetative life in common with plants and animals and an animal life that we share with the animals. We live from the earth, from the worlds of plants and animals, and obtain food, shelter, and clothing from them. We obtain our instruments from the mineral realm. We are from the earth; our rhythm of rest and work is attuned to the rotation of the earth. The earth exists for the sake of humanity and has to be cultivated and subdued by us (culture). Plants and animals are examples and lessons for us (the ant, lion, snake, dove, etc.). As Jesus showed, nature provides a parable of the eternal, of the kingdom of heaven. Nature, toward which we have many duties and rights, shapes our character and temper, teaches us, points us to God, and serves as the source of our science. Our relationships to nature are manifold, and also have a moral character. Rothe unites our relationship to persons and our relationship to nature under the general category of the moral or ethical.[141] This is incorrect. There is a difference between our relationship to other persons and our relationship to impersonal nature such as plants and animals. The latter can be regarded as ethical only in a broader sense; otherwise it would be immoral to butcher animals.

4. Religion and Morality[142]

Religion is a moral, spiritual phenomenon that belongs generally, formally, and psychologically to the moral dimension of life (in a psychic sense, morality is an act of the human will).[143] Furthermore, religion is governed by the moral law in all of its dimensions: knowledge, love (piety, religious practices), and worship.[144] Our attitudes and deeds, our entire life of the will, is also governed by law. In sum, religion is to morality (in terms of interhuman relations) what the first table is to the second table.[145]

We have considered the threefold relations in which people are involved and can now look at the mutual connections among these relations. Specifically, we shall consider the connection between religion and morality, and for this purpose can include our relationship to nature under our relationship to

141. GO: *sittlich*; Rothe, *Theologische Ethik*, §97.
142. DO: *Godsdienst en zedelijkheid*. See Kübel, "Sitte, Sittlichkeit"; Ritschl, "Religion und Sittlichkeit"; Fox, *Religion and Morality*; Kapp, *Religion und Moral im Christenthum Luthers*. Ed. note: Bavinck took the bibliographic information for Fox's *Religion and Morality* from a review of the book by William Brenton Green Jr. in the *Presbyterian and Reformed Review*.
143. DO: *Godsdienst*; *zedelijke, geestelijk verschinsel*.
144. LO: *cognitio*; *amor (pietas, religio)*; *cultus*.
145. Ed. note: This opening paragraph was a marginal note.

other people. We are excluding from our discussion those who deny one of
the two terms and for whom the issue of the relation between morality and
religion no longer really exists. On the one hand, there are ascetics, monks
who flee from the world and from other people, thus deny moral life, and
would turn all of life into religion. In France, for example, a nun is called *la
religieuse*. The Roman Catholic Church is generally inclined to this error,
wants to make everything ecclesiastical, and fails to recognize the independent
domains of art, science, or the state. On the other hand, there are the human-
ists (materialists, also pantheists, like Fichte) who ridicule God and religion
and dismiss them as childish fantasies or as a brain dysfunction. Recently
this issue has become enormously complicated, because religion and morality are not properly defined or distinguished, a problem that arises when one
starts from abstract ideas of religion and of morality instead of the concrete
and true religion and morality that the Christian tradition provides. It is as
impossible to find and describe an abstract thing called "morality" as it is to
find and describe "religion" as an abstraction. Those who pose the issue this
way are talking without making any progress. Both terms remain a variable
x, unknown quantities, because they have not been defined.

   1. Let me first give a concise summary of how pagans historically viewed
the connection between religion and morality.[146] Among the fetish worshipers,
religion is still the practice of magic and does not produce morality. Society
produces a moral code of loyalty, honesty, bravery toward others and for the
sake of others. When individuals begin to evaluate themselves according to
objective norms, their consciences obtain moral content. But religion and
morality are separate; sin and crime are distinct. But gradually they converge;
that is to say, religion prescribes and proscribes a set of actions as well. As a
result, religious and moral duties arise alongside each other. What is good in
one area is wrong in another; the religious domain is morally indifferent. Yet the
two areas converge, and a connection becomes established: self-sacrifice, the
limitation of selfishness, which religion requires, benefits morality. Among Se-
mitic and Indo-Germanic peoples the connection became much more intimate.

   Among the Semites, the gods still required child sacrifice, yet the gods were
nonetheless thought to be human—in other words, lords and kings; state and
church were one. Among the Indo-Germans, the gods were still powers of
nature; but they were nevertheless expressions of what is good and whole-
some, and increasingly became persons before whom oaths, marriages, and
hospitality were sacred. Thus moral action surpassed religious activity, Yet, a
large part of the moral life lay outside of religion, and vice versa. Among the

146. Cf. Schultz, "Religion und Sittlichkeit."

Egyptians, religion had a high position, and in their case, morality ethicized the gods. Among the Greeks, the gods were the guardians of measure, order, harmony, oaths, hospitality, and morals; morality here has religious motives. But for the rest, the gods often acted immorally and practiced adultery, theft, deceit, revenge, and the like. Philosophical ethics was therefore anti-religious. Among the Romans moral action also had religious motives. Public and familial life have a religious character. The religious state was supreme, and for this reason civic virtue was the highest form of morality. Among the Chinese, the state was the image of heaven, and the emperor was the standard for everything. Religion swallows up morality entirely. Among the Persians, there was a god for the good as well as an evil god. Religion and morality coincided. Among the Buddhists, there was, properly speaking, no such thing as moral action: there is not ethics, and everything belongs to ascetics. With Islam, God's will is absolutely everything; morality is determined by Allah.

What we see everywhere, then, is that religion increasingly determines morality. The two areas progressively merge. What is considered good in one area cannot be seen as evil in the other. Paul shows the relation in Romans 1:23: the gentiles had transformed God into a corruptible human; therefore God has given them up in the lusts of their hearts. Idolatry leads to immorality. Unnatural acts follow the divinization of nature. And the higher the conception of God, the higher the morality.[147]

2. In the present understanding of the connection between religion and morality, the issue is stated abstractly, so there is often a failure to make proper distinctions. According to Martensen, "The fundamental concept of the moral is therefore the unconstrained unity of man's will and God's will."[148] Religion is human dependence on God; morality is the freedom that develops from dependence into independence, the acceptance of the proffered communion with God, so that religion disappears as morality grows. The religious is passive, and the ethical is active. In faith, religion and morality are one. But both are developing: the religious *is* union with God, and the

---

147. Cf. Lamers, *Godsdienst en zedelijkheid*, 35–39.
148. Martensen, *Christian Ethics*, 1:12 (§4). Ed. note: Bavinck objects to this understanding of morality so prominent in his day because moral action increasingly displaces religion and worship. The direction is signaled by what follows in the sentence quoted here: the "unconstrained unity of man's will and God's will . . . signifies that man, in ministering adoration, makes his own person an instrument for the service of God; that in free devotion to the object of creation, and in conjunction with God, he brings the kingdom of humanity into the kingdom of God, which again requires that he, as the servant of the Most High upon earth, should make himself the lord of nature." Bavinck's gentle question at the conclusion of the paragraph should not lead us to overlook that thoroughly Pelagian and immanent vision of the religious life = moral life described here.

ethical strives to become one with God; the religious person has everything, the ethical person has to acquire it. (But, we should ask, if one already has union with God, does one still need to become one with God?)

According to Rothe, moral development is partly religious and partly ethical, which involves subduing nature and becoming a spirit or person. To the same extent, then, that human beings (as ethical beings) *spiritualize* themselves and become persons, they sanctify themselves, and God comes to live in them. God cannot live in matter, only in spirit.[149] It is necessary, then, that to a certain extent we first become spirit before God can indwell us. It is thus a religious development; as we increasingly become more ethical, we become more religious.[150] This religious development is initiated by God but is nevertheless mediated by the person, because piety is authentic communion, interaction between God and the person.[151] It is the case, after all, that even before persons are spirits, God acts on their nature and conditions and guides them toward the duty of orienting themselves in their relation to God. Religious development begins when a person agrees.[152]

We can make a few summary comments about Rothe's view at this point. (a) A person does not have a special religious organ; but religion exists because to be human is to be personal. (b) Religion, too, is mediated through human self-determination. (c) Religion, then, already *presupposes* a beginning of ethical development.

It is thus through that religious development that a divine consciousness and divine activity arise within a person.[153] Persons give themselves to God as instruments for his purpose, and that purpose is *solely* an ethical one.[154] The beginning of religion in us is determined by our ethical development (spirituality). Religion is real only in morality. Religion requires morality for truth, actuality, and concreteness. Morality is the primary product of the idea of communion with God. And morality requires piety to become perfect rather than just to exist.[155]

Several additional comments can be made: (d) Piety is indeed different from morality, but morality arises only in piety; religion is the soul of morality, although, like the soul, it does not have a separate existence. (e) Religion without morality is enthusiasm, fantasy, a phantasm of piety, empty, without

---

149. Rothe, *Theologische Ethik*, §114.
150. Rothe, *Theologische Ethik*, §115.
151. Rothe, *Theologische Ethik*, §116.
152. Rothe, *Theologische Ethik*, §117.
153. Rothe, *Theologische Ethik*, §118.
154. Rothe, *Theologische Ethik*, §121.
155. Rothe, *Theologische Ethik*, §124.

content. Morality without religion may be incomplete and abnormal, but it is not empty; on the contrary, it is something very real.

Some further observations about Rothe's view of the relation between morality and religion: (f) Morality is thus a precondition for religion—this in fact places humanity first and God second. (g) There is such a thing as morality without piety, but not the other way around. (h) Religion does not have its own life or separate existence, but is absorbed by morality, the church by the state, worship by art. Yet many moderns follow Rothe's position. According to Janet, morality is not complete without religion; religion is an essential element of humanity. Religion is not the theoretical foundation of morality, but nevertheless is the basis of morality's efficacy. Kant made God a postulate of morality. But Janet also says that to believe in virtue is to believe in God. Without God, virtue is an illusion; morality cannot exist without metaphysics.[156]

3. We first have to investigate the relation between objective religion and objective morality. The law of the Lord clearly tells us the relation between the first and the second table, our service to God and to our neighbor. (a) One heading appears above all the commandments, including the second table. God is also the lawgiver of the second table. (b) The law is one, it is an organism, and whoever violates one part of the law violates the entirety of the law (James 2:10). (c) The second table follows the first, not the other way around. As our Lord taught us: "So whatever you wish that others would do to you, do also to them, for this is the Law and the Prophets" (Matt. 7:12). "This is the great and first commandment. And a second is like it: You shall love your neighbor as yourself" (Matt. 22:38–39; cf. Luke 10:27). (d) "Love does no wrong to a neighbor; therefore love is the fulfilling of the law" (Rom. 13:10).

Both tables, then, constitute a single law, and in Holy Scripture they are always intimately conjoined and never divided. Both are issued by one lawgiver, both proceed from one principle, and both aim at one purpose. This is illustrated by the whole of Scripture. Samuel said, "To obey is better than sacrifice" (1 Sam. 15:22). The Lord said through Jeremiah, "If you truly amend your ways and your deeds, if you truly execute justice one with another, if you do not oppress the sojourner, the fatherless, or the widow, or shed innocent blood in this place, and if you do not go after other gods to your own harm, then I will let you dwell in this place, in the land that I gave of old to your fathers forever" (Jer. 7:5–7). Later Jeremiah records:

156. Janet, *La morale*, 596, 610–11; see further Cramer, *Christendom en humaniteit*, 203–31; Hoekstra, "Godsdienst en Zedelijkheid"; Pfleiderer, *Moral und Religion*; Weygoldt, *Darwinismus*, 65 (morality is independent, but religion supports, ennobles, and idealizes it); Kuyper, "Natuurlijke Godskennis," esp. pp. 72–87 (ET: Van Dyke, "Natural Knowledge of God").

> He judged the cause of the poor and needy;
>> then it was well.
> Is not this to know me?
>> declares the LORD. (Jer. 22:16)

Similarly, the prophet Ezekiel describes one who is "righteous and does what is just and right" as one who "does not eat upon the mountains or lift up his eyes to the idols of the house of Israel" and, at the same time, as one who "does not defile his neighbor's wife, . . . gives his bread to the hungry and covers the naked with a garment," and does not engage in usury. In sum, that person "walks in my statutes, and keeps my rules by acting faithfully—he is righteous; he shall surely live, declares the Lord GOD" (Ezek. 18:5–9). Many other Old Testament passages say the same: Psalms 40:7; 41:2; 51:19; Isaiah 1:12–20; 38:3; Hosea 4:1; 10:12; and especially Micah 6:8 (cf. Zech. 7:6; 8:16–17):

> He has told you, O man, what is good;
>> and what does the LORD require of you
> but to do justice, and to love kindness,
>> and to walk humbly with your God?

We find the same message in the New Testament:

Present your bodies as a living sacrifice, holy and acceptable to God, which is your spiritual worship. (Rom. 12:1)

Owe no one anything, except to love each other, for the one who loves another has fulfilled the law. (Rom. 13:8)

Religion that is pure and undefiled before God the Father is this: to visit orphans and widows in their affliction, and to keep oneself unstained from the world. (James 1:27)

If you really fulfill the royal law according to the Scripture, "You shall love your neighbor as yourself," you are doing well. (James 2:8)

And this is his commandment, that we believe in the name of his Son Jesus Christ and love one another, just as he has commanded us. (1 John 3:23)

The two tables therefore form a most intimate unity. But they are nevertheless two tables, never to be separated, but thoroughly to be distinguished. God himself distinguishes two tables of the law (Exod. 32:15; 34:1; Deut. 10:1; 1 Kings 8:9). In Matthew 22:38–39 they are distinguished as two commandments:

the first and great, and the second like it. The two tables are therefore never confused but are ever kept distinct in such a way that the first has the second as consequence. The first table has God as object, the second the neighbor. In a certain sense the second table also has God as object, but indirectly, in and behind our neighbor.[157] The neighbor should be loved in God and for the sake of God.

4. We shall now consider the relation between subjective religion and morality in the human person as subject. The fear of the Lord is the foundation of all morality (Prov. 14:2, 26; 15:16; 19:23). To walk before the face of God includes morality (Gen. 5:22; 6:9; 17:1). Godliness is the root of humility (Prov. 22:4), generosity (Prov. 19:17), wisdom (Prov. 9:10; 15:33), and science (Prov. 1:7). Furthermore, the fear of the Lord is to hate evil (Prov. 16:5). In the New Testament, faith is the principle of sanctification:

> Everyone who believes that Jesus is the Christ has been born of God, and everyone who loves the Father loves whoever has been born of him. By this we know that we love the children of God, when we love God and obey his commandments. For this is the love of God, that we keep his commandments. And his commandments are not burdensome. For everyone who has been born of God overcomes the world. And this is the victory that has overcome the world—our faith. (1 John 5:1–4)[158]

The fruit of faith is love:

> The aim of our charge is love that issues from a pure heart and a good conscience and a sincere faith. (1 Tim. 1:5)

> Whoever says, "I know him," but does not keep his commandments is a liar, and the truth is not in him, but whoever keeps his word, in him truly the love of God is perfected. By this we may know that we are in him: whoever says he abides in him ought to walk in the same way in which he walked. (1 John 2:4–6)

> For in Christ Jesus neither circumcision nor uncircumcision counts for anything, but only faith working through love. (Gal. 5:6)

> So also faith by itself, if it does not have works, is dead. But someone will say, "You have faith and I have works." Show me your faith apart from your works, and I will show you my faith by my works. (James 2:17–18)

---

157. Cf. Ursinus, *Commentary on the Heidelberg Catechism*, Q&A 93; Daneau, *Ethices Christianae*, 1:127, 170; Heidegger, *Corpus Theologiae Christianae*, 1:502 (XIV.ix).

158. Ed. note: 1 John 5:4b is one of Bavinck's favorite Scripture passages and the text of his only published sermon, "The World-Conquering Power of Faith."

Similarly, "every healthy tree bears good fruit, but the diseased tree bears bad fruit. A healthy tree cannot bear bad fruit, nor can a diseased tree bear good fruit. Every tree that does not bear good fruit is cut down and thrown into the fire" (Matt. 7:17–19; cf. 12:33; Luke 3:9; 6:43–45). A tree is known by its fruit.

The examples of people given in Scripture also demonstrate the same connection between faith and deeds: Lydia (Acts 16:14–15); Tabitha (Acts 9:36); Cornelius (Acts 10:2, 48); Zacchaeus (Luke 19:8); the church at Colossae (Col. 1:4); the church at Thessalonica (1 Thess. 1:3). New birth brings about changed lives: "And such were some of you. But you were washed, you were sanctified, you were justified in the name of the Lord Jesus Christ and by the Spirit of our God" (1 Cor. 6:11). Love is a fruit of the Spirit (Gal. 5:22); faith in Christ Jesus results in love for the saints (Eph. 1:15). Paul's prayer for the Ephesians is that their new faith may bring forth love, "that according to the riches of his glory he may grant you to be strengthened with power through his Spirit in your inner being, so that Christ may dwell in your hearts through faith—that you, being rooted and grounded in love, may have strength to comprehend with all the saints what is the breadth and length and height and depth, and to know the love of Christ that surpasses knowledge, that you may be filled with all the fullness of God" (Eph. 3:16–19; cf. Col. 1:4). Love is the highest virtue, the bond of perfection: "And above all these put on love, which binds everything together in perfect harmony" (Col. 3:14).

So Scripture teaches that also subjectively religion and morality cohere intimately and inseparably. The one demonstrates itself and is authenticated in the other. The one is the fruit of the other.

5. The church of all ages has taught this, including Gregory the Great, Bernard of Clairvaux, Lactantius, Augustine, Luther, and Calvin.[159] Zwingli showed the relation more psychologically and ethically.[160] For Zwingli, even the good works of the unbelievers were the fruit of faith. In answer to the question "What are good works?" the Heidelberg Catechism (Q&A 91) gives this answer: "Only those which are done out of true faith, conform to God's law, and are done for God's glory; and not those based on our own opinion or human tradition." And this is what all the Reformed teach. There is no morality except what proceeds from faith, but also there is no faith without morality.[161]

159. Gregory the Great, *Morals on the Book of Job* VII.23–24 (*PL* 75:780); Bernard of Clairvaux, *On Loving God* VIII (*PL* 182:987–89); Lactantius, *Divine Institutes* VI.10 (*ANF* 7:172–73); Augustine, *City of God* XIV.1 (*NPNF*[1] 2:262); Luthardt, *Die Ethik Luthers*, 49–60, 68–71; Lobstein, *Die Ethik Calvins*, 28–35; Ritschl, *Die christliche Lehre von der Rechtfertigung und Versöhnung*, 1:178; 3:154.
160. Bavinck, *De ethiek van Ulrich Zwingli*, 47–60.
161. Calvin, *Institutes*, II.viii–xi.

We can now summarize:

1. Religion and morality are two distinguishable entities.
    a. They are distinct in their connection: religion is original, morality is derived. The one is faith, the other is love, and faith and love are not the same.
    b. They are distinct in terms of where they reside, their content, and their expression. Religion operates in the arena of the mind and cultivates reverence, awe, fear, modesty, gratitude, prayer, humility, etc. Morality operates in another arena and cultivates other affections: justice, a sense of obligation, honor, and order.
    c. They are distinct in their outward expression. Religion in prayer, worship, church construction, and whatever belongs to the church; morality in life with people (love, self-denial, justice, duty, not coveting, not killing, not stealing, etc.). The religious sphere is thus a different one from the moral sphere; religion has an independent arena, a unique expression, expresses itself in its particular way, and is not absorbed by morality (contrary to Rothe).
    d. They are distinct in that the two tables describe especially the different expressions of these two kinds of life.
    e. They are distinct in object. In religion, God is the only and immediate object; in morality, the neighbor is the closest object.[162]
2. Religion and morality are never divorced.
    a. The two tables are one law: God is the author of the two commandments; God is one, and thus there is one, unbreakable law for religion and morality. The second commandment is like the first.
    b. The principle is one: the faith that grasps God produces love toward the neighbor. There is a psychological connection between faith and love, as we will see later.
    c. The object is one: in our neighbor, God is to be loved; our neighbor is to be loved in God, through God, and for God's sake. Indirectly, God is the object of the second table as well.

Such is the *normal* relation between religion and morality. But in what way has it become abnormal through sin? Sin leads to misconstruing the relation between religion and morality in two ways, both of which occur.

1. Religion and morality are absolutely separated. This was done by the fetish worshipers and more or less by all polytheists. After all, where there is

---

162. Cf. Ursinus, *Commentary on the Heidelberg Catechism*, Lord's Day 34, Q&A 93.

more than one God, there is also more than one law; one god gives this law, another gives that one. So laws in the religious arena can be entirely different than those in moral, civil, social, political, or family arenas. Each god has its particular arena (there is a god of theft, of commerce, of murder, etc.) and issues his own law for that arena, different from and often contradicting the law of another god for another arena. As a higher conception of the gods is formed, and the gods converge, the various arenas of life also move closer and greater unity results. This is also the position of proponents of *independent morality*,[163] whether they permit religion to exist alongside morality or completely reject it.

There are several arguments against this *separation* of religion and morality, but we should begin by recognizing that it contains a relative truth: religion and morality are two distinct things. They do not totally coincide. And there are two types or kinds of people: On the one hand, we find religious people full of fervor and admiration, with a rich emotional life, men, women, and children of faith and of prayer, and who yet morally, when it comes to nobility of character and temperament, rank low, are permissive of much, lacking order, discipline, and honesty. We find this among enthusiastic, fanatic, mystical, pietistic sects.[164] On the other hand, we find ethical people with a meager sense of wonder, fervor, and enthusiasm, poor in emotional life, but strictly moral, reserved, measured, virtuous. Such were the Stoics (the Pharisees) and many modern people who have lost the faith. Now it is certainly true that such people can accomplish much morally; there is a certain measure of independent morality. People can contain themselves, direct themselves, suppress their passions, and pursue the ideal of humanity (although this is not true God-pleasing morality and breeds pride, self-righteousness, and similar vices).

This tendency of religious and ethical people can also be found in the church. Many children of God, who enjoy much in fellowship with God, are much looser when it comes to morality than some who are ethically strict but enjoy

163. DO: *onafhankelijke zedeleer*. Ed. note: Bavinck refers here to a deistic desire to separate all morality and ethics from any religious roots. One writer of Bavinck's own day, citing this exact term from literature by Freemasons, tied it to the goals of all lodges in their vision for public education aimed at creating a Dutch national moral unity based on a common dedication to the golden rule and independent of any religious connection. See Ulfers, *De loge en de school*, 32.

164. Ed. note: Bavinck includes a general reference to "Anabaptists" here, failing to distinguish the peaceful and socially active followers of Menno Simons, for example, from revolutionary, millenarian Anabaptists such as John of Leiden in Münster and Thomas Müntzer, a leader of the German Peasants' Revolt in 1525.

God less.[165] There is therefore a relative truth in the separation of religion and morality; but only a relative truth—the separation itself is wrong; for five reasons:

    a. History demonstrates that religion and morality are related, as Paul indicated in Romans 1:23. A low concept of the gods is always accompanied by low concepts of morality.[166] It goes without saying: people who create and imagine a god for themselves who is cruel will be cruel themselves. People portray themselves in their gods.

    b. Monotheism has at least established the connection that what is good in the religious arena cannot be evil in the moral arena. The same God rules and legislates in both.

    c. Without metaphysics and religion, morality is rendered impossible, except in the form of utilitarianism. We therefore face mutually exclusive alternatives; either (a) good and evil are a priori, independent of our will and thought, and then there is metaphysics; or (b) good and evil become that a posteriori and are determined by us, in which case they are not properly good and evil, but only useful and harmful.[167]

    d. "To believe in virtue is to believe in God."[168] Virtue is an illusion without God because believing in the good includes believing that the good will rule, will triumph—otherwise, why do good? The good, therefore, must be an absolute authority that can and will overcome all opposition. This cannot be an idea but must be a power, a person, God. For this reason Kant made God a postulate of morality. A kingdom of humaneness cannot exist without God.

    e. Psychologically, although there are two arenas in the human person, and although conscience and God-consciousness are not identical, nevertheless both exist within one and the same person. We connect our conscience (the law of the moral life) with our God-consciousness involuntarily and spontaneously; we identify the giver of the moral law with the supreme power of our innate ideas.[169]

---

165. Kuyper, "Natural Knowledge of God," 95: "It is often seen that many people who are strict about duties, unbending on rights, chaste without blemish, praiseworthy in conduct, are nevertheless completely incapable of tender feelings like meekness and admiration and indifferent to any need of prayer. The converse is also seen. Many people who are lax about duties and far from keen about rights can sometimes show strong feelings of respect and enthusiasm, of admiration and devotion."

166. Lamers, *Godsdienst en zedelijkheid*, 34–39.

167. Lamers, *Godsdienst en zedelijkheid*, 11.

168. Janet, *La morale*, 610–11.

169. LO: *idea innata*. Ed. note: For a fuller discussion of innate ideas, see *RD*, 1:224; 2:53–54, 63–68, 70–72.

This brings us to the second way that sin can lead to misconstruing the relation between religion and morality.

2. Religion and morality are identified. This happens in the point of view that denies either God or the world. From one side the world is denied and viewed as sinful by the ascetics, and morality is then absorbed by religion. From the other side, pantheists, for whom the world is God, deny God. To live for the world is then to live for God; a specifically religious life with a particular content and form does not exist because there is no personal God. Religion is then absorbed in morality. This was done by Spinoza, Fichte, Hegel, Schleiermacher, and to some extent by Rothe. It was also more or less under the influence of this idea that the Mediating Theologians[170] soon dismissed the life of the soul, the mystical life with God, as quietism, sickliness, and fanaticism. They wanted the life of the church to be transformed entirely into morality—as by de la Saussaye—and rejected all religion except what could be immediately turned into morality. They even considered the ethical to be the essence of the religious. In the Netherlands, the so-called ethical movement[171] also suffers from this shortcoming and robs religious life of its proper content; it regards religious life only as a further description, determination, and modification of the ethical life (cf. Rothe). But the religious life is the properly meaningful life.[172] The ethical movement has extended the consequences of pantheism into the field of religion and morality, as Tholuck and Vinet previously did in the field of the divine and the anthropological.[173]

170. GO: *Vermittlungstheologie*. Ed. note: "Mediating theology," a school of nineteenth-century German theology influenced by Schleiermacher, sought to synthesize Christianity with modern idealistic philosophy into a rationally and morally defensible religion. Representatives include I. Dorner, J. Neander, Hans Martensen, K. Nitzsch, and J. Müller. See *RD*, 1:29–92.

171. DO: *ethische richting*. Ed. note: The "ethical" movement in the nineteenth-century Dutch Reformed Church represented a strongly Christocentric mediating theology that was strongly opposed to all forms of rationalism in the Christian life. The major representatives of this direction were Daniel Chantepie de la Saussaye (1818–74) and J. H. Gunning (1829–1905). The term "ethical" is necessary as a translation of the Dutch *ethische*, but it is potentially misleading for English readers, who should associate it with a word that more accurately describes the intention of these theologians, the word "existential." His criticism notwithstanding, Bavinck took this school seriously, even writing one of his earliest monographs on its leading theologian: Bavinck, *De theologie van Prof. Dr. Daniel Chantepie de la Saussaye*. According to Bavinck, de la Saussaye's error was to attempt a reorientation of Reformed theology along christological-anthropological lines (Bavinck, *Theologie van . . . de la Saussaye*, 10–19).

172. Kuyper, *De vleeschwording des Woords*, 225–35. Ed. note: This concluding chapter of the book was first published in *De Heraut*, no. 288 (July 1, 1883).

173. Ed. note: Friedrich August Gottreu Tholuck (1799–1877) was a German theologian and pulpit orator known for his evangelical piety; see Schaff, "Tholuck." Alexandre Rodolfe Vinet (1797–1847) was a Swiss Reformed theologian who sought to reconcile the spirit of modernity with the gospel by emphasizing the individual and the separation of church and state. See Rüegg, "Vinet."

Religion in its entirety is then absorbed by ethical phenomena. There is some truth in this, because religion and morality are very closely connected. But:

a. Holy Scripture strictly distinguishes them: the law contains two tables, and Jesus speaks of the First and the Second Commandment. Love toward God is always distinguished from love toward our neighbor and never identified with it. The two are always mentioned *alongside* each other. Leviticus 19:18 says "you shall love your neighbor as yourself," a command that is repeated in James 2:8, where it is called "the royal law" (cf. Matt. 5:43; 19:19; 22:39; Mark 12:31; Rom. 13:9; Gal. 5:14). Then there are passages that direct the child of God only to "love the LORD your God with all your heart and with all your soul and with all your might" (Deut. 6:5; cf. 11:1, 13, 22; 19:9; 30:6; Josh. 22:5; 23:11). And finally there are passages that link the two commands but still clearly distinguish them, as when Jesus summarized the law for the lawyer who questioned him about "the great commandment in the Law" (Matt. 22:36–40; par. Mark 12:29–31; Luke 10:25–28). There is a proper and distinct[174] love toward God, and another toward the neighbor.

b. This cannot be otherwise, because God and humanity are two different objects. The identification of religion and morality is the result of the identification of God and the world (pantheism). Although God and humanity are closely connected, and the world (humanity) is absolutely dependent upon God, nonetheless the world is something different from God. And as surely as the objects are different, the relations in which we stand to different objects must also be different; that is, religion and morality must be different.

c. It is true that love toward our neighbor is the proof and seal of love toward God. It is also true that I must love God in my neighbor and love my neighbor for the sake of God. Therefore morality in the broad sense may be called religion. I am called to serve God also in my profession and trade during the week.

Religion is therefore not a piece of life, but life itself. Our entire life must be serving God. But from this it follows that although the Sabbath can and should penetrate the other days, the other days must never penetrate the

174. Ed. note: "Proper and distinct" is our translation of the Dutch *eigen* ("own"). The word signifies what is properly characteristic of something, what intrinsically belongs to it, what is typical, what is its "own"; the translation "peculiar to" fits here, but the expression "peculiar love toward God" has too many misleading connotations today for it to be useful.

Sabbath. This is the mistake of the ethical movement. The Sabbath may not be pulled down to the level of the other days, but rather the other days should be elevated to the height of the Sabbath. In this dispensation, however, the Sabbath remains and should remain alongside the other days and exert an influence upon them without swallowing them up.

2

Humanity under the Power of Sin

The topic of sin properly belongs in dogmatics but also has to be discussed in ethics.[1]
We need to consider the nature and effect of the first sin on human consciousness and
on the condition or state of humanity. Sin is a turning away from God and a turning
to self, a condition described in Scripture as the "old self," "flesh," or the "natural
person" (in contrast with the "spiritual person"). "Flesh" is an ethical term signifying
enmity with God and not intended to restrict sin to bodily, material life. Similarly,
the contrast between "natural" and "spiritual" does not point us away from bodily
life toward some ethereal, spiritual life, but to the divide between those who have
been regenerated by the Spirit of God and those who have not. "Natural" people
are defined by their soul, their own mind and will, instead of by the Spirit of God.

The soul, spirit, heart, or "I" of our humanity is the center of our knowledge,
feeling, will, and conscience. All of these are darkened and corrupted by sin; as well,
our bodies in all of their parts are defiled by sin and can be used in the service of sin.
This state of natural humanity is called "death" and includes both physical and
spiritual death. Negatively, spiritual death is the absence of true life; it is alienation
from God. Positively, the spiritually dead person is still alive; in Holy Scripture death
is never nonbeing. The basic principle, the driving force of spiritually dead people is
not faith in God or love for him but selfish desire, a universal condition for all people
not regenerated by God's Spirit.

Human life is wholly corrupted and stained by sin, but there are grades or degrees
of sin. Sin can grow or develop in individuals and in nations and can be internal or
publicly manifest. The corruption of our knowledge—consciousness, reason, intellect,
conscience, imagination, memory—manifests itself by the way we have lost sight of

---

1. Ed. note: The title of this chapter is taken from Bavinck's marginal note: "*onder de macht*
[*heerschappij*] *der zonde.*" The manuscript had "In the Situation of Sin" (*In den toestand der zonde*).

the whole, the unity of truth in God, and are disconnected from real life. When we do not know God, who is the ground of all things, we truly know neither ourselves nor the world. Our minds become abstract, detached from life, both subjectively and objectively. Hence, the simplest godly person is wise; the most learned unconverted person is foolish.

The great variety of sins (along with the accompanying virtues) is usually drawn from the Decalogue. After all, the general character of sins is disobedience to God, lawbreaking, lawlessness. God's law is not arbitrary, simply an act of his will, but rests in all his perfections, in his being, in his divine mind. The moral law is thus one, one entity, an organism with a material and inner life-principle, the command of love. Though there are two commandments—love for God and love for neighbor—they are essentially one. Love is the organizing principle of the law, its summa, and therefore the organizing principle of the moral good. The good is determined by our relationship to God. We either worship the true God or we substitute another god in his place, a god for whom we live and to whom we dedicate ourselves. That substitute is the human Self, the "Ego" or "I." The organizing principle of sin is self-love or egocentricity. It is at the same time a turning away from order to disorder, to chaos, to revolution.

We can classify sins in a number of ways: inherited or original sin and actual sins; actual sins can be sins of omission or commission (two sides of the same coin). There is a difference between sins as such (expressly forbidden by God's law) and accidental sins that depend on circumstances. Starting with the conviction that egocentricity is the organizing principle of sin, we observe a twofold direction— of the flesh or of the human spirit—which produces a double array of sins, one downward and animal-like (sensual), the other upward and demonic. Sensual sins take pure, creaturely human desires and turn them into wicked passions and lusts. Spiritual sins are less public and may even accompany outwardly good deeds, but they are more serious. Although it is legitimate to assess the gravity or lightness of sins by certain criteria, this must never be done with excessive subtlety that risks diminishing the seriousness of all sins.

Finally, we distinguish the egocentric subject who covets from the object being coveted. Within the subject, we distinguish sins of the spirit from sins of the body; the objects of human desiring can be reduced to three broad areas: material things, the neighbor, and God.

§8. THE DEVASTATION OF THE IMAGE OF GOD IN HUMANITY[2]

We know what it is to be human according to God's original design, in the state of rectitude, and we also know what we are in reality now as sinners.

---

2. Ed. note: This heading reflects a combination of terms suggested by Bavinck. The manuscript itself reads simply "The Old Man" (*De oude mensch*); an interlinear insertion proposes

We will not discuss here the origin, essence, and nature of sin or the changed relation to God brought about by sin—namely, guilt and punishment of sin.[3] All of that is assumed here and will be treated insofar as it is necessary for our purpose. Vilmar includes the entire doctrine of sin in his *Ethics*, which is incorrect.[4] Nonetheless, sin must be discussed; it may not be passed over or treated merely in passing, as is done by many ethicists today. Our predecessors treated this subject better.[5] For instance, we must consider what we have become because of that sin—as it is revealed to us in God's Word. Furthermore, we need to examine the effect of sin on humanity in all areas of life; and then, finally, actual sins must be identified, classified, and discussed (the taxonomy of sins).

The First Sin and Its Consequences

Therefore, in ethics we first ask about the effect of sinning on human beings as human. Sin began in human consciousness when Adam and Eve were tempted by a *person*, and was completed by the will.[6] By that act they disobeyed God and showed contempt for his love. But how could this one act work such a great turnabout in them, have such a powerful influence on them, that suddenly they became unholy, sinners, powerless, fallen man and woman, fleshly, spiritually dead? Why were they not able to restore themselves in their

---

"natural" (*natuurlijke*) for "old," and a marginal note suggests a longer subject line: "The devastation of the image of God in humanity by sin. Or 'fallen humanity'" (*Den verwoesting van het beeld Gods in den mensch door de zonde. Of: de gevallen mensch*).

3. Cf. *RD*, 3:25–192 (chaps. 1–4).

4. Cf. Vilmar, *Theologische Moral*, 1:119–392; Vilmar's "Doctrine of Sin" (*Lehre von der Sünde*), which he also calls "A History of Illness" (*Krankheitsgeschichte*), is divided into two parts: §§9–16, "The Doctrine of Sin in General" (*Lehre von der Sünde im Allgemeinen*), and §§17–34, "The Doctrine of Sins in Their Appearance (about Sins)" (*Lehre von der Sünde in der Erscheinung* [*von den Sünden*]). The former is then further subdivided into sections on "The Fall into Sin" (*Sündenfall*), "Terms for Sin" (*Namen der Sünde*), "The Nature and Essence of Sin in General" (*Begriff und Wesen der Sünde im Allgemeinen*), "The Origin of Sin" (*Ursprung der Sünde*), "On Temptation" (*Von der Versuchung*), "The Consequences of Sin" (*Folgen der Sünde*), "Guilt" (*Schuld*), and "Original Sin" (*Erbsünde*). The second part is divided further into sections on "The Material Division of Sins: The Three Circles of Sins" (*Materielle Einteilung der Sünden: Drie Sündenkreise*), "Formal Division of Sins" (*Formelle Einteilungen der Sünden*), "On Sins of the Flesh" (*Von den Fleischessünden*), "On Sins Involving the Lust of the Eye" (*Von den Sünden der Augenlust*), and "On the Sins of Pride" (*Von den Sünden des Hochmuts*).

5. E.g., Driessen, *Evangelische Zedekunde*; Lampe, *Schets der dadelyke Godt-geleertheid*; Buddeus, *Institutiones Theologiae Moralis*; and Mosheim, *Kern uit de zede-leer der Heilige Schrift*.

6. Kuyper, *Work of the Holy Spirit*; Kuyper, *Concise Works of the Holy Spirit*, 65–69 (1.4.13); this chapter originally appeared in *De Heraut*, no. 309 (November 25, 1883).

consciousness and will after this one act and become good again? This is an important question, which is often not contemplated!

The first sin, with humans as with the angels, was an act, a free, conscious act; not a feeling, impression, or awareness but an act. That one act consisted of the following:

1. Eve allows the serpent to manipulate her consciousness, permits doubt to penetrate her consciousness, and allows herself to be charmed by the delusion that she will become something other, just as she feels she is able to become something other because her goodness is mutable.[7]

2. Through pride she is led to:

    a. *deny* the consequences of sin: "You will not die" (Gen. 3:4);

    b. *deny* the sin itself: "Your eyes will be opened" (Gen. 3:5); and

    c. *shift* the sin to God himself: "God himself will set you free; you shall become as God" (Gen. 3:5).

3. Infected by pride, now that her will is inclined, she turns to the tree (Gen. 3:6) and sees that it is:

    a. good for food—the lust of the flesh,

    b. a delight to the eyes—the lust of the eyes, and

    c. desirable for making one wise—the pride of life.[8]

4. Eve commits sin.

We see then that sin gains entrance through the *consciousness*, works on the *imagination*, arouses *yearning*, reaches for the ideal that is conjured up, and finally, having perceived it through the *senses* under the influence of that imagination, *grasps* for it. Thus, before the deed is accomplished, an entire process has occurred in a human being in one single moment. The whole person is affected by it, in spirit, soul, body, consciousness, feeling, and will.[9] This process proceeds as portrayed in James 1:14–15: "But each person is tempted when he is lured and enticed by his own desire. Then desire when it has conceived gives birth to sin, and sin when it is fully grown brings forth

---

7. LO: *mutabiliter bona.*

8. Ed. note: The progression described under no. 3 is taken from 1 John 2:16: "For all that is in the world—the desires of the flesh and the desires of the eyes and pride of life—is not from the Father but is from the world."

9. Ed. note: In the margin Bavinck added "Kempis, *De imitatione Christi* I:13" and "*primo occurrit menti simplex cogitatio, deinde fortis imaginatio, postea delectatio et motus pravus et assensio*" ("First, a mere thought comes to mind, then strong imagination, followed by pleasure, evil delight, and consent"). Kempis, *Imitation of Christ* 17.

death."[10] This is still how every concrete[11] sin originates. Our consciousness, assailed by doubt, conceives an idea; our imagination turns it into an ideal; our senses give form to that ideal in the sensory world; and our will tries to grasp it. The one sinful act is thus an act of the entire person in which all our powers and capabilities participate to a larger or smaller degree.

But there is more. This act (even though it was not repeated immediately) leaves behind within humanity a *condition* or *state*.[12] All Pelagians deny this. For them sin is an act of the will that does not affect people who sin; people remain the same and may subsequently just as easily choose to do a good deed. Sin, therefore, resides only in the deed; the self of the person always remains pure. Bellarmine could therefore say "all sins are voluntary."[13] It has even been claimed that the New Testament word for sin[14] indicates only such individual sinful acts. But Romans 7:8–11 clearly teaches that sin is an indwelling active power that resides in a person; in 7:17–20 this is called "sin that dwells within me."[15] Furthermore, in 7:23 the apostle speaks of "the law of sin that dwells in my members."[16]

That one sinful act of Adam and Eve was already a turnabout of the whole person: consciousness, feeling, and will. It was lawlessness[17] (1 John 3:4), disobedience to God, transgression of the law, putting oneself outside established boundaries, abandoning dependence on God, rejecting his lordship, and putting oneself alongside God as one's own god. Thus, it contained two elements:

1. *turning away from* God, enmity, hatred against God, scorning God, a refusal to surrender oneself—in other words, withholding oneself from God; and

2. *turning to self*, a commitment to self, a surrender to self—in other words, selfishness—a love of something other than God, namely, oneself; deification of self, glorification of self, adoration of self.

10. Vilmar, *Theologische Moral*, 1:121–22.
11. DO: *dadelijke*.
12. DO: *toestand*.
13. LO: *omne peccatum est voluntarium*; J. Müller, *Christian Doctrine of Sin*, 1:194–99; 2:259–306. Ed. note: Robert Francis Romulus Bellarmine (1542–1621) was a Jesuit cardinal and great defender of the Roman Catholic orthodoxy established at the Council of Trent (1545–63); his great apologetic work was *Disputationes de Controversiis Christianae Fidei*.
14. GrO: ἁμαρτία.
15. GrO: ἡ οἰκοῦσα ἐν ἐμοὶ ἁμαρτία.
16. GrO: τῷ νόμῳ τῆς ἁμαρτίας τῷ ὄντι ἐν τοῖς μέλεσίν μου; J. Müller, *Christian Doctrine of Sin*, 1:194–95.
17. GrO: ἀνομία.

The first act therefore involved a change of *condition* or state whereby humanity turned away from God and turned (was turned) toward the creature. The act is thus immediately and undeniably a change of condition, existing differently, standing in a different relationship to God than before, a turnabout in the relation to God.

The question now arises: Is this a momentary or a permanent condition? Is humanity able and willing to put an end to this? Is this condition of such a nature that humanity can alter it, just as the first condition of rectitude was altered? Pelagius said yes; sin has power only as the result of habit. We contend, however, that this is impossible, since by this one act the will has come to stand in an entirely different relation to God and is unable to want to change. The will has lost its real, material freedom (see below). Holy Scripture refers to the human person changed by sin as the *"old man"* or the *"old self"* (Rom. 6:6; Eph. 4:22; Col. 3:9) and as *flesh* (Gen. 6:3, 12), because "what is born of flesh is flesh" (John 3:6).[18] This language is especially characteristic of Paul (Rom. 7:5, 18, 25; 8:1–13; 9:8; 1 Cor. 1:26; 15:50; 2 Cor. 7:1; 10:2–3; 11:18; Gal. 2:20; 5:13; Eph. 2:3, 11; Col. 2:11). Language to describe the human condition after the fall includes "the *body* of sin" (Rom. 6:6; cf. v. 12; 8:10; Col. 2:11), "the *natural person*" (1 Cor. 2:14; 15:44, 45; James 3:15; Jude 19), and "by nature *children of wrath*" (Eph. 2:3).[19] Here the "natural person" is contrasted with the "spiritual person" (1 Cor. 2:15).[20]

Biblical Terms for Life under Sin

THE "OLD SELF"[21]

Let us examine these terms in greater detail, beginning with the expression "the old man" or "old self." This refers to the fallen human person in contrast to the renewed creature in Christ, the "new self."[22] We have here, therefore, the human condition in its sinful degeneration, or, to use another term, "flesh."[23] However, there is this one difference—namely, that the "old self" and the "new self" each flow forth from the activity of the flesh and the activity of the Spirit, respectively. In other words, they are the phenomena, the manifestations, of human nature itself, in the one case the fallen nature and in the other the new nature in Christ.

18. GrO: ὁ παλαιὸς ἄνθρωπος; σάρξ; τὸ γεγεννημένον ἐκ τῆς σαρκὸς σάρξ ἐστιν.
19. GrO: τὸ σῶμα τῆς ἁμαρτίας; ψυχικὸς δὲ ἄνθρωπος; τέκνα φύσει ὀργῆς.
20. GrO: ὁ δὲ πνευματικός.
21. GrO: ὁ παλαιὸς ἄνθρωπος.
22. GrO: ὁ καινὸς ἄνθρωπος.
23. GrO: σάρξ.

"FLESH"[24]

Let us now consider the biblical term "*flesh*."[25] Ammon, Baur, Hausrath, and Pfleiderer[26] all argue that Paul was a dualist because he held that sin has its origin and seat in sensuality, in matter. But this conflicts immediately with the following facts:

1. With Paul, the body is a temple of the Lord, and all its members must be dedicated to the Lord (Rom. 6:13, 19; 12:1; 1 Cor. 6:13, 15, 19, 20); this conflicts with all spiritualism that Paul would have had to cherish were he a dualist. 1 Corinthians 6:13 even states that the body is "for the Lord, and the Lord for the body."

2. Paul teaches the resurrection of the body in 1 Corinthians 15.

3. Paul is definitely not an ascetic; he considers marriage sacred and all food good (Col. 2:16; 1 Tim. 4:4).

4. Jesus also had flesh and nonetheless, according to Paul, was holy (2 Cor. 5:21), even though he was born of a woman (Gal. 4:4; cf. Rom. 9:5).[27]

5. Paul also accepts the idea of evil spirits who have no flesh at all.

Furthermore, the way Paul uses the term "flesh" precludes this derivation of sin from sensuality. For Paul, the term σάρξ has the same meaning it has in secular Greek and in the Septuagint, and as the Hebrew term בָּשָׂר.

1. It can mean the substance, the material stuff of our body (1 Cor. 15:39); all "flesh" is not the same kind of flesh.

2. It can mean the body itself, in contrast to the human person's "spirit,"[28] as in Colossians 2:5: "For though I am absent in body, yet I am with you in spirit"[29] (cf. 1 Cor. 5:3; 2 Cor. 7:5). Or it can be used in contrast with "heart"[30] (Rom. 2:29; Eph. 2:11; Phil. 1:22).

3. There is also a broader use of בָּשָׂר in the Old Testament than there is of σάρξ in secular Greek—namely, referring to all earthly creatures in

24. GrO: σάρξ; HO: בָּשָׂר.

25. See Cremer, *Biblico-Theological Lexicon*, s.v. "Σάρξ"; Cremer, "Fleisch"; J. Müller, *Christian Doctrine of Sin*, 1:321–23; Martens, "Israëlietische leerwijze bij Paulus"; Ernesti, *Die Ethik des Apostels Paulus*, 32.

26. Ed. note: Ammon, *Handbuch der christlichen Sittenlehre*; Baur, *Paul the Apostle*; Hausrath, *Der Apostel Paulus*; Pfleiderer, *Paulinism*.

27. GrO: γενόμενος ἐκ γυναικός.

28. GrO: πνεῦμα; HO: נֶפֶשׁ, לֵב, רוּחַ.

29. GrO: τῇ σαρκὶ ἄπειμι, ἀλλὰ τῷ πνεύματι σὺν ὑμῖν εἰμι.

30. GrO: καρδία.

which there is sensory life, the earthly creature as such, especially human beings. Σάρξ accents the difference with God by contrasting creaturely weakness, imperfection, and transience with God's eternality (see esp. Deut. 5:26; Jer. 17:5; Ps. 56:4). This use occurs in Paul only seldom (Rom. 3:20; Gal. 2:16; 1 Cor. 1:29).

4. But Paul now broadens the concept of σάρξ even beyond the Old Testament use and turns it into an ethical concept—namely, to indicate a general life orientation that has turned away from God and toward the world. From this we get terms and expressions like "of the flesh" (Rom. 7:14), "in the flesh" (Rom. 8:8), "live according to the flesh" (Rom. 8:13), and "walking according to the flesh" (2 Cor. 10:2–3; cf. 1 Cor. 3:3).[31]

The concept of flesh in Paul's thought is therefore the same as what John calls the "desires" of the "world" (1 John 2:16)[32]—that is to say, earthly-mindedness, a desire directed toward the creature instead of the Creator. In this sense "flesh" is opposed to "spirit," but not to the human spirit, which is a natural, created human reality (Col. 2:5).[33] The human spirit, too, is sinful, subject to corruption (2 Cor. 7:1) and must be sanctified just as the human "soul" and human "body" must be sanctified (Rom. 12:1–2; 1 Cor. 7:34; Eph. 4:23; 1 Thess. 5:23).[34] Rather, "flesh" is opposed to the Spirit of God, to the Holy Spirit (Rom. 8:3–9).[35] Paul continues in Romans 8 to describe this conflict using expansive expressions; the "flesh" is opposed to "the law of the Spirit of life in . . . Christ Jesus" (v. 2); "the Spirit of God [who] dwells in you" (v. 9); and "the Spirit of him who raised Jesus from the dead" (v. 11).[36] Therefore, in Romans 7:6 "the new way of the Spirit" is set over against the "old way of the written code."[37] To be "led by the Spirit" (Gal. 5:18; cf. vv. 5, 16–17, 22) is certainly identical to being "led by the Spirit of God" (Rom. 8:14).[38] "Flesh" therefore is the opposite not of the human spirit but of the Spirit of God, even though the human spirit is the seat of the Spirit of God (Rom. 8:9, 16).[39] This contrast between flesh and spirit is depicted by Paul especially in Romans and in Galatians 5:13–25, where

31. GrO: δὲ σάρκινός; ἐν σαρκὶ ὤν; κατὰ σάρκα ζῆν; and κατὰ σάρκα περιπατεῖν.
32. GrO: ἐπιθυμία τοῦ κοσμοῦ.
33. GrO: σάρξ; πνεῦμα; τὸ πνεῦμα ἀνθρώπου.
34. GrO: ψυχή; σῶμα.
35. GrO: σάρξ; τὸ πνεῦμα τοῦ θεοῦ; τὸ πνεῦμα ἅγιον.
36. GrO: ὁ νόμος τοῦ πνεύματος τῆς ζωῆς ἐν Χριστῷ Ἰησοῦ; πνεῦμα θεοῦ οἰκεῖ ἐν ὑμῖν; and τὸ πνεῦμα τοῦ ἐγείραντος τὸν Ἰησοῦν ἐκ νεκρῶν.
37. GrO: καινότης πνεύματος; παλαιότης γράμματος.
38. GrO: ἀγέσθαι τῷ πνεύματι; ἀγέσθαι τῷ πνεύματι θεοῦ.
39. GrO: σάρξ; πνεῦμα ἀνθρώπου; πνεῦμα θεοῦ.

"flesh" describes the entire human life in the state of sin, oriented to the things of this world. Among the fruits of the flesh (Gal. 5:19) are mentioned not only adultery and fornication but also idolatry, discord, rage, wrangling, and heresy—which are purely spiritual sins.

5. Thus, Paul is able ultimately to accept the closest connection between "flesh" and sin. He speaks of "sinful flesh" (Rom. 8:3) and of the body as "the body of the flesh" (Col. 2:11).[40] The body is not the source of sin but its seat; it is "sin that dwells in me"—that is, in my flesh (Rom. 7:20). In fact, "the mind that is set on the flesh is hostile to God" (Rom. 8:7)[41] because it does not and cannot obey the law. Here "flesh" designates our sinful, carnal, creaturely direction and way of life.

Paul's use of σάρξ points to a humanity turned away from God, hostile toward God and his Spirit, and unable to produce anything good on its own. It also means that sin consists in turning away from God toward the creature and must be measured by our relationship to God. The Pauline use of σάρξ may not and cannot be explained from anthropological perspectives or from secular Greek, but only as an expansion of the Hebrew notion of בָּשָׂר and from the depths of Paul's own religious consciousness.

"Natural Living Being"

We now turn to New Testament language for humans as natural living beings. The key terms are "soul" and an adjectival form of the word for soul modifying "man" or "human being."[42] These refer to:

1. life, breath, the life of a single living being, or
2. the living being itself as individual, as a person.

Now the "soul" is the subject, the carrier of life in the individual living being, but the "spirit" is the basis, the principle of life.[43] A human person *has* a spirit, but *is* a living soul.[44] Because God has breathed into us the "breath of life," the life-principle, we become "living beings."[45] The spirit joining with the body makes it a living being.[46] That is why Paul says, "The first man

---

40. GrO: σὰρξ ἁμαρτίας; σῶμα τῆς σαρκός.
41. GrO: τὸ φρόνημα τῆς σαρκὸς ἔχθρα εἰς θεόν.
42. GrO: ψυχή; ἄνθρωπος ψυχικός; HO: נֶפֶשׁ.
43. GrO: ψυχή; πνεῦμα; HO: רוּחַ.
44. HO: נֶפֶשׁ; רוּחַ.
45. HO: נֶפֶשׁ חַיָּה; רוּחַ.
46. HO: נֶפֶשׁ; רוּחַ.

Adam became a living being" while "the last Adam became a life-giving spirit" (1 Cor. 15:45).[47] The soul therefore characterizes what distinguishes us uniquely as human persons. Similarly, in the New Testament, the soul carries the spirit within itself and is its appearance and manifestation (Phil. 1:27). The term "soul," therefore, can be attributed only to the human spirit, while the term "spirit" applies also to God and the angels.[48] While soul and body can be separated from each other, spirit and soul can only be distinguished; the soul does not exist apart from the spirit. The "body" is the material organism animated by the "soul"; its substance, its matter, is "flesh."[49] "Flesh" refers only to what is earthly; "body" can be applied also to heavenly bodies (the sun and so forth; 1 Cor. 15).

We turn now to the derivative adjective of the Greek term for soul,[50] which can mean (a) being alive or (b) having a soul; it refers to the *natural* life of a human person. In the New Testament "natural" does not stand over against "bodily" but is contrasted to "spiritual"—that is, to someone who has the Spirit of God and lives.[51] A human being is a "living soul" (1 Cor. 15:45); the body that is animated by the soul is thus a "natural body" (v. 44).[52] But Christ is a life-giving spirit and therefore has a spiritual body received in and after the resurrection.[53] Adam had a "natural body," he was "from the earth" and had a mortal body that depended on eating, drinking, etc.[54] But Christ has a spiritual body, nourished by the Spirit, who quickens it continuously. Here "natural" most certainly does not include sin; before his resurrection, Christ also had a "natural body,"[55] an Adamic body, though without sin. Furthermore, the notion of "natural" does not rule out Adam possessing a "spirit"; on the contrary, he first became a living soul when God breathed "spirit"[56] into him. But that spirit was not immediately the life-principle of the body, for the soul was its power. Therefore, the spirit was only the indirect means.

The natural is therefore something different from the spiritual, and the former precedes the latter (1 Cor. 15:46).[57] The contraposition in 1 Corinthians 2:14 is different; there the contrast is not between the first and second Adam

47. GrO: ψυχὴν ζῶσαν; πνεῦμα ζῳοποιοῦν.
48. GrO: ψυχή; πνεῦμα.
49. GrO: σῶμα; ψυχή; σάρξ.
50. GrO: ψυχικός.
51. GrO: ψυχικός; σωματικός; πνευματικός.
52. GrO: ψυχὴ ζῶσα; σῶμα ψυχικόν.
53. GrO: πνεῦμα ζῳοποιοῦν; σῶμα πνευματικόν.
54. GrO: σῶμα ψυχικόν; χοϊκός.
55. GrO: σῶμα ψυχικόν.
56. GrO: πνεῦμα; HO: רוּחַ.
57. GrO: ψυχικός; πνευματικός.

but between the "psychical" and the "pneumatic" person.[58] The psychical or natural person has not yet been regenerated, has not yet received God's Spirit. These are the people who are characterized as "natural," those defined by their soul, their own minds and wills, instead of by the Spirit of God. Luther's translation of ψυχικός as "natural" is not literally correct (for then the text should read φυσικός = *naturalis*; ψυχικός = *animalis*), but the thought is correct. The natural as such is not sinful or carnal.[59] After all, Adam was also a natural man. But while psychical people, those who define themselves by their souls instead of by the Spirit of God, are contrasted with spiritual people, it is *actually* unregenerate, sinful people who can be said to be "natural," understood now as carnal (1 Cor. 3:1), in contrast to spiritual persons.[60] In the same way, Jude 19 speaks of "natural men" or "worldly people, devoid of the spirit."[61] These people are nothing more than and no different from what they are by nature; they do have a human spirit—otherwise the text would say "no spirit"—but do not have the Spirit of God as they should have.[62] In the words of James 3:15: "This is not the wisdom that comes down from above, but is earthly, unspiritual, demonic."[63] Now every natural person certainly is carnal, but not every carnal person can be said to be "natural" because the term "carnal" also applies to converts who allow themselves to be dominated by the flesh, as the Corinthians did (1 Cor. 3).[64]

Scripture on "Natural" or Fallen Humanity

Now, what does Holy Scripture teach us about these natural persons? We will first consider this in general terms.[65]

---

58. Ed. note: However, both 1 Cor. 2:14 and 15:46 use the same pair of contrasting adjectives, ψυχικός ("psychical," "natural") and πνευματικός ("spiritual"). In 15:46, modern translations render πνευματικόν as "spiritual" but differ on translating ψυχικόν. Most translate it as "natural" (ESV, KJV, NIV, NLT), but some choose "physical" (RSV, NRSV, CEV). Bavinck accepts the translation "natural," even though it is not literally correct, but observes that φυσικός is ordinarily used for "physical." To underscore Bavinck's point here, we introduced the translation "psychical."

59. GrO: ψυχικός; ἁμαρτωλός; σαρκικός.

60. GrO: ψυχικός; πνευματικοί; σαρκικός; σάρκινος.

61. GrO: ψυχικοί, πνεῦμα μὴ ἔχοντες.

62. GrO: πνεῦμα; μὴ πνεῦμα.

63. GrO: οὐκ ἔστιν αὕτη ἡ σοφία ἄνωθεν κατερχομένη ἀλλὰ ἐπίγειος, ψυχική, δαιμονιώδης.

64. GrO: ψυχικός; σαρκικός.

65. DO: *ziel, geest, hart, Ik*; cf. van den Honert, *De mensch in Christus*, 49–84; Vitringa, *Korte schets* (chap. 16, pp. 327–56, deals with spiritual death); Driessen, *Oude en nieuwe mensch*, 44–73; Mosheim, *Kern uit de zede-leer der Heilige Schrift*, 1:17–125 (I.i); Love, *Theologia Practica*, 505–64; Vilmar, *Theologische Moral*, 1:179–94; van Mastricht, *Theoretico-Practica Theologia*, I.iv.4, §§7–22 [2:328–36]; Borst, *Geestelicke geness-konst*, 130–39. Ed. note: In the

1. The *soul*, the *spirit*, the *heart*, the *I* of our humanity does not reside in the periphery of our being but penetrates to our very core.[66] In Holy Scripture the heart is the center of our knowledge, feeling, will, the seat of our conscience; from the heart "flow the springs of life" (Prov. 4:23). That heart and all its imaginations are evil by nature: "The LORD saw that the wickedness of man was great in the earth, and that every intention of the thoughts of his heart was only evil continually" (Gen. 6:5). "The fool says in his heart, 'There is no God.' They are corrupt, they do abominable deeds; there is none who does good" (Ps. 14:1). "The heart is deceitful above all things, and desperately sick; who can understand it?" (Jer. 17:9). We have hearts of stone (Ezek. 36:26). And Matthew 15:19 makes it very clear: "For out of the heart come evil thoughts, murder, adultery, sexual immorality, theft, false witness, slander." The heart therefore must be renewed (Ezek. 18:31), purified (Acts 15:9), and guarded through faith in Christ (Phil. 4:7). The ground, the bottom, of that heart is thus corrupt, an impure, dirty wellspring; this is why all human capabilities are also corrupt: they are aspects of that heart.

a. The *mind/understanding*[67] is darkened in spiritual matters: "They are darkened in their understanding, alienated from the life of God because of the ignorance that is in them, due to their hardness of heart" (Eph. 4:18; cf. 5:8). We do not know God: "For my people are foolish; / they know me not; / they are stupid children; / they have no understanding. / They are 'wise'—in doing evil! / But how to do good they know not" (Jer. 4:22). Understanding must therefore be illumined by the Holy Spirit (Ps. 119:18; 2 Cor. 4:3–6). "The natural person does not accept the things of the Spirit of God, for they are folly to him, and he is not able to understand them because they are spiritually discerned" (1 Cor. 2:14); "For we ourselves were once foolish, disobedient, led astray, slaves to various passions and pleasures, passing our days in malice and envy, hated by others and hating one another" (Titus 3:3); "The fool says in his heart, 'There is no God'" (Ps. 14:1).

In Holy Scripture, foolishness is rightly understood as a lack of divine insight, knowledge, wisdom. The mind has turned away from God and to the creature. We do have some knowledge of God, but as an image rather than as reality. The unregenerate person sees truths as images, as a painting;

---

margin Bavinck added: "here also the idea of κόσμος." For an explanation of the format we are using to cite van Mastricht's *Theoretico-Practica Theologia*, see the extended note in the introduction, §1, in the section "Reformed Churches" (pp. 8–9n48). The volume and page numbers come from the 1749–53 Dutch edition used by Bavinck.

66. Cremer, "Geist des Menschen"; Kuyper, *Principles of Sacred Theology*.

67. DO: *verstand*. Ed. note: In the margin Bavinck added the following Scripture references: 1 Cor. 1:23–24; 2:14; 2 Cor. 11:3; Gal. 1:6–7; Rom. 1:21–23; John 16:2.

the regenerate person sees them in God himself and imprinted on the heart. Knowledge of the former leaves one cold and does not nourish (like painted fruit); knowledge of the latter brings life.[68] The ideas we have of God are now always more or less false.

b. The *will* is also totally corrupted by sin:[69] "For the mind that is set on the flesh is hostile to God, for it does not submit to God's law; indeed, it cannot" (Rom. 8:7; cf. Rom. 7:15: "For I do not understand my own actions. For I do not do what I want, but I do the very thing I hate."). "All of us also lived among them at one time, gratifying the cravings of our flesh and following its desires and thoughts. Like the rest, we were by nature deserving of wrath" (Eph. 2:3 NIV). And then, there are all those places in the New Testament where we are called "slaves of sin": "We know that the law is spiritual; but I am of the flesh, sold under sin" (Rom. 7:14; cf. John 8:34).

Now the faculty of the will as such is not lost through sin; its spontaneity and freedom remain even after the fall. But the will always follows the mind. The mind has to know something first, then present it to the will, and then the will strives for it. That the mind comes first is necessary, because otherwise the will would not be a will but an unwitting, amoral, animal instinct.[70] The mind judges something and then (as practical reason,[71] conscience) evaluates it as good or evil. When reason deems it to be good, it arouses the will, else it disapproves. Before the fall the mind was good and thus distinguished well and caused the will to long for the good. The will was entirely good and inclined to do good. Moreover, the will had been created in such a way that it was natural for it to follow the good; it was a natural property of the will (not a superadded gift[72]); the will itself was holy, righteous, and therefore truly free. It was "will" in the true sense of the word. However, after the fall the mind is darkened and is unable to say what is truly spiritually good; it does not know the things of God and what is beneficial for itself. Now the will, which remains will, follows that erroneous, roaming mind and longs for the apparently good. Now, following that false idea, incorporated by Eve into her consciousness, the will tore itself loose from the ground in which it was planted and lost its material, true, natural freedom. What remained, however, is the will's capacity to follow what the mind designates as good, spontaneously and without coercion.

68. Driessen, *Oude en nieuwe mensch*, 49.

69. Cf. Étienne Gaussen according to de Moor, *Commentarius Perpetuus*, 2:1052–54; Gaussen (d. 1675) was professor of theology at the University of Saumur, 1664–75.

70. Ed. note: Cf. Bavinck, *Beginselen der psychologie*, 54–74, 160–78.

71. LO: *ratio practica*.

72. LO: *donum superadditum*.

As a result of the fall, therefore, the will remains as a human faculty, but its key ethical property, which was natural to it, was lost.[73] Thus the will is not indifferent, either before or after the fall. Formerly it followed the good voluntarily; now it follows the darkened mind voluntarily. Formerly it enjoyed true, material freedom; now, only formal freedom. Sometimes the will is merely indifferent—for example, when our mind evaluates something and finds as many reasons for as against it and thus does not know what is good and what is evil. In that case the will stands between the two, of course, and is unable to choose (e.g., a profession). But that is a deficiency in the will and not something lovely. If we do not immediately see what is good and are unable to know it even after lengthy consideration, then this is a great deficiency in our mind and will. This formal freedom that the will still possesses is equal to servitude; the will voluntarily follows the darkened mind and serves sin and Satan. From this it follows that the will cannot at one time turn to the good and at another time to evil. Pelagius believed this was possible because he considered the will as untouched, intact, and whole. But the will is now incapable of doing good. This is so for two reasons. (a) The will follows the darkened mind and therefore must first bring into that consciousness another way of thinking. That is, enlightenment by the Holy Spirit must occur. (b) The will itself, which has been torn loose from its material genuine freedom and has lost its innate, original inclination toward the good, having been diverted in another direction, is inclined toward evil and aims at what is evil. The will is attached to evil morally (as a sheep longs for a green sprig) and therefore must be turned around, repositioned, re-created, and new divine strength infused into it.[74] Of course, its inability is the result of sin: "Can the Ethiopian change his skin or a leopard his spots? Then also you can do no good who are accustomed to doing evil" (Jer. 13:23; cf. Gen. 6:5; Rom. 7:7–15). We are "so corrupt that we are totally unable to do any good and inclined toward all evil."[75] (See below regarding the good that a person is still capable of doing.)

c. *Feelings*[76] are the passions of hatred, wrath, love, etc., and have also been disoriented by sin: "But the wicked are like the tossing sea, for it cannot be quiet, and its waters toss up mire and dirt" (Isa. 57:20; cf. 2 Pet. 2:18–19). Materially, substantially, these passions are not sinful. Nor is sin found only in their excess, for then temperance and moderation would be sufficient, and Stoicism would yield the best morality. Instead, sin is found in the manner, the direction of those passions; their form is wrong. They are all animated,

---

73. De Moor, *Commentarius Perpetuus*, 2:1052–54.
74. Canons of Dort, III/IV, Rejection of Errors 6.
75. Heidelberg Catechism, Lord's Day 3, Q&A 8.
76. DO: *gevoel*.

formed, not by love for God, but by selfishness. Concupiscence is its formative principle (Rom. 7:10: "commandment"). This means, on the one hand,
that the objects/images that spirit and body deposit in the soul as the seat of
the feelings are impure, sinful, and corrupt; and, on the other hand, that the
feelings themselves are corrupt, reflect impurity, are blurred and muddled. As
a result, the passions are irregular, dissolute, inconsistent in their subjective
movements as well as in the objects with which they are engaged.

2. The *body*[77] is also defiled by sin. It is a body "enslaved to sin" (Rom.
6:6) and subject to death (Rom. 7:24). Sin thrashes about in it and works on
it; death and decay manifest themselves in it. That flesh, the body, is not the
source of sin, because then asceticism would be redemption. But the body
after the fall is the instrument of the sinful soul (mind, will, feelings). Human
beings now misuse the body for sin and as an instrument of unrighteousness (Rom. 6:12–13), as a tool for their desires. That is, from the will, sin
flows through the body to the outside and assumes form. And, conversely,
we have fellowship with the world through the body; through its senses the
body always provides new nourishment for its desires. Sin works through
the body from the inside out and from the outside in. All this takes place
through the body's organs.

The *eyes* do not see (Matt. 5:29; 18:9). Since "the eyes of both [man and
woman] were opened" (Gen. 3:7), the eyes no longer see (Deut. 29:4; Rom.
11:8), have a haughty look (Pss. 18:27; 101:5; Prov. 6:17) and an evil eye (Prov.
28:27), are not satisfied with seeing (Eccles. 1:8), and are blind (Isa. 35:5;
42:7) and full of adultery (2 Pet. 2:14) and lust (1 John 2:16). The eyes must
therefore be enlightened: "The precepts of the LORD are right, / rejoicing the
heart; / the commandment of the LORD is pure, / enlightening the eyes" (Ps.
19:8); "The LORD opens the eyes of the blind" (Ps. 146:8a); "Then the eyes
of the blind shall be opened" (Isa. 35:5a; cf. 42:7).

The *ears* do not hear: "But to this day the LORD has not given you a heart
to understand or eyes to see or ears to hear" (Deut. 29:4); "They have ears,
but do not hear" (Pss. 115:6a; 135:17a; Jer. 5:21); "The eye is not satisfied
with seeing, nor the ear filled with hearing" (Eccles. 1:8). The ears are dull
(Isa. 6:10; Zech. 7:11) and must be unstopped: "Then the eyes of the blind
shall be opened, / and the ears of the deaf unstopped" (Isa. 35:5); "The LORD
God has opened my ear, / and I was not rebellious; / I turned not backward"
(Isa. 50:5).[78]

---

77. DO: *lichaam*.
78. Ed. note: The following paragraphs on the hands, feet, neck, tongue, forehead, mouth,
nose, and knee have been modified and in some cases rearranged for flow and readability.

The *hands* are slow and weak and may cause us to stumble: "Strengthen the weak hands, and make firm the feeble knees" (Isa. 35:3; cf. Heb. 12:12); "If your hand or your foot causes you to sin, cut it off and throw it away" (Matt. 18:8; Mark 9:43). The hands must therefore be strengthened, cleansed, and lifted up: "Draw near to God and he will draw near to you. Cleanse your hands, you sinners, and purify your hearts, you double-minded" (James 4:8; cf. Ps. 24:4).

The *feet* are unstable (Pss. 38:17; 94:18; 121:3), run to evil (Prov. 1:16), turn to evil (Prov. 4:27; 6:18; Isa. 59:7), cause one to sin (Matt. 18:8), and are swift to shed blood (Rom. 3:15). They must therefore be turned to God's testimonies (Ps. 119:59), be held back from evil ways (Ps. 119:101), and have God's Word as a lamp (Ps. 119:105). They should guide into the way of peace (Luke 1:79).

The *neck* is hardened and turned away from God: "Circumcise your hearts, therefore, and do not be stiff-necked any longer" (Deut. 10:16 NIV; cf. 2 Kings 17:14); "For I knew how stubborn you were; / your neck muscles were iron, / your forehead was bronze" (Isa. 48:4 NIV); "For our fathers have been unfaithful and have done what was evil in the sight of the LORD our God. They have forsaken him and have turned away their faces from the habitation of the LORD and turned their backs" (2 Chron. 29:6; cf. Jer. 2:27; 17:23; 19:15).

The *tongue* is an instrument for all sorts of evil: injustice and deceit (Job 27:4; Pss. 109:2; 140:3; Mic. 6:12; James 3:5–8), flattery (Ps. 5:9; Prov. 6:24), boasting (Ps. 12:4), slander (Ps. 15:3), sins (Ps. 39:1), evil (Ps. 140:11), and lying (Prov. 6:17; 26:28; Jer. 9:3, 5). It is said to be against the LORD (Isa. 3:8) and sharp, like a deadly arrow (Pss. 64:3; 140:3; Jer. 9:8). It is therefore to be punished in the eternal fire (Luke 16:24; Rev. 16:10–11). Above all, the tongue must be guarded from evil (Ps. 34:14) and must declare God's righteousness (Pss. 51:15; 71:24). Then "the tongue of the righteous is choice silver" (Prov. 10:20), "a tree of life" (Prov. 15:4) that will "sing for joy" (Isa. 35:6; cf. 32:4; Acts 2:26; Rom. 14:11; 1 Pet. 3:10).

Likewise, the *forehead* reflects the human heart: demonstrating stubbornness, it is described as made of bronze (Isa. 48:4) or hard like flint (Ezek. 3:7–9). Unfaithfulness also shows on the brow: "Therefore the showers have been withheld, / and the spring rain has not come; / yet you have the forehead of a whore; / you refuse to be ashamed" (Jer. 3:3). A name on the forehead reveals a person's true identity: "And on her forehead was written a name of mystery: 'Babylon the great, mother of prostitutes and of earth's abominations'" (Rev. 17:5). The foreheads of the righteous must, therefore, be sealed: "Do not harm the land or the sea or the trees, until we have sealed the servants of our God on their foreheads" (Rev. 7:3; cf. 9:4; 14:1). God's name must be written on them: "They will see his face, and his name will be on their foreheads" (Rev. 22:4).

The *mouth* speaks arrogantly: "His mouth is filled with cursing and deceit and oppression; / under his tongue are mischief and iniquity" (Ps. 10:7); "They close their hearts to pity; with their mouths they speak arrogantly" (Ps. 17:10); "They open wide their mouths against me; / they say, "Aha, Aha! / Our eyes have seen it!" (Ps. 35:21); "Their mouth is full of curses and bitterness" (Rom. 3:14). Therefore, the mouth must be guarded with a muzzle (Ps. 39:1) so that it can speak God's praise (Pss. 34:1; 51:15; 71:8; 109:30) and be free from all foul talk (Eph. 4:29; Col. 3:8; James 3:10).

The *nose* can indicate pride: the wicked put their noses in the air (Ps. 10:4 and so forth).[79]

The *knees*, when weak, show a lack of spiritual vitality: "Therefore lift your drooping hands and strengthen your weak knees" (Heb. 12:12; cf. Isa. 35:3).

All parts of the body, all its organs, can therefore be used in the service of sin as instruments of unrighteousness. All the senses—sight, hearing, taste, smell, and touch—are corrupted; they long for what is sinful and convey that corruption to the spirit. In other words, the fall into sin did not merely occasion a loss of the spiritual life, our fellowship with God (Rome's view). But precisely because of that loss, the natural life in all its forms and dimensions is corrupted as well. This corrupted natural life includes

1. the *vegetative life*, which resides especially in the stomach and intestines; this tends toward intemperance, rowdiness, and the like;
2. the *animal life*, which includes excessive sleep, rest, wakefulness, and lechery; here sin resides especially in the sexual organs; and
3. the actual *rational life* of people, their minds, wills, and feelings—all of which are totally corrupted.

The state of natural humanity is generally called *death*: "For while we were living in the flesh, our sinful passions, aroused by the law, were at work in our members to bear fruit for death" (Rom. 7:5). Here death is understood in the general sense as the opposite of bearing fruit for God:[80] "The mind governed by the flesh is death" (Rom. 8:6 NIV).[81] This mind, "governed by the flesh," stands in opposition to "the mind governed by Spirit," which produces

79. Ed. note: Bavinck here follows the 1637 *Statenvertaling*: "De goddeloze, gelijk hij zijn neus omhoog steekt, onderzoekt niet; al zijn gedachten zijn, dat er geen God is" (lit., "The ungodly, as he puts his nose up, does not seek [God]; all his thoughts are that there is no God").

80. GrO: καρποφόρειν τῷ θεῷ.

81. GrO: τὸ φρόνημα τῆς σαρκὸς θάνατος.

"life and peace."[82] Our Lord also promised this life as a present reality to his followers: "Truly, truly, I say to you, whoever hears my word and believes him who sent me has eternal life. He does not come into judgment, but has passed from death to life. Truly, truly, I say to you, an hour is coming, and is now here, when the dead will hear the voice of the Son of God, and those who hear will live" (John 5:24–25). Paul sounds a similar note: "But God, being rich in mercy, because of the great love with which he loved us, even when we were dead in our trespasses, made us alive together with Christ" (Eph. 2:4–5). According to Cremer, the term "dead," in the expression "dead in our trespasses [and sins]," denotes "the state of those whose life is appointed to death as punishment of sin."[83]

Similar passages include the following:

And Jesus said to him, "Follow me, and leave the dead to bury their own dead." (Matt. 8:22; Luke 9:60)

"For this my son was dead and is alive again; he was lost and is found." So they began to celebrate. (Luke 15:24; cf. James 5:20: "Whoever brings back a sinner from his wandering will save his soul from death.")

Do not present your members to sin as instruments for unrighteousness, but present yourselves to God as those who have been brought from death to life, and your members to God as instruments for righteousness. (Rom. 6:13)

Awake, O sleeper, / and arise from the dead, / and Christ will shine on you. (Eph. 5:14)

We know that we have passed out of death into life, because we love the brothers. Whoever does not love abides in death. (1 John 3:14)

And to the angel of the church in Sardis write: "The words of him who has the seven spirits of God and the seven stars. 'I know your works. You have the reputation of being alive, but you are dead.'" (Rev. 3:1)

In the last example, the expression "but you are dead"[84] does not refer to moral inability but to inefficacy. According to Cremer, "death"[85] refers to the death that Scripture identifies as *the punishment pronounced by God*

82. GrO: τὸ φρόνημα τοῦ πνεύματος ζωὴ καὶ εἰρήνη.
83. GrO: νεκρός; νεκροὺς τοῖς παραπτώμασιν καὶ ταῖς ἁμαρτίαις; Cremer, *Biblico-Theological Lexicon*, 426, s.v. "νεκρός."
84. GrO: καὶ νεκρὸς εἶ.
85. GrO: θάνατος.

upon sin." "*Death* therefore is a very comprehensive term, denoting *all the punitive consequences of sin.*" Temporal death is central to this: "*The end of earthly life*, which is more immediately called death, *is always the point of the punitive sentence about which all the other elements in that sentence are grouped.* This it is that gives *the death of Christ* its significance; cf. Acts 2:24; Heb. 2:9; 5:7; Rom. 6:3, 4, 5, 9; 1 Cor. 11:26; Phil. 2:8."[86] Death[87] is therefore the opposite of life through Christ, and therefore the condition of those who live under that judgment (John 5:24; 1 John 3:14; Rom. 7:10, 13, 24; 8:2, 6). This is incorrect.[88]

This spiritual death consists of the following:

1. *Negatively*, the absence of *true* life, and in Holy Scripture this life is not a matter of abstraction, but refers to a concrete, content-full, authentic, and actual life that is found only in God and obtained through communion with Christ. Spiritual death thus means the absence of the spiritual (i.e., the holy, blessed, eternal life); it is alienation from the life of God (Eph. 4:18), being deprived of the glory of God (Rom. 3:28). It also means having lost the image of God, the knowledge of God, the love of God, faith and trust in God, and obedience to God. The substance of our thoughts, words, deeds—that is, the love for and knowledge of God, or the divine righteousness—has been lost; the form, although often also deformed, has remained in part as civic righteousness.[89] The appearance remains, the essence disappears. The righteousness, holiness—and thus also the blessedness—are lost. With respect to our duty, to what we must be, to the righteousness, love, knowledge of God; to the image of God—in a word, with respect to God and our true relationship to him, we are dead.

2. *Positively*, the spiritually dead person is still alive, however, and has life because in Holy Scripture death is never nonbeing. This spiritually dead person remains active, has and retains a spirit, a soul, and a body.[90] However, the basic principle, nature, direction, and fruit of this activity

---

86. Cremer, *Biblico-Theological Lexicon*, 284, s.v. "θάνατος." Ed. note: Cf. Cremer's comments on νεκρός: "Νεκρός corresponds with θάνατος as the state of man when he has suffered the penal sentence of death, and therefore like θάνατος it is often used in N. T. Greek to denote the state of men still living; and we may understand it of the state of those whose life is appointed to death as the punishment of sin; but *not*, as is so often supposed, of so-called 'spiritual death'" (426).

87. GrO: θάνατος.

88. See Philippi, *Kirchliche Glaubenslehre*, 3:384.

89. LO: *justitia divina; justitia civilis*; Vilmar, *Theologische Moral*, 1:182.

90. GrO: πνεῦμα; ψυχή; σῶμα.

has changed completely. Since we are in the flesh, we think, reason, imagine, and work out of our dead condition (Rom. 7:5; Eph. 2:1–2). The Ephesians were formerly dead and at that point were living according to the course of this world. Positively, spiritual death consists especially in living according to this world, according to the flesh, and, negatively, this life (in sin) is specifically spiritual death. Both sides of this spiritual death, the positive and the negative, are therefore not two but one; they coincide, they occur together at the same time. First Timothy 5:6 says, therefore, of a self-indulgent widow: she is dead "even while she lives," dead to righteousness, but living for sin. Romans 6:1–2 calls this positive aspect "continuing in sin" and "living in sin." Other texts speak of it as "walking [in disobedience]" (Col. 3:7); as "living according to the flesh" (Rom. 8:12–13); "living in sensuality, passions, drunkenness, orgies, drinking parties, and lawless idolatry" (1 Pet. 4:3; cf. 2 Pet. 2:10; 3:3; Jude 16–18). And this condition of living voluntarily in sin is also a condition of bondage to sin; sin has dominion over us, is our master. But believers are to consider themselves "dead to sin and alive to God in Christ Jesus" (Rom. 6:11).

This is a universal reality. All are under sin's dominion (Rom. 3:9; 6:16–23), "sold under sin" (Rom. 7:14), "imprisoned under sin" (Gal. 3:22).[91] To those who thought they were free because they were Abraham's children, Jesus said, "Truly, truly, I say to you, everyone who practices sin is a slave to sin" (John 8:34).[92] Paul speaks of being "captive to the law of sin that dwells in my members" (Rom. 7:23).[93] This is also evident when Scripture tells us that those who are in Christ have been delivered from Satan, "the prince of the power of the air" (Eph. 2:2; cf. 6:12; John 12:31; Acts 26:18; 2 Cor. 4:4; 2 Tim. 2:26; Heb. 2:14), and "from the domain of darkness" (Col. 1:13).[94] John speaks of all that is under the power of sin as "the world" and warns his readers: "Do not love the world or the things in the world. If anyone loves the world, the love of the Father is not in him" (1 John 2:15).[95]

The basic principle, the driving force of such a life is thus not faith, love for God, but concupiscent desire.[96] These desires, inclinations, and passions are not

---

91. GrO: πεπραμένος ὑπὸ τὴν ἁμαρτίαν; συνέκλεισεν . . . τὰ πάντα ὑπὸ ἁμαρτίαν.

92. GrO: δοῦλός ἐστιν τῆς ἁμαρτίας.

93. GrO: αἰχμαλωτίζοντά με ἐν τῷ νόμῳ τῆς ἁμαρτίας τῷ ὄντι ἐν τοῖς μέλεσίν μου.

94. GrO: τὸν ἄρχοντα τῆς ἐξουσίας τοῦ ἀέρος; ἐκ τῆς ἐξουσίας τοῦ σκότους.

95. GrO: μὴ ἀγαπᾶτε τὸν κόσμον μηδὲ τὰ ἐν τῷ κόσμῳ.

96. DO: *grondbeginsel, drijfkracht*; GrO: ἐπιθυμία; LO: *concupiscentia*; Vilmar, *Theologische Moral*, 1:183; de Moor, *Commentarius Perpetuus*, 2:1055.

sinful as such, but the direction in which they move makes them sinful; they do not focus on God, but on the *I* (selfishness), on the world. Their aim is not to glorify God, but to satisfy self; eating and drinking as such are not sins, but the manner makes them sinful; in the creature we are loving not God but self and the creature itself. The whole of human life is governed by this desire, in our individuality, in our civic life, socially, politically, morally, religiously, artistically, and scientifically. Augustine's words are true indeed: "The virtues of the pagans are splendid vices."[97] They have only the form, not the essence, the fabric, the substance of virtues, because they try to function as virtues apart from the living God. This desire is mentioned repeatedly in Scripture and is described with different terms: "covetousness" (Rom. 7:8), "passions of the flesh" and "desires of the body and the mind" (Eph. 2:3), "deceitful desires" (Eph. 4:22), "worldly passions" (Titus 2:12), "one's own desire" (James 1:14–15), "the desires of the flesh and the desires of the eyes and pride of life," all of which is "not from the Father but is from the world" (1 John 2:16).[98]

The *fabric*[99] of this life—what fills this life, its contents—is sin; it is wholly corrupted, stained by sin.[100] But in spiritual death, considered positively (not negatively, for then, as explained above, all the unregenerate would be dead), there are grades or degrees. There is growth in the life that is lived in sin—that is, growth as far as the human race is concerned.[101] The sin that Eve introduced into the world gradually increased within her, Adam, and their children, especially first in the Cainites and later also in the Sethites. The world was ripe for destruction (the flood). God intervenes repeatedly in history by way of judgments whenever sin's growth threatens to cause the human race to perish, and thus he bridles the power of sin through the flood, through the confusion of tongues at Babel, and the like. When such growth occurs among the nations, they must perish (the Babylonians, Assyrians, Greeks, Romans). In more recent times this is different because Christianity has the power to renew the nations (the Reformation, also of the nations, also in Roman Catholic countries). A similar growth of sin happens in the individual; no one body becomes suddenly bad.[102] That is why many live as respectable citizens; there is a difference between Socrates, Plato, and, for instance, Nero. Sin is a germ,

97. LO: *paganorum virtutes splendida vitia sunt.*
98. GrO: ἐπιθυμία; ταῖς ἐπιθυμίαις τῆς σαρκὸς ἡμῶν and τὰ θελήματα τῆς σαρκὸς καὶ τῶν διανοιῶν; τὰς ἐπιθυμίας τῆς ἀπάτης; τὰς κοσμικὰς ἐπιθυμίας; τῆς ἰδίας ἐπιθυμίας; ἡ ἐπιθυμία τῆς σαρκὸς καὶ ἡ ἐπιθυμία τῶν ὀφθαλμῶν καὶ ἡ ἀλαζονεία τοῦ βίου, οὐκ ἔστιν ἐκ τοῦ πατρὸς ἀλλ' ἐκ τοῦ κόσμου ἐστίν.
99. DO: *stof.*
100. Vitringa, *Korte schets*, 343.
101. Vilmar, *Theologische Moral*, 1:187–92.
102. LO: *nemo repente pessimus.*

present in every heart; but with some people, as a result of circumstances (including upbringing) conducive to sin, it comes to growth and development more than with others who enjoy a good upbringing, have a sedate character and a good temperament. The basic principle, the fabric, the fruit of all unregenerate people is one and the same, but its manifestation is different; there is always only a difference in degree, in form. With some this sinful life hardly manifests itself externally but remains completely internal; with some others it manifests itself in crankiness accompanied by an otherwise good attitude; with others in an outpouring of anger. These are people "who drink injustice like water" (Job 15:16). Many kinds of sin are the result: all kinds of sin—spiritual, character, attitudinal, carnal sins, etc.[103]

The *fruit*, the result, of this life is *death* for all—that is, *physical death*. This fruit includes also what precedes this death—namely, a preparatory disintegration process, a cancer[104] that is present in us from our conception. Our so-called development as individuals, as nations, also in art, science, and politics, is nothing but a slow death. Sin is the sting of death (1 Cor. 15:56), and that death begins with our coming into being. Within this death, thus considered, lie all disasters and ailments in the world that are not necessities of nature but the consequences of sin, which must therefore also be opposed. Culture therefore must be a struggle against sin and its consequences, an ethical rather than a physical battle.

Now, in order to understand clearly humanity in its natural condition (the "natural man"[105]), let us consider it particularly according to its capabilities and powers of soul, body, and spirit, and the influence that sin has had especially on them. Harmony and peace among them has been disrupted as sin dissolves everything; there is discord and conflict between conscience and being, reason and will, intellect and emotions, soul and body. Paul describes this dramatically in Romans 1:21–23:

> For although they knew God, they did not honor him as God or give thanks to him, but they became futile in their thinking, and their foolish hearts were darkened. Claiming to be wise, they became fools, and exchanged the glory of the immortal God for images resembling mortal man and birds and animals and creeping things.

This description fits all people in our natural state: "And you, who once were alienated and hostile in mind, doing evil deeds, he has now reconciled in his

---

103. See §9 below on the classification of sins.
104. DO: *tering*.
105. GrO: ἄνθρωπος ψυχικός.

body of flesh by his death, in order to present you holy and blameless and above reproach before him" (Col. 1:21–22). For unbelieving people "nothing is pure; but both their minds and their consciences are defiled" (Titus 1:15). These are people who "say to God, 'Depart from us! We do not desire the knowledge of your ways'" (Job 21:14). They are "blind guides," "blind fools" (Matt. 15:14; 23:16–19; cf. Luke 4:18; John 9:39–41). The light of the gospel comes into a darkness (John 1:5), a darkness that "we were at one time," but now we are "light in the Lord, children of light" (Eph. 5:8). Paul speaks of being "depraved in mind and deprived of the truth" (1 Tim. 6:5; cf. 2 Tim. 3:8). This comprehensive and thorough corruption from within is described well by our Lord: "What comes out of a person is what defiles him. For from within, out of the heart of man, come evil thoughts, sexual immorality, theft, murder, adultery, coveting, wickedness, deceit, sensuality, envy, slander, pride, foolishness. All these evil things come from within, and they defile a person" (Mark 7:22).

Intellect or knowledge in Holy Scripture is always practical, moral:

> Behold, the fear of the Lord, that is wisdom, / and to turn away from evil is understanding. (Job 28:28)

> The fear of the Lord is the beginning of wisdom; / all those who practice it have a good understanding. (Ps. 111:10)

> The fear of the LORD is the beginning of wisdom, / and the knowledge of the Holy One is insight. (Prov. 9:10; cf. 14:29)

> Good sense is a fountain of life to him who has it, / but the instruction of fools is folly. (Prov. 16:22)

The New Testament testifies that Christ is the one who brings truth, understanding, and life eternal:

> And this is eternal life, that they know you, the only true God, and Jesus Christ whom you have sent. (John 17:3)

> And we know that the Son of God has come and has given us understanding, so that we may know him who is true; and we are in him who is true, in his Son Jesus Christ. (1 John 5:20)

> Thanks be to God through Jesus Christ our Lord! So then, I myself serve the law of God with my mind.[106] (Rom. 7:25)

106. GrO: νοῦς.

The knowing aspect—consciousness, reason, intellect, conscience, imagination, memory—thus is totally corrupted by sin. The mind has been loosened from the will through sin; it has become immoral, one capability alongside others rather than within them. It is torn loose from life; the heart that is dead also kills the mind. Thus, we do have some knowledge of individual verities, but we do not know *the* truth, the system, the unity of all truth in God. We do not know God, who is the ground of all things, and thus we know neither ourselves nor the world. Our mind is abstract, detached from life, both subjectively and objectively. The simplest godly person is wise; the most learned unconverted person is foolish. Sin besots, blinds, darkens, by subjectively disconnecting the mind from true life (our being in God), by killing it, by removing reality from it, and by objectively disconnecting the objects of our knowledge (the world, ourselves) from God and by making them independent. We no longer see clearly and no longer see things in God and in his light (Ps. 36:9).

§9. THE ORGANIZING PRINCIPLE AND CLASSIFICATION OF SINS[107]

Here we are not discussing what sin is—that is, in relation to God, which is how we can first determine the nature of sin. Here, that issue is being assumed from dogmatics.[108] Our question is more specific: There are innumerable sins, appearances, forms, manifestations of the one sin. Is it possible to construct a system from that variety and number, and is there a connection between them all? In other words, is there an organizing principle[109] from which all sins can be objectively and substantively derived? This question really belongs in ethics[110] along with the description of individual sins. A rubric in ethics, specifically derived from Holy Scripture, must set forth an enumeration and elucidation of all sins. A faithful likeness of the world's true being must be held before the world, and all these sins must be traced to a common root.[111] Just as later we must unfold the image of a holy person, so now at the beginning we must describe the image of the sinful, natural

---

107. Luthardt, *Kompendium der theologischen Ethik*, §22, "Division of Sins" (*Die Unterschiede der Sünden*); cf. Laurillard, *De zeven hoofdzonden*; Zöckler, *Das Lehrstück von den sieben Hauptsünden*.

108. Ed. note: See *RD*, 3:25–192 (chaps. 1–4).

109. DO: *beginsel, reaalprincipe*.

110. Ed. note: Between the lines Bavinck inserted, "Therefore, a phenomenology of sin" (*Dus eene phaenomenologie der zonde*), and added a reference to Scharling, *Christliche Sittenlehre*, 184.

111. Vilmar, *Theologische Moral*, 1:248.

person and the world. Those two images must be juxtaposed—that is how the contrast becomes clear.

The Decalogue and Disobedience

Usually such a list of sins (along with the accompanying virtues) is drawn from the Decalogue. This is how Calvin does it in his *Institutes of the Christian Religion*.[112] He first shows how a commandment must be understood and explained. This involves proscribing internal as well as external conduct—that is, not only external stealing but also stealing in thought—just as Christ explained the law in Matthew 5:21–48. Christ showed that the law contains much more than what is expressed and included in the words.[113] In each commandment a part expresses the whole, and one must therefore ask not simply what is stated but also why it is given to us. Thus in each commandment something good (positive) is commanded, and the opposite evil is forbidden, and vice versa.[114] And for every kind of transgression, God has forbidden only the most terrible and shameful things in order to scare us off even more.[115] Whether these hermeneutical rules are valid or might instead lead to all kinds of arbitrariness, we will discuss later when we consider the Decalogue.[116] However, they have been followed by every Reformed interpreter, as we can see in Lord's Days 34–44 of the Heidelberg Catechism. In addition, see the second and third books of Lambert Daneau's *Ethices Christianae*, where virtues and vices are also arranged under the Ten Commandments.[117] Others organize them more freely and classify virtues and vices in terms of those against God, the neighbor, and ourselves and then discuss them together.[118] Driessen, in chapter 1, discusses various vices of the old nature (love of the world, covetousness, fleshly lust, pride, anger, unbelief, dissembling, ingratitude, etc.) apart from any system.[119] But all of these writers include, more or less completely, a description of sins in the discipline of ethics.

We know from dogmatics that the general character of sins is disobedience to God, lawbreaking, lawlessness (1 John 3:4).[120] All sin presupposes a law;

---

112. Ed. note: *Institutes*, II.viii.6–10.
113. *Institutes*, II.viii.8.
114. *Institutes*, II.viii.9.
115. *Institutes*, II.viii.10.
116. Ed. note: This material is covered in Book III, "Humanity after Conversion," in *RE*, vol. 2, *The Duties of the Christian Life*.
117. Ed. note: Daneau, *Ethices Christianae*.
118. E.g., Pictet, *De christelyke zedekunst*.
119. Ed. note: Driessen, *Oude en nieuwe mensch*.
120. GrO: ἀνομία; cf. *RD*, 3:133–36.

"where there is no law there is no transgression [nor imputation]" (Rom. 4:15). This text is often cited as proof that before the giving of the law on Sinai, God did not impute sin—imputation happened only after existing sin was considered sin. Then, appeal is also made to similar passages like Romans 5:13: "For sin indeed was in the world before the law was given, but sin is not counted where there is no law." Paul goes on to say, "Now the law came in [between the promise to Abraham and the fulfillment] to increase the trespass,[121] but where sin increased, grace abounded all the more, so that, as sin reigned in death, grace also might reign through righteousness leading to eternal life through Jesus Christ our Lord" (Rom. 5:20). In Romans 3:18–20 Paul says that the law addresses only those who are under the law—knowledge of sin comes only through the law (see also Gal. 3:19–25).[122]

Paul could not mean that there was no culpable sin deserving God's wrath prior to the law of Moses, because in Romans 5:13 he says that "sin indeed was in the world before the law was given," and as lawlessness (1 John 3:4) sin is always punishable.[123] God's wrath is manifested against the pagans as well (Rom. 1:18); they are "by nature children of wrath" (Eph. 2:3).[124] Moreover, the law is not the cause of sin (Rom. 7:7–16). The reference to "wrath" in Romans 4:15 cannot mean consciousness of wrath, and in Romans 5:13 the word "counted" cannot be interpreted as subjectively imputed to one's conscience.[125] For Paul says that Abraham obtained righteousness and became heir of the world through faith and according to the promise. One cannot obtain this or become this through the law (for then faith and promise would be in vain), because the law brings only wrath, since no human can fulfill the law. But "now" (Paul does not say "because") there was no law to which the fulfillment of the promise was linked; therefore, there was no transgression that would prompt God's anger and thus destroy the fulfillment of the promise. Thus, Abraham's inheritance and righteousness in no way depend on the law and its fulfillment. The promise is not destroyed through unbelief or sin (Rom. 3:3).[126]

121. GrO: νόμος δὲ παρεισῆλθεν ἵνα πλεονάσῃ τὸ παράπτωμα.

122. J. Müller, *Christian Doctrine of Sin*, 1:131–203; according to Cremer (*Biblico-Theological Lexicon*, 431, s.v. "Νόμος"), Rom. 5:13–14 provides clear evidence that νόμος without the definite article can also refer to the Mosaic law.

123. GrO: ἡ ἁμαρτία; ἀνομία.

124. GrO: τέκνα φύσει ὀργῆς.

125. GrO: ὀργή; ἐλλογεῖται; J. Müller, *Christian Doctrine of Sin*, 1:102–5.

126. Ed. note: Bavinck adds that Weiss is thus correct in his critique of Meyer and Philippi. He is undoubtedly referring to Bernhard Weiss, who prepared a thorough revision of the famous H. A. W. Meyer commentary on Romans in 1881; cf. Weiss, *Commentary*, vol. 3. "Philippi" is a reference to the German original of Philippi, *Commentary on Romans*.

In Romans 5:12 Paul wants to demonstrate that sin and death entered the world through one man, Adam. And now he says in verse 14 that there was sin in the world also from Adam until Moses (Cain, Sodom, etc.), but at that time there was no law in terms of which sin could be adjudicated as transgression deserving death.[127] Thus death is the result of Adam's deed. Therefore, according to Paul as well, all sin presupposes a law, especially the moral law, so called in distinction from the law of reason (logic), of nature, etc.—that is, that law which is instituted for human life and conduct. That law presupposes a Lawgiver. This cannot be Kant's autonomous "I"—for then our human nature would be torn into two parts, a commanding part and an obeying part, and why does the one command so sternly and the other feel obliged to obey? Nor can this be humanity itself, as claimed by Comte,[128] all Socialists, and Darwinists. This can only be God. God is the sole immediate object of our duty and obedience.[129] No person, no angel, no one other than God alone can obligate us to obey morally, in our conscience. Others can compel us, but that is exactly what is immoral; but when God commands something, then we feel instantly obligated to do it.

In order to find out the material principle in evil, we must first know the material principle in goodness. Evil can exist and be known only after the good is known. Thus we must ask: Is there a material principle in goodness, and if so, what is it? That such a principle exists must be denied by all who say that the moral law comes from a series of unrelated, arbitrary, atomistic commandments that rest only on an arbitrary act of God's will: "This I wish, thus I command, let my will stand in place of reason."[130] Thus also Scotus, who said something is good only because God wills it.[131] Thus there is no reason for it—evil would be good if God had desired this. The same view is held by Occam, Gabriel Biel, Pierre d'Ailly, and later by Descartes (however, for Descartes, thinking and willing are one with God), Pufendorf,

127. According to Weiss, *Commentary*, 3:45.

128. Ed. note: Auguste Comte (1795–1857) was a French philosopher of society and a founder of modern sociology who created a secular "religion of humanity," complete with liturgy, sacraments, and holy days, all dedicated to the "New Supreme Great Being"—i.e., humanity. See https://en.wikipedia.org/wiki/Auguste_Comte; https://en.wikipedia.org/wiki/Religion_of_Humanity.

129. J. Müller, *Christian Doctrine of Sin*, 1:100.

130. LO: *hoc volo, sic iubeo, stat pro ratione voluntas*. Ed. note: This is a saying attributed to the Roman poet Juvenal (Decimus Iunius Juvenalis [ca. AD 55–140]). The citation is from Juvenal's *Satires* VI.223; surprisingly, the context is not an imperial court but a household (lines 219–24; translation by George Gilbert Ramsay [1839–1921], a professor of humanities at the University of Glasgow; available online at https://en.wikisource.org/wiki/Satire_6).

131. J. Müller, *Christian Doctrine of Sin*, 1:95–96.

and others.[132] Such tearing of God's will from all his other perfections leads to skepticism.[133] On the other hand, it is also false that the moral law stands by itself and would be able to bind us even if there were no God.[134] The good does not exist in abstraction; it is impossible to love the good in itself. It is only because *the* All-Good One exists that the good also exists. The moral law rests thus in God, not as sheer will, but in all his perfections, in his being, in his divine mind.[135]

The moral law is thus one, one entity, an organism, and therefore has a material and inner life-principle. Jesus reduces all moral commandments, the whole law and the prophets, to two commandments: love to God and love to neighbor (Matt. 22:36–39; Mark 12:29–31). And these two are again essentially one: Jesus calls it the first and great commandment. The following passages reiterate this: "You therefore must be perfect, as your heavenly Father is perfect" (Matt. 5:48); "Love is the fulfilling of the law" (Rom. 13:10); "You shall be holy, for I am holy" (1 Pet. 1:16). Love is the organizing principle of the law, its *summa*.[136] And love, therefore, is also the organizing principle of the good. All virtue is one (Stoics), and the specific virtues, therefore, are all manifestations of love, they are all derived from love. Love of neighbor is thus essentially love of God.[137] The relation in which we subjectively stand toward God determines all our relations toward every creature (neighbor, world, Satan). And, objectively, it is God himself whom we love directly, for himself, and we love God indirectly in all creatures.

Sin is, then, the opposite of the good.[138] The good is determined by our relationship to God, and thus also the evil. Sin thus reverses our relationship

132. Ed. note: William of Ockham (1287–1347), Gabriel Biel (1420–95), and Pierre d'Ailly (1351–1420) were important figures in the nominalist movement or *via moderna* of late medievalism. René Descartes (1596–1650) was a French philosopher and mathematician and shaper of modern philosophy whose most famous philosophical statement is "I think, therefore I am" (*Cogito ergo sum*; French "Je pense, donc je suis"). Samuel von Pufendorf (1632–94) was a German jurist and philosopher who contributed significantly to modern discussions of natural law. See Seeberg, "Occam"; Tschackert, "Biel"; Tschackert, "Ailly"; Evans, "Descartes"; G. Frank, "Pufendorf," all in *Schaff-Herzog*.

133. J. Müller, *Christian Doctrine of Sin*, 1:97–98.

134. J. Müller, *Christian Doctrine of Sin*, 1:100–107. Ed. note: Müller attributes this view to the German rationalist philosopher Christian Wolff (1679–1754) and cites (100n1) Wolff's *Vernünftige Gedanken*, §20.

135. LO: *merum arbitrium*; *mens divina*.

136. J. Müller, *Christian Doctrine of Sin*, 1:108–10.

137. J. Müller, *Christian Doctrine of Sin*, 1:110.

138. Ed. note: In the margin Bavinck added: "Sin is not merely (a) ἄτη, bewilderment, infatuation, confusion of the mind (Homer); (b) ὕβρις, pride, transgression of boundaries, indulgence (the Greeks); (c) ignorance (Socrates); (d) a negative moment in the development of the Good (pantheism, Hegel); (e) an independent act of the will (Pelagius); (f) sensuousness, σάρξ (the

to God and therefore also to the world, to our neighbor, to Satan, and to ourselves. It is precisely because the pagans have not glorified God that they are abandoned to dishonorable passions and the like (Rom. 1:24–27).[139] People have turned away from God, their love has turned into hatred, and they have tried to dethrone God.

That is the negative side, however. Positively, who is now humanity's god? They must have gods for whom they live and to whom they dedicate themselves. Sin consists concretely in placing a substitute on the throne. That substitute is not another creature in general, not even the neighbor, but the human self, the "ego" or "I." The organizing principle of sin is self-glorification, self-divination; stated more broadly: self-love or egocentricity.[140] A person wants to be an "I," either without, next to, or in the place of God. Turning away from God is simultaneously a turning to self. Prior to this, God was the center of all human thought and action; now it is the person's "I." Humanity not only surrendered its true center but also replaced it with a false center. On the one hand, sin is a *decentralization* of all things away from God, a loosening, an undoing of bonds with God—atomism, individualism. On the other hand, it is at the same time also a concentration of everything around the human self, an attempt to subjugate everything to an individual "ego." Thus sin is not only a matter of turning away from the existing order—in effect, undermining order—but also an establishing of another order, which actually is a *dis*order. Sin produces not only an alternative or counterorder but an *anti*-order; in a word: *revolution*.[141]

Romans, Socinians, rationalists, Schleiermacher, Rothe, Scholten); or (g) ignorance (Ritschl) but active privation (*actuosa privatio*); sin is not a 'substance,' but it is reality." For a more thorough discussion of this point see *RD*, 3:136–38.

139. DO: *oneerlijke bewegingen*; J. Müller, *Christian Doctrine of Sin*, 1:131–32.

140. Ed. note: Between the lines Bavinck added: "φιλαυτία, not in an ethical sense only but in the broadest sense as 'wanting to be God.'" Parenthetically within the text, after the word *zelfzucht* (egocentric, egocentricity), Bavinck alluded to the etymological similarity of the Dutch words *zucht* (sigh), *zoeken* (seeking), and *ziekte* (sickness) and the German words *Seuche* (epidemic) and *Selbstsucht* (selfishness, egotism).

141. The following posit egocentricity as the foundation of sin: Tholuck, *Die Lehre von der Sünde*, 18, 28; J. Müller, *Christian Doctrine of Sin*, 1:136; Vilmar, *Theologische Moral*, 1:129–42 (§11); Philippi, *Kirchliche Glaubenslehre*, 3:3–12; Lange, "Selbstsucht"; Luthardt, *Kompendium der theologischen Ethik*, §20; Scharling, *Christliche Sittenlehre*, 165. Ed. note: In the margin Bavinck added: Augustine, *De civitate Dei* XIV.14; Thomas Aquinas, *ST* Ia IIae q. 77 art. 4; IIa IIae q. 25 art. 7; Melanchthon, Buddeus, et al. Bavinck affords only a qualified endorsement of the view that egocentricity is the organizing principle of all sin, adding in the margins:

> Identifying egocentricity as the organizing principle of sin is fine, but only if (a) it is taken in a very broad sense and includes the spiritual problems of haughtiness and unbelief, and (b) it is not understood as though all sins *logically* flow from this foundation. Egocentricity focuses on various things, places, everything—God, world, neighbor—in service to itself. The diverse forms of sin are determined by the many and diverse forms

Holy Scripture also teaches this. The fall occurred because of a desire to be like God. The prodigal son demands: "Give me the share of property that is coming to me" (Luke 15:12). Repentance begins with self-denial: "Whoever loves his life loses it, and whoever hates his life in this world will keep it for eternal life" (John 12:25). In the new life "none of us lives to himself, and none of us dies to himself. For if we live, we live to the Lord, and if we die, we die to the Lord. So then, whether we live or whether we die, we are the Lord's" (Rom. 14:7–8). Each one seeks the good of the other (1 Cor. 10:24, 33; Phil. 2:4). Christ "died for all, that those who live might no longer live for themselves but for him who for their sake died and was raised" (2 Cor. 5:15). Therefore, "It is no longer I who live, but Christ who lives in me" (Gal. 2:20). We are to look not only to our own interests but also to the interests of others (Phil. 2:4). Jesus even calls us to hate everything if we want to be his disciple, including our "own father and mother and wife and children and brothers and sisters, yes, and even our own life" (Luke 14:26). The highest manifestation of sin is the "man of lawlessness [or sin] . . . who opposes and exalts himself against every so-called god or object of worship, so that he takes his seat in the temple of God, proclaiming himself to be God" (2 Thess. 2:3–4). In the past, theologians were not as interested in the organizing principle of sin as in its beginning, in the origin of sin, and posited that origin in pride,[142] as Rome did, or in unbelief, as the Reformed did. They did not look for the organizing principle,[143] the source for classifying sins, because they found an order of treatment in the Decalogue. Nonetheless, they did classify sins.

Classification of Sins[144]

The fundamental classification made by both Reformed and Lutheran theologians, as well as others, identified sins as *inherited* or *original* sin and *actual* sins (2 Thess. 2:3).[145] Actual sins were then classified in various ways:[146]

---

of the Good. Furthermore, (c) sin can develop in such a way as to become satanic, pure hatred against God, but then only because he obstructs us.

142. LO: *superbia*.

143. DO: *reaalprincipe*.

144. Ed. note: Bavinck added a marginal note ("Vacation, March 1902") that provides a clue to his use of the manuscript for lecturing to his Kampen students. The spring and fall of 1902 were the last times Bavinck lectured on ethics. He left Kampen at the end of the year and began his professorate at the Vrije Universiteit, Amsterdam, where he did not lecture on ethics. See pp. xxxvi–xli of the introduction, on the de Jong manuscript. A slightly different classification, which includes many of the distinctions that follow, can be found in *RD*, 3:149–52.

145. LO: *peccatum originale et actuale*.

146. Heppe, *Reformed Dogmatics*, 348; Heidegger, *Corpus Theologiae Christianae*, 1:355 (X.61); de Moor, *Commentarius Perpetuus*, 3:313; van Mastricht, *Theoretico-Practica Theologia*, I.iv.3, §§10–35 [2:298–322]; Vilmar, *Theologische Moral*, 1:221–33 (§18).

according to their form—after the commandment—as sins of *omission* (James 4:17; Matt. 25:42; 1 John 3:17) and sins of *commission* (two sides of the same coin); or also sins *as such* (those expressly forbidden by God's law; e.g., lying) and *accidental* sins (in certain circumstances, in a certain manner).[147] In the latter instance a deed might be good in itself but not proceed from a good *foundation* (faith) or for a good *purpose* (to the honor of God), or not be carried out in a good *manner* (because of the circumstances). Considering sins in terms of the source from which they proceed, we can distinguish sins of thought/heart, sins of words, and sins of deeds.[148] Distinctions are also made between sins of the spirit and sins of the flesh; those that come under divine justice and those that are judged by external or civil law.[149] And then there are sins performed in weakness, in ignorance, and in anger and haughtiness.[150] Sins can also be classified according to their *object*: sins against God, against others, or against ourselves. Further distinctions are made between secret and public sins and between those committed by the unconverted and those committed by the regenerated.[151] These classifications all have their merit; they can show us how easily and how much human beings can sin. The problem with them is that they are developed from an idea and not from an organic point of view; they point to the quantity of sin but fail to reveal the inner connection of all sins.

In Vilmar's view, every sin is egocentricity[152] but is manifested in three areas of life, according to 1 John 2:16: "the desires of the flesh," "the desires of

---

147. LO: *ratione formae*; *per se*; *per accidens*.

148. LO: *cordis*; *oris*; *operis*.

149. LO: *spiritualia*; *carnalia*; *justitia divina* and *externa* (*justitia civilis*). According to Groen van Prinsterer, *Proeve*, 42, spiritual sin and fleshly sins reflect the two different pulls of sinful desires in humans—the former "heavenward," the latter "toward the earth." Consequently, all ethics outside of Christianity tends toward Stoicism or Epicureanism.

150. LO: *infirmitatis*; *ignorantiae*; *malitiae*.

151. LO: *adjuncta*; *regnantia*; *non regnantia*; *adjacentia*.

152. DO: *zelfzucht*; Vilmar, *Theologische Moral*, 1:210–13. Ed. note: When the manuscript was opened for the first time, a folded piece of paper was discovered between pp. 98 and 99 that contained Bavinck's notes on Vilmar as follows:

    Classification of sins, Vilmar, *Theologische Moral*, 1:249–392.

      [1.] Sins of the Flesh:

        a. Sexual sins: impurity, incontinence, passion (πάθος), unchastity (πορνεία), adultery (μοιχεία), unnatural lust, filthy speech, emancipation of the flesh.

        b. Sins of the belly: love of pleasure (ἡδονή), revelry, drunkenness, weakness, spaciousness.

        c. Sins of inertia and sloth (*acedie*): laziness, drunkenness, lassitude.

      2. Lusts of the Eye:

        a. Love of possessions: love of money, greed, search for ill-gotten gain, theft, robbery.

        b. Love of appearances (*Gestaltenlust*): self-love (φιλαυτία), inconstancy, vacillation, curiosity, sentimentality, superficiality, conformity to the world, double-heartedness.

the eyes," and "the pride of life."[153] Vilmar detects these three areas already in Satan's temptation of Eve (the tree is good for eating and attractive to the eyes, and it provides understanding), in the temptation of Jesus, and again in the narrative of Cain's descendants (Gen. 4:19–24). He relates all this to an anthropological trichotomy: sins of the body, sins of the soul, and sins of the spirit.[154]

The first of these, the lust of the flesh, occurs when the "I" surrenders to the material things of the world and consumes them—the body is the organ suited for the material of the world. The soul is the organ suited for the second, the lust of the eyes, which occurs when the "I" surrenders to the form, the appearance of the world, and all reality dissolves into form. The spirit is the organ for the third, the pride of life, in which all things are placed in subjection to the "I"—that is, when the "I" puts itself on par with God. Of course, these spheres do not lie separately alongside each other, but are intertwined within each other; each sin belongs in some sense to all three spheres, just as it does to the whole person.

Nevertheless, sins should be distinguished, and one person lives more in one of the spheres while another person lives in a different sphere. Similar distinctions have been made with respect to people groups: for example, the descendants of Ham have been associated with the first sphere (lust of the flesh), the Greeks with the second (lust of the eyes), and Romans with the third (pride of life).[155]

All this is an essentially attractive and true discovery. However, Vilmar's appeal to trichotomy, to Jesus's temptation, and to Genesis 4:19–24 is rather

---

    c. Love of knowledge: idle thoughts, hollow words, passion for science, art.
    d. Lying: deception, false oaths, unfaithfulness, lies of necessity.
    e. Tempting God: cursing, despairing, sorcery, superstition.
  3. Sins of Haughtiness (Pride):
    a. Against God: wickedness, pride, giving offense, suicide, blasphemy, the Blasphemy, the sin against the Holy Spirit.
    b. Against people: haughtiness, ostentation, vainglory, ingratitude—spiritual pride: infallibility.
    c. Mixed (against God and others): rioting, injury (*Verletzung*)—injustice, anger, hatred, envy, slander, strife, murder (war, etc.).

153. GrO: ἡ ἐπιθυμία τῆς σαρκὸς καὶ ἡ ἐπιθυμία τῶν ὀφθαλμῶν καὶ ἡ ἀλαζονεία τοῦ βίου. Ed. note: For the last of this threesome, in parentheses, Bavinck also provides a Dutch term, *pralerij* (from *pralen*, "to glory, to flaunt"), and a Latin term, *superbia*.

154. Ed. note: In the margin Bavinck added: "Luthardt, *Kompendium der theologischen Ethik*, §22 divides as follows: (1) unbelief: sins against God; (2) haughtiness/pride: laziness, jealousy, self-righteousness, envy, despising, hate, etc.; and (3) love of the world, divided further into (a) desire for possessions = lust of the eyes, (b) love of pleasure = lust of the flesh, and (c) longing for power/ambition = the pride of life."

155. Vilmar, *Theologische Moral*, 1:210–16.

far-fetched. To mention just one thing, the soul is not the organ suited for the form of the world.

The extent to which we agree with Vilmar will be shown in what follows. For now, we note that in 1 John 2:16 the apostle does not provide a classification of all sins.[156] John says that the love of the world and the love of God are mutually exclusive. This love of the world comprises three things:

1. the lust of the flesh—people try to possess and enjoy the goods of this world;
2. the lust of the eyes—they try to find satisfaction in what they see;
3. the pride of life—which leads to boasting.

These three are linked. Augustine already found in them a classification of all sins, as did Bede, who finds them back in the temptations of Adam and Jesus, and Lapide, who relates them to the Trinity.[157] Now it is true, John does not speak here of three distinct cardinal sins as Pascal does;[158] rather, John

---

156. Ed. note: On one of the loose pages found between pp. 98 and 99, after referencing Müller's discussion of obduracy, Bavinck wrote some notes critical of Vilmar.

   Hardening (*Verharding*), J. Müller, *Christian Doctrine of Sin*, 2:410–15 (*Die christliche Lehre von der Sünde*, 2:583–87)

   Against Vilmar: John does not intend this threefold division.
   1. They overlap each other (egocentricity violates the First Commandment and, as covetousness, the Tenth Commandment). Here there are two foundational principles—subject and object.
      a. The human person is the subject, but more in terms of his sensual or animal nature (sins of the flesh and animal-like sins).
      b. Object can either be God, the neighbor, or a creature.
   2. Sins involve a misuse of the creature.
   3. Human beings are not fulfilled in themselves; they "fill in" themselves with the world, with creatures.

While the first note about hardening is clearly tied to Müller, the source for the rest of the notes in critique of Vilmar's understanding of 1 John 2:16 is unclear; likely they are Bavinck's own. Müller discusses this passage in only one place (*Christian Doctrine of Sin*, 1:165–66), and neither there nor in his treatment of "hardening" does he deal with Vilmar.

157. Ed. note: Cornelius à Lapide (1567–1637) was a Flemish Jesuit exegete whose commentary on 1 John 2:16 connects the three desires of this verse to specific sins against the Trinity:

   This threefold desire is opposed to the Holy Trinity. Avarice to the Father, who is most liberal in communicating His essence and all His attributes to the Son and the Holy Spirit essentially, but to creatures only by way of participation. The lust of the flesh is opposed to the Son, who was begotten not carnally but spiritually from the mind of the Father, and who hates all carnal impurity. The pride of life is opposed to the Holy Spirit, who is the Spirit of humility and gentleness. Again, it is opposed to the three primary virtues, as lust of the flesh to continence, lust of the eyes to charity and kindness, pride of life to humility. (*Great Biblical Commentary of Cornelius à Lapide*, 6:381)

158. LO: *libido sentiendi, sciendi, dominandi*. Ed. note: In *Pensées*, no. 458, Pascal provides these three Latin phrases as explanatory commentary on 1 John 2:16.

is speaking only of three main forms of *love of the world*.[159] Not all sins are included in this; 1 John 2:2–11 speaks of lovelessness, and verses 20–22 speak of untruthfulness. The substance of Vilmar's claim had been denied earlier by Luther, Bengel, and Lücke (see also Lange and Meyer).[160] Idolatry, bearing false witness, and blasphemy cannot be included here. This means, therefore, that Vilmar is somewhat confused at times.

We follow a somewhat different classification. We do begin with the conviction that egocentricity[161] is the organizing principle of sin, noting the following qualifications:

1. Though egocentricity is foundational to all sin, this does not mean that every sin *subjectively* proceeds from egocentric motives. It is also possible to sin from a misunderstood love of neighbor or from misplaced zeal for God. Someone may steal, for instance, in order to provide bread for his children who suffer hunger; this is not from subjective, egocentric motives. But what we do intend to say is that *objectively* all sins may be traced back to egocentricity. We must therefore distinguish between an objective and a subjective organizing principle. The objective one is egocentricity, but, subjectively, motives may be quite diverse in different agents and circumstances. The objective organizing principle and subjective motivation for sins often differ.[162] Nevertheless, although this may not be conscious to the sinner, sin often proceeds from egocentricity, from the desire to exalt oneself.

2. This egocentricity is covetousness or concupiscence[163] and accompanies our birth (original sin) and is itself sin and the root of sin. Contrary to Rome, we teach that covetousness or concupiscence is sin. In itself, to desire is not sin; it was present in Adam (he desired food, drink, rest, and health [Gen. 2:24]) and in Christ (Matt. 4:2; John 4:7). There is a proper desire to serve God (Ps. 119:40; Luke 10:24; Rom. 7:22; Gal. 5:17; 1 Tim. 3:1). This is good. But covetousness consists of striving to obtain something for oneself apart from God. Wise people therefore consider coveting to be sin; egocentric desiring is

---

159. DO: *wereldliefde*.

160. Ed. note: Johann Albrecht Bengel (1687–1752) "was a Lutheran pietist clergyman and Greek-language scholar known for his edition of the Greek New Testament and his commentaries on it" (https://en.wikipedia.org/wiki/Johann_Albrecht_Bengel). Gottfried Christian Friedrich Lücke (1791–1855) was a German "mediating" theologian. For Lange, Bavinck does not cite a specific source but is likely referring to Johann Peter Lange, author of *Christliche Dogmatik* and numerous commentaries on books of the Bible, including the Gospel of John and the Epistle of James. With "Meyer," Bavinck is likely referring to Heinrich August Meyer's *Kritisch exegetisches Handbuch über die drei Briefe des Johannes*.

161. DO: *zelfzucht*.

162. J. Müller, *Christian Doctrine of Sin*, 1:149–51; cf. 189–91.

163. GrO: ἐπιθυμία; LO: *concupiscentia*.

sin.[164] Rome denies this and claims that we sin only when our will agrees with the desire. But the Tenth Commandment forbids covetousness (Matt. 5:28); Paul repeatedly calls it sin in Romans 7, and John says that it is not from the Father (1 John 2:16). We must struggle against it (Rom. 6:12).[165]

Egocentricity develops in a twofold direction—of the flesh or of the human spirit—and produces a double array of sins, from mild to more serious. That twofold direction, whether of the flesh or of the spirit,[166] is either downward toward the animal or upward toward the devil. A dual array of sins is born from egocentricity: one animal-like (sensual) and the other demonic. The latter is inexplicable for someone who derives all sin from sensuality. According to Rothe, people start out as sensual and egocentric, but as such this is not sin. It becomes sin only when this egocentricity is willed and established *in* and *by* the human personality. Sensual sin therefore is basic, but it can lead to spiritual sin. Rothe also acknowledges demons.[167]

Egocentricity and Sensual Sin

Now as far as the sensual array of sins is concerned, these can be easily deduced from egocentricity. Human beings of course have urges, inclinations that are focused on the external world, on matter and the form of things. It is these urges that our egocentricity turns into sensual sins. Originally these stood under the sacred will, were normed by God's law and intended as creaturely pointers to the Creator. Created things were therefore the medium. This is still true after the fall, but now God is no longer the goal; the human person has become his or her own goal, and the world has become their means. Pure passions now turn into urges, impulses, ardor; that is to say, we no longer meet the world actively but passively as it makes us dependent and enthralls us; we are now the world's servants. Because we cannot be satisfied with ourselves, except in an impoverished manner, we try to make that world subservient to

---

164. Ed. note: Bavinck carefully distinguishes "desire" (*begeeren*) from "coveting." Since the *Statenvertaling* uses the same word in Exod. 20:15 (*Gij zult niet begeeren*), Bavinck doubles up with the phrase "egocentric desiring" (or "desire as egocentricity"; *begeerlijkheid als zelfzucht*).

165. Cf. Kuyper, *Concise Works of the Holy Spirit*, 98: "Although there was in that fallen nature [assumed by Christ] something to incite Him to desire, yet it never became desire." In addition, "though the unbalanced powers of the soul which cause the darkening of the understanding, the blunting of the sensibilities, and the weakening of the will arouse the passions, yet even this could not result in sin if no personal ego were affected by this working. Hence sin puts its own mark upon this corruption only when the personal ego turns away from God, and in that disordered soul and diseased body stands condemned before Him."

166. LO: *peccata, carnalia et spiritualia.*

167. Rothe, *Theologische Ethik*, §§461–68; for a dissent from this, see J. Müller, *Christian Doctrine of Sin*, 1:146–49.

ourselves and derive satisfaction from it. Whether we want to use the world to satisfy our nobler passions—thirst for knowledge, love of art—or our baser passions, our aims are always egocentric. This is the source of "the love of the world" (1 John 2:17; Titus 2:12). All endeavors, honor, arrogance, greediness, lust, etc. presume a world, something outside the self that has to satisfy this self. Similarly, in a negative way, the sins of sloth, languor, and laziness are all merely particular forms of egocentricity. In fact, even hatred of the world and flight from the world are egocentric. They are nothing more than unsatisfied egocentricity that then withdraws from the world and into the self in anger and misanthropy.[168]

Egocentricity and Spiritual Sins

But the other aspect of sin, the demonic side, can also be explained by egocentricity. It is true that the demonic is more obviously and directly egocentric. For, in the case of loving the world, the world is always the medium, and thus the real aim, the satisfaction of the self, is more remote and therefore sometimes less conscious. Those sensual sins sometimes serve to restrain spiritual sins.[169] Those spiritual sins are less public, but much worse. The sin of lying, which is actually deceiving oneself (since sin is a lie), and thus self-deception, and subsequently a deceiving of others, can ultimately progress to even relishing lying itself without being egocentric.[170] (This then leads to the question whether egocentricity is really the organizing principle of sin.) The sin of pride, which is the naked expression of the principle of egocentricity, boasts of knowledge and virtue and develops into spiritual pride; it then progresses beyond egocentricity into terrible hatred of God, into intentional blasphemy, cursing, conscious hatred of God, and into delighting in this.[171] All these spiritual sins as well are forms of egocentricity. Hatred against humanity and against God is provoked, wounded egocentricity.[172]

All sins therefore display the same character: objectively, disobeying God, and subjectively, egocentricity. There is therefore really only one sin that comprises all others. In one sin we transgress all of God's commandments, we offend the entire organism of the law, and we attack the authority of the God who gave all the other commandments.[173] The Roman Catholic distinction

---

168. Philippi, *Kirchliche Glaubenslehre*, 3:4.
169. J. Müller, *Christian Doctrine of Sin*, 1:160–62.
170. J. Müller, *Christian Doctrine of Sin*, 1:162–64.
171. J. Müller, *Christian Doctrine of Sin*, 1:169–77.
172. J. Müller, *Christian Doctrine of Sin*, 1:172–75.
173. F. Turretin, *Institutes of Elenctic Theology*, 1:598 (IX.4.ix).

between *mortal sin* and *venial sin* is therefore incorrect.[174] By its nature no sin is forgivable. Every sin, even the smallest, deserves death, because (a) whoever does not uphold *everything* that is written is cursed (Deut. 27:26; Gal. 3:10) and (b) whoever stumbles at just one point of the law is guilty of breaking all of it (James 2:10).[175] Sins then are not independent from each other, as atoms, but in principle all other sins are contained in the one sin. No single sin is forgivable in and of itself—in other words, of no significance. Sin is forgivable only through the grace of God. There is only one exception to this: the sin against the Holy Spirit.[176]

That is the truth contained in the teachings of the Stoics. At the same time, however, as we have already noted, there are definite *degrees* of sin. One sin will reveal egocentricity more openly than the next.[177] The Stoics said that all sins are equal, equally serious. According to Augustine, the heretic Jovinian believed the same (although Jerome denied this), and according to Ambrose so did the Novatians.[178] Roman Catholic polemicists such as Robert Bellarmine[179] also accuse Protestants of this. It is true that every sin separates us absolutely from perfection and makes us lose our image of God absolutely; since there is no transition between good and evil, we find ourselves either on one side or the other. However, there is certainly development in sin, a worsening, a potential of sinking more deeply into sin. Holy Scripture clearly teaches us a basic distinction in Matthew 5:22 when our Lord says, "But I say to you that everyone who is angry with his brother will be liable to judgment; whoever insults his brother will be liable to the council; and whoever says, 'You fool!' will be liable to the hell of fire." Other Scripture passages teach the same:

> And she has rebelled against my rules by doing wickedness more than the nations, and against my statutes more than the countries all around her; for they have rejected my rules and have not walked in my statutes. (Ezek. 5:6)

174. LO: *peccata mortifera/mortalia; peccata venialia.* See de Moor, *Commentarius Perpetuus*, 3:308; van Mastricht, *Theoretico-Practica Theologia*, I.iv.3, §22 [2:310]; Calvin rejects this distinction altogether in *Institutes*, III.iv.28.

175. Just imagine that it was possible to commit one sin without in principle committing all other sins; would this one sin then condemn someone to eternal damnation?

176. Van Mastricht, *Theoretico-Practica Theologia*, I.iv.3, §§16–17 [2:300–305].

177. Van Mastricht, *Theoretico-Practica Theologia*, I.iv.3, §16 [2:300].

178. See de Moor, *Commentarius Perpetuus*, 3:305. Ed. note: Jovinian (d. ca. 405) was a former monk who turned against asceticism; he was condemned as a heretic in 390. Information about him is primarily derived from Jerome's *Adversus Jovinianum* (Healy, "Jovinianus"). Novatian (ca. 200–258) was a Carthaginian priest who became an antipope when Cornelius ascended to the chair of Peter in 251. He was declared a heretic because of his severe view about the restoration of those who had lapsed in the Decian persecutions that began in 250 (Chapman, "Novatian").

179. See n. 13 above.

Then he said to me, "Have you seen this, O son of man? You will see still greater abominations than these." (Ezek. 8:15)

Why do you see the speck that is in your brother's eye, but do not notice the log that is in your own eye? (Matt. 7:3)

Woe to you, Chorazin! Woe to you, Bethsaida! For if the mighty works done in you had been done in Tyre and Sidon, they would have repented long ago in sackcloth and ashes. (Matt. 11:21)

And that servant who knew his master's will but did not get ready or act according to his will, will receive a severe beating. But the one who did not know, and did what deserved a beating, will receive a light beating. Everyone to whom much was given, of him much will be required, and from him to whom they entrusted much, they will demand the more. (Luke 12:47–48)

Therefore he who delivered me over to you has the greater sin. (John 19:11)

The gravity or lightness of sin is determined as follows:

1. according to the *subject*, depending on the extent of knowledge, the firmness of the will, etc. (Hosea 4:14; Luke 12:48; Heb. 10:26; John 15:22);
2. according to the *object*, whether it is a sin committed immediately against God or against the neighbor (and, furthermore, whether it is committed against the authorities, parents, etc.);
3. according to the *nature of the sin*: in general, murder is a greater sin than theft and spiritual sins greater than sensual ones, etc.;
4. according to the *principle of intentionality*, whether a sin proceeds from anger, from weakness, from ignorance, etc.;
5. according to the *circumstances*: according to Proverbs 6:30, stealing in circumstances of poverty mitigates the sin.

But we need to mention here that this distinguishing between sins must not be done with excessive subtlety. In that case, we would tend to overlook and forget the sinful character of every sin.[180] No sin as such should ever be excused or justified. The same sinfulness exists in every sin. Nonetheless, there is a distinction;[181] for instance, whoever lusts after a woman or desires

180. Ed. note: In the margin Bavinck added "casuistry; penance morality (Liguori)." This is undoubtedly a reference to St. Alphonsus Maria de' Liguori (1696–1787), founder of the Redemptorist order (Congregation of the Most Holy Redeemer) in 1732 and important moral theologian who opposed "sterile legalism" and Jansenist rigorism.

181. Vilmar, *Theologische Moral*, 1:224.

someone's death has committed adultery or murder. Yet this is not the same as if someone had carried them out in actuality. As long as the sin resides in the mind and is not carried out in word and deed, there is still fear, shame, and reticence before God and his law, and there is still a restraint, a rein, a dam. Words are therefore worse than thoughts, and deeds worse than words. Whoever desires someone's death, gives voice to this desire, and then acts on it is a triple murderer. For then the sin takes on form, binds a person to itself more firmly, and makes turning back from it *much* more difficult.

When we assume that sin is egocentricity, then the principle of classification may be sought in the subject who covets as well as in the object being coveted. In other words, this leads to two questions: To what do egocentric persons subordinate everything, and to what do they subordinate themselves?

1. To what do egocentric persons subordinate everything? In general, to themselves, to self (ego, "I"). But this self or "I" comprises a great deal. No one is able to subordinate everything in its entirety to one's self. All people have something in themselves that they particularly favor and in which the ego is located and they find true life. All people have their own besetting sin. A person may subordinate everything to knowledge or desires (ambition) or feelings (passions of all kinds) or to the adornment of the body, or to carnality, and so forth. Regardless of the many organs and abilities we have, we will try to subordinate everything to these particular sovereigns. For that reason, there is infinite variety in sin. Two kinds of sin, however, stand out: sins of the spirit and sins of the body.[182]

2. The principle of classification may also be sought in the object, in response to the question: What is it that we humans seek to subordinate to ourselves? One may say: in principle, everything; egocentric people consider that everything exists for themselves. Yet there are differences. In one person egocentricity is focused on this, in the other on something else. There is endless variety that includes money, property, spouse, power, objects of beauty, liquor, honor, fame, and the list goes on. But it is possible to distinguish three broad areas: material things (money, possessions, property, etc.), the neighbor (lying, murder, adultery), and God (unbelief, idolatry, superstition). Of course, these three areas do not exist independently but devolve into each other: avaricious persons will err into lying, deception, killing of neighbor, and even, if God resists them, into lying to God and denying him. And yet we can distinguish, but not separate, these three areas. It should also be noted that every sin is sin against God, while sinning against the creature is most often also a sin against the neighbor.

182. LO: *peccata spiritualia; peccata carnalia.*

When we now combine 1 and 2, we see three areas in which egocentricity is manifest, in each according to its own facet (as sensual or as spiritual egocentricity), as follows:

1. Sins that subordinate the creature/material things to
   a. the spirit—possessiveness, avarice, thirst for knowledge;
   b. the body—finery, appetite, laziness;
2. Sins that subordinate the neighbor to
   a. the spirit—conceit, hunger for honor, hatred, anger, defamation, murder;
   b. the body—adultery, fornication, theft, deceit, etc.;
3. Sins that subordinate God to
   a. the spirit—unbelief, idolatry, blasphemy;
   b. the body—sorcery, spiritism, miracle-working, etc.

3

The Self against the Neighbor and God

In this chapter we are considering those sins of egoism in which people use the gifts of God's creation to serve themselves. Our basic division is between sensual sins and spiritual sins. The former involve food and alcohol as well as sins of inertia in which we fail to accept God's call to labor. Spiritual sins include love of money, abuse of language, and misuse of the neighbor's authority, life, chastity, property, and good name.

Sensual sins have pleasure at their core and involve immoderate use and abuse of God's good gifts. These sins are especially found among the rich and their feasts. Holy Scripture warns against gluttony and drunkenness, observing that these are pathways to poverty and ruin. Abuse of alcohol dulls our consciousness, which is the true mark of our humanity; that which is most noble in us is destroyed.

Sins of inertia are great dangers of riches and affluence. They not only harm our own souls but also lead to egocentric indifference to others: we eat, drink, and are merry while fires and floods destroy others. In addition to self-indulgence and hedonism, this sin also leads to complacency and, eventually, to complete apathy: "Why should we care about others when we ourselves have enough?" Such weariness with life and misanthropy has spread in our time and is even celebrated in literature.

Then there are also sins that take pleasure in form or appearance that is not based in reality. People are pleased with themselves, their physical appearance or strength, and vainly flatter themselves; they are also often hypersensitive with an overblown sense of honor that is too easily offended. Such people go out of their way to avoid adversity and suffering, often under the rationalizing guise of "self-respect." The other direction of these sins with respect to the form of things is instability, the dissatisfaction of creatures in their temporality, their transience. This is the great disease of our age—inconstancy, agitation, restlessness. We endlessly seek diversion and distraction in recreation, in entertainment, and even in speculative spiritualities such as spiritism. And, finally, we celebrate doubt and uncertainty as something good and noble. We have become individuals, naked and alone.

Unbelief is the root of all sin—failing to accept God as he is, not taking him at his word. Unbelief makes God out to be a liar, denying his truth and faithfulness. This unbelief can develop in either of two ways: making God equal to ourselves by bringing him down or by making ourselves equal to God by elevating ourselves. We do this in a sensual way when we misuse God for our own benefit, abusing his name, superstitiously playing with his providence, and misusing the Sabbath. Spiritual sins in this category are rooted in pride, in the desire to be like God rather than in surrendering to him and loving him. This is expressed in idolatry and blasphemy, especially the blasphemy against the Holy Spirit.

There is an order and law in the development of sin, already reflected in the first sin in Paradise: opportunity for sin is followed by external temptation; then come gradual compliance, rationalization, inclination of the heart, and completion of the deed. All sin begins with suggestion, followed by meditation, delighting in it, and, finally, yielding and acquiescing to it. In this way, every sin gives birth to more sin as sins become habitual or customary and are passed on from generation to generation. Contrary to Rome, we teach that not only the deed but also the crooked inclination (concupiscence) is sinful.

There is also a history, a development in the sin of the human race: of family, clan, people, humanity. Every age, clan, family, people, calling (business/agriculture, soldiers, students, fishermen, sailors), social position, era, century, environment, and climate/soil has its own sins. Scripture speaks of a "world" that is in the hands of the Evil One, with Satan as its head as the "god of this age." In this situation of sin, people occupy either (a) a state of bondage, in which they do not know that they are transgressors; (b) a state of security, in which they know they cannot save themselves and are comfortable with themselves as basically good and decent people; (c) a state of hypocrisy, in which they refuse to follow the divine stirrings of their hearts and break with sin's dominion, and in which they are outwardly respectable, but still rebels, and eventually become hardened; or (d) a state of hardening characterized by stubborn unbelief and a defiant refusal to be redeemed.

§10. SINS OF EGOISM IN THE NARROW SENSE

Sins of egoism are those sins in which people use creation, God's gifts, and the world[1] to serve themselves. They are especially (but not exclusively) those

---

1. GrO: κόσμος.

sins that were at one time called "sins against oneself."[2] When people are not satisfied with themselves and are impoverished because of sin, they seek satisfaction in creatures, in God's gifts. They surrender themselves to the world and take the world for themselves. Here we will differentiate between sensual sins and spiritual sins.

A. Sensual Sins

1. Sins Involving Food[3]

These sins have pleasure (James 4:1) at their core.[4] People are "lovers of pleasure" (2 Tim. 3:4) who revel in physical satisfaction, in taste.[5] This sin of taste can be derived from food or from drink and is the sin peculiar to Germanic peoples—especially the sin of drunkenness.[6] (Eastern people engage more in sexual sins.) The Greeks and Romans were initially known for moderation; carousing and drunkenness arose especially in the time of decline. The demand for bread and circuses and the hosting of expensive meals came in the period of the emperors.[7]

a. Preoccupation with food.[8] This sin occurs when people live in order to eat, when they find their purpose in eating. All attention is devoted to food, and the art of cooking becomes the most appealing skill. Eating can be elevated to life's highest purpose in all kinds of ways: moving dinner to an earlier or later hour to lengthen the eating time, preparing exquisite meals in an exotic manner, thrilling and tickling the taste buds, etc. This sin can begin in small

---

2. Pictet, *De christelyke zedekunst*, book 7; Stapfer, *De zeden-leer*, 3:301ff. (*Sittenlehre*, 3:104–812 [III.xi]). Ed. note: The title of Pictet's book 7 is "On the Duties and Virtues of a Christian with Respect to Oneself" ("*Van de pligten en deugden eens Christens met betrekking op zichzelven*").

3. DO: *Keel-en buikzonden, gastronomie* ("Throat and Stomach Sins, Gastronomy"). Ed. note: The classification comes from Vilmar, *Theologische Moral*, 1:261. Vilmar's heading is "*Bauchsünden* (gula)" (*gula* = throat, gluttony). Much of the material that follows echoes ideas and phrases from Vilmar, though Bavinck's treatment is his own.

4. GrO: ἡδονή.

5. GrO: φιλήδονοι εἶναι.

6. Ed. note: Bavinck takes this notion directly from Vilmar, *Theologische Moral*, 1:261–64.

7. LO: *panem et circuses*.

8. Pictet, *De christelyke zedekunst*, 639; van Mastricht, *Theoretico-Practica Theologia*, III.iv.2 [4:782–88]. Ed. note: Bavinck's reference is to "*Vierde deel*, Rotterdam/Utrecht, 1753, 557 (§ I.XVI)" (*Theoretico-Practica Theologia*, II.i.16), which seems incorrect. Van Mastricht deals with food sins in III.iv.2 [4:782–88]: "Concerning the Use and Abuse of the Stomach" (LO: *De alimentorum usu & abusu*; DO: *Van het gebruik en misbruik der dingen, die tot levens-onderhoudt geschiedt zyn*). For an explanation of the format we are using to cite van Mastricht's *Theoretico-Practica Theologia*, see the extended note in the introduction, §1, in the section "Reformed Churches" (pp. 8–9n48). The volume and page numbers come from the 1749–53 Dutch edition used by Bavinck.

ways, with a preference for certain foods or a craving to participate in the good life.[9] And this sin can then lead to gluttony and carousing, to serving the belly: "For such persons do not serve our Lord Christ, but their own appetites" (Rom. 16:18). "Their end is destruction, their god is their belly, and they glory in their shame, with minds set on earthly things" (Phil. 3:19). People become slaves to their bellies, which determines their laws. They seek honor in their shame—that is, in having good taste, in developing their palates. People of this sort, such as Apicius,[10] the emperor Geta,[11] and Elagabalus,[12] were known as gourmands.[13]

Holy Scripture warns against all this. The Old Testament's food prohibitions and meal offerings provide a defense against the abuse of food. The book of Proverbs warns us, "Be not among drunkards / or among gluttonous eaters of meat, / for the drunkard and the glutton will come to poverty, / and slumber will clothe them with rags" (Prov. 23:20–21; cf. Sir. 31:21–22; 37:29–31; Prov. 28:7). Jesus, who warns against carousing (Luke 21:34; cf. Paul in Rom. 13:13; Gal. 5:21; and Peter in 1 Pet. 4:3), portrays a rich man "who was dressed in purple and fine linen and who feasted sumptuously every day" as being in hell (Luke 16:19).

b. Sins involving strong drink/alcohol.[14] These sins also begin in a small way, such as enjoying a glass of gin, for example, and can then progress to

9. Ed. note: This is a paraphrase translation of Bavinck's term *pater gutleben*.

10. Ed. note: "Marcus Gavius Apicius is believed to have been a Roman *gourmet* and lover of luxury, who lived sometime in the 1st century AD, during the reign of Tiberius. The Roman cookbook *Apicius* is often attributed to him, though it's impossible to prove the connection" (https://en.wikipedia.org/wiki/Marcus_Gavius_Apicius).

11. Ed. note: Publius Septimus Geta (AD 189–211) was a Roman emperor who ruled with his father Septimus Severus and his older brother Caracalla from 209 until his death. According to the late Roman collection of imperial biographies, the *Historia Augusta*, Geta was a man of intemperate desires: "As a youth, he was handsome, brusque in his manners though not disrespectful, incontinent in love, gluttonous, and a lover of food and of wine variously spiced." "Life of Antonius Geta" 4.1 (*Historia Augusta* 2:39 [trans. Magie]).

12. Ed. note: Marcus Aurelius Antonius Augustus (commonly known as Elagabalus after the Syro-Roman sun god whose cult statue he brought to Rome) was Roman emperor from AD 218 to 222 and had a reputation for sexual debauchery. According to historian Edward Gibbon, "Elagabalus abandoned himself to the grossest pleasure and ungoverned fury, and soon found disgust and satiety in the midst of his enjoyments" (Gibbon, *Decline and Fall of the Roman Empire*, 1:187 [chap. 6]).

13. Ed. note: Bavinck includes in his list two other names for reasons not apparent to the editor: Publius Licinius Egnatius Gallienus Augustus (218–68, emperor from 253 to 268) and Mithridates. The latter name is clearly taken from the Persian deity Mithra, who was the inspiration for the Mithraic mysteries that became popular in the Roman Empire from the first to the fourth century AD. Bavinck may have intended a general reference to the cult, which was popular in the Roman army and therefore led to numerous Roman rulers naming themselves Mithridates.

14. Pictet, *De christelyke zedekunst*, 642.

truly enjoying wine and strong drink, to needing a drink, to regular drinking, and then to drunkenness and carousing. Noah and Lot are biblical examples that serve as warnings to us. These sins were not unknown in Israel. On the contrary! Consider Isaiah 5:11 and 22:

> Woe to those who rise early in the morning
> > to run after their drinks,
> who stay up late at night
> > till they are inflamed with wine. (Isa. 5:11 NIV)

> Woe to those who are heroes at drinking wine
> > and champions at mixing drinks. (Isa. 5:22 NIV)

Now the Hebrew word that is usually translated as "strong drink" [שֵׁכָר] was not strong drink in our sense (that is, compared to brandy or gin), but was made from roses, fruit, honey, and thistles.[15] The drink made from thistles was especially weak, but even that could cause a person to lose consciousness. And that is the appalling result of this sin: "Drunkenness is a small fury."[16] It dulls consciousness, both at the time and afterward; it removes the most noble element—namely, what is human in us. It is an attack on, a destruction of, the image of God, because self-consciousness is the true mark of humanity. Drunkenness makes us like animals. In a drunken person the soul is buried and the animal comes to the surface (in the nature of a pig or lion or ape, etc.).

Holy Scripture warns against drunkenness: "Wine is a mocker, strong drink a brawler; whoever is led astray by it is not wise" (Prov. 20:1). A striking description occurs in Proverbs 23:29–35;[17] "It is not for kings to drink wine, /

---

15. Gesenius, *Hebrew and Chaldee Lexicon*, s.v. "שֵׁכָר."

16. Ed. note: Bavinck cites the Greek proverb "ἡ μέθη μικρὰ μανία ἐστίν"; he is likely quoting Vilmar, *Theologische Moral*, 1:264.

17. Prov. 23:29–35 (NIV):
> Who has woe? Who has sorrow?
> Who has strife? Who has complaints?
> Who has needless bruises? Who has bloodshot eyes?
> Those who linger over wine,
> who go to sample bowls of mixed wine.
> Do not gaze at wine when it is red,
> when it sparkles in the cup,
> when it goes down smoothly!
> In the end it bites like a snake
> and poisons like a viper.
> Your eyes will see strange sights,
> and your mind will imagine confusing things.
> You will be like one sleeping on the high seas,
> lying on top of the rigging.

or for rulers to take strong drink" (Prov. 31:4); "Let us walk properly as in the daytime, not in orgies and drunkenness" (Rom. 13:13); "But now I am writing to you not to associate with anyone who bears the name of brother if he is guilty of sexual immorality or greed, or is an idolater, reviler, drunkard, or swindler—not even to eat with such a one" (1 Cor. 5:11; cf. 6:10). Among the works of the flesh are "envy, drunkenness, orgies, and things like these. I warn you, as I warned you before, that those who do such things will not inherit the kingdom of God" (Gal. 5:21); "And do not get drunk with wine, for that is debauchery, but be filled with the Spirit" (Eph. 5:18); "Deacons likewise must be dignified, not double-tongued, not addicted to much wine, not greedy for dishonest gain" (1 Tim. 3:8); "For you have spent enough time in the past doing what pagans choose to do—living in debauchery, lust, drunkenness, orgies, carousing and detestable idolatry" (1 Pet. 4:3 NIV). In our day these sins of the belly have been made more terrible by the invention of strong drink, by alcoholism, and by opium, a milky fluid with strong narcotic content made from the unripe seedpod of the poppy and used particularly by the Chinese and Javanese.[18]

c. Taken together, these two sins are found especially at banquets (Rom. 13:13; Gal. 5:21; 1 Pet. 4:3)[19] and especially during the imperial times of the fifteenth and sixteenth centuries. This also happened among our forefathers and is starting to happen again in honorary meals and dinners.[20]

2. SINS OF INERTIA[21]

This sin is, in its origin, a physical slowness, a flinching from exertion and effort; it is "taking it easy" and forgetting that we, like God, are called to labor. It is an aversion to labor, spiritually as well as physically; it is when we do nothing, loiter about, a "pleasant idleness."[22] This ideal is found today especially among Communists. Frequently this laziness results from or accompanies a soft lifestyle, springing from a luxurious upbringing, and with the sins associated with food. Paul, citing the Greek poet Epimenides, says

---

"They hit me," you will say, "but I'm not hurt!
They beat me, but I don't feel it!
When will I wake up
so I can find another drink?"

18. Ed. note: Bavinck cites as support for this Abraham Kuyper's antirevolutionary political platform, *Ons Program* (see esp. pp. 344, 899, 901, and 1016–23); ET: *Our Program*, 304, 318.

19. Pictet, *De christelyke zedekunst*, 637.

20. Vilmar, *Theologische Moral*, 1:261–67.

21. DO: *traagheidszonden*; Vilmar, *Theologische Moral*, 1:268; Pictet, *De christelyke zedekunst*, 677–81; van Mastricht, *Theoretico-Practica Theologia*, II.i.11 [4:543].

22. Italian original: *dolce far niente*.

that "Cretans are always liars, evil beasts, lazy gluttons" (Titus 1:12). Laziness is thus a great danger of riches, of affluence, of a certain culture, as it existed in the time of the Roman emperors.

This sin also leads to egocentric indifference to the suffering of others; to egocentric self-satisfying; to eating, drinking, and enjoying oneself; to saying, "The flood comes after us."[23] It leads to absolute eudaemonism, to sybaritic self-indulgence, such as was prevalent in the time of Roman emperors, in Europe before the Thirty Years' War, and before the French Revolution. It also leads to dumb, superficial complacency and narrowness, limitation, and also to cruelty—that is, to people who are not concerned about the suffering of others but are satisfied if they themselves have enough, caring nothing about anything else.

Thus, finally, this sin leads to complete apathy and indifference;[24] to being sated, dissatisfied, tired of life; to a boredom, usually paired with deep sadness; to being tired of oneself or bitter about one's lot in life. This may continue as hatred for all people, escape from the world, disgust with all creatures, doubt about everything and God, and, finally, suicide. This skeptical weariness with life has grown strong in our age and is being considered as a profound and more enlightened worldview rather than as a sickness and sin. This view is lauded and systemized in literature (Byron, Alfred de Musset, et al.); it is the melody of communist and socialist refrains. However, in its origin it is nothing but inertia of spirit and body, accompanied by pride that assumes that nothing is good enough for a person, that everything must serve them.

Holy Scripture warns against this sin:

> Go to the ant, O sluggard;
>   consider her ways, and be wise!
> ....
>
> How long will you lie there, O sluggard?
>   When will you arise from your sleep?
> A little sleep, a little slumber,
>   a little folding of the hands to rest,
> and poverty will come upon you like a robber,
>   and want like an armed man. (Prov. 6:6, 9–11)

---

23. FO: *Après nous le déluge*. Ed. note: In this form, the saying is attributed to the famous official mistress of Louis XV of France (1710–74), Madame de Pompadour (1721–64). In its more familiar form, "Après moi le déluge" ("After me comes the deluge"), it is usually attributed to the king himself. See Laguna, "Après moi."

24. GrO: ἀκηδία.

> I passed by the field of a sluggard,
>> by the vineyard of a man lacking sense,
> and behold, it was all overgrown with thorns;
>> the ground was covered with nettles,
>> and its stone wall was broken down.
> Then I saw and considered it;
>> I looked and received instruction.
> A little sleep, a little slumber,
>> a little folding of the hands to rest,
> and poverty will come on you like a robber,
>> and want like an armed man. (Prov. 24:30–34)

The New Testament provides similar wisdom: "Do not be slothful in zeal, be fervent in spirit, serve the Lord" (Rom. 12:11); "For even when we were with you, we would give you this command: If anyone is not willing to work, let him not eat. For we hear that some among you walk in idleness, not busy at work, but busybodies. Now such persons we command and encourage in the Lord Jesus Christ to do their work quietly and to earn their own living" (2 Thess. 3:10–12). Paul's instruction to Timothy not to "enroll younger widows" in the office of deacon includes this counsel: "Besides that, they learn to be idlers, going about from house to house, and not only idlers, but also gossips and busybodies, saying what they should not" (1 Tim. 5:13). And finally, the author of Hebrews: "We have much to say about this, but it is hard to make it clear to you because you no longer try to understand. . . . We do not want you to become lazy, but to imitate those who through faith and patience inherit what has been promised" (Heb. 5:11; 6:12 NIV).

3. SINS THAT TAKE PLEASURE IN FORM

These sins focus on the appearance of things apart from their reality. They are often not recognized as sins or are recognized as only minor sins. There are two types.

a. *Self-love.*[25] People love and are pleased with themselves and, for that reason, love other things related to themselves. People are first of all pleased with their own physical beauty, physical strength, and psychological endowments (e.g., a quick wit). Being pleased with one's own physical beauty occurs especially in women and leads to adorning of the body, flaunting oneself, using makeup (Isa. 3:16–24; 1 Tim. 2:9; 1 Pet. 3:3), to valuing everything according to external form. With men, it is more being pleased with strength,

---

25. GrO: φιλαυτία.

power, health of spirit, and body and expressed in sports and gymnastics. Both of these are sins of vanity. This sin leads also to wanting to please others; "pleasing oneself" (Rom. 15:1) leads to pleasing other people, to becoming a "people pleaser" (Gal. 1:10; Eph. 6:6; 1 Thess. 2:4).[26] With women this leads to teasing, flirting, and flattery; with men to gallantry and chivalry; and with both to flattery, to judging only with one's eyes, to being a respecter of persons, and to partisanship (James 2:1; Jude 16; Rom. 2:1; Prov. 24:13; etc.). In more extreme forms this sin leads to being easily offended, having an overblown sense of honor, hypersensitivity, quickly looking to defend oneself, and seeking one's own honor. Such people flee from the cross and from death (which may not be mentioned) and become preoccupied with saving and preserving their own lives and souls. In systems of morality, this principle is presented as "respect for oneself" and as maintaining the rights of humans—"O mortal, feel your worth!"[27]—and in this way leads to the terrible subjectivism of our age.

b. *Instability/inconstancy*.[28] The other direction of these sins with respect to the form of things is instability, the satisfaction of creatures in their temporality, their transience. Scripture often speaks about this: "But let him ask in faith, with no doubting, for the one who doubts is like a wave of the sea that is driven and tossed by the wind" (James 1:6); "He is a double-minded man, unstable in all his ways" (James 1:8); "Draw near to God, and he will draw near to you. Cleanse your hands, you sinners, and purify your hearts, you double-minded" (James 4:8). This instability, the result of a lack of steadfastness in oneself, consists generally of living by impressions, of being governed by feelings—which occurs especially in women, and also in religion—and is a weakness, lacking power. It is, most profoundly, a failure to believe in God's constancy.

26. GrO: ἀρέσκειν ἑαυτῷ; ἀνθρώποις ἀρέσκειν.

27. Ed. note: This is the first line of a hymn found in *Evangelische Gezangen*, no. 31, p. 59, to be sung to the melody of Ps. 65 (Peter Dathenus). Here is the entire first stanza (translated by John Bolt):

O sterveling! Gevoel uw waarde	O, mortal, feel your worth,
Wat u in' t stof nog vleit,	What still flatters you as dust,
Uw hart is veel te groot voor d' aarde	Your heart is much too great for earth,
Gij leeft voor d' eeuwigheid:	You live for eternity:
De tijd, die alles weg doet zinken,	Your greatness is not determined
Bepaald uw grootheid niet;	By time that sinks everything;
Gij ziet voor uw volmaking blinken	You see an endless horizon
Een eindeloos verschiet.	Shining for your perfection.

The translation of the last four lines involves some rearrangement to satisfy English grammatical sense.

28. GrO: ἀκαταστασία; DO: *onbestendigheid* ("instability, unsettledness, inconstancy").

Inconstancy[29] is also the great disease of our age—agitation, restlessness. This is manifested in many forms, for example, in seeking distraction and diversion,[30] in chasing exciting pleasure, in pursuing recreation over solitude, in being bored with oneself (Pascal). It is also apparent in excessive curiosity,[31] especially about hidden things (Deut. 29:29). Contemporary examples are *spiritism* and generally favoring the frivolity and superficiality of quantity over quality,[32] and therefore in the leveling and homogenizing found in the pantheistic merging of all things, which avoids thorough investigation into the essence of anything. It is also manifested in the antihistorical sense—in the perpetual reconstruction of history that tears people from their own history, from tradition, from the inheritance of previous generations. The result is a loss of piety and a severing of the bonds of the past (revolution) in exchange for subjective, self-pleasing egocentricity and individualism. Finally, it occurs in the intentional doubting of everything, the banning of faith, with each person standing naked and alone. Doubt has been made the beginning and condition of knowledge.[33]

B. Spiritual Sins

1. THE LOVE OF MONEY[34]

In 1 Timothy 6:10 the love of money is called the root of all evil.[35] Holy Scripture always warns against it:

> If I have made gold my trust / or called fine gold my confidence, / if I have rejoiced because my wealth was abundant / or because my hand had found much . . . (Job 31:24–25)

29. DO: *onbestendigheid*.
30. Pictet, *De christelyke zedekunst*, 661. Ed. note: Between the lines Bavinck added: "dancing, [card] playing, theater." This famous trio also earned the ire of Abraham Kuyper, who in his Stone Lecture on "Calvinism and Religion" (lecture no. 2), after insisting that the world order with God's creation ordinances is something that Calvinists, unlike Anabaptists, embrace rather than avoid ("Thus the fear of God is imparted to the whole of life as a reality—into the family, and into society, into science and art, into personal life, and into the political career"), makes the startling claim that "this admits of only one exception. . . . Not *every* intimate intercourse with the unconverted world is deemed lawful, by Calvinism, for it placed a barrier against the too unhallowed influence of this world by putting a distinct 'veto' upon three things, card playing, theatres, and dancing—three forms of amusement." Kuyper, *Lectures on Calvinism*, 72–74.
31. Pictet, *De christelyke zedekunst*, 739.
32. LO: *multa*; *multum*. Ed. note: Bavinck here reverses the classic Latin proverb *non multa, sed multum* ("not many, but much" or "not quantity, but quality"), attributed to Pliny the Younger (AD 61–ca. 113).
33. Ed. note: What Bavinck describes in this paragraph is uncannily similar to what is called "postmodernism" more than one hundred years later. The paragraph, and especially the last sentence, also expresses Bavinck's skepticism and concern about the Cartesian model.
34. GrO: φιλαργυρία.
35. Ed. note: Between the lines Bavinck inserted "ramp" = "disaster, calamity."

And he said to them, "Take care, and be on your guard against all covetousness, for one's life does not consist in the abundance of his possessions." (Luke 12:15)

No servant can serve two masters, for either he will hate the one and love the other, or he will be devoted to the one and despise the other. You cannot serve God and money. (Luke 16:13)

Again I tell you, it is easier for a camel to go through the eye of a needle than for a rich person to enter the kingdom of God. (Matt. 19:24)

Do not lay up for yourselves treasures on earth, where moth and rust destroy and where thieves break in and steal. (Matt. 6:19)

But those who desire to be rich fall into temptation, into a snare, into many senseless and harmful desires that plunge people into ruin and destruction. (1 Tim. 6:9)

Keep your life free from love of money, and be content with what you have, for he has said, "I will never leave you nor forsake you." (Heb. 13:5)

. . . not a drunkard, not violent but gentle, not quarrelsome, not a lover of money. (1 Tim. 3:3)

For people will be lovers of self, lovers of money, proud, arrogant, abusive, disobedient to their parents, ungrateful, unholy. (2 Tim. 3:2)

Put to death therefore what is earthly in you: sexual immorality, impurity, passion, evil desire, and covetousness, which is idolatry. (Col. 3:5)

For you may be sure of this, that everyone who is sexually immoral or impure, or who is covetous (that is, an idolater), has no inheritance in the kingdom of Christ and God. (Eph. 5:5)

This sin is universal, occurring among all nations and people, but especially in farmers[36] and businesspeople. The thirst for gold is general, occurring among all people, children and adults, increasing over time. The desire for money becomes a desire for the possession (not merely the use) of money, because money is the greatest power on earth—everything can

---

36. Ed. note: Bavinck's comment about farmers needs to be understood in the context of late nineteenth-century Dutch class structure with its clear distinction between wealthy, landowning "farmers" (*boeren*) and peasant farm laborers (*arbeiders*).

be obtained with money. Money is thus truly Mammon on earth, Satan's most powerful instrument of temptation.[37] Desire for money turns us away from God and toward the earth,[38] to its center, to the most noble that it affords. It is also incapable of being satisfied; everything eventually becomes nauseating, but the thirst for gold increases over time. The miser is tied to his gold, believing in its power, and gold is thus his god. Gold is not the only form of money; one can accumulate money also in property, a barn full of livestock, or a warehouse full of merchandise. Nor does the Greek word φιλαργυρία refer only to "covetousness," since it is also the root of squandering. For both, money is all that counts; one wants to accumulate it while the other wants to spend it. The one may be poor, and the other wealthy. (See the rich man in Luke 19:20–23; James 5:1; Matt. 19:22–24; Mark 10:22–27; Luke 18:22–27.)

The striving for money, miserliness—initially without dishonesty toward one's neighbor—eventually becomes greed.[39] Greed is indifferent toward the means of obtaining money, and eventually this leads to pinching pennies, depriving people of their livings (James 5), usury, deceit, and ill-gotten gain (Titus 1:7–11; 1 Pet. 5:2). Finally it leads to theft and robbery—that is, to sins against one's neighbor.[40]

2. SINS INVOLVING ABUSE OF WORDS (LANGUAGE)

The root of these sins is the vanity or futility of the mind (Eph. 4:17), the result of being cut loose from life, from the Word, from God's Logos. Thus words arise that are without content or vitality and ideas without reality. This is why Scripture speaks about "foolish talk" and "crude joking" (Eph. 5:4), "empty words" (Eph. 5:6), "gossips and busybodies" (1 Tim. 5:13), "irreverent babble" (1 Tim. 6:20), "empty talkers" (Titus 1:10), and "talking wicked nonsense" (3 John 10). And Jesus tells us that "on the day of judgment people will give account for every careless word they speak" (Matt. 12:36). By contrast, our "speech [should] always be gracious, seasoned with salt, so that you may know how you ought to answer each person" (Col. 4:6).

37. Kuyper, "Geldgierigheid is een wortel van alle kwaad" ("Love of Money Is a Root of All Evil"), a meditation on 1 Tim. 6:10; also see Kuyper, *E Voto Dordraceno*, 4:222, 279. Ed. note: In the margin Bavinck observes that faith in the power of money is reflected in men such as Cecil Rhodes (1853–1902), the British colonialist, businessman, mining magnate, and South African politician who founded the territory of Rhodesia and established the Rhodes Scholarship, and in trusts such as the Morgan.

38. Ed. note: Between the lines Bavinck added "*stof*" ("matter, dust").

39. GrO: πλεονεξία.

40. Covered in §11; cf. Pictet, *De christelyke zedekunst*, 747–55.

Such spewing of idle words comes to expression in daily interaction, in polite phrases with which we misuse language and empty words of their content. Talleyrand is correct when he says "language is created to conceal thoughts."[41] Such phraseology leads to excessive talking, to self-deception, and to the deception of others. The word continues to have great power over people and betrays them by leading them astray, into error and heresy. All great events have been called into being by a word (such as "revolution," "freedom," etc.). This happens in learning and science as well. People seek and love scholarship for themselves (egoism) instead of for God. Using vain words, ideas without content, or words in which one has placed faulty content gives rise to knowledge that is "demonic" (James 3:15), or to an "earthly wisdom" (2 Cor. 1:12), "to falsely called 'knowledge'" (1 Tim. 6:20), or the "wisdom of this world" (1 Cor. 3:19).[42] These result in a philosophy and a vain temptation that lead people astray with every "wind of doctrine" (Eph. 4:14).[43] Scholarship is no longer valued as a path to the truth because that is considered unattainable and is therefore reduced to desire, thirst, mere exercise. The same is true in art, the symbolized word. Art is reduced to form; it is no longer used to express the truth, to express the eternal, to express who we are. Its ideals and inspirations do not come from above, but from below. Only the figure, the form, and then, of course, the physical, the naked form, captivates—a coarse realism as in Zola, for example.[44]

§11. Sins against the Neighbor

Included in this category are all those sins in which one misuses for oneself the neighbor and all that belongs to the neighbor. One can abuse the neighbor's chastity and property in a kind of carnal egocentricity; abusing the neighbor's life, prestige, and good name is more demonic, spiritual.

41. FO: *la langue est faite pour cacher les pensées*. Ed. note: Charles Maurice de Talleyrand-Périgord (1754–1838) was a career civil servant during France's turbulent times from Louis XVI through King Louis Philippe. The saying is also given in another version and attributed to Stendhal (Marie-Henri Beyle [1783–1842]): "La parole a été donnée à l'homme pour cacher sa pensée" (http://www.linternaute.com/citation/4058/la-parole-a-ete-donnee-a-l-homme-pour-cacher-sa---stendhal/).

42. GrO: δαιμονιώδης; σοφία σαρκική; ψευδώνυμος γνῶσις; σοφία τοῦ κόσμου τούτου.

43. GrO: ἄνεμος τῆς διδασκαλίας.

44. Ed. note: Émile Édouard Charles Antoine Zola (1840–1902), French journalist, novelist, and playwright, was a leading exemplar of nineteenth-century literary naturalism, a movement that highlighted the dark side of life, human vice, and misery (Berg, "Zola").

1. The Neighbor's Chastity (Seventh Commandment)[45]

This involves sexual sins.[46] The first and most general form is "impurity" (Rom. 6:19; 2 Cor. 12:21; Gal. 5:19) and, even worse, "filthiness" (James 1:21).[47] In general, this uncleanness relates to all matters having to do with procreation, conception, and birth, all of which are mysterious. A boundary has been drawn around this mystery; it is shrouded, covered with a veil. It is to respect this mystery that shame is associated with this aspect of human life and is the reason for the purification laws of the Old Testament. Impurity comes from violating this mystery, from disrespecting it, from considering it as merely natural. This impurity begins with thoughts, but it also becomes a favored topic of discussion (among children, young men, and young women). It is fed and nurtured by the imagination, which turns abstract thought into images that are graphic, embodied, and living. The impure thought is expressed in words against which Scripture warns: "Do not let any unwholesome talk come out of your mouths" (Eph. 4:29 NIV); "You must also rid yourselves of all such things as these: anger, rage, malice, slander, and filthy language from your lips" (Col. 3:8 NIV); and "Bad company corrupts good character" (1 Cor. 15:33 NIV).

All this is aroused by words, by reading impure books, looking at images, and is expressed through indecent movements of the eyes, hands, gait, and the like. Scripture speaks directly to the manner in which we use and misuse our bodies. In protesting his innocence Job declares: "I have made a covenant with my eyes; / how then could I gaze at a virgin?" (Job 31:1). The psalmist prays: "Turn my eyes from looking at worthless things; / and give me life in your way" (Ps. 119:37). The wisdom literature of the Old Testament describes a wicked person this way:

> A worthless person, a wicked man,
>   goes about with crooked speech,
> winks with his eyes, signals with his feet,
>   points with his finger,
> with perverted heart devises evil,
>   continually sowing discord. (Prov. 6:12–14)

45. Ed. note: Bavinck included parenthetical references to specific commandments in the Decalogue only for no. 4 (the Fifth Commandment) and no. 5 (the Sixth Commandment) below. The explicit references to the Seventh Commandment (no. 1), the Eighth and Tenth Commandments (no. 2), and the Ninth Commandment (no. 3) were added by the editor.
46. Cf. the exposition of the Seventh Commandment in Calvin, *Institutes*, II.viii.41–44; Ursinus, *Commentary on the Heidelberg Catechism*, Lord's Day 41; Daneau, *Ethices Christianae*, 2:208–32 (II.xiv); Pictet, *De christelyke zedekunst*, 639, 652–57; van Mastricht, *Theoretico-Practica Theologia*, II.iii.5 [4:650]; Vilmar, *Theologische Moral*, 1:249.
47. GrO: ἀκαθαρσία; ῥυπαρία.

Scripture specifically also addresses women on this score:

> The LORD says,
>   "The women of Zion are haughty,
> walking along with outstretched necks,
>   flirting with their eyes,
> strutting along with swaying hips,
>   with ornaments jingling on their ankles." (Isa. 3:16 NIV; cf. 1 Tim.
>   2:9–10 for instruction to Christian women)

Nurtured in this way it becomes impurity (i.e., passion)[48] that yearns for satisfaction; this then turns a person into a slave, into an ox led to the slaughter (Prov. 7; Col. 3:5; 1 Thess. 4:5). This sinful lust was the cancer of the Roman Empire, and it continues even today.[49] It takes the form of fornication[50]—that is, sexual intercourse with unmarried women; here especially it becomes a sin against the neighbor. This sin also includes concubinage, which is a special form of fornication.

Holy Scripture contains serious warnings against this sin: "If there is a betrothed virgin, and a man meets her in the city and lies with her, then you shall bring them both out to the gate of that city, and you shall stone them to death with stones" (Deut. 22:23). Israelite men and women are forbidden to become cult prostitutes; cult prostitution is "an abomination to the LORD your God" (Deut. 23:17–18). The Old Testament prophets warn against this sin (Isa. 3; Hosea), as does the book of Proverbs (see chap. 7). The New Testament is equally clear and emphatic. The advice given to the gentile Christians by the Jerusalem Council (Acts 15) instructed them to "abstain from the things polluted by idols, and from *sexual immorality*, and from what has been strangled, and from blood" (v. 20, emphasis added). When Paul describes the "godless" and "wicked" in Romans 1, he observes that "God gave them up in the lusts of their hearts to impurity, to the dishonoring of their bodies among themselves, because they exchanged the truth about God for a lie and worshiped and served the creature rather than the Creator, who is blessed forever! Amen" (vv. 24–25). In consequence, "God gave them up to dishonorable passions" (v. 26) and "to a debased mind to do what ought not to be done" (v. 28). In 1 Corinthians, with astonishment, Paul chastises, "It

---

48. GrO: πάθος.

49. Ed. note: Bavinck added the abbreviated titles of two novels in parentheses at this point, Eugène de Mirecourt's *Eugène Sue* (Paris, 1855) and Émile Zola's *Nana* (Paris, 1880), as well as the title of an 1882 Dutch translation of Thomas Otway's play *Venice Preserv'd: Or, a Plot Discover'd* (London, 1682).

50. GrO: πορνεία; LO: *scortatio*.

is actually reported that there is sexual immorality among you, and of a kind that is not tolerated even among pagans, for a man has his father's wife" (5:1).

Sexual sin is especially serious because it defiles the body of Christ:

> Do you not know that your bodies are members of Christ? Shall I then take the members of Christ and make them members of a prostitute? Never! Or do you not know that he who is joined to a prostitute becomes one body with her? For, as it is written, "The two will become one flesh." But he who is joined to the Lord becomes one spirit with him. Flee from sexual immorality. Every other sin a person commits is outside the body, but the sexually immoral person sins against his own body. Or do you not know that your body is a temple of the Holy Spirit within you, whom you have from God? You are not your own, for you were bought with a price. So, glorify God in your body. (1 Cor. 6:15–20; cf. 1 Cor. 7:2; 10:7–8; 2 Cor. 12:21; Eph. 5:3; Col. 3:5; 1 Thess. 4:3; Heb. 12:16; 13:4; Rev. 21:8)

Fornication considers the neighbor an object and views one's own body in a similar light, forgetting that both belong not to us but to God. As Paul noted, while other sins are "outside the body"—there the world enters us—sexual sins are sins against our own bodies (1 Cor. 6:18) because the sin proceeds from the self, uses the body from the inside to the outside, and thus destroys the body with the body itself.

Adultery[51] is still worse. It is mentioned by itself in the Seventh Commandment because it is the apex of these sins. For this sin injures not only one's own body and our neighbor, but in also attacking marriage and family life assaults all of God's ordinances, overthrowing God's order for social life. In principle, adultery is revolution and makes society impossible. In our Lord's words: "Moses permitted you to divorce your wives because your hearts were hard. But it was not this way from the beginning. I tell you that anyone who divorces his wife, except for sexual immorality, and marries another woman commits adultery" (Matt. 19:8–9 NIV; cf. Lev. 20:10–11; Deut. 22:22; Rom. 2:22; 1 Cor. 6:19; 7:2; Gal. 5:19; Eph. 5:5; James 4:4; 2 Pet. 2:14). This sin also includes polygamy (Gen. 2:23; Matt. 19:5; 1 Cor. 7:2; Eph. 5:31).

But even here sin does not stand still. Eventually it leads to unnatural sins such as practices associated with pedophilia and homosexuality[52] (Rom. 1:27; 1 Tim. 1:10), common especially in the Greek world, where they were not condemned, even by Socrates and Plato, and later also in Roman culture. Also included are the sins of sodomy (Lev. 20:15), incest (Gen. 19:36; 35:22; 38:18;

---

51. GrO: μοιχεία; LO: *adulterium*.
52. GrO: ἀρσενοκοίτης.

2 Sam. 13:14; 16:21–22; Matt. 14:4; Mark 6:18; 1 Cor. 5:1–2), and onanism along with various "unspeakable sins" that are shameful even to name (Gen. 19:5; 38:9; Exod. 22:19; Lev. 18:22–23). All these sins come to expression in today's desired emancipation of the flesh, in publicly defended debauchery.

2. The Neighbor's Property (Eighth and Tenth Commandments)[53]

The most common form of this sin is *covetousness*, the longing to possess. This soon leads to the following:

a. *Dishonesty*,[54] which is often not considered a sin, allowing a person to commit it and remain respectable. This is a malady especially of the upper-middle classes and includes such actions as not returning what was borrowed (for instance, books) or keeping it too long. "The wicked borrows but does not pay back, / but the righteous is generous and gives" (Ps. 37:21). God's people are not to "withhold good from those to whom it is due, / when it is in your power to do it" (Prov. 3:27). This warning applies especially to those who provide loans to the poor; they must not charge interest, and "if ever you take your neighbor's cloak in pledge, you shall return it to him before the sun goes down, for that is his only covering, and it is his cloak for his body; in what else shall he sleep? And if he cries to me, I will hear, for I am compassionate" (Exod. 22:25–27; cf. Ezek. 18:7). This is the sin of those who do not repay debts, sins committed by fraudulent bankers and unjust stewards who withhold the wages of hired servants (Lev. 19; Deut. 24:13; James 5:4). In addition, we must include not returning what was found (Deut. 22:1), begging, and earning money through dishonest practices. In general, these sins involve an abuse of power by those who are the strongest and the wealthiest.

b. *Deceit, but under the guise of honesty*.[55] Today especially this involves dealing falsely with food and merchandise, selling something defective in place of something good (Lev. 27:9–10; Prov. 11:26; Amos 8:5–6) or selling with deceitful coin and weights (Lev. 19:35; Deut. 25:13; Prov. 10:2; 20:17; Ezek. 45:9–11; Mic. 6:11).

c. This develops into *swindling*,[56] especially in the business world, committed through shortchanging in all kinds of ways. But it also happens in other areas: intellectual theft, plagiarism, pretending that something is ours when it is not or is not yet. It also includes stealing animals (Exod. 22:1). In extreme

---

53. Pictet, *De christelyke zedekunst*, 498; van Mastricht, *Theoretico-Practica Theologia*, II.iii.6 [4:656].
54. DO: *oneerlijkheid*.
55. DO: *bedrog, maar onder schijn van eerlijkheid*.
56. DO: *dieverij*.

forms it involves depriving people of their rights and freedom, as in kidnapping, which is systematized in slavery (Exod. 21:16; Deut. 24:17; 1 Tim. 1:10).

d. *Theft*[57] is intentional misappropriation of the neighbor's property. Cheating is more a matter of taking credit for someone else's accomplishment, as expressed in Proudhon's "property is theft!"[58] (Eph. 4:28; Rom. 2:21; 1 Cor. 6:10; 1 Pet. 4:15). This sin was permitted in Sparta.[59]

e. The worst form is *robbery*,[60] which is practiced even by nations (England, Prussia) and in war is virtually approved. Temple robbery[61] is a special form of this particular sin (Josh. 7; Acts 5). God also owns property that is given and consecrated to him; to assail that property is to attack God himself (2 Chron. 28:21; Mal. 3:8; Prov. 20:23).

3. The Neighbor's Reputation and Good Name (Ninth Commandment)

Our neighbor's good name is more precious than great riches (Prov. 22:1) or fine perfume (Eccles. 7:1), and the Ninth Commandment protects it. The common basis of sins against the neighbor's good name is the lie, which in essence is a sin against God and oneself as well as against the neighbor. Fundamentally, it is not human but devilish,[62] as Jesus told his opponents: "You are of your father the devil, and your will is to do your father's desires. He was a murderer from the beginning, and does not stand in the truth, because there is no truth in him. When he lies, he speaks out of his own character, for he is a liar and the father of lies" (John 8:44). The apostle John points to the same thing in his epistle: "I write to you, not because you do not know the

57. DO: *diefstal.*
58. GO: *Erwerb*; FO: *la propriété, c'est le vol!* Ed. note: Bavinck attributed this saying to François Marie Charles Fourier (1772–1837), but it is usually credited to the French anarchist Pierre-Joseph Proudhon (1809–65), who wrote the following in his 1840 book *What Is Property? Or, an Inquiry into the Principle of Right and Government*:
> If I were asked to answer the following question: *What is slavery?* and I should answer in one word, *It is murder!*, my meaning would be understood at once. No extended argument would be required to show that the power to remove a man's mind, will, and personality, is the power of life and death, and that it makes a man a slave. It is murder. Why, then, to this other question: *What is property?* may I not likewise answer, *It is robbery!*, without the certainty of being misunderstood; the second proposition being no other than a transformation of the first? (Proudhon, *No Gods, No Masters*, 55–56)
The confusion is understandable since both men were radical French thinkers of the nineteenth century and were born in Besançon, France. Nonetheless, Fourier was a utopian socialist and Proudhon an anarchist.
59. Ed. note: In the margin Bavinck added: "Great and small both steal, but the great steal the most."
60. DO: *roof*; GrO: λῃστεία.
61. GrO: ἱεροσυλία.
62. Vilmar, *Theologische Moral,* 1:311–21 (§27).

truth, but because you know it, and because no lie is of the truth. Who is the liar but he who denies that Jesus is the Christ? This is the antichrist, he who denies the Father and the Son" (1 John 2:21–22).

In its essence, rather than accepting God's reality in a receptive mode, this sin involves positing empty reality using words, creating another reality, a thought world divorced from that which is. People do this in order to create "realities" that deny and reject the things of God. Lying is a self-conscious hiding of sin under images made up of words. People try to create themselves as different from who they really are, construct a different image of themselves for public view. This is self-deception, living in the lie; our very being becomes a lie. Worse, people lie to God when they present themselves to God as different from what they are (e.g., Ananias, Acts 5:4). This is at the same time the greatest evil and the greatest folly; it is hypocrisy and Pharisaism.[63] Lying to others presumes that they are beneath us, members of a lower class, and therefore not in communion with us in any way.[64]

Lies are classified into three categories: (a) *crafty lies*: simple lies, occurring merely out of desire for lying; (b) *playful lies*: "white" lies, in order to save oneself (e.g., Sarah, Gen. 18:15); and (c) *emergency lies*: lies of necessity to help another person or save someone from injury.[65] However, even when done for the sake of others, lying is still sin (Exod. 1:20–21).[66] "Do not lie to one another, seeing that you have put off the old self with its practices" (Col. 3:9).

Under lying as a general category, we can note particular sins such as suspecting others and thinking about them in a way that is contrary to the judgment of love:[67] "Judge not, that you be not judged" (Matt. 7:1); "[Love]

63. Pictet, *De christelyke zedekunst*, 547. Christian Science considers all reality an illusion, as did the Libertines in an earlier age.

64. DO: *levensgemeenschap*.

65. LO: *mendacium dolosum; mendacium jocosum; mendacium necessarium, officiosum.* Ed. note: Bavinck adds to this list "banter" and, citing Eph. 5:4, insists that this too is sin. How it fits in the catalogue of lies is not entirely clear. The classic threefold division that Bavinck uses here can be found in Aquinas, *ST* IIa IIae q. 110.

66. Ursinus, *Commentary on the Heidelberg Catechism*, Lord's Day 44. Ed. note: Bavinck provides the story of the Hebrew midwives who lied to Pharoah (Exod. 1:20–21) as proof here, but this may be difficult to square with the text of Exodus, because we are told that "God dealt well with the midwives. And the people multiplied and grew very strong. And because the midwives feared God, he gave them families." Bavinck is here faithfully reproducing the thought of Ursinus, who says the following in his commentary on Lord's Day 44: "Officious lies are often defended by bringing forward the Egyptian midwives, who lied to the king, and were nevertheless blessed of God; but God did not bless them because they had lied, but because they feared him and would not slay the children of Israel." While this may be technically correct (v. 17 points to their fear of God as the reason for not obeying the king's command), the narrator in Exod. 1 puts "So God dealt well with the midwives . . ." immediately after the report of their lie.

67. Pictet, *De christelyke zedekunst*, 525.

does not dishonor others, it is not self-seeking, it is not easily angered, it keeps no record of wrongs" (1 Cor. 13:5 NIV). To lie is to construe a false image of the neighbor, as the priest Eli did of devout Hannah: "Hannah was praying in her heart, and her lips were moving but her voice was not heard. Eli thought she was drunk" (1 Sam. 1:13). It is to give evil testimony in court, as the false witnesses did against Naboth (1 Kings 21:8) and against Christ (Matt. 26:60; cf. Prov. 6:16–19; Deut. 19:16–19). It is twisting someone's words, as the false witnesses[68] did at Jesus's trial when they testified, "This man said, 'I am able to destroy the temple of God, and to rebuild it in three days'" (Matt. 26:60–61; compare this with Jesus's actual words in John 2:19–21). The false testimony against Stephen (Acts 6:13–14) was similar.[69]

Deceit (Rom. 1:29; 3:13; 1 Pet. 2:1; 3:10; 2 Cor. 12:16) or *cunning* (2 Cor. 4:2; 12:16; Eph. 4:14) can occur in various forms and for various reasons.[70] Furthermore, hypocrisy occurs frequently in religion (1 Tim. 4:2; 1 Pet. 2:1; 2 Tim. 3:5). Unfaithfulness can escalate into treachery (2 Tim. 3:3–4; Rom. 1:31), as reflected in the kisses of Joab (2 Sam. 20:9) and Judas (Matt. 26:48–49). From a different perspective,[71] the lie is manifest in backbiting (public) and whisper campaigns (secret), in making public what must be kept private[72] or in simply speaking untruth about one's neighbor. "Do not go about spreading slander among your people. Do not do anything that endangers your neighbor's life. I am the LORD" (Lev. 19:16 NIV; cf. Pss. 15:1–3; 34:13; 64:3; 101:5). Scriptural examples include Doeg (1 Sam. 22:18–19) and Haman (Esther 3:8).

And then there is *slander*[73] (Rom. 1:30; 2 Cor. 12:20; James 4:11; 1 Pet. 2:1), which is already present when one gladly participates in talking about a neighbor's fault, when one takes pleasure in someone else's ruin or makes someone appear ridiculous.[74] It is even worse to rail against someone: "You shall not revile God, nor curse a ruler of your people" (Exod. 22:28). Scriptural examples include Shimei, who cursed King David (2 Sam. 16:5), Ahab (1 Kings 18:17), and the Pharisees who called Jesus "demon-possessed" (John 8:48; cf. Acts 2:13; 17:6). The New Testament also describes abusive, slanderous speech with the word "reviling" (1 Cor. 5:11; 6:10), and even "blasphemy" (slander, abusive speech: Col. 3:8; 1 Tim. 1:13; Titus 3:2; Eph. 4:31).[75] In both

68. GrO: ψευδομάρτυρες.
69. Pictet, *De christelyke zedekunst*, 541.
70. GrO: δόλος; πανουργία.
71. Pictet, *De christelyke zedekunst*, 525.
72. Ed. note: Bavinck references 1 Pet. 4:8 at this point for reasons that are not apparent.
73. DO: *achterklap*; GrO: καταλαλιά.
74. Vilmar, *Theologische Moral*, 1:383.
75. GrO: λοιδορία; βλασφημία.

cases, such speech attempts to turn the neighbor's good into evil. Thanks to the civilizing influence of our age, berating occurs a lot less frequently in our day than in former times.[76] Pictet provides a threefold response to those who would defend such speech by appealing to the scriptural examples of John the Baptist, Jesus himself, and the apostle Paul, all of whom berated others (Matt. 3:7; 23:23; Gal. 3:1; Acts 13:10):[77] (1) There is a great difference between us and Jesus, the apostles, and the prophets; they knew the people whom they berated in a way that is not accessible to us. (2) The Lord Jesus and the apostles were given power and authority not given to us. (3) The purpose and goal that Jesus and the apostles had in mind with their fierce denunciations differ greatly from what people generally have in mind when they berate others.

Finally, cursing one's neighbor[78] is God's prerogative alone and may be done by us only on God's authority. Scripture provides many examples of maledictions (Gen. 9:24–25; 49:3–4; Judg. 5:23; Pss. 69; 79; 109; Jer. 10:25; Lam. 3:65–66; Matt. 23; Acts 8:20; 1 Cor. 16:22; Gal. 1:8 9; 5:12).

4. The Neighbor's Authority (Fifth Commandment)[79]

The root and general character of this sin is pride, grandiosity[80] (1 John 2:16; 2 Tim. 3:2; James 4:16), the elevation of oneself above others, arrogance, the desire that everyone accommodate me and that nothing take priority over me. This sin has various forms:

a. *Self-will, arrogance* (Titus 1:7; 2 Pet. 2:10); always favoring one's own opinion, always imposing it, and refusing to acknowledge any authority of rank, position, age, experience, or office; the immodesty that treats others as if they belonged to a lower class.[81]

b. *Haughtiness* (Rom. 1:30; 2 Tim. 3:2); being proud of rank, social position, wealth.[82]

c. *Lawlessness* or *licentiousness* (2 Pet. 3:17); setting aside all discipline and thus arriving at fornication, seen especially in the "geniuses" (in

76. Ed. note: Between the lines Bavinck added: "Cf. Calvin, Molière."

77. Pictet, *De christelyke zedekunst*, 425. Ed. note: Bavinck omitted Pictet's three responses that follow; they have been supplied here by the editor.

78. Pictet, *De christelyke zedekunst*, 398. Ed. note: In the margin Bavinck added "cursing out, in military service. On this, see debate in Second Chamber [of the Dutch Parliament] on the Military Code, May 1902."

79. Vilmar, *Theologische Moral*, 1:348.

80. Ed. note: In the margin Bavinck added "every human being, an image of God."

81. DO: *eigenzinnigheid*; GrO: αὐθάδης.

82. DO: *hoovaardigheid*; GrO: ὑπερηφανία.

1770) who despised the world and its mores and considered themselves to be the norm.[83] It also comes to expression in cruel brutality (2 Tim. 3:3).[84]

d. *Boasting* (1 Cor. 3:21; 4:7) and *longing for fame or honor; vanity, conceit* (Gal. 5:26; Phil. 2:3), especially in the case of heroes (Lamech, Odysseus) and with all pagans, which then became the origin of dueling and the like.[85]

e. *Ingratitude* (2 Tim. 3:2); refusing to acknowledge oneself as needy, as being in want; considering gratitude as a form of self-abasement. (For example, Satan, who received everything from God, is the most ungrateful and hates God.)[86]

These sins, then, rise to the level of disdain and contempt, of discarding the neighbor, of rejecting authority in the family, society, and state. This leads to revolution and rebellion, insurgency, and anarchy and, on the other hand, to despotism and tyranny (Rom. 13:2; Titus 1:6–10; Rom. 1:30; 2 Tim. 3:2). This particular sin is a matter of discarding the law and pushing back against all limits while declaring human autonomy, rights, and freedom (2 Pet. 2:10; Jude 8–10).[87]

5. The Neighbor's Life (Sixth Commandment)

In general, sins against this commandment deny that our neighbors have equal rights as image-bearers of God (Gen. 9:6) and see them as hindrances, as being beneath us.[88] The result is *heartlessness*—a loss of natural affection, lovelessness (Rom. 1:31); the lack of all compassion and mercy; harshness; viewing the stranger as an enemy, as a barbarian, as someone of a lower order,

---

83. DO: *losbandigheid*; GrO: ἀθεσμία. Ed. note: Bavinck is referring to the importance placed on "genius" by the "Storm and Stress" (*Sturm und Drang*) movement in German literature and music primarily in the decade of the 1770s and represented by such figures as Goethe, Haman, Schiller, Haydn, and Mozart, among others. Heroes in literary works of the movement are driven to violent action not by noble or rational motives but by subjective desires. Goethe's introspective novel of hopeless love and eventual suicide, *Die Leiden des jungen Werthers* (*The Sorrows of Young Werther*, 1774), is one of the most famous exemplars of the movement. For recent discussion of this see Ehrich-Haefeli, "Die Kreativität de 'Genies.'" Also see Nicholls, *Goethe's Concept of the Daemonic*.
84. DO: *brutaliteit; wreed*; GrO: ἀνήμερος.
85. DO: *roemzucht*; GrO: καυχάομαι, καύχημα; κενοδοξία; Vilmar, *Theologische Moral*, 1:354.
86. DO: *ondankbaarheid*; GrO: ἀχάριστος.
87. Vilmar, *Theologische Moral*, 1:368.
88. Vilmar, *Theologische Moral*, 1:370.

of different descent.[89] Beyond this, *anger* and *dislike* develop. Wrath as such is not wrong since God himself displays wrath. However, in humans, anger is usually associated with what the Greeks called θυμός—that is, temper, agitation, and impetuosity—and Scripture warns against it (Job 36:18; Ps. 4:4; Prov. 29:22; Matt. 5:22; Eph. 4:26–31; Col. 3:8; James 1:19).

Jealousy is also attributed to God but without egocentric, personal, earthly admixtures.[90] *Bitterness* (Eph. 4:31; Heb. 3:8) is a kind of inner fury or wrath.[91] *Envy* (Prov. 14:30; Eccles. 4:4; Rom. 1:29; 1 Cor. 13:4; 2 Cor. 12:20; Gal. 5:20; Phil. 1:15; 1 Tim. 6:4; Titus 3:3; James 3:14; 4:5; 1 Pet. 2:1) is the desire to destroy the neighbor's happiness.[92] Envy often leads to gloating (Prov. 24:17; 1 Cor. 13:6).[93] *Hatred* (Lev. 19:17; Prov. 15:17; Matt. 5:23–24; 24:10; 1 John 2:9–11; Titus 3:3) is the desire to destroy the *person* of the neighbor, God's creature; it is to murder the neighbor in thought.[94] *Thirst for revenge* is forbidden because vengeance belongs to God (Prov. 25:21; Matt. 5:39; Rom. 12:17–19; 1 Pet. 3:9). Outward expressions of this sin, such as *quarreling, wrangling, dissension,* and *strife*[95] (Rom. 1:29; 13:13; 1 Cor. 1:11; 3:3), are wrath turned into words and deeds; so too fighting, murder—destroying the image of God. Blood feuds and duels are also condemned by this commandment.

§12. SINS AGAINST GOD

The root and basic form of this sin is unbelief[96]—that is, not accepting God as he is, and not taking him at his word, rather than simply believing him as he has revealed himself. Unbelief is really a negation of God, making him out to be a liar; it is a denial of his truth and faithfulness—thus a denial of God himself.[97] This unbelief can develop in either of two ways: (a) we try to make God equal to ourselves by bringing him down, or (b) we make ourselves equal to God by elevating ourselves.

89. GrO: ἄστοργος; LO: *hostis, hospes.*
90. GrO: ζῆλος; Pictet, *De christelyke zedekunst,* 734.
91. GrO: πικρία; GO: *Ingrimm*; Vilmar, *Theologische Moral,* 1:378.
92. GrO: φθόνος.
93. GO: *Schadenfreude*; Pictet, *De christelyke zedekunst,* 795. Ed. note: Between the lines Bavinck added: "La Rochefoucauld: in the misfortune of our best friends, etc." This is a reference to the French author of countless maxims, François de La Rochefoucauld (1613–80). The specific maxim is "In the misfortunes of our best friends we always find something not altogether displeasing to us" (http://www.brainyquote.com/quotes/quotes/f/francoisde151034.html).
94. GrO: μῖσος; Pictet, *De christelyke zedekunst,* 728.
95. GrO: ἔρις; ἐριθεία.
96. Van Mastricht, *Theoretico-Practica Theologia,* II.ii.6 [4:571].
97. Cf. Pictet, *De christelyke zedekunst,* 140.

1. Sins of a More Sensual Nature

These are sins in which one misuses God for one's own benefit—namely, careless use of his name (that is, using that name as an expletive for emphasis, to confirm one's own speech) and thoughtless, careless speaking of that name (that is, toying with God or joking with God like children do with each other on the playground). This is the sin not only of those who curse but especially of church leaders who misuse God's name in thoughtless prayer, special "sacred language" in preaching, praying, or pastoral calls. This sin escalates to testing God—that is, desiring that God reveal himself more clearly (Exod. 17:2–7; 1 Cor. 10:9), including desiring this from Christ (1 Cor. 10:9) and from the Holy Spirit (Acts 8:18–23; also see Num. 14:22; Deut. 6:16; Ps. 78:18–22; Mal. 3:15; Acts 15:10). This sin includes craving miracles (Matt. 16:1–4) and mighty deeds from God to satisfy our amusement and curiosity. Trickery or deceit[98] (Eph. 4:14) is a step further, playing with God, speculating with him to bring him to our side or turn him toward us (see Balaam in Num. 22–24). We try to use God especially in gambling,[99] which is a misuse of God's providence for one's own benefit, one's own purpose.

Here already we are on the path to superstition.[100] Superstition is the sum of a few remnants of an expired religion that continue alongside a new religion. In this case, we have pagan remnants among Christian people, such as belief in witches, ghosts, and werewolves. Modernists, that is to say, rationalists, explain Christianity, especially Israel's religion, as superstition.[101] Such superstition is a slippery slope. *Sorcery* is the attempt to incline God to us through all kinds of actions, formulas, and incantations.[102] Examples from Scripture include Simon the sorcerer (Acts 8:9), Bar Jesus (Acts 13:6), and the seven sons of Sceva (Acts 19:13–16). The New Testament condemns sorcery (Gal. 5:20; Rev. 9:21) and bewitching (Gal. 3:1). These are not really a matter of tempting God but of apostasy from God, latching on to evil powers and praying to them to perform something or other. Sorcery assumes the reality of Satan and evil spirits (Exod. 22:18; Lev. 20:6, 27). Other forms of this sin are

98. GrO: κυβεία; DO: *bedriegerij.*
99. Van Mastricht, *Theoretico-Practica Theologia*, II.ii.11 [4:605].
100. Vilmar, *Theologische Moral*, 1:324; Pictet, *De christelyke zedekunst*, 151; van Mastricht, *Theoretico-Practica Theologia*, II.ii.13 [4:614].
101. DO: *bijgeloof*; LO: *superstitio.*
102. Ed. note: Bavinck's term here is "theurgy" (*theurgia*), from the Greek θεουργία ("sorcery"). But the texts he cites use μάγος ("magician") in the first two instances and ἐξορκιστῶν ("exorcists") in the last. In the immediately following sentence Bavinck uses two addition terms, φαρμακεία ("sorcery") and βασκαίνω ("bewitch").

necromancy (1 Sam. 28:7) and fortune-telling—misusing God or evil spirits in order to know the future. The same is true for magic.[103]

To this we may add the misuse of the Sabbath—that is, in general, turning the service of God to one's own use and benefit.[104] The most terrible among these is hypocrisy (1 Tim. 4:2; 1 Pet. 2:1; 2 Tim. 3:5).[105] These take on a "form of godliness" but do not have it.[106] This can come to expression in gross or more refined forms.[107]

2. Sins That Are More Spiritual[108]

The root and basic form of this sin is especially pride, the desire to be like God (Sir. 10:12–13).[109] This sin resides in the spirit, is the opposite of surrender and love, and demands that everything be subject to it. The first form of this sin is idolatry[110] and is forbidden by the First Commandment (cf. Gal. 5:20; 1 Cor. 5:11; 6:9; 10:7; 1 Pet. 4:3). In itself it is a matter of indifference what one honors as God—whether it be a statue, one's own ideas, thoughts, or genius, humanity (Comte), the belly, or many other things. It is all idolatry—to embellish or have something else in which to place one's trust instead of the true God revealed in Jesus Christ.[111] This pride was found especially in Cain, Lamech, the tower of Babel, and whoever places "man-as-god" on the throne.[112] And this idolatry of humanity leads gradually to idolatry in a more specific sense (worship of images and the like), to the adoration and worship of human handiwork—the creature. This worship of images (the Second Command-ment) was the real sin of Jeroboam; it is self-willed religion[113] (Col. 2:23). It represents an attempt to seek salvation in ways other than those prescribed by God, such as through one's one reason or virtue. This unbelief also is manifest in those who are "offended" by Christ (Isa. 8:14; Rom. 9:32; 11:9;

103. Vilmar, *Theologische Moral*, 1:326.
104. Van Mastricht, *Theoretico-Practica Theologia*, II.ii.15 [4:623]; Pictet, *De christelyke zedekunst*, 227.
105. GrO: ὑπόκρισις; DO: *huichelarij*.
106. GrO: μόρφωσιν εὐσεβείας.
107. Vilmar, *Theologische Moral*, 1:315; Pictet, *De christelyke zedekunst*, 154; van Mastricht, *Theoretico-Practica Theologia*, II.i.8 [4:536].
108. Vilmar, *Theologische Moral*, 1:327.
109. LO: *superbia*.
110. GrO: εἰδωλολατρία; DO: *afgoderij*.
111. Heidelberg Catechism, Lord's Day 34, Q&A 95: "Idolatry is having or inventing some-thing in which one trusts in place of or alongside of the only true God, who has revealed himself in the Word."
112. Ed. note: Bavinck indicates that this is "according to Steketee's interpretation" (*lezing*); he likely has in mind Steketee, *Babel*.
113. GrO: ἐθελοθρησκία.

1 Pet. 2:7), which is unbelief in God's revelation combined with reluctance
and contempt (Matt. 11:6; 13:57; 26:31–33; Mark 6:3; 14:27, 29; John 6:61;
1 Cor. 1:23).[114] This sin presupposes that someone feels injured or insulted
(because of wisdom or wealth) by Christ's coming and action. This reaction
is very common among intelligent, proud, rich people, and it often escalates
to complaining, murmuring against God. Finally, it leads to hardened denial
of God, to imagining that there is no God and acting that out. Sometimes
this is ineffective, and then despondency arises, despair about God; often this
may also be the result of past sins, which cannot be undone. This despair
then frequently leads to suicide, as in the case of King Saul and Judas, as well
as Ahithophel (2 Sam. 17:23) and Zimri (1 Kings 16:18). In the pagan world,
suicide is thought to be permissible, sometimes even praised (Cato, Brutus).
The most terrifying forms of this sin of pride are "blasphemy" (2 Tim. 3:2),[115]
which is consciously, intentionally slandering and insulting God in Christ,
and perjury (1 Tim. 1:10), which is tempting God by using God himself as a
means to sin.[116] The worst of all these sins is blaspheming the Holy Spirit.[117]

Finally, we consider the development and history of sin, first, on the individual level,[118] which is shown already with the first sin in Paradise:

1. There is an *opportunity* for sinning, a *possibility* (posited by God objectively and subjectively through a probationary command and human
   free will).
2. There is *external temptation* which comes to us in three ways: (a) by
   Satan (Gen. 3:15; Job 1:7; Matt. 12:43–45; 13:19; Luke 22:31; John 8:44;
   2 Cor. 2:11; Eph. 2:2; 1 Pet. 5:8; Rev. 12:9), who for that reason is called
   the *Tempter* (Matt. 4:3; 1 Thess. 3:5); (b) by the *world* (John 15:19; 1 John
   3:13); and (c) by *our own flesh* (Rom. 7:23; Gal. 5:17; James 1:14).[119] The
   means used include delusions of grandeur, treasures, favors, friendship, sensuality, and indications of potential oppression, persecution, and slander.

114. GrO: σκανδαλίζεσθαι.
115. Ed. note: Readers of modern English versions (e.g., ESV, NIV, NRSV) might never
realize that Paul includes "blasphemers" in his list of "last day sinners," because these versions
translate βλάσφημοι as "abusive." The KJV has "blasphemers."
116. GrO: βλάσφημοι; ἐπιόρκοις.
117. Vilmar, *Theologische Moral*, 1:343.
118. Cf. Luthardt, *Kompendium der theologischen Ethik*, 81–83 (§21: "Die Entwickelung
der Sünde").
119. Ed. note: Bavinck's three sources of temptation are taken straight from the Heidelberg
Catechism's explanation of the sixth petition in the Lord's Prayer ("Lead us not into temptation"), which speaks of the Christian's three "sworn enemies, the devil, the world, and our own
flesh . . . [who] never stop attacking us" (Lord's Day 52, Q&A 127).

3. And then comes *gradual compliance, rationalization, inclination of the heart*, and *completion of the deed*.[120] And from this flows forth every subsequent sin (James 1:15), but with a difference. There is now within us a desire that provides a point of contact with sin; this starting point that dwells within us facilitates the pull of Satan and the world. Satan's playground in us is easier. All sin begins with *suggestion* (when sinful thoughts arise from within or without), followed by *meditation* (clinging to that thought and cherishing it in the imagination), *delighting* in it (enjoying it and being inclined toward it), and *agreeing* with it (yielding and acquiescing to it).[121]

There is still more. Every sin paves the way for additional sins; sin gives birth to more sin. "The curse of the evil deed is that, propagating still, it must ever bring forth evil" (Schiller).[122] Sin is a slippery slope. There is a law of sin's development. Every sin makes it easier for the next one to be committed. Every person is polluted by original sin, and thus (a) the possibility of all sins—that is, the root of all sins—lies in each one of us; and (b) thanks to our birth and the environment within which we are raised, the inclination to specific sins varies among people. Examples are a hereditary propensity to alcoholism or an environment filled with cursing. Our hereditary pollution develops in a certain direction, and when we walk in that direction we gradually pick up speed. This second inclination is a particular inheritance that must be distinguished from our general human inherited original sin, though they are connected.

The sins of drunkenness, lust, stealing, or other sins gradually become habit or custom. This is why we distinguish habit from deed and sinful nature or inclination from sinful deed.[123] Contrary to Rome's teaching, which does not count unacquiesced concupiscence as sin, we consider that sinful inclination itself to be sinful. Not only the *deed* but also the crooked *inclination* is sinful.[124] Not only the positive transgression but also the negative deficiency, the lack of original justice, is sin.[125] When someone commits a particular sin, then this becomes a

120. Ed. note: In the margin Bavinck provided an alternative progression: "doubt, unbelief—understanding, fascination, imagination, delighting, resolve of will, deed" (*twijfel, ongeloof—verstand, bekoring, verbeelding, delectatio, wilsbesluit, daad*).

121. LO: *suggestio*; *meditatio*; *imaginatio*; *delectatio*; *consensus*.

122. GO: "Das eben ist der Fluch der bösen Tat, daß sie, fortzeugend, immer Böses muß gebären." Ed. note: An aphorism from Johann Christoph Friedrich von Schiller (1759–1805), *Wallenstein 2*, *Die Piccolomini*, act 5, scene 1, spoken by Octavio Piccolomini.

123. LO: *habitus*; *actus*.

124. LO: *actio*; *inclinatio prava*.

125. LO: *carentia justitiae* (*originalis*).

vice,[126] a constant inclination to do evil, originating through continuing repetition of the sin. Passions must be controlled; they are not sinful in themselves.[127] Slander must be rooted out. Gradually seven sins came to be acknowledged as cardinal sins within Christian ethics: pride, greed, luxury, envy, gluttony, anger, and sloth.[128] Rome still acknowledges these seven. However, the most grievous sins, those against God, are not mentioned. The Reformers therefore enumerated differently: sins against God, against others, and against oneself.

There is also a history, a development in the sin of the human race: of family, clan, people, humanity. Every age, clan, family, people, calling (business/agriculture, soldiers, students, fishermen, sailors), social position, era, century, environment, and climate/soil has its own sins of sensuality and pleasure, ambition, pride, vanity, weakness, cruelty, indifference, anxiety, extravagance or miserliness, tribalism, socialism, and so forth. Eastern, western, southern, and northern nations, pagan and Christian nations all differ, as do youths and adults and the elderly, girls and women. This gives rise to sins of the family, of the clan, of the people, as well as of particular classes and professions. Scripture speaks of a world[129] that is in the hands of the Evil One, with Satan as its head as the god of this age (John 14:30; Gal. 6:14; 1 John 2:14–16; 5:19). And then these sins turn into what the Bible calls "sins that cry out to heaven": murder (Gen. 4:10), sodomy (Gen. 18:20), oppression of the poor (widows and orphans, Exod. 22:22–24), and withholding wages (Exod. 3:7; Lev. 19:13; Deut. 24:14; James 5:4).[130] And this is the process that occurs in the lives of the nations: moral strength followed by decay. For example, the descendants of Cain, humanity before the flood, the Canaanites in Canaan, Greeks, Romans (see Paul in Rom. 1–2), Jews (accursed throughout the entire world). The same occurs in more recent times: Paris (which da Costa called "Sodom"), Vienna, London. And so it will continue until the antichrist (Matt. 24:12; 2 Thess. 2:6; Revelation).

In the situation of sin, people occupy different states.[131]

1. The state of bondage:[132] Here people live unconsciously under the yoke of the law (Rom. 7:7), following their natural instincts, but do not know that they are transgressors.

126. DO: *ondeugd*; GO: *Laster*; LO: *vitium*.
127. DO: *hartstochten*; GO: *Leidenschaften*.
128. LO: *superbia, avaritia, luxuria, invidia, gula, ira, acedia*.
129. GrO: κόσμος.
130. LO: *clamitat ad coelum vox sanguinis et sodomorum, vox oppressorum, merces detenta laborum*. Luthardt, *Kompendium der theologischen Ethik*, 84 (§22.5).
131. Ed. note: Bavinck simply listed the four states of sin; they are taken from Scharling, *Christliche Sittenlehre*, 184–88 (§15).
132. LO: *status servitutis*.

2. The state of security:[133] Acknowledging that we cannot save ourselves, people give up trying, but live at rest in Zion, comfortable in their own acceptability as basically good and decent people.

3. The state of hypocrisy:[134] Persistently resisting the work of God within and refusing to follow the divine stirrings of one's heart by not breaking decisively with sin's dominion leads one to hypocrisy (Matt. 23:23–33). In their hearts people do want to confess that their consciences accuse them, but they are unwilling to repent, wanting rather to continue in their egocentric ways, according to the foolish promptings of their hearts. What shows outwardly is a virtuous respectability and the appearance of a God-blessed life. Eventually it is too much, and they enter the state of hardening.

4. The state of hardening:[135] Caught up in a web of lies and deceit, people finally begin to believe their own lies and shut themselves irrevocably to the truth. The Bible illustrates this with the example of Pharaoh and the sin against the Holy Spirit (Matt. 12:32; Luke 12:10). Stubborn unbelief becomes a condition from which redemption is impossible, because the person defiantly refuses to be redeemed.

133. LO: *status securitatis.*
134. LO: *status hypocriseos.*
135. LO: *status indurationis.*

4

The Fallen Image of God

Sin seeks to destroy and annihilate everything. But God did not allow that to happen because he had a different and higher purpose for humanity—namely, a people to proclaim his praise. God maintains his creation and tempers the inclination to evil. He did not need to do it; that he does is a gift. All of life and all of humanity are under judgment and fall within the purview of patience, of God's forbearance. Thanks to God's forbearance we have the gift of life itself, the capacities of our bodies and souls, including understanding and will, our feelings and passions.

What is impaired but not lost is the soul's mastery over the body; our bodies are often prisons for our souls and eventually our bodies completely fail our souls. What is lost completely is true knowledge in the mind and holiness in the will; we are spiritually dead and incapable of any spiritual good. Holy Scripture does not call the supernatural life that conforms to God "moral" but "holy," using words like "righteousness," "sanctification," "godliness," and expressions like "the fear of God." The ability to do the good, the supernatural, God-pleasing, eternal-life-deserving good, is totally lost.

At the same time, not only do we retain natural goods like eating, drinking, sleeping, and walking; some relative moral good also remains. We agree with Augustine that there can be no virtue without righteousness and no righteousness without faith, that the virtues of the pagans are but "splendid vices." Nonetheless, it is important to acknowledge gradations in evil even when pagans seek virtue to entertain themselves, to fulfill their desires, to exalt themselves in their own eyes. Acknowledging that certain pagan philosophers (Plato) said some sensible things about God and spiritual matters, Calvin judged that this only heightened their inexcusability; because they lacked faith they also lacked true knowledge and true virtue.

Furthermore, Reformed theologians believed that the moral virtues of the pagans came from the general operation of the Holy Spirit and did not arise from any innate ability of the human will. That is why some preferred to use the term "virtue" for pagan morality and reserve the term "good works" for Christian morality. The former is considered under philosophical ethics, and the latter under specifically Christian ethics. These two differ in their foundations, their norms, and their goals.

Human dominion over nature has been weakened and robbed of its spiritual character, but not eliminated; it has been impeded, but not destroyed. Science and scholarship bear witness to the human yearning for knowledge of earthly things. Philosophy and the natural sciences are gifts from God that must not be rejected or despised. Art in the broader sense of subjecting the earth and making it an instrument for the blessing of humanity is a power, like science, that can be used for or against God. Scripture, however, does point to progress in culture.

§13. THE IMAGE OF GOD IN FALLEN HUMAN BEINGS[1]

Sin is a corrupting and ravaging power. The principle and objective of sin do not permit sin to rest until it has totally and absolutely corrupted everything, all that exists. Sin would also destroy everything, since all that exists has substance as physical substratum, which is something good that God created and maintains. Sin is a destructive fury. It is nihilism![2] The "no" exists only through the "yes," but endeavors to destroy the "yes" and thus destroy itself. Sin devours everything else and itself.[3] Once sin had entered the human race, it would have totally corrupted and even destroyed and exterminated humanity if left to work undisturbed. But God did not allow that to happen; he had a different and higher purpose for our race. He wanted to prepare for himself a people taken from the corrupt mass of humanity,[4] a people to proclaim his praise, a body for the Son, a temple for the Holy Spirit. For this reason, God often acts in history to counter this destructive fury.[5] He reins in and bridles the destructive power of sin through punishments, pestilences,

---

1. Ed. note: In the margins Bavinck wrote "*grote vakantie 1902*" (big vacation 1902). This is another indicator that Bavinck used this manuscript for his final lectures to Kampen students in the spring and fall of 1902 before he moved to Amsterdam to take up his post at the Vrije Universiteit. See above, "Introduction to Herman Bavinck's *Reformed Ethics*," section on de Jong manuscript (pp. xxxvi–xli).

2. DO: *vernielingswoede* ("destructive rage").

3. J. Müller, *Christian Doctrine of Sin*, 1:293.

4. LO: *massa corruptionis*.

5. DO: *vernietingswoede* ("destructive rage"). Ed. note: This word is more intense than *vernielingswoede*, the term Bavinck used earlier. *Vernielingswoede* connotes ruin and degradation; *vernietingswoede* connotes annihilation, making into "nothing."

judgments, and devastations by natural forces. In this way, he moves nations and individuals to righteousness, penitence, national conversion, and seriousness of life, and limits and restrains dissoluteness. This happened in the time of Noah and at the building of the tower of Babel, it happened to Sodom and to the Canaanites, and it is also happening at present. These are all particular acts of God in history.

But God also works with the entire human race more generally. Immediately after the fall, God delayed both eternal and temporal death. God also mitigated spiritual death in various ways. Spiritual death consists of the inability to do good and the inclination to evil, to live for sin and unto death. In many ways, God tempers this inclination to evil. From the fall onward, human life and humanity itself have come under the purview of *common grace*.[6] It is not self-evident that humanity should exist. That we do exist and enjoy blessings is not simply grounded in the order of creation, because our sin forfeits our right to exist as well as the content of our life. Nevertheless, as we distinguish the two spheres of creation and redemption, common grace belongs to the sphere of creation. This fruit of common grace—being allowed to retain something of what we by nature possessed in Adam—we must not forget, is a gift of *grace*; it is not ours by right or covenant. It is in this sense that we also speak of natural theology, natural morality, and natural law. Even though we retain them only as gifts, they are remnants, graciously left behind for us, of what we once possessed by nature. Leaving them for us and giving them to us is an act of grace, but the content of the giving, the gift itself, is not a superadded gift, but a natural gift.[7] It can be expressed more clearly this way: all of life and all of humanity fall within the purview of *patience*, of God's *forbearance*.[8] This is better than seeing it under the purview of creation. The order of creation has been disturbed by sin and will never return. God's way of dealing with humanity after sin (and before salvation in Christ) is different than it was before the fall. Natural humanity is outside Paradise and not yet in the kingdom of God, but also not yet in hell. Humanity thus

---

6. Cocceius, *Summa Doctrinae*, IV.74, cited by Heppe, *Reformed Dogmatics*, 371: "Cocceius introduces his exposition of the doctrine of the covenant of grace (*De foed.* IV, 74), by declaring that of course God might at once have punished man with all evils. But the height of wisdom and power [*sapientia et potestas summa*] aided Him in His glorious plan for exercising mercy on man [*suppeditabat gloriosam rationem excercendi cum homine misericordiam*]. Accordingly, He resolved (1) to unfold his inexpressible mercy 'in vessels of mercy' [*voluit tum illam ineffabilem misericordiam* χαρά *et* χρηστότης], and (2) 'to employ an ineffable kindness and longsuffering towards the entire human race' [*inerrabili quadam beneficentia et patientia uti erga totum genus humanum*]."

7. LO: *donum superadditum; donum naturale.*

8. See Zahn, *Die natürliche Moral*, 114, 120, 147.

lives in an intermediate state, under the order of God's patience. Moreover, God does not simply allow something of his image to remain in us, and does not act only indirectly, but also directly. The sin in which we are lying makes direct acts by God necessary (his judgments, for example). All of this is best summarized under the purview of God's forbearance. But this should not be understood simply passively—that is, as forbearing, suffering, allowing, or permitting. It should also be understood actively, since *patientia* is related to *potentia*; in God everything is active, and God is actuality:[9] God causes us to exist, leads us, and directs us.

There is another insight here. This order of divine patience is an intermediate state between creation and re-creation, between the covenant of nature and the covenant of grace, and a state of preparation for the final state, as will soon be discussed. Paul views the entire pre-Christian period from this perspective. God put forward Jesus as a propitiation by his blood, "because in his divine forbearance he had passed over former sins" to "show his righteousness at the present time" (Rom. 3:25–26). If Paul is here speaking of Israel only (as Philippi thinks),[10] it would a fortiori be true of the pagan. We should view everything that follows in this chapter and in the next two chapters from this perspective.

We owe many things to this forbearance.

1. Life or Existence Itself

That we exist, that children are born, is not self-evident. Adam and Eve and all of us have deserved death at every moment. It is thanks to God's forbearance that Adam and Eve, instead of closing their eyes in death, cast their eyes down in shame. What Eve cried out in amazement in Genesis 4:2—"I have gotten a man *with the help of the* LORD"—can be said about every birth. Human life oscillates between God's forbearance and his wrath.[11] Every birth proclaims God's forbearance to us, and every death his wrath. The Spirit of God creates every new human life, pours life into the womb of death (Gen. 1:2; Job 33:4; Ps. 139; Zech. 12:1). "In him we live and move and have our

9. LO: *actus.*
10. Ed. note: Philippi, *Commentary on Romans*, 1:149: "But these were the sins of the people of Israel."
11. Ed. note: Bavinck's marginal note here reads, "Consider also the Macrobians" (*Denk ook aan de Makrobiërs*). The name is derived from the Greek Μακρόβιοι ("long-lived") and refers to "a legendary tribe of Aethiopia and kingdom positioned in the farthest land towards the western sunset in *ancient Libya* (Africa). . . . Their name is due to their legendary longevity, an average person supposedly living to the age of 120." Herodotus mentions them in his *Histories* 3.114; 4.197 (https://en.wikipedia.org/wiki/Macrobians).

being" (Acts 17:28). "The steadfast love of the LORD never ceases; his mercies never come to an end" (Lam. 3:22).[12] We have thus retained something of life, of the immortality bestowed upon Adam.

2. Soul and Body and Their Capacities

The substance of our being has totally remained; it has lost none of its strength, even though it has deteriorated. In this way, all its capacities have remained.[13] These include the following:

a. The *intellect*. That humans retain understanding is not something to be taken for granted.[14] This appears from the reality of mental illness. Although our power of thinking is weakened and, by living in sin, is dulled, enfeebled, and sometimes even suspended (in the mentally ill), it is not lost. We can still think, understand, evaluate, and make decisions. Even the intuitive, the prophetic, has not been totally lost, and shines brilliantly in the case of geniuses. Such differences between the mental powers of individuals prompt us to acknowledge them all as gifts.[15] All of this makes science possible, which is a great gift.

b. The *will*. The natural capacities of the will have also been affected by sin.[16] Just think of how a person can be either inflexible, stiff-necked, and willful or double-minded, indecisive, and unsettled. In one person, the will has become hardened, in another it has become enfeebled. Yet the will as a capacity has not been lost. We can freely and spontaneously, without compulsion, do what we do. We can even direct our will in accordance with our mind; that is, we can will only those things that the mind prescribes as good. This enables us to act rationally, reasonably, in accord with the voice of reason. And the original power of the will is occasionally present and is manifest in the heroic and vigorous energy of the great ones of our human race, such as reformers like the Buddha, world conquerors like Alexander, and scientists like Columbus and Galileo.

c. The *feelings*, the *passions*. These have also been affected by sin. They are excited by the wrong objects, express themselves too feebly or too strongly

---

12. Zahn, *Die natürliche Moral*, 114, 115.

13. The Belgic Confession (art. 14) says that we have retained only "small traces" of our excellent gifts; cf. Canons of Dort, III/IV.16.

14. Bavinck's marginal note: Calvin notes in *Institutes*, II.ii.12, that the human mind still has some desire to investigate truth, some natural love for the truth. One should also think here of traditional knowledge of God, which derives from Paradise. Knowledge and service of God long remained pure.

15. *Institutes*, II.ii.17.

16. Bavinck's marginal note: Not the will but the health of the will has been lost (*Institutes*, II.iii.5).

(when they become extreme, excessive, or unregulated), or are disharmonious and conflict with one another. Yet the emotive capacity has remained. We still have all the passions; love, admiration, compassion, hate, anger, and contempt are all still in us. They are substantively good, so long as they are directed in proper measure to the right goals. Even the glory of the passions has not been entirely lost.[17] Think of the power of a mother's love, love for one's fatherland, the artistic sense of awe (Plato), or noble inclinations.

d. The body as *instrument of the soul*. This, too, has suffered the influence of sin. The body has become independent; it absolutely refuses to be an instrument any longer. The flesh has become emancipated, and in many different ways has come to oppose the spirit (also in our natural state)—think especially of sexual life, which has become a power opposed to our will. For this reason, Paul could call the entire human person "flesh,"[18] naming the whole after the part. The body often refuses to make one or more of its members subservient to the soul, for example the eyes (blindness), or the feet (lameness). At that point, the body, instead of serving as an instrument, becomes a hindrance, an obstacle, a prison for the soul (something that Plato taught correctly). People have identified twelve thousand illnesses in which the body denies its service to the soul. Eventually the body refuses to serve altogether, weakens, ages, and dies, and our soul lacks the vital power to preserve that body and to renew it. Nevertheless, the body is still an organ; it is a weakened instrument, but not a lost one. Our soul still sees by means of the eye, thinks by using the brain, perceives through the senses, walks with the feet, rules and manages by the hand. The human ability to subject the body and make it subservient to the soul can still be seen in the asceticism of the Stoics and monastics.

3. Knowledge in the Mind and Holiness in the Will

These gifts have been lost. It is usually expressed this way: human beings are completely dead with respect to what is *spiritually good*. That is, they are unable to do any, even the smallest, *spiritual good* (what is supernaturally good or "good works"). After all, good works must proceed from a true faith,[19] must conform to God's law,[20] must be done for God's glory alone,[21]

17. GrO: ἐνθουσιασμός.
18. GrO: σάρξ; LO: *pars pro toto.*
19. "Whatever does not proceed from faith is sin" (Rom. 14:23); "Without faith it is impossible to please him [God]" (Heb. 11:6).
20. Deut. 11:32; 12:32; Ezek. 20:18–19.
21. 1 Cor. 10:31: "Whether you eat or drink, or whatever you do, do all to the glory of God."

and should not be based on our own opinions or on human traditions,[22] as the Heidelberg Catechism teaches.[23] Spiritual good is what spiritual people[24] perform, worked in them and through them by the Holy Spirit.

This good is called "supernatural" because it is not a fruit or goal of nature but of the supernatural life that the Holy Spirit has worked in us. God, or God's law, is the norm and standard of what is good. Only what entirely and in all its parts agrees with that standard is good. Holy Scripture does not call this "moral" but "holy," using words like "righteousness," "sanctification," and "godliness" and expressions like "the fear of God." Spiritual good, then, is what satisfies both the spiritual and the external sense of the law of God; what agrees with it in principle, in direction, in purpose; what therefore satisfies God himself. The doing of this good grants eternal life. But it is precisely the good in this sense that the natural person cannot fulfill, neither in its entirety nor even in stages by performing parts of it. The second of these options is impossible because the righteousness, the image of God—that is, total conformity to God's law—is an unbreakable unity. We cannot over time get closer and closer to the image of God, nor can it be repaired in stages.[25] This principle is absolute; it tolerates no imperfection; virtue is one and indivisible.[26] The first of these options—to fulfill the law in its entirety—is even more impossible, as everybody will agree. Natural persons do not *know*, do not understand, and do not comprehend the true, spiritual good.

The spiritual meaning of the law—to do everything from God, in accord with God's will, unto God—is hidden to natural persons. To know the spiritual good requires a heart provided by God: "I will give them a heart to know that I am the LORD, and they shall be my people and I will be their God, for they shall return to me with their whole heart" (Jer. 24:7); "I will put my law within them, and I will write it on their hearts. And I will be their God, and they shall be my people" (Jer. 31:33). God reveals himself to the little children: "Jesus declared, 'I thank you, Father, Lord of heaven and earth, that you have hidden these things from the wise and understanding and revealed them to little children'" (Matt. 11:25); "To you it has been given to know the secrets of the kingdom of heaven, but to them it has not been given" (Matt. 13:11); "Jesus answered him, 'Truly, truly, I say to you, unless one is born again he cannot see the kingdom of God'" (John 3:3). This is a work of God: "The

22. Deut. 12:32; Isa. 29:13–14; Ezek. 20:18; Matt. 15:7–9.
23. Heidelberg Catechism, Q&A 91.
24. GrO: πνευματικοί.
25. Hoedemaker, *De verhouding der ethiek tot de dogmatiek*, 22: "Het beeld Gods wordt niet bij benadering bereikt, niet by trappen hersteld."
26. LO: *simplex et una.*

Lord opened her [Lydia's] heart to pay attention to what was said by Paul"
(Acts 16:14; cf. 28:27–28).

The natural mind, governed by the flesh, not only does not understand God
(Rom. 3:11), but is hostile to God (Rom. 8:7). The cross is foolishness to the
world (1 Cor. 1:18–25) because the natural person cannot understand spiritual
realities (1 Cor. 2:7–14) and lacks light (2 Cor. 3:5; Eph. 1:17; 4:17–18; 5:8).
But beyond a failure of *understanding*, the natural person does not *want* to
do the truly and spiritually good, either:

> They say to God, "Depart from us! / We do not desire the knowledge of your
> ways." (Job 21:14)

> That which is born of the flesh is flesh. (John 3:6)

> No one can come to me unless the Father who sent me draws him. (John 6:44)

> You were dead in [your] trespasses and sins. (Eph. 2:1)

> For it is God who works in you, both to will and to work for his good pleasure.
> (Phil. 2:13)

The natural person does not *do* spiritual good:

> The evil person out of his evil treasure brings forth evil. (Matt. 12:35)

> For out of the heart come evil thoughts, murder, adultery, sexual immorality,
> theft, false witness, slander. (Matt. 15:19)

> Everyone who practices sin is a slave to sin. (John 8:34)

> Apart from me you can do nothing. (John 15:5)

> None is righteous, / no, not one; / no one understands; / no one seeks for
> God . . . / no one does good. (Rom. 3:10–12)

The ability to do the good, the supernatural, God-pleasing, eternal-life-
deserving good, is totally lost. Indeed, even the believer accomplishes not
a single perfectly good work. But the believer's good work can be good *in
principle*, because it derives from the Holy Spirit, from faith, and it takes
God's law as its standard, and it aims at God's honor. Then whatever is still
lacking is atoned for by Christ and supplemented by him. The fact remains,
however, that the spiritual good remains lost.

4. Natural Good and Moral Good

Eating, drinking, sleeping, and walking are all *natural goods*. This, in contrast to natural evil[27]—when someone cannot eat, see, or hear, for instance. Considered on their own, these deeds, acts, and states are neither good nor evil and do not, considered as such, come under the rubric of the moral law but the law of nature. They can indeed become moral or immoral by the way in which a person performs them, whether from a sinful inclination or for a sinful goal. Included, for example, are natural acts done out of lust or laziness. But, considered by themselves, they are not morally significant acts. Such natural goods have not been lost through sin. We can still eat, drink, sleep, and walk, for example. Yet such deeds have become weakened, and performing them has become difficult and now demands the sweat of our brow. Sometimes, because of sickness, natural goods are taken away entirely. Sin has therefore thoroughly affected also this terrain. But if one pictures concentric circles, with the spiritual as the center point, the moral as the next circle, and then the natural as the outermost circle, then sin has not destroyed the natural but only weakened it.

But *moral good* has also remained. We shall see later what this includes. For initial orientation on the topic one can consider the virtues of the pagans.[28] Some maintain that some pagans are saved.[29] The Pelagians thought that pagans had true and complete virtues. The Socinians and Curcellaeus[30] thought likewise, as did many Jesuits. The Christian church was less favorably inclined. Tertullian remarked that the pagans prohibit only external sins, but our law forbids also internal sins. And then he asks, "So then, where is there any likeness between the Christian and the philosopher? between the disciple of Greece and of heaven? between the man whose object is fame,

27. LO: *malum physicum*.

28. Alting, *Theologiae Problematica Nova*, 452–54 (VIII.9–10); Maresius, *Sylloge Disputationum*, 2:123–35; de Moor, *Commentarius Perpetuus*, 4:826–29; Pfanner, *Systema Theologiae Gentilis Purioris*, chap. 22, §33 (chap. 22 deals with the salvation of the gentiles); Trigland, *Antapologia*, chap. 17; F. Turretin, *Institutes of Elenctic Theology*, 1:683–85 (X.5; Latin text: *Theologiae Elenchticae*, I.753–56); Vitringa, *Doctrinae Christianae Religionis*, "Theologiae Elenchticae," IX.33–36; Vossius, *Historiae de Controversiis*, III.3; Vossius, *Opera Omnia*, 6:464–70; Witsius, *Economy of the Covenants*, 2:20–22 (III.12.lii–lviii); Witsius, *Twist des Heeren*, 214–50 (chap. 19); Wittewrongel, *Oeconomia Christiana*, 1:288–89.

29. Pfanner, *Systema Theologiae*, 491–92. Ed. note: Pfanner cites Justin Martyr, *1 Apology* XX (*ANF* 1:169–70); Clement of Alexandria, *Stromata* VI (*ANF* 2:480–519); Tertullian, *Answer to the Jews* I (*ANF* 3:151–52); Hilary of Poitiers, *Tractatus super Psalmos I* (*CSEL* 20:354–544, on Ps. 118); and Epiphanius (bishop of Salamis, ca. 310–403).

30. Ed. note: Étienne de Courcelles (Stephanus Curcellaeus [1586–1629]) was an Arminian Greek scholar and translator (https://en.wikipedia.org/wiki/%C3%89tienne_de_Courcelles).

156 HUMANITY BEFORE CONVERSION

and whose object is life? between the talker and the doer?"[31] Augustine says there can be no virtue without righteousness, and no righteousness without faith.[32] Nevertheless, Augustine acknowledges gradations of sin and virtue: "Fabricius will be punished less than Catiline, not because Fabricius was good, but because Catiline was more evil. Fabricius was less wicked than Catiline, not because he had true virtues, but because he did not deviate so much from the true virtues." Fabricius receives a lighter punishment than Catiline not because he is a good man but because the other is even more of a scoundrel. Fabricius was less impious than Catiline, because, although he possessed no true virtues, he did not greatly deviate from them.[33] The true good is a fruit of grace in Christ; therefore the virtues of the pagans, even if they enjoy some praise in human society, are not true virtues. Their will is unfaithful and impious and therefore not good.[34] Augustine therefore calls the virtues of the pagans "splendid vices."[35] Prosper said that, without serving the true God, whatever seems to be virtue is sin; none can please God without God.[36] Scholastics like Thomas connected the seven cardinal virtues with the three theological virtues. The Council of Trent anathematized anyone who taught that before regeneration no true virtues can be achieved.[37] Jansen taught something closer to Augustine: the pagans seek virtue to entertain themselves, to fulfill their desires, to exalt themselves in their own eyes.[38] And this stands to reason, because all who do not lift their eyes to God, to please God with their virtue, are seeking in virtue itself the end or purpose of the good, so that this is the desire they seek to fulfill. Virtue then becomes the purest ornament with which people adorn themselves.[39] The Roman Catholics recognize virtues among

31. Tertullian, *Apologia* XLV–XLVI (*ANF* 3:50–51).
32. Augustine, *Against Julian* IV.3.17 (FC 35:181).
33. Augustine, *Against Julian* IV.3.25 (FC 35:190).
34. Augustine, *Against Julian* IV.3.33 (FC 35:197–98).
35. Augustine, *City of God* XIX.25 (NPNF¹ 2:418–19).
36. Prosper of Aquitaine, *Call of All Nations* I.6 (ACW 14:31–33); see de Moor, *Commentarius Perpetuus*, 4:828.
37. According to F. Turretin, *Institutes of Elenctic Theology*, 1:683 (X.5: "Virtues of the Gentiles"). Ed. note: The sixth session of the Council of Trent, "On Justification," canon 7, reads: "If anyone shall say that all works that are done before justification, in whatever manner they have been done, are truly sins or deserving the hatred of God, or that the more earnestly anyone strives to dispose himself for grace, so much more grievously does he sin: let him be anathema" (Denzinger, no. 817).
38. Jansen, *Augustinus*, 2:253–56 (IV.11: "*De Statu Naturae Lapsu*"). Ed. note: Cornelius Jansen (1585–1638) was the Dutch Roman Catholic bishop of Ypres (Flanders) whose study of Augustine led him to emphasize predestination and grace, eventually leading to a condemnation of his views in a series of papal bulls (Tschackert, "Jansen").
39. Witsius, *Economy of the Covenants*, 2:28 (III.12.lxxiv).

the pagans. Bellarmine said that a person can fulfill certain moral virtues also without faith.[40]

Protestants, more in line with Augustine, thought differently. Luther wrote that Aristotle can give rules for only the natural, temporary, perishable life.[41] Natural moral theory emphasizes works (from the outside to the inside, *disposition* acquired through deeds),[42] whereas Christian moral theory emphasizes the person (first the tree is good, then the fruit). Natural theory does not relate good works to God. The ultimate ground and highest purpose is not God, but humanity, society, the state, the political end. Regarding Zwingli, see my *The Ethics of Ulrich Zwingli*.[43] Calvin guarded against any mixture of philosophy and Christian ethics.[44] He thought very unfavorably of the pagans, especially the Cynics, but also of the Stoics and Aristotle, particularly because of Aristotle's doctrine of free will. Only Plato, and occasionally Cicero, received a more favorable treatment.[45] In his *Institutes* Calvin distinguished between earthly, this-worldly things that concern the present life, and heavenly things that concern the knowledge of God, true righteousness, the mysteries of the kingdom of heaven.[46] According to Calvin, the natural person is still partially capable of performing things that belong to the first group; to some extent they can still know and will them.[47] The natural person is unable to know heavenly things, however. In these we are blinder than moles. But Calvin acknowledged that even with respect to heavenly things, some philosophers said some sensible things about God.[48] They had a little taste of God, but their situation was like that of a wayfarer who sees flashes of lightning in the night. The lightning does not bring wayfarers to the right path, but only plunges them into deeper darkness.[49] Pagans also do not know the law, certainly not the first table, but not even the second.[50] Some of them have lived very honorably. The grace of God has not delivered them from the corruption of nature, but has

---

40. See F. Turretin, *Institutes of Elenctic Theology*, 1:683 (X.5); Bellarmine, *Opera Omnia*, IV (1), 391–98 ("De Gratia et Libero Abitrio," V.9–10).

41. Luthardt, *Die Ethik Luthers*, 14–19.

42. LO: *habitus*; *actus*.

43. Bavinck, *De ethiek van Ulrich Zwingli*, 20–33 (chap. 2).

44. See Lobstein, *Die Ethik Calvins*, 6–14.

45. Bavinck's marginal note: Calvin acknowledges a certain operation of God's Spirit in pagans. See Schneckenburger, *Vergleichende Darstellung*, 1:231; also see Witsius, *Twist des Heeren*, 234–45.

46. *Institutes*, II.xiii.

47. *Institutes*, II.xiii.12–17.

48. *Institutes*, II.xiii.18.

49. *Institutes*, II.xiii.19.

50. *Institutes*, II.xiii.22; II.iii.3.

reined in this corruption.[51] Virtues like those of Camillus are worth nothing to God;[52] they are impure through a lust for glory, for example, even if they should be ascribed to the restraining grace of God. According to Lobstein, Calvin thought that Plato had some idea of the truth, of God, of the good, but this only served to lessen Plato's excusability; he lacked faith; he lacked true knowledge and true virtue; his knowledge and virtue were merely semblance and smoke.[53] Almost all the Reformed held to an essentially similar position. They fully acknowledged the virtues of pagans and affirmed their validity. They thought very highly of men like Camillus, Scipio, Cato, Seneca, Plato, and Socrates and often quoted their writings and beautiful maxims. They acknowledged that their virtues were objectively good, were praiseworthy as external deeds, were "not sins per se (and as to substance of the work), but by accident (and as to the mode of operation) in the essential conditions (on account of the various defects mentioned before)."[54] They further held that many pagans were examples to Christians and surpassed them; indeed, many pagans were even more advanced in these moral virtues than many believers, so that pagans often stand higher morally than the regenerate.[55] They believed two things about these moral virtues: (1) they originated only through the general operation of the Holy Spirit, through restraining grace, and could not be fulfilled by the human free will, without God, as Plato and Cicero themselves acknowledged.[56] Therefore, these virtues of pagans were not true virtues. (2) Nonetheless, God did on occasion graciously reward them temporally, only for this life; this is what happened to Ahab (1 Kings 21:27–28) and Nineveh (Jon. 3:5; cf. Matt. 12:41).[57]

But Reformed theologians did not go beyond this. The moral virtues of Plato and others resemble the true, spiritual virtues, in the same way that counterfeit pearls resemble genuine ones, or fake gold resembles real gold.[58] They cannot pass the test when assayed by the only true standard. Some have therefore preferred the term "virtue" when describing pagan morality and reserved the term "good works" for Christian morality.[59] The word "virtue"

---

51. *Institutes*, II.iii.4.

52. Ed. note: Marcus Furius Camillus was a fourth- or fifth-century BC Roman statesman whose character was celebrated by Livy and Plutarch; see, e.g., Livy, *History of Rome* 6.

53. Lobstein, *Die Ethik Calvins*, 7.

54. F. Turretin, *Institutes of Elenctic Theology*, 1:684 (X.5.vi).

55. See Witsius, *Twist des Heeren*, 214; cf. Wittewrongel, *Oeconomia Christiana*, 1:293–95.

56. F. Turretin, *Institutes of Elenctic Theology*, 1:683–85 (X.5.ii, ix); according to Turretin, Plato and Cicero also acknowledged this; cf. Wittewrongel, *Oeconomia Christiana*, 1:289.

57. F. Turretin, *Institutes of Elenctic Theology*, 1:684 (X.5.viii).

58. Wittewrongel, *Oeconomia Christiana*, 1:295.

59. De Moor, *Commentarius Perpetuus*, 4:817; Alting, *Theologiae Problematica Nova*, 733 (XVIII.4); Maresius, *Collegium Theologicum*, 295–96 (XII.9).

itself was not disapproved, because it is also used in Holy Scripture.[60] Paul asks us to "think about" whatever is true, honorable, just, pure, lovely, and commendable and summarizes all this with "if there is any excellence" (Phil. 4:8).[61] Peter tells us to supplement our "faith" with "virtue" (2 Pet. 1:5), and even speaks of the virtues of God ("that you may proclaim the 'excellencies' of him who called you out of darkness into his marvelous light" (1 Pet. 2:9).[62] But in Christian circles many prefer to speak of "good works" rather than "virtues" because

1. the Latin word *virtus* (from *vir* = "man") and the Greek ἀρετή (from ῎Αρης?)[63] were pagan in origin and meaning;
2. Holy Scripture uses the term infrequently; and
3. doing so preserves a terminological distinction between non-Christian[64] (philosophical) ethics and Christian ethics.

We distinguish four key differences between "virtues" and "good works," between philosophical and specifically Christian ethics:

a. In its *foundation*:[65] The virtues are rooted in the tenuous remnants of the image of God, preeminently in human reason. Some have located virtue in the desires (Epicurus) or in the passions, but the best philosophers (Socrates, Plato, Aristotle, the Stoics, Kant, Hegel, and others) have located it in reason, as the capacity for higher ideas.[66] Calvin therefore said: All philosophers say that the "reason which abides in human understanding is a sufficient guide for right conduct; the will, being subject to it, is indeed incited by the senses to evil things; but since the will has free choice, it cannot be hindered from following reason as its leader in all things."[67] Reason, they thought, is strengthened by good education and a study of philosophy, God's guiding providence, and grace. But wherever the virtues are located, they have no higher source than (fallen) nature (Rom. 2:14–15).[68] According to Calvin, the foundation of the

60. Ed. note: The Greek word ἀρετή, usually translated as "virtue," is found in each of the passages that follow; readers of standard English translations other than the KJV or ASV might miss this, however, with translations of Phil. 4:8 such as "anything excellent" (NIV) or "any excellence" (ESV, NRSV).
  61. GrO: εἴ τις ἀρετή.
  62. GrO: πίστις; ἀρετή; τὰς ἀρετάς.
  63. Ed. note: ῎Αρης (*Arēs*) is the ancient Greek god of war (Latin: Mars).
  64. DO: *heidense* ("pagan").
  65. DO: *beginsel*.
  66. See Betz, *Ervaringswijsbegeerte*.
  67. *Institutes*, II.ii.3.
  68. Witsius, *Economy of the Covenants*, 2:26 (III.12.lxviii).

philosophers' morality is free will, reason, and (especially in Stoic thought) nature.[69] They know nothing about the fall, about the corruption of our nature, about the need for regeneration. All their ideas about virtue and duty are splendid,[70] but they lack the foundation; they are a body without a head. A natural person can do no good that pleases God. By contrast, good works have the Holy Spirit as their author and are rooted in supernatural grace, in the faith that purifies our hearts internally, that first makes the tree good so that it can then produce good fruit: "Without faith it is impossible to please God" (Heb. 11:6; cf. Rom. 14:23).

b. The *norms* of the virtues are different from those pertaining to good works.[71] Pagan philosophers sought them in nature, in right reason, or in the morality of the community. Currently, they are sought particularly in what is ordinary for people, in the essence of the human person, or in what has utilitarian value for society. Sometimes philosophers also spoke of God's commandments (Epictetus and Seneca, for example, as explained by Witsius),[72] but they tried to derive these from nature, or reason, or the conscience, so that it was always a standard inherent in nature. Christian morality, however, has the perfect revealed law of God as its standard. No doubt some traces of this law remain in nature (see Rom. 2). Nonetheless, many parts of this law are entirely unknown, or only partially known (for example the First, Second, Third, Fourth, and Tenth Commandments). In any case, the spiritual meaning of the law is not understood by the unregenerate. But even if much more of God's law were naturally known—let us suppose that the whole moral law could be known by reason alone—even then there would be inadequate human ability to keep the law. The unregenerate may know the law externally but cannot do it; they may well display a likeness of the matter, but do not really have the substance itself. Philosophical morality is motivated only by compelling reasons and admonitions, which are weak before the power of the passions, and anyway they, too, lead people astray. Philosophy is a magnificent gift from God.[73] But Christian morality speaks of the love of God in Christ, holds up this love as an example, and, in ad-

69. Lobstein, *Die Ethik Calvins*, 8.
70. See Calvin's comments on Rom. 12:1.
71. Witsius, *Economy of the Covenants*, 2:30–38 (III.12.lxxx–ciii).
72. Witsius, *Economy of the Covenants*, 2:31 (III.12.lxxxi–lxxxii).
73. Ed. note: Calvin's clearest statement on this matter is found in a letter written to fellow reformer Martin Bucer: "Philosophy is, consequently, the noble gift of God, and those learned men who have striven hard after it in all ages have been incited thereto by God himself, that they might enlighten the world in the knowledge of the truth." Calvin, *Letters*, 2:213 = *Opera Omnia*, IX.B ["Epistolae"], 50 (letter 236); cf. *Institutes*, II.ii.15.

dition, provides power to fulfill the command of love. Christian morality is a doctrine of life, not merely a doctrine of language. God does not only command, he *gives*.[74] Further, while the pagans have only outstanding men and women as examples,[75] we have the patriarchs, the prophets, the apostles, the angels, yes, Christ himself.[76]

c. The *goal* of philosophical virtues is always situated within this life. When the purpose of this life is situated within this life itself, we are confronted with an antinomy. Life's purpose must be located beyond this life, and philosophical morality does not know that.[77] Thus, virtue is always sought for its own sake, for the sake of utility and advantage, for the sake of the fame that virtue brings, for the rewards that virtue may involve, for the sake of neighbors, but always within this life.[78] In Cicero's dialogue *The Nature of the Gods*, Cotta says that virtues are our own work, that we do not thank the gods for them.[79] By contrast, Christian ethics is not utilitarian, but directs everything to glorify God. It sees glorifying God as the goal of our lives.[80]

In summary.[81] In spiritual, heavenly matters, knowledge, will, and ability have been entirely lost. In moral and civil matters, in temporal, earthly matters, knowledge, will, and ability have been weakened, but not entirely taken away. There is therefore a certain good, measured by an earthly, temporal standard—and by natural persons themselves—that acquires temporal rewards. In themselves those virtues are good. But evaluated by the measure of God's holiness, the best virtues are splendid vices. They are completely wrong in their foundation, in the standard by which they are measured, and in their goal. This assessment of the philosophical virtues is severe but must be maintained on the basis of Holy Scripture and to hold high the exalted demand of the moral ideal. In the next chapter we will consider what morality is, from which foundation it flows (reason or feeling, for example), and what its value is.

74. Calvin's teaching, according to Lobstein: *Die Ethik Calvins*, 1:10–12; cf. *Institutes*, I.xvii.4; III.vi.2–4.
75. Seneca, *Moral Letters*, letters 6, 11, 20, 53 (vol. 1), 94, 103, 104 (vol. 3).
76. See, e.g., Witsius, *Economy of the Covenants*, 2:32 (III.12.lxxxvi).
77. *Institutes*, III.vii.1; III.vi.3; see Lobstein, *Die Ethik Calvins*, 10.
78. Witsius, *Economy of the Covenants*, 2:35–36 (III.12.xcvi).
79. Cicero, *De natura deorum* III.36.
80. 1 Cor. 10:31: "So, whether you eat or drink, or whatever you do, do all to the glory of God." Bavinck's marginal note: See also Heidelberg Catechism, Q&A 91, on perfection, pleasing God, and merit.
81. See Heppe, *Reformed Dogmatics*, 364–70; Polyander et al., *Synopsis Purioris Theologiae*, 1:416–19 (disp. XVII.18–24).

5. *Human Dominion over Nature*

Our dominion over nature has been weakened and robbed of its spiritual character, but it has not been eliminated.[82] Dominion has been impeded, not destroyed. Adam must now labor by the sweat of his brow against thorns and thistles, but he still wrests his food from the earth (Gen. 3). Human dominion now involves "fear and dread" of humans "upon every beast of the earth and upon every bird of the heavens, upon everything that creeps on the ground and all the fish of the sea" (Gen. 9:2). Animals and green plants have been given to us as food (Gen. 9:3).

Nonetheless, as Psalm 8 testifies, human royal dominion remains, together with wealth and culture, as part of God's rich provision, given to us to enjoy (1 Tim. 6:17). Dominion gives rise to culture, and culture has two parts:

a. *Science/scholarship*.[83] Knowledge of earthly things is possible, and there is a yearning to find out the truth about them. This is the basis of science and scholarship (law, medicine, mathematics, literature, and the liberal arts). These are the natural sciences,[84] with philosophy as their crown. These gifts of the Spirit should not be rejected or despised, for that would be to despise God himself.[85] Pagans themselves admit that philosophy, the arts, sciences, and laws were gifts from the gods. We cannot read the writings of the ancients without great admiration.[86] If by the Lord's will we can be helped by the activities of evil persons in the study of nature, in logic, in mathematics, let us then use these things. Zwingli said that whatever the pagans said that is good and beautiful, we accept and convert to the glory of our God. We decorate the temple of the true God with the spoils of the Egyptians.[87]

b. *Art* in the broader sense, the subjection of the earth, making the earth an instrument for humanity. The spiritual character of culture has been lost through sin. Culture itself has become a power, like science often becomes,

82. Van Mastricht, *Theoretico-Practica Theologia*, I.iv.4, §14 [2:650]. Ed. note: For an explanation of the format we are using to cite this work, see the extended note in the introduction, §1, in the section "Reformed Churches" (pp. 8–9n48). The volume and page numbers come from the 1749–53 Dutch edition used by Bavinck.

83. Calvin, *Institutes*, II.ii.13–19. Ed. note: We have used the double term "science/scholarship" because Bavinck's term *wetenschap* is broader than the English word "science," which is usually taken to refer to the natural or physical sciences.

84. Ed. note: Here too Bavinck is not restricting the term "natural sciences" to the "physical sciences" (physics, chemistry, biology) but is using it of the world of science and scholarship more broadly. "Nature" includes human beings, their abilities, and their activities.

85. Calvin, *Institutes*, II.ii.15. See also Calvin's commentary on Titus 1:12, in which he writes, "For since all truth is of God, if any ungodly man has said anything true, we should not reject it, for it also has come from God" (Calvin, *2 Corinthians, Timothy, Titus, Philemon*, 364).

86. Calvin, *Institutes*, II.ii.16.

87. Bavinck, *De ethiek van Ulrich Zwingli*, 28.

a fire fanned by Satan and used against God. It arose in the generations of Cain. The children of this world "are more shrewd in dealing with their own generation than the sons of light" (Luke 16:8). But for the rest, culture itself has increased, and in this there is doubtless progress. In Paradise, Adam and Eve were still clothed with animal skins (Gen. 3:21). By the time of Cain and Abel, we read of agriculture and animal husbandry; Cain and Enoch built cities; Lamech developed weaponry and the laws of war; Jabal made tents and led a nomadic life; Jubal created music; Tubal-Cain worked with iron; and Noah produced wine.[88] According to Holy Scripture there is progress in culture.

88. Zöckler, *Die Lehre vom Urstand*, 79.

5

Human Conscience

Although fallen human beings are spiritually dead, the sagas and saga complexes of peoples point to traditions of religious and moral wisdom that are as old as humanity itself. Included are kernels of truth concerning God, the soul, and conscience, particularly found in philosophy and in the great thinkers, that point to something present in human beings themselves which connects them to God. Tradition directs us to conscience.

Conscience is a general human phenomenon. Greco-Roman reflection on conscience was minimal so long as law, justice, and morality coincided with the objective law of the polis. In this case, subjective conscience played very little or no role in governing individual morality. With the collapse of the Greek city-states, people were directed to themselves and had to find moral certitudes within themselves; in that context, Cicero could write: "There is no greater theater for virtue than conscience."

The Old Testament has no specific word for conscience, but its "matter" is described by the important role given to the "heart." There are also clear testimonies concerning conscience (Joseph's brothers, David after the census, Solomon's dedicatory temple prayer). The idea of conscience is also found in Jesus's parable of the prodigal son and in the story of the woman caught in adultery. The apostle Paul frequently uses the Greek word for conscience and does so in a variety of ways. Gentile pagans and Jews as well as Christians are said to have a conscience; for none of them is the conscience an entirely reliable guide; our consciences are all darkened.

Christian reflection on conscience began in the early church (Tertullian, Clement of Alexandria, Chrysostom, and especially, Jerome), flourished in the Middle Ages (notably with Thomas Aquinas), and was highlighted among the early Reformers, whose actions were driven by conscience. The orthodox Protestant theologians of the seventeenth century, and particularly the Puritan writers (Perkins, Ames), carefully analyzed the movements of the conscience in order to provide practical spiritual guidance to Christians. They created and used careful distinctions between such dimensions and activities of the human soul as the law of the syntērēsis, *the witness of conscience, and judgment of the person. Modern thought, beginning with Kant, detached conscience from God and his law and placed it in the autonomous moral will. In modern philosophy, conscience is an enlightening, infallible, and undeceived star. Others (John Stuart Mill, Alexander Bain, Herbert Spencer) reduce conscience to social forces and see it as a product of nurture. Add into this mix the teachings of Charles Darwin's theory of evolution, and our contemporary world is filled with questions about conscience, including questions about the origin of conscience, whether it is religious or moral, positive as well as negative, and infallible or erring, and whether we have freedom of conscience or not.*

Etymologies can assist us in defining the notion of conscience. Included in the key terms are ideas of self-awareness, self-knowledge, and self-testimony about my conduct. Using our reason, we form judgments about our own conduct on the basis of God's law, which lies in our heart. This law of the conscience is called the "syntērēsis." It comes from God, to whom alone it is subject. To the degree that it is common to all people, it contains natural principles of religion, morality, and justice and is called a "natural conscience." For those regenerated by the Holy Spirit, enlightened consciences are those bound to the Word of God. No person or human authority may bind the conscience; only he who created and knows the conscience can bind and punish it.

Conscience in its proper sense is that power or activity in a person's understanding that, bound to the law of God in the syntērēsis, *judges the actions of a person observed by means of the consciousness, according to that law. It is we ourselves who do this judging; we accuse, convict and sentence, avenge and execute ourselves. Compelled to acknowledge God as God, we justify his judgment on us. This judgment is both religious and moral. The conscience judges everything about us, our actions, being, and thought. Nothing in us or done by us is outside God's law. Furthermore, conscience judges past acts, present acts, and future intended acts. The judgment is carried out as a practical syllogism where the* syntērēsis *(i.e., law or Word of God) provides the major premise and consciousness supplies the minor premise. The conscience draws the conclusion and renders judgment. This judgment accuses and condemns or exonerates and acquits.*

Consciences may be distinguished in various ways: as natural (pagan) or Christian (enlightened), as good or bad, as upright or erring, as assured or doubting, as strong or weak, as broad or narrow (scrupulous), as sleeping or alert. We are under obligation to have our consciences cleansed by the blood of Christ and strengthened by the Word of God. Conscience is universal, and God's moral law immutable and valid for all people. However, because our moral knowledge is darkened by sin, all of us have abnormal consciences. Conscience binds only the subject and no one else; we must respect each other's conscience, and all earthly authority must honor it. No one should ever be compelled against their conscience.

§14. THE CONSCIENCE

Introduction: Creation and Fall

The fall into sin did not formally remove from humans the substance of their knowledge of spiritual things—namely, of the knowledge and worship of God and of the moral law. They also retained the system of their ideas about the spiritual world, continuing to know who God was and what his law required. This knowledge and worship of God remained pure for a long time. Nevertheless, as a consequence of the fall, Adam died spiritually so that the system of ideas about the spiritual world was severed from its root in his heart. Thus torn asunder, this became a loose set of unconnected ideas languishing in his consciousness and doomed to wither away unless God were to plant again a spiritual life and a life-principle, a life-root, in his heart.

Adam was therefore in the same condition as an unregenerate Christian, one who has an intellectual knowledge of God, his law, and his word, but no spiritual knowledge, one for whom this knowledge lies loosely in the brain. But that knowledge of God that Adam still retained he did pass on; it remained pure in a few families and was thus salvific since the promise of Genesis 3:15 was also passed on along with it.[1] In this way the pure worship of God continued in the families of Abel, Seth, Enoch, and so forth. Even Melchizedek and Job apparently drew their true knowledge of God from the well of tradition. Thus, of its own accord, a tradition came into being that undergirded and undergirds all searching for and knowledge of God. This tradition became more or less tainted, was sometimes completely debased (eventually giving rise to paganism), separating itself from the invisible world, sinking into nature and divinizing it.

Indeed, tradition is a significant power and of great value. Out of reaction against Roman Catholicism, Protestants have often undervalued it. Tradition is the bond that unites people spiritually into one, in spite of separation by distance and time, so that we do not live spiritually and morally as isolated individuals. Instead, we all stand in a spiritual solidarity that reflects numerous

---

1. Ed. note: See *RD*, 3:241.

antecedents and connections with other people; it is the continuity of the spiritual and moral life.[2] Tradition is to the spiritual life what generation is to physical-biological life. It is manifest particularly in our religious life, which differs from our civic life, which is subject to countless changes. Religion creates community and pushes us toward unity and even uniformity. Thus we encounter the power of tradition in the sagas and their systems, which endure through the ages and are present in all peoples. These hark back to the primeval sagas,[3] which were fashioned from what was received from the Adamic and Noahic traditions by the tribes that came from a primeval home.[4] Tradition, therefore, is a binding power, stronger than natural bonds, something that Rome has understood well.[5] We must certainly derive many kernels of truth from the pagans by way of that tradition. But often too much has been derived from it. Some Christian apologists claim that all truth among pagans such as Plato was drawn from the Old Testament or the tradition that gave birth to the Old Testament. This is a mistake for two reasons: (1) those elements of truth concerning God, the soul, and conscience could not, any more than other spiritual knowledge, exist apart from a point of contact within the person, but are completely corrupted; and (2) those elements of truth we encounter most purely and clearly not in the sagas and religions of peoples but in their philosophy, among the thinkers, the people of reason. In this way, tradition itself directs us to conscience (and to reason).

Teachings about Conscience: A History[6]

GREEK AND ROMAN PHILOSOPHY

Greeks used the terms *syneidos* and *syneidēsis* for conscience; the Romans, *conscientia*. We do not encounter these terms at all first in Greek and Roman literature; they did exist, however, as did the matter itself, but only in the popular mind. The existence of the terms is apparent from the proverbs of Bias—"Good (or "clear") conscience"—and of Periander—"Freedom is a clear conscience."[7] (At the same time, are these sayings genuine?) We do not find the word *syneidēsis* in Socrates, Plato, or Aristotle at all. It is found first

---

2. Gunning, *Overlevering en wetenschap.*
3. GO: *Ursagen.*
4. DO: *urwoonplaats.*
5. Tschackert, "Tradition." Ed. note: An abbreviated version can be found in *Schaff-Herzog,* 11:437–38.
6. Kähler, *Das Gewissen.*
7. GrO: ὀρθὴ συνείδησις; ἀγαθὴ ἡ συνείδησις. Ed. note: Bias of Priene (sixth century BC) and Periander of Corinth (ruled over Corinth 627–587 BC) were two of the so-called Seven Sages of ancient Greece.

in Chrysippus, but then in the broader sense of consciousness.[8] It began to
be used in a philosophical sense near the start of the Christian era, especially
among Romans such as Cicero and Seneca. Subsequently, it was used among
Greek historians such as Dionysius of Halicarnassus (ca. 60 BC to 7 BC),
Diodorus Siculus (first century BC), and Plutarch (AD 46 to 120) and then
among the Hellenists.

This is an important observation. Why is there relatively little mention of the
conscience among the Greeks and Romans when it is such a universal human
phenomenon? And why did philosophy pay no attention to this important
factor in its early days and deal with it only later? Kähler attributes this to two
causes.[9] (1) For Socrates and Plato, ancient ethics was characterized by its inner,
indissoluble connection with the Greek polis.[10] Virtue was limited to this sphere,
and to be a good person was to be a good citizen. For the Greek, the norms for
morality, for the good, were objectively present in the laws of the polis and were
not specified by the acting subject in their conscience. As the people thought,
so thought the philosophical ethicists. In Plato's dialogue *Hippias Major*, when
Socrates is asked, "What is good?," he points to the polis: "That which is lawful
is just."[11] In other words, the law, justice, and morality coincide. Whoever observes the written and unwritten laws of the polis is perfectly righteous. Among
the gods as well, justice and law are one; morality and politics coincide. It follows from this that human conduct was always tested not by one's subjective
conscience but by the law of the polis. Therefore, not the conscience but this
law functioned to accuse or exonerate. (2) The Greek philosophical ethicists,
Socrates, Plato, and Aristotle, were intellectualists; this meant that they sought
the starting point and standard for conduct in human reason rather than in the

---

8. Ed. note: Chrysippus of Soli in Cilicia (ca. 279–ca. 206 BC) was a Greek Stoic philosopher.
Bavinck refers at this point to Diogenes Laertius, *Lives and Opinions of Eminent Philosophers*
7.85 ("Zeno"): "An animal's first impulse, say the Stoics, is to self-preservation, because nature from the outset endears it to itself, as Chrysippus affirms. . . . 'The dearest thing to every
animal is its own constitution and its consciousness thereof'" (trans. Hicks, LCL, 2:293). Cf.
the translation by Yonge (p. 290): "They say that the first inclination which an animal has is to
protect itself, as nature brings herself to take an interest in it from the beginning, as Chrysippus
affirms in the first book of his treatise on Ends; where he says, that the first and dearest object
to every animal is its own existence, and its consciousness of that existence [τὴν αὑτοῦ σύστασιν
καὶ τὴν ταύτην συνείδησιν]."

9. Kähler, "Gewissen," 151.

10. Ed. note: Bavinck uses the word "state" (*staat*) in this section; we have chosen to retain
the original Greek word *polis* because "state" fails to capture the meaning of key terms such
as τὴν σαυτοῦ πόλιν ("his own polis") and πολιτικῶν πράξεων ("activities for the common life
of the polis").

11. GrO: τὸ νόμιμόν δίκαιον εἶναι. Ed. note: In the opening of Plato's *Hippias Major*, Socrates
describes a "truly wise and perfect man" as one who in public affairs benefits his own polis
(τὴν σαυτοῦ πόλιν).

conscience. Proper thinking was extended and transposed into proper conduct. Thereby moral lapses became the result of intellectual error; knowing was and became virtue. Within this kind of ethic there was no place for conscience; reason was sovereign and the will had to follow.

All this changed with and through Alexander the Great. The life of the polis lost much of its significance, and objectivity became unstable. People were directed to themselves and had to find certitude, including moral certitude, within themselves. Individualism and cosmopolitanism gained the ascendency, and philosophy turned more and more to practical matters, coming down from its sovereign heights to answer questions of daily living (Stoicism, Epicureanism, etc.). Consequently, the conscience acquired a stronger voice in life and in philosophy. In Cicero's words: "There is no greater theater for virtue than conscience."[12] Especially with Cicero, conscience has a broad sense (consciousness) as well as a narrow sense (conscience). In his defense of his friend Titius Annius Milo, accused of murder (52 BC), Cicero appealed to conscience as overriding law: "The power of the conscience is great."[13] In his treatise *The Nature of the Gods*,[14] Cicero points out that evildoers are not always punished in this life and then adds this reflection:

> It is with reluctance that I enlarge upon this topic, since you may think that my discourse lends authority to sin; and you would be justified in so thinking, were not an innocent or guilty conscience so powerful a force in itself, without the assumption of any divine design. Destroy this, and everything collapses; for just as a household or a state appears to lack all rational system and order if in it there are no rewards for right conduct and no punishments for transgression, so there is no such thing at all as the divine governance of the world if that governance makes no distinction between the good and the wicked.[15]

A Latin proverb declares: "Conscience is a thousand witnesses."[16] Seneca and the Hellenists held similar views, especially Philo, who regards conscience primarily as punitive because our moral situation is especially imperfect. The most he will say is that it accuses.[17]

12. LO: *"nullum theatrum virtuti conscientia majus est"* (Cicero, *Tusculan Disputations* II.26 [trans. Yonge, p. 90]).
13. LO: *"magna est vis conscientiae"* (Cicero, *For Milo* 61 [trans. Yonge]). Ed. note: The full passage reads: "The power of conscience is very great, O judges, and is of great weight on both sides: so that they fear nothing who have done no wrong, and they, on the other hand, who have done wrong think that banishment is always hanging over them."
14. *De natura deorum.*
15. Cicero, *De natura deorum* III.35 (85) (trans. Rackham, pp. 370–73).
16. LO: *conscientia mille testes.*
17. GrO: ἐλέγχει.

CONSCIENCE IN SCRIPTURE

The Old Testament has no specific word for conscience, and the matter does not come up often. For Israel, the law fulfilled the task of the conscience; the focus of the conscience was not the acting subject, but God's will; the norms and thus the judge of all conduct were to be found only in the law. According to Oehler, "the good was placed before [Adam] objectively, in the form of a *command*."[18] And further, "by bringing man to a consciousness of the essential nature of a higher divine righteousness, the law roused the conscience from its slumber, taught men to recognize wickedness as sin, and so made the need of reconciliation with God to be felt."[19]

Nonetheless, the matter of the conscience is present in the Old Testament and is attributed to the heart. As Oehler puts it,

> The heart, as the central organ of the circulation of the blood, forms the focus of the life of the body. . . . But the heart is also the centre of all spiritual functions. Everything spiritual, whether belonging to the intellectual, moral, or pathological sphere, is appropriated and assimilated by man in the heart as a common meeting-place, and is again set in circulation from the heart. All vital motions of the soul proceed from the heart, and react upon it.[20]

The roots of our knowing, willing, and feeling spring forth from the heart and flow out to all life (Prov. 4:23). "In particular, the heart (Prov. xx:27) is the place in which the process of self-consciousness goes on,—in which the soul is at home with itself, and is conscious of all its doing and suffering as its own. The heart, therefore, is also the organ of the conscience, Job xxvii.6."[21] In Genesis 3 this is manifest in shame. According to Oehler, "When the woman, [Gen.] iii.2f., remembers the divine command, and knows that she is bound by it, and thus acknowledges its obligatory force, she has not yet sinned, and yet she shows that she has a conscience."[22] However, the question remains whether this should already be called conscience.

In the Old Testament, we find clear testimony concerning conscience: Joseph's brothers acknowledge their guilt with respect to their brother (Gen. 42:21); after cutting off a corner of Saul's robe, "David's heart struck him" (1 Sam. 24:5). Abigail pleads with David to forgive her husband Nabal's foolish

18. Oehler, *Theology of the Old Testament*, 158 (§73).
19. Oehler, *Theology of the Old Testament*, 183 (§84).
20. Oehler, *Theology of the Old Testament*, 153 (§71).
21. Oehler, *Theology of the Old Testament*, 153 (§71).
22. Oehler, *Theology of the Old Testament*, 158 (§73); cf. C. I. Nitzsch, *System of Christian Doctrine*, 207–8 (§98).

actions so that David would "have no cause of grief, or pangs of conscience, for having shed blood without cause" (1 Sam. 25:31); and, after he sinned in taking a census of the people, "David's heart struck him" (2 Sam. 24:10). In 1 Kings 2:44 Solomon tells Shimei, "You know in your own heart [i.e., you are conscious of] all the harm that you did to David my father." In his prayer dedicating the temple, Solomon asks God to attend to pleas made by anyone or all the people, "each knowing the affliction of his own heart," and forgive them (1 Kings 8:38). Similarly, the book of Job portrays the wicked as writhing in pain and filled with distress and anguish (Job 15:20–25); by contrast, Job clings to his integrity: "My lips will not speak falsehood, and my tongue will not utter deceit. Far be it from me to say that you are right; till I die I will not put away my integrity from me. I hold fast my righteousness and will not let it go; my heart does not reproach me for any of my days" (Job 27:4–6). This is a locus classicus. We also take note of those psalms in which the poet declares his innocence (Pss. 17:3; 18:32) and those in which he is profoundly aware of his guilt (6:2–7; 32:4; 51).[23] It is the heart that accuses: "Your heart knows that many times you yourself have cursed others" (Eccles. 7:22); "The sin of Judah is written with a pen of iron; with a point of diamond it is engraved on the tablet of their heart, and on the horns of their altars" (Jer. 17:1). The prophet Jeremiah cannot resist God's call: "If I say, 'I will not mention him, or speak any more in his name,' there is in my heart as it were a burning fire shut up in my bones, and I am weary with holding it in, and I cannot" (Jer. 20:9). The same prophet signals a *new covenant* "with the house of Israel after those days, declares the LORD: I will put my law within them, and I will write it on their hearts. And I will be their God, and they shall be my people" (Jer. 31:33). Whether hearts are bold or timid is ascribed to guilty and unburdened consciences, respectively: "The wicked flee when no one pursues, but the righteous are bold as a lion" (Prov. 28:1). Luther even translated "heart" as "conscience" in Joshua 14:7 ("I was forty years old when Moses the servant of the LORD sent me from Kadesh-barnea to spy out the land, and I brought him word again as it was in my heart") and in Job 27:6 ("I hold fast my righteousness and will not let it go; my heart does not reproach me for any of my days").[24]

In the New Testament, Jesus never speaks of the conscience, which is a great disappointment for the modernists. In Matthew 6:22—"The eye is the lamp of the body"—Jesus is referring to the capacity for the human mind to know the eternal, to reason, to the human spirit, and to the light of nature

---

23. J. König, *Die Theologie der Psalmen*, 376–79.

24. GO from the 1545 Luther Bible: "Und ich ihm Bericht gab nach meinem Gewissen; von meiner Gerechtigkeit, die ich habe, will ich nicht lassen; mein Gewissen beißt mich nicht meines ganzen Lebens halben."

(retained by humans after the fall).[25] The idea of conscience, however, can be found in the story of the prodigal son: "But when he came to himself . . ."[26] (Luke 15:17). The word *syneidēsis* is found in some of the text traditions of the Gospel of John (8:9). After Jesus says about the woman caught in adultery, "Let him who is without sin among you be the first to throw a stone at her" (v. 7), and Jesus writes on the ground, this follows: "And they which heard it, being convicted by their own conscience [*syneidēseōs*], went out one by one, beginning at the eldest, even unto the last: and Jesus was left alone, and the woman standing in the midst."[27]

It is the apostle Paul who more frequently uses the word *syneidēsis*:

And looking intently at the council, Paul said, "Brothers, I have lived my life before God in all good conscience up to this day." (Acts 23:1)

So I always take pains to have a clear conscience toward both God and man. (Acts 24:16)

Therefore one must be in subjection, not only to avoid God's wrath but also for the sake of conscience. (Rom. 13:5)

But some, through former association with idols, eat food as really offered to an idol, and their conscience, being weak, is defiled. (1 Cor. 8:7; cf. 8:12–9:27; 10:23–33; Rom. 14)

Paul defends his own conduct by appealing to his clear conscience (1 Cor. 4:4; 2 Cor. 1:12; 4:2; 5:11). In his charge to Timothy and his description of true faith and godly conduct, Paul repeatedly mentions conscience (1 Tim. 1:5, 19; 3:9; 4:2; 2 Tim. 1:3; Titus 1:15). In addition, we find the idea of conscience, as well as the word *syneidēsis*, in Hebrews 4:12; 5:14; 9:9, 14; 10:2, 22; and 13:18. The apostle Peter also uses it (1 Pet. 2:19; 3:16, 21).[28]

We will now sketch a summary of New Testament teaching on conscience.

We encounter the word *syneidēsis* first in the general sense of awareness or knowledge: "By the open statement of the truth we would commend ourselves

25. GrO: νοῦς; τὸ πνεῦμα; LO: *lumen naturae*. See Calvin, *Harmony*, 1:218; cf. Tholuck, *Ausführliche Auslegung der Bergpredigt*, 402.

26. GrO: εἰς ἑαυτὸν δὲ ἐλθών.

27. Ed. note: John 7:53–8:11 is not found in the oldest and most reliable manuscripts, as all readers of contemporary translations such as the RSV, NIV, and so forth know. Our translation of this verse comes from the KJV.

28. On conscience in Paul and other New Testament writers, see Ernesti, *Die Ethik des Apostels Paulus*, 22–24; Smeding, *Paulinische Gewetensleer*; Kähler, "Gewissen," 152–53; Kähler and Schultze, "Gewissen"; Kähler, *Das Gewissen*, 225–73, 281–85; Vilmar, *Theologische Moral*, 1:72–99; Cremer, *Biblico-Theological Lexicon*, 233–35, s.v. "συνείδησις."

to everyone's conscience in the sight of God" (2 Cor. 4:2); "Therefore, knowing the fear of the Lord, we persuade others. But what we are is known to God, and I hope it is known also to your conscience" (2 Cor. 5:11). Beyond this it acquires the significance of a testimony present to my consciousness concerning my circumstances and relationships, a critical self-awareness, in other words: "I am speaking the truth in Christ—I am not lying; my conscience bears me witness in the Holy Spirit" (Rom. 9:1); "For our boast is this, the testimony of our conscience, that we behaved in the world with simplicity and godly sincerity, not by earthly wisdom but by the grace of God, and supremely so toward you" (2 Cor. 1:12). In the third place, conscience has the meaning of moral obligation, being bound in our conduct by a conformity to God's law and will: "They show that the work of the law is written on their hearts, while their conscience also bears witness, and their conflicting thoughts accuse or even excuse them" (Rom. 2:15). Conscience is therefore a religious designation, as Peter demonstrates when he gives thanks for those who endure grief and suffer wrongfully "for conscience toward God" (1 Pet. 2:19 KJV)—that is, a conscience that bears witness in relation to God.[29] Similarly, civil authorities are "servants of God" to whom we are subject, "not only to avoid God's wrath, but also for the sake of conscience" (Rom. 13:5).[30] The inadequacy of the old covenant is described in terms of "gifts and sacrifices . . . that cannot perfect the conscience of the worshiper" (Heb. 9:9). Only "the blood of Christ, who through the eternal Spirit offered himself without blemish to God," is able to "purify our conscience from dead works to serve the living God" (Heb. 9:14; cf. 10:2).

Consequently, the conscience provides the judgment of human beings about themselves in their existing relationship to God, his law, and his will.[31] That law and will of God—in other words, God himself—in relation to which people consider themselves bound in their conscience and in terms of which they evaluate themselves in their conscience, is unchanging and remains eternally the same. But that law can change within the subject's conscience itself, according to the subject's level of development, moral nurture, and knowledge; that is to say, the conscience can interpret and impurely reflect that law, which itself is immutable. That results from the conscience itself being impure, corrupted by sin. The New Testament describes this unclean conscience in

29. GrO: διὰ συνείδησιν θεοῦ.
30. GrO: ἀλλὰ καὶ διὰ τὴν συνείδησιν.
31. DO: *oordeel*; Cremer, *Biblico-Theological Lexicon*, 234: "Συνείδησις is not merely the testimony to one's own conduct borne by consciousness . . . but, at the same time also that concerning duty, . . . namely, the obligation to divinely ordered action, even where God is not known. . . . Συνείδησις, accordingly, is *the consciousness man has of himself in his relation to God*, manifesting itself in the form of a self-testimony, the result of the action of the spirit in the heart."

various ways: "weak conscience" (John 8:9; 1 Cor. 8:7; cf. v. 10; 2 Cor. 7:1);
"whose consciences are seared" (1 Tim. 4:2); "their minds and their consciences
are defiled" (Titus 1:15). In the light of the Holy Spirit's work of applying
Christ's sacrifice, the contrast is palpable: "How much more will the blood of
Christ, who through the eternal Spirit offered himself without blemish to God,
purify our conscience from dead works to serve the living God" (Heb. 9:14);
"consciousness of sin" (Heb. 10:2); "sprinkled clean from an evil conscience
and our bodies washed with pure water" (Heb. 10:22).

This explains why consciences differ, also individually, among Jews, pagans,
and Christians. We first consider the pagan gentiles. According to Romans 2:14–
15, gentiles lack the positive revealed law (Torah) of Moses. Nonetheless, they
"by nature do what the law requires." Paul does not have in mind here the "doers
of the law" of whom he spoke in verse 13, those who are justified. If that were
the case, he would be saying that the pagan gentiles are saved (cf. v. 27). Pagans
do not keep the law in its deep spiritual significance and fullness (Rom. 7:14),
but they nonetheless externally obey the commandments in varying degrees.
Therefore, they have the "works of the law" (Rom. 2:15) just as the Jews do,
but nonetheless remain hearers rather than doers of the law. In this way pagans
show that they are obligated by nature[32] to the law and thus become a law for
themselves, giving them a positive law, the Mosaic law in the sense of individual,
external commandments. This is identical, says Paul, to the way Jews consider
the law of Moses, and for that reason the Jews with their law, as they understand
it, are no better off than gentiles. In fact, pagans derive the law from themselves,
showing that the "works of the law," the individual commandments of the law,
are written in their hearts (in contrast to being written on stone tablets, as with
Israel). And with those external deeds, which show the existence of the law
among pagans, their conscience agrees; that conscience also testifies accordingly
in connection with the law (here what is meant is the "subsequent conscience";
the law in their heart is the "antecedent conscience").[33] That personal conscience
is manifest in the public conscience, in the thoughts that combine to accuse or
exonerate them. In addition to personal conduct and personal conscience, this
public conscience is, so to speak, a third testimony and proof for the law having
been written in their heart. An important caution here: conscience is not identical with the law nor the seat of the law. Here too, among pagans, conscience
can excuse, and then it is classified as "good conscience."

The law is written in the heart, but the conscience is a being-bound to
this law and its testimony. Among the Jews, conscience was a being-bound

---

32. GrO: φύσει.
33. LO: *conscientia consequens*; *conscientia antecedens*.

to the objectively delivered Mosaic law, and its functioning involved that law. Concurring with that law leads to a clear conscience, a good conscience (Acts 23:1; 24:14–16; 2 Tim. 1:3). Nevertheless, this could perhaps be understood as Paul referring to a Christian conscience. Pagans and Jews can therefore have a "good" conscience—namely, one that does not condemn them—but this does not mean that it is pure. After all, the conscience can interpret the law falsely and give rise to a false security. The conscience, therefore, must be purified, and that has happened and is happening for believing Christians through the blood of Christ (Heb. 9:14). At that point, they receive a "purified conscience" (1 Tim. 3:9; 2 Tim. 1:3), a "good conscience" (Acts 23:1; 1 Tim. 1:5, 19; 1 Pet. 3:16, 21), a "clear conscience" (Acts 24:16). However, even among believers, the conscience is not immediately perfected or healthy. For many, the conscience remains weak (1 Cor. 8:7; 10:12; cf. 1 Cor. 10; Rom. 14) and must therefore be spared. It can still be bound to idols, to pagan laws and customs, from which it must gradually be set free to be bound solely and most strictly to God and his law. In other words, the activity of the conscience must be determined by the Holy Spirit alone (Rom. 9:1). The testimony of the conscience must be the witness of the Holy Spirit. Here we also need to appeal to 1 John 3:18–20, where the activity of the conscience is ascribed to the heart: "Whenever our heart condemns us, God is greater than our heart."

CHURCH FATHERS AND SCHOLASTIC THEOLOGIANS[34]

The church fathers provide very little about the conscience. In their opposition to pagans, they do not appeal to conscience but to objective revelation, to miracles and so forth. Tertullian's "testimony of the soul naturally Christian"[35] acknowledges an inclination to morality just as the soul, though enslaved to the body and to false gods, when it awakes and "comes to itself," spontaneously speaks of God, using such expressions as "God is great and good," "which God may give," "God sees," "I commend myself to God," and "God will repay me."[36] At the same time, such ordinary human morality is not sufficient; it must be Christian.

Nonetheless, here and there, we do find references to the conscience, even if only occasioned by the exposition of Holy Scripture, therefore primarily in exegetical works. Thus, especially in Clement of Alexandria, a good conscience keeps the soul pure and preserves it from ignorance.[37] Even more so

---

34. Kähler, "Gewissen," 153–55; Kähler and Schultze, "Gewissen," 242–43.
35. LO: *testimonium animae naturaliter christianae.*
36. Tertullian, *Apology* XVII (*ANF* 3:32).
37. Clement of Alexandria, *Miscellanies* VI.14 (*ANF* 2:506).

in Chrysostom, who says in a sermon on Genesis 27:42: "So let no one claim to be neglecting virtue through ignorance or through not having the way to it pointed out. In fact, we have an adequate instructor in our consciences, and it is not possible for anyone to be deprived of help from that source."[38] "For nothing is more pleasurable than a sound conscience, and a good hope."[39] And, on the other side of the coin: "For what pray is so painful as a bad conscience? or what more pleasing than a good hope? For there is nothing, assuredly there is nothing, which is used to cut us so deep, and press so hard on us, as the expectation of evil: nothing that so keeps us up, and all but gives us wings, as a good conscience."[40] The judgment of the conscience is not to be destroyed, because it is created within us by God. Conscience is an uncorrupted judge, from which we cannot escape. It cannot be bribed with money because it is divine, implanted within our souls by God himself. It is deaf to flattery, fear, or money. But, in addition to these general truths (found also among the pagans), Chrysostom believes that the conscience is an autonomous and autarchic source of moral insight, along with creation as the other original source of our knowledge of God.[41] With this, he points to a later motion, the so-called "antecedent" or "deontological"[42] conscience. In the West, preoccupied as it is with practice and anthropology, one might have expected more about the conscience. However, this is not the case. Augustine called the conscience an accuser, a witness to the depths of human depravity. A closer examination of conscience was made first by the medieval Scholastic theologians, especially after the publication of Alexander of Hales's *Summa Universae Theologiae*.[43]

Now, human persons were understood to have two faculties: intellect and will.[44] The former is manifest in two ways: as theoretical intellect[45] and as

38. Ed. note: John Chrysostom, *Homilies on Genesis* 54 (FC 87:92 [trans. Hill]; PG 54:472). For additional passages in Chrysostom on conscience, see Suicerus, *Thesaurus Ecclesiasticus*, 2:1154, s.v. "συνειδός." Laird (*Mindset, Moral Choice, and Sin*) examines Chrysostom's moral anthroplogy in detail and argues persuasively that the notion of γνώμη ("mind-set") as a faculty or power of the soul is the key to understanding Chrysostom. Calling attention to *Homilies* 11 and 13 on Romans (in addition to *Homily* 12), Laird claims that for Chrysostom, "the γνώμη controls the effect of the conscience (συνειδός). . . . In practice, conscience is subject to the whims and fancies of the γνώμη" (p. 74).

39. Ed. note: John Chrysostom, *Homilies on Matthew*, 2:726 (*Homily* 53, on Matt. 15:32).

40. Ed. note: John Chrysostom, *Homilies on Romans*, NPNF[1] 11:424 (*Homily* 12; Rom. 6:19); cf. *Homilies on 2 Corinthians*, NPNF[1] 12:286 (*Homily* 3; 2 Cor. 1:12).

41. John Chrysostom, *Homilies on Romans*, NPNF[1] 11:467–68 (*Homily* 16, on Rom. 9:20–21).

42. DO: *voorafgaand; bevelend*.

43. See *ST* Ia q. 79 art. 12; Ia IIae q. 94; Gass, *Geschichte der christlichen Ethik*, 1:383–92 (§122); Gass, *Die Lehre vom Gewissen*, 43, 216–28 (appendix on "Das scholastische Wort Synderesis").

44. LO: *intellectus*.

45. LO: *intellectus theoreticus*.

practical intellect.[46] These are not two different capabilities or powers;[47] rather, the former is directed to *the true* and the latter to *the good*. The practical intellect was called *synderesis* (or *syntērēsis*; "maintaining, protecting, observing"), "a term that is not frequently found in Greek literature, also not in the Greek fathers or in later Christian literature."[48] It was Jerome, in his exposition of Ezekiel, who is generally credited with introducing the term *synderesis/syntērēsis* into questions about morality.[49] With the interpreters of the early church, including Irenaeus and Augustine, Jerome takes the four creatures of Ezekiel 1:4–14 to be symbols of the four evangelists,[50] but also makes use of the creatures in a discussion of anthropology:[51]

> Most people interpret the man, the lion and the ox as the rational, emotional, and appetitive parts of the soul, following Plato's division, who calls them *logikon* and *thumikon* and *epithumētikon*, locating reason in the brain, emotion in the gall-bladder and appetite in the liver.[52]

46. LO: *intellectus practicus.*
47. LO: *diversae potentiae.*
48. Appel, *Die Lehre der Scholastiker*. See reviews of Appel by Rabus and F. Nitzsch. Ed. note: According to Gass, *synderesis* is an *"eingeführte Kunstausdruck"* ("borrowed neologism") that was "adopted" from the "academic Latin discourse of the Middle Ages" (*"lateinischen Gelehrten sprache des Mittelalters"*), but without the "explicit technical meaning" (*"ausdrücklichere technische Bestimmung"*) that it "demonstrably had in Greek" (Gass, *Die Lehre vom Gewissen*, 216). In a moral sense, συντήρησις has the idea of "holding fast to the law and commandments" (*Gesetz und Gebot*); Gass points to Luke 2:19; Matt. 9:17; Mark 6:20; and Luke 5:38 as examples (218). According to Muller, *Dictionary*, 294, s.v. *"synderesis/syntērēsis,"* *synderesis* or *syntērēsis* is *"the innate habit of the understanding which grasps basic principles of moral law apart from the activity of formal moral training . . .* used by the medieval scholastics as a synonym for the patristic term *scintilla conscientiae. . . . Synderesis* can be distinguished from *conscientia* in that the latter is an act while *synderesis* is a *habitus* or capacity."
49. Ed. note: Appel, *Die Lehre der Scholastiker*, 2: "Medieval theology brought back and grounded the doctrine of synteresis from Jerome's exposition of Ezekiel 1:4–10." Appel says that this significant term was "borrowed" (*entlehnt*) from Jerome and latinized.
50. Ed. note: Jerome, *Commentary on Matthew*, 55.
51. Ed. note: The remainder of this paragraph has been reconstructed and expanded by the editor. Bavinck provided only a few Latin fragments from Jerome's *Commentary* and mistakenly identifies *synderesis/syntērēsis* with the lion figure. In fact, after discussing the first three creatures (human, lion, ox) in terms of a Platonist tripartite anthropology (the reasoning, spirited, and desiring parts of the soul), Jerome links conscience to the eagle. It must not be overlooked that Jerome does not fully accept the Platonizing and allegorical Christian use of the Ezekiel vision (as Origen does, for example) but introduces it to point his readers to the importance of conscience, which he finds in the Pauline understanding of spirit (πνεῦμα). See Gass, *Gewissen*, 220–23.
52. LO: *anima rationale; anima irascitivium; anima concupiscitivium;* GrO: λογικόν; θυμικόν; ἐπιθυμητικόν. Ed. note: Jerome, *Commentary on Ezekiel* 1:7 (PL 25:22); the relevant passage in its context is provided by Gass, *Gewissen*, 220, and Appel, *Die Lehre der Scholastiker*, 2–3.

What about Ezekiel's fourth creature, the eagle? Jerome identifies this with the conscience, specifically the "spark of conscience, which [was] also in Adam's breast [understood as the seat of the affections], after he was cast out of Paradise, which is not extinguished, and by which, [still] nourished by pleasures or anger, we sometimes perceive, in something like a rational moment, that we sin."[53] Jerome goes on to speak of this as "conscience itself."[54] Jerome, therefore, understands *syntērēsis* simply as conscience. We do not know whether the word also had the meaning of maintaining or observing morality.[55] In fact, Cocceius denies this.[56]

Some scholars have argued that the term *syntērēsis* in Jerome's Ezekiel commentary is a textual mistake; it should be read as *syneidēsis*.[57] Erich Klostermann from the University of Kiel has recently discovered that three codices of Jerome's *Commentary* on Ezekiel do read *syneidēsis*.[58] In any case, Scholastic theologians used the term *synderesis/syntērēsis* for either a capacity (power) of the soul or as a natural habit of concrete activity.[59] In his *Summa theologiae*, Thomas raises the question of "whether synderesis is a special power of the soul distinct from the others."[60] In his response, he argues that it is not a "power" but a "habit":[61]

> Now it is clear that, as the speculative reason argues about speculative things, so that practical reason argues about practical things.[62] Therefore we must have, bestowed on us by nature, not only speculative principles, but also practical principles.[63] Now the first speculative principles bestowed on us by nature do not belong to a special power, but to a special habit, which is called "the understanding of principles,"[64] as the Philosopher explains (*Ethic.* vi, 6). Wherefore

53. LO: "*quae scintilla conscientiae in Adami quoque pectore, postquam ejectus est de paradiso, non extinguitur et qua, victi voluptatibus vel furore ipsaque interdum rationis similtudine nos peccare sentimus.*" Ed. note: This passage is found in Jerome's *Commentary on Ezekiel* 1:7 (*PL* 25:22); the relevant passage in its context is provided by Gass, *Gewissen*, 220, and Appel, *Die Lehre der Scholastik*, 2–3.

54. LO: *ipsa conscientia.*

55. According to Appel, *Die Lehre der Scholastiker.*

56. Ed. note: Bavinck refers simply to "Cocceius on 2 Tim. 1:15."

57. F. Nitzsch, "Über die Enstehung der scholastischen Lehre von der Synderesis."

58. Redaction, "Zur Synteresis-Frage."

59. LO: *intellectus practicus*; *potentia*; *habitus principiorum operabilium*. Ed. note: Bavinck indicates that this latter position was held by Thomas Aquinas and Saint Anthony of Florence (1389–1459), a Dominican who became Archbishop of Florence (1446–59).

60. *ST* Ia q. 79 art. 12.

61. LO: *potentia*; *habitus.*

62. LO: *ratio speculativa*; *ratio practica.*

63. LO: *principia speculabilium*; *principia operabilium.*

64. LO: *intellectus principiorum.*

the first practical principles,[65] bestowed on us by nature, do not belong to a special power, but to a special natural habit, which we call "synderesis."

In the same way, therefore, that we are born with the idea of true and false, so we are also born with the idea of good and evil. Simply as a habit, this *synderesis* is said to always incite one toward good and to oppose evil. Although it does not conduct specific activity, *synderesis* itself advances by protesting against that evil action.[66] The *synderesis* cannot sin; it cannot be extinguished, though it can be silenced. Even Satan retains it.

According to Thomas, the *synderesis* "is a habit containing the precepts of the natural law, which are the first principles of human action."[67] Scholastic theologians held firmly to this notion of *synderesis*, maintaining within it the human moral nature in the state of sin, and viewing it as the capacity to do good, in the same way that reason is the capacity to know the truth. Nevertheless, they did not for that reason deny the depth of sin, because this *synderesis* is inclined to the good in general, but it neither discloses the genuinely good (which is meritorious) nor leads one to perform it fully.

Synderesis is sharply distinguished from *conscientia*, which applies the *synderesis* to the particular and the concrete. Conscience is not a habit but an act.[68] In terms of a syllogism, *synderesis* is the major premise, and reason the minor premise, of an argument for determining whether a particular act is a duty or is to be repudiated. The conscience is therefore the "practical syllogism in the intellect."[69] From this, the conscience draws the conclusion—for example, this or that must be done or not. Those conclusions—that is, the functions of the conscience—are threefold: (1) to *witness*, whereby "we recognize that we have done or not done something," thus, merely consciousness; (2) to *bind*, or to "judge that something should be done or not done"; (3) to *incite*, whereby "we judge that something done is well done or ill done, and in this sense conscience is said to excuse, accuse, or torment."[70] Conscience, therefore, is always a "concluding knowledge," a derived, applied, subsequent knowing.[71]

65. LO: *principia operabilium*.
66. LO: *murmurare de male*; *ST* Ia q. 79 art. 12.
67. *ST* Ia IIae q. 94 art. 1.
68. LO: *habitus*.
69. LO: *syllogismus practicus in intellectu*. Ed. note: Bavinck's use of the term "practical syllogism" here needs to be distinguished from the way Reformed theology used it in connection with a believer's assurance of salvation being linked to the evidence of good works and sanctification in their life. On the moral syllogism linking *synderesis* and conscience, with conscience as a *concludens conscientia*, see Gass, *Gewissen*, 51. Gass attributes this all to Anthony of Florence, *Summa Moralis*, vol. 1, chap. 10.
70. LO: *testificatio*; *ligatio*; *concusatio*; *ST* Ia q. 79 art. 13.
71. LO: *concludens scientia*. Ed. note: See Gass, *Gewissen*, 51.

However, the conscience can frequently draw false conclusions (also because reason provides a false minor premise). In other words, the conscience can err, judging something to be evil when it is good or making wrong applications from premises or general principles that are good in themselves. This gives rise to consciences that are deceived, that doubt, that are overly scrupulous, perplexed, that are wrongly advised or are too accommodating. There is an ongoing, daily need for us to know with certainty how we should act. The medieval summaries of cases of conscience sought to meet that need.[72] These were manuals for the church's "confessors," which they could consult to find guidance from the collected writings of the church fathers. The confessors thus gained power of judgment over the consciences of their laity. They used painstakingly developed canon law to determine this. If the good that was required could not be determined, a person's doubting conscience could be pacified by giving a *probable* opinion.[73] This is the source of the terrible notion of *probabilism* that was developed later by the Jesuits. Here *synderesis* disappears completely, the conscience is regarded as a bias, and probabilism (with the authority of this bias) determines everything. It was Pascal's personal mission to oppose this.

The Scholastics, therefore, began by maintaining the moral human nature within the *synderesis*, but they separated and distinguished from it the conscience as something defective and erring. By means of that separation, the *synderesis* became inactive (a notion that contained a great truth). Meanwhile, the conscience, much too weak to stand on its own and be a guide, became subject to an alien authority.[74]

PROTESTANTS AND THE REFORMED TRADITION

The Protestant Reformation was an act of conscience, and in this way conscience is frequently discussed by Luther, Zwingli, and Calvin. Calvin defines conscience as a "sense of divine judgment,"[75] as a witness joined to them [human beings], which does not allow them to hide their sins from being accused before the Judge's tribunal." He adds that it is "a certain mean between God and man, because it does not allow man to suppress within himself what he knows, but pursues him to the point of convicting him."[76] Conscience provides "an awareness which hales man before God's judgment" and "is a

---

72. Ed. note: Such as Bartholomew of San Concordio (1262–1347), *Summa de Casibus Conscientiae.*
73. LO: *opinio probabilis* or *probabilior.*
74. According to Gass, *Gewissen*, 44.
75. LO: *sensus divini judicii.*
76. LO: *medium quoddam; Institutes,* III.xix.15; cf. IV.x.1.

sort of guardian appointed for man to note and spy out all his secrets that nothing may remain buried in darkness."[77] In the same way that "works have regard to men, so conscience refers to God."[78] Although "sometimes . . . it is also extended to men . . . properly speaking, . . . it has respect to God alone."[79] Calvin reiterates this in book IV of the *Institutes* in his discussion of church law: "For our consciences do not have to do with men but with God alone."[80] He adds: "While the whole world was shrouded in the densest darkness of ignorance, this tiny little spark of light remained, that men recognized man's conscience to be higher than all human judgments."[81] Calvin teaches us the following: (a) conscience is a knowledge of our deeds in relation to God, his judgment; (b) only God can bind the conscience and not any human person; (c) conscience is a witness, a guardian of our deeds; and (d) conscience stands above all human judgments. Conscience provides us with some knowledge of the moral law, but it is an incomplete and imperfect knowledge.[82]

Amandus Polanus divides the faculties of the soul into three: *vegetative*, including the *nutritive*, the *augmentative*, and the *generative*; *sensitive* (including *sense perception* and *movement*); and *rational*.[83] The last of these is divided into understanding and will, and the understanding is further divided into *theoretical* reason and *practical* reason, which is its proper work.[84] In addition, God created humans with an innate right reason and a true understanding of his will and works.[85] The author of this reason is the Logos of John 1:9, and its two norms are the inborn notion of fundamental principles—theoretical and practical—and conscience.[86] Conscience is a "certain notion of the divine will and actions in agreement with it or contrary to it, indelibly implanted in the mind, approving good actions, disapproving evil ones."[87] Peter Martyr

77. *Institutes*, III.xix.15.
78. LO: *ad Deum refertur*.
79. *Institutes*, III.xix.16.
80. *Institutes*, IV.x.5.
81. LO: *exigua lucis scintilla*; *Institutes*, IV.x.5.
82. Lobstein, *Die ethik Calvins*, 50–62; cf. *Institutes*, II.ii.24. Ed. note: Bavinck refers to a work titled *Ware Beschrijvinghe der Conscientien enz.* (1617, anonymous) and parenthetically asks, "Isn't this Remonstrant?"
83. LO: *vegetativa* (*altrix*; *auctrix*; *generatrix*); *sensitiva* (*apprehensiva* and *motiva*); *intellectiva*; GrO: λογικόν; Polanus von Polansdorf, *Syntagma Theologiae Christianae*, 324 (V, 32).
84. LO: *intellectus*; *voluntas*; *intellectus theoreticus/speculativus* = *ratio theoretica*; *intellectus practicus* = *ratio practica*.
85. DO: *ingeschapen*; LO: *recta ratio*; *vera notitia voluntatis et operum Dei*.
86. LO: *principia*; *conscientia*; Polanus von Polansdorf, *Syntagma Theologiae Christianae*, 1:2105 (V.xxxii).
87. LO: "*certa voluntatis divinae et actionum secundum vel contra illam facturum notitia, menti indelibiliter insita, actiones bonas approbans, malas improbans*" (Polanus von Polansdorf, *Syntagma Theologiae Christianae*, 1:2105 [V.xxxii]). Ed. note: Bavinck notes that Polanus cites

Vermigli put it this way: first comes *syntērēsis*, the natural knowledge of things concerning our conduct,[88] which provides the major premise (such as, fornication is sin). Conscience supplies the minor premise (what you want to do is fornication) and draws the conclusion: you should not do that.[89]

Conscience, however, is inadequate and needs to be enlightened by Holy Scripture and the Holy Spirit. Conscience can never make good that which in itself is sinful, even when someone acts with good conviction. Vermigli even speaks of "admirable powers of conscience."[90] Conscience is not only a judgment, deed, or activity, but it specifies a part, a natural power, a capacity of practical reason that is present in all rational creatures, including angels and humans, but not in God.[91] Its function consists in providing a judgment about things that have already been done (distinct from providing an idea, knowledge, and caution). In other words, these judgments pertain to things done by the subjects themselves, to one's own deeds (not the deeds of another— that is knowledge). Conscience is a *co*-knowing with God, who alone knows all that we do (unlike angels and other people). Conscience functions in a twofold manner: (1) *bearing witness* as to whether a deed has been performed or not (in Perkins's words: "Conscience is knowledge, knowledge joined with other knowledge"; i.e., "I know that I know");[92] and (2) *judging* whether evil or good has been done.[93] The conscience judges and must judge because it is bound; it stands under authority that drives it to that judging.

Only God and his word bind the conscience (Isa. 33:22; James 4:12).[94] Thus bound by God, the conscience in its own turn binds individual persons, while other people, authorities, the church and its laws can bind people only mediately and not truly.[95] The reasoning conscience functions in two ways:

Calvin and points to William Perkins. The unacknowledged(!) citation is from *Institutes*, III. xix.15; the Perkins reference is to *Anatomia Sacrae Humanae Conscientiae*. We will be providing references for both the Dutch translation of Perkins's work, *Eene Verhandeling van de Gevallen der Conscientie*, and the Latin text of *Anatomia*.

88. LO: *notitiae naturales agendarum rerum*.

89. Vermigli, *Loci Communes*, col. 296 (V).

90. LO: *admirabiles vires conscientiae*.

91. *ST* Ia q. 79 art. 13; Perkins, *Eene Verhandeling*, 69; *Anatomia*, 1199.

92. LO: *testimonium perhibere*; *cognitio*; *scientia*; "*Conscientia enim cognitio est, sive scientia, cum scientia coniuncta.*" Ed. note: Perkins uses two different words for knowledge, *cognitio* and *scientia*; according to Muller, *Dictionary*, 274, s.v. "*scientia*," they are synonymous, both referring to "knowledge in the most general sense of the term."

93. LO: *exercere iudicum*. Perkins, *Eene Verhandeling*, 70; *Anatomia*, 1199.

94. Perkins, *Eene Verhandeling*, 71; *Anatomia*, 1201.

95. Perkins, *Eene Verhandeling*, 77–89; *Anatomia*, 1210–30. Ed. note: The paragraphs that follow have been expanded beyond Bavinck's condensed version of Perkins in order to capture more fully some of the detailed nuances of his distinctions.

through the mind and through the memory.[96] The intellect makes use of ecclesiastical (canon) law and civil law. Memory arises from particular deeds,
either accomplished or only imagined, which the conscience judges by the
norms of the law. Here is the practical syllogism[97] by which the conscience
pronounces sentence:

> Major Premise: "All murderers are cursed," says the intellect.[98]
> Minor Premise: "You are a murderer," adds the conscience, assisted by
> memory.
> Conclusion: "Therefore, you are cursed," thus pronouncing judgment.[99]

The conscience judges both past and future conduct. In the case of past
deeds, conscience either *accuses* and *condemns*, or *exonerates* and *absolves*.[100]
The conscience accuses in this manner:

> Major premise: All murder is monstrous crime.[101]
> Minor premise: This deed you have done is murder.
> Conclusion: This act of yours is a monstrous crime.[102]

The next activity of the accusing conscience is *condemnation*, which it accomplishes in this way:

> Major Premise: All murderers doubly deserve death.[103]
> Minor Premise: You are a murderer.
> Conclusion: You doubly deserve death.[104]

The accusing and condemning conscience excites diverse emotions and passions
in human hearts, notably shame, sorrow, fear, despair, and consternation or

96. LO: *mente*; *memoria*; Perkins, *Eene Verhandeling*, 89; *Anatomia*, 1230.
97. Ed. note: Prior to introducing the syllogism, Perkins cites Rom. 2:15: "They show that
the work of the law is written on their hearts, while their conscience also bears witness, and
their conflicting thoughts accuse or even excuse them."
98. LO: *maledictus*; *mens*.
99. Perkins, *Eene Verhandeling*, 89; *Anatomia*, 1230.
100. LO: "*Conscientia iudicate, seu sert sententiam, vel de rebus praeteritis vel de rebus
futuris. De rebus praeteris dupliciter, vel accusando, et condemnando, vel excusando et ab-
soluendo. Rom. 2:15.*" Perkins, *Eene Verhandeling*, 89; *Anatomia*, 1231.
101. LO: *ingens scelus*.
102. Perkins, *Eene Verhandeling*, 89; *Anatomia*, 1231.
103. LO: *mortem promeretur duplicem*.
104. Perkins, *Eene Verhandeling*, 89; *Anatomia*, 1231.

restlessness (Isa. 57:20–21).[105] The final two emotions excited by the accusing and condemning conscience concerning deeds already done are exoneration and absolution.[106] The former is a judgment that something has been done well; the latter, that someone is free from the consequences and punishment of a misdeed and is judged and given immunity.[107] These two acts of the conscience produce (1) confidence and courage (Prov. 28:1) and (2) fame and joy.[108] Conscience also judges deeds that are still to be done, by a prior judgment, whether an act is good and pleasing to God. If so, the conscience gives a person permission to go ahead; this is the foundation of all "good works" (Rom. 14:23).[109]

Perkins distinguishes a good conscience from a bad one.[110] He also discusses the kinds of conscience: the proper nature of the conscience is to exonerate; this was its function in Adam and has begun in the regenerate.[111] That it accuses is a defect in it, a consequence of the fall.[112] There is thus a good conscience and a bad conscience.

Buddeus says that conscience is "the argument of human beings concerning their own actions with respect to God's law."[113] It is not God, but we ourselves who judge our acts by our conscience, albeit in accord with God's law.[114] It does not matter whether we call conscience an act, a disposition, or a capacity.[115] It is always a capacity but not always an act or disposition (sometimes it is asleep).[116] As a *knowledge of principles*[117] it is referred to as *syntērēsis* and is the rule, the norm, of conduct. As *knowledge of the fact*, conscience is and functions as a witness.[118] When the conscience assesses future acts, it is called the *antecedent conscience*; it persuades us of the good and dissuades us from

105. LO: *puder*, DO: *schaamte*; LO: *tristitia*, DO: *droefheid*; LO: *timor*, DO: *vreeze*; LO: *desperatio*, DO: *wanhoop*; LO: *perturbatio/inquietitudo*, DO: *ontsteltenis/ongerustheid*.

106. LO: *excusatio*, DO: *ontschuldinging*; LO: *absolutio*, DO: *ontslaan*.

107. LO: *qua rem bene factum*; "*Absolutio, est Conscientia actio, qua aliquem à culpa & consequenter etiam à poena liberum, & immune esse iudicat et pronunciat*" (Perkins, *Eene Verhandeling*, 90; *Anatomia*, 1233).

108. LO: *confidentia*, DO: *stoutigheid*; LO: *glorificatio*, DO: *roem*; LO: *gaudium*, DO: *blijdschap*.

109. LO: "*Principium est omnium rerum bonorum operum*"; Perkins, *Eene Verhandeling*, 91; *Anatomia*, 1233.

110. LO: *bona conscientia; mala conscientia*.

111. Perkins, *Eene Verhandeling*, 91; *Anatomia*, 1235.

112. Perkins, *Eene Verhandeling*, 104; *Anatomia*, 1257.

113. LO: *argumentatio hominis de actionibus suis ad legem relatis*; Buddeus, *Institutiones Theologiae Moralis*, 77 (I.iii, §2).

114. Buddeus, *Institutiones Theologiae Moralis*, 77 (I.iii, §2, note).

115. LO: *actus; habitus; potentia*.

116. LO: *dormire*; "*Sitne conscientia actus, an habitus, an potentia, frustra disputatur*"; Buddeus, *Institutiones Theologiae Moralis*, 77 (I.iii, §3).

117. LO: *notitia principiorum*.

118. LO: *scientia facti; testis*; Buddeus, *Institutiones Theologiae Moralis*, 77–79 (I.iii, §§3–5).

the evil.[119] Buddeus also notes that, according to Peter Chauvin, this capacity of the conscience to persuade or dissuade is what Socrates called "genius."[120] With respect to past deeds, we speak of a *consequent conscience*, supplying *approbation* of the good and *reprobation* of the evil.[121] Whether or not the conscience can err is a mere logomachy.[122]

According to Ames, "The conscience of man (for I do not intend to treat of the conscience of angels) is a man's judgment of himself, according to the judgment of God of him (Isa. 5:3)."[123] Conscience is not a "*contemplative judgment*, whereby truth is simply discerned from falsehood; but a *practical judgment*, by which that which a man knows is particularly applied to that which is either good or evil to him, to the end that it may be a rule within him to direct his will." There is debate about whether, as a judgment, the conscience is a power/capacity or habit/disposition. Calling Perkins's *Treatise of Conscience* "a peculiar work," Ames disputes Perkins's argument for thinking of conscience as "*A natural power or faculty*."[124] Furthermore, conscience is not a *habit*, contrary to Scotus, Bonaventure, and Durand.[125] It is not a habit because the proper work of a habit is "to make one do a thing readily,"[126] and conscience has "other operations, which belong properly to it, as to *accuse, comfort*, etc." Ames thus defines the conscience as "an act of practical judgment, proceeding from the understanding by the power or means of a habit." An act of judgment occurs either through "simple apprehension" or through a "discourse." Conscience "belongs to judgment discoursing because it cannot

---

119. LO: *conscientia antecedens; alii rei futurae bonam, suadentem, malam, dissuadentem.*

120. GrO: δαιμόνιον; Buddeus, *Institutiones Theologiae Moralis*, 79 (I.iii, §7, note). Ed. note: The reference is to Pierre Chauvin, *De Naturali Religione Liber*, I, 14. According to Buddeus, however, "many learned dispute" what Chauvinus claims here (*de quo tamen multa eruditi disputant*).

121. LO: *conscientia consequens; conscientiam rei praeteritae bonam adprobantem, malum, reprobantem vocant*"; Buddeus, *Institutiones Theologiae Moralis*, 80 (I.iii, §8).

122. LO: *meram*; GrO: λογομαχία; Buddeus, *Institutiones Theologiae Moralis*, 80 (I.iii, §8).

123. Ames, *Conscience*, 1 (I.i.1). Ed. note: The material from Ames that follows has been expanded considerably from Bavinck's manuscript, which is cryptic and filled with references that are not explored. Until further identified, the quotations from Ames are on pp. 2–4 (I.i.3–11); spelling has been updated to reflect modern (American) usage, but original punctuation has been retained.

124. Ed. note: Perkins considers the conscience a "natural power or faculty" because "the act of accusing, comforting, terrifying, etc.," cannot be ascribed to the conscience if it is itself an act. According to Ames, citing Rom. 2:15 as an example, this is a "weak" argument because in Scripture there are many effects "attributed to the thoughts themselves, which undoubtedly are acts" (Ames, *Conscience*, 2 [I.i.4]).

125. Ed. note: Ames is likely referring to Guillaume (William) Durand (1230–96), canon lawyer, author of *Speculum iudiciale* (1271–91), and bishop of Mende, France (https://en.wikipedia.org/wiki/Guillaume_Durand).

126. LO: *inclinare ad prompte agendum.*

do its act of accusing, excusing, comforting, unless it be through the means of some third argument, whose force appears only in a syllogism, by that which is deduced and concluded out of it." In sum: "Conscience in regard of the proposition is called a *Light*, and a *Law*; in regard of the assumption and conclusion, a *Witness*; but in regard of the assumption it is most fitly termed an *Index*, or a *Book*, and in regard of the conclusion, most properly a *Judge*. That which dictates or gives the proposition is called *Synteresis*, by the Schoolmen *Synderesis*. The assumption especially and peculiarly is called *Syneidēsis*, the conclusion is the *Krisis*, or Judgment." There are numerous syllogisms relating to conscience, but only this *practical syllogism*[127] "contains the whole nature of conscience. The proposition treats of the Law, the assumption of the fact or state, and the conclusion of the relation arising from the fact or state, in regard of the Law. The conclusion either pronounces one guilty, or gives spiritual peace and security."[128]

As a *habit*, *syntērēsis* is "only the principle of conscience"; it does not "make up any part of conscience, but only as conscience is in its exercise."[129] *Syntērēsis* is a *natural habit* to the degree that the "understanding of man is fitted to give assent to natural principles." As a shared understanding of the human species that is eventually accessible to the natural ability of each person, it is called an *acquired habit*. *Syntērēsis* differs only "in respect or apprehension from the Law of Nature, or from the Law of God, which is naturally written in the hearts of all men, for the law is the object, and *synteresis* is the object apprehended." While the "*synteresis* may for a time be hindered from acting, [it] cannot be utterly extinguished or lost. Hence it is that no man is so desperately depraved as to be void of all conscience." The *natural conscience*—"which acknowledges for law the principles of nature, and the conclusions arising from them"—needs to be distinguished from the *enlightened conscience*—which "in addition acknowledges what is prescribed in Scripture." From all this, "it appears that the perfect and only rule of conscience is the revealed will of God, where a man's duty is both shown and commanded." In conclusion, only the *law* of God—"the revealed will of God"—may bind the conscience. This means that although we are conscience-bound to obey human laws "in due and just circumstances," these laws do not bind our conscience. "The conscience is immediately subject to God, and his will, and therefore it cannot submit itself unto any creature without idolatry."

127. Ed. note: This *moral* practical syllogism tied to the work of the conscience is not to be confused with the so-called practical syllogism used to assure believers of their salvation.
128. Ames, *Conscience*, 4 (I.i.11).
129. Ames, *Conscience*, 5 (I.ii.3); quotations that follow are from pp. 5–7 (I.ii.2–15).

Ames states that the "office" of the conscience is twofold with respect to "necessary things": "to bind" and "to enforce to practice."[130] Conscience is bound by God and his will. "Conscience binds according as it is informed of the will of God: for in itself it has the power of a will of God, and so stands in the place of God himself." This binding is so powerful "that the command of no creature can free a man from it." This action of the conscience is a work of the *antecedent conscience*.[131] However, conscience can err.[132] Are we bound by an erring conscience? After making several subtle distinctions about the various kinds of errors that a conscience can make, Ames concludes the following about erring, overscrupulous consciences: "Conscience, though erroneous, binds always, so that he that goes[133] against it, sins. The reason is, because he that goes against conscience, goes against God's will; though not materially and truly; yet formally, and by interpretation; because what the conscience declares, it declares as God's will."[134] Errors of conscience may be *involuntary* and thus *blameless*, or *voluntary* and *blameworthy*. In the case of the former, conscience still binds us. In cases where the conscience puts before us two conflicting, binding obligations—such as lying to save one's own life or to fulfill the obligation of neighbor love—conscience still binds us, "but it does not bind us *to do so*." In this instance, someone with a well-formed conscience

can neither lie nor abstain from lying without sin. He cannot lie, because this is simply unlawful. He cannot abstain from lying, with such a conscience, because such manner of forbearance is forbidden by God, though forbearing it be commanded: for God requires not only that we do good, and abstain from evil; but likewise that we perform both these with a good conscience and not a bad one. Such a conscience does not *bind to do* what it says. First because there is no obligation to unlawful things. Secondly because conscience bids not to do, but by virtue of some command of God; but such a conscience is not grounded upon any command; for the Law of God can neither incline nor bind any man to sin.[135]

130. Ames, *Conscience*, 7 (I.iii.1); quotations that follow are from pp. 7–9 (I.iii.2–13).
131. Ed. note: When the conscience assesses future acts and persuades us of the good and dissuades us from the wrong.
132. Ed. note: The rest of the paragraph that follows is not in Bavinck's manuscript, which reads cryptically, "*Cap 4 kan dwalen* etc." ("Chap. 4 can err, etc."). Bavinck then goes on to elaborate this point with a discussion of van Mastricht's treatment of the topic. This material, taken from Ames, *Conscience*, 8–15 (I.iv.1–13), was added to complete Bavinck's discussion of Ames and to serve as a clarifying transition to his brief, dense discussion of van Mastricht.
133. Ed. note: To achieve greater clarity of meaning we have substituted "goes" here and in what follows for Ames's "does."
134. Ed. note: Ames provides an example of someone who mistakenly takes a private person for a king and therefore is conscience-bound as his subject.
135. Ames, *Conscience*, 13 (I.iv.10).

Van Mastricht provides us with a nice brief summary overview of the preceding: "Conscience is the judgment of humans about themselves, insofar as they are subject to God." It belongs to practical reason and judges according to a syllogism: the major premise is the *syntērēsis*; the minor premise, the *syneidēsis*; the conclusion, the *krisis*. The first one is *law*, the second is *witness*, the third is *judge*.[136]

MODERN RATIONALISM

In parallel with the eighteenth-century Enlightenment's emancipation of the natural person, rationalists detach conscience from God, his law, his Word, and place it on its own. The law lies encapsulated within the *syntērēsis*, needing only to be developed, enlightened. And that law within the conscience was the true, the good. This led to talk of the moral sentiment or sense, which needed to be detached from the emotions. This moral sentiment, once detached from God and his law, from all objective law, becomes purely moral and subjective. It was Rousseau who drew the consequence of this move and sought to return completely to nature. He regarded the natural human conscience, understood now as a moral sentiment, a feeling for the moral, as proof of an uncorrupted human nature. A superficial moralism was the result. Immanuel Kant brought about a change in this understanding by declaring the unconditional validity of duty. Kant considered the conscience as a courtroom drama between two persons: the accused and the judge. The individual consists of these two persons, whereby one is both personal lawgiver and personal judge (autonomy).[137] Thus, for Kant as well, conscience is detached from God and is only a moral instrument, not a religious one. Kant wants nothing to do with an erring conscience; the very notion must be banned. People can always be certain whether they have consulted their own conscience; this is the proper function of the conscience. Its material content may be wrong, but its formal operation cannot err. Conscience is for us an oracle of God and therefore absolute. Fichte defines conscience as "the immediate consciousness of that without which there can be no consciousness at all, the consciousness of our higher nature and absolute freedom," a consciousness of our particular duty.[138] Fichte also rejects the notion of an erring conscience and elevates conscience

<hr/>

136. LO of italicized words: *lex*; *testis*; *iudex*. Van Mastricht, *Theoretico-Practica Theologia*, II.iii.1 [4:525]; cf. Pictet, *De christelyke zedekunst*, 92–105 (I.ii.10–11); de Moor, *Commentarius Perpetuus*, 3:245–50; La Placette, *Christian Casuist*; Hoornbeeck, *Theologiae Practicae*, *Pars prior*, 284–304; Witsius, *Miscellaneorum Sacrorum, Tomus Alter*, 470–79.

137. Schopenhauer, *Die beiden Grundprobleme der Ethik*, 169, 292.

138. GO: *Bewußtsein*; *bestimmten Pflicht*. Ed. note: Bavinck provides no specific references for Fichte. The quotation is from his *System der Sittenlehre*, in *Sämmtliche Werke*, 4:147, cited

to an even higher level than Kant did. In the newer philosophy, conscience became an enlightening, infallible, and undeceived star. All the emphasis is placed on the formal function of judging by the conscience, which function is glorified; no attention is paid to its content.

In the philosophy that followed, however, the autonomy of the moral person was more detached, and more emphasis was placed on the social. Herbart defines conscience as "the innate compulsion to have an ideal, and acknowledging it as judge over oneself."[139] For Herbart, the ethical process is an aesthetic process.[140] Conscience applies not only to moral matters but is applied by Herbart to technical matters such as art and science. This generalizes and weakens the idea of the conscience. This is even stronger in Hegel's thought, where the good is identified with the nature of the will, of the completely realized will and not of the empirical will. That will is realized through thinking, through the process of thought.

Individual persons cooperate toward this, and therefore should have within themselves a germ of the final outcome. That germ is the conscience—namely, the affinity of the individual with the good. But that germ is flawed; conscience is valid for individual morality, but its standard, its ideal, is found in social ethics. The community exists far above the individual conscience and therefore need not always honor it. Schopenhauer criticizes and mocks Kant's theory of the conscience and calls it ridiculous;[141] the conscience does not deserve the deference Kant gives to it. It is not an infallibly commanding consciousness of duty, but only a "protocol of deeds"[142] that therefore follows the deed, and is empirical rather than intuitive and a priori. Whether the conscience approves or condemns depends on our sympathy or lack thereof. Since then, conscience is now understood by John Stuart Mill, Alexander Bain, and Herbert Spencer as a product of nurture, a result of social instincts.[143]

---

by Wood, "Fichte: From Nature to Freedom." Wood's essay is a valuable resource for understanding Fichte's view of the conscience.

139. GO: "*Die angeborene Nötigung, ein Ideal zu haben und als Richter über sich anzuerkennen.*" Ed. note: Bavinck provides no source for this quotation. Johann Friedrich Herbart (1776–1841) was a German philosopher and psychologist and the founder of pedagogy as a discipline. As an empiricist, Herbart rejected the notion of innate ideas as well as Kant's a priori categories of thought, concluding that "the world is a world of things-in-themselves [and] the things-in-themselves are perceivable" (Wolman, "Historical Role," 33, cited at https://en.wikipedia.org/wiki/Johann_Friedrich_Herbart). Herbart regarded ethics as a branch of aesthetics, dealing with relations among volitions (*Willensverhältnisse*) as either pleasing or displeasing.

140. See https://plato.stanford.edu/entries/johann-herbart/#AesEth; *Johann Friedrich Herbart's Sämmtliche Werke.*

141. DO: *bespottelijk*; Schopenhauer, *Die beiden Grundprobleme der Ethik*, 149.

142. GO: *Protokoll der Thaten.*

143. Cf. Pierson, *Eene Levensbeschouwing,* 71, 78, 101, 102, 185; Kuenen, "Ideaalvorming," 342; Spiess, *Physiologie der Nervensystems*, 346. Ed. note: Kuenen's essay is an extended review

The conscience plays an important role in Protestant theology, particularly in ethics. Schleiermacher did not pay specific attention to the conscience or give it a central place in his ethics. Those who came after him did discuss conscience frequently.[144] The main questions are these: (a) Is the conscience an original faculty, or is it produced by the environment, as Darwin suggested? Accompanying this question is another: does conscience have a general content or not? (b) Is conscience a religious faculty, or only a moral one? (c) Is conscience a negative faculty, or also a positive one; does it presuppose the fall into sin or not? Does conscience play an anticipatory role, or does it deal only with consequences? (d) Is it infallible, or can we also speak of an erring conscience? In general, what kinds of consciences are there? (e) What sort of freedom of conscience do humans enjoy?

Definition

1. ETYMOLOGY

According to Vilmar, the heart is the central midpoint of human being and living, and also the seat of self-consciousness.[145] The term συνείδησις (*syneidēsis*) comes from συνειδέναι ἑαυτῷ ("to be one's own witness" or "one's own consciousness coming forward as witness"). It does not come from συνειδέναι τινι (= "to know with someone"; i.e., to know something also

---

of Pierson's *Eene Levensbeschouwing*. Pierson responded with "Kantteekeningen op Prof. Kuenen's 'Ideealvorming.'" Bavinck calls attention to p. 458. John Stuart Mill (1806–73) was an English philosopher (utilitarian) and political economist whose views of individual liberty were influential in shaping modern liberalism. Alexander Bain (1818–1903) was a Scottish philosopher and "a prominent and innovative figure in the fields of psychology, linguistics, logic, moral philosophy and education reform. He founded *Mind*, the first-ever journal of psychology and analytical philosophy, and was the leading figure in establishing and applying the scientific method to psychology." Among his important publications was *Mental and Moral Science* (https://en.wikipedia.org/wiki/Alexander_Bain). Herbert Spencer (1820–1903) was an English sociologist who applied Charles Darwin's theory of evolution, particularly the doctrine of "survival of the fittest," to human society in a viewpoint that came to be known as "social Darwinism." His *Principles of Psychology* (1855) is a behaviorist precursor of B. F. Skinner (https://en.wikipedia.org/wiki/Herbert_Spencer).

144. See Rothe, *Theologische Ethik*, 2:1–7 (§171); Harless, *System of Christian Ethics*, 7–11; Vilmar, *Theologische Moral*, 1:65–115; Schenkel, "Gewissen"; Kähler, "Gewissen." For additional literature, see Ernesti, *Die Ethik des Apostels Paulus*, 22–23. Ed. note: Bavinck added in the margin references to Doedes, *De leer van God*, 85–96; Philippi, *Kirchliche Glaubenslehre*, 3:7–45; Elsenhaus, *Wesen und Entstehung des Gewissens*. Elsenhaus sets up the key questions with a discussion of Wundt and Rothe, then devotes large sections to Kant (22–38), Fichte (38–48), Hegel (49–65), Schleiermacher (66–78), Schopenhauer (79–92), and Herbart (93–130). Cf. the review of this volume by Wendt; also see Elsenhaus, "Beitrage zur Lehre vom Gewissen"; Oppenheim, *Das Bewissen*.

145. HO: לֵבָב; Vilmar, *Theologische Moral*, 1:67.

known by someone else, or even to know something about someone because I am an ear- or eyewitness to a person's guilt). In other words, conscience ("to be one's own witness") refers to what I know about myself, that my deeds are spiritually present to me, my "own consciousness coming forward as witness."[146] It has "primarily the same sense as τὸ συνειδός, denoting a consciousness arising out of and qualified by the conduct, or a consciousness estimating the conduct." "Next, however, it denotes an abiding consciousness, whose nature it is to bear witness to the subject regarding his own conduct, and that, too, in a moral sense." Here we have "the beginnings of our idea of 'conscience,' though approaching, but not yet embracing, its full force."[147] The use of *syneidēsis* in the sense that we speak of "conscience"—that is, as ethical consciousness—begins in the secular literature of the later Greek period. It was thus linked to *conscientia* (not only to know *with* someone, but to know *about* someone, because I was their witness). *Conscius* (conscious), therefore, means to be a witness, and also partner, in guilt. To continue, *conscire sibi* (to know oneself) is to be conscious because I am my own witness. Therefore, *conscientia* is simple consciousness and is still today the significance of the French *conscience*.

However, because our awareness of our being also pronounces a judgment over us, the consciousness that judges becomes our conscience; it becomes an ethical judgment. The words "consciousness" and "conscience" eventually merged together, were carried over into the ethical realm and restricted to it. Our notion of conscience (Dutch *geweten*) is not found in Ulfilas.[148] When the words now used in German and Dutch for conscience—*Gewissen* and *geweten*, respectively—evolved from Old High German to Middle High German, the root moved from a basic meaning of "inner consciousness" to the threefold significance of (1) knowledge; (2) knowing together, shared awareness; and (3) awareness of good and evil.[149] The general significance of knowledge remained with the word until the eighteenth century, but is now completely lost. Conscience is now something purely ethical. The prepositions *syn-* and *con-* (together, with) are a specific reference to "knowing together"

146. GrO: συνειδέναι ἑαυτῷ; Cremer, *Biblico-Theological Lexicon*, 233, s.v. "συνείδησις"; quotations that follow in this paragraph are from this source.

147. Cremer, *Biblico-Theological Lexicon*, 233.

148. Ed. note: Ulfilas (ca. 311–83) was a missionary to the Goths and the creator of the Gothic alphabet. He translated the Bible from Greek into Gothic (https://en.wikipedia.org/wiki /Ulfilas). Bavinck obviously has Ulfilas's translation in view here. The sentence that follows is a reconstruction of Bavinck's argument about the evolution of the meaning of the German and Dutch words for "conscience."

149. GO: *inneres Bewusstsein*; LO: *ingenium conscientia*. Ed. note: Old High German = up to AD 1050; Middle High German = AD 1050 to 1350.

with others, and then with oneself and not with God.[150] Conscience may in fact consist of a knowing-with-God, but that cannot be derived from the etymology of the word (contra Perkins).[151] It is a knowing-with-oneself; I am both the subject and the object in this knowing.[152]

2. CONSCIENCE AND INTELLECT

Conscience belongs to the *knowing* dimension of human life, to the sphere of the *intellect*. The words used (Latin: con-*scientia*; Dutch: ge-*weten*; German: Ge-*wissen*) already point to this. Conscience does not belong to the will, as Mosheim claimed: "Conscience is the will or the intent of the will that judges our relations to the world."[153] Nor does it belong to the realm of feelings, as C. A. Crusius believed: conscience "is the feeling of moral goods and evils."[154] It is possible to distinguish two directions in human knowing. The first is directed to knowledge of the truth as its goal (theoretical intellect or understanding, theoretical or speculative reason).[155] The second understands and engages in reasoning as an act—namely, it acts and effects that which it understands to be good; its goal is the act or effort (practical reason).[156] According to Thomas, "The speculative and practical *intellects* are not distinct powers," because "what is *accidental* to the *nature* of the object of a power, does not differentiate that power." The speculative intellect "directs what it apprehends, not to operation, but to the consideration of truth; while the practical intellect is that which directs what it apprehends to operation." In addition, "*Truth* and *good* include one another; for *truth* is something *good*, otherwise it would not be desirable; and *good* is something *true*, otherwise it would not be intelligible."[157] The intellect handles both theoretical and practical knowledge, because it is implanted in us. There is therefore a knowing that is both theoretical and practical: "Right reason [therefore is] a true knowledge of the will and works of God and of the order of divine judgments."[158]

---

150. GrO: σύν-. Ed. note: In the margin Bavinck added, "'Ge-' in 'geweten' is *not* 'with' but a simple perfect particle (*Groote Nederlandse. Woordenboek*, s.v.)"; Abraham Kuyper, untitled article, *De Heraut*, no. 579 (January 27, 1889), p. 3, col. 2.

151. Witsius, *Miscellaneorum Sacrorum*, 2:471.

152. Fr. H. R. Frank, *System der christlichen Wahrheit*, 503–12.

153. Mosheim, *Sitten-Lehre der Heiligen Schrift*, 230, cited by Kähler, "Gewissen," 155.

154. Crusius, *Kürzer Begriff der Moraltheologie*, 1:165–69, cited by Kähler, "Gewissen," 155.

155. LO: *intellectus theoreticus, ratio theoretica seu speculativa*.

156. LO: *ratio practica*. Polanus von Polansdorf, *Syntagma Theologiae Christianae*, 1:2102 (V.xxxii).

157. *ST* Ia q. 79 art. 11.

158. LO: *ratio recta = vera notitia voluntatis et operum Dei ut et ordinis judiciique divini*. Polanus von Polansdorf, *Syntagma Theologiae Christianae*, 1:2103 (V.xxxii).

Furthermore, this right reason which is a "true knowledge" is then "the form and norm concerning natural principles" which are "common notions implanted by God in the very nature of the human mind so that they can govern life and generate the sciences and the disciplines."[159] Thus there are two kinds of natural principles[160] implanted in the human mind: theoretical or speculative principles, which govern scientific work, and practical principles, which direct our moral life. According to Polanus, God's law is therefore written in the practical reason, just as the laws for thought are found in the speculative reason.[161] Polanus agrees with Thomas that reason[162] is not a faculty distinct from the intellect, because "to understand is simply to apprehend intelligible truth; and to reason is to advance from one thing understood to another." Angels have perfect knowledge of intelligible truth apart from discursive reasoning, but "man arrives at the knowledge of intelligible truth by advancing from one thing to another; and therefore, is called rational."[163] Reasoning is the way humans come to understand.

Moreover, we still possess conscience, which supplies our judgment about ourselves in (connection with) our relationship to God, according to the law of God, according to the right practical reason[164] implanted in us at our creation. Therefore, the conscience does not encompass the law of God within itself, but forms a judgment in accordance with that law of God which lies elsewhere (in the heart). Because the conscience does not judge the true and the false as such, but judges about the good and evil of the person's being, it belongs to the practical intellect. But now another question arises: Is conscience a distinct faculty within the practical intellect; is it a disposition/habit, a power/capacity, or an act?[165] Scotus, Bonaventure, and Durandus said that it was a disposition, a habit; for Perkins it is definitely a part of practical reason, a natural power, a capacity within it; and Schenkel considers it to be a separate faculty.[166] But, according to Thomas, "'Synderesis' is not a power

---

159. LO: *forma ac norma de principia naturalia; vera notitia; notitiae; a Deo naturae mentis humanae insitae; ut regant vitam et gignant scientias et disciplinas.* Polanus von Polansdorf, *Syntagma Theologiae Christianae,* 1:2103–4 (V.xxxii).

160. LO: *principia naturalia.*

161. LO: *ratio practica; ratio theoretica.*

162. LO: *ratio.*

163. *ST* Ia q. 79 art. 8.

164. LO: *ratio recta practica.*

165. LO: *habitus; potentia; actus.*

166. LO: *habitus;* DO: *hebbelijkheid; natuurlijke kracht, vermogen;* LO: *potentia.* Philippi, *Kirchliche Glaubenslehre,* 3:17. Ed. note: Durandus of Saint-Pourçain (ca. 1275–1332) was a French Dominican philosopher and theologian of the nominalist tradition (https://en.wikipedia.org/wiki/Durandus_of_Saint-Pour%C3%A7ain). The last reference here is to Daniel Schenkel (1813–85) and his *Die christliche Dogmatik,* 1:135–55.

but a habit [or disposition], bestowed on us by nature."[167] Taken together, the speculative intellect and the practical intellect constitute what we called above, with Polanus, "right reason."[168] Thomas goes on to say, "Properly speaking, conscience is not a power, but an act," a conclusion "evident both from the very name and from those things which in the common way of speaking are attributed to conscience."[169] Conscience, therefore, is not a testimony but a witness.[170] Conscience is not self-knowledge about ourselves, but God himself testifying within us. Sometimes we do not hear this very well; other times not at all. Conscience came only after sin.[171]

Conscience is not, however, a distinct capacity alongside others, but "the intellect itself ordered to specific actions."[172] Naturally, we always possess the faculty, the capacity, to evaluate our actions (otherwise we couldn't); however, that is not a distinct capacity alongside others but belongs to the intellect itself.[173] Thus the conscience is an act, a deed, an activity, flowing forth, however, from a disposition or habit.[174]

3. THE LAW OF CONSCIENCE: SYNTĒRĒSIS

Syntērēsis is a natural habit of concrete activity that contains the principles of practice or practical reason.[175] The law of nature is the content by which

---

167. LO: *synderesis non est potentia, sed habitus*; *ST* Ia q. 79 art. 12.

168. LO: *ratio recta.*

169. LO: *"conscientia, proprie loquendo, non est potentia, sed actus"*; *ST* Ia q. 79 art. 13. Ed. note: Thomas's argument begins with an analysis of the two parts of the word "conscience," which, he says, "may be resolved" into *"cum alio scientia,"* i.e., "knowledge applied to an individual case." He then lists the activities that are commonly attributed to conscience: "to witness, to bind, or incite, and also to accuse, torment, or rebuke." This application is made in three ways: (a) we recognize whether we have or have not done something; (b) "we judge that something should be done or not done; and in this sense, conscience is said to incite or to bind"; and (c) "we judge that something done is well done or ill done, and in this sense conscience is said to excuse, accuse, or torment." And since "all these things follow the actual application of knowledge to what we do . . . properly speaking, conscience denominates an act."

170. Ed. note: Kuyper, "God is meerder dan ons hart [God is greater than our heart!]," p. 1, col. 5: "Conscience is not a testimony [*getuigenis*], but a witness [*getuige*]; it is not knowledge [*wetenschap*] about ourself by ourself, but God himself testifying within us; sometimes we do not hear this very well, sometimes not at all." Bavinck and Kuyper both play on the Dutch words *getuigenis* and *getuige*; the former is inactive (like a written charge) and the latter is active (someone who bears witness). Cf. Kuyper, untitled article, *De Heraut*, no. 579 (January 27, 1889), p. 3, col. 2.

171. Kuyper, *"Van de Wet des Heeren* [Concerning the Law of God]."

172. LO: *intellectus ipse in ordine ad certas actiones.* Ed. note: Bavinck refers here to Witsius, *Miscellaneorum Sacrorum*, 2:471 (contra Perkins).

173. Buddeus, *Institutiones Theologiae Moralis*, 77 (I.iii.3).

174. LO: *habitus.* According to van Mastricht; Witsius; Ames, *Conscience*, 3 (I.i.6); and Vilmar, *Theologische Moral*, 1:84.

175. LO: *habitus principiorum operabilium; principia practica; ratio practica.*

the conscience evaluates our deeds.[176] Conscience needs a law to evaluate acts; the *syntērēsis* is that law. Perkins correctly observes that the conscience uses two assistants to come to a conclusion, the understanding and memory.[177] If we are to speak correctly, then, this *syntērēsis* does not belong to the conscience, but precedes it, is its necessary presupposition, without which the conscience cannot judge. To say that it is not itself part of the conscience[178] is to say that the law by which the conscience judges does not lie in the conscience itself but, as Romans 2:15 teaches, in the heart, in practical reason.[179] Strictly speaking, the conscience has no content; the lawbook by which it judges resides in the heart. Furthermore, the heart itself did not produce the law, is not itself the law, but is only the tablet for that law and is passive. This brings forth two questions: What is that law, and from whom does it come?

What is that law? There are those who say it is the law of nature,[180] which in its essence corresponds to the Ten Commandments. The biblical basis for this view is Romans 2:15, where Paul is speaking specifically of the law of Moses and claims that gentiles have "the work of the law"[181] written on their hearts. That is what the Christian church has always thought.[182] However, what has always been added is that this knowledge is incomplete and impure. Nonetheless, even then an additional objection arises. If the law of nature truly resides in us, albeit without clarity, why was it then revealed to Israel in such a ceremonious fashion? History provides us with an even greater objection. If the law of nature is indeed "natural" for all people, it should be the same everywhere. But what diversity![183] In Pascal's words: "A strange justice that is bounded by a river! Truth on this side of the Pyrenees, error on the other side."[184] Geographical borders change the entire moral law.

The whole of the Decalogue is not known among the pagans. This is obviously true with respect to the first four commandments, but also relates to the remaining six. Stealing, killing, harlotry, false testimony, and covetousness

---

176. LO: *lex naturae*. See Ames, *Conscience*, 5 (I.ii.4).

177. LO: *mente*; *memoria*. See Perkins, *Eene Verhandeling*, 89; *Anatomia*, 1230.

178. Ames, *Conscience*, 5 (I.ii.2).

179. LO: *ratio practica*. See Ames, *Conscience*, 5 (I.ii.2); Vilmar, *Theologische Moral*, 1:78.

180. LO: *lex naturae*.

181. GrO: τὸ ἔργον τοῦ νόμου.

182. Scholten, *De leer der Hervormde Kerk*, 270–303; Scholten deals with Zwingli and Calvin on pp. 288–96.

183. Flügel, *Das Ich*. One kind still has many varieties; therefore, even though the conscience is one, it develops in different directions under different circumstances, etc.

184. FO: "vérité en deça des Pyrenées, erreur au delà"; Pascal, *Pensées*, no. 294.

(Rom. 7) were viewed as permissible by many nations. Antiquity actually recognized only two crimes: murder of one's blood relatives and perjury.[185] There is no single moral command that all people considered obligatory.[186] This is the primary basis of Darwinism, which claims that conscience is entirely a product of circumstances, of the environment. Alternative circumstances would produce a different content. Nothing is necessarily good or evil a priori, but only becomes so through circumstances. All morality is a matter of convention; prostitution was permitted in Babylon, stealing in Sparta, assassination among Indians, polygamy and human sacrifice or cannibalism among many pagans. The Jews considered lighting a fire on the Sabbath to be impermissible, and some may stroll on Sunday without a sense of guilt, but not others. Some people have narrow consciences, others broad ones.[187] We must acknowledge that a good deal of the law of our conscience is circumstantial, introduced from the outside. Many Christian theologians argue, therefore, that the conscience possesses no material content.[188]

Vilmar argues that the ethical laws of the human world arise from the original revelation given to Adam and Eve, and that the basis of conscience was formed by the perspective or representation of the people, by the content and the course of ordinary human life.[189] Harless claims that there is no law that serves as the content of our conscience; instead, our own spirit is divine and must place and evaluate everything in relationship to God.[190] According to Harless, Paul does not say in Romans 2:15 that the law is written in the heart of the gentiles, but rather that "the work of the law" is.[191] This work, activity, or operation of the law involves judging and rendering a verdict. Thus, the gentiles, who are a law unto themselves, do not possess the positive law but do possess the *work* or *activity* of the positive law—namely, judging.[192] Others claim that the law of nature is only a very general rule without any specific application: "What you do not want others to do you. . . ." Here we need to observe the following:

---

185. Vilmar, *Theologische Moral*, 1:97.

186. E.g., Guyau, *Sketch of Morality*; see also van der Wyck, "'Fais ce que voudras.'"

187. Lecky, *History of European Morals*; Wake, *Evolution of Morality*; Hoekstra, *De ontwikkeling van de zedelijke idee*.

188. Including Rudolph Hofmann, *Die Lehre von dem Gewissen*; see Philippi, *Kirchliche Glaubenslehre*, 3:12–13. Kant sought the moral only in the formal. Rauwenhoff likewise in *Wijsbegeerte van den godsdienst*, 1:244–80. Opposing this view: van der Wyck, "Twee pleitbezorgers."

189. GO: *Gesammtanschauung*; Vilmar, *Theologische Moral*, 1:96, 100.

190. Harless, *System of Christian Ethics*, 56–58.

191. GrO: τὸ ἔργον τοῦ νόμου.

192. Harless, *System of Christian Ethics*, 60–62.

a. That even if *syntērēsis* had absolutely no content, no specific commandments, Darwinism would still not gain anything. But our experience is that what
is noble, lovely, etc., is universally regarded as such. Nowhere does conscience
encourage debauchery, malice, and so forth. While there is great difference among
people about what is good and what is evil, all people know that there is good.

b. Who alone can bind the conscience?[193] The conscience is not free but
bound; it is morally obligated to something. This is the law of God within
the *syntērēsis*. God himself stands above it, commands, presses the conscience
to judge, either to accuse or exonerate. God and God alone is the one who in
and through the *syntērēsis* binds the conscience, commands it, stands above
it, possesses power and authority over it. The conscience is immediately and
unconditionally subject only to God as its Lord. After all, he is its creator
and continues to maintain and regulate it. Furthermore, he alone knows our
conscience and sees through it with us, something no angel or other human
can do. Only God has the power to punish and to destroy it. "There is only
one lawgiver and judge, he who is able to save and to destroy. But who are
you to judge your neighbor?" (James 4:12). "For the LORD is our judge; the
LORD is our lawgiver" (Isa. 33:22). In addition, for all people in all times,
conscience has been bound first of all by the surviving natural principles of
morality and justice and of natural religion, given to us at creation and left to
us after the fall.[194] A conscience that has this natural knowledge[195] as content
in the *syntērēsis* is called a "natural conscience."

But second, among all people who know God's Word, conscience is absolutely bound to that Word, and believing in the gospel, therefore, is the
duty of everyone; unbelief is sin. Among those who do not know the Word,
the conscience is equipped to be bound to it, but is not actually bound (John
15:22; Rom. 2:12).[196] The conscience that is bound to the Word of God is
said to be enlightened. God binds the conscience in the *syntērēsis*, and the
conscience in turn binds and obligates the person. Therefore, God alone
binds the conscience. But there are also improper, indirect binders of the
conscience. First, there are human laws made by ecclesiastical or civil governments, which papists claim bind the conscience just as properly as the law
of God does. Furthermore, on the basis of a number of Scripture passages
(Deut. 17:12; Matt. 16:18; Luke 10:16; John 20:21; 21:16; Acts 15:28–29;
Rom. 13:2, 5), they contend that the church and worldly government may

193. Perkins, *Eene Verhandeling*, 71–72; *Anatomia*, 1201; Ames, *Conscience*, 6–7 (I.ii).
194. LO: *principia naturalia*; *religio naturalis*; Perkins, *Eene Verhandeling*, 72; *Anatomia*,
1201. This pertains to the essence of the conscience and not to its manner of presentation.
195. LO: *notitiae*.
196. Perkins, *Eene Verhandeling*, 75–82; *Anatomia*, 1201.

compel the conscience just as God does.[197] In opposition, the Reformed said that only the one who knows the conscience can bind and punish it. Other people can compel us, but no human being, prince, Satan, or angel can obligate us morally in the conscience; only God can. Nevertheless, human laws can bind us indirectly[198] by virtue of God's commandment and to the extent that they correspond to God's command. If they conflict with God's law, then the conscience may consider itself not to be bound and is obligated to passive resistance; we must obey God rather than other people (Dan. 3:28; Acts 4:19). Second, oaths and promises also bind the conscience, unless they are a bond of unrighteousness.[199]

4. Consciousness of Obligation and Judgment

Awareness of what one must do and of what one has done can also be called *conscientia* in a broad sense; Scholten even calls this the "conscience proper."[200] Nevertheless, properly speaking, it does not belong to the conscience and is not part of it. But, just as with the *syntērēsis*, this consciousness is used by the conscience (in the narrow sense) as an assistant so that it can come to a judgment.[201] To return once more to the example of murder that we used earlier, adding the notion of the *syntērēsis*, the major premise comes from the *syntērēsis*: "Every murderer is accursed"; the minor premise comes from our consciousness, our memory, our recollection: "You have committed murder." This accusation is the silent witness of our being and doing. This consciousness of having to do something or of having done something was naturally present in Adam before the fall, just as the *syntērēsis* was. But sin had a significant effect on the *syntērēsis* and this consciousness. Now the *syntērēsis* reproduces the law of God obscurely and can include mistaken content (idols). In addition, our consciousness is weakened and narrowed in the sense that we do a great deal that does not enter at all into our consciousness.[202]

197. Perkins, *Eene Verhandeling*, 78–82; *Anatomia*, 1201.
198. Perkins, *Eene Verhandeling*, 83; *Anatomia*, 1201.
199. Perkins, *Eene Verhandeling*, 86–89; *Anatomia*, 1201.
200. DO: *eigenlijke geweten*. Scholten, *De vrije will*, 214–15. Ed. note: Scholten takes pains to refute the idea that the conscience itself has knowledge of good and evil as a categorical imperative. It is reason that provides this knowledge; conscience only "declares to people whether or not they have acted (doing a good or an evil deed) in accord with the standard of good and evil that they have determined for themselves by their reason" (*De vrije will*, 215).
201. The *syntērēsis* logically precedes and is the presupposition for the conscience; it is the lawbook for the conscience, the foundational understanding, the reason (*ratio*) that is the treasury and protector of various fundamental rules. See earlier discussion of *syntērēsis/synderesis* in this chapter.
202. See discussion below on the erring conscience.

5. THREE QUESTIONS OF JUDGMENT: WHO? WHAT? HOW?

Conscience in its proper sense is that power or activity in a person's understanding that, bound to the law of God in the *syntērēsis*, judges the actions of a person observed by means of the consciousness, according to that law. We need to answer three questions: *Who* judges in the activity of the conscience? *What* does the conscience judge? And, *how* does the conscience judge?

Who Judges?

Who is the judging subject? Not God, although that is frequently the popular way of speaking, when conscience is described as the voice of God within us. There is a grain of truth here because conscience is God's gatekeeper within us, his substitute and lesser judge; conscience is the highest judge on earth, under God, standing above earthly rulers and judges, kings, and emperors. An appeal to conscience is therefore an appeal from all lower earthly courts to the highest court under God, and therefore "puts an end to all argument" (Heb. 6:16).[203] No one, neither an angel nor another person, may stand between God and someone's conscience. In our consciences we are bound directly to God, whose existence is disclosed to us in the *syntērēsis*. Nonetheless, we are not bound directly to God himself but indirectly via the judging subject. To state it more clearly: it is we ourselves who are the subject that judges us. The conscience is a particular part of our self-consciousness in which we function as subject and as object. In our conscience, we ourselves are the judge and the accused defendant. This was the understanding of all the Reformed thinkers like van Mastricht, Witsius, and Pictet: "Human beings judge themselves."[204] Ames says that "conscience is a man's judgment of himself, according to the judgment of God of him."[205] Buddeus specifically contests the idea that "God resides in our mind when it speaks intimately," but does say, "The mind of man, understanding and discerning the divine laws and judging his actions by them, has come to give this the name of conscience."[206] Conscience is a knowing-with-God, a judging that is done before the face of God, in the name of God, at the tribunal of God.[207] The subjects of the judging, therefore, are

---

203. GrO: πέρας ἀντιλογίας.

204. LO: *est iudicium hominis de se ipso.* Van Mastricht, *Theoretico-Practica Theologia,* II.iii.1 [4:525]; Pictet, *De christelyke zedekunst,* 92–101 (II.x); Witsius, *Miscellaneorum Sacrorum,* 2:473.

205. Ames, *Conscience,* 1 (I.i.1).

206. LO: "*Deus menti nostrae insidet cumque ea intime disserit*"; "*Mens hominis leges divinas intelligens expendens et ad eas actiones suas dijudicans, conscientiae nomine venit.*" Buddeus, *Institutiones Theologiae Moralis,* 77 (I.iii, §2).

207. LO: "*est iudicium hominis de se ipso; coram deo; nomine Dei, citat ad Dei tribunal*"; Witsius, *Miscellaneorum Sacrorum,* 2:473.

people themselves.[208] How miraculous this all is! God has appointed us to be our own judge.[209]

As judge[210] over ourselves when we sin, we serve as the accuser, the one who convicts and sentences us, the avenger and executioner.[211] We are obligated and bound by God to assess ourselves according to God's law and, if we sin, to acquiesce with God's judgment on us. In our conscience, we justify God contrary to our own will and desire; we are compelled to acknowledge God as God. It is as this judging subject that the conscience is called Judge: The conscience summons the guilty, listens to its witnesses, opens the lawbook (the *syntērēsis*), and judges and specifies the punishment accordingly. The conscience is a supreme court (Kant). This analysis now easily leads us to a question: Is the conscience a religious or a moral consciousness, or both? The *syntērēsis* as the direct consciousness of God, with God's moral law as its content, is thus (religiously) specified by God and has as its content the religious (first table) and the moral (second table). The conscience is bound to that law, judges in accord with that law, and judges in God's place, in God's name, and before God's face.[212] The *syntērēsis* is therefore entirely specified by God and is appropriately said to be "religious." However, it judges about the *moral* quality of a person's being and acting, and is therefore a moral consciousness. The human self-consciousness in our conscience, bound by God to his law and appointed as judge in his place (therefore religiously oriented), judges and must judge us ourselves (that is the moral dimension). The conscience is therefore religiously oriented and, for that reason, precisely moral.

What Does the Conscience Judge?

First, the conscience renders judgment about everything in a person, about the entire person; not merely about our actions but also about our being and state and our thoughts.[213] In other words, we feel obligated by our conscience to look at everything in relation to God and his law and to review it accordingly. Nothing within us or about us is excused or exempted from God and his law

---

208. Schenkel, "Gewissen," 137.

209. Ed. note: Bavinck uses the word *beoordeeler* ("one who judges, assesses, reviews"). It is important to highlight the specific dimension of reviewing and assessing here because Bavinck goes on to speak of a "judge" in a more expansive sense as the one who accuses, convicts, sentences, avenges, and executes.

210. DO: *rechter*.

211. DO: *veroordelaar, vonnisser, aanklager, wreker, beul*.

212. LO: *nomine Dei; coram Deo*.

213. LO: *de actionibus; de statu*. Witsius, *Miscellaneorum Sacrorum*, 2:473. Cf. van Mastricht; Buddeus, *Institutiones Theologiae Moralis*, 77 (I.iii, §7); Harless, *System of Christian Ethics*, 62–63.

in any of our capacities, gifts, powers, words, or actions; in our whole person we always stand under the law. Nothing in us or done by us is outside the law.[214]

But, second, here is a more important question: Does the conscience render judgment only about past, completed matters, or also about future ones? Stated differently, can we speak of an *antecedent* conscience as well as a *consequential* conscience?[215] According to Doedes,

> Conscience does not make people aware of their duty on any particular issue before the moment when they become aware of a conflict between their willing (or acting) and their moral obligation. Consciousness of moral obligation does not precede that which must be done and, therefore, does not speak in advance, but only after a person has willed or acted in conflict with the moral duty. Nonetheless, if the conscience is awake and time is sufficient, the conscience may restrain a person from completing acts that conflict with moral obligation. With sufficient time, a person may even be led by the conscience to choose an alternative. However, in neither case does this happen before the moment we come into conflict with our moral obligations.[216]

Now, to be sure, rendering a judgment about completed matters is surely the most important function of conscience[217] and is generally what people have in mind when they speak about conscience. Conscience is therefore primarily consequential. Nevertheless, the conscience is and becomes increasingly active before the act, before the conflict.[218] We imagine ahead of time how a future act will reflect in our moral consciousness, how our conscience will render judgment about it. That testimony of conscience precedes the act and provides warning or encouragement by forbidding or commanding me to do it. The *antecedent* conscience was therefore differentiated into suasion and dissuasion.[219] Many assigned the *daimonion* of Socrates[220] to this; however,

---

214. LO: *ex lex*.

215. LO: *conscientia antecedens*; *conscientia consequens*; Perkins, *Eene Verhandeling*, 90; *Anatomia*, 1201.

216. Doedes, *De leer van God*, 93.

217. Perkins, *Eene Verhandeling*, 89–90; *Anatomia*, 1201.

218. If Doedes understands "the moment of conflict" to refer to the moment when an act is presented before me and I ask whether that act is permissible, then he is correct.

219. LO: *suadens*; *dissuadens*.

220. Ed. note: Daemons (Greek δαίμονες, neuter δαιμόνιον) are benign spirits such as ghosts, guardian angels, or forces of nature. In Plato's *Symposium* love is characterized as a daemon. Bavinck here refers to a key passage in Plato's *Apology of Socrates* where Socrates appeals to an inner voice that prevented him from doing wrong: "Hitherto my divine monitor [*daimonion*] has constantly been in the habit of opposing me even about trifles, if I was going to make a slip or error in any matter" (*Apology* 40 b–c, in *Euthyphro, Crito, Apology, Symposium*, 55 [trans. Jowett]).

most today consider it to be a refined personal sense of what he could and was permitted to do, a clear consciousness of the boundaries established by his personal individuality.[221] God has given us this prior knowing en route, to show us the course we must follow. And this prior knowing has great authority, for everything that is not from faith (even though in itself it may be good) is sin. One may never do something unless one knows it to be something good. (An Anabaptist who out of fear swears an oath to the government is sinning.) A good opinion or confidence is not enough; firm assurance in the conscience is needed.

How Does the Conscience Render Judgment?

The conscience renders judgment in the form of a syllogism. The conscience is the practical syllogism in the intellect in which the major premise is the law or Word of God, the minor premise is the truth of the matter, and the conclusion is the application of approbation or condemnation (Melanchthon).[222] The *syntērēsis* (i.e., the law or Word of God) provides the major premise, and consciousness[223] supplies the minor premise. The conscience draws the conclusion and renders judgment. This judgment either accuses or exonerates (Rom. 2:15).[224]

First, accusing and condemning.[225] This function of conscience begins immediately after the action and consists in accusing—"You have done wrong"—and condemning—"You deserve punishment." The results of that accusing function of conscience especially include shame,[226] an unpleasant feeling about a misdeed, sadness (regret, depression), fear (Prov. 28:1; Wis. 17:11–15), despair (doubt about salvation and forgiveness; e.g., Ahithophel and Judas).

Second, exonerating and acquitting.[227] This is followed by a quiet conscience, courage, and joy and raises the question whether conscience speaks only negatively in disapproval and accusation or also affirmatively in exoneration. According to Doedes, conscience speaks only negatively—that is, only when wrong is committed. Conscience says only no and does not say yes. When an act is good, the conscience is silent, remains at rest. This restful

---

221. Buddeus, *Institutiones Theologiae Moralis*, 77 (I.iii, §7); cf. Vilmar, *Theologische Moral*, 1:101.

222. Philippi, *Kirchliche Glaubenslehre*, 3:13.

223. LO: *memoria*.

224. Ed. note: The Dutch text engages in a wordplay: "*be*schuldigend" or "*ont*schuldigend"; guilt (*schuld*) is the key notion here.

225. Perkins, *Eene Verhandeling*, 89; *Anatomia*, 1201.

226. Scholten, *De vrije wil*, 210, describes shame as "unpleasant feeling about a mistake" (*onaangenaam gevoel over een misslag*).

227. Perkins, *Eene Verhandeling*, 90; *Anatomia*, 1201.

conscience can be viewed as a good testimony, and that it is; but then that good testimony is not provided by the conscience, but by the rest, by the silence of the conscience. This is true;[228] it can also be observed that the pleasant feelings of joy and courage that follow a good deed are seated in the emotions, not in the understanding or conscience. But Doedes says more than this. The statement "I am not aware of doing anything wrong" is preferable to "I am aware of having acted morally." Why? Because one can think, be convinced, and can demonstrate that one has acted morally, but consciousness of duty tells us nothing. This claims too much. After someone has sinned, their conscience does not declare positively and loudly: "You have acted morally." A completely clear consciousness of having acted rightly is always absent, is always more or less obscured, weakened. But apart from sin, moral action is properly accompanied by a firm consciousness of being moral, just as knowledge accompanies awareness thereof (I know that I know). And that brings us to this question: Does a holy person (Adam before the fall; Jesus; the saints) also have a conscience?

God does not have a conscience. The expression "conscience of God" (1 Pet. 2:19; "conscience toward God," KJV) is an objective genitive;[229] God is the object of our human conscience. After all, a conscience is a judgment about someone's being and acting in accord with a law and assumes therefore that the individual is subject to the law. That cannot be said about God. God does not stand under the law, but is himself the law. He is the Lawgiver and not a subject. He is righteousness itself.[230]

Animals also have no conscience, because they are not subject to a moral law, have no law, and therefore cannot transgress any law. Conscience can exist therefore only in rational creatures, in angels and human beings. The devils have a thorough knowledge of the law of God—that is, intellectual knowledge (even as they know that there is a God)—but the law of God no longer resides in their heart, neither entirely nor partially, as it does with us. Similarly, they know intellectually that they act contrary to what God's law requires of them; they have a very clear awareness of being in conflict with God. But they do not have an actual conscience that accuses them, any actual awareness of sin and guilt. They have no repentance, only regret. They are conscience-less—in other words, entirely separated from God, not physically but ethically.

---

228. Vilmar, *Theologische Moral*, 1:90.

229. Ed. note: That is why modern translations render it "conscious of God" (NIV) or "mindful of God" (RSV, ESV). Grammatically, the genitive "love of God" can be an objective genitive (*our* love to God) or a subjective genitive (God's love to *us*).

230. Perkins, *Eene Verhandeling*, 90; *Anatomia*, 1201; Buddeus, *Institutiones Theologiae Moralis*, 77–78 (I.iii, §§3–4).

We turn now to human beings. A *syntērēsis* was certainly present in Adam and in Jesus, and this was entirely pure; the foundational practical principles (= the law of nature) lay completely pure and clear within them.[231] Similarly, their *consciousness* of their own being and doing was completely clear and transparent; their entire (ethical) being was reflected faithfully and completely in their ethical consciousness. With us there is a gap between being and consciousness; the latter is smaller than the former because sin darkens our consciousness. Nevertheless, upright persons know (God and therefore) themselves clearly and transparently. Third, they had a *consciousness*, the firm, clear consciousness (not merely an opinion, a conviction, or even a confidence) of having acted morally. Contrary to Doedes, a holy deed is accompanied with infallible or holy consciousness, just as the truth possesses the consciousness of the truth. Otherwise the truth would turn into an antinomy, creating a nontruthful consciousness. In addition, then the elect would not be able to be assured of their election. Paul says "we know" (are conscious) that "if the tent that is our earthly home is destroyed, we have a building from God, a house not made with hands, eternal in the heavens" (2 Cor. 5:1). The question simply comes down to this: May this consciousness of having acted morally be called "conscience"? This is the proper way of asking the question, rather than "Did Adam have a conscience before the fall?" Vilmar claims that the possibility of having a conscience is identical with the possibility of sin; conscience is the consciousness of one's limits. The presence of a conscience requires sin as its basis; the first expression of a conscience can be found in the description of Adam and Eve after their sin: "Then the eyes of both were opened, and they knew that they were naked" (Gen. 3:7). Conscience is thus first negative, a consciousness of having done wrong.[232] Schenkel says that conscience is the relatedness of human self-consciousness to God, which, because of sin, is no longer directly one with God, but can only relate to God indirectly. Conscience is the differentiating of God-consciousness and self-consciousness and a "symptom of disorder/disease"; it is the point at which the person still stands in relation to God after sin.[233] Our answer to the question "May this consciousness of having acted morally be called 'conscience'?" must be "No." First, because that "infallible" consciousness in Adam, in Jesus, and in those saints who acted morally is completely absent in what we call conscience. The conscience is a judge, but this assumes injustice. In the

231. LO: *principia operabilium* = *lex naturae*.
232. Vilmar, *Theologische Moral*, 1:89–90.
233. GO: *Symptom der Erkränkung*; Schenkel, "Gewissen," 137–38.

state of integrity, conscience was silent, faith spoke. Furthermore, what we have already identified as the condemning role of conscience was completely missing in Adam. The law's demands in the conscience are those of a "guilt-ruler" toward guilty subjects.[234]

Second, in Adam the consciousness of God's will and law (*syntērēsis*) coincided precisely with the consciousness of having acted according to that law. Adam himself willed and did precisely what God commanded him in the *syntērēsis*.

Therefore, the law was viewed not as a lawbook over against him but within him. Adam himself stood within the law, which was the immanent life energy of his will. In a word, Adam was conscious of his own will being perfectly in harmony with God's will. But today that harmony is broken; the unity between what ought to be and what is, is gone. The law, already placed within our heart, stands over against us and lies before us. Conscience is the bond that still binds us in sin to the law, but precisely the need for such proves that "should" and "would" are no longer one but two.[235] The law still binds us in our conscience; otherwise we would have walked away entirely and fled from the law. The law makes demands in the conscience like a creditor does to a debtor.[236]

Nevertheless, we may state it somewhat popularly that Adam and Jesus each had a conscience. This is so, in the first place, because it is in the conscience that we take note of the bond that ties us to God. Hegel said that our moral consciousness of the obligation to do God's will comes through the law as well as the consciousness to agree with that will. Second, we can say this because the conscience remains the continuing testimony of God within us. This testimony did not come after the fall but is a surviving remnant of the original testimony in Adam that was his communion with God. At the same time, it must be said that the form, orientation, and function of this testimony have radically changed. What was originally a communion of love for God on the part of Adam and Eve is now, on the one hand, precisely the denial of communion. On the other hand, though that communion no longer exists, what does remain is a reminder of what did exist, and a reminder that, in spite of our having separated ourselves from God, he has not abandoned us. God holds us firmly and binds us under his law so that we might not sink completely into sin but continue to have an ethical connection to God, to the eternal, and to heaven.[237]

234. DO: *schuldheer*; *schuldenaar*; Philippi, *Kirchliche Glaubenslehre*, 3:20–22.
235. GO: *sollen*; *wollen*.
236. Philippi, *Kirchliche Glaubenslehre*, 3:20–22.
237. Philippi, *Kirchliche Glaubenslehre*, 3:17–20.

6. Kinds of Conscience[238]

Consciences come in many kinds. We will consider them in a series of contrasting pairs.

Natural (Pagan) and Christian (Enlightened) Consciences

The natural or pagan conscience has the law of nature[239] and natural civil law as its content. By contrast, a Christian or enlightened conscience renders judgment according to the Word of God.

Good and Bad Consciences

A good conscience exonerates while a bad conscience accuses. In a certain sense, relatively speaking, the natural person can also have a good conscience. This is not, however, an objectively good conscience because the standard or norm can be wrong, the consciousness might not correctly reflect the person's being, and the conscience can draw a false conclusion. Only a regenerated person (and, if one wishes, Adam and Jesus) can have an objectively good conscience, at least in principle. A bad conscience accuses and can also be present in believers. In this case, the adjectives "bad" and "good" describe the conscience according to its results.

Upright and Erring Consciences

The upright conscience renders correct judgments. But can we speak of an erring conscience? Does such a conscience exist? This is denied by Braun, who states that if it did exist, God would be a deceiver.[240] Others such as de Moor, Witsius, Buddeus, Ames, and Hoornbeeck all dispute this.[241] In recent times it was denied also by Rothe, who argues that the conscience is the act of God within us, is absolutely infallible and unerring, although we can be deceived about its pronouncement.[242] Schenkel claims that conscience is infallible insofar as it is based on God.[243] In other words, it is infallible in its essence but not empirically in its manifestation.

238. Perkins, *Eene Verhandeling*, 92. Buddeus, *Institutiones Theologiae Moralis*, 79–80 (I.iii, §§6–9); Ames, *Conscience*, 9–21 (I.iv–vi); Pictet, *De christelyke zedekunst*, 93–101 (II.x); Schenkel, "Gewissen," 139–42.

239. LO: *lex naturae*.

240. J. Braun, *Doctrina Foederum*, 93–95 (I.ii.5, §6), cf. 104–5 (I.ii.5, §17); cf. Cocceius, *Summa Theologiae*, 270–71 (XXII.15); Momma, *De Varia Conditione et Statu*, 210–11 (II.11 §60).

241. De Moor, *Commentarius Perpetuus*, 3:246–50; Witsius, *Miscellaneorum Sacrorum*, 2:470–72; Buddeus, *Institutiones Theologiae Moralis*, 80 (I.iii, §8); Ames, *Conscience*, 9–16 (I.iv); Hoornbeeck, *Theologiae Practicae*, 1:293.

242. Rothe, *Theologische Ethik*, 1:267 (§147); Fichte also denies this; cf. Janet, *La morale*, 331–48.

243. GO: *weit es auf Gott bezogen ist*. Schenkel, "Gewissen," 139.

But, in the first place, Holy Scripture clearly teaches the reality of an erring conscience:

> The heart is deceitful above all things, / and desperately sick; / who can understand it? (Jer. 17:9)

> However, not all possess this knowledge. But some, through former association with idols, eat food as really offered to an idol, and their conscience, being weak, is defiled. (1 Cor. 8:7)

> . . . if his conscience is weak. (1 Cor. 8:10; cf. v. 12; 10:28–29)

> . . . through the insincerity of liars whose consciences are seared. (1 Tim. 4:2)

> To the pure, all things are pure, but to the defiled and unbelieving, nothing is pure; but both their minds and their consciences are defiled. (Titus 1:15)

In the second place, experience proves it. Conscience can err in the very commandment that it sets forth, as when occasionally it prescribes idolatry among pagans.[244] It can also err in our awareness of our own act or in rendering judgment. And formally, it is then also true that conscience can become weakened or strengthened; it can sleep, be awakened, or be seared. It can even incorporate entirely mistaken material content and thereby must itself take on a distorted form. Braun and others claimed that the conscience was infallible but then ascribed any error not to the conscience but to opinions, presuppositions, miscalculations, and the like. However, this is logomachy, mere quarreling about words. We define conscience simply as a person's self-judgment. Whenever we separate ourselves from the erring part of our conscience, we surely retain the non-erring part. However, to identify then the non-erring part alone as "conscience" is wholly arbitrary. With Braun and others, this is related to Descartes's argument that understanding in itself cannot err (therefore neither can the conscience) but proceeds from the will. In addition, the conscience is a witness, a judge in God's name, but it does not exercise its function infallibly. The question whether an erring conscience still binds us is difficult. Ames says that it certainly does, and so does the apostle Paul (1 Cor. 8:9–13).[245] The conscience always binds in such a way that to act against it is to sin. This is not a sin in the material sense of breaking a commandment of God, but in the formal sense. In this

---

244. De Moor, *Commentarius Perpetuus*, 3:247.
245. Ames, *Conscience*, 11–12 (I.iv.6); cf. Schenkel, "Gewissen," 140.

case a person does nothing evil but does act culpably because conscience has declared an incorrect command as being God's will. When we sin against our conscience, we believe that we are sinning against God, and in that case we really do sin against God.[246] A parallel would be an insult directed against a private person whom the insulter believed to be a king, though he was not (Ames).

Whoever despises the conscience despises God himself. But when conscience judges that we must do what is impermissible, it binds us but does not obligate us in the sense that we sin when we neglect to do what it prescribes. Because God commits us only to the good, the conscience that prescribes evil must be an erring conscience needing to be set aside. The conscience can turn a good deed into a crime, when it (erroneously) binds a person who commits it, but can never turn a crime, neither in the material nor certainly in the formal sense, into a good deed.[247]

But then Ames addresses an objection: "If an erroneous conscience does so bind that we may neither follow, nor not follow it without sin, then there lies a kind of necessity of sinning on those that do thus err, which cannot stand with the equity of God's Law."[248] In other words, the case can arise where one must sin: on the one hand, by doing what an erring conscience prescribes, one sins against God's commandment; on the other, by not doing it, one sins against the conscience formally. This means that one sins either materially or formally.[249] Response: Yes, unless one can set aside and better instruct the erring conscience.

Assured and Doubting Consciences[250]

A conscience is identified as doubting when, in answering the question of whether a particular act is permitted or not, it does not know how to answer.[251] In former times such a doubting conscience was generally accepted, and Jesuit casuistry built upon that acceptance the doctrine that one had to

246. Pictet, *De christelyke zedekunst*, 96 (II.x).
247. Pictet, *De christelyke zedekunst*, 97 (II.x).
248. Ames, *Conscience*, 14 (I.iv.13).
249. Ed. note: On the question of whether it is "a greater sin to go against such an erroneous conscience, or to do according to it"—materially following the conscience or formally refusing to follow it—Ames adds this wise counsel: it depends on the gravity of the respective sins ("greatness of sin according to the quality of the thing to be done or omitted"). Someone who refuses to attend worship for conscience's sake because of a "lewd and naughty preacher" sins more in refusing to worship God and honoring his conscience; another whose refusal is tied to the presence of idolatry would sin more by neglecting his conscience (*Conscience*, 15 [I.iv.13]).
250. LO: *certa*; *dubia*.
251. Ames, *Conscience*, 16–19 (I.v).

trust in advance that the conscience had decided according to probability.[252] Nowadays many deny the existence of a doubting conscience. It is said that because conscience is knowledge—even more than that, it is *con*sciousness—it is therefore *doubly certain*,[253] completely knowing, normed with indubitable certainty.[254] This too is logomachy, for the conscience (always certain in itself as consciousness) is also identified as conscience in that situation where one cannot obtain firm knowledge, where the conscience, the judgment, can also be weak or darkened.[255] Rothe says that all the cases of conscience built on the doubting conscience should be removed and that, where conscience is genuinely skeptical, where it does not know, there it is obligated conscientiously to abstain: "When you doubt, do not act."[256]

According to Ames,[257] "First, in such things as are necessary to salvation, and God's worship, no opinion can be sufficient, though it have never so great certainty of reason; because faith is required to these and faith takes only the infallible word of God." However, he then adds, "In such things, which are more remote from their principles, diligent care is to be had, that we also get a certain persuasion, or belief of them, out of the Scriptures; but if that cannot be obtained, it is lawful in our actions to follow some such opinion, as is tried by the rule of Scripture." And further, "Using all diligence to be certain (though we be not) it is lawful in many things to follow that opinion, which is most profitable." With respect to a doubting conscience, Ames distinguishes *speculative* doubt from *practical* doubt. The former "is that, which is *not* immediately conversant about a practice or action"; the latter "is that, which is *immediately* conversant about some particular action." We are to respond to speculative doubt by making "diligent enquiry" so that "we may perceive the truth and not *doubt*." Here is the reason: "For the more certain our knowledge is, touching those things which we do, the more *confident* we are in doing, and more joyful when we have done them." That being said, "Oft times it is lawful to do a thing, though a *speculative doubt* remain,

---

252. Ed. note: This is the Jesuit doctrine of "probabilism," where in difficult matters of conscience and moral ambiguity all that is needed is a probable case for a specific act to be right.

253. Ed. note: "Doubly certain" is our attempt to capture Bavinck's emphasis on *be* in *bewustzijn*. *Bewustzijn* is a loan translation (calque), a literal root-for-root translation from the Latin *con-scientia* ("to know with"). Bavinck is thus intensifying the certainty of the knowledge by emphasizing "with."

254. LO: *scientia; con + scientia*; Schenkel, "Gewissen," 139–40.

255. As Schenkel himself acknowledges: "Gewissen," 139–40.

256. LO: *casus conscientiae; conscientia dubia; quod dubitas ne feceris*; Rothe, *Theologische Ethik*, 264–69 (§147); Pictet, *De christelyke zedekunst*, 98 (II.x).

257. Ed. note: What follows in this paragraph are passages from Ames, *Conscience*, 16–19 (I.v). This section is a considerable enlargement of Bavinck's original.

because he that does so, does not necessarily do either against a *doubting* conscience, nor without a persuaded conscience; for notwithstanding that *speculative* doubt he may assuredly conclude with himself; that, that which he does, ought to be done." The case of *practical doubt* is quite different: "It is not lawful to do anything against a *practical* doubt; that is, a doubt whether the thing to be done is lawful." Ames lists four reasons: (1) it cannot be done out of faith (Rom. 14:23); (2) someone who sins against a practical doubt "does not sufficiently abhor sin" because "he willingly and wittingly exposes himself to the danger of sinning"; (3) such a person "is not fully enough addicted to God's will" by acting "against the law of friendship" and "the law of love to God"; and (4) "In things doubtful, the safest way is to abstain; for herein is no danger of sinning." Indeed, the safest and best choice is "when you doubt, do not act."

Strong and Weak Consciences[258]

According to Ames, "A good conscience admits of degrees, for which cause it is by the apostle distinguished into a *weak* and a *strong* conscience" (Rom. 15:1). A strong conscience is one that "is *established* in the truth" (Rom. 14:5; cf. 2 Pet. 1:12), which "knows that an idol is nothing" (1 Cor. 8:4, 7 NIV), bears the weak (Rom. 15:1), and is not offended (Rom. 14:3). A weak conscience has been improved by faith, but, nonetheless, still depends on someone other than God and something other than his Word (Rom. 14:15). Consequently, it still considers some things unclean (1 Cor. 8:7; Rom. 14:14), is quickly saddened (Rom. 14:15), is easily offended (Rom. 14:15, 21; 1 Cor. 8:9, 12), and condemns others (1 Cor. 10:29; Rom. 14:3, 15). The distinction between a free and an unfree conscience is closely connected with this distinction between strong and weak.

Broad and Narrow (Scrupulous) Consciences[259]

Having been weakened by forgetting the function of judging, a broad conscience is a weakened conscience that permits everything. In contrast, a narrow or scrupulous conscience is always judging, always asking whether something is good. Such a conscience never discerns the good immediately and clearly, but is quickly frightened and becomes timid. A weak or scrupulous conscience

258. Ames, *Conscience*, 38–40 (I.xiii). Ed. note: What follows in this paragraph is all taken from chapter I.xiii. The specific Scripture references are from Ames.
259. Ed. note: Ames covers this distinction under the rubric "Of a Scrupulous Conscience" (*Conscience*, 19–21 [I.vi]). Ames helpfully points to different sources of weak, scrupulous consciences: they may come (a) from God as punishment or testing, (b) from "the suggestion of the Devil," (c) because of melancholy or other bodily condition, or (d) "from the society of scrupulous men."

must be distinguished from the tender conscience that is horrified by sin and cannot bear it in the least.

Sleeping and Alert Consciences

Perkins draws the basic distinction between an alert or alive conscience and a dead one. Dead consciences can be viewed in two stages: a slumbering or sleeping conscience and a seared conscience. The former is inoperative until the sinner faces a major crisis such as sickness or fear. Perkins gives the example of Joseph's brothers, who were not troubled by the evil they had done to Joseph until, in Egypt, they risked losing their brother Benjamin (Gen. 42:21). A seared conscience (1 Tim. 4:2) is inactive with respect to all sins, even the very worst. By contrast, an active or awake conscience is fully functional and either accuses or exonerates. Consciences can also be clean or unclean, and at rest or restless (or disturbed, as, e.g., with Franciscus Spira).[260]

7. OUR DUTY TO AND CARE OF OUR CONSCIENCE[261]

Our first obligation to our conscience is to have our unclean, evil, restless consciences cleansed by the blood of Christ (Heb. 9:14). A true conscience comes only through faith; its accusations can be stopped only by the cross, where God's law was fully satisfied. Once we have obtained an objectively good conscience, it must also be made subjectively good. We accomplish this, first of all, by bringing the Word of God more and more into the *syntērēsis* and freeing it from all laws that conflict with it. Christ must be the content of our conscience. The subjective standard in our conscience must be brought increasingly into correspondence with the objective standard. Christ must liberate our conscience from every external authority and make it acknowledge God's will as the only valid authority. In a word, the law of God must

---

260. Ed. note: Franciscus Spira (1502–48) was a native of Padua, Italy. He left the Roman Catholic Church and became openly critical of Rome and an enthusiastic advocate for the Reformation and its evangelical faith. Under intense pressure from the Inquisition, fearing for his family, position, and possessions, he publicly recanted his conversion in 1548. Tragically, believing he had now forfeited his salvation and was a reprobate, he was thrown into the deepest of melancholies and died within six months. His story spread rapidly through Europe, and numerous Protestant polemicists (including John Calvin) used it as a warning against backsliding and the temptation of despair. The full title of a famous four-author Latin text dating back to 1550/51 captures what was seen to be at stake: *The History of Franciscus Spira, Who Fell into a Dreadful State of Despair Because, Having Once Assumed a Profession of Evangelical Truth, He Had Afterwards Recanted and Condemned the Same.* The Spira story also served as the inspiration for Nathaniel Woodes's play *The Conflict of Conscience.* See Sullivan, "Doctrinal Doubleness"; Westerink, *Melancholie en predestinatie.* A resource that would have been available to Bavinck is Westhoff, "Francesco Spiera."
261. Perkins, *Eene Verhandeling,* 106–10.

be written in our heart. In the second place, we must work at clarifying our consciousness, so that with increasing purity it reflects our situation, our dispositions, and our deeds. To use an image, we must keep polishing the mirror of our consciousness. We do that by avoiding sin, because sin anesthetizes the consciousness, while holiness clarifies it. And, finally, we must free the judging work of our conscience from all passions and influences that would hinder us from hearing it submissively. In this way we obtain a conscience that is *independent* (taking only the standard of God's will into account), *clear* (sensitive, tender—so that all our being is directly reflected in our consciousness), and *powerful* (the conscience is the highest power within us).

8. FREEDOM OF CONSCIENCE

Conscience is universally human; an absolutely conscience-less person does not exist. Conscience can, of course, be silenced (for a time), but it can never be extinguished. But conscience possesses an individual character; there are as many consciences as there are people. The moral law is one, immutable, and valid for all people. At the same time, different people interpret the moral law, each in their own way; they assimilate it in accord with their own nature, with the groups to which they belong, and with the societies in which they live. Another important consideration: sin darkens our knowledge of the moral law; all of us have *abnormal* consciences. If they were normal, all people would hear the same moral law, but in fact no one has perfect knowledge of the moral law, and the consciences of people vary in purity, clarity, and strength.

Nonetheless, whatever its condition may be, conscience always dictates what it prescribes or proscribes (even if an act is sinful) in the form and under the rubric of the law of God. Whoever sins against conscience believes that a sin is being committed against God and his law. Freedom of conscience flows from our recognition of this reality. The following points should be observed.

First, conscience binds only the subject and no one else. As the apostle Paul noted: "Why should my liberty be determined by someone else's conscience?" (1 Cor. 10:29). That is to say, we must respect each other's conscience and consider conscience sacred. We must also take care not to offend each other's conscience.[262]

Second, conscience limits all earthly authority such as that of the church and the state. Neither may compel us to do what our conscience forbids us to do, lest we damn ourselves by sinning against God or against him whom

---

262. Ed. note: At this point Bavinck added a footnote reference to "see dictaat Kuenen. Rothe there." This is a reference to Bavinck's own notes of lectures on ethics dictated by his Leiden professor Abraham Kuenen. These notes have been preserved and are in the Bavinck Archives.

we honor as God.[263] This does not mean that the church and state should not require anything that is forbidden by the consciences of its members. In that case, no community would be possible. Individuals who disagree with the law and have conscientious objection to it should not be compelled. They may offer passive resistance, but not the active resistance of rebellion.

263. Pictet, *De christelyke zedekunst*, 100.

6

The Sinner and the Law

As a sign of God's forbearance, an order of lawfulness remains even after the fall into sin. Human moral nature, including the conscience, continues to guide and bind people, albeit imperfectly. That we remain under the law is a sign of God's favor to us; he has not left us entirely to our own devices and instincts. Human beings have not become beasts; they are still guided by natural law. This reality is taught by the apostle Paul in Romans 1–2 and testified to by philosophers and by the laws and practice of nations.

While it is true that all people have a sense of this natural moral law, with its sense of obligations to God and to the neighbor, all expressions of this law apart from biblical revelation are but pale approximations of the real thing. Outside of revelation it is not clear that God is the author of the law that binds our conscience; reasons for obeying it other than those that come from divine authority will fail to satisfy and hold us fully accountable. Reason cannot do it; Kant cannot explain why people should obey the categorical imperative of the practical reason. Appeals to logic (Hegel), to social hierarchies (parents, the state), or to evolutionary processes are also unable to account for the unconditional validity and authority of the moral law.

When we start with revelation as the disclosure of God's will for his creatures, we base the authority of the moral law on God himself. The good, which is identical to God's will, binds us and imposes duty on us. Similarly, we possess virtue as we desire and do that which is good. The moral law speaks to us in our conscience with an unconditional and all-encompassing authority and shows us how God wants his people to be as well as how they are to act. The Decalogue is the summa of the law; the rest of the Old Testament and the New Testament are its explanation and commentary.

The law of God in the Old Testament has three parts: ceremonial, judicial, and moral. All three are fulfilled in Christ. This law is spiritual and unchangeable, and its purpose is to govern the entire person, inwardly as well as outwardly. The moral law needs to be distinguished from the law of thought, from civil law, and also from natural law. God's law has three functions: a civil use to restrain evil, a pedagogical use to convict us of sin and judgment, and a teaching use as a rule of life to guide believers.

All people have a sense of natural law and natural morality and experience the conflict between good and evil, even when they do not understand it as clearly as those whose minds are illumined by the word of God. However, moral dispositions are also shaped by differences of social class, environment, and personal temperament. Nurture has the task of developing this disposition and forming it into moral character. It is each person's responsibility to become virtuous; important virtues such as wisdom, courage, temperance, and righteousness are developed and exercised in community. The important communities are marriage, family, friendship, work, art, church, and state.

This natural morality is not produced by Christianity but grew from the root of natural, created humanity. Nonetheless, Christianity has influenced, modified, and improved natural morality. From the perspective of God and his kingdom, natural morality has absolutely no value; it does bring us a step closer to the kingdom of heaven. It does have great value from an earthly perspective: it leaves humanity without excuse; it restrains persons; it alleviates life's burdens and makes human life bearable, even to give it some joy so that it is not yet a hell on earth. Natural morality also serves the church and individual believers by being the presupposition of faith, a preparation for the spiritual life. Regenerate people are double persons: Christians are no longer flesh, Christ lives in them and they in Christ, but they still live in the flesh and struggle against it. The purpose and task of ethics is therefore to describe how regenerate people are to manifest their eternal heavenly life in the form of the temporal earthly life.

§15. THE LAW

Our human moral-rational nature has remained, even in the state of sin.[1] This moral-rational nature is manifest in the human moral instrument, the conscience.[2] In the first part of this chapter we shall see that conscience is bound to the law, and in the second part we shall explore how this law is actualized in the individual, in the state, and in society and cultivates civil

1. See §13.
2. See §14.

order.[3] The order of God's forbearance can be characterized in one word: *lawfulness*.[4] Here we see how the order of creation before the fall is distinct from the order of grace in the church of Christ.[5] In a certain sense, prior to the fall there was no positive command, no objective law placed before humanity.[6]

The law was the immanent, life-directing movement of the will: people acting in accord with their rational natures manifested the law, which became public in the lives and conduct of people. "Ought" and "want"[7] coincided completely; people were permitted to do what they wanted. Only one boundary was put into place for that human will—namely, the prohibition "Thus far and no further!" However, this changes after the fall: God now binds those who are fleeing from him, in their conscience, to the law, still written in their hearts. Through conscience, God places us under the law. This is the way it has to be. First John 3:4 tells us that "sin is lawlessness";[8] it violates and puts aside all God's laws; it is absolute, thoroughgoing willfulness. The character of sin is that it does not rest until it has shaken off all law and can do anything it wills to do. It wants to be absolutely unruly and absurd. This would result, however, in completely dehumanizing people, in turning us into animals, since animals, after all, do not submit to moral laws but live according to their instincts. God however, had a purpose for humanity; he wanted to re-create it.[9] In order to do this, God had to guard the very humanity of people, and he does this by bringing humanity under the law. Lawfulness is the character of God's patient ordering, the means by which humanity is guarded and prepared for re-creation, for the grace in Christ.

Adam stood *in* the law (cf. Christ in Ps. 40: "I delight to do your will, O my God, and your law is within my heart"). Because of the fall, the law came to

---

3. LO: *justitia civilis*.

4. DO: *wettelijkheid*.

5. Wichelhous, *Die Lehre der Heiligen Schrift*, 387.

6. Ed. note: Bavinck added a marginal reference here to Marckius, *Historia Paradis Illustrata*, 390 (II.vii, §3): "against Alting: Adam must have had consciousness of the good. Alting rejects the covenant of works." Marckius cites Alting on Heb. 8:6.

7. GO: *sollen und wollen*.

8. GrO: ἡ ἁμαρτία ἐστὶν ἡ ἀνομία.

9. Ed. note: Bavinck uses different words to describe the renewing, restoring work of God's grace in Christ with respect to creation/nature: *restauratie* ("restoration"), *herstel* ("restoration"), and *herschepping* ("re-creation"). Two key points need to be underscored: *restauratie* and *herstel* both mean "restoration," but (a) the former suggests "mere" restoration or repristination, while (b) the latter points to full renewal and re-creation. In the passage that follows, Bavinck uses the words *herscheppen* and *herschepping*, in contrast with *schepping* ("creation"). We are translating *herscheppen* and *herschepping* as "re-create" and "re-creation." For more on this, see Veenhof, "Nature and Grace in Bavinck," esp. A. M. Wolters's translator's preface, p. 12.

stand *above* and humanity to stand *under* the law. Ever since then, the moral
ideal hovers over us, out of reach. Sin requires law and its power to uphold
order in conscience, society, public opinion, the state, and so on, so that sin
can be held in check and not morally destroy the human race completely.[10] We
need to consider the following matters with respect to this law: terminology,
author, content, object, and purpose or use.

Terminology[11]

We call this law the "moral law"[12] because it concerns morality. The moral
law is the rule for human being and doing, also for religious being and doing.
It is more common to speak of "natural law,"[13] so called, according to some,
because it came forth from God's nature and was natural to humanity as it
ought to be. According to others, it is called "natural" because it is known—at
least with regard to its substance—out of and through nature, without special
revelation, and obligates humans without mediation by anyone or anything.[14]
Jurists speak in the same way of "natural justice, which Nature teaches all
living creatures."[15] They distinguish this from the common "law of the nations" and the "civil law" based on the law of the state.[16] Rothe disputes
the term "natural law," because rather than directly recognizing this law in
their natural condition, human beings are shut off from clear and complete
awareness of it by their natural sinfulness.[17] Awareness of the law is now
only achieved through salvation.[18] The need for the law does naturally lie
within us, but not the power to discover it. It is not a so-called rational law.
On the contrary, it is a positive law, which sets itself over against humans
by external authority. It is a divine law revealed by God, though mediated
by human beings.

Harless acknowledges that pagans do know *that* God exists but do not
know what God *is* or what God *wills*.[19] The pagan world "is nowhere of
such a nature as to correspond to God's revelation of Himself in His word.
And with respect to the *quid velit*, we find only a relative approximation."[20]

---

10. Wichelhous, *Die Lehre der Heiligen Schrift*, 388–90.
11. DO: *Naam*; de Moor, *Commentarius Perpetuus*, 2:586–88.
12. LO: *lex moralis*.
13. LO: *lex naturae*.
14. Marckius, *Historia Paradis Illustrata*, II.viii, §4.
15. LO: *jus naturae quod Natura omnia animalia docuit*.
16. LO: *jus gentium; ius civile*; de Moor, *Commentarius Perpetuus*, 2:586.
17. Rothe, *Theologische Ethik*, 2:478–84 (§§800–802).
18. GO: *Erlösung*.
19. LO: *quod sit Deus; quid sit; quid velit Deus*.
20. Harless, *System of Christian Ethics*, 110.

Now surely the natural law and Decalogue differ[21] in manner of revelation, in extent, purity, clarity, and foundation ("I am the LORD your God"). However, one may speak of the natural law as something known from nature because[22] (a) all human beings experience obligations toward God and to their neighbor, regardless of what those obligations are and how they must be fulfilled; *and* they feel bound to obey the moral law when they know it; (b) Paul teaches the reality of the natural law in Romans 1:19–20; (c) our conscience confirms this; (d) philosophers such as Cicero testify to it;[23] (e) the nations with their natural and national law bear witness to it; (f) the church fathers all testify to it;[24] (g) without natural law the moral world order, the moral order of God's kingdom,[25] and human dependence on God would completely collapse (against the libertines [Calvin][26] and atheists like Hobbes). The natural law and the Decalogue differ from the law prior to the fall in that they are negative, consisting of prohibitions: "Thou shalt not . . ." So they presuppose sin, the doing what is forbidden.

Author

The law, to which our conscience binds us and subjects us, needs to rest in God and is based on his authority. For the "ought"[27] of the law presupposes a will higher than ours or than that of those who are equal to us, to which our will and that of others is subject. "*Thou* shalt" presupposes an "*I* am the LORD" who pronounces the law. Other humans cannot compel us; we feel ourselves to be free with respect to them. Neither can angels. The law needs to be based on divine authority.[28] The law cannot be derived and explained from any of the following: (a) our own ego ("I"), which lays down the law for itself, because it cannot say *why* I must do this or that or *why* I do what I do; (b) the authority of parents, the state, or society (Darwin and his followers); since other human beings do not naturally have any authority over us, we feel bound to these authorities only insofar as God's authority rings

---

21. Cf. Alting, *Theologia Problematica Nova*, X.476–78; de Moor, *Commentarius Perpetuus*, 2:589.

22. Ed. note: Bavinck lists only five points, a–e; since (d) and (e) each have several additional reasons, we have separated them.

23. Cicero, *De legibus* I.15–16. Ed. note: Bavinck adds: "except for the Cyrenians," a sect mentioned by Cicero in *Tusculan Disputations* III.13, 15, 22, 31.

24. De Moor, *Commentarius Perpetuus*, 2:589; Marckius, *Historia Paradis Illustrata*, 389 (II.viii, §2).

25. LO: *regnum Dei morale*.

26. Calvin, *Treatise against the Anabaptists and the Libertines*.

27. GO: *Sollen*.

28. Stahl, *Fundamente einer christlichen Philosophie*, 84–99 (III, §§32–38).

through them; (c) the world and nature (Stoics), over against which we feel free and are allowed to control as much as we can. The moral law ought to have the same cause as the conscience, which, like a divine judge, holds us accountable to the law and pronounces sentence on us.

Even the pagans experienced this. Cicero states that "Law is not a product of human thought, nor is it any enactment of peoples, but [is] something eternal which rules the whole universe by its wisdom in command and prohibition. . . . Wherefore that Law which the gods have given to the human race has been justly praised."[29] However, for the pagans, this law of God has no instrument by which it reveals itself other than the right reason of the philosophers.[30] The ultimate source of moral knowledge is reason. To reconstruct the moral law through reason is the problem for pagans and more recent moral philosophers. This is a problem for which they think a solution can be found. However, due to the depravity of reason, it is, in fact, impossible. Rationalism, supranaturalism, Kant, and the materialists have clearly demonstrated this.[31] The Christian church, Christian philosophy, and theology based the moral law only on God's authority. It was not called "natural law," as if it rested on and in human nature.[32] However, Hugo Grotius (1583–1645), and especially Christian Wolff (1679–1754), brought a change in this way of thinking.[33]

Hobbes continued to base moral law on God's authority, but Wolff, just like Grotius, completely abstracts from God and declares: "What is good will remain good even without God. The atheist ought morally to act in the same way as the theist, since the actual ground for moral behavior is situated in the physical nature, not in God. Such is the case with nature obligating us to marriage as well, connecting lust with cohabitation."[34] Now there is some truth here in that atheists will likely behave in much the same way as the theists, but not if they consistently apply their theory in practice. Kant similarly loosens the tie between God and the good, situating its binding power in reason, in the inexplicable categorical imperative of the practical reason. It cannot be explained how autonomous people can give themselves such a law. Consequently, Hegel finds the source of knowledge and sanction

---

29. Cicero, *De legibus* II.4, in Cicero, *"De republica," "De legibus,"* 381.

30. LO: *recta ratio*. See Betz, *Ervaringswijsbegeerte*.

31. Ed. note: Bavinck discusses both (naturalistic) rationalism and supranaturalism in *RD*, 1:284–312, 355–65.

32. Harless, *System of Christian Ethics*, 88–95, 110 (§§12, 14).

33. Vilmar, *Theologische Moral*, 1:59–94.

34. Ed. note: Bavinck indicates this as a quotation but provides no reference. It is likely taken from Wolff's famous 1721 oration "On the Practical Philosophy of the Chinese," in which he insisted that morality does not depend on revelation or on God's commands but is obtained from the general rule or law of nature.

of the moral law in logic, in thinking. After all, the whole of nature, all of reality, flows forth from the logical laws of thought or categories. Logic is the essence of all things, also of people.[35] This all leaves the unconditional validity and authority of the moral law unexplained, as is the case for deducing its authority from parents, the state, and so on, as advocated by Alexander Bain and Herbert Spencer.[36] The law that binds us is itself "the good" which is the norm for the will. It presupposes the majesty and the unconditional right of the good. Not only does the formal law itself—the character of the commandment, the "ought"—lay claim on us, but its content does as well.[37] The moral law is precisely this: the good as an external authority over against us.

The good, which is identical to God's will, binds us and imposes *duty* on us.[38] Similarly, we possess *virtue* as we desire and do that which is good.[39] The moral law speaks to us in our conscience with an unconditional and all-encompassing authority: This moral law ought to be your very own nature and being. You will never shed it![40] That the moral law is based on God's authority can readily be deduced from the nature of authority and from the content of the moral law. Moreover, we know from the Holy Scriptures that the heading of the law is "I am the LORD your God" (Exod. 20:2). The moral law is acknowledged throughout the whole Bible as God's law, even by Jesus himself, who explicitly speaks of biblical commandments as God's commands and words (Matt. 15:4). Therefore, the law cannot be undone, only fulfilled (Matt. 5:17; cf. Rom. 7:23, 27; 8:2).[41] When modern thinkers posit an evolutionary origin for biblical law and deny its divine source, they need to be challenged, as Harless has done: "The law of God in Israel is not the product of a development-process in the people of Israel in which they had gradually become conscious to themselves of what is right and good in the relation, whether of man to man, or man to God. On the contrary, God testifies His will in gradual revelation, in opposition to the spirit predominating amongst the people."[42]

This is evident from its content but also in the way that the law does not just show us how we ought to relate to God and to our neighbor. Instead, first and foremost, it shows us how God wants his people to be, contrary to the spirit of the nations that surround them. Everything here is brought

---

35. Stahl, *Fundamente einer christlichen Philosophie*, 87–90.
36. Ed. note: On Bain and Spencer, see chap. 5, n. 143 above.
37. J. Müller, *Christian Doctrine of Sin*, 1:37–42.
38. DO: *plicht*.
39. DO: *deugd*.
40. Stahl, *Fundamente einer christlichen Philosophie*, 84–99 (§§32, 33).
41. Harless, *System of Christian Ethics*, 102 (§13).
42. Harless, *System of Christian Ethics*, 111 (§14).

under the norm of the godly will. All the relationships between people and God and among his subjects are regulated.[43] The source of knowledge of the moral law, therefore, cannot be only our conscience and reason—although they are very valuable—but Holy Scripture in its entirety. This means not only the Pentateuch but also the prophets and the New Testament. The Decalogue is only the summa of the law; the Old and New Testaments are the explanation and commentary.[44]

Content

We distinguish three parts in God's law: the ceremonial law, the judicial or forensic law, and the moral law.[45] The first two have not been abolished or removed by Jesus—he did not abolish anything—but have been fulfilled in and through him. The shadows vanish when the body is present. What was merely a type in the Old Testament is now exactly what is completely spiritualized and realized. The form has changed; the essence is the same. All sacrifices and priests culminate and find their full realization in the one sacrifice and in the one high priest, in the same way that all the prophets and Davidic kings find their purpose realized in Christ. Yes, even the civil law of Israel is fulfilled in Christ and in his church. It has become spiritual truth. Laws concerning war, tithing, pledges, and marriage still have a spiritual meaning for the church, even today, and are written for our benefit.[46]

We are concerned here only with the moral law. According to some this law is based solely on God's will: something is good only because God says it is good.[47] For others the law is based entirely on God's being.[48] And for a third group[49] the moral law is based partly on God's nature—such as the first table of the Decalogue—and partly on God's free will, as is the case with needing to celebrate the Sabbath on the seventh day, the prohibitions of polygamy and theft, and so on. These laws presuppose that God has first voluntarily ordained

---

43. Harless, *System of Christian Ethics*, 105–8 (§§13, 14).

44. Vilmar, *Theologische Moral*, 1:51.

45. LO: *lex ceremonialis; lex judicialis; lex moralis*.

46. Vilmar, *Theologische Moral*, 1:53.

47. F. Turretin, *Institutes of Elenctic Theology*, 2:10 (XI.2.x); de Moor, *Commentarius Perpetuus*, 2:614 (XI.xxviii). Ed. note: Bavinck repeats the examples given by Turretin: "Occam, in 2 q. 19+; Gerson, 'De Vita Spirituali Animae,' (1) in *Opera Omnia* [repr. 1987], 3:5–16; Peter of Ailly, in 1. Q. 14+." Turretin also includes "Almayno, *Acutissimi clarissim . . . Moralia*, Pt. 3:15 [1525], pp. 103–4."

48. Maresius, *Systema Theologicum*, 319–20 (VII.14); Turretin, *Institutes of Elenctic Theology*, 1:233 (III.18); 2:10 (XI.2.x); Turretin, *Institutio*, II.11; de Moor, *Commentarius Perpetuus*, 2:615 (XI.xxviii).

49. Marckius, *Compendium Theologiae*, 218 (XI.xxviii).

that the human race would procreate and would have property. These commandments could be held in abeyance temporarily; occasionally dispensation from the law could be granted, for example, from monogamy.[50] Dispensation was also granted for such things as deceit (2 Kings 10:19). Marckius denies these but does find examples of dispensation in Levites killing Israelites (Exod. 32:27–28; Num. 25:7–8), Moses killing the Egyptian (Exod. 2:12), and Abraham sacrificing his son (Gen. 22:2).[51] Other examples include stealing from the Egyptians (Exod. 3:21–22; 12:35–36), killing the Canaanites (Deut. 7:2), and possibly Hosea marrying a prostitute (Hosea 1:2).

Insofar as the moral law rests on God's nature, it is also unchangeable.[52] The law is spiritual, as Jesus (cf. Matt. 5 and 23) and the faithful (cf. Ps. 119:96; Rom. 7:14) understand it to be. Jesus summarizes the moral law in Matthew 22:37 with this command: "You shall love the Lord your God with all your heart and with all your soul and with all your mind." In his understanding of murder he also includes anger (Matt. 5:22, 28), and he sees the whole law culminating in perfect obedience: "You therefore must be perfect, as your heavenly Father is perfect" (Matt. 5:48). These guidelines follow from this point for interpreting the law: (a) all prohibitions include their opposite as a commandment, and vice versa—divorce is prohibited, so chastity is commanded; (b) under the heading of a virtue or vice all corresponding items are included—for example, the commandment to honor one's parents encompasses love and obedience, including that toward other authorities; (c) with an external sin, its source and cause are also condemned—for example, the prohibition against murder includes anger (cf. Matt. 5:22; 1 John 3:15) and even the pretense of anger (cf. 1 Thess. 5:22).[53] That is precisely why the law is perfect and the only rule of life (Ps. 19:8), so that everyone who obeys the law will have eternal life (Lev. 18:5). Nothing, then, can be added to it or taken away from it, because the law orders us to love God and our neighbor, which is everything and includes everything.[54] For this reason we must reject the "evangelical counsels" of Roman Catholicism, the triad of obedience, poverty, and chastity.[55]

---

50. De Moor, *Commentarius Perpetuus*, 2:616 (XI.xxviii).

51. De Moor, *Commentarius Perpetuus*, 2:614 (XI.xxviii).

52. De Moor, *Commentarius Perpetuus*, 2:630 (XI.xxx); this section is directed against the Socinians and Roman Catholics, especially the Jesuits.

53. Calvin, *Institutes*, II.viii.6–10; Turretin, *Institutes of Elenctic Theology*, 2:34–37 (XI.6); de Moor, *Commentarius Perpetuus*, 2:636–38.

54. De Moor, *Commentarius Perpetuus*, 2:638.

55. LO: *consilia evangelica*; de Moor, *Commentarius Perpetuus*, 2:638; Vilmar, *Theologische Moral*, 2:101. Ed. note: Bavinck also mentions the journal *Protestantsche bijdragen tot bevordering van christelijk leven en christelijke wetenschap*, founded in 1870 and edited by

Object

The law controls the entire person, inwardly and outwardly, and not only our deeds as the Pelagians claim, and also Schleiermacher.[56] According to Schleiermacher, because the law can only measure outward conduct—deeds, acts— and cannot "determine and measure . . . *the inward, the disposition of the mind*," it cannot bring awareness of sin.[57] However, the law also regulates the essence, the nature of a human person.[58] Notwithstanding, there is some truth in Schleiermacher's statement. The law orders or prohibits and is therefore always directed toward the will. Thus the law always focuses first on deeds, those that are produced by the human *will*. The moral law is indifferent to whether we are tall or short, healthy or sick, strong or weak, beautiful or ugly, or any number of other qualities found among humans. The law's object is in fact the human will, which is the seat of morality—that which is good or evil. The law regulates human deeds, and, to the extent that who we are (our essence and nature) comes from our deeds, the law regulates this as well. We are not responsible for those things over which we have absolutely no influence (our temperament, inclinations, and so forth). However, because we sinned in Adam, our sinful nature is included. Our being, our inclinations, the condition and actions of our soul and mind, to the degree that they are acts of the will (whether in us or in Adam), are subject to the moral law along with the will and our deeds.[59] Moral law must therefore be distinguished from the *law of thought*;[60] the law of thought is only for our thinking, for the mind, and definitely not for the will and the heart, which have a completely different law. So the law of thought rules over only a small part of our being human, ought to be confined to that area, and should therefore never become the law for everything and everyone (cf. Hegel).

The law of thought also does not bind completely; it does not obligate us in our conscience. We do not experience guilt when we make a mistake in logic, and we do not ask forgiveness. However, the law of thought, and reason itself,

---

Daniel Chantepie de la Saussaye and Nicholas Beets, but cites no specific passage. Bavinck also fails to mention J. Müller's discussion of the *consilium evangelicum* in *Christian Doctrine of Sin*, 1:51–58.

56. J. Müller, *Christian Doctrine of Sin*, 37–51. Ed. note: On Schleiermacher, see esp. pp. 43–51.

57. Ed. note: J. Müller, *Christian Doctrine of Sin*, 48. Ed. note: Müller points out that there is no good reason that the perfect form of morality cannot be "denoted by the law" and that "it is just this exhibition of the perfect" that Schleiermacher's ethics rejects. "In ethics there are only laws in so far as they express the *real action* (*wirkliche Handeln*) of the reason on nature" (p. 49).

58. Marckius, *Historia Paradis Illustrata*, 414; Cloppenburg, *Disputationes Theologicae XI*, I.xxii; Cloppenburg, *Exercitationes super Locos Communes Theologicos*, "Loci de status homine ante lapsum," disp. II, "De lege naturae."

59. J. Müller, *Christian Doctrine of Sin*, 43–45.

60. DO: *denkwet*.

stands under the moral law. The moral law, addressing our will—which is the center of our person—obligates us as whole persons, including the faculty of reason. So then we do feel guilty about error when it is not only logically wrong but also morally wrong. Our reason ought to operate and think formally and morally, in accordance with moral law. Concurrence with the moral law can never, therefore, be in conflict with the law of thought. What agrees with the one also agrees with the other. However, the opposite is not the case: one can think correctly and still sin against the moral law, because the moral law does not order reasoning itself (which can be correct) but only the quality of moral reasoning, the "how" of the reasoning. Therefore, every error in understanding is not yet a moral mistake, and is also not rooted in a moral mistake, as J. H. Gunning asserts.[61] So infallibility in understanding does not correspond with moral infallibility. The moral law is the center of all laws, regulating the entire human person: mind, will, feeling, and all powers.

The moral law needs to be distinguished from *civil law* (jurisprudence) as well; although they are related, morality and justice are not the same.[62] Justice must be based on the moral and ought not to be in conflict with it, but they are not identical. With justice, we are in the public sphere, in the terrain of the state and not the terrain of the inner life. Justice ought to and may be maintained with violence and coercion. Morality cannot be compelled, because we cannot bend the human will. Justice, therefore, is the moral in that the moral is situated in the public sphere—in the state.[63]

Finally, the moral law must be distinguished from the *natural law*.[64] In the past, the word "law" pointed solely to the positive law of the state or also to the law of nature given by God. "The 'law of nature' meant an ethical rule that was known by nature."[65] This changed in the sixteenth and seventeenth

61. Ed. note: Johannes Hermanus Gunning (1829–1905) was a Dutch Reformed minister and theological professor at the University of Amsterdam. He was a well-known proponent of the so-called *ethische theologie* of Daniel Chantepie de la Saussaye (1818–74), an antimodernist movement in the national Dutch Reformed Church (the Nederlandse Hervormde Kerk) that sought existentially to reconcile head and heart. Bavinck's source may have been Gunning, *Overlevering en wetenschap*, 134–37. Cf. Gunning, *Jezus Christus*, 17–33. The latter can also be found in Gunning, *Verzameld Werk*, 171–258.

62. DO: *rechtswet*.

63. See §16 below.

64. DO: *natuurwet*; E. Zeller, *Über Begriff und Begründung der sittlichen Gesetze*; also in *Vorträge und Abhandlungen*, 189–224.

65. LO: *lex naturae*; *RD*, 1:369. Ed. note: We are taking Bavinck's own lead here by inserting key elaborations of his point from his *Reformed Dogmatics*; a marginal note in his manuscript calls for inserting an "excerpt" from *Gereformeerde Dogmatiek*. The quoted passages that follow in this paragraph are from this same page. Bavinck follows the passage we have just cited with a lengthy quotation from Wilhelm Wundt (1832–1920), the German physician who was a key figure in the founding of modern psychology: "In the seventeenth century God legislated

centuries when "this term was transferred in a very metaphorical sense to
nature, for no one enacted those laws of nature and no one has the power
to obey or transgress them. That is the reason why even today there is much
disagreement about the concept and meaning of the 'laws of nature.'"[66] Schleiermacher's essay "On the Distinction between Natural Law and Moral Law"
attempted to show that the natural law was still an *obligation*, which is fully
realized nowhere, while the moral law is no longer an obligation, though it is
already partly realized.[67] According to Schleiermacher, "the moral law is not
to be set over against natural law, but it develops by means of an ascent from
the lower to that highest individual natural law."[68] The moral law, therefore,
is merely potentialized natural law, the law for human intellectual life. Similarly, "vegetation is a new law for the elementary life of the earth; the animal
world is a new law for the vegetation; the intellectual life of humanity is a
new law for the animal world, vegetation, and elementary life."[69] Humanity
gradually detects and fulfills this moral law as the law of its intellectual life.
This is nothing other than pantheism. There is a fundamental distinction
between natural law and moral law. There is no "ought" in natural law; it
may be violated without punishment, applies to all creation, and is a law of
impersonal being.[70] The moral law has obligations that *must*[71] happen, it
punishes offenses, it employs no physical coercion, and, unlike natural law,
it focuses on the personal, not on the impersonal: it addresses the will.

Purpose or Function

Three uses of the law are distinguished:

1. *Civil* use.[72] Here the law is used to "check all the unbridled passions of
people with the reins of its own external control."[73] The law is a bridle that

---

the laws of nature; in the eighteenth, nature itself decreed them; and in the nineteenth century
the individual natural scientists furnish them."

66. *RD*, 1:369; Cf. Christ, *Die sittliche Weltordnung*, 25.

67. GO: *Sollen.*

68. GO: *Steigerung*; F. Schleiermacher, "Über den Unterschied zwischen Naturgesetz und
Sittengesetz," cited by R. Rothe, *Theologische Ethik*, 3:359n1 (§800). Ed. note: Rothe provides
as a reference, "G W, III., B.2." In a footnote Rothe refers to J. T. Beck, *Die christliche Lehr-
Wissenschaft*, I.136–37.

69. Vilmar, *Theologische Moral*, 1:61–62; cf. C. I. Nitzsch, *System of Christian Doctrine*,
208 (§99); J. T. Beck, *Die christliche Lehr-Wissenschaft*, 136–43. Ed. note: Vilmar describes
this vision as "a fundamentally thoroughgoing pantheistic notion of law" (*im Grunde völlig
pantheistischen Gesezesbegriffes*).

70. GO: *Sollen.*

71. GO: *soll.*

72. LO: *usus politicus.*

73. Polyander et al., *Synopsis Purioris Theologiae*, disp. XVIII.41.

tames and restrains the raging animal within people. People can no longer fulfill the law in a spiritual sense. However, they can bring their actions into conformity with the law. When the rich young man came to Jesus and said, "All these [commandments] I have kept" (Matt. 19:20), Jesus does not contradict him. Paul claims that when it came "to righteousness under the law," he was "blameless" (Phil. 3:6). Though this was true with respect to a human court, it was untrue for God's. A correct and true disposition is lacking: I do not obey the commandments out of love for God and neighbor, and thus I do not fulfill them. That being said, external conformity of one's actions with the law can be present. It is precisely because of this that we are able to deceive ourselves so terribly, thinking that we can fulfill the law and go in search of eternal salvation in our own righteousness. In this situation we consider ourselves to be rich and lacking nothing (cf. 1 Cor. 4:8; Rev. 3:17). The civil use of the law, therefore, often results in pride, haughtiness, and legalistic virtue. This is not the fault of the law: it is the fault of those who use the law wrongly. In that case, there are "*works* of the law," but there is no "*heart* of the law"—frequently, the greater the external compliance, the greater the inner disharmony and distance.[74]

2. *Pedagogic* or *convicting* use.[75] Here the law functions in two ways: first, it convicts us of sin (Rom. 3:19, 20; 4:15; 5:20; 7:7–20); second, it convicts us of judgment and punishment (2 Cor. 3:7; Rom. 4:15; Heb. 12:29). It is through the law that we become aware of the ideal that God desires concerning what we ought to be and will be. To be precise, the law does not teach us that we cannot fulfill the law; we learn this from experience. Similarly, the law does not teach us that we can fulfill it; even less so does the law provide power or life. The law gives nothing; it only demands.

The law states only, unrelentingly: this is how you ought to be, and if you are not, then you are guilty and punishment awaits you. The first thing the law teaches us to know is sin in its actual character as guilt before a holy God,

74. GO: *Werke des Gesetzes*; *Herz des Gesetzes*; Harless, *System of Christian Ethics*, 113, 117–23.

75. LO: *usus paedagogicus*; *usus elencticus*. Ed. note: The passages that follow are taken from Hollaz, *Examen*; Philippi, *Kirchliche Glaubenslehre*, "Die Lehre von den Gnadenmitteln," 5/2:4n. Philippi's note refers back to H. F. F. Schmid, *Doctrinal Theology*, 519. Bavinck's brief summaries have been filled in with larger sections from Hollaz by way of Schmid, 515–16. Further definition of both the *elenctic* and *pedagogic* uses follows: "The *elenchtical* use consists in the manifestation and reproof of sin, and also in the demonstration of the most severe divine judgment. Rom. 3:20." "The *pedagogic* use of the Law consists in indirectly compelling the sinner to go to Christ. Although the Law formally and directly neither knows nor teaches Christ, yet by accusing, convincing, and alarming the sinner, it indirectly compels him to seek for solace and help in Christ the Redeemer. Wherefore the Law is our Schoolmaster, to bring us unto Christ. Ga. 3:24" (Schmid, *Doctrinal Theology*, 515–16). The text is from Hollaz, *Examen*, 1021.

who functions as our Judge in the law. Second, the law works fear. The experience of Israel, where people loved the law (Pss. 19; 119), does not conflict with that. For the law, we must remember, was that of *Israel's* God. And he became *their* God not through the law but through promise.[76] However, as the law of the Judge, the law arouses fear, rage, and cursing; it leads to despair.[77] With this function, the law becomes the disciplinarian (leading us to Christ, Gal. 3:24).[78] "The law itself does not direct us to Christ, for the law knows nothing of Christ but functions in the same sense as the disease drives us to the doctor, namely, indirectly, since with it there is no salvation."[79]

3. *Teaching* use among believers.[80] This use "consists in the instruction and direction of all internal and external moral actions. Thus, the law is a perpetual rule of life, Matthew 5:17."[81]

§16. NATURAL MORALITY[82]

This section will provide a brief sketch of natural morality. This is possible because Christians in particular can discern better than others with the light of the Word what is in nature and thereby have learned to distinguish between nature and grace.[83] When people awaken to consciousness of the self, they immediately become aware that they are not who they should be. There is a law in their heart, a law that stands above them and opposes the law within their members. This former law undergirds their consciences, guiding them to choose between what is (relatively) good and evil. This gives rise to a struggle. The natural moral life is a life of conflict between good and evil. That is the

76. Harless, *System of Christian Ethics*, 118–19.

77. DO: *vertwijfelen.*

78. GrO: παιδαγωγός. Ed. note: Most recent translations (NIV, ESV, ISV) translate παιδαγωγός as "guardian"; only the NRSV translates it as "disciplinarian," which is in accord with Bavinck's *"tuchtmeester."*

79. F. A. Philippi, *Kirchliche Glaubenslehre*, 5/2:4n; H. F. F. Schmid, *Doctrinal Theology*, 519: "The divine Law is not the causative or conferring means of salvation to fallen humanity, but it is only the pedagogic means to a sinner seeking the causative means of salvation, Gal. 3:24. The Law leads to Christ not directly, but as disease leads to the physician, indirectly and on account of the manifested inability of obtaining salvation by the Law." The original Hollaz passage is *Examen*, 996.

80. LO: *usus didacticus.* Ed. note: Section 15 of Bavinck's manuscript ends here, which seems abrupt until we remember that we are still in Book I, "Humanity before Conversion," and that Bavinck will be devoting Book III to "Humanity after Conversion" and a thorough discussion of the Decalogue. This will be the content of vol. 2.

81. H. F. F. Schmid, *Doctrinal Theology*, 516. The original passage from Hollaz is *Examen*, 1021.

82. LO: *justitia civilis.*

83. Zahn, *Die natürliche Moral*, 3.

character of the moral. People feel called to this struggle. They feel that this is their moral task and that they need to be free to direct themselves in accord with reason.

The moral disposition, however, is shaped by differences of social class, environment, and personal temperament.[84] In relation to nature, nurture has the task of developing this disposition and forming it into moral character (consciousness). This happens especially when children are brought up under the moral law, learn to obey it, and begin of their own accord to do habitually what they ought to do by virtue of the commandment. This is how moral consciousness awakens and grows strong within people, who then feel conscience-bound to the law or moral idea. They sin who act contrary to this moral idea, initially out of weakness, later out of frivolity, and eventually out of malice. During this process, the conscience becomes silent, struggle ceases, the person sinks away, and the end is pessimism, the cry of moral lostness. On the other hand, they become accustomed to following the moral idea, encounter conflict, and surely suffer defeat often. However, through repentance they are led back to the moral idea. And in this way, in the process of falling and rising, the moral disposition that is eagerly devoted to the moral idea and is manifest in virtues is born. The moral character is an individual matter. Though it shares virtues in common that ought to adorn everyone, moral character applies these virtues in a way that is appropriate to each individual person. A finished moral character that no longer needs to struggle against sin and that always follows the moral idea has never existed. In this life, the moral is always a struggle.

The Greeks associated the virtues that manifest the moral character of natural humanity especially with wisdom, based on natural love for truth as the fruit of study and science.[85] Reason must rule.[86] This was followed by courage (manliness), based on self-respect, a sense of honor, and self-worth, which express themselves in great and noble deeds.[87] This is what we would

---

84. Ed. note: Parenthetically Bavinck added the four classic personality types that hark back to the Greek physician Hippocrates and were tied to the notion of four bodily "humors": the sanguine (optimistic and social), choleric (short-tempered or irritable), melancholic (analytical and quiet), and phlegmatic (relaxed and peaceful).

85. GrO: σοφία.

86. Ed. note: Bavinck's discussion of the classic virtues is brief and follows a different order than is traditional. He also indicates no sources; the major classic texts are Plato, *Republic* IV.426–35; Aristotle, *Nicomachean Ethics*; and Thomas Aquinas, *ST* Ia IIae qq. 56–67; IIa IIae qq. 45–170. Classically, the four cardinal virtues are, in this order, prudence, justice, fortitude (courage), and temperance. Bavinck treats wisdom as the first, followed by courage (ἀνδρεία), which he links with *virtus* ("power, manliness") rather than the usual *fortitudo*. Bavinck does not include prudence (φρόνησις) in his list.

87. GrO/LO/DO: ἀνδρεία; *virtus*; *mannelijkheid*.

call magnanimity,[88] manifest in actions that display selflessness and even self-sacrifice. A third virtue was temperance,[89] characterized by suppression of the passions, lucidity of spirit, moderation, and self-control, which needs little and is content. Finally there was justice or righteousness,[90] desiring to give others their due, a sense of fairness, and a zeal for justice and righteousness that often includes compassion.

Human beings, however, do not exist in isolation but display moral character and virtues in the moral spheres of human society. Viewed objectively, those communities exist outside and above individual persons. The highest good is not individual moral perfection but the moral perfection of humanity. In fact, the one cannot be achieved without the other.

The first community is marriage, to which we are drawn by sensual love. But a sense of shame already demonstrates that sensual love has to support what is moral. Marital love is moral when the lovers honor each other and love the human person in the other. Marriage is based on free choice and the permission of the parents. It should be entered into publicly, since ill-considered zeal and passionate love are thereby forced to maturity and are calmed. The moral idea of marriage requires monogamy and indissolubility, unless it has in fact been broken by adultery.

Community exists next in the family, especially in the love of parents and children. Parents are the givers and their children the receivers; parental love is the greater. Parents are to nurture their children, initially by requiring unquestioning obedience, but eventually training them to obey freely. Parents have authority and power over the children, who in turn show piety toward their parents. A sense of freedom, equality, justice, and righteousness takes shape in the circle of brothers and sisters. In this way family becomes a microcosm, a little world of the various relationships that multiply through association with other families: grandparents, uncles and aunts, cousins, all of whom give character to the family circle.

A still wider sphere is then formed by friendship, which is of great significance in natural morality. Friendship is not based on natural disposition, as marriage is, but on a disposition and a need nonetheless. The goal of friendship is not effort but relaxation,[91] an exercise of love and enjoyment. In friendship we seek to complement ourselves. It is therefore particularly important at a young age, when we are still being formed; in later life we maintain friendships

88. DO: *grootheid van ziel*.
89. GrO: σωφροσύνη.
90. GrO: δικαιοσύνη.
91. Ed. note: In Dutch, there is a play on the words *inspanning* ("effort, exertion") and *ontspanning* ("relaxation").

rather than establish them. Among pagans, friendship is manifested particularly in hospitality toward guests.

Our occupations form yet another sphere. Even when no bonds of love or friendship draw people together, commonality in the life of work, sustaining life and subduing the earth, often binds people together. Work communities vary greatly, and an array of unique virtues are deemed appropriate to each of them. Yet all these virtues are based on the moral ideal, on loyalty, honesty, and honor. In part, these virtues are more external and serve to maintain life. This notion of moral community implies that the relationship between employer and employee should be free: employees are not merely a labor force but human persons.

Temporal life has great value in itself for humanity and also in the goal of life that lies beyond us. Bodily life must be sustained not only in its being—within which we suffer, due to immorality, among other things—but also in its well-being and health. This makes moderation in food and drink obligatory. The body is serviceable for work, and work serves health, which can sometimes be strengthened further by exercise. Property, too, must be respected. Property is what people have and what they use to live. It is the product of striving for dominion; the earth is the property of humanity. Some possession is indispensable; otherwise all freedom is lost and no love can be practiced. For loving is giving, and when one has nothing, one can give nothing. Property must be acquired through work or obtained by a gift or inheritance.

Some work communities are societies of a more interior and spiritual kind, especially communities of science and the arts. Science is the fruit of striving after consciousness of the self and after freedom. Science is knowledge of reality, and since reality is often deceptive, science seeks to know the truth in order to govern reality and to understand the past, the present, and ourselves. Scholars have the task of serving humanity, and to the extent that humanity requires an increasing division of labor, an increasing number of scholars is needed. Their task is a moral one.

Art is to be determined in accord with the consciousness of self. Art is to direct the will to realize the moral idea as the highest expression in all its acts and works. The good that a person does is the beautiful. But the beautiful also has value in itself; the harmony in the diversity speaks to us, both by image and by sound, and especially by word. Art, as well, however, serves the moral idea and works to complete humanity as the supreme work of art. Art is the sister of the true and of the good.

These communities are ultimately enclosed within the religious community and the state. Natural morality knows nothing of a church and can say nothing about the ultimate basis and purpose of this life. Natural morality, however, demands liberty of conscience and thus freedom of religion. It would be immoral to bind consciences, because natural morality must remain silent especially about life's ultimate questions. Death is a mystery to natural morality, and life is a secret, but natural morality must forbid homicide and suicide. Natural morality must leave religious life free and not make pronouncements about truth or falsehood.

Finally, the state is the organization of society with its own people and language. With the sword as its symbol, the state must maintain justice; its power is the law. The state compels by force in order to confine sin within the domain of the private life and thus has great moral value. The government is the conscience of the state. The state has to defend itself internally and externally, the latter by war as a last resort. Everyone has an obligation toward the state that includes bravery and compassion toward others. The highest ideal of natural morality is a world empire, a kingdom of love and fraternity for all humanity; yet it is imperative that the relative independence of nations and kingdoms continues to exist. If that world empire were attainable, it would surely be the highest good, the ideal, realized on earth for everyone.

All of the above—moral character, morality, virtue, family, household, nurture, friendship, occupation, science, art, and the state—are products of natural morality. Notice that I am not claiming that these have not been influenced, modified, and improved by Christianity. Christianity has had, and still has, a great influence on how people understand morality, nurture, science, and the state. But all of the above also exist among pagans. These things have therefore not been created by Christianity but have grown from the root of the life of natural humanity and continue to grow from that root. If this were not the case, the rejection of Christianity would result in their immediate disappearance.

Finally, in conclusion, we can easily determine the value of natural morality.

1. Viewed from the perspective of God's kingdom, natural morality has absolutely no value in God's eyes. It does not bring us a single step closer to the kingdom of heaven. Stated better, it may perhaps bring us closer to the kingdom of heaven, but it can never bring us in. A wide chasm lies between the most highly developed moral life and the smallest seed of spiritual life. To obtain spiritual life, it is precisely the natural moral life that has to be entirely surrendered, put to death, and crucified with Christ. In that case, virtues are nothing but splendid sins.[92]

---

92. LO: *peccata splendida*. Ed. note: This term is often attributed to Augustine (*City of God* XIX.25), but this has been disputed; see Irwin, "Splendid Vices?"

2. Viewed from an earthly perspective within time, however, natural morality and its fruits have very great value. Not recognizing their value is narrow-minded, petty, and superficial Methodism and quietistic pietism—anything but Reformed. The value of natural morality is threefold:

a. It leaves humanity without excuse. Even a community of robbers must acknowledge justice, and thieves hate laws, "not because they do not know them to be good and holy; but raging with headlong lust, they fight against manifest reason."[93] Even the greatest evil seeks to cloak itself in the garment of goodness and hide under it.[94] Every person's own conscience testifies to natural morality.

b. It restrains humans, or rather the wild creatures within humans. Natural morality is like a cordon drawn around the cruel monsters within the human heart, like a cage around human lusts. For many people it even creates an unusual satisfaction in doing good and avoiding evil. This is evident from noble persons like Plato, Seneca, and Plutarch and from the laws of Solon, Draco, and Lycurgus; many are examples to Christians and surpass the converted in outward virtues.[95] In short, it serves to make possible the existence of humanity, to prevent it from sinking into bestiality, to maintain its capability for being saved, and to keep the human kingdoms, republics, and mutual dwelling places of humanity orderly.[96] In the words of Goethe, "Giant Evil bursts forth, as soon as the wise regulations / Self-impos'd by man, are ever so slightly remitted."[97] The moral world order is the realm above the mechanism of cause and effect embedded in nature. It is a realm of freedom and yearning, rather than one of compulsion, and maintains itself in the conscience, in the state, in religion, in art, in history, in God's government of the world.

c. It makes human life bearable, ameliorates life, even gives some joy so that life is not a hell on earth. The practice of virtue always gives some joy, peace, and happiness. The love for truth is satisfied to some extent by science.[98] Technology supplies humanity with some advantage in the struggle against the elements of nature. Medicines supply some advantage against sicknesses, logic against error, jurisprudence against injustice. And in the terrain of natural morality, there is still some reason for optimism, and pessimism is weakness of character and lack of courage.

93. Calvin, *Institutes*, II.ii.13.
94. Wittewrongel, *Oeconomia Christiana*, 1:293.
95. Wittewrongel, *Oeconomia Christiana*, 1:291, 293.
96. Wittewrongel, *Oeconomia Christiana*, 1:293.
97. Goethe's "*Hermann and Dorothea*," 42 (trans. Teesdale); GO: "*Losgebunden erscheint, sobald die Schranken hinweg sind Alles Böse, das tief das Gesetz in die Winkel zurücktrieb*" (Goethe, *Hermann und Dorothea*, 45).
98. Calvin, *Institutes*, II.ii.15.

3. Natural morality also has great value for the church and for individual believers:

a. Natural morality is the presupposition of faith. The world is the field in which the seed of the Word, prepared by the Holy Spirit, is sown, germinates, and bears fruit (Matt. 13:38). Regeneration presupposes natural birth, re-creation presupposes creation, and Scripture presupposes nature.[99] The world, the earth, is the foundation of the church; without the one the other would be impossible, just as revealed theology is impossible without natural theology.[100]

b. Natural morality is even a kind of preparation for the spiritual life; natural morality is given so that it may gradually equip and lead some people somewhat toward greater grace. For, although we are dead in sins and trespasses, and have of ourselves no capacity in this world to do anything supernaturally good, God does not treat us like lifeless creatures, pieces of wood and brick, or like mindless beasts.[101] God has therefore left within humanity principles of religion and civic virtue that furnish the basis upon which he may, according to his wise and gracious decision, sometimes want to work further. In this sense, nature and grace are not opposed, but nature is the terrain in which grace works to re-create.[102] God has left within us fragments of his image, to be like seeds from which the image of God may afterward, through the grace of renewal, sprout and bud again. In this way, there is a general preceding grace and a general work of the Holy Spirit, which leads to particular grace and prepares for it.[103] This is to be seen not only in all individuals but also in God's works among the pagan nations before Christ (such as the Greeks and Romans), and it is still happening today in all of humanity: natural life is the field, and, depending on the extent to which that field has been tilled by the Holy Spirit, the seed cast into it bears fruit, or is choked, or is lost. Whether the faith is a temporal faith, a miraculous faith, a historical faith, or a saving faith depends on the depth of the furrows in the field and the depth to which the seed is sown. The field varies, and so therefore the effect of the Word. The Holy Spirit prepares the field, tills the soil, and penetrates that soil deeply and lastingly (think of the impressions of our youth). The beginning

---

99. Zahn, *Glaubensgewißheit und Theologie*, 26.

100. LO: *theologia revelata*; *theologia naturalis*.

101. Ed. note: Bavinck does not indicate a source here, but he clearly echoes Canons of Dort, III/IV.16: "This divine grace of regeneration does not act in people as if they were blocks and stones."

102. Van Mastricht, *Theoretico-Practica Theologia*, I.iii.9 §39 [2:99]. Ed. note: For an explanation of the format we are using to cite this work, see the extended note in the introduction, §1, in the section "Reformed Churches" (pp. 8–9n48). The volume and page numbers come from the 1749–53 Dutch edition used by Bavinck.

103. LO: *gratia preveniens*.

of faith is therefore different for everyone, because the process that leads to regeneration varies.

c. The life of natural morality remains in the believer and in the church. It remains the vessel into which the spiritual life is poured and by which it is carried. We are not entirely regenerated in this life. Our character, intellect, will, heart, body, mood, status, and situation all remain the same. The regenerate person is a double person, with a spiritual and a moral life. It is like new wine in an old wineskin! In the spiritual life as such there is nothing earthly or temporal, only what is heavenly and eternal. For example, the spiritual life contains no marriage, household, family, children, brothers, sisters, fatherland, state, occupation, science, or art. In Christ there is no male or female, etc. All these are rooted in the moral life.

To summarize: The Christian continues to live in the flesh (Gal. 2:20). Christians are no longer flesh: Christ lives in them; their "I" ("ego") lives in Christ, but they still live in the flesh. The calling of the Christian, then, is not to use the spiritual life to kill the natural moral life through asceticism or to castigate it with scourges, like some of the monks did. The calling of the Christian is also not to go to the other extreme and to say with the antinomians, "I am not flesh; that was my former nature." But the spiritual life should animate the moral life, control it, subject it, and make it its instrument, as we read in Galatians 2:20: "Christ . . . lives in me. And the life I now live in the flesh I live by faith in the Son of God." The purpose and task of ethics (especially in our third book)[104] is therefore to describe how regenerate people are to manifest their eternal heavenly life in the form of the temporal earthly life.

104. Ed. note: Book III, "Humanity after Conversion," in vol. 2, contains Bavinck's discussion of the Ten Commandments.

BOOK II

CONVERTED HUMANITY

7

Life in the Spirit

In this chapter, we move from the morality of sinful people who follow the guidance of natural law to those who have been renewed by the Spirit of Christ. This new life is variously described as being "in Christ," "crucified with Christ," "new creations," "children of light," or simply as "spiritual" rather than "fleshly."

This is a state of grace over against the law. It is also a state of liberty, having been set free from the slavery to sin. Above all, it is the state of life as opposed to death in sin. Life is more than being: it is an activity, a life-force, whether that be vegetative life, the sensory life of animals, or the rational life of human beings. Most importantly, life is the promise of the gospel; a spiritual life differs from vegetative, sensory, or rational life essentially, qualitatively. It has its own distinctive life-principle.

Only the Triune God has life in himself; all creaturely life is derived from and dependent upon God. While the drive for self-preservation characterizes all vegetative and sentient life, the spiritual life is characterized by love for God, in Christ, through the Holy Spirit. Its fundamental principle is not found within the natural life but first arises through denial, self-crucifixion, renunciation, and loss of our soul. Love, poured into our hearts by the Holy Spirit and fruit of the Spirit, gives stature and form to the spiritual life.

Because love for God is its foundation, spiritual life itself consists of fellowship with God, with Christ, with fellow believers. Spiritual life is a communal life; it cannot exist on its own, for then it languishes and dies. This threefold communion is fellowship with the Father, fellowship with Christ, and fellowship with the Holy Spirit. The believer experiences the life of God himself: from the Father through the Son in the Spirit and, conversely, in the Spirit through the Son to the Father.

This spiritual life is a hidden life, invisible, not yet embodied. Scripture speaks about our "inner being," our heart, our mind, and our spirit. The heart is the seat of the spiritual life; our rationality, emotions/feeling, and will are all rooted in our heart. It is where "God's love has been poured . . . through the Holy Spirit who has been given to us."

This internal, hidden life is not yet complete; we live by faith, in the state of grace, which is not yet the state of glory. This is not to deny that the spiritual life spreads itself to some degree across the entire soul. Believers now want to do the good. The new life in Christ is life indeed, eternal life, conscious life of a renewed mind, a free life, and a blessed life.

The spiritual life has its objective origin in election. Subjectively, even Reformed theology acknowledges preparations, antecedents to conversion, such as hearing the word, going to church, cultivating a sense of sin, hope of pardon, and the like. These acknowledge God's providential guidance until the Holy Spirit regenerates a person. The "preparations" are part of the general work of God the Holy Spirit; regeneration is particular and irresistible.

Spiritual life follows the pattern of all life and consists of separating, dividing, assimilating—and appropriating to itself. Conversion is a sincere and steadfast renouncing of all sin by a born-again person. Regenerated persons reveal themselves immediately and positively by believing, trusting that God's testimony is true. To believe is to say "Amen" to God's Word. Even more, it is trust in the person of Christ.

Some Christians emphasize the knowledge of faith, others the trust of the heart. The former risk dead orthodoxy; the latter, confusing faith with experience and diminishing the importance of Scripture. Head and heart belong together; both are essential.

§17. THE NATURE OF THE SPIRITUAL LIFE

In Book I we considered humanity before conversion—namely, what humanity should be (the image of God), what it is in the state of sin, and what it has retained of the image of God in sin. Now we turn to the beginning and progress of conversion; in other words, the nature, birth, growth, and perfection of the spiritual life and our ignorance of it. Nonetheless, understanding is necessary, especially for shepherds, who must recognize (diagnose) spiritual life, nurture it, and, when it is sick, restore it; they are physicians of the soul, and must therefore know the soul in its "state, its way and its condition."[1]

There is a gradual transition between Book I and Book II. Following the light of conscience and law, human beings are able to achieve a moral walk,

1. See Vitringa, *Korte schets*.

some civic righteousness. But even with all that, humans remain dead in a spiritual sense. There is, however, a life other than the moral one: a spiritual life.

1. Biblical Terms for the State of the Spiritual Life[2]

The spiritual life is presented in Holy Scripture with a variety of terms and images. The apostle Paul speaks of himself as a "man in Christ" (2 Cor. 12:2) because God has revealed his Son in him (Gal. 1:16).[3] Paul, who has himself "been crucified with Christ," so that "it is no longer I who live, but Christ who lives in me" (Gal. 2:19–20), prays for the Galatian Christians that Christ might be formed in them (Gal. 4:19).[4] He reminds the Corinthians that they are his children, begotten in Christ through the gospel (1 Cor. 4:15), and thus "new creations" (2 Cor. 5:17).[5] However, believers who consider themselves "dead to sin and alive to God in Christ Jesus" (Rom. 6:11) but remain "infants in Christ" cannot be considered "spiritual."[6] Instead, Paul calls them "fleshly" (1 Cor. 3:1).[7]

For believers such as Paul, "to live is Christ" (Phil. 1:21).[8] The task of gospel ministry by chosen leaders is to "build up the body of Christ" unto maturity, "to the measure of the stature of the fullness of Christ, so that we may no longer be children" (Eph. 4:13–14).[9] The apostle Peter instructs his readers to "grow in the grace and knowledge of our Lord and Savior Jesus Christ" (2 Pet. 3:18).[10] Once again, referring to Timothy as "my child," Paul encourages him to be "strengthened in the grace of Jesus Christ" (2 Tim. 2:1).[11] Jesus instructs his disciples, "Abide in me," adding, "and I in you" (John 15:4).[12] Apart from Christ, his disciples "can do nothing"; but he assures them, "If you abide in me, . . . ask whatever you wish, and it will be done for you" (John 15:5, 7).[13] Those who "have received Christ as Lord" (Col. 2:6) are "rich in him" (1 Cor. 1:5) and "blessed in Christ with every spiritual blessing in the heavenly places"

2. Vitringa, *Korte schets*, 2 (I §1); Lampe, *Schets der dadelyke Godt-geleertheid*, 40–61; van den Honert, *De mensch in Christus*, 1:467–68.
3. GrO: ἄνθρωπον ἐν Χριστῷ; ἀποκαλύψαι τὸν υἱὸν αὐτοῦ ἐν ἐμοί.
4. GrO: Χριστῷ συνεσταύρωμαι; ζῶ δὲ οὐκέτι ἐγώ, ζῇ δὲ ἐν ἐμοὶ Χριστός; μέχρις οὗ μορφωθῇ Χριστὸς ἐν ὑμῖν.
5. GrO: καινὴ κτίσις.
6. GrO: εἶναι νεκροὺς μὲν τῇ ἁμαρτίᾳ ζῶντας δὲ τῷ θεῷ ἐν Χριστῷ Ἰησοῦ; νηπίοις ἐν Χριστῷ; πνευματικοῖς.
7. GrO: σαρκίνοις.
8. GrO: ἐμοὶ γὰρ τὸ ζῆν Χριστός.
9. GrO: τοῦ πληρώματος τοῦ Χριστοῦ; ἵνα μηκέτι ὦμεν νήπιοι.
10. GrO: αὐξάνετε δὲ ἐν χάριτι καὶ γνώσει τοῦ κυρίου ἡμῶν καὶ σωτῆρος Ἰησοῦ Χριστοῦ.
11. GrO: τέκνον μου; ἐνδυναμοῦ ἐν τῇ χάριτι τῇ ἐν Χριστῷ Ἰησοῦ.
12. GrO: μείνατε ἐν ἐμοί, κἀγὼ ἐν ὑμῖν.
13. GrO: χωρὶς ἐμοῦ οὐ δύνασθε ποιεῖν οὐδέν; ὃ ἐὰν θέλητε αἰτήσασθε καὶ γενήσεται ὑμῖν.

(Eph. 1:3).[14] They are, therefore, seated "in the heavenly places in Christ Jesus" (Eph. 2:6).[15] Thus kept in Christ, we receive "the peace of God which surpasses all understanding" and "guards our hearts and minds in Christ Jesus" (Phil. 4:7).[16] These are the "blessed . . . who die in the Lord" (Rev. 14:13).[17]

This state into which believers have entered through Christ is called the state of *grace* (Rom. 6:14–15), over against that of the *law*, because God's grace is its only foundation. This state derives its being, its existence, and its life from grace alone; only God's grace in Christ through the Holy Spirit has prepared it and gives it being. It is called the state of grace also in distinction from the state of righteousness (of long-suffering) and the state of glory. As such, it lets us know the condition in which the image of God is again gradually restored in us. Called forth from a former state of darkness, believers are now "children of *light*" (Eph. 5:8; 1 Thess. 5:5; 1 Pet. 2:9).[18] As children of light we are those who "walk in the light" (1 John 1:7), "put on the armor of light" (Rom. 13:12), "abide in the light" (1 John 2:9–10), and have fellowship with other believers (1 John 1:7).[19] The state of grace is a state of *light* because it is fellowship with the One who is Light (Matt. 4:16; Luke 2:32; John 1:4; 8:12; 9:5; 12:35–36, 46), with God who is Light (1 John 1:5) and "dwells in unapproachable light" (1 Tim. 6:16).[20] That is to say, it is fellowship with him who is the truth and who with the truth drives out the ethical darkness of error, lying, and ignorance and enlightens us.

All this has our consciousness in view. With the eye on the will, we can speak of the state of *liberty*. Jesus Christ came to proclaim liberty to the captives (Isa. 61:1–2; cf. Luke 4:19), and "creation itself will be liberated from its bondage to decay and brought into the freedom and glory of the children of God" (Rom. 8:21 NIV).[21] Freedom is a profoundly pneumatological reality: "Now the Lord is the Spirit, and where the Spirit of the Lord is, there is freedom" (2 Cor. 3:17).[22] Having been "called to freedom" (Gal. 5:13),[23] we

14. GrO: παρελάβετε τὸν Χριστὸν Ἰησοῦν τὸν κύριον; ἐπλουτίσθητε ἐν αὐτῷ; ἐν πάσῃ εὐλογίᾳ πνευματικῇ ἐν τοῖς ἐπουρανίοις ἐν Χριστῷ.

15. GrO: συνεκάθισεν ἐν τοῖς ἐπουρανίοις ἐν Χριστῷ Ἰησοῦ.

16. GrO: ἡ εἰρήνη τοῦ θεοῦ ἡ ὑπερέχουσα πάντα νοῦν φρουρήσει τὰς καρδίας ὑμῶν καὶ τὰ νοήματα ὑμῶν ἐν Χριστῷ Ἰησοῦ.

17. GrO: Μακάριοι οἱ νεκροὶ οἱ ἐν κυρίῳ ἀποθνήσκοντες; van den Honert, *De Mensch in Christus*, 1:467.

18. GrO: σκότος; τέκνα φωτός; υἱοὶ φωτός.

19. GrO: ἐν τῷ φωτὶ περιπατῶμεν; ἐνδυσώμεθα δὲ τὰ ὅπλα τοῦ φωτός; ἐν τῷ φωτὶ μένει.

20. GrO: φῶς οἰκῶν ἀπρόσιτον.

21. GrO: αὐτὴ ἡ κτίσις ἐλευθερωθήσεται ἀπὸ τῆς δουλείας τῆς φθορᾶς εἰς τὴν ἐλευθερίαν τῆς δόξης τῶν τέκνων τοῦ θεοῦ.

22. GrO: ὁ δὲ κύριος τὸ πνεῦμά ἐστιν· οὗ δὲ τὸ πνεῦμα κυρίου, ἐλευθερία.

23. GrO: ὑμεῖς γὰρ ἐπ' ἐλευθερίᾳ ἐκλήθητε.

are instructed to "stand firm, therefore, and . . . not submit again to a yoke of slavery" (Gal. 5:1). This liberty must not be misused: "Live as people who are free, not using your freedom as a cover-up for evil, but living as servants of God" (1 Pet. 2:16).

This state is called "free" in contrast to the slavery of sin (John 8:34; Rom. 6:7) and of the law (Gal. 4). Furthermore, it is free because it is a state of the *Spirit*: "That which is born of the Spirit is spirit" (John 3:6);[24] "For the desires of the flesh are against the Spirit, and the desires of the Spirit are against the flesh" (Gal. 5:17);[25] "It is the Spirit who gives life;[26] the flesh is no help at all. The words that I have spoken to you are spirit and life" (John 6:63). The imperatives follow from this indicative: Romans 8:1–4 (NIV): since "the law of the Spirit who gives life has set you free from the law of sin and death," believers are called to walk "not according to the flesh but according to the Spirit";[27] Romans 8:5, 9 (NIV): "Those who live in accordance with the Spirit have their minds set on what the Spirit desires" because they "are in the realm of the Spirit"; Galatians 5:18, 25: believers are "led by the Spirit" and "live by the Spirit."[28] This freedom in the Spirit is set over against the covenant defined by "letter" (2 Cor. 3:6) and the "spirit of slavery" (Rom. 8:15) under the law of the Old Testament.[29] Our Lord makes the same point using the image of health in Matthew 9:12: "Those who are well have no need of a physician, but those who are sick." Similarly, this state is described using images of purity, holiness, and beauty.

Most frequently, however, this state is called a state of *life* as opposed to the former state of death in sin. See, for example, Ephesians 2:1–3:

> And you were dead in the trespasses and sins in which you once walked, following the course of this world, following the prince of the power of the air, the spirit that is now at work in the sons of disobedience—among whom we all once lived in the passions of our flesh, carrying out the desires of the body and the mind, and were by nature children of wrath, like the rest of mankind.

God in Scripture calls us again and again: "Listen to the statutes and the rules that I am teaching you, and do them, that you may *live*" (Deut. 4:1; cf. 30:6). It is the prayer and vow of the psalmist: "Let your mercy come to me, that I may *live*; for your law is my delight" (Ps. 119:77); "I will walk before the LORD in the land of the *living*" (Ps. 116:9). Similarly, the prophet Isaiah:

24. GrO: τὸ γεγεννημένον ἐκ τοῦ πνεύματος πνεῦμά ἐστιν.
25. GrO: ἡ γὰρ σὰρξ ἐπιθυμεῖ κατὰ τοῦ πνεύματος, τὸ δὲ πνεῦμα κατὰ τῆς σαρκός.
26. GrO: τὸ πνεῦμά ἐστιν τὸ ζῳοποιοῦν.
27. GrO: μὴ κατὰ σάρκα περιπατοῦσιν ἀλλὰ κατὰ πνεῦμα.
28. GrO: πνεύματι ἄγεσθε; ζῶμεν πνεύματι.
29. GrO: γράμμα; πνεῦμα δουλείας.

"O Lord, by these things men *live*, and in all these is the *life* of my spirit. Oh restore me to health and make me *live*!" (Isa. 38:16). Ezekiel calls the people to repent and live: "For I have no pleasure in the death of anyone, declares the Lord GOD; so turn, and *live*" (Ezek. 18:32); "Say to them, As I live, declares the Lord GOD, I have no pleasure in the death of the wicked, but that the wicked turn from his way and *live*; turn back, turn back from your evil ways, for why will you die, O house of Israel?" (Ezek. 33:11).[30]

Life is the promise of the gospel:

> Truly, truly, I say to you, whoever hears my word and believes him who sent me has eternal *life*. He does not come into judgment, but has passed from death to *life*. (John 5:24)

> We were buried therefore with him by baptism into death, in order that, just as Christ was raised from the dead by the glory of the Father, we too might walk in newness of *life*. (Rom. 6:4)

> For through the law I died to the law, so that I might *live* to God. I have been crucified with Christ. It is no longer I who *live*, but Christ who *lives* in me. And the *life* I now *live* in the flesh I *live* by faith in the Son of God, who loved me and gave himself for me. (Gal. 2:19–20)

> But God, being rich in mercy, because of the great love with which he loved us, even when we were dead in our trespasses, made us *alive* together with Christ. (Eph. 2:4–5)

We call this new life *spiritual* life, in distinction from another kind of life, because it is a life *from*, *through*, and *in* the Holy Spirit of God:[31] "If we *live* by the Spirit, let us also keep in step with the Spirit" (Gal. 5:25).

2. The Distinctive Way of This Life[32]

Life is a self-activating movement outward from within.[33] Life is more than *being* (stones and other objects also *exist*); life is not merely a state but

---

30. Ed. note: The emphasis in these preceding verses and in the next paragraph was added.
31. Ed. note: Emphasis of prepositions added.
32. Ed. note: Bavinck provides a single source here—"cf. Drummond"—without further identification. A number of Drummond's works fit the general topic of life and spiritual life: *Eternal Life*; *Changed Life*; *Natural Law in the Spiritual World*, especially the section on "Eternal Life," pp. 201–50; *Ideal Life*. The most likely possibility is *Natural Law in the Spiritual World*, which was translated into Dutch according to Warner et al., eds., *Library of the World's Best Literature*, 9:4897 (s.v. "Henry Drummond").
33. GO: *selbstthätige, von innen ausgehende Bewegung*. Löber, *Das innere Leben: Beitrag*, 2.

also a deed, activity, action, movement. Life is always an activity, an activity of an inner all-animating, all-controlling, organized, internal foundational principle that people call a *life-force*.[34] And this activity must be thought of as continuous, as a state. Of course, there are various kinds of life: the vegetative life of plants, the sensory life of animals, and the rational life of humans. In all three cases life is an activity that comes from a hidden, internal, mysterious, inexplicable fundamental principle that cannot be explained from a mechanical point of view. It is in the continuity of this activity that something is said to live. The vegetative life still remains entirely in a state of bondage, is bound to its place, is not able to move, and has no power or command over itself; it lacks not only consciousness but also a sense of existence. Nevertheless, in spite of that, it grows. The sensory life of animals is on a higher level; here we have sensations of existence and of freedom; the animal is no longer bound to one place, but moves about as it ascends to consciousness and freedom, although it stops at the threshold. But living human beings enter the sacredness of consciousness and freedom, are aware of it, and even govern their lives with free wills. The self is subject to the *I*. Plants sleep, animals dream, humans are monads who are awake (Leibniz).[35] Nonetheless, the lower life stages[36] are incorporated in the higher ones; humans share the vegetative life (in stomach, intestines), also the sensory life of animals (in senses, body). In addition to that, humans possess reason. That rational life now comes to expression in various life-spheres: in marriage, family, society, state, art, and science. From it, therefore, flow multiple forms, manifestations, and areas of the single human rational life. Life itself then becomes richer and fuller as it advances. These stages of life are differentiated not only in consciousness and feeling, as pantheists

34. LO: *vis vitalis*.

35. Ed. note: Gottfried Wilhelm Leibniz (1646–1716) rejected "the Cartesian doctrines that all mental states are conscious and that non-human animals lack souls as well as sensation." The key difference between animal souls and human (rational) souls, among other things, is the capacity of the latter for self-consciousness, abstract thinking, and acting freely. "Leibniz is a *panpsychist*: he believes that everything, including plants and inanimate objects, has a mind or something analogous to a mind. More specifically, he holds that in all things there are simple, immaterial, mind-like substances that perceive the world around them. Leibniz calls these mind-like substances 'monads.'" Leibniz's hierarchy of monads begins with "bare monads" such as plants, which "lack all sensation and consciousness." Leibniz compares their mental state "to our states when we are in a stupor or a dreamless sleep." "Animals, on the other hand, can sense and be conscious, and thus possess souls. God and the souls of human beings and angels, finally, are examples of minds because they are self-conscious and rational. As a result, even though there are mind-like things everywhere for Leibniz, minds in the stricter sense are not ubiquitous" (http://www.iep.utm.edu/lei-mind/).

36. DO: *levensstufen*.

and materialists assert,[37] but also in content and fullness. The life-force, the fundamental principle itself, differs not only in quantity but also in quality. There is not merely one substance, but a variety. The rational life differs from the vegetative and sensory not only in feeling, consciousness, and reflex, but in its foundational principle—namely, the *life-force*; it is life of a different kind.

The *spiritual life* differs from all of these not only in degree, but essentially, in quality. There are similarities, of course, because we are speaking about life; the spiritual life, therefore, is also an activity, a fundamental principle, a continuity. But it differs specifically *also* from the rational life. However much it differs from them, it does not exclude the previously mentioned kinds of life and is not ill disposed toward them. The spiritual life can and may be associated with them and even adopt them as instruments for itself by completing, purifying, and perfecting them for the glory of God. Thus it does not exclude the vegetative and sensory life; otherwise even eating, drinking, marriage, etc. would not be permitted, and asceticism, self-flagellation, or even suicide would be a duty. Even the rational life in all its spheres (state, art, etc.) is not excluded from the spiritual life but assimilated by it, made subservient to it, and regulated, purified, and completed by it. The spiritual life completely excludes and is diametrically opposed only to the life of sin that follows the will of the flesh and its desire (Eph. 2:3; 1 Pet. 4:3).[38] In a word, it opposes the "natural man" (1 Cor. 2:14), the distinctively human life not shared by God, Christ, or the angels, because the latter is a continuous activity flowing from an organizing, controlling, energizing, principle of life characterized by selfishness and lust, in coarser or finer form.[39] The natural life also affects the vegetative, sensory, and rational life of human beings in all its spheres—subjugates, inspires, and thus corrupts, empties, and corrodes life. The spiritual life is diametrically opposed (Gal. 5:17) to this natural life wherever it presents itself. The fundamental principles of both are antipodes.

3. The Foundational Principle of the Spiritual Life

The spiritual life has its own life-principle that is distinguished from all other kinds of life. Of course, no creature has an absolute self-originating life; all creaturely life is derived, its originating principle is "secondhand." We can only speak of a foundational, originating principle within life as something

---

37. Such as G. W. F. Hegel (1770–1831), Arthur Schopenhauer (1788–1860), Karl Robert Eduard von Hartman (1842–1906), Charles Darwin (1809–82), and Herbert Spencer (1829–1903).

38. Vitringa, *Korte schets*, 4–12 (I §§4, 5, 8).

39. GrO: ἄνθρωπος ψυχικός.

that is assumed by life itself. There is only One whose life absolutely arises from himself, who has life in himself, who is absolutely *the* beginning, a beginning not provided by anything outside himself, who is the life-force itself, absolutely free and conscious, life and source of life at the same time. This is the Triune God.[40] All creaturely life is derived, not original; only God has life in the full sense of the word. "For with you is the fountain of life; in your light do we see light" (Ps. 36:9). The life of creation comes from God and is mediated by the Logos ("In him was life, and the life was the light of men," John 1:4), who has life in himself: "For as the Father has life in himself, so he has granted the Son also to have life in himself" (John 5:26).

Nonetheless, we may speak of a relatively independent life of our own and therefore also of a creaturely life-principle. Pantheism does not allow for that since it teaches that God's life and that of creatures are one. But the Holy Scriptures do allow for such a relatively independent life. Although there is no spark of life in any creature except from and through God, nevertheless, God's life is different from that of creatures. Our life is created; God's life is not. And thus we can speak of a life and life-principle of its own. The principle that forms and designs the spiritual life, organizes and governs it, is the direct opposite of the natural life. If the latter is characterized by selfishness and lust, the former is characterized by love for God, in Christ, through the Holy Spirit.[41] The drive for self-preservation, to conserve and persist in existence, is the foundation of all vegetative and sentient life (Spinoza).[42] And because of sin this has also become the principle of all of life itself; self-preservation became the life-principle of the family, of society and state, even of art and science, which, as it is said, must be practiced for themselves. The principle of all of life, therefore, is found within the province of that life itself, encompasses it, but does not reach beyond it. This natural state perishes and ceases with that life itself. Self-preservation[43] has become the principle of all of life because all life is conscious (since sin) of having become subject to death; it resists death with all its strength and seeks to maintain itself, although to no avail. This is what it means to be held "in slavery by the fear of death" (Heb. 2:15). The *fear* of death has become the *principle of life*.

The spiritual life is altogether different. Its fundamental principle is not found within the natural life but first arises through denial, self-crucifixion, renunciation, and loss of our soul. It is, therefore, not selfish either, always thinking of self-preservation; it is not preoccupied with this life. It is not

40. Löber, *Das innere Leben: Beitrag*, 2.
41. Vitringa, *Korte schets*, 8–9 (I §6).
42. GO: *Selbsterhaltungstrieb*; LO: *se in suum esse conservare/perseverare*.
43. GO: *Selbsterhaltung*.

natural but supernatural and spiritual, not external but internal, not internally focused but reaching beyond time and this earth. It is itself spiritual—that is, invisible; it is fed from the spiritual and reaches out to the spiritual. The foundation, content, and aim of this life is spiritual, and anyone who shares in it is a "spiritual person" (1 Cor. 2:15; 3:1; Gal. 6:1)—that is, one who is led by the Spirit of God (Rom. 8:14) has the indwelling Spirit (Rom. 8:11).[44] "Spiritual persons" are the opposite of "people of the flesh" (1 Cor. 3:1) and also of "natural people" (1 Cor. 2:14).[45] For the foundational principle of the spiritual life is the love of God in Christ poured out upon us through the Holy Spirit (Rom. 5:5). The "love of God"[46] here is an objective genitive (love with God as its object), paralleling passages such as Deuteronomy 6:5; 11:1, 13, 22; Matthew 22:37: "You shall love the Lord your God with all your heart," etc. Love here is a spiritual principle, not only poured out into our hearts by the Holy Spirit and fruit of the Spirit (Gal. 5:22), but itself also spiritual by nature. This means that it is not fruit of the field of our natural life. Nor is it the greatest deed of the human spirit, of our personality, that has surrendered self and after that does not live for self, that does not withdraw into self but gives liberally and sacrifices self for others. Its object is also spiritual: God himself in Christ, the invisible eternal One. The love of God is therefore stripped of all that is sensuous, earthly, and impure and is now pure and holy. And this principle now flows into all of life, into all the thoughts and deeds of the spiritual person. Love of God gives stature and form to the spiritual life; it organizes and inspires it, turning it into one beautiful organic whole which functions as the foundational *life-force.*[47]

4. The Essence of the Spiritual Life

Because love for God is its foundation, spiritual life itself consists of fellowship with God, with Christ, and with fellow believers. Love strives after and is fellowship, a fellowship that is only possible through and in love. Hatred separates; love binds. Because there is no love for God in the vegetative, sensory, rational, or psychological life, there is also no fellowship with God. Love and fellowship—κοινωνία—assumes persons, rational beings—that is, those who know themselves and give themselves to each other. Spiritual life is a communal life; it cannot exist on its own, for then it languishes and dies. This threefold communion is as follows:

44. GrO: πνευματικός.
45. GrO: σαρκίνοις; ἄνθρωπος ψυχικός.
46. GrO: ἡ ἀγάπη τοῦ θεοῦ.
47. LO: *principium organicum; vis vitalis.*

1. Fellowship with the *Father*. First John 1:3: "Our fellowship is with the Father and with his Son Jesus Christ." The purpose of this fellowship is "that they may all be one, just as you, Father, are in me, and I in you, that they also may be in us, so that the world may believe that you have sent me" (John 17:21). Godliness flows forth of itself from the exercise of this fellowship and the desire to strengthen it. This fellowship is no empty sound or form but the highest reality: concrete fellowship between people on earth. It consists in the knowledge, the firm consciousness we possess, that God knows us personally, in Christ has shown us grace, and now as Father fulfills all the good pleasure of his goodness for us (2 Thess. 1:11), loves us, leads us, and so forth. Furthermore, because God's Spirit "bears witness with our spirit that we are children of God" (Rom. 8:16), we believe and feel all of this in our heart. We embrace him by faith and love, see him with the eye of the soul, experience him and reach out to him, live and walk in him. Fellowship with the Father, therefore, assumes election, justification, and consists of (a) God's love, grace, etc.; (b) God giving himself to us, and us, from our side, taking God into our heart, mind, will, feeling, imagination; (c) giving ourselves completely to God with our mind, soul, and all our strength; and (d) God, from his side, accepting us in love.

2. Fellowship with *Christ*. We were chosen (to be) in Christ (Eph. 1:4), begotten in him (1 Cor. 4:15), crucified and died with him (Rom. 6:6; Gal. 2:20), buried with him (Rom. 6:4), planted in him (Rom 6:5), raised with him and live with him (Rom. 6:8; Gal. 2:20; Col. 3:1), and seated with him in heaven (Eph. 2). And now believers are one with him: Christ is their life (Phil. 1:21), they abide in him (John 15:4), they have put on Christ (Gal. 3:27), and they bear the image of Christ. He is in them (2 Cor. 13:5), dwells in them (Eph. 3:17), lives in them (Gal. 2:20), is one flesh with them (Eph. 5:30), and he and they are one in spirit (1 Cor. 6:17; Rom. 8:9, 11). And this intimate fellowship is represented by the images of vine and branches (John 15), head and members (Rom. 12:5; 1 Cor. 6:11; 12:12), foundation and stones (Eph. 2:20; 1 Pet. 2:4–5), body and nourishment (John 6:33, 35), husband and wife (Ezek. 16:8; Isa. 62:4, 5; Hosea 2:16; Ps. 45; Eph. 5:32; 1 Cor. 6:16–17), and king and subjects (Ps. 2:6; Zech. 9:9). This fellowship also consists of a mutual interchange between Christ and believers: we receive and take on the whole Christ and give ourselves entirely and completely to him (2 Cor. 8:5). However, this is no Christification or deification of the believer, no blending, no exchanging of Christ and the believer, but a spiritual fellowship. This is not merely a moral fellowship (agreement of mind and will) but a substantial and real fellowship of Christ's person and our persons, the closest union of Christ and us, through and in love, as in marriage.

3. Fellowship with the *Holy Spirit* (2 Cor. 13:14), and secondarily with each other (1 John 1:7; 1 Cor. 12:12–31; Eph. 1:22–23; 4:16). The purpose of human life is fellowship with God; to live in him is life's goal. The spiritual life is to live in fellowship with the Triune God[48]—that is, *in* the Holy Spirit, *through* Christ, *with* the Father. This fellowship is *one*—that is, divine—and yet different with respect to the three persons. First there is the fellowship of the Holy Spirit convicting of sin, righteousness, and judgment; then that of Christ adopting us and granting us his benefits; thereafter that of the Father adopting us as his children in and because of Christ. The spiritual life always moves among these three persons and is therefore a genuinely rich life, rich in diversity, without monotony. The believer experiences the life of God himself: *from* the Father *through* the Son *in* the Spirit and, conversely, *in* the Spirit *through* the Son *to* the Father. The spiritual life is therefore a life of God (Eph. 4:18), a life that originates from God, is granted by grace, unites us with God, is worked in us immediately through the Holy Spirit, and has the spiritual life of God himself as model and example. The spiritual life of believers is a shadow, an impression[49] of the most perfect life of God himself, so that it is said that they share in the divine nature (2 Pet. 1:4).[50]

5. The Seat of the Spiritual Life

The spiritual life is a hidden life (Col. 3:3), invisible, not yet embodied. Therefore Paul speaks of our "inner being/man" being strengthened or renewed (Eph. 3:16; 2 Cor. 4:16), and Peter of "adorning the hidden person of the heart" (1 Pet. 3:4).[51] This expression stands opposed to "flesh"[52] and to all that is not our true self. It points to that which is described with subtle nuances as "mind," "heart," and "spirit"; in other words, to the divine, spiritual, human essence.[53] The spiritual life is spoken of as the "inner being/man" to the degree that the Spirit (living from the Spirit) comes to expression in the mind.[54] The "outward being/man" is not the "old [sinful] man/self" (Rom. 6:6; Eph. 2:15; 4:12–14) but that which hides the spiritual life, the "inner man."[55] Paul's command to "not be conformed to this world, but transformed by the renewal of your mind" indicates that the mind, the consciousness, especially

48. Löber, *Das innere Leben: Beitrag*, 4, 26.
49. DO: *afdruksel*.
50. Vitringa, *Korte schets*, 16.
51. GrO: ὁ ἔσω ἄνθρωπος; ὁ κρυπτὸς τῆς καρδίας ἄνθρωπος.
52. GrO: σάρξ; Cremer, *Biblico-Theological Lexicon*, 147, s.v. "ἄνθρωπος."
53. GrO: νοῦς; καρδία; πνεῦμα.
54. GrO: πνεῦμα; νοῦς; Cremer, *Biblico-Theological Lexicon*, 148.
55. GrO: ὁ ἔξω ἄνθρωπος; ὁ παλαιὸς ἄνθρωπος.

the ability to reflect, the organ of moral thought and recognition (Rom. 7:25), is the seat of the spiritual life.[56] This parallels the "conscience" (Titus 1:15) as an organ of the spirit and is therefore located in a part of the heart; the "mind" is a function of the "heart."[57] Compare Ephesians 4:23: "Be renewed in the spirit of your minds."[58] The *soul/life* has its origin in the *spirit*, and its organ (both as to its conscious and as to its unconscious side) is the *heart*.[59] The heart is the concentrating and mediating organ of all circumstances and activities.[60] Thus the sequence is spirit–soul–heart: foundation–subject–organ.[61] Rationality, emotion/feeling, and will, then, are rooted in the heart.[62] The heart, therefore, is the seat of the spiritual life, as is indicated by biblical references to "the hidden person of the heart" (1 Pet. 3:4) and circumcision being "a matter of the heart, by the Spirit, not by the letter" (Rom. 2:29). It is in the heart that "God's love has been poured . . . through the Holy Spirit who has been given to us" (Rom. 5:5), where Christ lives by faith so that we are "rooted and grounded in love" and "may have strength to comprehend with all the saints what is the breadth and length and height and depth, and to know the love of Christ that surpasses knowledge" (Eph. 3:16–19), where God sends "the Spirit of his Son . . . crying, 'Abba! Father!'" (Gal. 4:6), where God, who "puts his seal on us," gives us his Spirit as a down payment/guarantee (2 Cor. 1:22).[63]

Precisely for the reason that the seat of the spiritual life is internal, this life itself is hidden and therefore also incomplete. The believer lives by faith (Hab. 2:4) in the state of grace and not yet in the state of glory.[64] This is not to deny that the spiritual life spreads itself to some degree across the entire soul. The *mind*, formerly darkened, receives some light as God opens "the eyes of hearts" unto enlightenment (Eph. 1:18; cf. 2 Cor. 4:4). This enlightenment is "the light of the knowledge of God's glory displayed in the face of Christ" (2 Cor. 4:6 NIV).[65] In that way believers receive clear, pure knowledge of God and his attributes, of themselves as sinners, of Christ as prophet, priest, and king. And they know all this not from the letter, in metaphor, but from the events themselves with application to self. They know it in the *will*, initially

56. GrO: μεταμορφοῦσθε τῇ ἀνακαινώσει τοῦ νοός; νοῦς.
57. GrO: συνείδησις; νοῦς; καρδία; Cremer, *Biblico-Theological Lexicon*, 343, s.v. "καρδία."
58. GrO: ἀνανεοῦσθαι δὲ τῷ πνεύματι τοῦ νοὸς ὑμῶν.
59. GrO/HO: ψυχή/נֶפֶשׁ; πνεῦμα/רוּחַ; καρδία/לֵב.
60. Cremer, *Biblico-Theological Lexicon*, 343.
61. GrO: πνεῦμα–ψυχή–καρδία; Cremer, *Biblico-Theological Lexicon*, 503–4, s.v. "πνεῦμα."
62. GrO: νοῦς; καρδία.
63. GrO: ἀρραβών.
64. LO: *status gratiae*; *status gloriae*.
65. GrO: φωτισμός τῆς γνώσεως τῆς δόξης τοῦ θεοῦ ἐν προσώπῳ Χριστοῦ.

living "in the passions of [their] flesh, carrying out the desires of the body and the mind . . . , [being] children of wrath" (Eph. 2:3), but then those who "were once slaves of sin" became "obedient from the heart to the standard of teaching to which [they] were committed, and, having been set free from sin, [became] slaves of righteousness" (Rom. 6:17–18). Now their desire is in the law (Ps. 1:2), prompting them to seek out God's will (Acts 9:6)[66] and say: "Teach me to do your will, / for you are my God! / Let your good Spirit lead me / on level ground!" (Ps. 143:10).

Believers now desire to know "the good and acceptable and perfect will of God" (Rom. 12:2). They want to *do* the good (Rom. 7:18) in their passions and emotions and even in the instrument of their bodies.[67] The throat is an open sepulchre (Rom. 3:13), but now God's praise is in the mouth (Ps. 149:6). The tongue is an uncontrollable evil (James 3:5–6), but now God is extolled with the tongue (Pss. 51:14; 66:17; 119:172). The mouth was full of impurity (Rom. 3:14), but now God establishes his strength out of the mouth of babes (Ps. 8:2); their feet were swift to shed blood (Rom. 3:15), but are now shod with the preparation of the gospel (Eph. 6:15).[68]

6. Attributes of the Spiritual Life[69]

a. *Life indeed.* It goes without saying that this is *life*, as Holy Scripture often calls it. All other life is temporary, transient, fleeting, and subject to death (even without sin); the vegetative, sensory life cannot last on its own, not even in human beings. Physical life cannot be immortal of itself, not even in Adam, in whom it might have been eternalized through the spiritual. The rational life, the soul-life, of humans is not real life; it exists, but sin impoverishes it, wears it down, and emaciates it. Only the spiritual life is now true, genuine life.

b. *Eternal life.* Our fellowship with God immortalizes us, safeguards us against death. Therefore we need not fear death (John 3:36; 8:51). This fellowship with the Eternal One is unbreakable.

c. *Conscious life.* Conscious life begins with enlightenment, consists in the renewal of the mind,[70] and is mediated through faith (accepting the truth of God). It is not a dark, vague, mystical feeling; not delusion or fanaticism; not

---

66. Ed. note: Bavinck's appeal to this text will not be clear to those who use modern translations because the first of two sentences present in the KJV is missing: "And he trembling and astonished said, Lord, what wilt thou have me to do?"

67. Van den Honert, *De mensch in Christus,* 1:479.

68. Driessen, *Oude en nieuwe mensch,* 293.

69. DO: *eigenschappen.*

70. GrO: νοῦς.

religious emotion and impulse. Instead, it is a clear, lucid conscious life.[71] Its seat is not feeling, but the heart, the mind.[72] From there conscious life does manifest itself in feelings that are satisfied and pleasantly affected by it; this is the blessed life. However, it is not mediated by feeling but by faith, intellect, and will. The emotional life does not come first in the spiritual life, but second. Even where emotional life is missing, spiritual life continues to exist. Not feeling but believing is first and foremost.

d. *A free life.*[73] The spiritual life is *free* because we have been set free from servitude to sin (Rom. 6:11; cf. vv. 17–18; Eph. 4:3; 1 Pet. 4:2–3) and from the curse of the law (Rom. 6:14; Gal. 2:19; 3:10). Now that we are free from any creature—death, life, angels, demons, the present, the future, any powers, height, depth, or anything else in all creation (Rom. 8:38–39)—everything belongs to us: "The world or life or death or the present or the future—all are yours" (1 Cor. 3:21–22). Because we are only subject to God, Christ alone is our master, and his will coincides completely with the will of God. Our wills are free when they are in full harmony with God's will. Everything becomes an agent of the believer's *I*, of the spiritual life as it finds its goal again in the glory of God: "And whatever you do, whether in word or deed, do it all in the name of the Lord Jesus, giving thanks to God the Father through him" (Col. 3:17).

e. *A blessed life.*[74] Finally, the spiritual life is a blessed life, with gladness and joy in our hearts (Ps. 4:7) that no one can take away (John 16:22). The truth comforts and fully satisfies the human heart; that is, it creates harmony. It is a life of peace (Rom. 5:1), of love and joy (Gal. 5:22), even in the midst of tribulation (Rom. 5:3).

§18. THE ORIGIN OF THE SPIRITUAL LIFE

Objective and Subjective Causes

The first objective cause of the spiritual life is election, which is the fountain of all blessings (Rom. 8:28). The Father gave the elect to the Son from eternity (John 6:37; 17:24). The second objective cause, the meritorious cause, is the

---

71. Vitringa, *Korte schets*, 3 (I §2).

72. GrO: νοῦς. Ed. note: Bavinck makes a simple parenthetical reference to "Schleiermacher" at this point; clearly he meant "contra Schleiermacher"; see the latter's *Christian Faith*, 5, proposition §3: "The piety which forms the basis of all ecclesiastical communions is, considered purely in itself, neither a Knowing nor a Doing, but a modification of Feeling, or of immediate self-consciousness."

73. Löber, *Das innere Leben: Beitrag*, 27.

74. DO: *zalig leven*. Löber, *Das innere Leben: Beitrag*, 27.

obedience of Christ,[75] "who abolished death and brought life and immortality to light through the gospel" (2 Tim. 1:10). This is signified and sealed in baptism, the washing of regeneration (Titus 3:5), as the following passages reveal:

> Unless one is born of water and the Spirit, he cannot enter the kingdom of God. (John 3:5)

> I will sprinkle clean water on you, and you shall be clean from all your uncleannesses, and from all your idols I will cleanse you. And I will give you a new heart, and a new spirit I will put within you. And I will remove the heart of stone from your flesh and give you a heart of flesh. (Ezek. 36:25–26)

> On that day there shall be a fountain opened for the house of David and the inhabitants of Jerusalem, to cleanse them from sin and uncleanness. (Zech. 13:1)

The images of water and fountain certainly denote the blood of Christ, and the apostle John tells us that Jesus "came by water and blood" (1 John 5:6), which is to say, regeneration, cleansing, and reconciliation.[76] The third objective cause is the Holy Spirit: "he saved us, not because of works done by us in righteousness, but according to his own mercy, by the washing of regeneration and renewal of the Holy Spirit" (Titus 3:5; cf. John 3:5: "born of water and the Spirit").

God the Father is also mentioned because the Triune God is the author of all life:

> . . . who were born, not of blood nor of the will of the flesh nor of the will of man, but of God. (John 1:13)

> Know that the LORD, he is God! / It is he who made us, and we are his; / we are his people, and the sheep of his pasture. (Ps. 100:3)

> For we are his workmanship, created in Christ Jesus for good works, which God prepared beforehand, that we should walk in them. (Eph. 2:10)

---

75. Vitringa, *Korte schets*, 33 (III §3).

76. Ed. note: In the annotations to the *Statenvertaling*, the note on "fountain" in Zech. 13:1 reads: "A fountain: Or spring, well, that is, the grace of God in forgiving sins through the blood of Jesus Christ, with which we are washed." The note on "through water and blood" in 1 John 5:6 reads: "The apostle has in view here the water and blood that poured out of the pierced side of Christ, which only John mentions (John 19:34–35); and retells it here in order to disclose what is hidden in it, namely, that what flows from him is the water of the Holy Spirit by which we are purified and regenerated, and that our reconciliation with God and the forgiveness of our sins is obtained through the shedding of his blood on the cross."

> Of his own will he brought us forth by the word of truth, that we should be a kind of firstfruits of his creatures. (James 1:18)

Christ also is called the life-giving Spirit (1 Cor. 15:45).[77] Within the economy of the Trinity, regeneration is the work of the Holy Spirit (John 3:5; 6:63; 1 Cor. 6:11; 2 Cor. 3:3, 6). Paul tells the Corinthians that they "are a letter from Christ delivered by us, written not with ink but with the Spirit of the living God, not on tablets of stone but on tablets of human hearts" (2 Cor. 3:3; cf. Jer. 31:33; Ezek. 36:26). After all, the Holy Spirit has given life and motion also to the universe (Gen. 1:2; Job 26:13). Regeneration is spiritual, to make holy; to whom can this be attributed better than to the Holy Spirit? The Holy Spirit is the author also of all rational, moral life; wisdom, power, courage, bravery, intellect come from him. He is therefore the Spirit of life (Rom. 8:2), the author of all that is spiritual in humanity. It is the distinctive characteristic of the Holy Spirit to influence the human spirit. All spirituality, intellectual competence, inclination, and activity depend on the Holy Spirit, the source of all spirituality.

We turn now to the subjective causes of the spiritual life, the manner in which human spiritual life originates.[78] We first consider the matter of preparations for the new birth. Ordinarily, a great deal precedes regeneration—conviction, repentance, shame, fear, longing for rest, etc. Is this now preparation, a good disposition as such for the new birth?[79] The Remonstrants said that regeneration required in advance that one acknowledge one's spiritual death and bemoan it, long for redemption, before the actual rebirth took place.[80] Reformed theologians, however, would have nothing to do with such a preparatory grace.[81]

The question needs to be posed correctly. An actual preparation in the sense of using the light of nature by the free will of humans (Pelagius) or

77. GrO: πνεῦμα ζῳοποιοῦν.

78. Vitringa, *Korte schets*, 45–77 (IV); van Eenhoorn, *Eusooia*, 1:220ff.; van Aalst, *Geestelijke mengelstoffen*, 369ff.; 298ff.

79. LO: *dispositio per se bona*. De Moor, *Commentarius Perpetuus*, 4:482–84; Owen, *Doctrine of Justification by Faith*, chap. 1; Kuyper, *Concise Works of the Holy Spirit*, 299–303 (II.17); cf. Kuyper, *De gemeene gratie*, 3:216–23. Ed. note: Bavinck's reference here adds "v." = "following" without specifying the ending page; issues of common grace as "preparatory grace" continue through p. 383.

80. Episcopius, *Arminian Confession*, 11.4, "Apology."

81. LO: *gratia praeparans*. Trigland, *Antapologia*, chaps. 25–26; van Mastricht, *Theoretico-Practica Theologia*, I.vi.3, §§19, 28 (3:229–30, 239); Witsius, *Economy of the Covenants*, 1:360–72 (III.5.ix–xxviii). Ed. note: For an explanation of the format we are using to cite van Mastricht's *Theoretico-Practica Theologia*, see the extended note in the introduction, §1, in the section "Reformed Churches" (pp. 8–9n48). The volume and page numbers come from the 1749–53 Dutch edition used by Bavinck.

through the means of grace (Remonstrants, Lutherans) does not exist, of course. Remonstrants require that one longs for righteousness through Christ while still in a sinful condition. But this would confuse spiritual and moral life, death and life, nature and the supernatural. There is no gradual transition between death and life. For this reason, all Reformed thinkers hold that regeneration is the absolute beginning of the spiritual life. Yet it is possible to speak of preparation in a different way, as Perkins did.[82] Ames also did so in his *Cases of Conscience*, where he devotes a chapter in his second book to the question of "how the sinner ought to prepare himself to conversion."[83] British theologians at the Synod of Dort spoke similarly of "antecedents to conversion" such as the hearing of God's Word, going to church, awareness of God's will, a sense of sin, fear of punishment, thought of liberation, and hope of some pardon.[84] Divine grace does not work through sudden enthusiasm; it assumes predispositions.[85]

All of this can become stifling. Others disputed this notion strongly, for in the reprobate, these are not preparations of grace, neither inherently nor according to God's purpose.[86] And in the elect, they are already signs of the calling, converting, regenerating grace and its fruit, although that is difficult to prove. Nonetheless, even among the elect there is much that often precedes the actual rebirth.[87] Witsius also acknowledges that the entire life of the elect until their rebirth is particularly under God's guidance in a special way: they are richly endowed, which serves the rebirth later; they are safeguarded against blaspheming the Holy Spirit and begin to understand the truth theoretically, etc. There is nothing against speaking of preparations as long as rebirth/regeneration remains the absolute beginning.[88] This is to be understood in the same sense as the wood being dried so that it later burns (but all of this through fire).[89] This sense is parallel to God creating dust on the first day and

---

82. See Perkins, *Aureae Casuum Conscientiae Decisiones*, I.69–101 (chap. 5).

83. Ames, *Conscience*, II.iv.1–7. This preparation includes self-examination based on "seriously looking into the Law of God," resulting in a "conviction of conscience" (Rom. 1:20, 32; 2:20; 7:7), concluded by despair arising from our inability to save ourselves (Rom. 7:9, 13), followed by "a true humiliation of heart, which consists of grief and fear because of sin," which "brings forth conversion" (Matt. 9:12).

84. LO: *antecedancis ad conversionem; notitia voluntatis divinae; sensus peccati; timor poenae; cogitatio de liberatione; spes aliqua veniae.*

85. LO: *per subitum enthusiasmum; predispositiones. Acta Synodi Nationalis*, 128.

86. LO: *praeparationes ad gratiam.* Witsius, *Economy of the Covenants*, 1:362–66 (III.6.xi–xv).

87. Comrie, *ABC of Faith*, chap. 1, "Putting On" ("*Aandoen*"), 3–6.; cf. Comrie, *Stellige en praktikale verklaring*, 358 (Q&A 20–23); Heppe, *Reformed Dogmatics*, 510–42.

88. Van Aalst, *Geestelijke mengelstoffen*, 368.

89. Kuyper, *Concise Works of the Holy Spirit*, 307 (II.18). Ed. note: Bavinck borrows the wood and fire analogy from Kuyper, but to make a different point. Kuyper points out the error

later forming everything from it, and to Christ's going to Nain and touching and making the bier to stop before raising the young man from the dead (Luke 7:14).[90]

It would be better to call these antecedent acts instead of preparatory acts, since what precedes does not prepare. In the same way, Zacchaeus wanted to see Jesus and climbed into a tree (Luke 19:1–10). In Acts 2, through the preaching, the crowd is moved, perplexed. In Acts 16 the jailor experiences the earthquake, is anguished and distraught. Consider Paul's preparations: surrounded by light, falling to the ground, blindness, etc. Daily experience also teaches this: almost no conversion happens without prior external and internal events. External: heavy blows, rich blessings, hearing a sermon, etc. Internal: sinners come to themselves, see their misery, become afraid of punishment, start searching Scripture, and long for deliverance. It is true, all of this may happen to the reprobate and be lost again entirely, being stifled by worldly cares. But with many of the elect (and Witsius forgets this), it penetrates ever deeper, it stays, until the time of love arrives and God grants life. However, once again, these preparations may not be commingled with spiritual activities; they are not a lower stage of the spiritual life (just as the sun gradually rises), but are specifically to be distinguished from it; they are not the organizing principle of the life of grace. The spiritual life never develops gradually from it, is not earned by it. Sometimes God regenerates apart from all those preparations, at once, suddenly. But ordinarily this preparation precedes, and that is why we must observe the outward means of grace: going to church, reading God's Word, searching our souls in the light of conscience and Scripture, testing ourselves. God binds his blessing to the use of these means. To this extent we can agree with Prof. Shedd that someone who proceeds in this manner will probably be born again and converted.[91] At any rate, we must do what we can, taking the path God uses for conversion.

The distinction between these actions and the spiritual activities consists objectively in that the former are brought about by the general grace of the Holy Spirit—though they are still the particular fruit of grace and not the product of our nature or will. This grace is granted to all people through the gospel to a greater or lesser degree, so that all unconverted people have experienced those activities more or less. Everyone knows such moments. The

---

of modern theologians who think that "preparatory grace is like the drying of wet wood, so that the spark can more readily ignite it," and notes that the analogy breaks down because, while it is true that "wet wood will not take the spark [but] *must* be dried before it *can* be kindled," none of this applies to divine grace, which can, because it is omnipotent, kindle any kind of wood.

90. Van Aalst, *Geestelijke mengelstoffen*, 368.

91. Shedd, *Dogmatic Theology*, 2:516–17.

spiritual activities, however, are the result of the particular, irresistible grace of the Holy Spirit. And subjectively, these preparatory activities take place in our conscience; they are the life of sin in our conscience (Rom. 7:9). At the same time, they are not salvific and do not make someone fit for salvation.[92] These activities take place on the periphery of our lives, on us, around us.[93] The spiritual activities occur in the heart, in the center, within us, in our "I." And these activities certainly have a different meaning for the elect than for the reprobate. In addition to church attendance, listening to the proclamation of God's Word, theoretical knowledge of the truth, and so forth, there are additional preparatory activities. These consist in the following:

1. *Special guidance in our daily walk:*[94] Conceived by and born from a particular set of parents, in a particular generation, people group, country, and time, we receive a specific upbringing, education, and character formation and a particular intellectual, moral, and physical development; we also fall into certain sins, yield to all kinds of evil, etc. Everything is antecedent. Frequently, there are special adversities, disasters, deaths, judgments, diseases, that lead us to become serious and thoughtful, awaken our conscience, unsettle our insensitivity, impress us with God's wrath, etc. As long as everything goes smoothly, we forget the Lord, we think he is favorable toward us, and we cast off convictions of conscience. "But Jeshurun grew fat, and kicked; / you grew fat, stout, and sleek; / then he forsook God who made him / and scoffed at the Rock of his salvation" (Deut. 32:15).[95] Sometimes, but less frequently, there are special blessings that awaken us to a feeling of our own unworthiness and God's goodness. Sometimes it comes through hearing a serious sermon, through a powerful text, an admonition, etc.

2. *Subduing our stubborn nature.* Here the recalcitrance and stubbornness of our nature is broken.[96] William Perkins argued that with "the outward means of salvation, especially the ministry of the word," God often "sends some outward or inward cross to break and subdue the stubbornness of our nature that it may be made pliable to the will of God."[97] Scriptural examples include King Manasseh (2 Chron. 33:11–12), the Philippian jailor (Acts 16), and the response of the Jews to Peter's preaching (Acts 2:37). At some point the carelessness stops and concern about salvation ensues.[98]

---

92. Comrie, *ABC of Faith*, 56.
93. DO: *aan ons; om ons.*
94. Van Eenhoorn, *Eusioia*, 220–29.
95. Vitringa, *Korte schets*, 70–71.
96. DO: *weerspannigheid en hardnekkigheid onzer natuur.*
97. LO: *Fractio naturalis contumaciae et flexilitas voluntatis.* Perkins, *Whole Treatise*, I.v, pp. 50–51 (spelling modernized).
98. Ames, *Conscience*, II.iii.

3. *Serious consideration of the law.*[99] The preceding having occurred, "God brings the mind of man to a consideration of the law, and therein generally to see what is good, and what is evil, what is sin and what is not sin."[100] This inquiry is to be made with serious intention leading to self-examination and self-evaluation; looking at our own face in a mirror, we must not forget who we are (James 1:23–24).

4. *Consideration of sin.*[101] "Upon a serious consideration of the Law, God makes a man particularly to see and know, his own peculiar and proper sins, whereby he offends God."[102] This is more than the general conviction that we are sinful, which does not produce sincere remorse and leaves one completely cold. Instead it is often an insight into a few special individual sins that disturbs us. As Paul says, "I would not have known what sin was had it not been for the law" (Rom. 7:7 NIV). This is the so-called convicting grace, which must be distinguished from regenerating grace. Scripture refers to this phenomenon in a number of places: "They hate him who reproves in the gate, and they abhor him who speaks the truth" (Amos 5:10); "Then he opens the ears of men / and terrifies them with warnings" (Job 33:16); "And when he [the Holy Spirit] comes, he will convict the world concerning sin and righteousness and judgment" (John 16:8); Scripture, which is "breathed out by God," is "profitable for teaching, for reproof, for correction, and for training in righteousness" (2 Tim. 3:16). In convicting grace, the Holy Spirit convicts seriously minded people that their state is cursed and that their sins are accursed; in other words, the Holy Spirit impresses on them the severity of God's wrath and the "fear of the Lord" (taken as an objective genitive, 2 Cor. 5:11).[103] Penitence is included in this preparation, in distinction from repentance.[104]

5. *Fear of legal punishment, despair.*[105] Continuing the previous point, Perkins adds: "Upon the sight of sin, he smites the heart with a legal fear, whereby when man sees his sins, he makes him to fear punishment and hell,

---

99. LO: *seria legis consideratio.*
100. Perkins, *Whole Treatise*, 51.
101. LO: *consideratio peccatorum.*
102. Perkins, *Whole Treatise*, 51.
103. GrO: τὸν φόβον τοῦ κυρίου. Vitringa, *Korte schets*, 67–68; van Aalst, *Geestelijke mengelstoffen*, 377.
104. LO: *poenitentia; praeparationes; resipiscentia.* This is the view of Calvin and Beza; see *RD*, 3:522–28. Ed. note: The Reformers used *resipiscentia* instead of *poenitentia* to translate the New Testament Greek word *metanoia*. *Resipiscentia* was used in a more restrictive sense and "indicated *poenitentia* only in the sense of the penitence or contrition characteristic of conversion to Christ and of the effects of the gracious work of the Spirit in sinners" (Muller, *Dictionary*, 264, s.v. "*resipiscentia*").
105. LO: *legalis metus poenarum desperatio.*

and to despair of salvation, in regard of anything in himself."[106] This is Paul's point in Romans 7:9–11: "I was once alive apart from the law, but when the commandment came, sin came alive and I died. The very commandment that promised life proved to be death to me. For sin, seizing an opportunity through the commandment, deceived me and through it killed me." Other elements include the insight that the Lord Jesus is necessary, the longing for deliverance, and a desire to be converted (because one is unhappy, miserable, etc.).

These are the general, ordinary preparations for receiving grace. We are speaking only of the normal route.[107] It is different for pagans, who are sometimes turned around powerfully by preaching; all these preparations come together in the moment of new birth. It is also different for sinners who are suddenly plucked from a godless life as burning wood from the fire (Jude 23). It is different again with children who already received grace in their early youth and who later grow and are strengthened in grace, such as Jeremiah, John the Baptist, and Timothy. But they also experience the essential elements in the preparations described above.

The Struggle toward Rebirth

However, after one receives these preparations, the process can go in two directions. After all, with such a preparation there will be a struggle between the convicting Spirit in one's conscience and the flesh.[108] The Spirit knocks on the door of one's heart and calls to conversion, to distance oneself from the world and its allurements. Even imperfect desires to be converted arise within the person. They would want to be converted, but the flesh and the world are opposed; they would have to surrender so much pleasure, so much sweetness, and sacrifice advantage. The flesh advises keeping the door of the heart closed. In this way, a struggle ensues, anxiety, doubt.[109] If one now follows the flesh, then one opposes, distresses, and grieves the Holy Spirit. And those who continue to resist are often like a dog that "returns to its own vomit, and the sow, [which] after washing herself, returns to wallow in the mire" (2 Pet. 2:22). Such people turn around after going halfway, return to their sin, and silence their conscience. They love the present world (2 Tim.

106. Perkins, *Whole Treatise*, 51.
107. Ed. note: Bavinck is clearly thinking here of a situation within Christendom, where someone lives within a broader sociocultural environment in which the Christian gospel is public knowledge.
108. Vitringa, *Korte schets*, 69–71.
109. GrO: διστασία ("doubt"). Ed. note: Bavinck's source for this Greek word is not known, and the word does not appear in Liddell and Scott's *Greek-English Lexicon*. Undoubtedly it is derived from the verb διστάζω ("to doubt, be uncertain").

4:10), plunge into ever cruder sins, and thus sometimes blaspheme the Holy Spirit (Heb. 6) after having tasted the heavenly gift. Others adopt a middle course,[110] turn from coarse sins, become staid and religious in their walk, attend church, and become zealous advocates for the church, missions, etc. This is how they are described in Psalm 58:2–5:

> In your hearts you devise wrongs;
> > your hands deal out violence on earth.
> The wicked are estranged from the womb;
> > they go astray from birth, speaking lies.
> They have venom like the venom of a serpent,
> > like the deaf adder that stops its ear,
> so that it does not hear the voice of charmers
> > or of the cunning enchanter.

Such people often become hypocrites; they bend their heads like a bulrush, torture their souls the whole day with fasting, and spread sackcloth and ashes over themselves. Among them we often find the critics, the nitpickers, those who never came to the point of being born again and missed all spiritual life, but still use the standard of preparatory experience and boast about it. They are like a foolish child who is too busy to be born (Hosea 13:13); like a cake that has not been turned over, they are half-baked (Hosea 7:8).

The elect, however, are saved from such lapsing. Sometimes, for a short time, or even for a longer time, they are kept standing in this preparatory conviction. But then comes the moment of regeneration. Until that point we were keeping part of the house for ourselves, in order to hold on to one or another sin, but then convicting grace makes room for regenerating grace.[111] This regeneration, "the new creation, the raising from the dead, the making alive so clearly proclaimed in the Scriptures . . . God works in us without our help."[112] Without any cooperation on our part, God begins this regeneration in us by his irresistible grace, penetrating our conscience through to our heart and pouring into us a new life-principle. This enlightens our understanding, judgment, conscience, and memory so that the darkness disappears and we evaluate ourselves, God, and Christ differently.[113] The scales fall from our eyes (Acts 9:18). God bends and turns around our will, so that sinners cannot resist, and drives them to Christ; he re-creates their inclinations and passions

110. Vitringa, *Korte schets*, 70.
111. Vitringa, *Korte schets*, 73.
112. Canons of Dort, III/IV.12.
113. DO: *oordeel*; *geweten*; *geheugen*. Myseras, *Der vromen ondervinding*. Ed. note: The second section of this tract deals with regeneration (*wedergeboorte*).

and rekindles in them a love for God and Christ. He opens the heart, as he did with Lydia (Acts 16:14), rips away the lock of the heart (Hosea 13:8), which until now was closed through prejudgments, and conquers the power and mastery of the flesh. The "new person" is born and the old has passed away (2 Cor. 5:17).

We do not know how this happens. Rebirth is as mysterious as natural birth. The wind blows where it wishes, etc. (John 3:8). We cannot analyze it, any more than we can analyze the act of creation and the origin of humanity and each person. How this work of grace begins is unfathomable to us.[114] There is here an absolutely new beginning that we cannot understand. We do not know how life comes to the soul—whether it is carried in from the outside or created from within. But this is what we do see and experience: he who was dead is now alive (Rev. 1:18). We know this from God's Word: the living word is the means by which it happens; it is an imperishable seed.[115] We are not able to understand this either: How can truth become a means to life? Truth and life are so different from each other, and yet they are one in God, in Christ. However, the Word does not work by itself to create life; the Word creates life only as it is borne into the heart by the Holy Spirit and becomes powerful and fruitful. The Word is the hammer, but the Holy Spirit must wield it in order to break our hearts. The Word is a sharp-cutting sword, but the Holy Spirit must do the cutting.

But now the question arises: Is that life itself, which is granted in regeneration, already born out of and in communion with Christ? Most theologians say yes. There is no participation in Christ's benefits (including regeneration) unless we participate in him (Calvin).[116] But the only way to come into fellowship with Christ is by faith; this assumes a spiritual act, and it thus already assumes spiritual life, rebirth.[117] Thus we arrive at this proposition: the initial life in regeneration is produced through and from the Holy Spirit, and that life is manifest in the work of faith, and that faith grasps Christ.[118] Mystical union arises (logically) after regeneration, simultaneously with and through faith.[119] Becoming one with Christ, we therefore already have the organizing principle of life. But this life-principle[120] now draws, as it grows, all its power, strength, and nourishment from Christ. And in order to be grafted into him

114. Vilmar, *Theologische Moral*, 2:5, 6.
115. Vitringa, *Korte schets*, 51.
116. Calvin, *Institutes*, III.i.2.
117. Van Aalst, *Geestelijke mengelstoffen*, 298.
118. Witsius, *Miscellaneorum Sacrorum*, 2:788–91; Kuyper, *Concise Works of the Holy Spirit*, 343–54 (II.25–26).
119. LO: *unio mystica*.
120. DO: *levensbeginsel*.

who is the olive tree, we must already be living twigs. One does not ingraft dead branches.

There is, however, an objection to this idea: there appears to be some spiritual life outside Christ.[121] Yes, insofar as that spiritual life is poured out into us before the mystical union with Christ, but not as though this came into existence outside Christ. The initial life-principle is the work of the Holy Spirit, who proceeds from Christ. We may speak here of a passive union but not of one that is active from our side. Christ is the meritorious cause[122] of this also—he has earned the Holy Spirit, this faith, etc. for us. Besides, this objection remains: no matter how early the mystical union begins, it cannot begin before the faith that imparts it. Faith is thus imparted before the mystical union. Thus there is an "initial grace" which assumes absolutely nothing in us, not even the mystical union—that is, the "drawing of the Father"—the convicting and regenerating grace of new birth, and the granting of faith.[123] The "second grace" does assume something within us—namely, faith, mystical union, justification, sanctification, etc.[124]

More specifically, this life is an imprint of the life of God.[125] Not every kind of life is brought forth through regeneration, but only the spiritual life, such a life as is also found in the One who brings forth. God is the author of the spiritual life, and it must therefore conform to his life. After all, God is the author of all life, but we do not for that reason say that everything (animals, plants, and people) is born of God or is his child. But we who participate in this life are God's children, born of him, according to 2 Peter 1:4: "He has granted to us his precious and very great promises, so that through them you may become partakers of the divine nature."[126] For our spiritual life is to be in conformity with God's life, an imprint of his life, which must be the archetype, the example, for ours. God's life consists in that perfect activity of God through which he perfectly knows and loves himself and lives according to his holy nature in blessedness.

Our spiritual life is similar to and an image of that blessedness. The spiritual person once again is God's image, knows God, judges purely, and pursues God and fellowship with him. In this way we are blessed and live to God's honor. The spiritual person, therefore, is not estranged from the life of God.

121. Van Aalst, *Geestelijke mengelstoffen*, 303. Ed. note: In a marginal note Bavinck wrote, "No, because the Holy Spirit creates that first beginning of life in us from Christ. Thus there is passive union, but still no active union on our part."

122. LO: *causa meritoria*.

123. LO: *gratia prima*; *tractio Patris*.

124. LO: *gratia secunda*.

125. DO: *afdruksel van het leven Gods*. Vitringa, *Korte schets*, 48–51.

126. GrO: γένησθε θείας κοινωνοὶ φύσεως.

§19. The First and Basic Activity of the Spiritual Life

All life is activity and immediately reveals itself as such. This is also true of spiritual life. What then is the basic, remaining activity of all life? It consists of separating, dividing, assimilating—and appropriating to itself. This is already the law of the lowest form of organic life—plants. The plant rejects whatever is strange, whatever does not serve as food, but assimilates related material for life: for its growth it needs life, warmth, water, electricity, air (dampness, dew, and rain), metal and nonmetal substances—in a word: heaven and earth. It assimilates, absorbs, and transforms these things into organic elements for its own life; the plant, therefore, is at the same time independent and dependent. And through that separation and appropriation it grows, matures, and produces seed and fruit. It is the same in the animal world.[127]

Human life follows a similar pattern: breathing in oxygen and breathing out nitrogen, absorbing food and eliminating non-nourishing elements. Our moral life also absorbs related perceptions, feelings, and observations, and our conscience sheds heterogeneous elements.[128] It is the same in the spiritual life. As soon as that life is created in us though rebirth, it reveals itself immediately and perpetually in a rejecting and appropriating activity.[129] The first is called conversion, and the second faith. The two elements are paired together, in reciprocal action, usually united especially after the moment of rebirth. The tears then shed are tears of remorse as well as of joy and love. Sometimes the one or the other emotion takes over. If remorse is dominant, then there is deep dismay and consternation, and then often doubt. "Could I, such a great sinner, be saved?" or "O God, this is too great for me, an unworthy one." If the second emotion is dominant, then people are in the time of first love, full of impatience and diligence, wanting to convert everyone, wanting to become ministers or missionaries. Such people "have a zeal for God, but not according to knowledge" (Rom. 10:2). They may make comments to experienced Christians whom they consider to be indifferent and lacking in love.[130] Then later these people realize that with that fervor there was much passion and "strange fire," that they must also serve God with their reason, and that they are not holy nor can be holy. And with that disappointment it sometimes happens that people doubt their conversion, dismiss all their spiritual experiences, and doubt everything. And in this way faith can again lead to conversion and conversion to faith.

127. Löber, *Das innere Leben: Beitrag*, 36.
128. Löber, *Innere Leben: Beitrag*, 37.
129. Löber, *Innere Leben: Beitrag*, 123.
130. Van Eenhoorn, *Eusooia*, 1:244.

1. Separating Activity, Commonly Called "Conversion"[131]

We understand conversion to be a sincere and steadfast renouncing of all sin by a born-again person. This immediately reveals the spiritual life. But we do have to make a distinction here. A certain conviction, a parting from sin also took place already before rebirth, as preparation. There is a great, specific difference between this renouncing of sin *before* and *after* regeneration. Sorrow before regeneration can also be experienced by reprobates, as shown by Cain, Ahithophel, Saul, Judas, the Ninevites, Felix (Acts 24:25), Agrippa (Acts 26:28). This general conviction has its origin in the Spirit as God (not as the Spirit of Christ) and his common grace and enlightenment. It is mostly brought on by judgments, illnesses (sickbed confinement), and pestilences, and it concerns mostly grave and public sins (not so much the hidden ones), as well as shameful and harmful matters; most of the time it is out of fear for punishment, debasement, hell. It benefits the mind and the conscience but leaves the heart unchanged. It is often observed that this general conviction, this "worldly grief" (2 Cor. 7:10), produces death.[132] It leads people to recoil from God; in Isaiah's words: "The sinners in Zion are afraid; / trembling has seized the godless: / 'Who among us can dwell with the consuming fire? / Who among us can dwell with everlasting burnings?'" (Isa. 33:14). They take satisfaction in external improvement of life (like the young man in Matt. 19) or seek distraction in the world, like Cain, who builds a city, like Judas, who looks for a noose, like the dog that returns to its own vomit (2 Pet. 2:22). In the end this general conviction differs from genuine conviction in that it turns into despair or greater godlessness or mere external conversion.

True conviction that is godly sorrow, however, has the following characteristics: (a) It is a work of the Holy Spirit as Spirit of Christ (John 16), the Spirit, therefore, who is the fruit of Christ's intercession (John 14:16–17), of his merits (John 16:14). And the Holy Spirit works it through the law (Rom. 3:20; Rom. 7) or through the gospel (not only through the law; it is not true that the gospel only promises while the law only commands),[133] through heavy trials (Ps. 119:67, 71; Luke 15) or rich blessings (Gen. 16:13; 32:10), and then further through regeneration and enlightenment. (b) This true conviction is internal most of the time; it penetrates into and arises from the heart. It pertains to *sin*, to the sinful condition in which we are conceived (Ps. 51:5),

---

131. GO/DO: *Ausscheidende werkzaamheid*. See Löber, *Innere Leben: Beitrag*, 20; van Aalst, *Geestelijke mengelstoffen*, 355ff.; Ames, *Conscience*, II.viii ("Of Repentance"); Myseras, *Der vromen ondervinding*, 9–19; Martensen, *Christian Ethics*, 284–307 (§§90–99); Vitringa, *Korte schets*, 82ff.

132. GrO: τοῦ κόσμου λύπη.

133. Van Aalst, *Geestelijke mengelstoffen*, 202–15.

to sin's dominion over us (Rom. 6:14; 7:24). Included are sinful deeds in our thinking, our words and deeds, our hidden and public sins, the small sins and the large (Ps. 19:13). In a word, it is about sin as sin and not in the first place because a deed is harmful, shameful, or improper or because we are fearful of punishment or hell. It is about sin as that which angers the God of steadfast love and mercy (Ps. 51:1). Psalm 51:4: "Against you, you only, have I sinned / and done what is evil in your sight, /so that you may be justified in your words / and blameless in your judgment"; Genesis 39:9: "How then can I do this great wickedness and sin against God?" It continues with acknowledging *punishment* for sin, because God's curse rests on all who fail to "confirm the words of the law by doing them" (Deut. 27:26), and he will inflict vengeance "in flaming fire . . . on those who do not know God and on those who do not obey the gospel of our Lord Jesus" (2 Thess. 1:8). It is all about one's own impotence and loss of life, to the glory of God himself. It is for a person to acknowledge that without Christ they are "dead in trespasses and sins . . . having no hope and without God in the world" (Eph. 2:1, 12); they are "wretched, pitiable, poor, blind, and naked" (Rev. 3:17). All this is the substance of their sorrow.

All who are born again need to know this sorrow to some degree, although it may not be quite as strong and instantaneous for those who have been taught from youth or who were converted through an evangelical gospel ministry.[134] It is not possible to indicate the size and extent of this sorrow, which can vary significantly as long as it is great enough to drive us to Christ. Time and duration of such sorrow cannot be defined either. Sometimes it takes a long time because of lack of knowledge about the way of salvation, or unbelief, or serious struggle; sometimes it takes very little time, as with Zacchaeus or Paul (three days, Acts 9:9). A question still lingers here: After regeneration, after being saved, do people then still have knowledge of their misery?[135] Yes, they do, but then they *see* themselves as they were and are in the natural state of sin. In the moment that we experience this true sorrow, we do not yet *know* that we are regenerated, nor do we believe it. The rebuffing and rejection of sin can occur only when the sin has become a heterogenic element—that is, when we ourselves recognize within ourselves an *I* who is not in the grip of sin but seeks to be released from it and for that reason shoves it aside and banishes it. Conversion as a dying of the "old self"[136] presupposes a new person who dies to sin, the world, etc. This conversion

---

134. Van Aalst, *Geestelijke mengelstoffen*, 364.
135. Van Aalst, *Geestelijke mengelstoffen*, 378.
136. Heidelberg Catechism, Q&A 88.

is therefore the rejecting activity of the new person rebuffing what is sinful and evil, hating it, and fleeing from it. In banishing, abjuring, and expelling sin we bury the "old man." Because sin clings to everything, to our *I*, to our intellect, will, emotions, passions, body, soul, to all our faculties, strength, hand, eye, ear, foot, and also to our spouse, children, house, money, goods, world, this conversion is truly a dying of the "old *man*," an act of our full, complete humanity and not just in part. We must let our *I* be crucified (Gal. 2:20), absolutely deny our *self* (Matt. 16:24), be crucified to the whole world (Gal. 6:14), die to all that is seen (2 Cor. 4:18), despair of all things created. There must be an absolute unbelief in all that has been created as if any creature could give support, be the footing, grant security, and offer some deliverance. We must consider our own life and soul as loss and everything as burdensome baggage.

2. *Appropriating Activity*[137]

Spiritual persons who have been regenerated, who are born of the Holy Spirit through passive mystical union with Christ, reveal themselves immediately and positively by believing. This is indeed the one, great, lasting, positive activity of the spiritual person and, according to Jesus, the work God commands: "This is the work of God, that you believe in him whom he has sent" (John 6:29). Believing is psychological. It is to accept someone else's testimony, to be persuaded of the truth of that testimony on the basis of confidence in the person who provides the testimony. Believing thus has as its object a word, a promise, a testimony, and, as ground, support, and basis, the trustworthiness of a *person*. As the locus classicus for saving faith—1 John 5:9–11—makes clear, faith is a conviction that God's testimony is true because God himself is trustworthy. The object of faith, therefore, is God's testimony—namely, the testimony he has given concerning his Son: that he is God and Savior, that eternal life is in him "who became to us wisdom from God, righteousness and sanctification and redemption" (1 Cor. 1:30). God himself is the ground, support, and basis of that testimony. We must believe God's testimony for no other reason than it is *he* who gives it. To believe is to say "Amen" to God's Word.

If this now is the essence of faith, then those among the Reformed who maintained that consciousness is the seat of faith were right. What then follows in the Christian life does not belong to the essence of faith but to its fruits. The truth and veracity of that faith (i.e., that it truly means what it says) is

---

137. GO/DO: *Aneignende werkzaamheid*. Löber, *Innere Leben: Beitrag*, 154–80; Eenhoorn, *Eusooia*, 235, 247ff.; van Aalst, *Proeve des geloofs*; Ames, *Conscience*, II.vi.

then *demonstrated* in this double move: (a) abandoning the thought that life is to be found in something other than the Son (in self, money, goods, family, any creature), for this would be unbelief; and (b) seeking life in the Son alone because God says that it is in the Son alone. The abandoning mentioned in (a) is *conversion*. That which is mentioned in (b) is in a narrower sense what Scripture calls *faith*: hungering for God, seeking God, going to God, coming to God, trusting in God, and believing in Christ. For this, the actual object is not so much God's testimony as the person of the Lord himself, of God himself in Christ. In order to distinguish it, let us call this faith in the narrower sense that is indicated in (b) *trust*.

We could also reason this way: faith is accepting God's testimony regarding his Son on the basis of God himself. In order for us to accept this testimony regarding Christ we must already trust God, consider him trustworthy. The basis for faith in someone must precede believing in their testimony because we will accept someone's testimony only if and after we have come to know them as trustworthy. Believing God's testimony regarding Jesus precedes faith in God. Here is what happens when we connect these two thoughts: (a) we consider God trustworthy with ourselves as liars, (b) we accept his testimony regarding his Son, and (c) we trust in (that is, come to, hunger for, etc.) that Son. To which this must be added: (d) to be adopted as a child we go to the Father again through the Son by counting him as righteous. Now there are two views that belong to the essence of faith that do not exclude each other and that also appear in Scripture side by side. The one is that of rational people, the other of people who rely more on feelings, the former of intellectuals and the latter of those more ethically inclined, of head people and heart people. For one, the essence of faith is what we mentioned under (b): accepting God's testimony regarding his Son on the basis of God himself. The seat of faith is consciousness; its essence is knowledge (John 17:3). And for the other, the essence of faith is what we mentioned under (c): trust in Christ. The seat of faith is the heart (Rom. 10:10); the essence of it is trust, as we see time and again in the Old Testament, etc.

Those who are of the first opinion (the rationally inclined) are in danger of confusing saving faith with historic faith, of cultivating dead orthodoxy. Those of the second opinion run the danger of disparaging the importance of accepting God's testimony, of confusing saving faith with feeling and experience, and of cultivating a passive, sensitive antinomianism that feeds on experience and relies less on the Word. The first represents the dangers of Catholicism, the second of mysticism. In this case, those who rely on feelings and pious experience have a more accurate perception of the spiritual life. They use better distinctions, referring to faith that is "refuge-seeking," "salvation-embracing," "trusting," and secure.[138] The first engage in deeper study of God's Word. Our catechism connects these two: to believe is to *know* and to *trust*, to *accept* God's Word and to *trust* in Christ.[139] That is the right way. A twofold act is at play in faith: the more we accept God's Word and agree with it, the more we also learn to trust the person of Christ; and conversely, the more our trust in Christ increases, the more we cling to the Word. Through the Word we get closer to Christ himself, but then also through Christ we get ever deeper into the Word. Faith therefore (in the full sense of the word) has a twofold object: the Word of God concerning Christ (accepted, agreed to, and known), and Christ's person himself as an object of trust.

The two objects are very closely related because, after all, Christ is, so to speak, the living Scripture, the living Word, and Scripture is the written Christ. The Scriptures are the very testimony concerning Christ. This Scripture is necessary in the present dispensation, but will disappear someday. Faith as acceptance of Scripture (God's testimony regarding Christ) will someday cease, but now it is the only means to arrive at trust in Christ (which will remain always, also in heaven). For this reason trust in Christ is the permanent element in faith and also its essence. By agreeing with Scripture and honoring it, we put our trust in Christ; the one automatically cultivates the other; the two belong together. And trusting Christ, we agree evermore with Holy Scripture; the formal supports the material principle, and vice versa. This is faith.

How is this now the appropriating organ of the spiritual person, and in what way does this process of appropriation happen? Faith has conversion as its converse—namely, expelling, banishing, and distrusting self and all creatures. Faith, on the other hand, is trusting in God. Faith serves as the appropriating organ for the believer in the same way as it happens with a child. A child lives by faith, and this is how we live on this earth where we grow up. In heaven we will have become adults and will do away with what once was childish. A child who lives by faith does not work for a living but lives in the quiet, unconscious confidence that its parents will provide food. The child never doubts this; it goes without saying that parents provide for the child's needs. So it is with believers: they do not work and toil for their salvation, but believe that God will take care of it. And it is precisely out of that faith

138. Ed. note: Bavinck inserted a parenthetical note here, "See the following chapter." Following this instruction strictly would bring us into vol. 2; however, the topics indicated here are also covered in chaps. 9–12 of this volume.

139. Ed. note: Without naming it, Bavinck has in view here Heidelberg Catechism, Q&A 21: "What is true faith? True faith is not only a *sure knowledge* by which I hold as true all that God has revealed to us in Scripture; it is also a wholehearted trust, which the Holy Spirit creates in me by the gospel, that God has freely granted, not only to others but to me also, forgiveness of sins, eternal righteousness, and salvation."

that they live. The child always receives food in its time, and a child's faith is never betrayed. The believer receives salvation, peace, glory, and food when it is needed, and does not feel betrayed. Both live by faith.

However, that faith is not the food itself nor does faith earn the food. Faith is thus not life itself, but the Father provides the food, the food gives life, and the Father gives it out of love, without paying attention or giving any thought to merit. In the same way, just as in the life of a child its faith is the means by which it lives off the bread that it receives from its parents, so it is with the spiritual life. If the child does not believe and starts to work itself for its food, it gets nothing; it cannot earn anything and would die if it had to rely on itself. However, parents provide food because it is their child, because they know it is their obligation to look after the child, and they do that of their own accord, out of love. Thus, when we believe as children—that is, when we depend on our Father—then we live and will live. Then God gives everything in his time and at the right time.

Believing, therefore, is *the* work, the only, complete, sufficient, always necessary work of the Christian. Never anything else or anything more than to believe. To believe in all circumstances, for our earthly and temporal as well as for heavenly and eternal good. Faith does not bind, force, or obligate the Father to give. No, the Father gives voluntarily, out of love, and yet for the child faith is required. The Father could also give without faith (as far as his power is concerned), but this he does not want to do; he wants the child to be a child and to remain a child and have faith. In that way faith is the assimilating organ. Actually, we do not *take* or obtain food through it. Faith is opening our heart—it is a passive organ. God has to give first, then we receive.

What does faith appropriate? Christ, who is the object of faith. And, to be sure, first his person, according to both his divine and his human natures. The mystical union or joining of our essential *I* with the divine-human essential *I* continues to grow in intimacy; the Spirit binds us ever closer together, but in such a way that the boundaries between Christ and us are never eliminated. In addition, we appropriate to ourselves Christ and all his merits, all the benefits of the covenant of grace—wisdom, righteousness, sanctification, full redemption, peace, joy, full bliss, the whole image of God. Now these are altogether moral qualities, not substances; we become new creations. Jesus himself says that he is the bread of life, that people must eat his flesh and drink his blood—in other words, himself—and they will have eternal life (John 6:48–58). Jesus is speaking of his flesh that he will give for the life of the world—that is, his sacrificed flesh and his blood shed on the cross. His blood is now proof of payment for our sins—deliverance from death and punishment; his flesh is the food that communicates life—resurrection.[140] In other words, he surrenders flesh and blood in death as a peace offering, so that believers receive forgiveness and life. This also is to be understood spiritually, not physically.[141] The result of this eating—that is, this believing—is that one has eternal life (v. 54) and remains in Jesus (v. 56) (which is the mystical union) and his teachings.[142] All of this also, the appropriation by faith, takes place indirectly—that is, through word and sacrament.

Here also faith as trust is strengthened again by faith as accepting the testimony (John 5:38). His word must remain in us, and we must remain in his word (John 8:31; 14:23). Thus in the Lord's Supper, the cup is sharing in the blood of Christ (1 Cor. 10:16), and the bread is sharing in his body. Accepting the testimony (faith in the narrower sense) serves therefore temporarily to help increase faith as trust in the person of Christ. The true endorsement of God's testimony drives people, of its own accord, to Christ. Knowledge of the Word becomes, then, knowledge of Christ himself. Studying the portrait makes us know and recognize the person himself.

The result of this appropriation by faith of Christ and his merits is the growth of the new man. This growth takes place organically, not mechanically. That is, the moral qualities (righteousness, sanctification, peace) are not poured out mechanically into us (although they are imputed to us at once in justification) but are gradually assimilated by us by faith. Just as food when chewed enters the body and is gradually absorbed into the bloodstream and thus becomes part of our organism, so it is also in the spiritual realm. It happens similarly in the realm of science and the arts: someone's opinions have to be processed and reflected upon before they become ours. God's Word has to be meditated upon before it becomes our thought, and therefore also Christ and his merits, accepted by faith, must be processed in struggle and pain and assimilated before they become ours. Thus the new man, who does not live by bread but by the Word of Christ, grows. And this is a new, complete *person*, not just in part, because in regeneration the entire man with all his faculties and abilities is re-created in principle. And as this new person grows, he shows ever more clearly the traits of the image of God that, imprinted at once, gradually appear more noticeably (like a father's image in a child).

140. Godet, *Commentary on John*, 2:39–42.
141. See the annotations of the *Statenvertaling*.
142. Van Andel, *Jezus' leer*, 43–55.

8

Life in the Spirit in the Church's History

Historically, the Christian church has repeatedly met the challenge of lapses in holy living by its members with reform and renewal movements. These began with monasticism in the early church, a monasticism which needed and underwent reform in the Middle Ages. The monastic orders helped create a dual morality in Catholicism: "precepts" for the laity and "counsels of perfection" for those committed to the "religious" life.

The Reformation repudiated these stages in the spiritual and emphasized the universal vocation of all believers. The Anabaptists, however, had different ideas, separated nature and grace, and tried to remake the world into a spiritual kingdom. The Anabaptists were Protestant monastics, and their vision led to Pietism and Puritan precisionism. Reformers such as Zwingli, Calvin, and à Lasco worked hard at creating ordered church communities with disciplined Christian living.

The church has always been challenged by one-sided understandings of the Christian life. Restricting religious life to feelings leads to mysticism; narrowing it to imagination and empiricism results in fanaticism; limiting it to speculation and reflection results in gnosticism; overemphasizing activity leads to Pharisaism or nomism; limiting it to confession leads to orthodoxism. Mystical union with Christ is at the heart of the Christian faith; mysticism is a degeneration arising from a renunciation of the historical and ecclesiastical dimension of the faith and drawing everything from within oneself. Quietism, asceticism, and even zealotry are frequently the outcome. Mysticism rests upon legitimate religious desires and can be properly expressed in genuine inner experience. It goes astray when people blur the boundary between themselves and God, either by seeking to enlighten their consciousness (mysticism) or awaken their conscience (enthusiasm). Mysticism moves through three stages: contemplation (or asceticism), inner illumination, and union of the soul with God.

Mysticism found a home in Western Christianity through the writings of Pseudo-Dionysius the Areopagite, in thirteenth- through fifteenth-century Germany, among reformers such as Wycliffe and Hus, and among the Anabaptists. All churches have their peculiar forms of mysticism that react against the externalization of the church.

Though the term is variously used, Pietism seeks to move the church beyond reformation of doctrine to reformation of life. While mystics often become quietists, Pietists tend to activism, to mission work, to education, to philanthropy. Important Pietists include Lutherans Philipp Jakob Spener and August Hermann Francke, English Puritans Thomas Cartwright, William Perkins, John Owen, Richard Baxter, and many more. In the Netherlands, during the so-called Further Reformation, we need to mention Jean Taffin, Willem Teellinck, Wilhelm à Brakel, Jodocus van Lodenstein, and Gisbert Voetius. William Ames is the "bridge" between the English and the Dutch.

The excesses of Dutch "Golden Age" life in the seventeenth century led many pious Christians to adopt a puritan lifestyle, shunning theater and dancing and enjoining strict Sabbath observance and fasting. Family life was strictly organized around religious practices nurtured by faithful family visitation. Mystical excess was also introduced into the Dutch Reformed church by Jean de Labadie, who emphasized mental prayer and contemplation leading to union with the Triune God. Labadism influenced the Netherlands by promoting the existence of conventicles as "little churches within the church." Under the influence of Labadism and Pietism, Friedrich August Lampe introduced a multistage piety to the Netherlands with key distinctions: seeking, hungry faith; clinging, struggling faith; refuge-seeking faith; appropriating faith; dependent, confident faith; and assured faith.

Special mention needs to be given to Count Nikolaus Ludwig von Zinzendorf and the Brethren Congregation (Brüdergemeine), or Moravian Church, known for its worldwide mission activity and distinct community. The body of Christ is regarded as an association, a society rather than a church bound by its confession. This confused the natural and spiritual orders. In critique we point to faith as primarily a matter of feeling, a denial of faith's objectivity, promotion of unhealthy separation and group mentality, loss of the covenant idea, religion reduced to the "things of God" and divorced from daily life, excessive inwardness, and loss of biblical normativity.

Methodism sought to do for the Anglican Church what mysticism sought for the Roman Catholic Church and Pietism sought for the Lutheran (and Reformed) churches—namely, to extend the Reformation into everyday life. John Wesley's conversion and life of service is inspiring. Doctrinally, he subscribed to the Anglican

Thirty-Nine Articles but dissented on predestination and perseverance. His views on regeneration (prevenient grace) and sanctification (perfectionism) were also outside of Reformed orthodoxy. Methodism indirectly affected the Netherlands at the beginning of the nineteenth century through the international revival movement known as the Réveil, which profoundly influenced Groen van Prinsterer, Abraham Kuyper, and the Dutch Reformed Churches. Methodism's weakness is that it regards conversion as sudden, momentary, and immediate and thus devalues the church, baptism, and Christian nurture. It also runs the risk of allowing sanctification to be absorbed into the task of converting others. The Salvation Army is the natural consequence of Methodism.

§20. MYSTICISM, PIETISM, AND METHODISM[1]

Reform Movements

We begin with a brief overview of the ways the church has historically viewed the Christian life.[2] Reformations occurred in Roman Catholic regions already before the time of the Protestant Reformation, including those of Pope Gregory VII (ca. 1015–85),[3] Francis of Assisi (1181–1226), Peter Waldo (ca. 1140–ca. 1205),[4] and the Congregation of Windesheim.[5] This reformation of

1. Ed. note: Bavinck treats the material of this chapter in more detail and in a slightly different manner in two essays on the imitation of Christ. See Bolt, *Theological Analysis*, appendices A and B, pp. 372–440. In the margin, Bavinck wrote and then scratched out: "The stages of the spiritual life."

2. Kuyper, *Drie kleine vossen*; Murisier, *Les maladies du sentiment religieux*; Lobstein, review of *Les maladies du sentiment religieux*.

3. Ed. note: Gregory VII was pope from 1073 to 1085 and best known for his role in the Investiture Controversy, a contest between the church and the state for control over the appointment of church officials such as bishops. The defining moment of his power struggle with Holy Roman Emperor Henry IV came in January 1077, when Gregory made Henry wait in penitence before the gate of the Castle Canossa in Emilia-Romagna, Italy, during a blizzard.

4. Ed. note: Peter Waldo was a wealthy merchant from Lyons who founded the Waldensians, a lay movement that emphasized voluntary poverty and adherence to scriptural teaching, rejecting the Roman Catholic doctrines of transubstantiation and purgatory. A Waldensian church, begun in the twelfth century, continues to the present as the Waldensian Evangelical Church in Italy (https://en.wikipedia.org/wiki/Peter_Waldo; https://en.wikipedia.org/wiki/Waldensian_Evangelical_Church).

5. Acquoy, *Het klooster te Windesheim*. Ed. note: The Congregation of Windesheim "is a branch of the Augustinians. It takes its name from its most important monastery, which was located about four miles south of Zwolle on the IJssel, in the Netherlands. This congregation of canons regular, of which this was the chief house, was an offshoot of the Brethren of the Common Life and played a considerable part in the reform movement within the Dutch and German Catholic Church in the century before the Protestant Reformation" (https://en.wikipedia.org/wiki/Congregation_of_Windesheim).

monasticism in the Middle Ages was actually considered a reformation of Christianity in general, especially because for Roman Catholics monasticism represented the true, ideal Christian life. The Middle Ages are full of such monastic reformations. Especially noteworthy among these are the reform of the Benedictine Order in Cluny (vow of silence) and the founding of the Franciscan Order (vow of poverty).[6] Both were aimed at separating the orders from the world.[7] The monastic orders were the cause of the distinction of a twofold morality, one for priests and the other for laity, a distinction between "counsels of perfection" and precepts. The monastic life was considered to be a higher order. But here, too, there were stages: from asceticism to contemplation and mysticism.[8] In addition to their regular orders of "Friars Minor" and "Poor Clares" (the women's Order of Saint Clare), the Franciscans created the secular "Third Order," the members of which were allowed to remain in the world.[9]

The Reformation abolished these stages[10] in the spiritual life altogether. It affirmed the same ideal of perfection for all Christians and a single moral code. The Reformation had a totally different understanding of the relationship of believers (the church) to the natural areas of life (family, occupation, state, society, etc.). The latter were not to be shunned but sanctified. Biblical texts that spoke of turning the other cheek, giving away one's goods, etc. were interpreted "with a grain of salt."[11] But the Reformers did believe that progress in the spiritual life was accompanied by struggle and suffering, that it was not complete all at once but was a process. The two basic elements and activities of the spiritual life were also specified: repentance and faith.[12] In addition, all of life was seen to consist of self-denial and cross-bearing.[13] But actual stages of the spiritual life do not exist as yet [in Protestant understanding].

---

6. Ed. note: Cluny Abbey, founded in 910, was the originating source of a series of monastic reforms within the Roman Catholic Church that sought to restore traditional monastic life. The Order of Friars Minor (commonly known as the Franciscan Order) was founded in 1209 by Francis of Assisi (1181/82–1226).

7. Ritschl, *Geschichte des Pietismus*, vol. 1, *Der Pietismus in der reformierten Kirche*, 13–18.

8. Gass, *Geschichte der christlichen Ethik*, 1:130–31.

9. LO: *fratres minors*. Ed. note: The Secular Franciscan Order, also known as Brothers and Sisters of Penance, was given a rule by St. Francis in 1221. After the death of Francis, members of this "Third Order" began to live in common and follow a more ascetical way of life. In 1447, a papal decree created the Third Order Regular of St. Francis of Penance (https://en.wikipedia .org/wiki/Franciscans).

10. DO: *trappen*. Ed. note: For the most part we will be translating *trappen* as "stages" to avoid the impression that Bavinck is describing successive steps in the spiritual life rather than different levels or orders.

11. LO: *cum grano salis*.

12. LO: *poenitentia; fides*.

13. Calvin, *Institutes*, III.vii–x.

The Anabaptists, who led the Reformation astray, had different ideas.[14] They wanted a congregation of saints, a kingdom of God (chiliasm) with strict separation of the converted and the unconverted (rebaptism). They also separated nature and grace,[15] church and state, spiritual and worldly matters (separatism). And then in the church itself they held property in common, a kind of spiritual and physical communism, and organized all this into its own kingdom,[16] establishing it with fanaticism. Thomas Müntzer, born in 1490, a mystic by nature and an admirer of Johannes Tauler,[17] introduced a community of goods in Allstedt (Germany) in 1523, and members of the community had to experience penitential anxiety and the peace of being graced.[18] In Switzerland the Anabaptist movement was led by Balthasar Hubmaier (1480–1528), Conrad Grebel (1498–1526), and Felix Manz (1498–1527). Anabaptism was Protestant monasticism;[19] it prescribed everything: clothes and their length and size, rules for eating, drinking, sleeping, resting, and rising. In this they were the precursors of the later Pietists and precisionists.[20] They used the name "Father" (after all, they were his born-again children), just as the Moravians used the name "Savior" and the rationalists the term "Heaven." Nevertheless, great emphasis was placed on cultivating, nurturing, and caring for the spiritual life.[21] Zwingli viewed the civil parish and the church parish as one. The city council, advised by the ministers, was in total control and appointed a consistory and a marriage court to maintain Christian discipline. The church, therefore, was not autonomous; the ministers, resembling prophets, only preached. However, Zwingli did try to work on the spiritual level in the church in two ways. First, through *synods*, called by the council, meeting biannually. Here the ministers, in the presence of nine council members, dealt with what was in the interest of the church and supervised each other's life and doctrine. Second, through *prophecy*, where five times a week, the Old and New Testament were explained from the original

14. Goebel, *Geschichte des christlichen Lebens*, 1:134–38; the fundamental ideas are summarized on pp. 174–95.

15. Anabaptists refused to swear oaths, participate in war, serve in the office of magistrate, or marry unbelievers.

16. By means of an inner word, visions, dreams, enthusiasm, and revelations.

17. Ed. note: Johannes Tauler (ca. 1300–1361) was a German Dominican mystic, preacher, and theologian who emphasized the soul's personal relationship with God in a Neo-Platonist manner (https://en.wikipedia.org/wiki/Johannes_Tauler).

18. Goebel, *Geschichte des christlichen Lebens*, 1:147.

19. Bullinger's judgment; see Goebel, *Geschichte des christlichen Lebens*, 1:157–59.

20. Ed. note: "Precisionist" is a translation of the Dutch *fijnen* and denotes those who were noted for their scrupulous abstention from anything that might give the appearance of sin.

21. Lutherans relied heavily on discipline that assumed the nurture of the nation to morality. See Ritschl, *Geschichte des Pietismus*, 1:71.

languages for ministers and students, and, in a subsequent hour, expounded in an edifying manner for the people.

Calvin held to four offices.[22] (1) Pastors were appointed by the other pastors, subject to the approval of the council and the congregation. These pastors met weekly (the pastoral conference) to guard each other's purity. (2) Doctors of theology (professors). (3) Presbyters/elders. Two were chosen from the Small Council, four from the Council of Sixty, and six from the Council of Two Hundred. All were confirmed by the Small Council subject to approval by the pastors. The elders, together with the pastors, formed the *consistorium*.[23] (4) Deacons. Excommunication from the congregation also involved banishment from the city.

John à Lasco,[24] born in 1499, was a church superintendent in Emden, East Frisia, and then in London from 1549 to 1553. He instituted presbyteries, church discipline, and weekly gatherings of pastors.[25] His London church order included (1) professors or prophets who conducted prophecy once a week; (2) pastors, chosen by the congregations, though the final decision was made by the consistory; (3) elders, chosen by cooptation; and (4) deacons. Stern discipline was exercised along the following steps: (a) admonition before the consistory, (b) admonition before the congregations, and (c) excommunication, subject to the approval of the entire congregation.

22. Goebel, *Geschichte des christlichen Lebens*, 1:313–19.

23. Ed. note: When Calvin returned to Geneva in 1541 from exile in Strasbourg, Genevan civic life was "controlled by a hierarchy of councils": (a) "The General Council of all citizens and bourgeois, men who were at least twenty years old and who possessed substantial property or practiced honorable professions. . . . This General Council met once a year in February, to elect the members of the other councils and a number of standing committees for the coming year." (b) The Council of Two Hundred (and the Council of Sixty) "met on special occasions to handle certain problems of general importance. . . . One of its more important functions was to consider occasional appeals for pardon, presented by people who had been convicted of crimes by the Small Council." (c) The Council of Sixty "was an older institution, and most commonly was called to consider problems in relations with other governments." (d) "At the apex of this hierarchy was the Small Council of twenty-five citizens, which met almost every day, serving as an executive committee. . . . The presiding officers of the Small Council were four men elected every year and given the title of syndics." Kingdon, *Adultery and Divorce in Calvin's Geneva*, 12–13.

24. Ed. note: John à Lasco (Jan Łaski, 1499–1560) was a Polish evangelical reformer who pastored a church in Emden, East Frisia, before going to England and becoming the superintendent of the Strangers' Church of London in 1550. Church government in theory and practice were his main contribution to the Reformed Churches. The Dutch theologian and statesman Abraham Kuyper began his scholarly career with a University of Groningen prize essay comparing the ecclesiologies of à Lasco and John Calvin. He was awarded the gold medal prize for the work on October 11, 1860. Six years later (March 1866) Kuyper published the 1,540-page *Opera* of à Lasco (https://en.wikipedia.org/wiki/Jan_%C5%81aski; de Bruijn, *Abraham Kuyper*, 29, 50).

25. LO: *coetus*.

Mysticism[26]

A person who was initiated into the mysteries (i.e., religious-political secret teachings with solemn practices) was called a "mystic."[27] Spiritual dramas received the name *misteres*, from *ministerium* (ministry), which was later confused with *mystères* (mysteries). Mysticism became the name of a specific form of religious life, especially in the Christian-ecclesiastical domain. Many now confuse mystic, mysticism, quietism, pietism, fanaticism, zealotry, etc. The rationalists rejected all this, once and for all. But since Schleiermacher there has been a turnaround in this respect.[28] Sick manifestations appear in religious life when the balance of all those relational human functions (in whose harmonious constellation[29] religion ought to provide fulfillment of life) is upset. Restricting religious life to feelings leads to mysticism; narrowing it to imagination and empiricism results in fanaticism; limiting it to speculation and reflection results in gnosticism; overemphasizing activity leads to Pharisaism or nomism;[30] limiting it to confession leads to orthodox*ism* (34). Nitzsch further distinguishes "mysticism" from "the mystical"[31] and says the following: "Generally, the error under consideration is expressed by the phrase: To run wild in gloomy feelings (or even to revel in them); in which this much at least is admitted, that the question certainly turns upon feeling, contemplation, and in general upon the mode of cognizing what intuition is, whenever the discussion turns upon the mystic, or mysticism, and upon internal experience" (34n1). Where does the notion of "the mystical" as a distinct dimension of human life come from? "The term is derived from the Greek worship, the most important part of which consisted in solemn self-communications of a Deity." In Greece "the Supreme Being had not only bestowed upon a country and a people, at once and originally, some essential constituents of

---

26. Lange, "Mystik," 152–64; Preger, "Theologie, mystische"; cf. Moll, *Johannes Brugman*, 1:37–45; Gass, *Geschichte der christlichen Ethik*, 1:415–29; Preger, *Geschichte der deutschen Mystik*; Görres, *Die christliche Mystik*; Groen van Prinsterer, *Proeve*, 33–36; Luthardt, "Das 'mystische Element'"; Fritzsche, *Über Mysticismus und Pietismus*.

27. GrO: μυστικός.

28. Cf. C. I. Nitzsch, *System of Christian Doctrine*, 33–39 (§15). Ed. note: In the next three paragraphs Bavinck summarizes or restates many of Nitzsch's points. On occasion, for the sake of clarity, we will cite directly and more extensively from Nitzsch than Bavinck originally did; page references will be provided in parentheses within the text.

29. DO: *harmonisch samenzijn*.

30. Ed. note: The English translators of Nitzsch's *System der christliche Lehre* mistakenly translated *Nomismus* as "nominalism."

31. Ed. note: This is our not entirely satisfactory attempt to capture the difference between the two Dutch terms *mysticisme* and *mystiek*; the former is the aberration of the latter, a distinct dimension of human life. "Mystical" as we are using it here ("the mystical") must be understood as a noun denoting this dimension, rather than as an adjective.

civilization, such as law and usage, agriculture and the cultivation of the vine, and the active faculties associated with these . . . but, more than this, He had also instituted permanent rules, and bequeathed them to man, from the very foundation of Theophany . . . [so that] virtuous individuals might partake in the blessing of a full consecration to a higher life" (34–35). To the degree that achieving this higher life was a human effort, these "consummations were called τέλη, τελεταί [final acts]; in so far as they were, in the highest sense, representative and executive actions, they were denominated ὄργια [works]; and finally, when they were concealed and included and demanded a denial of common experience, meditation, speech and act, they were designated μυστήρια [mysteries]." The word μύω means to close one's eyes, to wink; μυέω is to "place a person in that condition, i.e., to bring him from a state of non-sight to sight, or the reverse—to a state of secret experience." Finally, a "mystic" [μύστης], "in this point of view, is one who is experienced, one who is initiated," and "the matters, actions, and the conditions appertaining to them, were styled Mysteries" (35).

"The mystical therefore, when taken in an objective sense, is always Divinity, in the act of communicating itself to man by means of an external or internal medium; as, for instance, by a sacrament. On the other hand, in a subjective view, it is an especial experience, perception, and discovery of the same, subjected to peculiar conditions and processes." While human beings have a capacity to receive such communications, practices that are "essentially with this capacity" include "a certain self-restraint, ascetic self-denial, and self-renunciation, arising partly from sensuous, partly only from mental idiosyncrasy, in order that, while still a member of a common, earthly and temporal state, [a person] may become acquainted with, and participate in, that which is uncommon." From this it follows, according to Nitzsch, that "every religious and believing man, as such, is a Mystik; for he who has no consciousness of the Deity is unable either to discern or venerate Him; and whoever gives God merely a passing thought, unaccompanied by love and purity of heart, is incapable of livingly apprehending Him; far less is he, who desires to see Him sensibly, capable of discerning Him spiritually" (35). Nitzsch concludes that "the living energy of religion is always Mystical; and the Christian notions of illumination, of revelation, incarnation, regeneration, of the sacrament and of the resurrection, are essentially mystical elements." Mysticism then, "is a partial domination and degenerated form of the Mystical tendency" (35–36).

Mysticism arises when "internal perception may already be defective, by renouncing the historical and ecclesiastical element of true religion; as for example, whenever Christians seek after and pretend to an internal light independent of God's word; or when they reject and contemn the sacrament, in order to indulge a preference for prayer" (36). Inwardness becomes "still farther defective, when, in the form of exclusive sensitiveness, it opposes the claims of thought, divests itself of action, and prematurely desires a violent gratification, partly of intuitive love, and partly of Divine rest." The result is that "instead of intellectual contemplations, there arise empirical fantasies; instead of rest in God, indolence and *quietism*; and what is worse than all, instead of love for God, there is evinced a wanton and impure coquetry with natural beauty, and yet, notwithstanding this, there exists a pietistic and ascetic sternness toward the purely human and rational" (36). This is essentially Sack's position.[32] According to Hase, "the common, characteristic shortcoming of mysticism is the exclusion of knowledge and the generally human as legitimate in religious life." The religious life is then "more or less abandoned to zealotry; surrendered to fantasy and enthusiasm, and flung by the will into fanaticism, to a knowledge of the spiritual realm apart from the mediation of human reasoning—theosophy."[33] For Lange, "the mystical is always the inner life of religion, but mysticism is a one-sided domination and degeneration of the mystical."[34]

Religion is a healthy interaction between objective God-consciousness and subjective self-consciousness. Mysticism then is the relationship of the subjective life to the God who reveals himself. Mystics want to submerge themselves in God, sacrifice themselves, their *I*, to contemplation of God, and lose their own self-consciousness. Soon they lose the idea of a personal God and become pantheistic; they become quietistic and want peace and silence. The Christian lives in fellowship with Christ, but this fellowship here is always a matter of faith, resting on the word.[35] Contemplation[36] will be enjoyed only in the hereafter, and then this fellowship will depend no longer on the word but on itself. But some do not honor this ordinance of God and seek already now to have immediate fellowship with God so that they may taste, experience,

---

32. Sack, *Christliche Polemik*, 283–303 ("Vom Mystizismus"). Ed. note: Bavinck likely took over this reference to Sack directly from C. I. Nitzsch, *System of Christian Doctrine*, 36.

33. GO: *Überglauben*; Lange, "Mystik," 152.

34. Lange, "Mystik," 153. Ed. note: This translation attempts to capture the fine distinction and play on words here between the German *Mystik* (translated as "the mystical"; i.e., a dimension of human religious experience) and *Mystizismus* ("mysticism"), which is its aberration. The original reads: "Die innerliche Lebendigkeit der Religion is allezeit Mystik—Mystizismus ist eine einseitige Herrschaft und Ausartung der Mystik."

35. Heppe, *Geschichte des Pietismus und der Mystik*, 1.

36. Ed. note: Bavinck is speaking of what is historically known as the "vision of God" (*aanschouwen*), a level of full fellowship with God that is an eschatological promise (1 John 3:2) yet to be realized.

and contemplate him. Subsequently things happen to the soul that rest not upon the word but on human nature and willing. Faith is replaced by love, through which one seeks unity with God, even a merging with or sinking into the depths of the Deity. This is mysticism, which has a practical and a speculative side. Contemplation in love unites one with God and makes God knowable. The inner word is thus the fountain of knowledge. This love also purifies the heart, teaches it to slay selfishness and to follow Christ in all of life. Enlightenment follows purification, and eventually losing oneself in God. Contemplative mysticism is expressed in "mental prayer," in distinction from audible prayer.[37] Mysticism regards Christ merely as an example; sanctification is actually, first of all, a matter of reconciliation.[38] In other words, the line is blurred between the objective justification obtained by Christ's death, on the one hand, and the subjective application or appropriation of that work to the believer, on the other. The death of Christ and the work of the Holy Spirit are regarded as two separate aspects of justification.[39] From this we see that mysticism is really at home within Roman Catholicism, among other reasons, because Catholicism does not provide the Christian with a personal living communion with Christ.[40] This creates a true longing for such a relationship, and people try to obtain it through asceticism, contemplation, meditation, and prayer. Protestantism satisfies this longing completely because it teaches such a personal relationship.[41]

37. LO: *oratio mentalis*; *oratio vocalis*.

38. DO: *heiligmaking*; *verzoening*. Ed. note: The Dutch word *verzoening* is used to translate "atonement" as well as "reconciliation." The sentence that immediately follows has been inserted by the editor for better understanding of Bavinck's point. Whether to tie the life of holiness and sanctification to justification was the great issue between John Calvin and Roman Catholic cardinal Jacopo Sadoleto. Sadoleto wrote a letter to the people of Geneva in which he argued against the Reformation slogans of *sola gratia* and *sola fide* on the basis of the principle that "faith without works is dead" (James 2:17). In response, Calvin insisted that "works" must be severed from justification lest the gospel truth that we are saved not by works but by grace be lost. See Calvin and Sadoleto, *Reformation Debate*.

39. Ed. note: Bavinck here states the position defended by Cardinal Sadoleto and made binding dogma by the Roman Catholic Council of Trent (1545–63); two anathemas in the *Decree on Justification* of the sixth session of the council (January 1547) state this explicitly: "If any one shall say that by faith alone the sinner is justified, so as to understand that nothing else is required to cooperate in the attainment of the grace of justification, and that it is in no way necessary, that he be prepared and disposed by the action of his own will; let him be anathema" (canon 9; Denzinger, no. 819). "If any one shall say that men are justified either by the sole imputation of the justice of Christ, or by the sole remission of sins, to the exclusion of the grace and the charity which is poured forth in their hearts by the Holy Spirit and remains in them, even that the grace by which we are justified, is only the favor of God; let him be anathema" (canon 11; Denzinger, no. 821).

40. DO: *persoonlijke levensgemeenschap*.

41. Erbkam, *Geschichte der protestantischen Sekten*, 14–98.

Mysticism rests upon a legitimate basic religious desire that actually has always been present in the Christian religion and that pervades the church. It must therefore arise from the very core of the human spirit. Philosophy tried it first when in mysticism it detected vestiges of its own speculation. Mysticism was veiled philosophy and was judged accordingly, for example, by Hegel. But this was not possible; the mystical was explored and came to be just what it did not want to be: conceptual thought. Others conceived of mysticism as exclusively practical, as a piety of the heart, and as such a part of every Christian, as it should be. This was the view of Gottfried Arnold.[42] Mysticism, then, is not in the first place understanding, knowledge, theory, or speculation but praxis, experience, and immediate self-perceived life.[43]

However, it is then praxis of a special kind which, although resting on a basic general religious desire, is not available to all people. The basic character of mysticism is immediacy of fellowship with God, not so much in thought (which is always mediated) but in the *personal* spiritual life, as a person communicating with a person (through ears, eyes, body, etc.; which is not direct like instant self-consciousness). Mysticism thus proceeds from the premise that in religion it is possible for the personal God and human beings as persons to have an actual relationship of mutual giving and receiving. In addition, mysticism moves in the area of inner, real experience. It always describes the personally experienced religious conditions of the soul; otherwise it becomes brooding and self-deception. Therefore, it cannot be simulated theoretically.[44] Erbkam says that there is an actual difference between true mystical conditions and those in which mysticism is merely an exchanging of God and the proper self; the former are *religious* conditions, and the latter are not, because they are pantheistic.[45] The mystical process is then as follows: the "ego" (*I myself*) enters into fellowship with God, but here the *I* is passive and God active; the soul surrenders to God; the *I* yields and retreats from its central position in the organism. And God assumes his place and sees, hears, and wills through our organs; the soul has become an *affect* of God.[46] This condition may be compared best to clairvoyance, dreaming, in which our *I* rests, but not our organs, which then are servants of the soul's embodied nature. In mysticism, the soul has become the organ of God and creates religious conditions.[47]

---

42. Arnold, *Historie und Beschreibung der mystischen Theologie*, cited by Erbkam, *Geschichte der protestantischen Sekten*, 17n.

43. GO: *unmittelbares selbstempfundenes Leben*.

44. Ed. note: Bavinck uses the verb *nabootsen* ("to copy"), in clear distinction from *navolging* ("to follow, imitate").

45. Erbkam, *Geschichte der protestantischen Sekten*, 24, 26.

46. Erbkam, *Geschichte der protestantischen Sekten*, 28.

47. Erbkam, *Geschichte der protestantischen Sekten*, 39–45.

Now there are two dimensions to personality: self-consciousness and self-determination.[48] Therefore, there are also two forms of mysticism. One is predominantly *enlightenment*, the other *awakening*; the former strengthens the self-consciousness, the latter the conscience; the former is communication of God's love, the latter of God's majesty.[49] The former is active in images, uses visions, is an inner seeing, contemplation; God is presented here especially as Light; his influence is called inner radiance.[50] This is an internal hearing and obeying; God works here especially by way of divine inner speech, and the content of this mysticism is the internal word; God speaks: the soul responds. The former opens the internal eye and shows heavenly visions; the latter opens the internal ear and makes the person hear divine voices. The former is properly called "mysticism," the latter "enthusiasm."[51] There is reciprocity between both of these forms, which, in turn, creates prophecy and ecstasy.

In mysticism, there is a process, there are various steps.[52] But there is no agreement on the number of steps, and there is no uniform terminology. Basically, there are these three stages:[53]

1. *Purgative/purification*: Contemplation (in the first main form of mysticism) or asceticism (the second main form of asceticism) prepares a person for the union of their soul with God. In contemplation, people wrench themselves away from the outside world, lose themselves consciously in their selves; in asceticism they loosen their wills from all external stimuli.

2. *Illuminative*: In the second stage,[54] the divine influence begins as radiation of the divine light or inspiration of the divine Spirit; thereby the personality,

---

48. DO: *zelfbewustzijn; zelfbepaling* = GO: *Selbstthätigkeit*.

49. GO: *Erleuchtung; Erweckung*; Erbkam, *Geschichte der protestantischen Sekten*, 46.

50. DO: *instraling*; Erbkam, *Geschichte der protestantischen Sekten*, 47.

51. Erbkam, *Geschichte der protestantischen Sekten*, 49.

52. GO: *Stufen*. Ed. note: Here we are translating *Stufen* and the Dutch *trappen* as "steps" because Bavinck is describing a *process* with successive steps.

53. Ed. note: In order to link Bavinck's descriptions with the broader literature on mysticism, we are inserting here the classic terms for the "threefold path," which dates back to the Christian monk and ascetic Evagrius Ponticus (AD 345–99): "purgative," "illuminative," and "unitive." The descriptions that follow these terms, however, are Bavinck's alone. His terminology and description of the threefold path are slightly different from the traditional understanding based on the anthropological division of body, soul, and spirit (Devine, "State or Way"). At this point Bavinck added in a marginal note a reference to W. à Brakel, *Christian's Reasonable Service*, 2:640–42, "A Warning against Pietists, Quietists, [and others]." Here is how à Brakel describes the difference between truly godly people and "mystics": it is as "the difference between imagination and truth; between worldly and heavenly; between seeking an unknown God and serving the true God; and between being engaged without, and contrary to, the Holy Scriptures (dabbling with invisible things), and living according to the written Word of God" (2:642).

54. LO: *stadium*.

the individual *I*, is suppressed; God is at work; the only thing that remains is a general sense of being alive.

3. *Unitive:* Then comes the "inward perception,"[55] when one completely and only feels; the union of the soul with God is felt and experienced. This is often called a "becoming like God," a transformation of the soul; then one is alone with God, and God with us; one revels in a fellowship of love; God is the bridegroom, the soul is the bride. God is the fire that consumes and warms the soul. One swims in an ocean of blessedness. It is especially here that self-deception often occurs; what actually happens is that God becomes a passive bride, while the soul becomes an active bridegroom (this has come to fruition in the devotion of Mary).[56] The mystic enjoys spiritual inebriation expressed in different ways: tears, laughter, jubilation, shouting, silence, and the like. On this level mysticism is then described as a "savory knowledge of God, a most savory contemplation of God, experiential wisdom."[57] The danger of this stage exists especially in wanting to perpetuate this blessed condition artificially. This results in a mysticism that lacks all clarity or (with the second main form) a quietism that lacks purity and often becomes sensual.[58] Mysticism then attaches itself to the person of Jesus Christ, whose continuous life in fellowship with God it seeks to imitate. Intellectual mysticism uses as an example especially the transfiguration on Mount Tabor; ethical mysticism uses as its example especially the death by crucifixion on Calvary. However, in mysticism, Christ often becomes nothing more than a reflex of a person's own subjective consciousness and loses objective significance; for the mystic, the entire objective world becomes a reflex of the internal.

There was mysticism in the Brahmanism of India; it became a world religion in Buddhism. Egyptian priests were aware of it, and it was present in the Greek mystery religions and later in Neo-Platonism. With the Jews, it was present among the Essenes, in Kabbalism,[59] and in the teachings of Spinoza. In Islam, it is found in Sufism.[60] Mysticism, especially in its ethical

---

55. LO: *sensio.* Ed. note: This may have been intended as *sentio* ("to perceive, sense, discern, feel").

56. Erbkam, *Geschichte der protestantischen Sekten,* 57.

57. LO: *sapida Deo notitia, contemplatio, sapientia experimentalis;* Erbkam, *Geschichte der protestantischen Sekten,* 59.

58. Erbkam, *Geschichte der protestantischen Sekten,* 87.

59. Ed. note: Kabbalism arose within the mystical tradition of Judaism during the twelfth and thirteenth centuries AD in southern France and Spain. It "is a set of esoteric teachings meant to explain the relationship between an unchanging, eternal, and mysterious 'אֵין סוֹף' (Ein Sof = Infinity) and the mortal and finite universe (God's creation)" (https://en.wikipedia.org/wiki/Kabbalah).

60. Lange, "Mystik," 155–57.

form, appears in Christianity first in heretical Montanism;[61] asceticism is
the starting point of this mysticism, and ecstasy its content. Montanism
attached itself to Manichaeism, which has accompanied and troubled the
church in East and West in various sects and under various names. Finally,
it is found in gnosticism, which derives its material and images from mysticism, and in philosophy, which takes its systematic form of speculation
from it. Real mysticism thus originated in monasticism, and Egypt is the
birthplace of monasticism; mysticism was born there in the monasteries.
Its first representative is Macarius (ca. 300–391), whose mysticism remains
hidden in the swaddling clothes of asceticism without having a specific main
form as yet. Then follows Pseudo-Dionysius the Areopagite (late fifth–sixth
century), who is the first methodical teacher of mysticism and gave it its
language and its manual.[62] He sees Christianity as a Platonic mysteriosophy.
The highest aim of Christianity is *divinization* and *union*. This is reached
through three steps: *purification*, *illumination*, and *contemplation*.[63] Pseudo-
Dionysius already uses the term "mystic"[64] and borrows many words from
the Greek mysteries. In the West, John Scotus Eriugena (ca. 815–ca. 877) is
the first to translate and comment on the works of Pseudo-Dionysius, but
he is more of a philosopher than a mystic. The blossoming period of mysticism begins in the twelfth century with Bernard of Clairvaux (1090–1153),
who was led to it by the dryness of Scholasticism, by the drive for cultural
advance that was present at the time in all spheres of life.[65] At the same time
(under the influence of Pseudo-Dionysius), a mystical school developed in
the Abbey of St. Victor in Paris. William of Champeaux (ca. 1070–1121)
founded a school there in 1108–9, and the most important representatives of
this school were Hugo (ca. 1096–1141), Richard (d. 1173), Walther (d. 1180),
Bonaventure (1221–74), and Jean Gerson (1363–1429). These represent the
Franco-Gallic mysticism of the twelfth through fourteenth centuries. Mysticism was essentially a reaction against Scholasticism; its slogan was "God
is known to the extent that he is loved."[66] Seven steps are usually assumed
in the mystical path; the sixth is contemplation, and in the seventh one
becomes a child of God, experiences ecstasy of the spirit.[67] The journey

61. Erbkam, *Geschichte der protestantischen Sekten*, 110.
62. Ed. note: Pseudo-Dionysius's two major works are the *Celestial Hierarchies* and the
Ecclesiastical Hierarchies.
63. GrO: θέωσις; ἕνωσις; κάθαρσις; φωτισμός /μύησις; ἐποπτεία. Ed. note: In the margin
Bavinck wrote, "ἐποπτεύω: a seeing becoming, the highest good in the Elysian Mysteries."
64. GrO: μυστικός.
65. GO: *Bildungstrieb*. Neander, *Vorlesungen*, 274–89.
66. LO: *tantum deus cognosticur quantum diligitur.*
67. Lange, "Mystik," 159.

is conditioned by seven virtues resting on seven affections and opposing seven sins.

Mysticism found its true home and highest blossoming in Germany in the fourteenth and fifteenth centuries. It had its beginning already in the twelfth century with Abbess Elisabeth of Schönau (ca. 1129–64) and Hildegard of Bingen (ca. 1098–1179), abbess of the monasteries of Rupertsberg and El-bingen. Mysticism was also manifested in the numerous sects of the time: in the Waldensians, who began in the twelfth century, in the pantheistic Breth-ren of the Free Spirit, founded by Amalric of Bena (Amaury de Bène; d. ca. 1204–7) in the thirteenth and fourteenth centuries, in the Friends of God in the fourteenth century, and in the Brethren of the Common Life, founded by Gerard Groote (1340–84).[68] In the fourteenth century this mysticism was advanced by the poor conditions in the church and also by the Black Death.[69] The main representatives are Meister Eckhart (ca. 1250–ca. 1328), who was associated with the Brethren of the Free Spirit and was pantheistic; Henry Suso (ca. 1295–1366), who was connected to the Friends of God; Johannes Tauler (ca. 1300–1361), associated with the Friends of God and the Waldensians; Jan van Ruysbroeck (ca. 1293–1361); Denis the Carthusian (Dr. Ecstaticus, 1402–71); and the *Theologia Germanica*, most likely from the second half of the fourteenth century. A mystical current also ran through John Wycliffe (ca. 1320–84), Jan Hus (ca. 1372–1415), Savonarola (1452–98), and Wessel van Gansfort (1419–89), as well as through the Reformers. But the real mysti-cism continued after the Reformation in Andreas Carlstadt (ca. 1480–1541), Sebastian Franck (ca. 1499–ca. 1542), Caspar Schwenkfeldt (1490–1561), Valentin Weigel (1533–88), and among the Anabaptists Thomas Müntzer (1489–1525), Nicolaus Storch (d. ca. 1536); Conrad Grebel (1498–1526), Felix Manz (ca. 1498–1527), George Blaurock (ca. 1491–1529), Balthasar Hubmaier (ca. 1480–1528), and Melchior Hofmann (ca. 1495–ca. 1543). Mysticism is especially prominent in Jakob Böhme (1575–1624).

68. GO: *Gottesfreunde*; LO: *Devotio Moderna*. Ed. note: Bavinck also cites David Dinant (ca. 1160–ca. 1217) as a cofounder of the Brethren of the Free Spirit. This is unlikely; although Dinant was a pantheist, like Amalric of Bena, founder of the Amalricians, "the details of his system and the sources of his pantheistic teaching can not be ascertained with certainty. At all events, he is not dependent on Amalric of Bena, but was rather influenced by Aristotelian writings and Jewish and Moorish comment on them" (Haupt, "David of Dinant"). The Friends of God "was a medieval lay mystical group with the Catholic Church and a center of German mysticism. It was founded between 1339 and 1342 in Basel, Switzerland. It grew out of the preaching and teaching of Meister Eckhart, and especially his Dominican spiritual heirs the preacher John Tauler and the writer Henry Suso" (https://en.wikipedia.org/wiki/Friends_of_God).

69. Ed. note: The Black Death (bubonic plague), which peaked in Europe in the years 1346–53, killed an estimated 75 to 200 million people, 30 to 60 percent of Europe's population (https://en.wikipedia.org/wiki/Black_Death).

In the seventeenth century this mysticism lost its influence and degenerated into all sorts of sectarian excesses such as chiliasm, theosophy, fanaticism, and spiritualism.[70] In the Protestant church a reaction arose around 1650 against orthodoxy. In the Lutheran Church this included Arndt, Andreae, Muller, and Christian Scriver; in the Reformed Church it came to expression in Jean de Labadie. All of these can be connected to Jansenism and the later Pietism.

Mystical sects also existed in the Reformed churches: Collegiants, Levellers, the Hebrewers and Verschoorists, etc.[71] All churches—the Roman Catholic Church, the Greek Orthodox Church, the Lutheran and Reformed churches—have their peculiar forms of mysticism with respect to the externalization of the church.

Pietism[72]

The term "pietist" is used in a variety of ways. Sometimes it is restricted to the movement initiated by Philipp Jakob Spener (1635–1705) and August Hermann Francke (1663–1727) for renewal in the Lutheran churches of Germany during the period roughly from 1677 to 1747.[73] This is too narrow; the Württemberg Pietism also belongs to it.[74] On the other side the name

---

70. Ed. note: Bavinck associates the four named errors with, respectively, Johann Wilhelm Petersen (1649–1727), Johann Georg Gichtel (1638–1710), Quirinius Kuhlmann (1651–1720), and Johann Conrad Dippel (1673–1734).

71. Ed. note: The Collegiants "were an eclectic religious sect, formed in 1619 [after the Synod of Dort] among the Arminians and Anabaptists in Holland. They were so called because of their meetings (colleges) held the first Sunday of each month, at which everyone had the same liberty of expounding the scripture, praying, etc." (https://en.wikipedia.org /wiki/Collegiants). The Levellers "were a political movement during the English Civil War that emphasised popular sovereignty, extended suffrage, equality before the law, and religious tolerance" (https://en.wikipedia.org/wiki/Levellers). Bavinck mentions the "Hebreeërs and the Verschoor isten" separately, but they are different names for the same phenomenon. A certain Jacobus Verschoor (1648–1700), having been refused candidacy for ministry in the Dutch Reformed Church after several attempts in different jurisdictions, began his own conventical meetings outside the structure of the organized churches. Set in a climate of severe criticism of the clergy in the Dutch Reformed Church and promoting law preaching, including women, the sect derived its name "Hebrewers" from its criticism of the "official" Dutch *Statenvertaling* Bible and read the original Hebrew and Greek in its worship services (*Christ. Encycl.*[1] 2:490–91, s.v. "Hebreën [Secte der]").

72. Tholuck, "Pietismus"; Riggenbach, "Pietismus"; van Andel, "Piëtisme"; Pierson, *Eene levensbeschouwing*, 9–31.

73. Ed. note: Spener's influential work of devotion and call for church reform, *Pia Desideria* ("Pious Desires" or "Heartfelt Desire for God-Pleasing Reform"), was first published in 1675 and is generally credited with launching Lutheran Pietism.

74. Ed. note: Spener and Francke are associated with the cities of Frankfurt and Halle, especially with the founding of the University of Halle in 1604; Ritschl, however, also mentions

is used very broadly and comprises mysticism, separatism, etc. Ritschl also speaks of Pietism in the Reformed Church, and also derives the Secession[75] from it. Furthermore, he himself deduces Pietism from Anabaptism and from the mystical sects of the Middle Ages. Pietism is a peculiar phenomenon in the Lutheran Church and not in the Roman Catholic Church. Nonetheless, contrary to Tholuck and Riggenbach, the same phenomenon, with slight modification, is also found beyond the Lutheran churches, in the Reformed churches.[76] Pietism strives for perfection, seeks to complete the unfinished Reformation of the sixteenth century (which was limited only to doctrine) and bring renewal to everyday practical affairs through revival and cultivation of piety. Pietism, therefore, assumes a dead orthodoxy, doctrine without life. It thus addresses the remnants of Catholicism that remain in Protestant churches, particularly the significant moral shortcomings of Protestants. This reformation tries to reach piety through the practice of godliness.[77] It did not encroach upon church doctrine, but doctrine had to be experienced. Piety is not the same as orthodoxy; religion is a matter of the heart and does not require church approval; it simply has to be lived in fellowship with Christ. Only the person who is born again knows God and understands his Word, while an unregenerated person is only a slave to its letter. The born-again person then needs to grow spiritually, take Christ as example, and consider suffering and cross-bearing as training toward godliness.

Ascetic practices (fasting, prayer, meditation, reading of Holy Scripture) and religious meetings/conventicles are the means to cultivate the godly life. According to Lange, pietism emphasizes the subjective life in the same way that the mystic accentuates the divine life in us.[78] Pietists want to express the divine in their lives always and everywhere; pietism sinks away into the self[79] and does not rest in God, but pays attention to the subject, who has to appropriate the divine and has to display this in his daily walk. It often tries, therefore, to obtain and retain the divine by way of homemade, subjective

---

Michael Müller (d. 1702), Johan Wolfgang Jäger (1647–1720), Christoph Reuchlin (d. 1704), and Andreas Adam Hochstetter (d. 1717) as members of a "group with pietistic inclinations" and associates them with the city of Württemburg ("*diese Gruppe des kirchlich gesinnten Pietismus in Württemburg*"). Ritschl, *Geschichte des Pietismus*, 3:6.

75. Ed. note: Bavinck is referring to the *Afscheiding* (Secession) of 1834 from the National Dutch Reformed Church (the Nederlandse Hervormde Kerk) and the formation of the Christian Reformed Church (Christelijke Gereformeerde Kerken), of which he was a member and professor at its theological school in Kampen.

76. See Tholuck, "Pietismus"; Riggenbach, "Pietismus."

77. LO: *praxis pietatis*.

78. Lange, "Mystik," 159.

79. DO: *verzinkt*.

self-torment. Mystics lose themselves in God and become quietists; pietists lose God in themselves, always consider themselves, but are also active, engage in mission work, in teaching, in education of the people, etc.; in one word: philanthropy.

Spener and Francke brought Pietism into the Lutheran Church, but there were pietists before Pietism: Arndt, Weigel, Böhme, Müller, Scriver, Gerhard, Andreae, Calixtus. There were even publications with the title *Pia Desideria* ("Pious Desires") before Spener published his famous tract in 1675.[80] Spener, born in 1635, read works in practical theology from English writers and Arndt's *True Christianity*, published between1605 and 1610. He was influenced by Jean de Labadie in Geneva and founded "Schools of Piety" in 1670.[81] Valentine Ernst Löscher rebuked Spener for making intellect dependent on the will and orthodoxy on the pious life.[82] Pietism was a movement within the church and, at the same time, against the church. Pietists said that being orthodox was not sufficient; something else has to happen. In this way, they created a dividing line *within* the church between the converted and the unconverted. The covenant idea was not decisive; people had to have had certain experiences. What kind of experiences? "Inward penitential struggle," followed by a "breakthrough" and "sealing."[83]

Years later, in the 1730s, Prussian monarch Frederick William I "not only protected the pietist movement but positively promoted it. Francke's students [at Halle] were given special preference in appointments to the ministry, and, after 1536, all candidates for the clergy were required to study for at least two years at the University of Halle."[84] That is when this edification exercise became a method, a requirement; the ascetic practices, the entire care of the soul, acquired a systematic-statutory character. Pietism thus encouraged indifference with respect to doctrine and subjectivism with respect to the church. Ironically, this is the exact same judgment arrived at by the Enlightenment. Pietism reacts against scholastic technical terminology, limits itself to fundamental truths, and challenges superstitious adulation of the confessions. It also despises church doctrine, emphasizes the subject and a subjective relationship

80. Ed. note: Bavinck's manuscript reads, "Before them [Spener and Francke] there were others who discredited scholastic theology, who desired tolerance (Calixtus), who published *pia desideria* (pious desires)." Bavinck cites as his source Tholuck, "Pietismus," 646–47, and then lists the following as "pietists before Pietism": George Calixtus (1586–1656), Johann Arndt (1555–1621), Valentine Weigel (1555–1621), Jakob Böhme, Christian Scriver (1629–93), Georg Müller (1603–84), and Johann Gerhard (1582–1637).
81. LO: *collegia pietatis*.
82. Riggenbach, "Pietismus," 682.
83. GO: *Busskampf; Durchbreukung; Versiegelung*.
84. Gorski, *Disciplinary Revolution*, 111.

to God, thereby forming a "church within the church" and separatism. Pietism produces many conversion stories (virtually unknown in previous times),[85] leaves the church to its own devices, but stresses revival, confirmation, and so forth of the individual soul. Two hundred and sixty heresies were attributed to Spener, and his influence spread to Württemberg and to Tübingen, where "schools of piety" were introduced in 1705. Johann Albrecht Bengel (1687–1752) and Friedrich Christoph Oetinger (1702–82) emerged from this and introduced a theosophical-intellectual element.[86]

We will now consider the Reformed churches.[87] In England a double reformation took place, one from above that was hierarchical (Henry VIII, Elizabeth I, et al.) and one from below (Knox) that was presbyterian and Calvinistic.[88] Proponents of the latter, called Puritans since 1564, lived especially in London and Cambridge, where Thomas Cartwright (1535–1603) became Lady Margaret's Professor of Divinity in 1569. Persecution of the Puritans began already in 1571; they had seceded, assembled together, appointed presbyteries, and established "prophesyings" where Scripture was explained with practical applications and matters of conscience and so forth were discussed.[89] The "Brownists" or "Independents," named after Robert Browne, who founded a congregation in Middelburg in the Netherlands in 1581 and returned to England in 1589, were a distinct branch of Puritans.[90] When the Brownists were persecuted, they fled to the Netherlands. Among their number were Francis Johnson, Henry Ainsworth (1569–1622), and John Robinson (d. 1625). The origin of Pietism within the Reformed Church is to be found among this group.[91] Prime movers are William Whitaker (1547–95), professor in Cambridge, and William Perkins (1558–1602), also professor in Cambridge. Perkins conceived of theology as the science of living blessedly forever, thus entirely practical. He wrote about matters of conscience, about spiritual abandonment, about the origin and development of the spiritual

85. Tholuck, "Pietismus," 655.

86. Ed. note: A recent study of Bengel and Oetinger (who was drawn into Swedenborgianism) sees them as precursors of German Idealism: Heinze, *Bengel und Oetinger*.

87. See Heppe, *Geschichte des Pietismus und der Mystik*; W. à Brakel, *Christian's Reasonable Service*, 2:640–42; Beard, *Reformation of the Sixteenth Century*, 300–336.

88. Ed. note: Bavinck wrote in the margin, "became refugees during the time of Mary (1553–58), fled to Zurich, Basel, Geneva, and Frankfurt, among other places."

89. Weingarten, *Die Revolutionskirchen Englands*, 18. Presbyteries were appointed in protest against remnants of Roman Catholicism in the Anglican Church (vestments, bishops, absolution, etc.).

90. Weingarten, *Die Revolutionskirchen Englands*, 2.

91. Ed. note: Bavinck wrote in the margin, "England does not produce many works of dogmatics; there is, however, study of the church fathers and the text of the New Testament" (Beard, *Reformation*, 330).

life—ordering it in accord with the example of Christ—about struggles of the flesh and spirit, about living well and dying well, about determining if one is converted, and so forth. His books were translated into German, French, Dutch, and Spanish. Perkins was particularly influential in England and had many followers in the Anglican Church and among the Puritans, such as Paul Baynes (d. 1614), John Smith (d. 1616), Thomas Brightman (1557–1607), Francis Rous (1579–1659), Edward Leigh (d. 1671), and Richard Sibbes (1571–1635), lector in Cambridge, prolific writer of practical theology. Lewis Bayly (d. 1632) wrote *The Practice of Piety* (fifty-first edition in 1751), which was also translated into Dutch and German.

There is a long list of Perkins's contemporaries:[92] George Downame (ca. 1563–1634); Daniel Dyke (d. 1614); Jeremias Dyke (d. 1620), also in the Netherlands; Nicholas Byfield (1579–1622); Thomas Hooker, born in 1586, who had to flee to the Netherlands and eventually went to America, where he became a minister in Hartford (d. 1647); Joseph Hall, born in 1574, member of the Synod of Dort, bishop of Norwich (d. 1656); Thomas Taylor (1576–1632); John Ball (1585–1640); Anthony Burgess (d. 1664); Jeremiah Burroughs (ca. 1600–1646); Richard Capel (1586–1656); John Preston (1587–1628); Arthur Hildersham (1563–1631); William Gouge (1575–1653); Thomas Gouge (1605–81); Samuel Ward (1577–1640); Joseph Symonds (d. 1614); Henry Scudder (ca. 1585–1652); Thomas Watson (1620–86), rector of the church in Walbrooke, later minister at Crosby Hall; Stephen Charnock (1628–80); Thomas Adams (1583–1652); John Howe (1630–1705); William Bradshaw (1571–1618); Richard Greenham (ca. 1542–94); Philip Nye (1595–1672); William Guthrie (1620–65), who wrote a book on assurance, *The Christian's Great Interest*; Thomas Goodwin, born in 1600, eventually converted, became minister at Cambridge, went to the Netherlands in 1639, returned to Oxford in 1649 (d. 1679); John Owen, born in 1616, greatly respected, preached for the House of Commons on the day of Charles I's beheading, friend of Cromwell (d. 1683)—he was the great dissenter, produced eighty pieces of writing, and was esteemed by all parties including those of the high church; Richard Baxter,[93] born in 1615, vicar at Kiddermister, died in 1691, a man of peace, who openly condemned Cromwell's deed,[94] tried to reconcile episcopalians and presbyterians, wrote *The Saints' Everlasting Rest* and *Call to the Unconverted*, among some 180 books; John Bunyan, born in 1628, became a Baptist in 1653, started to preach in

92. Ed. note: The lists of names in this and subsequent paragraphs follows Bavinck's order. For a helpful brief introduction to most of these figures, see Beeke and Pederson, *Meet the Puritans*.
93. Weingarten, *Die Revolutionskirchen Englands*, 162–63.
94. Ed. note: Bavinck speaks simply of "*Cromwells daad*" without specification; undoubtedly he has in mind Cromwell's leadership of the revolt against and regicide of Charles I.

1655, imprisoned in Bedford from 1660 to 1672 (d. 1688); Christopher Love, born in 1611, councilor, minister, accused before Parliament in 1651 of high treason for trying to mobilize troops against the present government, having proclaimed Charles Stuart (eldest son of Charles I) king, having supported the Scots against Cromwell, and having carried on written negotiations from March 1650 to June 1651 with Charles II (Stuart) and the Scots and was beheaded on August 23, 1651, on the same day that Charles II entered Worcester at the head of the Scots.[95]

And there are many more such writers: Richard Alleine (1611–81); Joseph Alleine (1634–68); William Whately (1583–1639); Samuel Rutherford (1600–1661), nobleman by birth, minister in Anwoth, Scotland, preached against popular sins, was brought to trial because of his treatise *Apologetical Exercises on Behalf of Divine Grace, against James Arminius and His Followers, and the Jesuits* (1636)[96] and because he refused to acknowledge the court of bishops as a court of Christ; he was imprisoned in 1636, released in 1638, and became professor of divinity at St. Andrews (declining an appointment to Utrecht); accused of high treason in 1661 but could not appear for trial because of illness and died;[97] Richard Rogers (1551–1618); Timothy Rogers (1658–1728);[98] and George Hopkins (1620–66). Richard Baxter mentions these in his *Body of Practical Divinity.*[99] The Puritans (who were the majority) experienced a very vibrant spiritual life in the period from roughly 1600 to 1660.

The teaching of these writers about the practice of godliness can briefly be summarized as follows:[100]

- They are and remain entirely Reformed in their understanding of doctrine; they teach all the characteristic Reformed doctrines—predestination, election, human inability, etc.—without deviation.
- But this truth has to be lived; truth must become praxis, and godliness must be practiced and demonstrated in everyday life.

95. Neal, *History of the Puritans*, 2:122–25. Ed. note: Charles II was defeated by Oliver Cromwell at the Battle of Worcester on September 3, 1651, and fled into European exile until the restoration of the monarchy in 1660.

96. *Exercitationes Apologeticae Pro Divina Gratia . . . Adversus Jacobum Arminium ejusque asseclas, & Jesuitas . . .* (Amsterdam, 1636).

97. Neal, *History of the Puritans*, 3:89–91. See also Crookshank, *History of the State and Sufferings of the Church of Scotland*, 1:139–40.

98. Ed. note: We have substituted John Rogers's son Timothy here for his father, "a nonconformist minister in the Diocese of Durham" (Beeke and Pederson, *Meet the Puritans*, 509), because of difficulty in obtaining biographical information about the father.

99. Baxter, *Christian Directory.*

100. Heppe, *Geschichte des Pietismus und der Mystik*, 52–73.

- The point of departure is the proposition that every person is either in the natural state or in the state of grace; there is no state in between. Everyone therefore must know the state they are in and the time they transitioned from the one into the next.
- For that reason, great emphasis is placed on self-examination.
- Proper self-examination requires distinguishing marks. These then are counted and developed, by the dozen, and include spiritual poverty, sadness, love of God's Word, love of people, love of righteousness, a longing to die, and more.[101]

To prevent people from considering themselves converted too soon and being lost because of such rash self-deception, it is especially pointed out how far it is possible for a reprobate to go and what one may experience without having obtained this special grace; that is, natural man is portrayed at his very best. Yet, on the other hand, it is also pointed out how small a beginning of grace may be present in the soul (so that troubled souls will not leave feeling defeated and without comfort). In other words, Christians are also portrayed at their worst and shown how far they can possibly stray. To be born again, to be converted, is a miracle to which we can contribute no more than Adam could in being created or a child in being born. This spiritual life, the life of faith, is in essence a life in fellowship with God, with Christ. Its essence is mystical union.[102] This is described very realistically, particularly through the imagery of bridegroom and bride (the soul), and furnished with ideas from the Song of Solomon[103] such as the eating and drinking of Christ and so forth.[104] This is the mystical dimension of Reformed theology that occasionally is pulled in the direction of mysticism and expressed all too realistically.

However, it is not enough that this life exists; it also has to grow and mature.[105] To this end, under the category of ascetic theology or "ascetics,"[106] various

101. Heppe, *Geschichte des Pietismus und der Mystik*, 58.
102. LO: *unio mystica*.
103. Heppe, *Geschichte des Pietismus und der Mystik*, 68.
104. Heppe, *Geschichte des Pietismus und der Mystik*, 61.
105. Therefore, there are stages in the spiritual life: longing, accepting, sealing, etc. (Heppe, *Geschichte des Pietismus und der Mystik*, 57–58).
106. LO: *asketica*. Ed. note: The term *asketica* was used by van Mastricht in the concluding section of *Theoretico-Practica Theologia*, III, and by Voetius in Τα Ασκητικα. According to Joel Beeke,

> Voetius understood "ascetics" to be the systematizing of that part of theological doctrine which describes how genuine, biblical piety is to be experienced and practiced.... Voetius dealt with how to cultivate a continual life of prayer, repentance, faith, and conversion; how to approach and attend and reflect on the Lord's Supper, how to pray and give thanks, both at state time and extemporaneously.... He dealt with an array of practical subjects

means are proposed: reading of Holy Scripture, the singing of a psalm, kneeling and praying at certain times. Sundays in particular are to be devoted to this;[107] all labor must cease, preparations have to be made on Saturday evenings. On Sundays, only the Bible may be read; it is important to rise early, examine oneself, and prayerfully prepare for the preaching. After the sermon is preached, it must be contemplated and discussed at home; the remainder of the day is to be spent in prayer, singing, reading, visiting the poor, and the like. In addition, fasting and penance (the intentional reflection on and confession of sins) serve as extraordinary means. Also included are meditation on life and death[108] in which the spirit is focused on a specific topic and immerses itself in it. This is to be a solitary practice, and its prime goal is union of the soul with Christ. This meditation comes close to the edge of mystical contemplation. With all these writers, godliness is something that must be practiced systematically, in accord with strict rules. The spiritual self, the condition of the soul, is thus constantly the object of reflection. Religion is to be truly busy with eternal things, with thinking about God, not just occasionally but throughout the day.[109] This creates a rich experience of God, which is its purpose, a deep spiritual psychology, an understanding of the soul in all its conditions and changes, a most detailed scrutiny of self and self-knowledge. Of course, this also creates a need to discuss this self-examination with like-minded people.

It is self-evident that all this gives rise to conventicles, religious meetings, fellowships, leading to "little churches within the church" (*ecclesiolae in ecclesia*). It thus clearly risks becoming separatist by separating "believers" and "unbelievers" in the church. At the same time, we note that this does not necessarily lead to quietism. On the contrary, it is precisely these men who wrote about the praxis of godliness who urged and admonished people to live an active life, who themselves were inspiring preachers, were zealous in making home visits, maintained church discipline, and did much to evangelize the people, especially the lower classes, and who established catechism instruction classes and schools.[110]

This same practical theology also arose here in the Netherlands.[111] Jean Taffin (1509–1602) served as the chaplain to William of Orange from 1573

---

of concern to those truly converted to God: Sabbath-keeping, daily life, spiritual strife, temptation, spiritual desertion, and communion of saints. He provided guidance on how to face martyrdom and how to die well. (Beeke, *Gisbertus Voetius*, 28–29)

Bavinck discusses ascetics and ascetic theology in §§1 and 3 above and in chap. 12 below.

107. Heppe, *Geschichte des Pietismus und der Mystik*, 66–72.
108. Heppe, *Geschichte des Pietismus und der Mystik*, 70–72.
109. Heppe, *Geschichte des Pietismus und der Mystik*, 66.
110. Heppe, *Geschichte des Pietismus und der Mystik*, 51–52.
111. Heppe, *Geschichte des Pietismus und der Mystik*, 95–105.

to 1585, then served the Walloon church in Haarlem, then ministered in Amsterdam. His two most important works are *The Marks of God's Children* and *The Amendment of Life*.[112] Gottfried Cornelius Udemans (ca. 1580–ca. 1649) published *Christian Reflections (and Prayers)*[113] (1608) dealing with matters of sin, God's benefits, gratitude, etc. He also published *Jacob's Ladder*, in which he distinguishes eight rungs on the correct road to heaven: repentance, knowledge, faith, confession, godly life, patience, joy, and perseverance.[114] Other important works include *The Practice of Faith, Hope, and Love* (1612), *Heaven's Siege* (1633), *Spiritual Compass* (1617, for seafarers), *Merchant's Chase* (1637), and *Spiritual Rudder* (1638).[115] Undoubtedly, more writings of this sort were published. But the flourishing period of the practice of godliness was inspired by English authors and brought to the Netherlands by Teellinck, à Brakel, Lodenstein, Martinus in Groningen, and Koelman.

Willem Teellinck was born in 1579 and, after obtaining a doctorate in law at the University of Poitiers (France) in 1603, went to England in 1604, where he spent time among the Puritans. "His lodging with a godly family . . . and his exposure to Puritan godliness—lived out through extensive family worship, private prayer, sermon discussions, Sabbath observance, fasting, spiritual fellowship, self-examination, heartfelt piety, and good works—profoundly impressed him and was used for his conversion."[116] He then studied theology at Leiden "for two years under Lucas Trecatius, Franciscus Gomerus, and Jacob Arminius."[117] His longest ministry was in Middelburg (1613–29), where he died. His best-known book is *The Path of True Godliness*.[118] In addition, he left behind 127 manuscripts, which were excerpted in an anthology produced by Franciscus Ridderus, *Uit de Geschriften en Tractaten van Mr. Willem Teellinck*.[119] He urged people to live a godly life during the period of struggles between Remonstrants and Counter-Remonstrants, was diligent in combating carnivals and excess in such matters as clothing, and favored strict celebration of the Sabbath and the Lord's Supper.

Puritanism was carried over from England by William Ames, who was born in 1576 at Ipswich, Suffolk, studied under William Perkins, and, after encountering opposition as a fellow at Christ's College, Cambridge, went into exile in the Netherlands, where he became a professor in 1622 at the new University

112. Taffin, *Marks of God's Children*; Taffin, *Amendment of Life*.
113. DO: *Christelijcke bedenckingen (en gebeden)*.
114. DO: *verbreking, kennis, geloof, belijden, godzalig leven, geduld, vreugde, volharding*.
115. Udemans, *Practice of Faith, Hope, and Love*; DO: *Hemels belegh*; *Geestelijk compas*; *Koopmans jacht*; *Geestelijk roer*.
116. Beeke and Pederson, *Meet the Puritans*, 782.
117. Beeke and Pederson, *Meet the Puritans*, 783.
118. Teellinck, *Path of True Godliness*.
119. Beeke and Pederson, *Meet the Puritans*, 786.

of Franeker, Friesland. With Perkins, Ames defines theology as "the doctrine of living for God," as a "godly work." He lectured on practical theology and advised students to study the entire content of the Holy Scriptures and not only the "common topics" of theology, lectionary readings, prayers, and testing.[120] Ames's two major works are *The Marrow of Theology* and *Conscience, with the Power and Cases Thereof.* Gisbert Voetius (1585–1676), encouraged by the work of Willem Teellinck, Thomas à Kempis, Lewis Bayly, and others, became acquainted with the piety of English Puritanism, especially William Perkins, and wrote *Proof of the Power of Godliness* (1627) and *Meditation on the True Practice of Godliness or Good Works* (1628).[121] He lectured on ascetic theology or "ascetics" and wrote about spiritual abandonment and *Spiritual Exercises.*[122] Johannes Hoornbeeck (1617–66), who also conceived of theology as practical, wrote a book on how to die well (1651), a work on homiletics that van Oosterzee calls "the first original treatise on Homiletics, strictly speaking, published on Dutch Soil" (1645), and a two-volume practical theology in 1663.[123] Other writers and works include Herman Witsius, *Practical Theology*; C. Vitringa, *A Brief Outline of Christian Ethics or, Concerning the Spiritual Life and Its Characteristics*; Ewout Teellinck, *Fire and Cloud-Column* (1622) and *Christian Complaint* (1618); Franciscus de Wael, *Incense-Offering, or The Practice of Prayer* (1637); Daniel Souter, *Trumpet of Comfort*; J. Hondius, *Black and White Register of a Thousand Sins and Comforts* (1679).[124]

Consequently, a puritan lifestyle arose in many circles; dancing and theater attendance (Voetius) were shunned, days of fasting were introduced, Sunday observance was very strict, family life was organized around religion with the practice of family visitation (W. Teellinck, Wittewrongel), and many exercises and conventicles were held. Thus far this practical bent proceeded in a healthy way. Voetius knows that he is not a mystic, detects mysticism in de Labadie, and claims that de Labadie introduced it into the Reformed Church and that until that time it had been absent.[125]

120. LO: *doctrina Deo vivendi*; GrO: θεουργία; LO: *loci communes*; *lectio*; *oratio*; *tentatio*; Ames, *Marrow of Theology*, I.1.
121. DO: *Proeve van de kracht der godzaligheid*; *Meditatie van de ware practijcke der godsalicheydt of der geode werken.*
122. Voetius and Hoornbeeck, *Spiritual Desertion*; Voetius, *De praktijk der godzaligheid.*
123. DO/LO: *Euthanasia ofte welsterven*; *Tractatus de ratione concionandi*; *Theologicae practicae*; van Oosterzee, *Practical Theology*, 146.
124. Witsius, *Practicale godgeleertheid*; Vitringa, *Korte schets*; E. Teellinck, *Vuur- en Wolkkolom*; Teellinck, *Christelicke clachte*; de Wael, *Revk-offer*; Souter, *Troost-basuyn*; Honidus, *Zwart en wit register*; source: van der Hoeven, *Catalogus*, 53, no. 1653.
125. On dancing, see Ritschl, *Geschichte des Pietismus*, 1:105–11; on Voetius and mysticism in the Dutch Refomed Church, see Ritschl, 122–30.

But in 1655 Francis Rous (1579–1659) published his *The Innermost Reign of God*, which gathered into one volume three tracts, *The Heavenly School*, *The Great Seat*, and *The Mystical Marriage of Christ with the Church*.[126] Rous was a Puritan who referred to Bernard of Clairvaux, Pseudo-Dionysius the Areopagite, Hugo of St. Victor, and others in developing his mystical spirituality.[127] Perhaps a mystical trait appears already also in Willem Teellinck's *Soliloquium*, although Voetius certainly did not think so.[128] This mystical, pietistic trend becomes more pronounced in his son, Johannes Teellinck, who died in 1663. Theodorus Gerhardus à Brakel (1608–69) already at the age of sixteen reveled in the love of God and was unwilling to become a minister until he had received a direct call. His publications, *The Spiritual Life* and *Steps (or Stages) of the Spiritual Life*, are concerned with how the spiritual life can go beyond conversion and faith.[129] These are the lowest stages, but based on them one can ascend through meditation to contemplation, to the beatific vision, to the standpoint of immediacy, seeing visions and hearing voices.[130]

Jodocus van Lodenstein (1620–77) studied under both Gisbertus Voetius and Johannes Cocceius in Franeker;[131] he was a very serious person, single, who observed moderation in all things such as eating, drinking, and sleeping. He misunderstands the natural (weddings, the birthday of his mother) and insists that all of life must be "worship."[132] For those whose doctrine is correct he wants reformation of life.[133] He judged that monasteries, vespers, and fasting should not have been done away with completely but modified. He reproves literature and opulence; blessedness consists of a contemplative life, of pure beatific vision and losing oneself in it, of being enlightened by the Holy Spirit.[134] Flowing forth from this is the will to love God, a godly life filled with all kinds of virtues. The day must begin and end

---

126. LO: *Interiora Regni Dei*; *Academia Coelesti*; *Grande Oraculum*; *Mysticum Matrimonium Christi cum Ecclesia*. Ed. note: For a helpful discussion of Rous, his relation to Bernard of Clairvaux, and his influence on the development of a mystical bent in Herman Witsius, along with valuable bibliography, see de Reuver, *Sweet Communion*, 266–69.

127. Ritschl, *Geschichte des Pietismus*, 1:128. Ed. note: De Reuver sums up Rous as follows: "Rous was an English politician of a Presbyterian-Puritan stripe, an erudite person, whose mystical spirituality radiated an undeniably Bernardian spirit" (*Sweet Communion*, 267). De Reuver also mentions Basil, Cyprian, and Jean Gerson among the writers to whom Rous appealed (*Sweet Communion*, 269).

128. According to Ritschl, *Geschichte des Pietismus*, 1:124–30.

129. T. à Brakel, *Het geestelijke leven*; à Brakel, *De trappen*.

130. Heppe, *Geschichte des Pietismus und der Mystik*, 184.

131. Ed. note: This is an interesting historical tidbit, considering the great ecclesiastical rivalry between the two men and their respective followers.

132. DO: *godsdienst*.

133. Proost, *Jodocus van Lodenstein*, 123.

134. Proost, *Jodocus van Lodenstein*, 136.

with meditating on God's deeds, and sometimes with reading, thinking and finding solitude, reading Scripture, prayer, and meditation; this should take place especially on days of prayer and fasting and on Sundays. The essence of the Christian life consists in unmediated fellowship with Jesus, as bride with bridegroom.[135] In addition, Lodenstein insisted on church discipline and firmly opposed the reading of set formal prayers, refusing even to read the liturgical form for baptism.[136] Assuming a true union with Christ in the Lord's Supper, he believed that allowing everyone to partake desecrated Holy Communion. Influenced by Jean de Labadie, Lodenstein stopped administering the Lord's Supper after 1673, contending that a reformation of morals had to take place first.[137] Opposed to feast days, he was willing to preach on them but devalued them by not celebrating the Lord's Supper on them. He was a strong advocate of Sunday observance, just as Voetius was (against Gomarus, Cocceius, and Burman);[138] he wanted people to prepare on Saturdays, fast on Sundays, go to church, pray, and so forth throughout the day. In polity, he worked zealously for the autonomy of the church and defended Koelman, who had been deposed by the authorities for failing to read the forms and celebrate the feast days. For him, the Spirit and not the letter was important; a Reformed Christian without the Spirit is an atheist. "O Lord, preserve us from the letter which kills thousands, or put the stamp of your Spirit on it!"

Jean de Labadie was born near Bordeaux in 1610 and educated in a Jesuit college where there was some influence of Spanish mysticism.[139] He was dismissed from the college because of illness in 1639, preached in Paris and Amiens, and gradually drew closer to the Reformed confession, moving to the Reformed Church of Montauban on October 16, 1650. The mystical element in de Labadie consists in the high value he placed on mental prayer,[140] by which one senses and tastes God. The goal is union with God—that is, conformity to God, changing into God. God, the three persons in all their

---

135. Proost, *Jodocus van Lodenstein*, 147.

136. Proost, *Jodocus van Lodenstein*, 156.

137. Proost, *Jodocus van Lodenstein*, 167.

138. Proost, *Jodocus van Lodenstein*, 176.

139. Ed. note: Bavinck began this paragraph with a very brief reference to "Anna Maria von Schurman (Schotel), born in Cologne in 1607," but does not develop her biography. Heppe, *Geschichte des Pietismus und der Mystik*, 271; Ritschl, *Geschichte des Pietismus*, 194–267. Bavinck adds a cryptic reference here to "Van Berkum," which is to either H. van Berkum, *De Labadie en de Labadisten: Eene bladzijde uit de geschiedenis der Nederlandsche Hervormde Kerk* (Sneek, 1851), or H. van Berkum, *Antoinette Bourignon: Een beeld uit de kerkelijke geschiedenis der XVIIde eeuw* (Sneek, 1853).

140. LO: *oratio mentalis*.

perfections, is the object of contemplation. Therefore, there is nothing higher than contemplation in which we possess God, become holy, free, and blessed like God.[141] God's word and the sacraments may be means of grace, but without meditation these channels would be very dry. There are various ways of supernatural contemplation: God can overpower us, pull us up; the soul can withdraw into itself, in its depth, and seek God there.[142] It is also possible through dreams, visions, inner speech, and immediate union of God with the soul. The last-mentioned is the highest, the state of glorification. This sanctification must take place through separation from the world. The love for God must be totally disinterested; true self-denial is to love God even if he rejects us.[143] The highest good is for human beings to no longer have their own will in the presence of God; his will must be the only will. The life of the Christian must be an expression of Christ and his sufferings; it consists of contemplation, self-denial, and love toward God through which the soul flows into God as brooks flow into the sea.[144] In this way our Christian self, our *I*, becomes the self of Christ and of God.[145] De Labadie was deposed from the ministry in 1669 for his theological views and sought to establish a totally new apostolic church outside the existing one, an "evangelical congregation." He founded a house church in Amsterdam, was persecuted, and in 1670 fled with his pupil Anna Maria van Schurman and his congregation to Herford, Germany, where he founded another house church. Communion of property was introduced in Herford, and the Lord's Supper was celebrated with kisses, and so forth.

Labadism had quite an influence on the nation by promoting the existence of conventicles.[146] Of course, conventicles and catechetical instruction in the practice of godliness existed before this. The 1629 South Holland Synod [of the Dutch Reformed Church] discussed them and assigned their regulation to the church consistories. Koelman and Voetius advocated for them,[147] and de Labadie had established them during his ministry in Middelburg (1666–69). More detailed rules for conventicles were added at the Synod of Schoonhoven in 1669. Lay preachers were present everywhere with all sorts of ideas, including Hattemism,[148] Labadism, and Pietism. Consequently, many pious people

141. Heppe, *Geschichte des Pietismus und der Mystik*, 271.
142. Heppe, *Geschichte des Pietismus und der Mystik*, 274–76.
143. Heppe, *Geschichte des Pietismus und der Mystik*, 279–83.
144. Heppe, *Geschichte des Pietismus und der Mystik*, 329.
145. Heppe, *Geschichte des Pietismus und der Mystik*, 330.
146. Cf. Heppe, *Geschichte des Pietismus und der Mystik*, 395.
147. Vos Az., *Geschiedenis der vaderlandsche kerk*, 2:55–57.
148. Ed. note: "Hattemism" refers to the followers of Pontiaan van Hattem (1645–1706), who was accused of heterodoxy and deposed from the ministry in 1683. His Christocentric

became ill disposed toward the church and withdrew from it. A synod in Groningen took measures that created aversion to all set prayers, and people were taught that Christians could know with a high degree of certainty, though not infallibly, that they had been converted. Thus, only the truly regenerated were permitted access to the Lord's Table, and only the converted were allowed to pray the Lord's Prayer. In the form for baptism the expression "are sanctified" had to be changed to "are being sanctified" or "having been sanctified," or with the addition of "according to the covenant." Labadistic and pietistic influences penetrated into various circles, congregations, and ministers,[149] including Jacob Borstius (1612–80); Simon Oomius (1628–1706); Benedictus Pictet (1655–1724); W. A. Saldenus (1627–94): J. Verschuir (1680–1737); Sicco Tjaden (1693–1726); Joh. Everardi (1672–1731), minister in Emden, who liked to talk about experiences, figures, embraces, etc.; and Willem à Brakel (1635–1711), who in his *The Christian's Reasonable Service* took a firm stance against mystics and Pietists but nevertheless included pietistic elements here and there.[150]

Labadism and Pietism had particular influence on Friedrich August Lampe (1683–1729), who had been awakened to a serious Christianity by Lodenstein.[151] Lampe studied in Franeker under the Cocceian professors Vitringa, Van der Waeyen, and Roëll. These professors had been influenced by Labadism as well as the Cocceian protest against the reigning scholasticism in favor of biblical theology and had adopted the true (i.e., serious) piety of the Cocceian theology, which distinguished itself from the "pure" or "green" Cocceian party in Leiden.[152] Under their influence and the support of ministers such as David Flud of Giffen (d. 1701), Lampe became a very committed Cocceian, having experienced a very difficult conversion after much struggle. Lampe made a sharp distinction between those born again and those who were not, and although he did not exclude the latter from the congregation (as de Labadie had done), he nevertheless strongly *urged* them to abstain

---

thinking led him to overemphasize the love of God, deny his wrath, and seek union with God in a quietist fashion (S. van der Linde, "Hattem, Pontiaan van," *Christ. Encyl.*[2] 3:378–79).

149. Ed. note: Bavinck adds a number of titles for these authors that we have not included here; most are obscure and inaccessible. One reference, however, is valuable for helping to date Bavinck's manuscript: Saldenus, *Een Christen vallende en opstande*, published in 1884. This reference is given in the main text and is not a later marginal note.

150. W. à Brakel, *Christian's Reasonable Service*, 2:639–99 (§43).

151. DO: *ernstige*; Goebel, *Geschichte des christlichen Lebens*, 2:398–435; Thelemann, "Lampe"; Heppe, *Geschichte des Pietismus und der Mystik*, 236.

152. Ed. note: Henricus Groenewegen (ca. 1640–92) "was committed to preserve the system of Cocceius against the slightest modification either practically or doctrinally. This ultraconservative Cocceian wing was generally called 'Green' [*Groen*] after Groenewegen" (Gerstner, *Thousand Generation Covenant*, 135).

from the Lord's Supper. In his sermons, he always addressed the two groups separately, believing that those who differ from one another as light from darkness cannot be spoken to in the same manner. Both need to be admonished and reproved, but distinctly.[153]

Furthermore, he also distinguished five classes among unconverted: the ignorant, the reckless, the common people who are Christian in name only, the hypocrites, and those who are persuaded. Among the converted he distinguishes weak from the strong believers. But then Lampe speaks of five steps or stages in the internal call:[154] (1) external use of the means of grace; (2) attentiveness to the Word; (3) internal, living conviction of one's own sinful condition through the Holy Spirit, the truth of the Word of God. These three are also still part of the external call. But the last two are not: (4) enlightenment; (5) inclination of the will. Lampe further distinguishes a weak and a strong faith as distinct stages/steps.[155] Each of these also has two parts. Weak faith is understood to include (a) a longing for Jesus and (b) entering the road and going to Jesus. Strong faith includes (a) appropriating Jesus unto oneself and (b) the assurance of being in the state of grace. This faith is preceded by fright, being crushed by the law, anguish, darkness, and attacks by Satan, a little light that shines in the soul but that is first thought to be Satan as an angel of light, and the breakthrough of the light, refreshing experiences of God's mercy.[156]

Mysticism, Pietism, and Cocceianism (Lampe's theology) have thus over time created a certain idea of the way of salvation that is cherished among the pious, especially in Holland. In the broad sense this idea can be sketched as follows.[157] The beginning of grace is the conviction, consisting in the crushing of the heart by the law, in darkness and attacks by Satan: I am lost. But then God sends some light and shows the way of escape in Christ. In other words, he enlightens our mind, our memory, our judgment, our conscience; he bends our will; he changes our affections. All this is convicting and regenerating grace, the work of the Holy Spirit. It is fellowship with the Holy Spirit. But after this, faith awakens (God pours it forth), and does so in several steps/stages:[158]

153. Goebel, *Geschichte des christlichen Lebens*, 2:416.

154. DO: *trappen*; Lampe, *De verborgentheit*, 243–52 (VII.xiv–xix). Ed. note: This is a Dutch translation of *Geheimnis des Gnaden-bunds*.

155. Lampe, *De verborgentheit*, 313–14 (VIII.xxvi–xxvii).

156. Lampe, *De verborgentheit*, 313–23 (VIII.xxviii–xxxiii); Heppe, *Geschichte des Pietismus und der Mystik*, 238.

157. See Myseras, *Der vromen ondervinding*.

158. Ed. note: Bavinck cites no specific sources for the steps/stages that follow, though they can be found in Lampe, *De verborgentheit*, 316–36 (VIII.xxx–xli).

1. *Expectant, longing, thirsting, hungry* faith (Mic. 7:7: "I will look to the LORD; / I will wait for the God of my salvation; / my God will hear me"; Luke 18:13: "'God, be merciful to me, a sinner!'").[159]

2. *Clinging, struggling* faith (Matt. 15:27: "Yes, Lord, yet even the dogs eat the crumbs that fall from their masters' table"; Gen. 32:26: "I will not let you go unless you bless me").[160]

3. *Refuge-seeking, pending* faith (Matt. 11:28: "Come to me, all who labor and are heavy laden, and I will give you rest"; Isa. 45:22: "Turn to me and be saved, / all the ends of the earth! / For I am God, and there is no other").[161]

4. *Appropriating* faith, consisting of negotiation of the soul with Jesus and eventual surrender of the soul to Jesus to be saved by him (Matt. 8:2: "And behold, a leper came to him and knelt before him, saying, 'Lord, if you will, you can make me clean'"; John 1:12: "But to all who did receive him, who believed in his name, he gave the right to become children of God").[162]

5. *Dependent, supported, confident* faith, *trusting*,[163] followed by

6. *Assured* faith (2 Tim. 1:12: "I know whom I have believed, and I am convinced that he is able to guard until that Day what has been entrusted to me").[164]

All of this pertains to the activity of the soul in relation to the Lord Jesus, the Second Person of the Trinity. Negotiation with the third member of the Trinity, the Father, then follows. This consists of justification and establishing a covenant. Justification from God's side, in the tribunal, takes place in the moment when faith, in its first step, is poured in; justification in a person's conscience takes place when faith becomes trusting, accepting faith. With covenant-making an additional distinction is made. There is an agreeing to the covenant that takes place when the soul longs for Jesus (i.e., the first step of faith), but this step is frequently followed by a drifting away when people discover that they are lost. When people arrive at trusting faith and experience justification in their conscience, a solemn covenant ceremony, a marriage with the Lord takes place. (This solemn covenant ceremony must not be identified with earlier agreeing to the covenant; saying "yes" to Jesus is like a betrothal.)

159. DO: *uitziend*; *verlangend*; *dorstend*; *hongerend*.
160. DO: *aanklevend*; *worstelend*.
161. DO: *toevluchtnemend*; *komend*.
162. DO: *aannemend*.
163. DO: *leunend*; *steunend*; *vertrouwend geloof*; *betrouwen*.
164. DO: *verzekerd*.

This is followed by the "confirmation" of the covenant, which, so to speak, brings conversion to completion.[165] Now the mystical marriage begins, interrupted repeatedly by sin, struggle, temptation, but nevertheless a beginning of growth and maturation in grace. The believer now experiences a life of love, of fellowship in the Holy Spirit with Jesus and the Father. The sealing of the Holy Spirit is born from this life of love with Jesus.[166]

In the Netherlands, the followers of Johannes Verschoor (who were called "Hebrewers" after 1680)[167] belonged to the mystical sects. They taught that everything was inevitable, that God himself had no freedom, that there was no difference between good and evil, and that Christ's death is only a revelation of God's willingness to forgive. The followers of Pontiaan van Hattem (the so-called "Hattemists") believed the same. Both taught that (a) to believe is to trust; (b) forgiveness, justification, etc. took place already when Christ died; and (c) the believer is in Christ and Christ in him, and therefore the believer has nothing to fear because God is all and does all, and human beings do nothing. This was a form of Spinozistic, pantheistic mysticism. Others of this sort include Willem Deurhoff (d. 1717), a cabinetmaker, who had studied Descartes, acquired followers beginning in 1680, and taught that all spirits (souls) and bodies (material) were only modifications of a substance God had created with the creation. Frederik van Leenhof published *Heaven on Earth* in 1703 and taught that we should always be cheerful, even in the greatest of adversities, and that religion is joy because everything depends on God, in whom we live and have our being.[168] A dispute about his teaching led to his dismissal from the ministry in 1711. Johan Eswijler was a private citizen who published *Beneficial Conversation* (also given the title *Meditation for a Solitary Soul*).[169] This was initially approved by ecclesiastical officials but later retracted because it contained pantheistic traits. Notwithstanding, many of Voetius's followers highly praised it. Then there was the mystical sect called Knobbelhouwers in Rotterdam and its surroundings.[170] Antoinette Bourignon (1616–80) left the Roman Catholic Church and became a

---

165. DO: *bevestiging.*
166. Myseras, *Der vromen ondervinding*, 68–72.
167. Ypey, *Geschiedenis van de kristelijke kerk*, 7:290–312; Heppe, *Geschichte des Pietismus und der Mystik*, 375–84; Wybrands, "Marinus Adriaansz. Booms"; B. Glasius, "Jacob Verschoor," in Glasius, *Godgeleerd Nederland*, 2:500–504.
168. DO: *Hemel op aarde.*
169. DO: *Nuttige zamenspraak; Zielseenzame meditatie.*
170. Ed. note: The sect's name indicates a "hacking of the knot" (as in cutting the "Gordian knot" perhaps). The sect is mentioned in works on Pietism, but not much is known about it except that its members sought divine guidance by inner light rather than external words, including Scripture. See Heppe, *Geschichte des Pietismus und der Mystik*, 383; Stoeffler, *Rise of Evangelical Pietism*, 162.

Pietist, but did not join the evangelical church. Beginning in 1662 she started receiving revelations and visions and insisted on strict renunciation of the world and self-resignation to the divine will, finding direction by inner light, prayers of the heart without words.[171] Peter Poiret (1646–1719), during an illness in 1672, promised God that he would write a book justifying faith philosophically and published his *Rational Reflections* in 1677.[172] He was acquainted with the writings of Tauler and à Kempis, corresponded with Anna Maria van Schurman, became acquainted with Antoinette Bourignon, and became a contemplative mystic instead of a philosopher, accompanying Bourignon on her travels until her death in 1680. He published both his own mystical work and that of others with the following ideas: true knowledge of God can be obtained only through internal enlightenment, through union with him; this is a matter of feelings and not the intellect. God needs to impart his light, life, and salvation to our soul (which is dark by itself).

We can mention a few more: Gerhard Tersteegen (1691–1769), in high demand as a traveling teacher, was a quietist mystic.[173] Willem Schortinghuis (1700–1750) wrote the very influential and contentious *Intimate Christianity* (*Het innige Christendom*, 1740), which was hesitantly approved by the theological faculty in Groningen (Van Velzen, Gerdes, Driessen, Verbrugge).[174] However, the book was condemned by the 1742 Dutch Reformed Synod of Appingedam because of its many mystical expressions. Experiential knowledge and agreeable enjoyment of the truth are necessary and can be known only through feeling and experience. The person who has not been granted grace knows only sounds; the one who has been granted this knows its meaning. We are nothing (I will not, cannot, know not, have not, am unworthy). Others denounced the book because it taught that it was not the Word that

---

171. One of her followers, Jan Swammerdam, in a treatise for Louis XIV, wrote: "Most High Majesty, I present to Your Excellency, here the almighty finger of God in the anatomy of a louse" (Huet, *Het land van Rembrand*, 2/2:57). Ed. note: To place this quotation in perspective, it is helpful to know that Huet's discussion of Jan Swammerdam is found in a chapter titled "Science and Literature" and follows two sections on the Dutch mathematician, physicist, and astronomer Christiaan Huygens (1629–95). By contrast, Swammerdam, a biologist, turned his scientific observations to the microscopic, to the smallest creatures and features (red blood cells) of God's world. For Swammerdam, "studying the Earth's creatures revealed the greatness of God; scientific pursuits were pious activities" (https://en.wikipedia .org/wiki/Jan_Swammerdam).

172. LO: *Cogitationes rationales*.

173. Goebel, *Geschichte des christlichen Lebens*, 3:289–447.

174. Schortinghuis, *Het innige Christendom*. Ed. note: For a version of *Het innige Christendom* in modern Dutch along with an exploration of Schortinghuis's analogues, see de Vrijer, *Schortinghuis en zijn analogien*.

provided knowledge but internal enlightenment and that assurance was only possible through immediate enlightenment. Schortinghuis was condemned in 1745 by the Synod of Overijsel. The ministry of Gerardus Kuypers (1722–98) in Nijkerk (1749) was accompanied by strange religious phenomena: kissing, embracing, jumping, dancing, headshaking, shoulder pulling, stuttering, knees knocking, etc. Such phenomena were also found in the congregation of de Labadie.[175]

The Brethren Congregation from Herrnhut (the Moravian Church)[176]

Historically affiliated with the old Bohemian-Moravian brother community dating back to 1457, the revived Brüdergemeine in the eighteenth century was a continuation of Pietism. "In 1722, a small group of Bohemian Brethren (the 'Hidden Seed') who had been living in northern Moravia as an illegal underground remnant surviving in a Catholic setting of the Hapsburg Empire for nearly 100 years, arrived at the Berthelsdorf estate of Nikolaus Ludwig von Zinzendorf" (1700–1760) and shortly after "established a new village called Herrnhut, about 2 miles from Berthelsdorf."[177] Educated as a youth for six years at Halle in one of August Hermann Francke's schools, Zinzendorf sought to apply Pietist ideals practically through proclaiming Jesus (the universal religion of the Savior) by way of books, letters, and travel. On May 12, 1727, Zinzendorf issued the Charter for Herrnhut as a "renewed fraternity," a unified civil and spiritual community ruled by twelve elders with Zinzendorf as local lord and head.[178] "The charter members of this community were Moravian and Bohemian Protestants who had been driven from their homes by the Counter Reformation."[179] Celebration of the Lord's Supper followed on August 13 along with the institution of the *Stundengebet*—during which each person prayed one hour for the community—and the official founding of the community.

Zinzendorf "wanted the Moravian colony to form a special group within the Lutheran church of Saxony" where they would participate in the life of the Lutheran church. Nonetheless, in addition to having its own distinct organization (the twelve elders), "this special 'congregation' should meet for daily worship by itself. In these special gatherings, they introduced the love-feast,

---

175. Goebel, *Geschichte des christlichen Lebens*, 2:181–435 (II/3); also Ritschl, *Geschichte des Pietismus*, 2:367, 369.

176. GO: *Brüdergemeine*; *Herrnhutter*. Burkhardt, "Zinzendorf und die Brüdergemeine"; Schulze, "Zinzendorf's christliche Weltanschauung"; Schneckenburger, *Vorlesungen*.

177. See https://en.wikipedia.org/wiki/Moravian_Church.

178. However, the civil and spiritual communities were separated again in 1729.

179. Qualben, *History of the Christian Church*, 366.

and feet-washing, and the fraternal kiss."[180] Young men and young women lived apart, children were considered to belong to the whole community and separated by sex. In 1729 Zinzendorf realized that he had been converted since his youth and came to the conviction that Christ's death is central to the doctrine of salvation, that the reference to ransom[181] in Matthew 20:28 does not refer only to being declared just but also to being released and changed internally. Christ's *person* therefore comes first, not his work *in abstracto*. Opposition to the community came from the Pietest centers of Halle and Wittenberg as well as the government. Zinzendorf was banished from Saxony in 1736 and went to Wetterau (east of Frankfurt am Main).

The community engaged in significant mission activity, sending "out missionaries to the West Indies in 1732 and to Greenland in 1733. Zinzendorf secured ordination for his missionaries by introducing the episcopacy into his organization. Jablonsky, a court-preacher at Berlin and a former bishop of the Moravian church," ordained Zinzendorf "as a Lutheran Minister in 1724 . . . and as Bishop of the Community of Moravian Brethren in 1737."[182] The Community of Moravian Brethren was now in fact an autonomous church alongside the Lutheran Church, though full legal autonomy did not come until 1742, when it was "formally recognized by the Saxon government" as the "Unity of the Brethren."[183] The true "community of Jesus,"[184] most openly displayed in the Community of the Brethren, can be found in all churches. Theologically, the group taught that feeling comes first, then grace, and from grace faith and love flow forth on their own. Zinzendorf, who was called *papa*, saw the Trinity as a family: the Father is father, the community his daughter-in-law, and the Holy Spirit the mother of the community. His preaching concentrated on the wounds of the Savior, especially those in his side. Over time, people began to live extravagantly, luxuriously, and fantasy was given free play as a source of knowledge of Jesus. A romantic period ensued during which fanaticism reigned, characterized by sensual representation and love for the Savior as a man, a regarding "of Christ according to the flesh" (2 Cor. 5:16). A healthy reversal took place in 1750; in order to cover debts a communal property was created. Zinzendorf, who died in 1760, had a vivid imagination and a clear intellect; he was a man of action, a dominating person with a strong, heartfelt love for Christ and one evangelical

180. Qualben, *History of the Christian Church*, 367.
181. GrO: λύτρον.
182. Qualben, *History of the Christian Church*, 367. Ed. note: Qualben adds here that this act "established a formal connection with the Hus[s]ite church."
183. Qualben, *History of the Christian Church*, 367.
184. GO: *Gemeine Jesu*.

goal: to win people for Christ. It was with this love that he embraced all who shared his goal and gathered them into a community that serves Christ in everything, including as a civil community.

August Gottlieb Spangenberg (1704–92) completed the organization of the Unity of the Brethren and helped formulate its doctrines, especially in his work *Idea fidei fratrum* (1782). The Community of Moravian Brethren also published a catechism (third edition in 1860) and a hymnbook in 1775.[185] Their characteristic beliefs are as follows:

1. The Trinity is a family. The Father: the congregation is the Son's bride, the daughter-in-law of the Father, and the Holy Spirit is mother of the church. The church is the wife of Jesus. Jesus—that is to say, the abstract godhead of Jesus and not his humanity—is the object of faith and love. Worship of Jesus is realistic, as the veneration of Mary is in Roman Catholicism.

2. Jesus, the husband of the believing woman, is feminine; love rather than faith is central. The person of Jesus—that is, his divinity—stands in the place of doctrine and dogmas. The inspiration of Scripture is denied; inner feeling is the source of revelation. The doctrine of justification recedes. A gradual growing in love replaces the "inward penitential struggle" followed by a "breakthrough."[186]

3. This community is the "face"[187] of the church. It is a community that seeks union with other Christians but is nonetheless its own fellowship. This communion is one large family with Jesus as its head and segregation of the sexes. Ecclesial fellowship is associational, a society rather than a church bound together by its confession. The natural and spiritual orders are confused; the spiritual is materialized.

Here in summary are the community's key principles: love is primary (not faith); Christ and not God is the object of faith; the Trinity is a model family; justification is internal as much as forensic; the overall approach is sensual-mystical and involves feeling and fantasy; the church's purpose is to win souls; the church community is the "face" of the true church, and the "Community of Jesus" can also be found in Lutheran and Reformed churches;[188] civil and church communities are merged, and Jesus is to be the center of both with all people serving him; and the church is an association, a society, not a community bound by a confession.

---

185. *Kleines Gesangbuch der evangelischen Brüdergemeine* (Gnadau: Buchhandlung der Brüder Unität, 1875); *Liturgienbuch der evangelischen Brüdergemeinde* (Gnadau: Buchhandlung der Brüder Unität, 1882).

186. GO: *Busskampf; Durchbruch.*

187. GrO: πρόσωπον.

188. GrO: πρόσωπον; GO: "Gemeine Jesu."

Critique

However justified mysticism and Pietism were in their objection to rationalism and dead orthodoxy, both of which locate the seat of faith in the intellect, they are themselves also one-sided. Here are six points of critique:

1. Mysticism and Pietism put the seat of faith in feeling and thus do not embrace the fullness of our humanity. That which most affects and arouses feelings gets the emphasis.

2. This results in a denial of the faith's objectivity—that is, the Word, the letter, the sacraments, the church, and even doctrine (e.g., satisfaction).

3. Another consequence is the formation of a pernicious group (club) mentality. The converted separate themselves, live apart, and leave family and world to fend for themselves. They are salt not within but alongside the world.

4. The covenant idea is lost altogether. The converted and the unconverted each live their own lives totally detached from one another. Mutual contact takes place only mechanically and not organically.[189] The unconverted are left to their own devices.

5. This also has adverse results for the converted. Religion is limited to being busy with the things of God (reading, praying). Daily work becomes a matter of necessity alone rather than a holy calling. Sunday stays disconnected from the rest of the week; faith is not tested *in* the world. Christians become passive, quietistic.

6. By constantly attending to self-contemplation, people make their experience the norm for everyone else, and unhealthy, unscriptural elements enter. Simplicity and the childlike character of faith give way to sentimentality. Experience guides the exegesis of Scripture and even becomes the source of knowledge, materially as well as formally.

Methodism[190]

Methodism sought to do for the Anglican state church what mysticism sought for the Roman Catholic Church and Pietism sought for the Lutheran (and Reformed) Churches—namely, to extend the Reformation into everyday life. The state church in England provided a dismal picture in this respect, and

189. Ed. note: We have translated *geweldadigen* (lit., "violent") with "mechanically and not organically" to reflect what seems to be Bavinck's intention here. The importance of the notion of "organic" in opposition to "mechanical" in Bavinck's (and Abraham Kuyper's) thought cannot be overemphasized. See Eglinton, *Trinity and Organism*.

190. Schöll, "Methodismus"; de la Saussaye, *De godsdienstige bewegingen*, 109–14; Möhler, *Symbolik*, §§75–76; Schneckenburger, *Vorlesungen*, 103–51; Boehmer, "Pietismus und Methodismus."

the Puritans also had slumped into idleness after the Act of Toleration (May 24, 1689), with many of them becoming Deists or Quakers.[191] John Wesley was born on June 17, 1703, to parents who were really Nonconformists but who joined the Anglican Church. He studied in Oxford, where he read Thomas à Kempis and Jeremy Taylor (1613–67).[192] At that time he already disagreed with the doctrine of predestination, which he considered a threat to the moral life. With his brother Charles he established a "Holy Club," whose members lived disciplined lives and were dedicated to reading the New Testament, to prayer, to fasting, and to visiting the sick and the poor.

It is here that the derisive term "Methodist" was first applied. One of the members of the club was George Whitefield (1714–70), whose evangelistic preaching later fueled the Great Awakening in Britain and America. John and Charles Wesley went to Georgia (America) as missionaries in 1735, became acquainted with the Moravian Brethren, and returned to England in 1738, wondering about the assurance of their salvation. In John Wesley's own words: "I went to America to convert the Indians; but, oh, who shall convert me?"[193] After returning to England Wesley underwent his great life-changing experience in the Aldersgate chapel on May 24, 1738. Here is how he describes it in his journal:

> In the evening I went very unwillingly to a society in Aldersgate Street, where one was reading Luther's preface to the Epistle to the Romans. About a quarter before nine, while he was describing the change which God works in the heart through faith in Christ, I felt my heart strangely warmed. I felt I did trust in Christ, Christ alone, for salvation; and an assurance was given me that He had taken away my sins, even mine, and saved me from the law of sin and death.[194]

Now Wesley began to preach in London along with Whitefield, always within the Anglican Church. But on February 17, 1739, Whitefield preached in an open field for the first time, since the churches were closed to them. That same year the first Methodist chapel was established in Bristol. The name "Methodist" was not new; in former days it designated a theoretician, someone who followed a very strict method in science or practice; in the

---

191. Ed. note: The Act of Toleration was an act of Parliament that granted freedom of worship to so-called Nonconformists—i.e., those who dissented from the Church of England (Baptists, Congregationalists).

192. Ed. note: Jeremy Taylor "is sometimes known as the 'Shakespeare of Divines' for his poetic style of expression, and he is frequently cited as one of the greatest prose writers in the English language" (https://en.wikipedia.org/wiki/Jeremy_Taylor).

193. Wesley, *Journal of John Wesley* (entry for January 24, 1738).

194. Wesley, *Journal of John Wesley* (entry for May 24, 1738).

seventeenth century it became a common name for those who followed a new trend in religion. It was first applied to Wesley and his followers in Oxford, and they adopted it as a badge of honor (as identifying a person who lives according to the biblically established method). And thus it continued, Wesley preaching in London to crowds of twenty thousand to thirty thousand people. However, internal disagreement arose because of antinomian and quietistic influences. A parting of the ways between the Methodists and the Moravians occurred in 1740, and Whitefield separated from Wesley over the doctrine of divine election in 1741. Beginning in 1741–42, Wesley appointed assistants, lay preachers, who met in annual conferences starting in 1744. Upon joining the Methodist chapels, members had to promise (a) to avoid all sin such as cursing, Sabbath desecration, drunkenness, alcohol, usury, gossip, opulence, etc.; (b) to do good; and (c) to use the means of grace (reading, sacraments, fasting, etc.). They were divided into four societies: (1) the awakened (who met the conditions for joining); (2) the blessed (band societies, for whom the rules were stricter: their "yes" had to be "yes," they were not allowed to smoke, had to practice moderation, etc.); (3) the enlightened (even higher standards); and (4) the penitents, who had fallen from grace but had returned. In addition, all these societies were subdivided (since 1742) into classes of twelve persons, each with a class leader as head. A number of these societies were combined into a circuit—already nine by 1748—with an assistant (superintendent) at its head. There were also stewards for external matters. Daily hours of meditation and prayer were observed, with occasional love-feasts[195]—a practice taken over from the Moravians—and monthly night watches. Beginning in 1755 they also renewed their covenant on the first Sunday of the year; beginning in 1762 they held prayer meetings, and in the same year they began to dedicate the last Fridays of August, November, February, and May to fasting. In 1784 Wesley issued a *magna carta*, a constitution for Methodists, in which all authority was assigned to the conference. In that same year, the separation from the state church began as well. Wesley himself ordained a few preachers and placed a few of the chapels and preachers under the protection of the Act of Toleration, and thereby in fact became a dissenter. Wesley died in 1791.

For the most part Wesley subscribed to the Thirty-Nine Articles of the Anglican Church, but dissented on the doctrines of predestination—which he conceived of conditionally—and perseverance, which he denied. He also had different takes on regeneration and sanctification. He believed that regeneration is preceded by prevenient grace, which evokes a deep sense of sin and guilt,

195. GrO: ἀγάπαι.

of deserving judgment, showing that that righteousness and peace cannot be obtained by works.[196] This deep, sudden feeling of sinfulness is necessary for someone to then receive the feeling of justification. Heart-wrenching, shocking preaching and hymns are used to get there. All this must be *felt* and lived through. Being able to state the day and hour of one's conversion is the proof of conversion. Methodism engages in bookkeeping of regeneration. Consciousness of sin comes to a conclusion here; this experience is not true of those who are converted.

This sense of sin, guilt, and judgment is followed by the offer of salvation in Christ, which must be accepted by faith. The power of the new life is given in the moment of rebirth, which is a *sudden* conversion (cf. Wesley himself).[197] Conversion is a conscious act, the most intense moment of our moral life; but, just as with our natural birth, it is accompanied by great distress and often severe shaking of the body. Wesley turned this experience into a general norm. Therefore much effort was put forth in the preaching to bring about this *sudden* conversion, while Wesley's followers paid close attention to emotional reactions.

Converts are then called to fulfill their moral task. The goal here is Christian *perfection* (appealing to Ezek. 36:25; Matt. 5:48; John 17:20, 23; 1 John 4:19; Eph. 5:25–27; 1 Thess. 5:23), and this goal can be achieved in this life.[198] Perfection, however, does not consist of absolute, sinless perfection, but in loving God with one's whole heart, soul, mind, and strength, and the neighbor as oneself. This love must have complete rule over sinful thoughts, words, and the flesh. Perfection is therefore a purely ethical (nonintellectual) and relative perfection. Furthermore, this perfection is usually granted shortly before death and may also be lost.

Wesley's accomplishments are significant: he reinstituted the diaconate, resumed mission work to the pagans and is the father of domestic missions; he visited prisoners and children that had been neglected; he improved the

196. LO: *gratia praeveniens.*
197. The essence of faith consists of assurance, although this assurance coincides with the direct act of faith (Schneckenburger, *Vorlesungen,* 115). Wesley also rejected the doctrine of predestination. Methodists receive assurance in their feelings through immediate witness of the Holy Spirit, but only for the present (not that they are *eternally* saved). Conversion is the main thing, resulting in an excessive zeal for conversion reflected in preaching that focuses on sin and penitence (*boetepredikaties*), designed to rouse sinners awake. The effect is to diminish the importance of home nurture; gradual, organic development of the spiritual life is not desired; the inner life of the soul is externalized; evangelical freedom becomes legal coercion; active life does not permit the quiet life of the affect to come into its own; and means of grace are not appropriately valued, much less the church.
198. However, perfection *cannot* be proven, but depends on self-testimony, which itself depends on the testimony of the Holy Spirit in the soul.

Sunday schools initiated by Robert Raikes;[199] he cared for the poor, began street preaching and the distribution of tracts and Bibles, and opposed the slave trade. Wesley created in the Protestant church an evangelizing order of preachers whose aim was to convert and to save others. Methodism soon spread, to Scotland in 1741, Ireland in 1747, and America in 1770. After Wesley's death, disagreements arose among the Methodists, and a number of additional societies appeared, largely as a result of the hierarchy of the conference.

Methodism did not have much direct influence in the Netherlands. But at the beginning of the nineteenth century (around 1825), Methodism sent out missionaries to Geneva[200] and French Switzerland along with colporteurs. Services were held and led to persecution in Geneva and the Canton of Vaud (German Waadt).[201] A revival (*réveil*)[202] took place and a free church was established in Vaud. This *réveil* had a methodistic flavor, though later on it was also partly influenced by the Swiss theologian Alexandre Rodolphe

199. Ed. note: Robert Raikes (1736–1811) was an English philanthropist and Anglican layman who, with his friend Rev. Thomas Stock (1750–1803), began the Sunday School movement in England in 1780. Schooling some 1,250,000 children by 1831, these Sunday Schools are a precursor to the modern "common schools" tradition (https://en.wikipedia.org/wiki/Robert_Raikes; https://en.wikipedia.org/wiki/Thomas_Stock).

200. De la Saussaye, *De godsdienstige bewegingen*, 141.

201. Ed. note: The Canton of Vaud is located in Romandie, the French-speaking western part of the country; its capital and largest city is Lausanne.

202. Ed. note: We have included Bavinck's use of the French word "réveil" here because of its important historical significance for the Dutch Reformed Church—particularly for the Secession Christian Reformed Church, of which Bavinck was a member—and for the "awakening" of Abraham Kuyper and Dutch neo-Calvinism. The Réveil ("Awakening" or "Revival") was an international renewal movement that has its roots in the ministries of Scottish Presbyterian minister Thomas Chalmers (1780–1847), who became the mover and leader of the Free Church of Scotland. From Scotland it moved to Geneva, where Scottish Baptist layman Robert Haldane (1764–1842), who was founder of the "Society for the Propagation of the Gospel at Home" and who had become an effective church planter (along with his brother James, establishing some eighty-five churches in Scotland and Ireland), visited in 1816. Haldane began Bible studies with theological students, notably the significant "Society of Friends" (Société des Amis), which included César Malan (1787–1864), Jean-Henri Merle d'Aubigné (1794–1872), François Samuel Robert Louis Gaussen (1790–1863), and the brothers Frédéric (1794–1863) and Adolphe Monod (1802–56). From Geneva the Réveil spread to France and reached Germany and the Netherlands. The Dutch Réveil can trace its beginnings to the baptisms of two Portuguese Jewish converts to Christianity, Abraham Capadose (1795–1874) and Isaac da Costa (1798–1860), in 1822 and 1821, respectively. Both men had been tutored at the University of Leiden by the Dutch poet Willem Bilderdijk (1756–1831), who championed a more conservative and evangelically Christian worldview (including the Dutch monarchy) against the "liberal" ideas of the French Revolution. His "antirevolutionary" posture greatly influenced another of his Leiden followers, the Dutch historian and statesman Guillaume Groen van Prinsterer (1801–76), who in turn was the major spiritual and intellectual influence on Abraham Kuyper. See M. Elisabeth Kluit, "Réveil," *Christ. Encycl.*[2] 5:627–29; the standard work on the Réveil is Kluit, *Het Protestantse réveil*.

Vinet (1797–1847).[203] It had an impact on the Netherlands, particularly in the aristocratic circles,[204] through the writings of Gaussen, Auguste Rochat, Merle d'Aubigne, Gonthier, Bonnet, A. Monod, and others. This methodistic trait of the *réveil* came to expression in our country in the work of domestic missions, the "Heldring Foundation,"[205] the Society for Christian Reading Materials (*Vereeniging voor Christelijke lectuur*), missions, the seminary of Da Costa, orphanages, and the like.

Methodism has an aggressive character, seeks only conversion, and looks for the seat of faith in the will (Pietism in feelings, rationalism in the intellect). But it regards conversion as a sudden, momentary, and immediate act. Therefore, it also misunderstands the church, baptism, and Christian nurture. In addition, it runs the risk of allowing sanctification to be absorbed almost entirely in the task of converting others.[206] This is the reason for blind zeal without understanding, for all those committees, and for penitential sermons. Everything must be geared toward missions; children, young men and women, must establish societies, evangelize, and mobilize all efforts to make converts, and with tracts and Bibles to conquer the world by storm. The natural consequence of all this is the Salvation Army. The result is that all secular areas, science, art, literature, politics, are abandoned to the world. It is important to abstain from smoking and drinking, among other activities, because they all belong to the world. By putting the *will* in the foreground in order to oppose quietism and predestination, Methodism lacks a harmonious anthropology of the whole person.

---

203. Ed. note: Vinet advocated complete freedom of conscience and the formal separation of church and state, leading a secession from the Swiss Reformed Church and the formation of the Free Church (L'Église Libre) (https://en.wikipedia.org/wiki/Alexandre_Vinet).

204. See de la Saussaye, *La crise religieuse en Hollande*.

205. Ed. note: Reformed pastor Otto Gerhard Heldring (1804–76) was an active participant in the *réveil* whose concern for the unfortunate of society, starting with homes for young women who were pregnant against their will, led to shelters, homes, and schools for orphans and at-risk children (*Christ. Encycl.*² 3:420–21, s.v. "Heldring, Otto Gerhard," "Heldring-Stichtingen"). Today, the Ottho Gerhard Heldring Stichtung "is a Dutch orthopaedic institution in Zetten, Netherlands. It is a private (nongovernmental) managed centre for youth with severe behaviour and also often psychiatric problems" (https://en.wikipedia.org/wiki/Ottho_Gerhard_Heldringstichting).

206. Ed. note: The tentative nature of this sentence comes from the question mark (?) Bavinck inserted between the lines of his otherwise strong statement that sanctification *is* "completely taken up in converting others" (*geheel opgaan eigenlijk in bekeering van anderen*).

9

The Shape and Maturation of the Christian Life

The life of Christ is the shape, the model toward which our spiritual life must grow. Jesus himself teaches that we who bear God's image are to imitate him in our mercy, our compassion, and our love. Angels, prophets, model believers such as Paul are also held before us as examples. Above all, Scripture speaks of the imitation of Christ in word and deed; we are to follow him, to be in spiritual fellowship with him, to forsake everything for his sake, to trust him and obey him. In this following, we must never forget that he is our teacher, leader, and example while we learn, follow, and imitate. We do not simply accompany him on his journey, traveling side by side. No, Jesus leads the way and we follow after him. To imitate Jesus is to enter into fellowship with his suffering, with his path of passion. This requires self-denial and cross-bearing, a willingness to lose our life in order to find it in him. Jesus is supremely our example in love and suffering, and the hallmark of our participation in Christ's suffering is patient endurance.

This imitation of Christ has been understood and practiced in a variety of ways throughout the history of the Christian church. Martyrdom was the earliest notion of this imitation, but as persecution came to an end, it was replaced by the monastic ideal. Monastic life was regulated by Benedict of Nursia in the West and by John Cassian in the East. Monasticism in the Middle Ages underwent necessary reform, and individual monasteries became associated with and governed by orders. The thirteenth century also saw the rise of mendicant orders, which intensified their vows of poverty, chastity, and obedience by abandoning all possessions. Pain-inducing chastisements such as flagellation (for penance) spread in the fourteenth century, especially during the years of the Black Death.

This is also the context within which we can understand the appearance of the stigmata—those bodily manifestations of Christ's own wounds in the hands, feet, and side. This phenomenon is said to have occurred in a total of some eighty people, all of them Roman Catholic, including several Dutch women in the fourteenth century. More recently, there have been several well-attested cases in the nineteenth century. Undoubtedly, there is deception, imagination, and exaggeration in the phenomenon of the stigmata, but its factuality is firmly attested. It should be explained on the basis of the power of the human soul on the body. What is required for the appearance of the stigmata is a fervent, glowing power of imagination that internalizes Christ's wounds in the same way that people can imagine themselves into real illness.

This same power of imagination led people to consider the imitation of Christ as a series of circumstances, deeds, and expressions that had to be copied literally. We find better, more spiritual, understandings of this imitation in Bernard of Clairvaux, Bonaventure, Johannes Tauler, and especially Thomas à Kempis and his classic Imitation of Christ. *Protestants also usually understood this imitation more spiritually in terms of various virtues such as obedience to God, love, humility, goodness, uprightness, suffering, and holiness. Furthermore, people sought the norm for the Christian life in the law of the Ten Commandments and not in the person of Christ, although self-denial and cross-bearing are the heart of Calvin's discussion of the Christian life. Nineteenth-century theology celebrated Jesus as an example but began to vacillate because Jesus was not sufficiently involved in human social activities (marriage, politics) to be a universal example. At best he is regarded as the supreme human person, harmonious in character, joining the masculine and the feminine, the contemplative and the active, all the while experiencing a rich emotional life, a holy pathos. We follow him by letting his "spirit" guide us.*

In our view, the imitation of Christ as the form of the spiritual life does not consist in slavish repetition of Jesus's earthly life, or in considering him as the model mystic, or in being animated by his "spirit." Rather, it consists of acknowledging him as Mediator and Redeemer, being united with him through the Holy Spirit and led into a life of self-denial and cross-bearing, shaping our lives in accord with Christ. Thus we are restored as image-bearers of God in knowledge, righteousness, and holiness. This life is fully shaped by the law of God, in which we find moral freedom.

There is development and maturation in the spiritual life. Christians are not to remain "infants," to be of "little faith," but to grow "in the grace and knowledge of our Lord and Savior Jesus Christ," to become mature, complete. This maturation must be both intensive and extensive. It reorients our lives to "becoming citizens of heaven." This is a growth in knowledge, in love, and in hope. All this is a gift of the Holy Spirit and is characterized by personal communion with God in Christ. We need to acknowledge variation and degree in spiritual growth; there are differences in knowledge, in wisdom, in holiness, and in hope. These should not be thought of as "levels" or "stages." In all this, we are to heed the apostle's words: "I say to everyone among you not to think of himself more highly than he ought to think, but to think with sober judgment, each according to the measure of faith that God has assigned."

§21. THE SHAPE OF THE CHRISTIAN LIFE: THE IMITATION OF CHRIST

In the seventh chapter we considered the nature of the spiritual life (§17), its origin (§18), and its first and basic activity (§19). In chapter 8 we warned against the side paths of mysticism, Pietism, and Methodism. We will now proceed in an orderly fashion. The one side of our spiritual life's basic activity was faith—appropriating Christ. Christ, however, is not only our prophet, priest, and king; he is also our example and ideal. His life is the shape, the model, that our spiritual life must assume and toward which it must grow. The New Testament regularly speaks of this.

Imitation in Scripture

Scripture also speaks of an imitation of *God* (Eph. 5:1).[1] The Greek verb μιμηταί means "to imitate," "to copy," and must be distinguished from another verb, ἀκολουθέω ["to follow"].[2] The idea of imitating God is already found in the Old Testament. In Numbers 14:24 God says of Caleb, "My servant Caleb . . . has followed me fully" (cf. 32:11–12), and Deuteronomy 13:4 commands:

---

1. GrO: μιμηταὶ τοῦ θεοῦ; from μιμέομαι ("to imitate, emulate, follow"). Key New Testament passages include 1 Cor. 4:16: "I urge you, then, be imitators of me [μιμηταί μου]"; 1 Thess. 1:6: "You became imitators of us and of the Lord [καὶ ὑμεῖς μιμηταὶ ἡμῶν ἐγενήθητε καὶ τοῦ κυρίου]"; 1 Thess. 2:14: "For you, brothers, became imitators of the churches of God in Christ Jesus [ὑμεῖς γὰρ μιμηταὶ ἐγενήθητε, ἀδελφοί, τῶν ἐκκλησιῶν τοῦ θεοῦ]"; 2 Thess. 3:7, 9: "For you yourselves know how you ought to imitate us [δεῖ μιμεῖσθαι ἡμᾶς] . . . to give you in yourselves an example [τύπον] to imitate [εἰς τὸ μιμεῖσθαι ἡμᾶς]"; Heb. 6:12 (NIV): "Imitate those who through faith and patience inherit what has been promised [μιμηταὶ δὲ τῶν διὰ πίστεως καὶ μακροθυμίας κληρονομούντων τὰς ἐπαγγελίας]"; Heb. 13:7: "Remember your leaders, those who spoke to you the word of God. Consider the outcome of their way of life, and imitate their faith [μιμεῖσθε τὴν πίστιν]"; and 3 John 11: "Beloved, do not imitate evil but imitate good [μιμοῦ . . . τὸ ἀγαθόν]."

2. Ed. note: The subtlety of Bavinck's point here is hard to capture adequately in translation. Bavinck distinguishes two Dutch words, *volgen* ("follow") and *navolgen* (lit., "follow after" or "imitate, copy"). In what follows, except when retaining the words of Scripture, we will translate *volgen* as "follow" and *navolgen* as "imitate."

"It is the LORD your God you must follow.[3] . . . Keep his commands and obey him" (NIV). Elijah challenges the Israelites: "If the LORD is God, follow him"[4] (1 Kings 18:21). In the Old Testament imitating God is mostly a matter of listening to him, walking in his ways.

In the New Testament Jesus sets God before us as a personal example in Matthew 5:48: "Be perfect, therefore, as your heavenly Father is perfect" (NIV).[5] He specifies this further in Luke 6:36: "Be merciful, just as your Father is merciful."[6] As "dearly loved children" we are called to be "imitators of God" (Eph. 5:1).[7] Ephesians 4:32 commands: "Be kind to one another, tender-hearted, forgiving one another, as God in Christ forgave you."[8] Repeatedly in the Old Testament we encounter the command: "Be holy, for I am holy" (Lev. 11:44–45; 19:2; 20:26; 21:8). Peter tells his readers, "Just as he who called you is holy, so be holy in all you do," and he grounds it in the Levitical command: "For it is written, 'Be holy, because I am holy'" (1 Pet. 1:15–16 NIV). This imitation, it is obvious, does not take place on the metaphysical plane (i.e., the incommunicable attributes of God) but in the sphere of the ethical, in God's holiness, goodness, and mercy (i.e., in the image of God in which we participate thanks to regeneration). Such an imitation is possible because we who are his beloved children are his image (Eph. 5:1). We are to be imitators of God in the same way that children imitate their parents—that is, not their authority, governing, majesty, and all their conduct and relationships. Our imitation of God is real but not entirely clear because God is invisible. God's example is not visible or tangible; it is completely real as an idea and ideal.[9]

In the second place, Scripture sometimes speaks of imitating *angels*. Jesus taught us to pray, "Your will be done, on earth as it is in heaven" (Matt. 6:10b; cf. Heb. 12:22). We are also to imitate other human beings, such as prophets (James 5:10) and persevering believers "who through faith and patience inherit the promises" (Heb. 6:12). The apostle Paul repeatedly speaks of his readers imitating him:[10]

> You know what kind of men we proved to be among you for your sake. And you became *imitators of us and of the Lord*, for you received the word in much affliction, with the joy of the Holy Spirit. (1 Thess. 1:5–6)

3. HO: אַחֲרֵי יהוה אֱלֹהֵיכֶם תֵּלֵכוּ; אַחֲרָי.
4. HO: לְכוּ אַחֲרָיו.
5. GrO: τέλειος.
6. GrO: οἰκτίρμων.
7. GrO: μιμηταὶ [τοῦ] θεοῦ.
8. GrO: χρηστοί, εὔσπλαγχνοι, χαριζόμενοι ἑαυτοῖς . . . ἐχαρίσατο ὑμῖν.
9. Witsius, *Prakticale godgeleertheid*, 64–68 (chap. 8, "Van de navolging van God").
10. Ed. note: Emphasis is added in the Scripture passages that follow.

For you yourselves know how you ought to *imitate us*, because we were not idle when we were with you . . . that we might not be a burden to any of you. It was not because we do not have that right, but to give you in ourselves *an example to imitate*. (2 Thess. 3:7–9)

I urge you, then, be imitators of me. (1 Cor. 4:16)

Be imitators of me, as I am of Christ. (1 Cor. 11:1)

Hebrews 13:7 provides general advice: "Remember your leaders, those who spoke to you the word of God. Consider the outcome of their way of life, and *imitate their faith*." Of course, this imitation is not intended absolutely, as the qualifications in the preceding passages make clear.

The "prophets who spoke in the name of the Lord" (James 5:10) are "an example of suffering and patience." Others are examples of faith (Heb. 13:7), of "faith and patience" (Heb. 6:12), of having "worked night and day" (2 Thess. 3:7–9). To imitate Paul is to imitate Paul "and the Lord" (1 Thess. 1:6) or to follow his example "as I follow the example of Christ" (1 Cor. 11:1 NIV). What is in view here are the specific ethical, Christian virtues of faith, long-suffering, suffering, etc., and all of them circumscribed by the imitation of Christ (1 Cor. 11:1).[11] According to Dr. Palmer, "Apart from 1 John 2:6 and 3:3, there is only one dimension of Jesus that is held before us for imitation, namely his suffering in obedience to the Father, his love for the neighbor, and the patience needed for this."[12]

Most often Scripture speaks of the *imitation of Christ*[13] (which Jesus himself demands). It is not only his words that must be followed, but also his deeds. Speaking and doing, revelation and being, doctrine and life are one with him and cannot be separated; Jesus *is* what he *says*. Jesus himself does God's will and therefore counts all who do God's will as his brother, sister, and mother (Matt. 12:50). He who is "gentle and lowly in heart" (Matt. 11:29) and teaches others to be the same repeatedly demands imitation. The key word in the New Testament is ἀκολουθέω. According to Cremer, ἀκολουθέω comes "from κέλευθος, a *going, journey, path, way* (perhaps connected with the German *gleiten*, 'to glide or slide,' which is not to be confounded with the compound *geleiten*, whence *Begleiter*); ἀκόλουθος, '*attendant*' (α copulative),

11. See Bosse, *Prolegomena*.
12. C. D. F. Palmer, "Das Vorbild Jesu," 678. Ed. note: The author Bavinck has in mind is likely Christian David Friedrich Palmer (1811–75), professor of evangelical theology at Tübingen. He was influential in Mennonite circles. See http://www.gameo.org/index.php?title=Palmer,_Christian_David_Friedrich_(1811-1875).
13. DO/LO: *navolging Christi*.

accordingly = to be an attendant, to accompany, to go with or follow, as brothers in arms (Xen. *Hell.* V.3.26 and often, parallel to σύμμαχος εἶναι), as soldiers, in contrast with πολεμαρχεῖν, as servants (Plut. *Alc.* 3)."[14] "Literally, to *accompany, follow, follow after*, Matthew 4:20, 22, 25. . . . Construed with the dative; also μετά τινος = to *accompany, go with*, Luke 9:49, Revelation 6:8, 14:13; ὀπίσω τινος, Matthew 10:38, Mark 8:34."[15] In a moral and spiritual sense it means to follow or to obey, also in secular Greek. And this is how it should be understood in the New Testament, where in "the Gospels and Revelation 14:4, [it refers to] the scholars and disciples of Christ, not, however, because in ancient times instruction was given *ambulando*, as is stated in all lexicons hitherto without any confirmatory examples."[16]

Nevertheless, we do take note here of the demand that Jesus specifically places before his disciples. Jesus places this call before individuals: to Matthew, "Follow me" (Matt. 9:9);[17] to the rich young man, "If you would be perfect, go, sell what you possess and give to the poor, and you will have treasure in heaven; and come, follow me" (Matt. 19:21); to the disciples, "Follow me, and I will make you fishers of men" (Matt. 4:19, cf. John 1:37–42, 44). He also states this in general to all who want to be his disciples:[18]

And *whoever* does not take his cross and follow me is not worthy of me. (Matt. 10:38)

If anyone would come after me, let him deny himself and take up his cross and follow me. (Matt. 16:24)

And calling the crowd to him with his disciples, he said to them, "If anyone would come after me, let him deny himself and take up his cross and follow me." (Mark 8:34)

And he said to all, "If anyone would come after me, let him deny himself and take up his cross daily and follow me." (Luke 9:23)

I am the light of the world. Whoever follows me will not walk in darkness, but will have the light of life. (John 8:12)

If anyone serves me, he must follow me. (John 12:26)

14. Cremer, *Biblico-Theological Lexicon*, 79–80, s.v, "ἀκολουθέω."
15. Cremer, *Biblico-Theological Lexicon*, 80.
16. Cremer, *Biblico-Theological Lexicon*, 79–80.
17. GrO: ἀκολούθει μοι.
18. Ed. note: Emphasis added in the Scripture passages that follow.

Occasionally someone comes and volunteers to follow Jesus, as in Matthew 8:19: "And a scribe came up and said to him, 'Teacher, I will follow you wherever you go.'" In Luke 9:57, "As they were going along the road, someone said to him, 'I will follow you wherever you go.'" Jesus responds: "Foxes have holes, and birds of the air have nests, but the Son of Man has nowhere to lay his head" (9:58). Another responds to Jesus's call to follow him, "Lord, let me first go and bury my father" (9:59). Jesus says to him: "Leave the dead to bury their own dead. But as for you, go and proclaim the kingdom of God" (9:60). Another says to Jesus, "I will follow you, Lord, but let me first say farewell to those at my home," to which Jesus replies, "No one who puts his hand to the plow and looks back is fit for the kingdom of God" (9:62).

We draw the following conclusions from the preceding passages:

1. The imitation of Christ consists specifically in *literally following Jesus*, accompanying him on his travels throughout Palestine. This involves a fellowship in his external life and his destiny (Matt. 8:18; 9:9; 19:21; Luke 9:57–62). But this does not exhaust the idea of imitation; in fact it could not exhaust it. Imitation had to rest upon, be a revelation of or a pull toward, a deeper, inner relation to Jesus, a love for Jesus. Such a life of denial, cross-bearing, and complete opposition to the world could only be desired by those who sought to deny themselves for Christ's sake.

2. The imitation of Christ, therefore, is *a spiritual life-relationship*[19] *with Jesus*. This is clear from Jesus's own words. When asked by the rich young man, "Teacher, what good deed must I do to have eternal life?" Jesus replies, "If you would be perfect, go, sell what you possess and give to the poor, and you will have treasure in heaven; and come, follow me" (Matt. 19:16, 21; Mark 10:17–21). To follow Jesus is therefore the way to gain eternal life. Conversely, "whoever does not take his cross and follow me is not worthy of me" (Matt. 10:38). Stated in other words, "Such a person I will reject, I do not know." And in Luke 9:62: "No one who puts his hand to the plow and looks back is fit for the kingdom of God." Following Jesus, therefore, is the condition for gaining eternal life, for entering the kingdom of heaven, for being worthy of Jesus.

3. Precisely because the imitation of Christ is a spiritual communion, Jesus demands that we *forsake everything for his sake*. The rich young man had to sell all he possessed (Matt. 19:21), Matthew had to leave his tax-collector's booth (Matt. 9:9), and the disciples had to leave their ships and nets (Luke 5:11). When Jesus commented that "foxes have holes, and birds of the air have nests, but the Son of Man has nowhere to lay his head" (Luke 9:58), he was referring not to self-denial with respect to possessions, not to his poverty,

19. DO: *geestelijke levensgemeenschap.*

but to his self-denial with respect to rest and security. This is clear from the examples that follow: for someone who wants to follow Jesus, there is no time to bury one's dead or take leave of one's family (9:59, 61). Negatively, self-denial means forsaking the world; positively, cross-bearing means exchanging the world for a cross. That is the condition for the imitation of Christ. Self-denial and cross-bearing are not so much two components of the imitation of Christ as they are the two accompanying circumstances of imitation; they are not the heart of it.

4. The heart of imitation consists of a *spiritual, believing communion with Christ*,[20] in trusting him, in obeying him. Even external denial of the world and bearing one's cross are not yet true imitation. This is clear from the way Jesus distinguishes spiritual following from simply physically accompanying him on his travels. He called many to follow him who did not accompany him in the same way that his disciples did. This is also clearly taught in John 8:12, where Jesus tells *all* the people, including the Pharisees, "I am the light of the world. Whoever follows me will not walk in darkness, but will have the light of life." It is taught, above all, in the parable of the good shepherd, where Jesus distinguishes "his sheep"—namely, those who "hear my voice, and I know them, and they follow me"—from those who have seen the "works that I do in my Father's name" but do not believe (John 10:25–26). This spiritual communion is also spoken of in John 12:26: "If anyone serves me, he must follow me; and where I am, there will my servant be also. If anyone serves me, the Father will honor him." Similarly, Matthew 10:38 and 16:24 (with the parallel passages) signify a spiritual communion only.

5. At the same time, spiritual communion as such does not fully capture what is involved in the imitation of Christ but needs to be *qualified*, described more narrowly. Imitation is not a communion of two equals, but specifically one of teacher and pupil, of leader and follower, of example and imitator. Even as he describes what it is to follow him spiritually and prescribes it for us, Jesus also always intends to present himself as example. That is apparent in the formulas associated with "to follow," "with me," "after me."[21] Imitation does not simply mean "accompanying" or "traveling side by side." No, Jesus leads the way, and we follow after him. To imitate Jesus is to enter into fellowship with his suffering, with his path of passion. The requirements Jesus places on following him make this clear:

a. *Self-denial*. Everything has to sacrificed: the young man's riches, the disciples' boats, one's whole life (Matt. 16:25), everything (Matt. 19:21), love

---

20. DO: *geestelijke, geloofsgemeenschap met Christus.*
21. GrO: ἀκολουθεῖν; μετ' ἐμοῦ; ὀπίσω μου. Ed. note: See discussion earlier in this chapter.

for parents and even one's own life. Luke 14:26: "If anyone comes to me and does not hate his own father and mother and wife and children and brothers and sisters, yes, and even his own life, he cannot be my disciple." This self-denial must all be for the sake of Christ (Matt. 16:25; 19:29; Luke 21:12; John 15:21). That it is all for the sake of Christ becomes even more clear for the second requirement.

b. *Cross-bearing.*[22] The image is of course borrowed from Jesus's own crucifixion and undoubtedly chosen deliberately by Jesus with an eye to his own death (Matt. 10:38; 16:24; Mark 8:34; 10:21; Luke 9:23; 14:27). This image indicates that the imitation of Christ is accompanied with the greatest defamation, rejection, and oppression by the world. For that reason, the imitation of Christ is also an entry into his glory. Great rewards of "a hundredfold" and "eternal life" await those who have "left houses or brothers or sisters or father or mother or children or lands, for my name's sake" (Matt. 19:29). Furthermore, "Whoever finds his life will lose it, and whoever loses his life for my sake will find it" (Matt. 10:39; cf. 16:25). To follow Jesus is to "have the light of life"; those who follow Jesus will be where he is and be honored by the Father (John 12:26); they will go where he is going (John 13:36).

6. Following Jesus does have a *literal* significance. This does not mean that we accompany him on his journey, because that is no longer possible for us. But it is also not merely something spiritual, such as observing his commandments and obeying him. There is a mystical significance to imitation; through self-denial and cross-bearing in faith we enter into a fellowship with his suffering and glory. The imitation of Christ presupposes the mystical union,[23] a life unity with Christ.

This is the imitation of Christ that was the content of the apostles' preaching. For Peter, the new life of recently regenerated Christians that needed to be fed and nourished by Christ was to be guided by his example (1 Pet. 2:21).[24] Peter's audience "had been called" to endure in suffering "for doing good," and Peter instructs them: "For to this you have been called, because Christ also suffered for you, leaving you an example, so that you might follow in his steps."[25] Peter describes Christ's example as follows: "He committed no sin, neither was deceit found in his mouth. When he was reviled, he did not revile in return; when he suffered, he did not threaten, but continued entrusting himself to him who judges justly" (vv. 22–23). Jesus, therefore, is

22. GrO: λαμβάνειν τὸν σταυρὸν ἕαυτοῦ.
23. LO: *unio mystica.*
24. GrO: ὑπογραμμός; Weiss, *Biblical Theology,* 1:218–19 (§46c).
25. GrO: ἵνα ἐπακολουθήσητε τοῖς ἴχνεσιν αὐτοῦ.

an example in holiness and patience in his suffering. Peter repeats and summarizes this in the next chapter: "For it is better to suffer for doing good, if that should be God's will, than for doing evil. For Christ also suffered once for sins, the righteous for the unrighteous, that he might bring us to God" (3:17–18). And then this: "Since therefore Christ suffered in the flesh, arm yourselves with the same way of thinking, for whoever has suffered in the flesh has ceased from sin" (4:1) This last phrase means that whoever suffers in the flesh for Jesus's sake, for righteousness' sake (3:14, 17), no longer serves sin. Believers who have this fellowship in Christ's suffering are called to *rejoice*,[26] because "insofar as you share Christ's sufferings . . . you may also rejoice and be glad when his glory is revealed" (4:13). Once again, to imitate Christ is to take him as an ethical example, to share in his suffering, to be mystically united to him. Through that suffering, in communion with Christ, believers receive God's favor (2:19–20), and through the testing of their faith (4:12) obtain "the outcome of your faith, the salvation of your souls" (1:7–9).

Returning to the apostle Paul, already in 2 Thessalonians 3:5 he prays that the Lord "may direct your hearts to the love of God and the steadfastness of Christ"[27] after lauding the Thessalonians in his first letter (1:6) for being "imitators of us and of the Lord, for you received the word in much affliction, with the joy of the Holy Spirit." "Paul did not, like the original apostles, look up from the picture of the earthly life of Jesus, which they themselves had seen, to the divine glory of the exalted Lord; he looked back from the radiant light of this glory, in which Christ had appeared to him, to His earthly life."[28] Nonetheless, Paul does draw details from Jesus's earthly life: born from David's line (Rom. 1:3; 9:5; Gal. 3:16); raised on the third day (1 Cor. 15; along with Jesus's postresurrection appearances); especially his death and passion (Rom. 6:6; 1 Cor. 1:18–2:5; 2:8; 2 Cor. 1:5, 7; Phil. 3:10; Col. 1:24; Gal. 2:20; 3:13; 5:11; 6:12, 14); and Christ's institution of the Lord's Supper (1 Cor. 11:23–25). Paul also calls attention to Christ's sinlessness (2 Cor. 5:21) and his meekness and gentleness.[29] Paul himself is an imitator of Christ (1 Cor. 11:1). Christ is our example in becoming poor though he was rich (2 Cor. 8:9), an attitude that must be ours as well (Phil. 2:5–8).

And Christ is our example in love. After instructing the Ephesian Christians to be "imitators of God, as beloved children," Paul tells them to "walk

---

26. GrO: χαίρετε.
27. GrO: τὴν ὑπομονὴν τοῦ Χριστοῦ.
28. Weiss, *Biblical Theology*, 1:403.
29. GrO: πραΰτης; ἐπιείκεια.

in love, as Christ loved us and gave himself up for us, a fragrant offering and sacrifice to God" (Eph. 5:1–2). However, Paul's understanding of the imitation of Christ goes deeper than gentleness. In baptism we are brought into a living communion with Christ (Rom. 6:3; Gal. 3:27). We are given the Spirit, who unites us with Christ and makes us one spirit with him (1 Cor. 6:17) as he is formed in us (Gal. 4:19). We are now *in Christ*, and Christ is *in us* (Gal. 2:20; 3:28; 2 Cor. 13:5; Col. 3:11; Eph. 3:17; Phil. 1:8, 21). But that life begun in Christ by faith must progress; those who are "infants in Christ" (1 Cor. 3:1) need to "put on the Lord Jesus Christ" (Rom. 13:14) and become mature in him.[30] The communion with Christ that began with being crucified and buried with Christ (Gal. 2:19; Rom. 6:1–6, 8) must become a fellowship of suffering with Christ: "if children, then heirs—heirs of God and fellow heirs with Christ, provided we suffer with him in order that we may also be glorified with him" (Rom. 8:17). Paul considers the life-threatening dangers he faces "every hour" (1 Cor. 15:31) as a daily death, as "always carrying in the body the death of Jesus" (2 Cor. 4:10), "always being given over to death for Jesus' sake" (2 Cor. 4:11). Believers "share abundantly in Christ's sufferings" (2 Cor. 1:5), and the purpose of this participation is "that I may know him and the power of his resurrection, and may share his sufferings, becoming like him in his death" (Phil. 3:10). Paul even rejoices in his sufferings for the sake of the Colossian believers because "in my flesh I am filling up what is lacking in Christ's afflictions for the sake of his body, that is, the church" (Col. 1:24). With respect to the "trouble" he has received, Paul tells the Galatians: "I bear on my body the marks of Jesus."[31]

The hallmark of this participation in Christ's suffering is *patient endurance* (Rom. 8:25; 12:12; 2 Cor. 6:4; 12:12).[32] In believers it is *affliction* that produces patient endurance, which in turn produces character, which in its turn produces hope (Rom. 5:3–4).[33] It is through fellowship in his suffering that "the God of endurance and encouragement" equips us "for all endurance and patience with joy" (Rom. 15:5; Col. 1:11).[34] That is the reason believers ought to "boast in their sufferings" (Rom 5:3–5; cf. 8:18; 2 Cor. 4:17; 6:4).[35] Sharing in Christ's suffering is a surety of our participation in his glory (Rom. 5:5; 8:17). Thus, there is also a participation in his resurrection and

30. GrO: νήπιος; τέλειος ἐν Χριστῷ.
31. GrO: τὰ στίγματα τοῦ Ἰησοῦ.
32. GrO: ὑπομονή.
33. GrO: θλῖψις; δοκιμή; ἐλπίς.
34. GrO: θεὸς τῆς ὑπομονῆς καὶ τῆς παρακλήσεως; πᾶσαν ὑπομονὴν καὶ μακροθυμίαν μετὰ χαρᾶς.
35. GrO: καυχώμεθα ἐν ταῖς θλίψεσιν.

life (Rom. 6:5–11), even for our mortal bodies (Rom. 8:11). We also share in his ascension (Eph. 2:6) and in the revelation of his glory (Col. 3:4). In sum: "And we all, with unveiled face, beholding the glory of the Lord, are being transformed into the same image from one degree of glory to another" (2 Cor. 3:18).

In the Epistle to the Hebrews, Christ, "who learned obedience by what he suffered" (5:8), is said to be able "to sympathize with our weaknesses" because he "in every respect has been tempted as we are, yet without sin" (4:15). He was "made like his brothers in every respect, so that he might become a merciful and faithful high priest in the service of God, to make propitiation for the sins of the people" (2:17). He was like us and faithful to his call (3:2) and is therefore "able to help those who are being tempted . . . because he himself has suffered when tempted" (2:18). Jesus is "the founder and perfecter of our faith, who for the joy that was set before him endured the cross" (12:2)[36] and was "made perfect through suffering" (2:10). In John's Revelation, faith is manifested especially in patient endurance (2:3).[37] Even death for the Word of God (6:9; 20:4) is not to be feared (2:10; 12:11). Jesus's word is said to be "the word of patient endurance" (3:10), of which he himself is the example (1:9). And finally, John tells us that those who say they abide in Christ "ought to walk in the same way in which he walked" (1 John 2:6). This means purifying themselves (3:3) and not sinning (3:6).

The Imitation of Christ in Church History: Martyrs, Monks, and Mystics

This imitation of Christ has been understood and practiced in a variety of ways throughout the history of the Christian church. The literature of the first Christians is characterized by an upbeat, joyful tone, deep personal feelings, and an indifference to this world and to death.[38] Conflict with the world soon followed along with martyrdom in the second and third centuries. This conflict was regarded as a struggle (Col. 2:1; Phil. 1:30; 1 Thess. 2:2; 1 Tim. 6:12) or as warfare (2 Cor. 10:4).[39] Martyrs are conquerors for God's cause in the presence of other people and angels, the bodyguards of the Christian army, the "impenetrable column against which the power and fury of the enemy was ineffectually hurled. The Christians were killed but their dying was life and their defeat was triumph; their death-days were regarded and

---

36. GrO: ἀρχηγός; τελειωτής.
37. GrO: ὑπομονή.
38. Gass, *Geschichte der christlichen Ethik*, 1:58.
39. GrO: ἀγών; στρατεία.

remembered as birth-days."[40] Martyrs were considered the most authentic *imitators* of Christ on his road of suffering.

This is the earliest notion of the imitation of Christ in the Christian church. Sometimes the pathos was overwrought and an authentic longing for death turned into a fanatic desire for the glory of martyrdom. Martyrs became the highest, truest Christians, their disposition deduced from the deed as such. In this way the Christian ideal acquired a pathological character; the essence of the Christian life consisted in suffering and dying, and death was its consummation.[41] This remained true for some time; faith/endurance is the highest virtue, and Tertullian, Cyprian, and especially Origen praise martyrdom to the highest heavens. Increasingly the imitation of Christ became a continuation of the mediatorial suffering and dying of Christ and gained merit. The suffering and dying of believers earned them a share in the saving and atoning benefits that flow from Christ's sacrifice. Thus the way was prepared for the notion that good works are meritorious.[42] Patience and self-control, that is to say steadfastness and joy in suffering, become the highest virtues.[43] Patience and endurance are the cause of the good; impatient drive is the original sin (Tertullian).

But circumstances changed, and with them so did the Christian ideal. The Christian church was recognized by the state, and its suffering from persecution came to an end. Many entered the church without genuine conviction, and its purity was lost. The church faced the luxury of toleration, and the Christian ideal was dragged lower and sank. Consequently, monasticism arose after the rule of Constantine[44] with the goal of holding high the Christian ideal for small circles rather than for all members of the church. This gave rise to a double morality of *precepts* for all and *counsels of perfection* for monks. The way for this had been prepared by the premium placed on fasting, by Tertullian's repudiation of second marriages for clergy, the preference for celibacy, the despising of wealth and possessions,[45] and the emphasis on works of justice and mercy—that is to say, the operative morality that ends up in asceticism.[46] The monks are the successors to the martyrs. They were directed by circumstances to copy and be the deputies of the martyrs. The

---

40. Ed. note: This passage, an elaboration of Bavinck's claim in the manuscript, is taken from his "De navolging van Christus," 105, translated in Bolt, *Theological Analysis*, 376.

41. Gass, *Geschichte der christlichen Ethik*, 1:64–68.

42. Gass, *Geschichte der christlichen Ethik*, 1:83–86.

43. GrO: ὑπομονή; σωφροσύνη.

44. According to Gass (*Geschichte der christlichen Ethik*, 1:124), this happened around 340; others place it in the decades 360–80.

45. Gass, *Geschichte der christlichen Ethik*, 1:92–100.

46. Gass, *Geschichte der christlichen Ethik*, 1:104.

monastic life was soon called the greatest struggle (2 Tim. 4:7; Heb. 12:4), the divine or highest philosophy, the life of a God-lover, angelic, and so forth.[47] In Chrysostom's words, the monk is the true king who is rich in his poverty and fruitful in his childlessness.[48] Monks sought to achieve the Christian ideal of perfection through ascetic practices, denying the body so that the soul might live, detaching themselves from the body of the world so that the soul might be bound to heaven. Ascetic practice consisted of *poverty* (detachment from riches and pleasure), *chastity* (not marrying, putting to death sensual desires), and *obedience*.

Monks consider Mary and Martha along with John the Baptist as precursors and want to be *imitators* of Jesus,[49] to engage in warfare (2 Cor. 10:4; 1 Tim. 1:18) under him as king.[50] They understand imitation as a slavish copying of Jesus in his personal life's journey; Jesus is the perfect monk who was poor, rejected marriage, and wandered through the land, feet unclad, in obedience to his Father.[51] Imitation consists of copying the external life of Jesus and then only in some of the outward circumstances of his life, which are exaggerated as well.

A new conception of the imitation of Christ arose in the Middle Ages. Monastic life was regulated by Benedict of Nursia (ca. 480–ca. 543/47) in the West[52] and by John Cassian (ca. 360–435) in the East as an extraordinary institution for achieving Christian perfection; each monastery was autonomous. This all changed with the establishment of the Cluny Abbey in 910. From there a monastic reform movement spread through France and Italy with the abbot of Cluny retaining authority over the new monasteries established by the Benedictine Order. These monasteries, which were "congregations" bound and subject to the order, soon spread over the whole of Europe and as far as Palestine. The orders became a power, with a founding principle, "mother" monasteries, and their own immediate subjection to the pope. In the meantime, the orders of knights added the use of the sword to their vows along

---

47. GrO: ἀγών; ἡ κατὰ θεὸν φιλοσοφία; ὑψηλὴ φιλοσοφία; βίος φιλόθεος; ἰσάγγελος. Gass, *Geschichte der christlichen Ethik*, 1:126.

48. Ed. note: See Hunter, *Comparison between a King and a Monk.*

49. Gass, *Geschichte der christlichen Ethik*, 1:145, 149.

50. GrO: στρατεία. Cf. Lucius, "Das mönchische Leben."

51. DO: *nabootsing.* "Just as the Lord lived His life in obedience, so they desire to imitate Him by expressing outwardly obedience in their daily walk, pledging themselves to submit implicitly to monastic rules and the commands of their superiors. Just as the Lord had not where to lay His head, they desire to imitate Him by the endurance of poverty throughout the whole circumstances of their lives; and as the Lord lived in celibacy, they desire to imitate Him by abjuring marriage and family life, and cutting asunder all the ties which through these bind a man to the world." Martensen, *Christian Ethics*, 1:296.

52. Gass, *Geschichte der christlichen Ethik*, 1:145.

with poverty and chastity. Another unique development of the Middle Ages, in the thirteenth century, was the appearance of the *mendicant orders*.[53] These orders observed the three monastic vows of poverty, chastity, and obedience, but intensified them by *abandoning all possessions*. Because they were dependent for their life and livelihood on the gifts of others, these orders demonstrated the monastic ideal in the midst of *society*. The one dimension of monastic life—namely, living apart from society—was abandoned in order, *in* society, to bring the monastic ideals more strongly to awareness and legitimacy. In addition to abandoning their possessions and living on love offerings, they added to the negative crucifixion of the flesh (depriving themselves of food and drink, sleep, clothing, houses, speaking, marriage), also taking on positive chastisements, understood through the athletic metaphor of "practice" and regarded as "carrying in the body the death of Jesus so that the life of Jesus may also be manifested in our bodies" (2 Cor. 4:10).[54]

Other phenomena such as self-wounding, blood-letting, castration, flagellation (self-flagellation in the eleventh century), girdles of thorns, and chain-dragging (by the Flagellants) had appeared earlier. However, these positive chastisements were imposed by the mendicant orders and systematized into a variety of forms and degrees.[55] A Flagellant movement broke out in the thirteenth century, with "the first recorded incident in Perugia [Italy] in 1259, the year after severe crop damage and famine throughout Europe."[56] Flagellants included people of noble birth, the marginalized, women, and even children, flagellating and slashing themselves for thirty-three days (to match the thirty-three years of Jesus's life) as they traveled over land and through cities. The movement spread to Carinthia,[57] Styria,[58] Austria, Bohemia, Hungary, and even to Poland. In the fourteenth century Flagellant pilgrimages grew in number, especially during the height of the Black Death (1348–49). By April 1349 they covered the whole of Germany. Pope Clement VI officially condemned them on October 20, 1349.[59] The practice of flagellation as penance was initiated, or perhaps at least brought into practice, by the hermit Peter

---

53. Gass, *Geschichte der christlichen Ethik*, 1:280–83.
54. GrO: ἄσκησις; τὴν νέκρωσιν τοῦ Ἰησοῦ ἐν τῷ σώματι περιφέροντες, ἵνα καὶ ἡ ζωὴ τοῦ Ἰησοῦ ἐν τῷ σώματι ἡμῶν φανερωθῇ.
55. Cf. Zöckler, *Kritische Geschichte der Askese*. Ed. note: In a marginal note Bavinck added a reference to the later appearances of Madame Guyon (1648–77) and the Trappists.
56. See https://en.wikipedia.org/wiki/Flagellant.
57. Ed. note: Carinthia (German *Kärnten*; Dutch *Karinthië*) is the southernmost state in Austria.
58. Ed. note: Styria (German *Steiermark*; Dutch *Stiermarken*) is one of the federated states of Austria, located in the southeastern part of the country.
59. Herzog, "Geißler."

Damian (ca. 1007–1072/73) and his disciple Dominic Loricatus (995–1060), who wore a coat of chain mail next to his skin as a hair shirt.[60] During the recitation of the Psalms, the penitent received one hundred lashes for each psalm. One cycle of the entire Psalter (fifteen thousand lashes) covered five years of penance (three thousand lashes per year).[61] The monastic orders invented all sorts of pain-inducing chastisements in order to copy the sufferings of Christ.

This was a way of expressing the "worthlessness of earthly and bodily life, the triumph of the spirit over the flesh, the narrowness of the heavenly path, and the appropriation and copying of Christ's loving sacrifice."[62] Imitating Christ was regarded as following after Christ's suffering, repeating his suffering and death,[63] as a memorial and repetition of that suffering. This is the context within which we must understand the so-called stigmata, which we first encounter with Francis of Assisi (1182–1226).[64] While Francis was praying and fasting on the mountain of Verna in September 1224, on the day of the Feast of the Exaltation of the Cross, Francis had a vision of Christ "as a seraph, a six-winged angel on a cross. This angel gave him the gift of the five wounds of Christ."[65] Francis himself spoke of this, another monk with him bore witness, and many others, Clare, Pope Alexander IV, along with numerous residents of Assisi, saw the stigmata. Their authenticity was affirmed by Pope Gregory IX in three papal bulls. The same pope declared Francis a saint on July 26, 1228, and the Franciscan order later commemorated the day he received the stigmata. Up to forty additional parallels were adduced between Francis and Jesus. Both performed miracles, were said to have been predicted in the Old Testament, prophesied, were crucified, and were exalted above the angels.

The stigmata are also said to have occured in others, a total of some eighty people, all of them Roman Catholic.[66] Gertrude van der Oosten (Gertrude of

60. LO: *lorica hamata*.

61. Vogel, "Damianus."

62. Gass, *Geschichte der christlichen Ethik*, 1:284.

63. Ed. note: It is difficult adequately to capture Bavinck's play on words in translation (*een na-, over-, weer-lijden van Christus lijden*), particularly since the second term, *overlijden*, means "to die."

64. Engelhardt, "Franz (Franziskus) von Assisi"; Sabatier, *Life of St. Francis*, 287–96. Imbert-Gourbeyre, *Les stigmatisées*; Jelgersma, *Het hysterisch stigma*.

65. Chesterton, *St. Francis*, 131. Ed. note: This account comes from Francis's companion, Brother Leo.

66. Hamberger, "Stigmatisation." Ed. note: Bavinck wrote in the margin, "Görres, *Die christliche Mystik*, counts a number of false reports in addition to the sixty to seventy genuine ones." Bavinck's source is Zöckler, "Louise Lateau," 8. Zöckler, in turn, refers to Görres, *Die christliche Mystik*, 2:410–86. An English translation of this section is readily available in Görres, *Stigmata*.

Delft, d. 1358) was a Dutch Beguine who on occasion had milk flow from her virgin breast and who received the full stigmata after intense contemplation on the most severe and horrific torments of the Savior on the cross.[67] Her prayers that they be removed were answered: the bleeding stopped, but the scars remained.[68] Lidwina of Schiedam (1380–1433), a beautiful girl with numerous suitors already at the age of twelve, broke a rib on her right side while ice skating.[69] This was the beginning of thirty years of intense suffering during which she ate very little. On the advice of her confessor, Jan Pot, she began a practice of meditating on the sufferings of Christ. After an eight-year apprenticeship in accordance with the received or traditional form, she became a "visionary."[70] According to Jacob Brugman, Lidwina also received the five stigmata, which closed after her prayer, but a careful look at Brugman's account suggests that all of this was *visionary* and not actual.[71] Others who are reported to have received the stigmata include Teresa of Ávila (1515–82) and Catherine of Sienna (1347–80).[72] Like her namesake in the early church who was martyred under the Roman emperor Maxentius (ca. 278–312; emperor from 306 to 312),[73] Catherine had a ring

67. Ed. note: The Beguines and Beghards "were Christian lay religious orders that were active in Northern Europe, particularly in the Low Countries in the 13th–16th centuries. Their members lived in semi-monastic communities but did not take formal religious vows. That is, although they promised not to marry 'as long as they lived as Beguines,' to quote one of the early Rules, they were free to leave at any time. Beguines were part of a larger spiritual revival movement of the thirteenth century that stressed imitation of Christ's life through voluntary poverty, care of the poor and sick, and religious devotion" (https://en.wikipedia.org/wiki/Beguines_and_Beghards). On Gertrude, see Görres, *Stigmata*, 70–71. Görres does not mention the "milk miracle" with which Bavinck leads his description of Gertrude. Bavinck's source for this is Moll, *Johannes Brugman*, 2:105.

68. Moll, *Johannes Brugman*, 2:106. Ed. note: Johannes Brugman (d. 1453) was a Franciscan German friar who wrote two biographies of Lidwina; on the basis of the first, Thomas à Kempis produced his *St. Lydwine of Schiedam*. Moll discusses Brugman's biographies in *Johannes Brugman*, 2:107–42.

69. Ed. note: Bavinck says that she broke her leg, but most other sources (including Moll, *Johannes Brugman*, 2:110) indicate that she broke her rib. See also Albers, "St. Lidwina" (http://www.newadvent.org/cathen/09233a.htm). Lidwina is believed to be one of the first documented cases of multiple sclerosis; she is the patron saint of skaters.

70. LO: *secundum traditam sibi formulam*; DO: *schouwster*.

71. Moll, *Johannes Brugman*, 2:140.

72. See Zöckler, "Katharina von Siena."

73. Ed. note: Bavinck does not identify this earlier Catherine but clearly has in mind Catherine of Alexandria (d. early fourth century), who is "one of the most popular early Christian martyrs and one of the Fourteen Holy Helpers. She is not mentioned before the 9th century, and her historicity is doubtful. According to legend, she was an extremely learned young girl of noble birth who protested the persecution of Christians under the Roman emperor Maxentius—whose wife and several soldiers she converted—and defeated the most eminent scholars summoned by Maxentius to oppose her. In the Middle Ages, when the story of her mystical marriage to

placed on her finger by Christ himself as a sign of betrothal to him. "In Pisa, in 1375 . . . she received the stigmata (visible, at her request, only to herself)."[74] Stigmata also appear in our days. Anne Catherine Emmerich (1774–1824), born in Coesfeld, Münster, received the stigmata in 1811 [or 1813].[75] In answer to prayer, bleeding ceased at the end of 1818, and the wounds closed,[76] although the wounds became red and occasionally bloody on Fridays. Similarly, Maria von Mörl (1812–68) from Caldaro (Kaltern) in Tyrol, Italy, received her stigmata in 1833 and on Thursday evenings and Fridays experienced "clear blood [that] flowed in drops from the wounds."[77] The most recent example is Louise Lateau (1850–83),[78] who first received the stigmata (on her left side, her hands, and her feet) on April 21, 1868. Later, as also experienced by other stigmatics such as Anne Catherine Emmerich, she received an additional wound on her shoulder (on which Christ carried his cross) and a wreath of wounds on her forehead (from the crown of thorns). These wounds "appear without apparent cause on the night of Thursday to Friday and disappear the next night. It will do this until her death in 1883."[79] Other phenomena include ecstasy, insensitivity to pain (even to electric shocks), visions, cessation of sleep and food deprivation for three years (except for communion),[80] and being able to distinguish consecrated bread from unconsecrated or a priest from a layman.

Undoubtedly, there is deception, imagination, and exaggeration in the phenomenon of the stigmata, but its factuality is firmly attested. How do we explain it? The Roman Catholic Church considers them miracles, but they should be explained on the basis of the power of the human soul on the body. The soul is involved in the formation of the body in its entirety, a fact that is manifested in many ways. Spiritual depression comes to expression in

Christ was widely circulated, she was one of the most popular saints" (http://www.britannica.com/biography/Saint-Catherine-of-Alexandria).

74. Noffke, *Catherine of Sienna*, 5. Ed. note: Bavinck gave 1370 as the date of the stigmata, but this fuses it with another event of that year, Catherine's "mystical death"—"four hours during which she experienced ecstatic union with God while her body seemed lifeless to observers" (Noffke, 4). Bavinck also says that the stigmata were only "internal (in her feeling)."

75. Ed. note: Bavinck provides 1811 as the date, but reports of the stigmata began in early 1813 (https://en.wikipedia.org/wiki/Anne_Catherine_Emmerich).

76. Ed. note: Bavinck gives 1819 as the date.

77. Ed. note: The quotation, along with several details not given by Bavinck, is from http://www.mysticsofthechurch.com/2010/07/maria-von-morl-stigmatic-ecstatic.html.

78. Zöckler, "Louise Lateau."

79. See https://en.wikipedia.org/wiki/Louise_Lateau.

80. Ed. note: A canonical investigation of Louise was opened in 1868. It concluded that "there was no conscious deception in the stigmata and the ecstasies." But "abstention from food and the cessation of sleep were not medically attested by the commission" (https://en.wikipedia.org/wiki/Louise_Lateau).

bodily [ailments], some of which are permanent. A major scare (frightening anxiety) can result in a person's hair turning gray; pregnant women who are frightened give birth to children who bear an imprint of the particular fright.[81] What is required for the appearance of the stigmata is a fervent, glowing power of imagination[82] that can internalize the known object (e.g., Christ on the cross). This has to be accompanied by a weak, particularly susceptible and tender body.[83] Imagination is a wondrous faculty, and we can imagine ourselves into real illness. Operating through our nerves, the imagination impresses its object on a receptive body. The visions, ecstasies, apparitions, revelations, appearances of Jesus and Mary, angels, light, and similar phenomena, all of which were especially prominent in the thirteenth and fourteenth centuries, must also be attributed to the enormous power of the imagination. Those two centuries were characterized by sentimentality, youthful, fresh living, and a drive toward action. Innumerable "Lives of Jesus" appeared everywhere.[84] All of them were written in living colors, with a practical goal not only to think deeply about his life but to represent it, visually to internalize it. It was important to *see* Jesus walking, suffering, hanging on the cross.[85] These "Lives of Jesus" were read daily and repeatedly in a single week; for example, the flight to Egypt on Monday, preaching in the synagogue of Nazareth on Tuesday, fellowship with Mary and Lazarus on Wednesday, the passion on Thursday, Friday, and Saturday, and the resurrection on Sunday. Then the cycle was repeated from the beginning.[86] The imitation of Christ is the great all-determining basic idea of this mystical literature,[87] the means to holy living and for drawing us away from the world toward that which is higher, toward contemplation, to climb toward the vision of patriarchs, prophets, martyrs, even on occasion to a vision of Jesus and God himself.[88] All devout men and women of that day, in the monasteries of Diepenveen, Deventer, Windesheim, and Zwolle, strove to become Christ-formed or God-formed.[89]

81. Ed. note: The belief that a child's appearance was influenced by the experiences of the pregnant mother dates back to the Greek physician Galen and continued into the twentieth century.

82. DO: *gloeiende verbeeldingskracht.*

83. Hamberger, "Stigmatisation"; cf. Perty, *Die Anthropologie*, 2:428–32. Ed. note: Bavinck indicates that his source for this reference is Zöckler, "Louise Lateau," 9n; Moll, *Johannes Brugman*, 2:88–90.

84. Moll, *Johannes Brugman*, 2:1–97.

85. Moll, *Johannes Brugman*, 2:56–58.

86. Bonaventure, according to Moll, *Johannes Brugman*, 2:59.

87. Moll, *Johannes Brugman*, 2:63.

88. Moll, *Johannes Brugman*, 2:67.

89. Moll, *Johannes Brugman*, 2:72.

However, for many the imitation of Christ amounted to nothing more than a mere repetition of single deeds and circumstances of Jesus. A few understood it better,[90] but most conceived of the imitation of Christ as a series of circumstances, deeds, and expressions that had to be copied literally. Some went into churches or chapels to look for a "despised little corner" so that they could be like Jesus, who was born "in a house full of holes." Others walked on the street with bowed heads and eyes cast down as Jesus had done on his way to the cross.[91] Reading about Jesus before the council, people would slap themselves, flog themselves as he was flogged, and extend their arms as he was crucified. All this led naturally to stigmata and to visions.[92]

A powerful imagination having been aroused, people really believed that they heard Jesus's own voice, saw him "bloodied and flogged"[93] as though he were being flogged right in front of them, saw him crying in the manger right before them.[94] That these visions were subjective is evident from the fact that everyone sees these objects just so with an imagination shaped by their own knowledge and individuality.[95] Nonetheless, one can find here and there a purer, more spiritual grasp of the imitation of Christ. Examples are Bernard of Clairvaux, Bonaventure, Tauler, and especially Thomas à Kempis, author of *The Imitation of Christ*.[96] This work has a weak, sentimental tone, is written in Netherlandish Latin, monotonous and repetitive but lyrical. Its main theme is asceticism, flight from the world, the vanity of all things. Every part of it proclaims the cross and is an education about the way of the cross. Christ is the expression of that cross, his entire life a martyrdom. The imitation of Christ is about conforming to that suffering and imitating it, and this happens through love. But Thomas also turns attention to the ethical, to the necessity of imitating Christ's humility and tenderness. Thomas is practical: it is more important to have a good conscience and to keep God's commandments than to know definitions and understand the Trinity. This is the genuine imitation of Christ.[97]

90. Moll, *Johannes Brugman*, 2:36.
91. Moll, *Johannes Brugman*, 2:73–74.
92. Moll, *Johannes Brugman*, 2:79–88.
93. Moll, *Johannes Brugman*, 2:82.
94. Moll, *Johannes Brugman*, 2:85–87.
95. Moll, *Johannes Brugman*, 2:88–97.
96. Gass, *Geschichte der christlichen Ethik*, 1:426; Bähring, *Thomas von Kempen*, 251–56; Abraham Kuyper, *E Voto Dordraceno*, 1:70–77 (Lord's Day 21, originally published in *De Heraut*, no. 564 [October 14, 1888]). Ed. note: Bavinck includes in this list "the author of the sermon" and refers to "Moll, 1:34–36." The "author" is Johannes Brugman, and Moll includes the sermon in question in *Johannes Brugman*, 1:250–59 (appendix 5).
97. Gass, *Geschichte der christlichen Ethik*, 1:427–29.

Imitation of Christ among Protestants[98]

Protestants usually understand this imitation in terms of various virtues such as obedience to God, love, humility, goodness, uprightness, suffering, and holiness.[99] Witsius distinguishes between an imitation of Christ in his humanity and as Mediator (only insofar as believers are also prophets, priests, and kings), and an imitation of God.[100] Not a great deal is said about the imitation of Christ because people sought the norm for the Christian life in the law of the Ten Commandments and not in the person of Christ. For the most part it was discussed only in treatments of cross-bearing and self-denial (Calvin), as well as in discussions of our mystical union with Christ, in which we participate in his death and resurrection.[101] Jesus is merely an example for Socinians, Remonstrants, and rationalists, and not his person but his teaching and commandments. The nineteenth-century Groningen "school" of theology also thought of Jesus as an example.[102] God is the Great Educator, and this education is accomplished especially through Christ, who has revealed divine truth, true human happiness, the moral ideal. Therefore, Jesus is also the demonstration of God's love. Similarly, T. Cannegieter, who put it even more strongly: "Jesus is the normal person."[103]

98. Witsius, *Prakticale godgeleertheid*, 130 (chap. 17); Pictet, *De christelyke zedekunst*, 333–36 (IV.xiv); Buddeus, *Institutiones Theologiae Moralis*, 340; Ridderus (d. 1683), *Het leven van onzen Heere Jesus Christus*; Vitringa, *Korte schets*, VII; van Leeuwarden, *De bevestigde Christen*, 211; Voetius and Hoornbeeck, *Disputaty*, IV.130–32; Schneckenburger, *Vergleichende Darstellung*, 1:143–44; 2:242.

99. Pictet, *De christelyke zedekunst*, 333–36 (IV.xiv).

100. Witsius, *Prakticale godgeleertheid*, 130 (chap. 17).

101. LO: *unio mystica*; Calvin, *Institutes*, III.vii–viii.

102. Ed. note: We are using "school" to capture the conventional Dutch word "richting" (lit., "direction"). This school was a Schleiermacher-influenced reaction against theological intellectualism and rationalism. The true seat of religion was believed to be found in feeling rather than reason. Its slogan was "Niet de leer, maar de Heer" (lit., "not doctrine but the Lord," which in the Dutch language has a rhyming quality lacking in English). Its inspiration came from University of Utrecht philosophy professor (1804–39) Th. W. van Heusde, whom Bavinck describes as a charismatic teacher influencing "a circle of students in Utrecht and another circle in Groningen." Bavinck adds,

> Soon afterwards, in a very remarkable manner, many of these students were settled in close proximity to one another, in the city and Province of Groningen, as professors and ministers. J. F. Van Oordt and P. Hofstede de Groot were called to chairs in the University in 1829, Pareau in 1831. Van Herwerden became minister of the church of Groningen in 1831, Amshoff in 1832, etc. In 1835 some twelve of them organized an association which published a periodical, *Waarheid en Liefde* (*A Periodical for Cultured Christians*), 1837–72. In addition to this they formulated their ideas in manuals, covering all branches of theology. Their *Compendium Dogmatices et Apologetices* was published in 1845. (Bavinck, "Recent Dogmatic Thought," 213)

See also Roessingh, *De moderne theologie*, 26–44; Roessingh, *Het modernisme*, 55–60; ten Zijthoff, *Sources of Secession*, 104–6; Pareau, *Initia Institutionis Christianae Moralis*.

103. Cannegieter, *De zedelijkheid*, 66–69, 118–20, 160–62, 165–69; Hugenholtz, *Studiën*, 2:32–33.

Modernist theologians[104] let go even the idea of Jesus as an example, because they also gave up on his sinlessness and therefore no longer saw in him the moral ideal, since it is not possible to embody an ideal for everyone. Nonetheless, Jesus does embody an ideal—namely, as the founder of a religion—but not *the* ideal and therefore not a universal example.[105] Furthermore, Jesus was a man uninvolved in societal and political matters, unmarried, and therefore unable in countless areas of life and for numerous people to serve as an example. In other words, he was limited, one-sided in character, in calling, and so forth. By contrast, recent ethicists have begun increasingly to speak of the imitation of Christ, precisely because the norm of the moral law disapppears more and more.[106] Some conceive of Christ especially as an example,[107] while others argue that Jesus, as an itinerant teacher, could teach only in his day and not now. He does not fit into any of our current vocations and offices (minister, professor, and so forth).[108] And still others emphasize that he was indeed a specific character, an individual.[109] He was a *man* and not a woman, a Jew, and he developed in a specific direction and did not make use of all his gifts. Christ as a person is indeed a foundation for ethics, but not his example. He penetrates everyone; truth is not a matter of being a copy of Jesus; it is to share his family likeness.[110] One cannot derive homiletics, catechesis, or missions from his example; Timothy is a far better source.

Modern people have no moral ideal, no example; they are only infatuated with progress toward a misty ideal. They are, therefore, restless, empty, without authority, disconnected, and emancipated. Someone who does not need a Savior also needs no moral example,[111] but it is only in Christ that we know what it is to be human. Christ can be imitated only by those who believe in him as Savior; if he were only an example, he would frighten us away, accuse us. As example, Christ must be above us and yet be like us, a true human being. Christ is not only a great man, but is unique among all the "great men"; he alone founded a world religion, he alone is the Giving One. His organizing

104. Ed. note: Bavinck inserts a parenthetical reference here to lecture notes (*dictaat*) from his Leiden teacher Abraham Kuenen.

105. Thus Strauss, according to Ritschl, *Die christliche Lehre von der Rechtfertigung und Versöhnung*, 3:350, 389.

106. See D. G. Monrad, *World of Prayer*, 37–56; cf. Martensen, *Christian Ethics*, 1:237–41 (§71).

107. De Wette, *Sittenlehre*, §68.

108. Palmer, "Das Vorbild Jesu," 690.

109. Ullmann, *Sinlessness of Jesus*, 62–82; Ullmann, *Sündlosigkeit Jesu*, 62–82; C. F. Schmid, *Biblical Theology*, 71–76. Cf. Martensen, *Christian Ethics*, 1:237.

110. Cf. Schleiermacher, *Die christliche Sitte*, 291.

111. Cf. Martensen, *Christian Ethics*, 1:142.

principle was unique: freedom and love; his goal was to establish the kingdom of God; his means were merely his own person. He is the turning point of history who provides and unfolds his example in the midst of many contrasts. In him, the ideal of moral freedom is fulfilled; in him is no discord with the law; he was sinless.[112] He possesses a completely harmonious character[113] of general and particular love, the masculine and the feminine, the lion and the lamb, a contemplative and practical nature; he engaged in conflict and acted freely without passionate emotions, while still experiencing a rich emotional life, a holy pathos. Always his own master, he remained faithful, balancing righteousness and love, sorrow and joy; he is the true human, the key individual, universally human and yet a particular individual.[114] But also the moral ideal of love is fulfilled in him, in relation to us and in his obedience to the Father, with respect to protecting (receiving) and active (giving) love, active and tolerant love.[115] The ideal of *personal righteousness* also is fulfilled in Christ, the example of glory (including the miracles).[116] In conclusion, the imitation of Christ is a life lived according to Christ's example, in Christ's power. Christ is an example, not as mediator, but in what from his disposition we must carry forward in everything—namely, love.[117] This applies not only to the "religious," preachers, martyrs, and monks. What is needed is conformity to Christ's will; a monk lives for self.[118]

Christ is not an example merely in his disposition, as rationalism contends, excluding him as Redeemer.[119] Nor can we follow the mystics, for whom Christ is an example only of the mystical union with God.[120] Martensen also conceives of the Christian life as an imitation of Christ and divides this imitation into two chief virtues, love and liberty.[121] The new life not only contains a more normal unfolding of the law but also has an objective norm that stands above and is external to us.[122] By means of this, God brings his personal will to clearer awareness in our hearts. In Christ, the law is and remains the norm

112. Martensen, *Christian Ethics*, 1:247–49.
113. Martensen, *Christian Ethics*, 1:252.
114. Martensen, *Christian Ethics*, 1:257.
115. Martensen, *Christian Ethics*, 1:260, 273.
116. Martensen, *Christian Ethics*, 1:280–83.
117. Martensen, *Christian Ethics*, 1:293–94.
118. Martensen, *Christian Ethics*, 1:296–98.
119. Martensen, *Christian Ethics*, 1:299.
120. Martensen, *Christian Ethics*, 1:300. Ed. note: At this point Bavinck inserts the name "Kierkegaard." Martensen discusses Kierkegaard on pp. 302–7 (§§99–100).
121. Martensen, *Christian Ethics*, 1:191–202 (§§59–62: "The Kingdom of God and the Kingdom of Humanity: Redemption and Emancipation"); Martensen discusses the imitation of Christ on pp. 293–302 (§§95–98).
122. Harless, *System of Christian Ethics*, 299–305 (§32).

for believers (Rom. 10:4; Col. 2:17). The imitation of Christ consists in Christ taking shape within us; Christ is not an example in a legal sense, except for the unconverted.[123] According to Beck, the imitation of Christ is an entry upon his path of atonement.[124] The Christian life-journey has Christ as its content (substance), as its foundational law, so that the life of Christ becomes ours only through our abiding in him. This is a life that develops toward Christ; the Christian life is nothing other than a transformation into the image of Christ. Christ as our example presupposes his likeness to us ("flesh," σάρξ), but also our likeness to him ("spirit," πνεῦμα). Christ is an example only for believers; the Spirit makes us to be like Christ in his cross, death, resurrection, etc., first inwardly and then outwardly.[125]

Imitation of Christ as the Form of the Spiritual Life

Imitation of Christ as the form of the spiritual life does not consist in (1) the repetition of Jesus in one's manner of life, as monks believed: in poverty, chastity, and obedience. Therefore, also not in reenacting his suffering, in suffering again as the martyrs conceived it. In a word, the imitation of Christ is not a matter of copying, mimicking, or simulating Christ. This is apparent from the fact that those who want to be like Jesus in this way are actually quite different from him.[126] Though they appear outwardly to be like Jesus, inwardly they are far from him. After all, Jesus lived for humanity, suffered and died for them; the monk and the martyr who seek death live for themselves, are preoccupied with themselves. This view thus leads to externalism, to superficiality, to outward conformity without inner relationship. The imitation of Christ is not limited to the religious even though during his travels on earth it often consisted of a specific forsaking of family and occupation, following and preaching Jesus; this cannot be everyone's calling. Christ wants not only renunciation of the world but also to conserve the world, to save the world (John 3:17). Asceticism is only one exercise of virtue, an exercise that has no content other than the exercise itself.

Nor does it consist (2) in the dominant view of many mystics, like Eckhardt, Tauler, Suso, and Ruysbroeck. They do regard Christ as the true God-man, but not as Redeemer;[127] actually he is only an example of the mystical

---

123. Vilmar, *Theologische Moral*, 2/3:92–94.
124. J. T. Beck, *Vorlesungen*, 1:90.
125. J. T. Beck, *Vorlesungen*, 1:118–22; cf. 2:92–96 and 58–61, where Christ is called the law, the norm of the new life.
126. Martensen, *Christian Ethics*, 1:293.
127. DO: *Verzoener.*

union with God, an example of love, patience, and prayer. They have greater sympathy with Jesus, just like the women on the road to the cross, and they weep about and with him (Francis of Assisi) rather than being bowed under the consciousness of guilt and seeking justification in him. In the sentimental Middle Ages the goal was to preach about the suffering of Christ as movingly as possible; whoever cried the most was deemed the most pious. This is no imitation of Christ, but traveling alongside him.

The imitation of Christ also does not consist (3) in a rationalistic keeping of his commandments, in the modern notion of being animated by his "spirit." This completely sets aside the example of Jesus as a person and has no clue how to deal with Jesus's call to "forsake everything for my name's sake." Jesus as a person becomes a matter of indifference, as J. G. Fichte noted; in this case the imitation of Christ is completely lost.

Here is what constitutes the imitation of Christ:

1. The imitation of Christ means acknowledging Christ as Redeemer, as Mediator. This is the condition for the imitation of Christ. Anyone who needs no Redeemer also needs no example. Modernists[128] have no savior and also no ideal; they "take a shot in the dark," have no purpose, are restless and driven, or become indifferent. A holy person like Jesus can never be an example unless he is first our Savior. Otherwise, he would frighten us away, just as the law that he fulfilled presses us down rather than lifts us up.

The imitation of Christ, therefore, is only possible in faith. Christ is the example not for everyone but only for those who are regenerated. Imitating him is the only form of the spiritual life. Therefore, our lives can be directed *to* Christ only when they proceed *from* him and abide *in* him. The mystical union with Christ is the foundation of the imitation of Christ.

2. Inwardly, the imitation of Christ consists in Christ taking shape within us (Vilmar), our entering into permanent communion with him, particularly in the fellowship of his suffering. As such, it has two parts: self-denial and cross-bearing. The Holy Spirit conforms us to Christ in his suffering, death, resurrection, and glorification. To be sure, we do not follow Christ as Mediator; the mediatorial work is his alone. An abstract separation of Christ's virtue into those we should follow and those we should not is impossible. Christ was always Mediator, but always was the moral ideal as well. Therefore, we must imitate him in everything, albeit in our own way, with our own individual personality, status, social class, and calling. In addition, we may not say that Christ is to be imitated only as a human person and not as God; again, this is an impossible, abstract separation. Christ is

---

128. Martensen, *Christian Ethics*, 1:237.

to be imitated as he presents himself, as the God-man, in his entire being, walk, and conduct.

3. Most characteristically, the imitation of Christ consists in shaping our lives in accord with Christ. Stated differently, the content, the material of our life comes from Christ; but now the shape of this life must take on the shape of Christ's own life. If the material of our life were physically the same as that of Christ, then its shape would have to be exactly the same as his; that is, then we would be God-men, Mediators, Christs, as the mystics and "ethical theologians" believe.[129] If the material of our life were nothing more than our actual natural life, awakened by Christ's example, then its shape would be simply a following of Christ's example, as the rationalists believe. The material of our lives differs from or corresponds to the life of Christ in the same way and in the same respect as its shape differs from or corresponds to the shape of Christ's life.[130] Now the material of our life is not physically the same life in Christ (as if Christ's own life overflowed in ours in a pantheistic, mystical manner), but is ethically the same, not of the same substance but of the same qualities. That is to say, even as Jesus is the Son of God, so we are also God's children; we are conformed to the image of the Son (Rom. 8:29). God re-creating us in his image is what Christ has earned and acquired for us. The content of our life, therefore, is nothing other than the image of God—namely, knowledge, righteousness, and holiness, which are ethical qualities that correspond to those in Christ, who is the perfect Image of God.

So then, in the same way that the material content of our life coincides with Christ, so must its form (shape). The image of God must be manifest in us in the same form, come to outward expression in the same way, as with Christ. The shape of our life is not physically, substantially, like the form of Christ; if it were, then copying and repeating the life journey of Jesus would be the highest, the best imitation, and the monk and martyr would, as such, be the best Christians. On the other side, our life is not only outwardly like that of Christ, as the rationalists posit, but is acquired through Christ and arises in us only through faith—that is, by connection to the person of Christ through mystical union. For that reason, the shape of our life does not consist of following the spirit of Jesus, of a disposition (rationalists, modernists). The imitation of Christ is, therefore, not a copy of the person of Jesus; it is

129. Ed. note: Bavinck is referring to a specific school of nineteenth-century Dutch theology represented by Daniel Chantepie de la Saussaye (1818–74) and J. H. Gunning (1829–1905). The Dutch term *ethische theologie* does not mean "moral theology" but is more appropriately understood as "existential" since these theologians regarded intellectualism as the greatest obstacle to a living faith in Christ and following him. See also chap. 6, §16, above.

130. DO: *vorm*; LO: *forma*.

not a Christification of believers. At the same time, it is also not a matter of conforming to his commandments apart from his person. The true imitation of Christ stands between these two. This consists of shaping the life that exists only in and from communion with Christ in accord with his moral example; it is acquiring a Christ-*shape*[131] in us, so that others can know Christ from and through us. This correspondence of our life's shape with that of Christ manifests itself in a variety of virtues,[132] but especially in righteousness and love. Righteousness or holiness is complete agreement with the law—that is, with moral freedom. For us believers, the law no longer stands over against us abstractly, but in Christ; in Christ the law is our norm (Harless). Christ is the moral ideal, the living law. As the moral ideal, he is love, love for God and people, because love is the fulfillment of the law. He is the union of receiving and giving love, of active and enduring love, of contemplative and practical love. The apostles continually point to these virtues, especially patient endurance and suffering (Rom. 8:17; 2 Cor. 4:10; Gal. 6:17; Phil. 3:10; 2 Thess. 3:5; Heb. 12:2; 1 Pet. 2:21–25; 3:17–18; 4:1, 13), love (2 Cor. 8:9; Eph. 5:2; Phil. 2:5–11), and holiness (1 Pet. 2:21–25). And in this sense Christ is indeed an example and can be that example for everyone; he is a fully harmonious character, a union of masculine stability and femininity, of strength and tenderness, of contemplation and practice, of sorrow and joy, always master of himself, faithful, both universally human and yet particularly individual.[133]

§22. THE GROWTH OF THE SPIRITUAL LIFE

Spiritual Development

There is development in the spiritual life.[134] Holy Scripture teaches this. The Old Testament supplies little information on the subject. In the Psalms it is not so much the stages of the spiritual life, but its various circumstances that come into view (see chap. 10). It is mostly strong believers who speak there, who nonetheless find themselves in various situations in which their faith is strong (Pss. 121; 138), oppressed (Pss. 4; 7; 26; 64), or in doubt (Pss. 77; 88), and others. There are places in the Old Testament [where the shepherd metaphor] speaks to this: "He will tend his flock like a shepherd; he will gather the lambs in his arms; he will carry them in his bosom, and gently

131. DO: *gestalte.*
132. Vitringa, *Korte schets*, 113–16 (VII §§6–10).
133. Martensen, *Christian Ethics*, 1:316–19.
134. Schneckenburger, *Vergleichende Darstellung*, 2:166–82 (§10: "Das christliche Leben in seiner graduellen Entwicklung und die evangelische Vollkommenheit: Lehre von der Heiligung").

lead those that are with young" (Isa. 40:11). In Ezekiel 34 the Lord rebukes
the false shepherds of his people who take care only of themselves, and says,
"I myself will be the shepherd of my sheep, and I myself will make them lie
down, declares the Lord GOD. I will seek the lost, and I will bring back the
strayed, and I will bind up the injured, and I will strengthen the weak, and the
fat and the strong I will destroy. I will feed them in justice" (Ezek. 34:15–16).
The prophet Isaiah comforts the afflicted with messianic hope: "A bruised
reed [the poor crushed by guilt] he [the Messiah] will not break, and a faintly
burning wick he will not quench" (Isa. 42:3). "The Spirit of the Lord GOD is
upon me . . . he has sent me to bind up the brokenhearted . . . that they may
be called oaks of righteousness, the planting of the LORD, that he may be
glorified" (Isa. 61:1, 3).

In the New Testament, 1 John 2:12–14 is the locus classicus. In the previous verses John has described the main characteristics of the new life as a
"walking in the light." Now he proceeds to exhort the congregation and
addresses them as children [τεκνία, παιδία], youth [νεανίσκοι], and fathers
[πατέρες]. Some have understood these terms to refer not to a difference in
natural age but rather to the stages and periods of the Christian life.[135] But a
difference in age is certainly meant (Calvin, Erasmus, Meyer, annotations of
the *Statenvertaling*),[136] which would nonetheless entail a weaker or stronger
degree of spiritual life. But note that John does not speak of four stages of life
in the strict sense (so that τεκνία and παιδία would both refer to children) but
three. In verse 12, "children" is used in a general, all-inclusive sense (Calvin,
Luther, Meyer);[137] otherwise the sequence would be children, fathers, and
youth, which is illogical. But, according to some, "children" here refers to
three distinct groups: fathers, youth, and children, while others contend that
only two groups are in view (Meyer).

The argument against three goes as follows: (a) In verse 14, "I have written
unto you, fathers . . . young men" (KJV), only two groups are distinguished;
there is no mention of children; and (b) verse 13c must certainly be read as "I
have written [ἔγραψα] to you, children" rather than "I write to you, children"

135. Vitringa, *Korte schets*, 128–30 (VIII §3). Ed. note: Bavinck only provides the names
of Clement, Oecumenius, Cajetan, and Grotius; the specific references have been supplied by
the editor. Clement of Alexandria, *Miscellanies* VII.10 (*ANF* 2:538–40); Oecumenius, *Commentariorum in Novum Testamentum* (PG 119:635–38); Cajetan, *Epistolae Pauli*, 222; Grotius,
Annotationes, 8:159–61.
136. Calvin, *Gospel of John and 1 John*, 250; Erasmus, *In Novum Testamentum Annotationes*, 765–66; Huther and Meyer, *General Epistles*, 513–14.
137. GrO: τεκνία. Ed. note: See the preceding note for Calvin and Meyer. Luther does not
specifically address the meaning of τεκνία in v. 12 in his *Lectures on 1 John* (*Luther's Works*,
30:244).

[which would be γράφω ὑμῖν, παιδία]. And if we distinguish two groups in this way, it becomes "I write to you, children [γράφω ὑμῖν, τεκνία, v. 12], and more specifically to the fathers and youth among you" (v. 13a, b); "I have written to you, children [ἔγραψα ὑμῖν, παιδία, v. 13c—also used in a general sense, just as in v. 18 = τεκνία], and, more specifically, to the fathers and youth" (v. 14). It is strange that Calvin, who in verse 13 distinguishes three groups among the τεκνία (while in fact there are only two) judged verse 14 to be redundant and inserted by unskilled readers and copyists.[138] "Now I write" [γράφω] in verses 12 and 13a, b and "I have written" [ἔγραψα] are used interchangeably in verses 13c and 14. But "I have written" [ἔγραψα] refers not to an earlier letter but to this same First Epistle of John. John intends to say, "I am writing, I am busily engaged in writing to you fathers and youth (to please walk in the light), yes, as I just now wrote to you already in the first chapter and in verses 1–11 of the second chapter of this letter." And now John continues, "I am writing to you, little children [in general], to walk in the light because your sins are forgiven for his name's sake" (the forgiveness of sins is basic to the Christian life), and more specifically "to you fathers [that is, the older ones], because you [have learned to] know him [Christ, not God] who is from the beginning"[139] (cf. John 1:1). The older ones, who had profound insight into who Christ was, definitely possessed this knowledge. John writes and has already written to the youth to walk in the light, "because you have overcome the evil one" (which the older ones certainly had also done, but which the strong youth had only recently done, so that they had to take care lest they lose hold of this victory) and because (as is added in 2:14) "you are strong"—namely, in the Spirit (not in their own strength)—because "the word of God abides in you."

The result is then, first of all, that John makes a distinction according to age, but at the same time there is also a corresponding degree of spiritual life. He assumes, however, not three but only two groups: youth and fathers. Second, he does not portray the youth as weaker in the faith; on the contrary, they are strong; yet they are different from the fathers since their fight against Satan is more intense, and they must see to it that they retain the victory, while the fathers, who have obtained the victory for quite some time already, rely more on Christ and increase in their knowledge of Christ. He mentions no distinction between a refuge-seeking faith and confident faith or anything of that nature, but he does distinguish between militant and reposing faith.

In 1 Corinthians 3:1–3 Paul says that the Corinthians are still "of the flesh"—that is, born of flesh (John 3:6), which is even stronger than "fleshly"

---

138. Calvin, *Gospel of John and 1 John*, 251–53.
139. GrO: ὁ ἦν ἀπ' ἀρχῆς.

(1 Cor. 3:3).[140] They are infant children, mere "beginners," in contrast to being
"mature" in Christ, so that they still have to be fed with milk (the simple
introductory teaching of the gospel) and not with solid food (the higher,
more advanced teaching and wisdom, as, e.g., in 1 Cor. 15, found among the
mature, 2:6–16).[141] They were weak and continued to be weak, not because
of their weak, narrow-minded faith or the like, but because there was envy
and strife among them and because they walked according to their human
nature, with individuals saying, "I am of Apollos," and the like. In the words
of the apostle Peter, "So put away all malice and all deceit and hypocrisy and
envy and all slander. Like newborn infants, long for the pure spiritual milk,
that by it you may grow up into salvation" (1 Pet. 2:1–2).[142]

In Hebrews 5:12–14, the author intends to explain how Christ is a priest
in the order of Melchizedek (v. 10) and says that this involves many things
that are hard to explain (v. 11), but he bemoans the fact that his readers are
so slow to learn, when by this time they ought to be teachers: "For though
by this time you ought to be teachers, you need someone to teach you again
the basic principles of the oracles of God,"[143] that is, the rudiments, the
elementary things going back to the beginning—that is to say, the basic fun-
damentals of God's words. Consequently, you have become people who need
milk (elementary instruction in Christianity, such as catechism) and not solid
food (further instruction in the essence of Christianity, the maturation we
discuss in the next section of this chapter). This is inadequate because "anyone who lives on milk, being still an infant, is not acquainted with the teaching about righteousness"—that is, is inexperienced in the gospel, namely, in
Christianity.[144] By contrast, solid food is for the mature, "who by constant use
have trained themselves to distinguish good from evil."[145] This is a reference
not to narrow-minded faith but rather to lack of knowledge, inexperience
in Christian doctrine, and thus a lack of practice in distinguishing between
what is good and what is evil—that is, in intellectually distinguishing pure
doctrine from that which is harmful.

That there is development in the spiritual life is further shown when Jesus
refers to those of little faith:[146] "If that is how God clothes the grass of the
field, which is here today and tomorrow is thrown into the fire, will he not

140. GrO: σάρκινος; σαρκικός.
141. GrO: νήπιος; τέλειος; γάλα; βρῶμα; σοφία; τέλειοι.
142. GrO: ἀρτιγέννητα βρέφη τὸ λογικὸν ἄδολον γάλα.
143. GrO: τὰ στοιχεῖα τῆς ἀρχῆς τῶν λογίων τοῦ θεοῦ.
144. GrO: νήπιος ἐστιν; ἄπειρος λόγου δικαιοσύνης, v. 13.
145. GrO: στερεὰ τροφή; τέλειοι; διὰ τὴν ἕξιν τὰ αἰσθητήρια; πρὸς διάκρισιν καλοῦ τε καὶ
κακοῦ, v. 14.
146. GrO: ὀλιγόπιστοι.

much more clothe you—you of little faith?" (Matt. 6:30; Luke 12:28). During the storm on the Sea of Galilee, Jesus asked his disciples, "You of little faith, why are you so afraid?" (Matt. 8:26). Similarly to Peter, walking on the sea, "You of little faith, why did you doubt?" (Matt. 14:31). And when the crowd following him was hungry, again to the disciples: "You of little faith, why are you talking among yourselves about having no bread?" (Matt. 16:8). This "little faith" contrasts with the "great faith" that Jesus found in the centurion (Matt. 8:10; Luke 7:9) and in the Canaanite woman (Matt. 15:28). For Jesus, people of little faith are not those who doubt their own status, but those who lack confidence in God's or Jesus's power and love. The distinction between infants and the mature is similar.[147] The term "infant"[148] can be used in a positive sense: "I thank you, Father, Lord of heaven and earth, that you have hidden these things from the wise and understanding and revealed them to little children" (Matt. 11:25; par. Luke 10:21). Here and in Matthew 21:16 ("Out of the mouth of infants and nursing babies / you have prepared praise"), the term has the positive sense of "simple," "childlike." However, it can also be used in a more or less unfavorable sense: "When I was a child, I spoke like a child, I thought like a child, I reasoned like a child. When I became a man, I gave up childish ways" (1 Cor. 13:11); "The heir, as long as he is a child, is no different from a slave, though he is the owner of everything. . . . In the same way we also, when we were children, were enslaved to the elementary principles of the world" (Gal. 4:1, 3). Romans 2:20 is definitely unfavorable: "an instructor of the foolish, a teacher of children."[149] Similarly, Paul in 1 Corinthians 3:1 ("I . . . could not address you as spiritual people, but as people of the flesh, as infants in Christ") and Ephesians 4:14 ("No longer be children, tossed to and fro by the waves and carried about by every wind of doctrine").[150] And in the passage from Hebrews we have already considered (Heb. 5:13), anyone who lives on milk is inexperienced, a child.

Toward Spiritual Maturity in Christ

The contrasting term to "infant" [νήπιος] in the New Testament is τέλειος, which has several layers of meaning: (a) *perfect* in a moral sense, irreproachable (Matt. 5:48; 19:21; Rom. 12:2; Col. 1:28; 4:12; James 1:17, 25; 1 John 4:18); (b) *complete*, with nothing lacking, grown up, over against "partial"[151] (James

147. GrO: νήπιοι; τέλειοι.
148. GrO: νήπιος.
149. GrO: ἄφρονες; νήπιοι.
150. GrO: πνευματικοῖς; σαρκίνοις; νηπίοις; νήπιοι.
151. GrO: ἐκ μέρους.

1:4; 1 Cor. 13:10). Thus Paul speaks of attaining "to the unity of the faith and of the knowledge of the Son of God, to mature manhood, to the measure of the stature of the fullness of Christ" (Eph. 4:13); he tells the Corinthians to "not be children in [their] thinking" (1 Cor. 14:20) but to think as those who are mature (Phil. 3:15).[152] To such Paul imparts wisdom (1 Cor. 2:6), something he was unable to do for those who were not "spiritual people," but "people of the flesh," "infants in Christ" (1 Cor. 3:1).[153] The mature[154] are therefore those who are children with regard to evil (1 Cor. 14:20), who are able to tolerate solid food, the wisdom of Christ, who are mature in their thinking. These are therefore not so much adults in the moral sense as adults in terms of understanding. It is a perfection according to the measure of our growth.[155]

And finally, growth in the spiritual life is possible and necessary according to admonitions found throughout all of Scripture. We are to "grow in the grace and knowledge of our Lord and Savior Jesus Christ" (2 Pet. 3:18; cf. 1 Pet. 2:2), to "be strengthened with power[156] through his Spirit in [our] inner being" (Eph. 3:16). God will "restore, confirm, strengthen, and establish" us (1 Pet. 5:10), to be renewed inwardly day by day (2 Cor. 4:16), to be "renewed in knowledge" (Col. 3:10), to be "transformed by the renewal of [our] mind" (Rom. 12:2), by the Holy Spirit (Titus 3:5), with increasing glory, which "comes from the Lord who is the Spirit" (2 Cor. 3:18), to press on to take hold of that for which Christ Jesus took hold of us (Phil. 3:12).[157] This development therefore presupposes the first principle of spiritual life—that is, regeneration. Development is possible, because although the new person is perfected at once, this newness is only partly realized; but this does not happen in stages. New persons in Christ are at once complete; no single piece of the new person in Christ is missing; they are a new *whole person* (not a partially new person, Col. 3:10). The very *I* of a new person dies and lives with Christ (Gal. 2:20); in the regenerated person there arises immediately a new consciousness, will, feeling, spirit, soul, body, albeit all of these in principle. The spiritual life is an organism. But the new person is not perfected *in stages*; we are perfected, but never perfect here on earth. The new life thus reveals itself like all organic life on earth, as a "formative drive," "a creative drive."[158] For the Reformed,

152. GrO: ἄνδρα τέλειον; μὴ παιδία γίνεσθε ταῖς φρεσίν; ὅσοι οὖν τέλειοι, τοῦτο φρονῶμεν.
153. GrO: σοφίαν δὲ λαλοῦμεν ἐν τοῖς τελείοις; σαρκίνοι; νήπιοι ἐν Χριστῷ.
154. GrO: τέλειοι.
155. Kuyper, "Volmaakt in trappen of in deelen?" Ed. note: Kuyper's meditation is loosely based on Col. 1:28: "Him we proclaim, warning everyone and teaching everyone with all wisdom, that we may present everyone mature in Christ."
156. GrO: κραταιωθῆναι.
157. GrO: καταρτίσει; στηρίξει; σθενώσει; θεμελιώσει; μεταμορφοῦσθε.
158. GO: *Bildungstrieb; als plastischer Trieb.* J. T. Beck, *Vorlesungen*, 2:6.

the organic life of those who are born again cannot be terminated, contrary to the Lutherans, who deny the doctrine of perseverance.[159]

The Christ in us, that new life, is something emerging, something not perfectly complete, as it is in Christ himself; it can be amplified in strength, power, growth, size, dimension. This development generally consists of the following aspects:

1. It is both *intensive* and *extensive*. Intensively it is pure development. Development is a middle voice,[160] it has an unfavorable as well as a favorable meaning. In a sinner it is broken and must be restrained. But the new humanity needs to develop, or rather to mature. This new person is good, pure, created in God's image (Col. 3:10); this person cannot sin (1 John 3:9) *because* (not insofar as) this person is born of God. Extensively, growth consists in this: as the new self grows, less territory is left to the old self, which is banished from the center of the heart and pushed back to the periphery. After all, the old self is no longer the governing principle, since Christ lives in the heart (Eph. 3); the old self is no longer the master, initially cast out from the heart to the perimeter, from the fortress to the ramparts (John 12:31). Yet that old humanity is much more advanced in development than the new humanity; it is much older, more developed and cunning, and it attacks the new self. It does so in part as evil desire (James 1:15) to tempt us to sin, partly as affliction and suffering (1 Pet. 5:9) to at least weigh us down and prevent our growth.[161] The new humanity must develop itself in opposition to this and so ward off temptation, earnestly seek to do what is good (2 Pet. 1:5), and bear affliction with patience.[162]

2. This growth occurs in and through Christ and in and through him in God. The new life of regeneration is itself called "Christ in us" (2 Cor. 13:5; Col. 1:27). It is no longer living for oneself, but a life lived by faith (Gal. 2:20). This growth thus consists of Christ increasingly taking shape in us. Paul tells the Galatians that he is "again in the anguish of childbirth until Christ is formed in [them]" (Gal. 4:19).[163] In fact, we have been "predestined [by God] to be conformed to the image of his Son" (Rom. 8:29).[164] Thus, we are "being transformed into the same image" (2 Cor. 3:18).[165] From this it follows then that neither this growth nor (re)birth is our own work, but both are equally

159. Schneckenburger, *Vergleichende Darstellung*, 1:250 (§13).
160. LO: *vox media*.
161. GrO: ἐπιθυμία; θλῖψις; πάθημα. J. T. Beck, *Vorlesungen*, 2:9–10.
162. GrO: σπουδή; θλῖψις; ὑπομονή.
163. GrO: μορφωθῇ Χριστὸς ἐν ὑμῖν.
164. GrO: συμμόρφους.
165. GrO: μεταμορφούμεθα.

God's gracious doing. Sanctification is also God's work. Spiritual growth is therefore a process of dying and being resurrected in communion with Christ (Rom. 6; Eph. 2). Dying with Christ is not a destruction of our personal self but only pertains to the sin in the self, in one's soul and body, insofar as they serve sin; we have died to sin (Rom. 6:2, 10).[166] This dying is therefore the separation of the self from sin and its fellowship—that is, it is a dying-*off* (Col. 2:20; 1 Pet. 2:24).[167] This dying is not a physical but a moral event, although it has a physical dimension insofar as the physical, the body, is the moral organ of sin.[168] And furthermore, it is a dying to the whole world (Gal. 6:14) so that the *I* becomes completely isolated, separated from the entire sin-organism and sin-connection within and outside us. This dying to the old humanity requires a complete self-denial that is an ongoing crucifying of the old self. Crucifixion is not yet death but a means of putting to death, and specifically a judicial means;[169] the old humanity lies under the curse and must therefore be put to death (Gal. 5:24; Rom. 6:6; Gal. 2:19; 3:13; 6:14). In addition to self-denial, the followers of Jesus must also take up their cross (Matt. 16:24). And this crucifying is then associated again with abstaining from sin, from sinful deeds, the deeds of the body ("If by the Spirit you put to death the deeds of the body, you will live," Rom. 8:13).[170] Similarly, "I discipline my body and keep it under control" (1 Cor. 9:27); "Put to death therefore what is earthly in you: sexual immorality, impurity, passion, evil desire, and covetousness, which is idolatry" (Col. 3:5). And Jesus tells his disciples: "If your right eye causes you to sin, tear it out and throw it away. For it is better that you lose one of your members than that your whole body be thrown into hell" (Matt. 5:29). And thus the old humanity is first separated from us, put in opposition to us (objectified), and then resisted—that is, put in subjection, crucified, tied down (not put to death, for this only happens when we die physically), and finally put to death in its outward manifestation. The old humanity is therefore subject to suffering, oppression, and death: we carry the death of Christ in us (2 Cor. 4:10–12; cf. 1 Cor. 4:9–13); "Our outer self is wasting away" (2 Cor. 4:16); we are "to put off [our] old self" (Eph. 4:22); we "have put off the old self" (Col. 3:9).[171] And in this way we are saved, set free from our former ways, from the way of life that was handed down to us (1 Pet. 1:18; Eph. 4:22).

---

166. GrO: ἀπεθάνομεν τῇ ἁμαρτίᾳ.

167. GrO: ἀπο-θανεῖν.

168. J. T. Beck, *Vorlesungen*, 2:14–15; Beck refers to the body as the *seelisches Organ*, the spiritual or mental organ.

169. J. T. Beck, *Vorlesungen*, 2:17–18.

170. GrO: τὰς πράξεις τοῦ σώματος.

171. GrO: νέκρωσις; διαφθείρεται; ἀποθέσθαι; ἀπεκδυσάμενοι τὸν παλαιὸν ἄνθρωπον.

Converse to this, yet coupled to it, is the process of being raised with Christ.[172] The dying process is only possible because we have already been born again. Christ lives in us. The new person in us detaches from the old self, and thus makes our dying to be like the dying of Christ. Being raised with Christ (Col. 2:12) is not identical with being born again. To be raised is only possible when there is life first. Life first is instilled within us, and then we die to the old self, while we are raised in the strength of the new life, and after this a new way of life begins. God "made us alive together with" Christ and raised us together with Christ (Eph. 2:5–6) so that we may "walk in newness of life" (Rom. 6:4–5), "that I may know him and the power of his resurrection" (Phil. 3:10).[173] Thus, in regeneration we first receive a new life-principle internally, in our spirit, in our self, our *I*. That new self reveals itself negatively in self-denial, crucifixion, and putting to death the members of our body and likewise, positively, in putting on Christ, in rising, and in subjecting the members of our body to righteousness. The new self puts on Christ, in whose fellowship it was born (Rom. 13:14); it is rooted in Christ (Gal. 2:20) through faith (Eph. 3:17), so that this faith is not a magical but a moral operation, and then this new self rises in the power of Christ and with Christ (Rom. 6:5; Eph. 2:5–6). In other words, one puts on the new self (Eph. 4:24), and the new life is revealed in the various spheres of life,[174] in speaking and acting. From now on we offer the members of our body and the self as instruments[175] of righteousness (Rom. 6:13) to God unto sanctification (v. 19). And thus the new self begins a new way of life, puts off lying, speaks the truth, does not get angry, repudiates adultery, etc., and puts on inner deeds of mercy and loving-kindness (vv. 12–14). That is to say: the entire organism of our personality (soul, spirit, body, etc.) must be an instrument of righteousness, governed by the Spirit and not by the flesh (Rom. 8:1, 4, 12–14); it must be dedicated to God as a living, holy sacrifice, well pleasing to God (Rom. 12:1). The result is a totally new way of life, in which one's citizenship[176] is in heaven (Phil. 3:20). Indeed, if we have been raised with Christ, we are seated with him in heaven, for, as Jesus said, "Where I am, there will my servant be also" (John 12:26), and "[I] will draw all people to myself" (v. 32). Born of God and sharing in Christ and the Holy Spirit (Eph.

---

172. J. T. Beck, *Vorlesungen*, 2:21.

173. GrO: συνεζωοποίησεν; συνήγειρεν.

174. GO: *Lebenssphäre*.

175. Ed. note: Taking his translation directly from the *Statenvertaling*, Bavinck uses the word *wapenen* ("weapons") here. The Greek word is ὅπλα, and "in classical Greek the word referred to the weapons of the Greek soldier. Paul thinks of the members of the Christian's body as weapons to be used in the Christian warfare against evil" (Wuest, *Word Studies*, 1:107).

176. GrO: πολίτευμα.

1:3; 2:6), we are not ideally but really born as citizens of heaven, God's children (Rom. 8:16), like him (Col. 3:10), brothers of the older brother (Rom. 8:29). Jerusalem is our mother (Gal. 4:26); we are of heaven just as the Lord is from heaven (1 Cor. 15:47–49). The Spirit of Christ, who gave us a new birth, sanctifies us and thus prepares us for the world above by granting us heavenly blessings (Eph. 4:8), filling us with Christ and granting us gifts (Eph. 4:8, 10), imparting grace upon grace (John 1:16). Thus believers set their hearts on things above (Col. 3:1–10; 2 Cor. 4:18) and look for—that is, desire—the city that is to come (Heb. 13:14). They have, therefore, a completely different way of life and are strangers here and sojourners (Heb. 11:13; 1 Pet. 2:11); even though they belong to heaven, they still work on earth as light and salt (Matt. 5:14–16; 1 Pet. 1:1–2, 11).

How the Spirit Works

3. In the preceding we described the course of growth according to the main events in the life of Christ, our example. Now the question is: In which *strength* is this growth realized?[177] Objectively, this power consists of being strengthened in the inner person by the Spirit (Eph. 3:16). But the working of this Spirit within us is multifaceted: as the Spirit of wisdom (Eph. 1:17), as the Spirit of holiness (Rom. 1:4; 2 Thess. 2:13; 1 Pet. 1:2). And thus, subjectively, the growth of the spiritual life is a growth in all virtues, in all human faculties (mind, will, feelings, etc.). Faith is the root here, the agent of all virtues. With regard to our intellect, this Spirit, this faith, especially produces knowledge and wisdom (Philem. 6); with regard to the will it produces holiness and love (Gal. 5:6); and with respect to feelings it produces peace, joy, hope, patience (Rom. 15:13). Thus, this growth consists in the strengthening of faith in knowledge, love, and hope, being strengthened by the Spirit of wisdom, holiness, and glory.

a. Faith becomes *knowledge*. Knowledge ranks very highly in Holy Scripture.[178] Scripture rejects not only folly (Mark 7:22) but also imagined, proud, external, formal knowledge detached from reality and life; worldly, fleshly wisdom that wants to judge the divine by human standards (1 Cor. 1:17–31); false knowledge (1 Tim. 6:20); and deceptive philosophy (Col. 2:8, 23).[179] But knowledge of God's truth in Christ, and thus a wisdom that judges what is earthly by heavenly standards, rates very highly in Scripture. Scripture certainly rejects a subconscious Christianity that resides only in feelings. The saying "It is

177. J. T. Beck, *Vorlesungen*, 2:33–55.
178. W. à Brakel, *Christian's Reasonable Service*, 2:270–74 (chap. 32).
179. GrO: κενὴ φιλοσοφία.

the heart that makes the theologian"[180] is only half true. "Pectoral theology" (cf. van Oosterzee),[181] separated from the mind, does not exist. Faith is absolutely not indifferent with regard to knowledge. On the contrary, already in the Old Testament, learning and knowledge are esteemed very highly: one prays for it (Ps. 119:66); it is more valuable than fine gold (Prov. 8:10); and without it the nation perishes (Isa. 5:13; Hosea 4:6). (Simply observe the words "learning, wisdom, knowledge.")[182] The Spirit is a Spirit of wisdom and knowledge (Isa. 11:2). And in the New Testament, in Philemon 6, Paul prays "that the sharing of [Philemon's] faith may become effective for the full knowledge of every good thing that is in us for the sake of Christ Jesus."[183] Faith is made strong and confirmed through knowledge. Truth that is known[184] sets us free from sin (John 8:32). Paul prays that "the God of our Lord Jesus Christ" may give the Ephesians "the Spirit of wisdom and of revelation in the knowledge of him, having the eyes of [their] hearts enlightened, that [they] may know what is the hope to which he has called [them]" (Eph. 1:17–18).[185] Similarly to the Philippians (1:9): "And it is my prayer that your love may abound more and more, with knowledge and all discernment."[186] Paul considers everything "as rubbish" compared to "the surpassing worth of knowing Christ Jesus [his] Lord" (Phil. 3:8). This knowledge has a definite moral element, as Paul indicates in the following passages: "I want you to be wise as to what is good and innocent as to what is evil" (Rom. 16:19). "Do not be children in your thinking.[187] Be infants in evil, but in your thinking be mature" (1 Cor. 14:20).[188] Second Peter 3:18: "Grow in the grace and knowledge of our Lord and Savior Jesus Christ." Indeed, 1 John 5:20: "The Son of God has come and has given us understanding,[189] so that we may know him who is true." And to know God in Jesus Christ is to have eternal life (John 17:3).

The *content*, the object of this knowledge, is thus God himself in Jesus Christ, the One who is true. It is therefore theological and at the same time

180. LO: *Pectus est quod theologum facit.*
181. Ed. note: Van Oosterzee, "Pectoraal-Theologie"; van Oosterzee, *Christian Dogmatics*, 1:82–85; cf. van Oosterzee, *Practical Theology*, 39–48. The professors of Chicago Theological Seminary identified van Oosterzee as a "pectoral theologian" and noted that the motto "*Pectus est quod theologum facit*" is from J. A. W. Neander (*Current Discussions in Theology*, vol. 4 [Chicago and New York: Revell, 1887]).
182. DO: *wetenschap; kennis.*
183. GrO: ἐνεργής; ἐν ἐπιγνώσει παντὸς ἀγαθοῦ; εἰς Χριστόν.
184. GrO: γινώσκω.
185. GrO: ἀποκάλυψις; ἐπίγνωσις.
186. GrO: ἐπίγνωσις and αἴσθησις, that is, inner contemplation.
187. GrO: ἀκέραιοι; μὴ παιδία γίνεσθε ταῖς φρεσίν.
188. GrO: ἀλλὰ τῇ κακίᾳ νηπιάζετε, ταῖς δὲ φρεσὶν τέλειοι γίνεσθε.
189. GrO: διάνοια.

soteriological knowledge. The object of this knowledge is truth in its fullest sense (essence) and power for life[190] as it exists in a person (God). And then it is whatever the Christian can expect in God: "the hope to which he has called you, . . . the riches of his glorious inheritance" and "the immeasurable greatness of his power toward us who believe, according to the working of his great might that he worked in Christ" (Eph. 1:17–19). In a word, therefore, the object of this knowledge is the supernatural content of Christianity.

The *quality* of this knowledge is not an unfruitful knowing, not knowledge that is unrelated to life; its object is not just the historical *that*, but the *who*, and the *what is*—that is, the nature, the quality of the object itself (not merely a word that describes the object).[191] This object does not simply present itself in a literal, historical outward form, but manifests its own spirit and being to the knowing person and gives life, since it is a living object itself. This knowledge is thus life (John 17:3), and gives and creates life in us; this knowledge is also wisdom, the knowledge of how to live wisely (Eph. 5:15–17), such as how the wise "make the best use of the time" (v. 16). The "wisdom from above is first pure, then peaceable, gentle, open to reason, full of mercy and good fruits, impartial and sincere" (James 3:17). The darkness, sin's web of deceit and fraud, gives way to this knowledge, this enlightenment; its light immediately manifests itself in good works (Matt. 5:14–16); "Walk as children of light (for the fruit of light is found in all that is good and right and true), and try to discern what is pleasing to the Lord" (Eph. 5:8–10); believers have been "called out of darkness into [God's] marvelous light" (1 Pet. 2:9). The knowledge of the Scriptures makes believers wise unto salvation and equips them for every good work (2 Tim. 3:15–17; cf. 2 Pet. 1:3).

This knowledge is *received* from the Holy Spirit, who teaches all things (John 14:26), guides into all truth (16:13), and takes from what is Christ's and makes it known. As he warns his readers about the coming of the antichrist and those who "went out from us, but they were not of us; for if they had been of us, they would have continued with us," John writes: "But you have been anointed by the Holy One [this anointing is itself the Holy Spirit received from Christ, "the holy one," John 15:26],[192] and you all have knowledge. I write to you, not because you do not know the truth, but because you know it, and because no lie is of the truth" (1 John 2:19–21). John did not write them to acquaint them with the truth about Christ, but precisely because they did know it, and thus to confirm them in it. This thought is repeated in verse 27:

190. DO: *levenskracht*.
191. GrO: εἰδέναι; ὅτι; τίς; τί ἐστιν.
192. GrO: χρῖσμα ἀπὸ τοῦ ἁγίου.

because Christians as believers have the anointing of the Holy Spirit, who guides them into all truth, they do not need anyone to teach them. There is nothing new that can be preached to them; that which they have heard and possess by faith can only be explained to them more clearly. Those who are trying to lead them astray have no support here whatsoever; John does not put Word and Spirit in contrast to each other, but instead says, "Let what you heard from the beginning abide in you" (v. 24). He alternates this with "the anointing that you received from him abides in you" (v. 27). The Spirit therefore reveals nothing apart from or above the Word, but only explains the Word (John 16:13) and guides and points the way into all the already existing truth,[193] which is in Christ.

The *activity* of the Spirit by which he teaches us is called enlightenment.[194] Paul speaks of "having the eyes of your hearts enlightened,[195] that you may know what is the hope to which he has called you, what are the riches of his glorious inheritance in the saints" (Eph. 1:18). This enlightenment takes place at regeneration, but continues as well. It enables a person to understand the truth according to its spiritual meaning and content and not merely to know it in its form (to know and understand).[196] The Holy Spirit unlocks the content of the truth to our consciousness and thus reveals the truth; therefore the Holy Spirit is called the Spirit of wisdom and revelation (Eph. 1:17).[197] The Holy Spirit gives enlightenment to our eyes—that is, takes the cover away and all at once opens our eyes so that we see the eternal realities of God's Word (law and gospel, sin, Christ, God, righteousness, grace). With that we can arrive at a knowing and understanding (Eph. 1:18)—namely, a saving knowledge; theology is a saving science.

b. Faith and *love*. Christ is given not just for wisdom but also for righteousness and holiness (1 Cor. 1:30). Paul tells the Corinthians, "But you were washed, you were sanctified, you were justified in the name of the Lord Jesus Christ and by the Spirit of our God" (1 Cor. 6:11). Christ consecrated

---

193. GrO: ὁδηγήσει ὑμᾶς ἐν πάντῃ τῇ ἀληθείᾳ. Ed. note: Here Bavinck has altered the Greek text, which reads: ὁδηγήσει ὑμᾶς ἐν τῇ ἀληθείᾳ πάσῃ (not πάντῃ). It is worth noting that πάντῃ is not an alternative text-critical reading; Bavinck's rendering is also a dative prepositional phrase, and so there is no difference in meaning, although the original order placed the emphasis on the "all": "into the truth, all." Bavinck likely reconstructed the text from memory, and his order is the more natural one, demonstrating an impressive facility with a biblical language among his other gifts. My thanks to my Calvin Seminary colleague and New Testament professor Dean Deppe for his assistance on this.

194. DO: *verlichting*; Vilmar, *Theologische Moral*, 2/3:47–50 (§37); J. T. Beck, *Vorlesungen*, 2:37.

195. GrO: πεφωτισμένους.

196. Vilmar, *Theologische Moral*, 2:47–48.

197. GrO: πνεῦμα σοφίας καὶ ἀποκαλύψεως.

himself so that we might be sanctified (John 17:17, 19). This sanctification is the fruit of the Spirit of sanctification (Rom. 1:4; 2 Thess. 3:13; 1 Pet. 1:2). "The fruit of the Spirit is love, joy, peace, patience, kindness, goodness, faithfulness, gentleness and self-control" (Gal. 5:22). God gave us a Spirit of power, of love and self-discipline (2 Tim. 1:7). Among all these fruits of the Spirit, all those virtues, love is the greatest (1 Cor. 13:13). It is the bond of perfection (Col. 3:14), the fulfillment of the law (Rom. 13:10).[198] As the fruit of the Spirit, its principle and foundation is God's love for us (1 John 4:10, 16, 19): we love him because he first loved us; "As the Father has loved me, so have I loved you. Abide in my love" (John 15:9). This love of God for us is poured into our hearts by the Holy Spirit (Rom. 5:5); it is thus introduced into us, internalized. God's love does not remain outside us, stirring our feelings and moving them only from the outside; rather, he enters us: "So we have come to know and to believe the love that God has for us.[199] God is love, and whoever abides in love abides in God, and God abides in him" (1 John 4:16). The Holy Spirit who comes to live in us is the Spirit of love (2 Tim. 1:7)[200] and thus works in us mutual love, not as a fleeting mood or sentiment, but as a lasting principle of the heart, so that the person loves God above all with one's whole heart and strength. The result, the manifestation of that love, is obedience to all of God's commandments with delight and eagerness: "For this is the love of God, that we keep his commandments. And his commandments are not burdensome" (1 John 5:3). They are not burdensome because they are written on the heart (Heb. 8:8–10; Jer. 31:31–33). Just as wisdom makes us understand God's will and unlocks the spiritual meaning of the law, so this love gives us the strength to carry it out with delight and eagerness; we have hearts of flesh rather than stone (Ezek. 11:19; 36:25–27; Jer. 32:39–41).

Our love is shown by keeping God's commandments (John 14:21). Scripture in fact emphasizes this quite strongly, so that we will mature and increase in love and every virtue. This is what mainly constitutes spiritual growth. Our faith must be shown in works (James 2), and works through love (Gal. 5:6).[201] When Paul refers to "speaking the truth in love" in Ephesians 4:15, he does not mean *practicing* the truth, but *being* true, speaking the truth.[202] The phrase "in love" does not belong to "speaking the truth" but rather with what follows: "Growing into him let us, being true, grow in love until we attain to

---

198. GrO: σύνδεσμος τῆς τελειότητος; πλήρωμα νόμου.
199. GrO: τὴν ἀγάπην ἣν ἔχει ὁ θεὸς ἐν ἡμῖν.
200. GrO: πνεῦμα ἀγάπης.
201. GrO: δι' ἀγάπης ἐνεργουμένη.
202. GrO: ἀληθεύοντες δὲ ἐν ἀγάπῃ; ἀληθής; DO: *betrachten.*

the stature of him who is the head."[203] Paul's prayer for the Philippians (1:9) is that this love in them "may abound more and more, with knowledge and all discernment."[204] All the letters of the apostles are full of admonitions to live holy lives, to increase in all kinds of virtues: righteousness, holiness, love, gentleness, patience (Rom. 1:14; Eph. 4–6; Phil. 3–4, etc.). This is what chiefly constitutes the growth of the spiritual life. Most God-fearing people experience a decline, stagnation; they do not advance, do not conquer their sins, do not fight against their character defects, their sins of temperament. The best ones mainly engage in introspection, self-examination, questioning their state and condition, but do not diligently pursue the greatest gifts. To always engage in self-reflection makes people narrow-minded and petty, whereas if they would work more in faith through love, they would obtain proof of their faith by its fruits and so arrive at assurance.

c. Faith and *hope*. Besides growth in knowledge and love (all kinds of virtues), the Christian must also grow in hope. We are also born again into a living hope through the resurrection of Jesus Christ (1 Pet. 1:3); that is, through regeneration we are born into, inserted into the life of Christ, so that his life also becomes ours and his resurrection, his ascension, also awaits us—and we are thus born into the living, powerful expectation of eternal life. In hope we thus cling to the complete redemption and salvation granted us in Christ. Christ is the object of this hope (1 Thess. 1:3), and it is fulfilled at his appearing (1 Pet. 1:3–6, 13).[205] This hope is worked in us by the Holy Spirit, who continuously testifies that we are the children of God (Rom. 8:14–16) and therefore heirs (v. 17), and it holds before us the glory of the hope that does not put us to shame, especially in and during our suffering (Rom. 5:5). Thus also in our oppression and suffering we rejoice because of that hope (Rom. 5:2–5), expecting with certainty the revelation of the children of God (Rom. 8:17–25), and are saved in hope (v. 24). The Spirit as Spirit of hope is therefore the guarantee of our complete redemption (Eph. 1:14; 4:30; 2 Cor. 5:5). This hope in turn produces in us *joy* and *peace* (Rom. 15:13) in the midst of all our suffering, for our glory is sure (1 Pet. 5:10); it also produces *endurance* and *perseverance* (Heb. 6:11–12; 10:36–39). To make progress in these things, then, is part of the growth of our spiritual life: "May the God of hope" (the object and author of hope) "fill you with all joy and peace in believing, so that by the power of the Holy Spirit you may abound in hope" (Rom. 15:13). The example of Christ's perseverance is constantly brought to

203. GrO: ἐν ἀγάπη; ἀληθεύοντες; αὐξήσωμεν εἰς αὐτόν. Ed. note: Bavinck here is criticizing the *Statenvertaling*, which understands Eph. 4:15 as saying, "But practicing the truth in love . . ."
204. GrO: αἴσθησις.
205. GrO: ἀποκάλυψις. Vilmar, *Theologische Moral*, 2/3:134–36 (§50).

our attention (1 Pet. 2:21–25; 4:13; 2 Thess. 3:5, etc.). The race must be run with perseverance (Heb. 12:1), suffering must be endured with patience (Rom. 5:3; 12:12), we are to be joyful in hope (Rom. 12:12).

Variation and Degree in Spiritual Growth

4. Thus far we have described how the growth of the spiritual life should happen according to the Scriptures, what course it should take for all persons. Nevertheless, though there is one ideal for all, there is a difference in how it works out individually. To each is given in their own measure; not everybody progresses equally in faith, knowledge, love, and hope, just as not every person is converted in the same manner. Paul instructs everyone "not to think of himself more highly than he ought to think, but to think with sober judgment, each according to the measure of faith that God has assigned" (Rom. 12:3); for "grace was given to each one of us according to the measure of Christ's gift" (Eph. 4:7).[206] Just as rebirth and conversion differ among people, so growth of the spiritual life differs in highly energetic people as opposed to the melancholy, between those who are more intellectual and those who are more emotional, between the nonchalant and the tenderhearted. There are also varieties of gifts (1 Cor. 12).

But it is also the nature of spiritual growth that there are different degrees of faith, knowledge, love, etc. There are stages: those who are only beginners, and those more and farther advanced, the more deeply initiated, instructed, and grounded.[207] There is a difference in *knowledge*, in spiritual discernment of spiritual matters (1 Cor. 2:15). Faith immediately includes knowledge, however little; this knowledge is frequently dim at first, confused, poor in content and extent, mixed with prejudice and worldly wisdom. This was true, for example, even with the disciples, with the two men on the road to Emmaus, with converted Jews (the entire Petrine school), so that they remained infants[208] for a long time (1 Cor. 3:1; Heb. 5:12–6:3). By contrast, however, the one who is in Christ *knows* the essence of God in Christ, who has revealed himself in this dispensation; *understands* the hidden things of the kingdom of heaven that Christ established; is able to *judge* what contradicts it (Phil. 1:10); can *test and approve* the good will of God (Rom. 12:2); *tests* the spirits (1 John 4:1); and has the *gift of discernment* (1 Cor. 12:10). There is a difference in *wisdom*—that is, in the practical wisdom of everyday life, in the ordering of all of life to the honor of God. This is the fruit of life experience;

---

206. GrO: μέτρον πίστεως; κατὰ τὸ μέτρον τῆς δωρεᾶς τοῦ Χριστοῦ.
207. See Vitringa, *Korte schets*, 136–37 (VIII §§7–8).
208. GrO: νήπιοι.

it is knowledge applied to life. There is difference in *holiness*, first in resisting temptation from without as well as from within ourselves, in subduing the old nature within us with its desires, passions (envy, pride, anger, all sorts of sins of character and temperament and the heart). And then, on the other hand, people differ in growing in the fruits of the Spirit (Gal. 5:22), in adding virtue to faith (2 Pet. 1:5), and in overcoming the evil one (1 John 2:14). Finally, there is a difference in *hope*, patience, long-suffering, gentleness, and endurance. For hope is the fruit of experience.[209]

This does not mean experience in our ordinary sense (soul experience);[210] rather, it indicates testing, self-examination (1 Cor. 11:28), "a severe test of affliction" (2 Cor. 8:2). It is thus a matter of proving through endurance, of being put to the test, of being verified, authenticated, of proving the genuineness by which authenticated faith is seen. And this testing in turn is the fruit of patience, which in turn is the fruit of affliction.[211] Thus, when God sends hardship, he thereby puts our faith to the test. And if in that hardship we remain steadfast and endure it without grumbling, then the fruit is that we stand approved.[212] And thus there is further a difference in all sorts of virtues such as trust, patience, gentleness, contentment, and so forth. But it is good to note here: the growth, condition, and measure of our spiritual life is determined not by all kinds of arbitrary human standards—whether we have experienced or lived through this or that, whether we are still with the Spirit or already with the Son and the Father, or whether our bones have already been broken and we have looked through the crevice—but by the measure of our faith as it shows itself in knowledge, love (all sorts of virtues), and hope (patience). This is the true, pure measure of the spiritual life, its gauge and scale.

5. On the basis of this teaching of Scripture and some other passages (to follow), the Pietists in the Lutheran and Reformed churches have constructed an entire system of spiritual steps or stages. They categorize the unconverted into the ignorant, the reckless, nominal Christians, hypocrites, and the convinced. Among the converted they make further distinctions among gifted ones, the concerned (with a faith that looks ahead longingly) and the strugglers (who flee to Jesus with a refuge-seeking faith), the trusting (with accepting, sustaining faith), and the assured.[213] And among the last group there are the firmly initiated, the well-founded, the established, and the sealed Christians.

209. GrO: δοκιμή: "test, ordeal."
210. DO: *zielservaring*.
211. GrO: δοκιμή; ὑπομονή; θλῖψις.
212. GrO: ὑπομονή; δοκιμή.
213. Ed. note: Bavinck's reference here is "Lampe, etc." See Lampe, *De verborgentheit*, 313–39 (VIII.xxvi–xlviii).

In these circles, the aforementioned texts are appealed to (in addition to the Psalms; see the next chapter) as well as passages such as 1 John 2:12–14; 1 Corinthians 3:1–3; 1 Peter 2:1–2; and Hebrews 5:12–14, along with the contrast between infants and the mature (treated at the beginning of this chapter).[214] None of these Scriptures teach a system of successive steps as is assumed in those pious circles.

Now it should be noted that (a) *acts* of faith should not be confused with steps. It is true that faith hungers, thirsts, longs for, takes refuge, trusts, etc. Those are attributes[215] and operations of faith that are also found in the most advanced persons. It is a mistake to see these operations as part of a mathematical sequence from which even the Holy Spirit may not deviate. Such categorizing of the process of conversion, of the religious experience, is unwholesome for new beginners, who are rebuffed by it; it binds the Holy Spirit, nurtures pride among the more advanced, and subjects everything and everyone to criticism.

(b) One comment: steps in the development of faith, the assurance of faith, and the sealing of faith will be discussed in the next chapter because of their importance. The other steps of faith, such as hungering, taking refuge, taking hold of salvation, etc., are not steps; even at its earliest stage faith apprehends salvation, and at its highest it still remains a faith that takes refuge, hungers, etc. Whoever has taken all these steps may still be an infant[216] according to Scripture (1 Cor. 3) if that person has little knowledge, love, good works, or hope. Scripture never speaks of little or great faith by itself, detached, without knowledge, love, or hope. The error in this doctrine of stages consists in thinking of one's own faith (one's own conversion and its stages) as having many steps. Faith in Christ as Surety is single, undivided; it may be weak or strong, but does not take refuge without embracing salvation. Believing, then, is not a virtue in a separate category, isolated from the other virtues and growing by itself. But faith grows in, by, with, and from the other virtues. In addition, the person who is "assured and sealed" yet poor in love and patience is still an infant. The question is: How many assume they are mature, when in fact they are infants?[217]

(c) Thus, there are stages, or steps in the spiritual life. There are infants, youth, fathers, and the mature.[218] But the standard for assessing these is not

214. GrO: νήπιοι; τέλειοι.
215. Witsius, *Prakticale godgeleertheid*, 9; F. Turretin, *Institutes of Elenctic Theology*, 2:560–64 (XV.8).
216. GrO: νήπιος.
217. GrO: τέλειοι; νήπιοι.
218. GrO: νήπιοι; νεανίσκοι; πατέρες; τέλειοι.

the arbitrary criterion of pious experience but that of Holy Scripture. Infants are those who still have little understanding (Matt. 11:25), who are still in the flesh, unable to digest deep truths (such as predestination, Christian liberty, the Sabbath), who still need milk. Youth are not those who are anxious or without assurance, but those who are still engaged in their fight against Satan and who still face many battles. Fathers are those whose faith is firm and who continue to put their confidence and trust fully in Christ. The mature do the same; they are adults who understand the truths and live them.

10

Persevering in the Christian Life

If I believe today, can I be sure I will still believe tomorrow? Next year? On my deathbed? If I say that God preserves his elect, can I be confident that I am among the elect? On the other hand, can those who are truly converted ever fall away?

These questions have troubled Christians from the time of the apostles and received theological exposure by Augustine in his conflicts with the Pelagians. Since then, believers have struggled to find assurance of their salvation, often oscillating between being overly anxious and finding no security on the one hand, and the casual consolation of cheap grace on the other.

After Augustine, the church became Pelagian. Roman Catholic scholastic theology taught that apart from special revelation no assurance is possible. The Remonstrants and Lutherans also fail to provide full certainty. Starting with Zwingli, however, and then especially after Calvin, the Reformed tradition taught a full, confident assurance in the perseverance of the saints, one that nonetheless did not exclude all experiences of doubt and anxiety. This assurance does not derive from some private revelation beyond or outside the Word but from faith in the promises of God, from the testimony of the Holy Spirit that we are God's children, and from a serious and holy pursuit of a clear conscience and good works. Although our faith derives its stability from God's promise, it can nonetheless be strengthened by considering such "good works" as "testimonies of God dwelling in us." Any valid use of the "practical syllogism" starts with faith. But believers may not rely on good works or begin with them; this results only in uncertainty.

In the early days of the Reformation, in a time of revived, powerful faith manifested in powerful deeds, people were assured of their election; this is the assurance that the Reformed confessions refer to as "reward." Over time, however, more and more people who believed still lacked assurance, and a fatal distinction was made between faith and the assurance of faith, between "refuge-taking" faith and "refuge-seeking" faith. To console anxious believers, spiritual writers tried to point out that much of what anxious people experienced within was not from themselves and was not experienced by unbelievers. In fact, their experiences of uncertainty were similar to those of all or many true children of God—namely, that faith could be very weak and still be present. Not satisfied with this, some began to seek immediate assurance, a direct illumination from God. This was contrary to Reformed theology, which teaches that though the testimony and sealing by the Holy Spirit are supernatural, they are tethered to the Word: this testimony is in and through faith and consists of the Holy Spirit testifying with our spirit.

The question of assurance is an ancient philosophical question and includes assurance about ourselves and that which is external to us. We want to know if we can be sure of what we know. Faith is essential to all human knowing, not only the assurance of our salvation. The latter depends on and is drawn from the assurance of present grace; our election is tested by faith, not the other way around. We are assured by faith—in the promises of God, by the testimony of the Spirit. This faith is an agreement in mind and trust in the heart that God's promises are true for me; I am conscious of my own faith as a gift sealed by the Holy Spirit, also through my own works as its fruit. We can be absolutely and infallibly sure of our salvation; our past election and future glory are assurances drawn from the present experience of grace, in which we realize our adoption as God's children. The same Spirit who makes us conscious of our adoption is also the pledge and guarantee of our future glory and confirms and seals it until the final day. This sealing is objective and subjective; it is our sanctification and our awareness of our renewal as image-bearers of God. Assurance of faith is a direct act of faith based on God's promises; the feeling of assurance is a reflexive act of faith that rests upon the reality of Christ in us. The Holy Spirit adopts, leads, and seals believers.

Contrary to what some pious people think, sealing and assurance are not a special, extraordinary revelation but a testimony of the Holy Spirit mediated by the Word (text), our faith, and the leading of the Spirit in doing good works. Sealing, however, is not identical with conversion, the infusion of faith, regeneration, but a moment of development (worked by the Holy Spirit) in the spiritual life distinguished from those other moments. This does not happen at the same time in all persons; ignorance of the Word, unbelief, lack of good works may stand in the way.

When the initial joy and confidence of Reformation faith waned, people turned to self-examination using "marks" of grace. This did lead to extremes of easy and false assurance, which in turn elicited indifference, on the one hand, and hyperscrupulousness fueling anxiety and doubt, on the other. A healthy approach reminds believers not to be fooled by appearances of piety in "almost Christians" and seeks to help believers avoid becoming overwhelmed and discouraged by believing that only heroic faith can save. True faith includes trust and assurance and comes from the inner testimony of the Holy Spirit and from a serious and holy pursuit of a clear conscience and good works.

§23. SECURITY AND SEALING[1]

Perseverance in Christian History

In the early Christian church, people lived in faith[2] and were secure in their faith. Reflection about that arose only later. With respect to the generally accepted notion of free will, the possibility of apostasy was widely taught, and absolute assurance was not. Augustine taught that predestination was the same as election[3] and that the elect are certainly converted, while the others were certainly condemned as unconverted. Appealing to Romans 8:29–30, Augustine concludes, "Of these who are predestinated, . . . not one shall perish with the devil."[4] But Augustine separated conversion and perseverance.[5] Even the truly

---

1. Ed. note: The Dutch heading of this section plays on two words, *verzekering* and *verzegeling*; we have tried to retain some of this with our assonance of "security" and "sealing." In the body of the chapter we have usually translated *verzekering* as "assurance"; it should be noted that the Dutch word *zekerheid* can be translated as "certainty" as well as "assurance," and in contemporary usage *verzekering* is also used for "insurance." The opening of Bavinck's discussion demonstrates that this complex of ideas is closely connected to the doctrine of perseverance. As will become evident, it is this larger matrix of terms, all directed to a Christian believer's "security" in salvation, that is Bavinck's concern in this chapter. The following outline is provided here to help the reader trace Bavinck's argument; it highlights the seven key characteristics of assurance as Bavinck understands them.

    Perseverance in Christian History
    The Reformed Tradition
    Experiential Challenges
    An Examination of Assurance
     1. Definitions
     2. The Foundation: Present Grace
     3. Possibility of Absolute Assurance
     4. Testimony and Sealing of the Holy Spirit
     5. The Word
     6. Faith
    Anxiety and the Marks of Faith
     7. Good Works as Fruit of Faith

2. Ed. note: Bavinck includes here a marginal reference to "*De Heraut*, nos. 567–68, also about anxiousness." The respective issues are November 4 and November 11, 1888; the references are to Abraham Kuyper's reflections on the Heidelberg Catechism, Lord's Day 20, chaps. 4 and 5, which were republished in Kuyper, *E Voto Dordraceno*, 1:93–107.

3. Augustine did acknowledge that faith, once it was present, possessed inherent assurance. Cf. Heidegger, *Corpus Theologiae Christianae*, 2:420–21 (locus XXIV, §100).

4. Augustine, *On the Holy Trinity* XIII.xvi.20 (*NPNF¹* 3:178). Ed. note: Bavinck likely took over this reference from Schweizer, *Die protestantischen Centraldogmen*, 1:41.

5. LO: *perseverantia*.

converted could fall away. However, only the elect who fell could be converted again; others could not. It is not clear how Augustine reconciled the notions that faith and conversion proceed only from faith and nonetheless that the non-elect share in true faith and can lose it. Speaking of the promise to Abraham in Romans 4:19–21, Augustine writes, "He does not say, 'What He foreknew, He is able to promise'; nor 'What He foretold, He is able to manifest'; nor 'What He promised, He is able to foreknow': but 'What He promised, He is able also to do.' It is He, therefore, who makes them to persevere in good, who makes them good. But they who fall and perish have never been in the number of the predestinated."[6] Augustine said: God has judged that it is better to mingle some nonpersevering people among the saints, because assurance does not profit the saints in the trials of this life; by looking at others who fell away they would think, "That can happen to us as well," and thereby would be guarded against sins.[7] According to Augustine the non-elect can come to conversion, but must then also come to apostasy. This teaching of Augustine has nothing of practical benefit, for the elect are certainly saved, and the reprobate who are converted still fall away. The final result is not affected, but Augustine takes away the comfort of believers. Thus, the gift of perseverance[8] is given by God only to a few, to the elect, not to the converted in general.

After Augustine, the church became Pelagian.[9] Scholasticism denied the absolute assurance of salvation but nevertheless acknowledged the practical syllogism.[10] Thomas teaches[11] that perseverance is a special virtue, because "to persist long in something difficult involves a special difficulty. Hence to persist long in something good until it is accomplished belongs to a special virtue. . . . Perseverance is a special virtue, since it consists in enduring delays in the above or other virtuous deeds, so far as necessity requires."[12] Understood as "the act of perseverance enduring until death," perseverance "needs not only habitual grace, but also the gratuitous help of God sustaining man in good until the end of life."[13] For Thomas, assurance lies

6. Augustine, *Treatise on Rebuke and Grace* XXXVI (*NPNF¹* 5:486). Ed. note: Bavinck likely also took over this reference from Schweizer, *Die protestantischen Centraldogmen*, 1:41.

7. LO: *securitas*. Vossius, *Historiae de Controversiis*, 581; Schweizer, *Die protestantischen Centraldogmen*, 1:41; Wiggers, *Versuch einer pragmatischen Darstellung*, 1:303–18.

8. LO: *donum perseverantiae*.

9. See Hoornbeeck, *Theologiae Practicae*, 2:70.

10. LO: *certitudo salutis*. Heidegger, *Corpus Theologiae Christianae*, 2:420–21 (locus XXIV, §100).

11. Ed. note: Bavinck's source for the Thomas material that follows, as well as the reference to Duns Scotus in the next footnote, is Seeberg, "Melanchthon's Stellung," 134n3.

12. LO: *specialis virtus*; *ST* IIa IIae q. 137 art. 1.

13. *ST* IIa IIae q. 137 art. 4; cf. Ia IIae q. 112 art. 5. Ed. note: Bavinck writes in the margin, "Is it true that Duns Scotus (*Sentences*, IV dist. 14 qu. 4 §3) considered assurance possible? (Thus, *Neue Kirchliche Zeitschrift*, 8.2, p. 134 [i.e., Seeberg, "Melanchthons Stellung"])."

in the knowing alone.[14] According to Heidegger, Thomas says that we can "know with certainty that Christ is in us, but he ineptly adds: 'according to the intellect, but not according to the effect.'"[15] Similarly, Bellarmine says that hope consists of "humans firmly holding on to what they hope for," although the person is not certain "intellectually" whether what is hoped for will be certainly attained.[16] In fact, hope does not at all include this kind of certainty; if it did, it would no longer be hope.[17] All the Scholastics say that no assurance is possible other than through revelation, in signs, by an angel, or by God's Spirit in us, for God's predestination is in God himself and thus is hidden to us.[18] This was how it was made known to Paul and several others. This teaching was established at the Council of Trent.[19] The ninth chapter of the sixth session, "Against the vain confidence of heretics," says: "For, just as no pious person should doubt the mercy of God, the merit of Christ, and the virtue and efficacy of the sacraments, so everyone, when he considers himself and his own weakness and indisposition, may entertain fear and apprehension as to his own grace [canon 13], since no one can know with a certainty of faith, which cannot be subject to error, that he has obtained the grace of God."[20] Canon 16 of this decree states this emphatically: "If anyone shall say that he will for certain with an absolute and infallible certainty have that great gift of perseverance up to the end, unless he shall have learned this by a special revelation; let him be anathema."[21] This is judged to be a benefit rather than a loss since it

14. LO: *in cognitione*; *ST* IIa IIae q. 18 art. 4.

15. LO: *certo nos cognoscere, quod Christus in nobis sit, sed inepte addit: secundum intellectum, non effectum* (Heidegger, *Corpus Theologiae Christianae*, 2:414 [locus XXIV, §81]; cf. 2:420–21 [locus XXIV, §100]). Ed. note: Bavinck took the reference to Thomas, as well as the Bellarmine reference that follows, directly from Heidegger, who provides no specific citation for either. The idea but not the specific language is found in *ST* Ia IIae q. 112 art. 5.

16. LO: *adhaesio hominis ad rem speratam*; *ex parte intellectus*.

17. Heidegger, *Corpus Theologiae Christianae*, 2:415 (locus XXIV, §85).

18. Ed. note: Bavinck cites as his source a summary of Jerome Zanchi's views by William Perkins in *Alle de Werken*, 3:273. The summary by Perkins, *A Brief Discourse*, accompanies his *A Case of Conscience, the Greatest That Ever Was*, which is a dialogue between the apostle John and the church based on 1 John. Where possible, subsequent references to *Case of Conscience* will be to the original English text, with Bavinck's Dutch references provided in parentheses following.

19. Ed. note: Prompted by, and in direct response to the Protestant Reformation (i.e., as a Counter-Reformation), the Roman Catholic Council of Trent met from 1545 to 1563. Its most significant work was likely that of the sixth session (January 1547), which produced the "Decree on Justification."

20. Denzinger, 231 (no. 802).

21. LO: *perseverantia in finem*. Denzinger, 259 (no. 826). Ed. note: Bavinck added in the margins, "At the Council of Trent, some—Catharinus, Vega, Marinarius—were pleading for possible assurance (Heidegger, *Corpus Theologiae Christianae*, 2:421 [locus XXIV, §101]; Hoornbeeck,

arouses in believers a salutary fear and striving for vigilance. The Roman Catholic Church could not teach this certainty of salvation[22] because then the church's mediatorial role would be lost and the individual could find certainty outside the church. This conviction that the certainty of faith born from good works is always conjectural was held by all Roman Catholic dogmaticians, including Bellarmine, the Spanish Jesuit Benedict Pereira (Pererius, 1536–1610), the Dutch Catholic Willem Hessels van Est (Estius, 1542–1613), and others.[23] For Möhler, even the act of reflecting on whether what one has and does is pure often makes it unclean. He writes: "I believe that in the presence of someone who under all circumstances was certain of his salvation, I would scare myself in the highest degree and I would likely not be able to resist the thought that something diabolical was going on."[24]

The Remonstrants also taught that there was nothing other than conditional certainty and that it was beneficial to doubt that in the future we would always be who we are now.[25] To be sure, there is a distinction between Rome and the Remonstrants. Rome denies that one can be certain that one has forgiveness, both for now and for the future. Remonstrants like Limborch, for example, say that we can be certain now that we believe, have forgiveness, etc., but not whether we will continue to remain standing in the future. The Lutherans are also partly in this group. Luther could obtain no assurance in the works imposed on him in the monastery.[26] He came up against the reality that the pope, appealing to Ecclesiastes 9:1,[27] forbade possessing certainty. Along with

---

Theologiae Practicae, 2:69). According to F. Turretin, *Institutes of Elenctic Theology*, XVII.3, some Catholics distinguish between certainty of faith (*fidei*) and certainty of hope (*spei*)."

22. LO: *certitudo salutis.*

23. De Moor, *Commentarius Perpetuus*, 2:92.

24. GO: "Ich glaube, daß es mir in der Nähe eines Menschen, der seiner Seligkeit ohne alle Umstände gewiß zu sein erklärte, im höchsten Grade unheimlich würde, und des Gedankens, daß etwas Diabolisches dabei unterlaufe, wüßte ich mich wahrscheinlich nicht zu erwehren" (Möhler, *Symbolik*, 196–97 [§20]).

25. De Moor, *Commentarius Perpetuus*, 2:93: "*Remonstrantes similiter negant, dari ullum sensum Electionis in hac vita nisi conditionatum; & laudabili ac utile esse ducunt dubitare, an ii semper futuri simus, qui nunc sumus, ut est in Collatione Hagiensi* pag. 298, 340, 342, 346"; similarly, van Limborch, *Theologia Christiana*, 1:754–57 (VI.vii); cf. J. H. Scholten, *De leer der Hervormde Kerk*, 2:514–15. Ed. note: De Moor's reference to Bertius is to Petrus Bertius, *Scripta Adversaria Collationis Hagiensis Habitae Anno MDCXI; inter Quosdam Ecclesiarum Pastores de Divina Praedestinatione & Capitibus ei Adnexis* (Leiden, 1615, 1616). Pagination in both editions is identical and given page numbers are a problem; pagination starts anew after p. 320 and ends with p. 169. Pages 340, 342, and 346, therefore, do not exist. However, that next section has dual numbering with numbers beginning at 287 also found in the margins. Marginal page numbers 298, 340, 342, and 346 are found on pages 12, 57, 58, and 63 of the new numbering, respectively.

26. Köstlin, *Luthers Theologie*, 1:29–30; 2:469–71.

27. Ed. note: In the margin Bavinck cites Eccles. 9:1: "The righteous and the wise and their deeds are in the hand of God. Whether it is love or hate, man does not know; both are before

Augustine, Luther required that one must examine whether one has faith. And now, in order to arrive at that certainty, Luther pointed objectively to the richness of God's grace in Christ, forgiveness, and the life that he offers in Christ (and also in the sacraments)—which must be accepted by faith alone, without any works. He pointed subjectively to the testimony of the Spirit within us (Gal. 4:6), to the desire for, and love toward, Christ and his commandments. But although he said that people could be assured of their faith in the present, he denied that for the future.[28] People must take care that they do not fall; they do not know whether they will persevere, even though they firmly believe that God wills their salvation, and it is simply their fault if they fall. The Lutheran symbols agree with that and teach that justification and faith ultimately can be lost,[29] and thus absolute certainty is not possible. According to Buddeus, people can be certain of their salvation *as long as* they believe and make proper use of the means of grace.[30] Philippi opposes asking whether one is elect or not. One must remain on earth and hold to God's revealed will; predestinationism leads to superficial assurance or miserable doubt.[31] Lutheranism points to the gracious will of God and to the faithful use of the means of grace, thereby moving toward repeated grasping of faith. But, according to predestinationism, regeneration is the proof of election. Those who doubt their regeneration have no other proof, and people can hardly be certain that their regeneration is genuine since false regeneration resembles genuine regeneration so closely. The Lutheran teaching thereby sails between the Scylla of doubt and the Charybdis of false assurance.[32]

In distinction from this, the doctrine of the perseverance of the saints and, on its basis, the assurance of salvation, was taught by Zwingli and especially by Calvin, for whom "the knowledge of faith consists more in assurance than in comprehension."[33] This faith is "sure and firm," it is "a full and fixed

---

him." He then adds an explanation and counterpoint: "Entirely in God's hand, he knows not whether he will love or hate; not whether he discovers God's love or hatred: the expression is too general for that."

28. Ed. note: In the margin Bavinck added: "Exactly as Melanchthon did; see J. A. Möhler, *Symbolik*, §20."

29. LO: *finaliter*. Hofmann, *Symboliek*, 300–302 (§95).

30. Buddeus, *Institutiones Theologiae Dogmaticae*, 1175–77 (V.ii, §10).

31. Philippi, *Kirchliche Glaubenslehre*, 4/1:81–84.

32. This is in agreement with Schneckenburger, *Vergleichende Darstellung*, 1:90, 233–87; 2:71–74, 178; Stahl, *Die lutherische Kirche und die Union*, 200–210; 231–33.

33. LO: *perseverantia sanctorum*; *fidei notitia certitudine magis quam apprehensione continetur certitudo salutis*; *certitudine*; *apprehensione*. Cf. Bavinck, *De ethiek van Ulrich Zwingli*, 50, 53, 54, 56; Calvin, *Institutes*, III.ii.14. Ed. note: Bavinck quotes extensively from the Latin text of the 1559 *Institutes*; translations and narrative transitions that follow are from the editor, with assistance from the Battles, Allen, and Beveridge translations.

certainty"; in fact "no one is truly a believer unless he is firmly persuaded that God is a propitious and benevolent Father to him, one who promises him all things from his goodness."[34] Similarly, "no one is a believer who does not lean on the security of his salvation" and "confidently [triumph] over the devil and death."[35] Nevertheless, this assurance of faith does not exclude all doubt and anxiety.[36] Believers must always fight against their distrust.[37] Consider Psalm 42:5–6: "Why are you cast down, O my soul, / and why are you in turmoil within me? / Hope in God; for I shall again praise him, / my salvation and my God."[38] The nature of faith, however, always comes to the surface again and must arm itself with God's Word against doubts and attacks. Faith is thus ineradicable; it always continues to smolder beneath the ashes.[39]

Calvin contends vigorously, therefore, against Roman Catholic uncertainty, moral conjecture, and doubt, which conflict entirely with the nature of faith and with the testimony of the Spirit within us, with Christ in us.[40] Indeed, in view of Romans 8:38 we can also have assurance for the future.[41] The Scholastics err because they view faith "as a bare simple assent arising from understanding," whereas it is also "confidence and assurance of heart."[42] In this way Calvin describes faith repeatedly as a gift of the Spirit and thus certain

---

34. LO: *certa, firma; plena et fixa certitudo; vere fidelis non est nisi qui solida persuasione Deum sibi propitium benevolumque patrem esse persuasus, de ejus benignitate omnia sibi pollicetur*; Calvin, *Institutes*, III.ii.15–16.

35. LO: *fidelis non est nisi qui suae salutis securitati innixus, diabolo et morti confidenter insultet*; Calvin, *Institutes*, III.ii.16; cf. *Institutes*, I.vii.5, in relation to Scripture.

36. LO: *certitudo; subitatio; sollicitudo*.

37. LO: *diffidentia*; Calvin, *Institutes*, III.ii.17.

38. Ed. note: Bavinck referred to Ps. 42; the specific verses were added by the editor.

39. Calvin, *Institutes*, III.ii.18, 21.

40. LO: *coniectura moralis; dubitatio*. Ed. note: Though Bavinck does not cite it here, the term *coniectura morali* comes from *Institutes*, III.ii.38, where Calvin speaks of it as "that dogma of the Schoolmen" (*scholasticum illud dogma*). With respect to *dubitatio*, Bavinck refers to *Institutes*, III.ii.24, at this point and undoubtedly has in mind Calvin's opening reference to "that gross doubt which has been passed down in the Schools" (*craffam illam dubitationem, quae in scholis tradita fuit*).

41. Calvin, *Institutes*, III.ii.38–40.

42. LO: *nudum ac simplicem ex notitia assessensum arripiunt; cordis fiducia et securitas*; Calvin, *Institutes*, III.ii.33–36. Ed. note: Bavinck's chief concern is to draw a contrast between faith as mere "assent" or "knowledge" (*notitia*) and a more robust understanding of faith that incorporates knowledge but also affirms certainty and assurance of the "heart" (*cordis*). The Heidelberg Catechism's definition of faith captures this well: "True faith is not only a sure knowledge by which I hold as true all that God has revealed to us in Scripture; it is also a wholehearted trust, which the Holy Spirit creates in me by the gospel, that God has freely granted, not only to others but to me also, forgiveness of sins, eternal righteousness, and salvation. These are gifts of sheer grace, granted solely by Christ's merit" (Lord's Day 7, Q&A 21).

and firm,[43] even though it still needs to be strengthened by sacraments.[44] The assurance of faith is sought by Calvin in all the passages cited, especially in the promise and grace of God, in Christ, in the Holy Spirit who works faith, seals us, testifies with us, and so forth. There is no moral conjecture that needs to be deduced from works.[45]

That is not to say that Calvin wants us to investigate what God has decided for the world. In his commentary on 2 Thessalonians 2:13 he writes, "We have no reason to ask what God decreed before the creation of the world in order to know that we have been elected by Him, but we find in ourselves a satisfactory proof if he has sanctified us by his Spirit and enlightened us to faith in His gospel."[46] Whoever wishes to investigate God's hidden decree "plunge[s] into an endless labyrinth"; we must "be satisfied with the faith of the gospel and the grace of the Spirit by which we have been regenerated."[47] For our assurance, we are given "signs or tokens of our election"—namely, "sanctification of the Spirit and belief of the truth."[48] For Calvin, good works are the fruit of faith and thus of election. Faith, which itself flows from election and regenerates us, is the root of all good works.[49] Although our faith derives its stability from God's promise, it can nonetheless be strengthened "by the consideration of the works" because they are "testimonies of God dwelling in us."[50] But believers may not rely on good works or begin with them; this results only in uncertainty.[51] A tree is known by its fruit, and the goal of election is holiness of life.[52] That is Calvin's argument against Trent.[53]

The Reformed Tradition

This teaching became Reformed doctrine. According to Georg Sohn, "faith is never unknown to itself"; it always includes assurance, even about oneself; doubts do not proceed from faith, but from the flesh.[54] Jerome Zanchi also

43. Calvin, *Institutes*, I.vii.5; II.iii.8; III.i.4; III.xiv.8.
44. Calvin, *Institutes*, IV.xiv.7–8.
45. LO: *coniectura moralis*; Calvin, *Institutes*, III.ii.38.
46. LO: *sed in nobis reperiemus legitimam probationem, si nos Spiriti Sancto suo sanctificaverit, si in fidem evangelii sui illuminaverit*. Calvin, *Romans and Thessalonians*, 410, translation altered; Lobstein, *Die Ethik Calvins*, 25.
47. Calvin, *Romans and Thessalonians*, 410.
48. LO: *signa electionis*; Calvin, *Romans and Thessalonians*, 409.
49. On election as the basis of faith, see Calvin, *Institutes*, II.iii.8; III.ii.9; III.iii.1; III.xi.1; III.xvii.1; III.xxii.10; IV.xiii.20; Lobstein, *Die Ethik Calvins*, 28.
50. LO: *operum consideratio; testimonia Dei in nobis habitantis*; Calvin, *Institutes*, III.xiv.18.
51. LO: *vitae sanctimonia*; Calvin, *Institutes*, III.xiv.18–20; III.xv.8.
52. Calvin, *Institutes*, III.xxiii.12.
53. Schweizer, *Die protestantischen Centraldogmen*, 1:243–49.
54. LO: *fides numquam se ipsam ignorat*. Sohn, *Methodus Theologiae*, in *Operum*, 2:979–80.

defended the doctrine of assurance.[55] According to the Heidelberg Catechism, "Christ preserves me and assures me by his Holy Spirit of eternal life."[56] Ursinus explains these words by telling us that "this assurance is obtained, in the first place, from the testimony of the Holy Spirit working in us true faith, and conversion, bearing witness with our spirits that we are sons of God . . . ; and secondly, from the effects of true faith, which we perceive to be in us."[57] According to the Canons of Dort, "assurance of their eternal and unchangeable election to salvation is given to the chosen in due time, though by various stages and in differing measure. Such assurance comes not by inquisitive searching into the hidden and deep things of God, but by noticing within themselves, with spiritual joy and holy delight, the unmistakable fruits of election pointed out in God's Word—such as a true faith in Christ, a childlike fear of God, a godly sorrow for their sins, a hunger and thirst for righteousness, and so on."[58] Furthermore, concerning the "preservation of those chosen to salvation and concerning the perseverance of true believers in faith, believers themselves can and do become assured in accordance with the measure of their faith."[59] How does this happen? "Accordingly, this assurance does not derive from some private revelation beyond or outside the Word, but from *faith* in the promises of God which are very plentifully revealed in the Word for our comfort, from the *testimony* of 'the Holy Spirit testifying with our spirit that we are God's children and heirs' (Rom. 8:16–17), and finally from a serious and holy *pursuit* of a clear conscience and of good works."[60] Yet "scripture testifies that believers do not always *experience* this full assurance of faith and certainty of perseverance."[61] It also needs to be said that the doctrine of assurance of perseverance does not make "true believers proud and carnally self-assured" but "is rather the true root of humility, of childlike respect, of genuine godliness, of endurance in every conflict, of fervent

55. Schweizer, *Die protestantischen Centraldogmen*, 1:448–50; see Perkins's summary of Zanchius in *A Case of Conscience*.
56. Heidelberg Catechism, Lord's Day 1; cf. Q&A 21: "deep-rooted assurance"; Q&A 53: "[Christ] is given to me personally . . . and remains with me forever"; Q&A 54: "the Son of God . . . gathers, protects, and preserves for himself a community chosen for eternal life . . . and of this community I am and always will be a living member"; Q&A 56: "God . . . will never hold against me any of my sins. . . . In his grace God grants me the righteousness of Christ to free me forever from judgment."
57. Ursinus, *Commentary on the Heidelberg Catechism*, 19.
58. Canons of Dort, I.12; cf. Rejection of Errors I.7: "The Synod rejects the errors of those: Who teach that in this life there is no fruit, no awareness, and no assurance of one's unchangeable election to glory, except as conditioned upon something changeable and contingent."
59. Canons of Dort, V.9.
60. Canons of Dort, V.10.
61. Canons of Dort, V.11.

prayers, of steadfastness in cross-bearing and in confessing the truth, and of well-founded joy in God."[62] By contrast, the Roman Catholic and Remonstrant doctrine takes away the comfort of believers and introduces papal doubt into the church again.[63]

We also find this healthy, genuinely Reformed sensibility in numerous dogmaticians such as Keckermann, Bucanus, and Wollebius.[64] While God alone knows the number of the elect, a believer "may have the most undoubted certainty . . . of his own election—not of course *a priori*, i.e., not by useless poring over the mystery of the divine counsel of grace, but only *a posteriori*, i.e., the moment he is converted and born again."[65] We can know we are elect a posteriori, via the *means* of election, which "are mainly the Word, and the Sacraments . . . faith in Christ, the witness of the H. Spirit and zeal in sanctification (in good works)."[66] This was also the view held by Johannes Cocceius, J. H. Heidegger, Amandus Polanus, and the *Synopsis of Purer Theology*.[67] Polanus mentions four divine testimonies: witness of the word, witness of the sacraments, testimony of conscience, and the testimony of the Holy Spirit.[68] Heppe, who at this point cites Caspar Olevian, Frans Burman, Heidegger, and Cocceius, also holds this view.[69]

Van Mastricht[70] describes the derivation of assurance by way of a syllogism: the major premise is obtained through faith: whoever believes is saved;[71] the minor premise is obtained through feeling and experience: I believe. The

62. Canons of Dort, V.12.

63. Canons of Dort, Rejection of Errors, V.5: "The Synod rejects the errors of those: Who teach that apart from a special revelation no one can have the assurance of future perseverance in this life. For by this teaching the well-founded consolation of true believers in this life is taken away and the doubting of the Romanists is reintroduced into the church."

64. Heppe, *Reformed Dogmatics*, 175–78 (VIII.21).

65. Heppe, *Reformed Dogmatics*, 176.

66. LO: *media electionis*; Heppe, *Reformed Dogmatics*, 176. Ed. note: We have amplified Bavinck's quotation here; it is from Bartholomew Keckerman.

67. Heppe, *Reformed Dogmatics*, 177–78; Heidegger, *Corpus Theologiae Christianae*, 1:149 (V.vii); Polyander et al., *Synopsis Purioris Theologiae*, disp. XXIV.61.

68. LO: *testimonia divina*; see Heppe, *Reformed Dogmatics*, 177–78. Ed. note: Polanus von Polansdorf distinguishes "outward" testimonies from "inward" ones; the witness of the gospel and that of the sacraments belong to the former; conscience and the inner testimony of the Holy Spirit belong to the latter (*Syntagma Theologia Christianae*, IV.9).

69. Heppe, *Reformed Dogmatics*, 581–89 (XXIII); Burman, *Synopsis Theologiae*, VI.x.17; Heidegger, *Corpus Theologiae Christianae*, 2:409–14, 419–25 (XXIV.lxix–lxxxi, xcvi–cxii); Cocceius, *Summa Theologiae*, XLIX.15.

70. Van Mastricht, *Theoretico-Practica Theologia*, I.ii.1, §55 [1:160]; I.vi.1, §16 [3:179]; I.vi.22 [1:183]. Ed. note: For an explanation of the format we are using to cite this work, see the extended note in the introduction, §1, in the section "Reformed Churches" (pp. 8–9n48). The volume and page numbers come from the 1749–53 Dutch edition used by Bavinck.

71. Cf. Mark 16:16.

conclusion of the syllogism points to the means of assurance: the increase and testing of faith.[72] According to Turretin, "The question is not, is election perceptible to us *a priori*; rather election is perceptible only *a posteriori*; not by ascending into heaven that we may inquire into the causes of election and unroll the book of life (which is prohibited); but by descending into ourselves that we may consult the book of conscience and, observing the fruits of election in ourselves, ascend from the effects to the cause."[73] The most certain way we obtain assurance is by means of "a practical syllogism, of which the major [premise] is read in the word, the minor [premise] into the heart."[74] One can be "certain (not as to a continuous and uninterrupted act, but as to the foundation and habit, that can never be lost), not only of his present but also of his future state."[75] Turretin lists five reasons: "(1) believers can know from faith, from the Holy Spirit, that they are God's children; (2) God writes the law in their heart; (3) it is confirmed by the testimony and sealing of the Holy Spirit; (4) the practice and example of the saints (who were certain of their own election and salvation) teaches that certainty is not only possible, but necessary"; (5) "the effects of faith demand this certainty" and include "confidence" (Eph. 3:12), "full assurance" (Heb. 10:22), "boasting" (Rom. 5:2), and "unspeakable joy" (1 Pet. 1:8).[76] This certainty of salvation "is not founded immediately upon the word of God (saying that I believe and repent), yet it does not cease to be built upon it immediately (inasmuch as it describes the nature, properties, and effects of true faith and repentance, from which we can easily gather the verity of our own faith and repentance)."[77] At the same time, someone who lacks this assurance can nonetheless have true faith.[78]

Roman Catholics distinguish an "assurance of faith," leaning on God's Word and infallible, from an "assurance of hope," which is uncertain.[79] In contrast, the Reformed teach that believers can be assured through divine, infallible assurance.[80] This assurance has three dimensions: "past election that

---

72. Van Mastricht, *Theoretico-Practica Theologia*, II.i.57 (1:161–62).

73. F. Turretin, *Institutes of Elenctic Theology*, 1:373–74 (IV.13.iv).

74. F. Turretin, *Institutes of Elenctic Theology*, 1:374 (IV.13.iv).

75. LO: *quoad fundamentum et habitum*; F. Turretin, *Institutes of Elenctic Theology*, 1:374 (IV.13.viii). Ed. note: In keeping with Turretin's "we affirm," we have stated as a positive proposition what he posed as a question.

76. LO: *effecta fidei*; GrO: πεποίθησις; πληροφορία; καύχησις; χαρᾷ ἀνεκλαλήτῳ. F. Turretin, *Institutes of Elenctic Theology*, 1:374–77 (IV.13.ix–xv).

77. F. Turretin, *Institutes of Elenctic Theology*, 1:378 (IV.13.xix).

78. F. Turretin, *Institutes of Elenctic Theology*, 1:379 (IV.13.xxvii); cf. 2:616–31 (XV.17.i–xxxvii).

79. LO: *certitudo fidei*; *certitudo spei*. F. Turretin, *Institutes of Elenctic Theology*, 2:616–17 (XV.17.i).

80. LO: *certitudine divina, infallibile*.

we may know that we belong to the number of the elect; present grace that we may be certain of the grace of God and of our faith (namely, that we truly believe and are in the grace of God); and future glory that we be persuaded of the possession of the glory and happiness promised by God."[81] The first and third depend on the second; the second is not *directly* in God's Word but is deduced from what people observe in themselves: "the testimony of the Holy Spirit and the vision of the heart; in the serious self-examination of itself and the experimental [experiential] sense of the peculiar marks and effects of grace (such as grief for sin, desire of grace, repentance and the desire for holiness, abnegation of the self and the love of God above all things and the like)."[82] Assurance flows forth from (1) "the nature of faith"; (2) "the testimony and seal of the Holy Spirit"; (3) "the examples of the saints"; (4) "the prayers of the saints"; (5) "the fruits of the Spirit and of faith"; and (6) "the absurdities which follow the opinion of our opponents."[83] Hoornbeeck deduces it also from the nature of faith and the testimony and sealing of the Holy Spirit.[84] Many Roman Catholics also join us in acknowledging assurance.[85] The means of assurance are: guarding oneself against sin and against doubt, choosing the Spirit's side when facing temptations, meditating on the covenant of grace, exercising virtues, self-examination, use of the sacraments, and so forth.[86]

Experiential Challenges

This assurance was emphasized especially by the practical writers in England (Whitaker, Perkins, Bayly, Taylor, and others).[87] This emphasis was entirely in agreement with Reformed doctrine. Assurance, certainty of salvation, is the highest goal. Calvin defined faith as "a firm and certain knowledge of God's benevolence toward us, founded upon the truth of the freely given promise in Christ, both revealed to our minds and sealed upon our hearts by

81. LO: *electio praeterita*; *gratia praesens*; *gloria futura*. F. Turretin, *Institutes of Elenctic Theology*, 2:618 (XV.17.vi).

82. F. Turretin, *Institutes of Elenctic Theology*, 2:618 (XV.17.vi).

83. F. Turretin, *Institutes of Elenctic Theology*, 2:620–26 (XV.17.xii–xxiii).

84. Hoornbeeck, *Theologiae Practicae*, 2:64–68.

85. Hoornbeeck, *Theologiae Practicae*, 2:68–70.

86. Ames, *Conscience*, IV.ii; E. Erskine, "Assurance of Faith"; R. Erskine, "Believer's Internal Witness."

87. Ed. note: William Whitaker (1548–95); Lewis Bayly (ca. 1575–1631), author of *Practice of Piety*; Jeremy Taylor (1613–67), author of *The Rule and Exercise of Holy Living* and *The Rule and Exercise of Holy Dying*; see Perkins, *Eene Verhandeling*, in *Werken*, 3:265–72. In the margin Bavinck added a reference to Marshall, *Gospel-Mystery*, and left a reference to "Chr. Love, *Van de verzekering van onze roeping en verkiezing* ["Concerning the certainty of our calling and election"]; et alia."

the Holy Spirit."[88] Our Heidelberg Catechism also speaks this way.[89] In the works of these practical writers, therefore, people were urged not to rest until they knew themselves to be elect. In the early period of Reformed spirituality writers always pointed out that assurance of election was never a priori, outside of time and the Word, outside of the historical. Instead, assurance was obtained by means of a practical syllogism, from the nature of faith, the testimony of the Holy Spirit, and good works. In the early days of the Reformation, in a time of revived, powerful faith life, when that faith manifested itself in powerful deeds, this worked well and people were assured of their election. This is the assurance that our confessions—the Belgic Confession, the Heidelberg Catechism, and the Canons of Dort—refer to as "reward."

But when that robust period was past, when faith and its expression were no longer as naïve and immediate, then difficulties arose. An increasingly greater number of people emerged who did believe, who were converted, but nonetheless lacked assurance. Thus a distinction was made between faith and the assurance of faith. Faith is "the firm persuasion of the truth of God's revelation or that truth itself considered as the object of belief."[90] To this "objective, doctrinal definition of *fides*" is added the "act of faith"—that is, "faith as it occurs or is actualized in the human believing subject."[91] This act of faith is an operation of both the intellect and the will. In addition, within the act of faith, a further distinction was made between "a direct operation of faith" and a "reflexive act of faith."[92] The direct operation of faith "is faith receiving, or more precisely, having its object." Simply put, "an individual believes the promises of the gospel." By contrast, "the reflex or reflective act of faith, is the inward appropriation of the object according to which the individual knows that he believes." The writers of the Dutch Further Reformation began to distinguish "refuge-taking faith" from "assured faith," thereby giving rise in the church to a large number of refuge-taking, anxious believers.[93] The question now became: How can these people be given "space" and brought to

---

88. Calvin, *Institutes*, III.ii.7.

89. See Heidelberg Catechism, Lord's Day 7, Q&A 21.

90. Muller, *Dictionary*, 115, s.v. "*fides*."

91. LO: *actus fidei*. Ed. note: We have expanded Bavinck's discussion of these distinctions with direct quotations from Muller, *Dictionary*, 21–23, s.v. "*actus fidei*."

92. LO: *actus directus fidei*; *actus reflexus fidei*.

93. DO: *toevluchtnemend geloof*; *verzekerd geloof*. Ed. note: The terms "Further Reformation" and "Dutch Second Reformation" are used to translate the Dutch "Nadere Reformatie," which refers to a period of renewal and revival in the Dutch Reformed Church resembling English Puritanism and German Pietism. Two of its leading figures were the Utrecht professor Gisbertus Voetius (1589–1676) and the pastor Wilhelmus à Brakel (1635–1711), author of the influential *The Christian's Reasonable Service* (*Redelijke Godsdienst*). See Beeke, *Assurance of Faith*, 62, 128, 333, 351n, 373.

assurance?[94] This was a difficult question for the practical writers, especially for the following reasons:

1. The question had to be asked. It did not arise in Lutheran churches or among the Remonstrants. There, people simply believed and were satisfied with that. In the Reformed Church, however, everything depended on election, the fountain of all benefits. Hence the question, the main question, is whether one is elect. If one is assured of that, everything is in order. In the Reformed Church the matter is not yet finished when people are assured that now, at this moment, they believe. No, the big question is not about today but about yesterday and tomorrow. The real object of assurance, therefore, was past election—"Am I among the elect?"—and the assurance of future glory promised to us.[95]

2. Now everyone continually warned against attempting to attain assurance about that past election and future glory by speculating about God's decree, going beyond the Word and experience; that is to say, going beyond the historical, the present. The present therefore became the authenticating *stamp* of the past and the secure *guarantee* for the future.[96] So the question became: Is the present fixed and firm enough to carry the edifice of assurance for the past and the future?

3. This gave rise to an enormous difficulty. Assurance can be constituted only from the present—in other words, from the experience of faith, regeneration, justification, sanctification, and testimony of the Holy Spirit that a believer possesses. But what if it is precisely those realities that are in doubt! It is good and well to say that faith, regeneration, and the rest are signs of election. But what about those who are uncertain about whether they possess them? An explanation had to be provided for how people could discern whether they truly had faith, were regenerated, and so on. This is how people entered upon the path of the marks—that is, the data, the benchmarks of faith, conversion, and regeneration. This shifted the question. Initially the question was: How can we know if we are elect? The answer: from faith, conversion, and regeneration. The new question became: How do we know if we have faith, conversion, and regeneration?

94. DO: *ruimte*.
95. LO: *electio praeterita*; *gloria futura*.
96. Ed. note: Bavinck engages in a wordplay in his pairing of "waar*merk*" ("mark of truth") and "waar*borg*" ("guarantee of truth").

4. The answer to that question in turn generated additional great difficulties. For while there was true faith, there was also temporary faith; in addition to true conversion there was also false conversion. In fact, even the reprobate could experience many things, including (according to Heb. 6) the gift of the Spirit, illumination, the powers of the coming age, etc.! The issue became one of indicating a specific essential distinction between regenerated people at their worst and unregenerated people at their best.[97] It was necessary to find an essential difference between the richest and best experiences of the unregenerated and the experiences of the regenerated. This is surely the case objectively. But it is difficult to demonstrate, and people came up with subtle, sophisticated, splendid, and often sharp psychological distinctions.[98] How could anxious people ever succeed? How could they ever come to assurance on the basis of all those marks? Would they not move even farther off the path? Suppose they had one mark but lacked the others, or experienced some of the marks, but somewhat differently than the writer had described them; in this way they went from bad to worse. And the worst was that in so doing they had surrendered themselves entirely to the "Ancient Writers" and had lost the thread of Scripture; numerous marks were established arbitrarily, constructed on false exegesis, and the experience of one person was made to be the standard for another.

5. But let's leave that aside! The assurance that was obtained thereby was not absolute but built upon the fallible perspective of one's own circumstances. The major premise of the practical syllogism—whoever believes is saved—was certain, but the minor premise—I believe—was uncertain, since one could be mistaken. How then could one reach an infallible conclusion? O how many doubters could render that minor premise uncertain! Brakel provides a variety of reasons that give rise to believers raising doubts about their salvation.[99] People doubt their election, fear that they are not converted, because they do not know the time of their conversion, do not consciously experience a transition from death to life, and are not "as sore broken upon viewing [their] sins" as other Christians report being. Since people are of "the opinion that assurance is considered to be of the essence of faith, or at least that faith is always

---

97. Van der Groe, *Toetsteen der waare*.

98. Concerning marks, see van Aalst, *Geestelijke mengelstoffen*, 1:71; W. à Brakel, *Christian's Reasonable Service*, 2:307–40 (chap. 33); Heppe, *Geschichte des Pietismus und der Mystik*, 58.

99. W. à Brakel, *Christian's Reasonable Service*, 4:209–33. Ed. note: Quotations that follow in the text are taken from these pages. In the English edition, this is chap. 94; in the Dutch, it is chap. 52. Bavinck's original has been amplified for clarity.

accompanied by assurance, [they] reason as follows: If my faith were true saving faith, I would be assured of my saving interest in Jesus and of salvation itself. There are times, however, when I cannot even find the infallible marks of grace—faith and repentance—from which I would dare to conclude that I have true grace. And if I occasionally observe such marks in me, I nevertheless cannot come to this conclusion. I fear that I do not rightly understand the spiritual meaning of these marks as they are presented in the Word of God, and that which I discern in myself is not spiritual in the sense that Scripture delineates this to be."[100] The "magnitude of the matter" overwhelms people, and the idea that they are numbered among the elect is deemed "to be too great and un-believable"; it would be "presumptuous" to come to such a conclusion. People say that they are unable to pray and that their prayers are not heard. Others fear that their religion is only intellectual, historical, or temporary faith, proceeding from an "enlightened mind." Then there are those who, having sensitive consciences, suspect themselves of hypocrisy because in their service of God they are very conscious of themselves. Sin is present in their lives; they judge themselves for having "an evil, abominable, and defiled heart" and wonder if they have unknowingly sinned against the Holy Spirit.[101] Experiencing "spiritual darkness and deadness," people say, "I am more dead and insensible than the most ungodly person, and thus I have neither spiritual life nor grace. My case is more hopeless than that of the most ungodly sinner." Finally, people doubt because they see no spiritual growth in their lives.

To answer these concerns, spiritual writers tried to provide conso-lation by making some distinctions, pointing out that much of what anxious people experienced within was not from themselves and was not experienced by unbelievers. In fact, their experiences of uncertainty were similar to those of all or many true children of God—namely, that faith could be very weak and still be present. Sometimes this consolation became flattery; anxious persons were pampered and often proceeded to view themselves as genuinely true believers who were lionized by others. In any case, anxiety became systematized.

6. Notwithstanding all these refined distinctions, marks, and consolations, many people did not achieve the goal of assurance they desired. This explains why godly folk increasingly asked for an unmediated assurance.

---

100. Cf. van Aalst, *Geestelijke mengelstoffen*, 384ff.

101. This fear was especially found among Reformed folk; see Schneckenburger, *Verglei-chende Darstellung*, 1:260–63.

This was contrary to what proper Reformed theology taught. After all, the testimony and sealing of the Holy Spirit were supernatural but not unmediated, not a special revelation, but tethered to the Word; it was a testimony *in* and *through* faith, testifying *with* our spirit.[102] People gradually came to posit an *im*mediate assurance in the following sense:[103] Some are affected immediately and extraordinarily in such a way, with such radiant light within their soul, that they can say, "I have seen God face to face" (Gen. 42:30); with Paul they are taken up into the third heaven and led by the king into his inner chamber (Song of Sol. 2:4). Among pious people one encounters many who boast of such an immediate assurance, who have seen Jesus, who were surrounded in the middle of the night by a light, who suddenly received in their heart a joy and heavenly delight and walked for several days in that light. Other forms of immediate assurance[104] consist in the Holy Spirit sealing us with biblical texts that he impresses powerfully upon our soul as if a voice called from heaven: "I have loved you with an everlasting love" (Jer. 31:3) or "I have called you by your name" (cf. Isa. 43:1) or "I have engraved you on the palms of my hands" (Isa. 49:16) or "I am your shield and your reward shall be very great" (cf. Gen. 15:1). Writers mention other sealing texts such as Isaiah 27:1: "In that day the LORD with his hard and great and strong sword will punish Leviathan the fleeing serpent, Leviathan the twisting serpent" (a woman in Franeker).[105] Myseras distinguishes both of these forms of *im*mediate or direct assurance from the *mediate* or indirect assurance by the Holy Spirit as guarantee and seal. Similarly, but not as strongly, van Aalst also speaks of *im*mediate assurance when God comes into the soul with his light.[106] Lampe agrees: *im*mediate assurance takes place when the Lord suddenly causes the light of his glory to rise in our mind, when our heart is aroused in love, and so on.[107] Further Reformation writers Bernardus Smytegeldt (1665–1739) and Johan Verschuir (1680–1737) also held such views.[108] Those who travel

---

102. See later in this chapter for further discussion of the Spirit's testimony and sealing. Ed. note: Cf. *RD*, 1:561–600; 3:593–95; 4:270.

103. Myseras, *Der vromen ondervinding*, 72–75 (§ XI).

104. Ed. note: The source is Myseras, *Der vromen ondervinding*, 73.

105. Ed. note: Here Bavinck is likely drawing from his own experience as minister in Franeker, Friesland, 1880–82.

106. Van Aalst, *Geestelijke mengelstoffen*, 389.

107. Heppe, *Reformed Dogmatics*, 587 (XXIII.12); but especially Lampe, *De verborgentheit*, 571–629.

108. Ed. note: Bernardus Smijtegelt was author of *The Christian's Only Comfort (Des Christens eenige troost)* and *The Bruised Reed (Het gekrookte riet)*; this latter image, taken from

along this path are but a step removed from fanaticism, from enthusiasm.[109] To this was added the idea that before people gave their heart entirely to Jesus, they needed to be taught in a special way that Jesus's invitation to them was different from the general invitation extended to the reprobate.[110] People were speaking an unnatural language.[111]

An Examination of Assurance[112]

1. *Definition(s)*. What is assurance? First, in general.[113] How to attain assurance is an old question in philosophy. The Stoics found it in immediate evidence, in that which is manifestly evident—for example, that $2 \times 2 = 4$. Epicurus found it in observation: what is observed is true, all the rest is false. Descartes saw it in thinking: "I think; therefore I am."[114] And the materialists nowadays once again locate it in observation. With respect to assurance, we need to distinguish assurance regarding ourselves from assurance of things outside ourselves.

a. Assurance regarding ourselves.[115] A person has consciousness, is simultaneously object and subject. Assurance regarding ourselves exists when the subject, apart from any reasoning, coincides and incorporates itself *immediately*, directly, at once, with the object, as being identical; when I say I am that *I*, I thus recognize that the subject and the object are one and the same *I*. This cannot be proven, cannot be deduced; for that coincidence occurs *im*mediately; the *I* posits itself before, and independently of, everything. That *I* am *I* is a matter of faith; so too, that *I* exist. *I* cannot be otherwise. Anyone who doubts that, anyone who doubts whether *I* am *I* and that *I* exist, cannot be logically refuted, but is sick and must be healed; doubt is

---

Isa. 42:3 ("A bruised reed he will not break, and a faintly burning wick he will not quench; he will faithfully bring forth justice"), was a favorite among spiritual writers in the seventeenth century, both on the continent and in England; see Sibbes, *Bruised Reed*. Johan Verschuir was author of *Waarheit in het binnenste*.

109. Cf. Buurt, *Beschouwende godgeleerdheid*, 5, §1334.

110. Cf. Buurt, *Beschouwende godgeleerdheid*, 5, §1236.

111. Cf. Buurt, *Beschouwende godgeleerdheid*, 5, §1196.

112. Ed. note: In the remainder of this chapter Bavinck explores seven dimensions of assurance, beginning with "definition" (no. 1). Although we are inserting additional subheadings at different spots, we are retaining Bavinck's structure and clearly identifying his seven points. All subheadings, however, including the italicized summary statements that lead each of Bavinck's seven points, have been added by the editor.

113. Heidegger, *Corpus Theologiae Christianae*, 2:409 (locus XXIV, §70); Burman, *Synopsis Theologiae*, VI.x.17.

114. LO: *cogito ergo sum*.

115. Ed. note: The paragraph that follows and pp. 53–68 of Bavinck's *Philosophy of Revelation* mutually complement each other.

a psychological or soul sickness. I thus have assurance regarding myself if I incorporate me immediately with myself, join me to myself, rest in or believe in myself. Self-consciousness is an immediate knowing[116] regarding myself, and thus regarding the circumstances in which I live, regarding my actions. In a certain sense, it is also an immediate knowing regarding my eternal existence, my immortality. The *I* cannot imagine its destruction, cannot posit its nonexistence.

b. Assurance regarding things outside us.[117] We are not only conscious of our selves but also have consciousness, knowledge of things, outside us. Those fall upon our consciousness as onto a mirror; those things outside us are God and the world (spiritual and material things). God impinges upon my consciousness, casts his image onto my mirror, casts his "idea" in my soul, testifies within me of his existence. I have assurance of God's existence if my *I* coincides *im*mediately with the testimony of God in my consciousness. In the same manner I have assurance regarding the foundations of the sciences, including mathematics.[118] The innate ideas[119] are immediately evident, without demonstration, but nonetheless unconstrained, automatically accepted by me as needing to exist. The objects of the sciences are established for me on the basis of my own (spiritual or sensory) observation—nature, morality, justice, etc.—or on the basis of the testimony of another—for example, history. In a word: the "thatness," the existence of all things, myself, God, and the world, is certain for me only if I immediately join, conjoin myself, God, and others to the *I*, the consciousness of myself, God, and others.[120] In other words, assurance regarding the existence of all things is possible only through faith, accepting the testimony that my *I* itself, or God, or the sensual things, or the spiritual world, or others provide to my consciousness. The existence of things is thus certain through the testimony of my consciousness; that is the certainty of knowledge.[121]

116. Doedes, *Inleiding tot de leer van God*, 8.
117. Ed. note: Cf. Bavinck, *Philosophy of Revelation*, 68–82.
118. LO: *principia*.
119. Ed. note: Cf. *RD*, 1:223–33.
120. Ed. note: The point Bavinck is making in this dense sentence is clarified by his explanation in *The Philosophy of Revelation* that human consciousness of self is a disclosure, a revelation that is inseparably intertwined with our conscious experience of reality. "The ego is not an aggregate of parts, not a mass of phenomena of consciousness, afterwards grouped together by man under one name. It is a synthesis, which in every man precedes all scientific reflection, an organic whole possessing members. It is complex but not compound" (*Philosophy of Revelation*, 61). In other words, becoming aware of our identity as selves is a process that takes place together with our growing awareness of God and the world. Reality is of one piece, and so is our consciousness of it.
121. LO: *certitudo intelligentiae*.

c. Assurance that we have true knowledge[122] about what we know exists (the "whatness" of things). How can we have a scientific sort of certainty? Objectively through proofs, through logical argument, but subjectively in that knowing always includes immediate consciousness of what is to be known; when I know, I know also simultaneously that I know; in other words, as soon as I know, I immediately join myself to what is known and believe that I know. What is known is the content of my consciousness; it has become part of my self; the *I* who believes in myself also believes in that content of my consciousness. At bottom, all assurance regarding myself and things outside of me is thus a believing in my own consciousness, in myself, and the content of my "self." Doubt arises when I am not joined to myself, when there is a division[123] between my *I* as subject and as object; when something inserts itself between my consciousness and the testimony of God and the world in that consciousness.

d. This scientific certainty, mediated only by belief in ourselves (belief in a general sense), is essentially distinct from the assurance of salvation, which is a certainty of faith—that is, saving faith.[124] This latter certainty is born of saving faith, is possible only through saving faith, and is the fruit of saving faith. Assurance of salvation is impossible apart from this special faith; without that faith, assurance is merely a delusion by which one is deceived. This faith consists especially in (i) an agreement in the mind and at the same time a trusting in the heart, whereby one embraces the promises of God in his Word, applies them to oneself, leans firmly upon them; and (ii) an experiential knowledge, feeling, consciousness of the reality that one believes; this consciousness is born from faith, from the Holy Spirit as seal, and from good works (see below).

The assurance of salvation[125] is therefore a conclusion that is drawn from these two premises and rests upon a practical syllogism. The major premise is drawn from Scripture and states that whoever believes has forgiveness, life, salvation, etc., and this is entirely and completely a matter of pure, unadulterated faith. The minor premise, "I believe," is not purely and only a matter of faith, but of faith in our faith, a matter of experience, feeling, cognizance. This explains why the syllogism and thus also the conclusion, the assurance, are of mixed nature and character, born from both faith and experience.[126]

122. LO: *scientia*.
123. GrO: διάστασις. Ed. note: Bavinck has δίστασις.
124. LO: *certudo salutis*; *certudo fidei*; *fides salvifica*.
125. LO: *certudo salutis*.
126. W. à Brakel, *Christian's Reasonable Service*, 4:215; Burman, *Synopsis Theologiae*, VI.x.19; van Mastricht, *Theoretico-Practica Theologia*, I.ii.1, §55 [1:160]; I.vi.1, §16 [3:179]; I.vi.22 [1:183]; Heidegger, *Corpus Theologiae Christianae*, 2:409 (locus XXIV, §70).

There can be no objection to the major premise; it is certain and can be certain because God himself says in Scripture: "Whoever believes and is baptized will be saved."[127] We can be absolutely and infallibly certain of that. The major premise, in any case, can introduce no doubt or uncertainty into the conclusion. The difficulty lies in the minor premise: Can one know absolutely and infallibly that one believes and will continue believing? If Scripture had stated, "God will save Peter, Paul, you, and you," then the minor premise would also be infallible. But Scripture does not say that. The minor premise must therefore be validated from within ourselves, from our own experience. Not only that I believe now but also that I will persevere. For, as we have seen, according to the Reformed, assurance has three dimensions: (a) past election: we know that we are elect; (b) present grace: we have the grace of faith; and (c) future glory: we are heirs of salvation.[128]

2. *The Foundation: Present Grace.* Now it is paramount that the assurance of past election and future glory depend on and are drawn from the assurance of present grace, which is the bond between both: the fruit of election, on the one hand, and the means and gateway to glorification, on the other. Those who believe may deduce from that and decide on the basis of God's Word that they will both persevere and be saved.[129] So the belief that I will be saved, and in addition that I am elect, is to be derived only from the present grace and is thus always mediated, a conclusion that goes like this: God says that whoever believes is elect and will persevere. I believe. And therefore it is so.[130] *Im*mediate assurance of election and glorification, apart from faith, apart from present grace, does not exist. The belief that I am elect, am glorified, is always mediated by the belief in the doctrine of the perseverance of the saints. Lutherans will join Reformed Christians in saying "I believe," but because Lutherans do not confess the doctrine of perseverance (not finding the minor premise in Scripture), they can never reach the conclusion "I will be saved" apart from the qualifier "if I keep on believing." Being elect and being glorified are thus never made known to nonbelieving persons but only to believers through and in and from faith. In order to attain assurance of election and glory, one must climb up to that from present grace (and do so through rational argument that knows that perseverance is a doctrine of Scripture). The Reformed Church has constantly warned against striving to attain the assurance of election and salvation apart from present grace. Faith may not be tested by election, but

127. Mark 16:16.
128. LO: *electio praeterita*; *gratia praesens*; *gloria futura*. F. Turretin, *Institutes of Elenctic Theology*, 2:618 (XV.17.vi).
129. LO: *perseverantia sanctorum*.
130. LO: *atqui ergo*.

election is tested by faith.[131] Many pious people want to attain knowledge as to whether they are elect first through immediate, special revelation, and from that conclude that the faith that is in me, no matter how weak it may be, must therefore be genuine, and I am saved. This is tempting, and would be a conclusion from election to faith, from God to us; but Scripture forbids that, and it never leads to any other result than fanaticism. The secret things belong to the Lord; one can never attain knowledge about who is elect except from present grace; what functions with validity here is not the deductive, but the inductive, method. An *im*mediate assurance of election and salvation, a special revelation that supplies those apart from faith (not through and from faith), which makes it known to our understanding, consciousness, without going through the heart, an intellectual assurance without an ethical one (in the heart, in the will), in the head apart from the heart, *does not exist*. Here, consciousness is built upon experience. Therefore, all the Reformed have warned against any attempt to attain knowledge of one's election apart from faith.[132] This assurance is possible only by means of a practical syllogism. All the weight ends up falling on the minor premise. The question becomes: Can I know absolutely and infallibly that I believe, am regenerated, possess grace, and am forgiven?

3. *Possibility of Absolute Assurance*. This absolute assurance is possible on the basis of the minor premise, as is illustrated by many examples in the Old and New Covenants.[133] Abraham believed "in hope . . . against hope that he should become a father of many nations. . . . He did not weaken in faith . . . but he grew strong in his faith . . . fully convinced that God was able to do what he had promised" (Rom. 4:18–21).[134] Jacob said: "I wait for your salvation, O LORD" (Gen. 49:18). And David wrote,

> I have set the LORD always before me;
>> because he is at my right hand, I shall not be shaken.
> Therefore my heart is glad, and my whole being rejoices;
>> my flesh also dwells secure.
> For you will not abandon my soul to Sheol,
>> or let your holy one see corruption. (Ps. 16:8–10)

131. W. à Brakel, *Christian's Reasonable Service*, 4:209–10.

132. Calvin, *Romans and Thessalonians*; Canons of Dort, I.12; V.9; Keckermann, Bucanus, and Wollebius, in Heppe, *Reformed Dogmatics*, 176; F. Turretin, *Institutes of Elenctic Theology*, 1:374 (IV.13.xiii).

133. Heidegger, *Corpus Theologiae Christianae*, 2:418–19 (locus XXIV, §91); F. Turretin, *Institutes of Elenctic Theology*, 1:374 (IV.13.xiii); 2:624–29 (XV.17.xix).

134. GrO: παρ' ἐλπίδα ἐπ' ἐλπίδι; πληροφορηθείς. Ed. note: Bavinck makes the point that πληροφορηθείς literally means "actually make full, fulfill (2 Tim. 4:5, 17) and is used intransitively in this place: 'be full of something, be fully persuaded,' as in Rom. 14:5; Col. 4:12."

And this:

> Even though I walk through the valley of the shadow of death,
>   I will fear no evil,
> for you are with me; . . .
> Surely goodness and mercy shall follow me
>   all the days of my life. (Ps. 23:4, 6)
>
> In you, O LORD, do I take refuge;
>   let me never be put to shame. (Ps. 31:1)

The psalmist confesses:

> For God alone my soul waits in silence;
>   from him comes my salvation.
> He alone is my rock and my salvation,
>   my fortress; I shall not be greatly shaken. (Ps. 62:1–2)

Many psalms express the believer's faith/trust[135] (Pss. 56:4, 9; 57:2–3; 62:5–7; 121:1–2; 125:1–2). Paul especially confesses his confident assurance:

> There is therefore now no condemnation for those who are in Christ Jesus. (Rom. 8:1)
>
> For I am sure that neither death nor life, nor angels nor rulers, nor things present nor things to come, nor powers, nor height nor depth, nor anything else in all creation, will be able to separate us from the love of God in Christ Jesus our Lord. (Rom. 8:38–39)
>
> I have fought the good fight, I have finished the race, I have kept the faith. Henceforth there is laid up for me the crown of righteousness, which the Lord, the righteous judge, will award to me on that day, and not only to me but also to all who have loved his appearing. (2 Tim. 4:7–8)

These all have this assurance, and not through special revelation (as some might argue, without any basis at all). Paul derives this assurance (Rom. 8:38) from election (vv. 28–29); he is speaking not only of himself but also about *us* (Rom. 5:1; 8:1, 28–29, 35–36), about all believers. The same faith is granted to all believers, not in the same measure but in the same essence: the same forgiveness and salvation. Abraham and Paul possessed that assurance not through special revelation but through faith; it was an assurance of faith, not

---

135. DO: *geloofsvertrouwen.*

of special revelation; it was from faith in the promises of God in his Word and the testimony of the Holy Spirit in us.[136]

4. *Testimony and Sealing of the Holy Spirit.* The minor premise, "I believe, I am regenerate, I possess forgiveness," is established in the first place through the *testimony and sealing of the Holy Spirit.* Just as the Son was sent by the Father to testify about the Father and to glorify him (John 1:18; 17:4; Rev. 1:5), so in turn the Holy Spirit was sent by the Son to testify about the Son, to glorify him (John 15:26; 16:13–15). This testimony consists of applying and appropriating the person of Christ to the church. For that purpose, the Spirit regenerates (John 3:5) and grants faith (1 Cor. 12:3; "the S/spirit of faith," 2 Cor. 4:13).[137] The Spirit also teaches (John 14:26) and leads into the truth (John 16:13); that is, he places within us the testimony of the truth of God, of his promises, of Christ, of Holy Scripture, so that we cannot doubt these (John 15:26; 16:13–15). God reveals that Jesus is the Christ (Matt. 16:17) and teaches us (John 6:45). The Spirit opens the eyes and illumines the mind (Eph. 1:17–18); he gives the light of the knowledge of the glory of God in Jesus Christ (2 Cor. 4:3–6); he anoints us so that we have no need for anyone to teach us (1 John 2:20, 27). From this, we see clearly that the Holy Spirit testifies within believers about God, his Word, his promises, Christ, etc., making everything infallible, indubitable to their consciousness (the testimony of the Holy Spirit in relation to Scripture).[138]

The object of this testimony is God and his truth. But here we are dealing with a slightly different testimony—namely, with the testimony that the Holy Spirit provides within believers about his own work in them (about their faith, regeneration, and forgiveness). The question becomes: Does this testimony exist, and in what does it consist? Paul teaches the following.[139] Baptism, whereby one enters the church, occurred in Jesus's name (1 Cor. 1:13–16) and thus presupposed faith in Christ. In baptism, the believer receives the symbolic guarantee of the forgiveness of sins or justification obtained by Christ's suffering, accepted and received in faith, for God justifies the believer (Rom. 3:22, 28). In that baptism (1 Cor. 12:13) we now receive God's Spirit (called the "Holy Spirit" in Rom. 5:4; 1 Cor. 6:19; 2 Cor. 6:6; 13:13; the "Spirit of God" in 1 Cor. 3:16; 6:11; 7:40; 2 Cor. 3:3; Rom. 8:11, 14; and identical with the "Spirit of Christ," Gal. 4:6; 1 Cor. 2:16; 2 Cor. 3:17; Phil. 1:19). It is this Spirit who assures believers of their justification. For after we have been adopted in faith as children (of which baptism is the proof and seal), God

---

136. LO: *certitudo fidei*. Heidegger, *Corpus Theologiae Christianae*, 2:417–18 (locus XXIV, §91).
137. GrO: πνεῦμα [τῆς] πίστεως.
138. LO: *testimonium Spiritus Sancti*; Calvin, *Institutes*, I.vii.4–5.
139. Weiss, *Biblical Theology*, 1:453–61 (§84).

grants us the Spirit of adoption (Rom. 8:15; Gal. 4:6).[140] This adoption, which is an objective act of God happening when we believe, obtains significance for our consciousness only through the Holy Spirit, who makes us to know that adoption subjectively and testifies within us that we are adopted. The Spirit's communication is not concurrent with, but presupposes and is the seal of, adoption as an objective act of God;[141] the "spirit of adoption" (Rom. 8:15) is not the Spirit who works adoption (which God does) but who applies it. That Spirit makes us conscious of our adoption by crying out within us, "Abba, Father"[142] (Mark 14:36; Rom. 8:15); the Spirit himself, as it were, cries out through us as the instrument, shouts, "Abba, Father." The juxtaposition of the Aramaic and the Greek does not signify that the Spirit of Jews and gentiles is one and the same (thus Augustine, Luther, Calvin, Bengel). Rather, calling upon God as Abba was so customary that it was used by Christ and taken over from him by gentiles untranslated; the word was deepened with the address to God in their own language. Similarly, we read in Romans 8:15–16: "For you did not receive the spirit of slavery/bondage [i.e., a spirit that fits with slavery, a slavish Spirit] to fall back into fear,"[143] but a "spirit of adoption," which is then the fruit of the testimony of the Spirit of God.[144] But regarding Galatians 4:6, and considering the two verses that precede Romans 8:15 as essential context and where we definitely read about the objective Spirit of God, it is better to see "the spirit of slavery" as referring to God's Spirit and then equivalent to a Spirit of God, like that which would dominate and belong within slavery. Paul is merely stating what the Spirit of God is not. God's Spirit is not a spirit of slavery/bondage but of "adoption," *in* which we cry: "Abba Father."[145] In Romans 8:16 it is "the Spirit himself"—again clearly the Spirit of God—who, in contrast to our crying "Abba Father," "bears witness with our spirit that we are children of God."[146] Our own spirit does that by

140. GrO: πνεῦμα υἱοθεσίας.

141. Contra Ritschl, *Die christliche Lehre von der Rechtfertigung und Versöhnung*, 2:353.

142. GrO: κράζω; ἀββᾶ, ὁ πατήρ.

143. Ed. note: We have moved this from the main text to a footnote for the sake of clarity: "Here the word spirit (πνεῦμα) surely does not refer to the Spirit of God, who never fits with slavery, but, subjectively, the spirit of the human being's spiritual disposition, as slaves (δουλεία), produces that within us; so too 'a spirit of stupor' (πνεῦμα κατανύξεως, Rom. 11:8), 'of cowardice' (δειλίας, 2 Tim. 1:7), 'of faith' (πίστεως, 2 Cor. 4:13?), 'of gentleness' (πραΰτητος, Gal. 6:1), 'of wisdom' (σοφίας, Eph. 1:17)." The question mark following the reference to 2 Cor. 4:13 is Bavinck's own.

144. GrO: πνεῦμα δουλείας; πνεῦμα υἱοθεσίας. On the likely parallelism of the subjective disposition as well, see Philippi, *Commentary on Romans*, 1:415–16.

145. GrO: ἐν ᾧ κράζομεν. Here it is the "we" who call out loudly with confidence, not fearfully or indecisively. Meyer, *Romans*, 315–16.

146. GrO: αὐτὸ τὸ πνεῦμα συμμαρτυρεῖ. This means: bears the same witness as our own spirit and does so simultaneously with our own spirit.

means of crying "Abba Father," and the Holy Spirit agrees with that, bears simultaneous witness to that.

How does the Holy Spirit do so? Some[147] say: when our spirit says, "I am God's child," then the Holy Spirit says, "You are God's child" (Luther). Others say: the Holy Spirit testifies by applying to us the general promises of the gospel (Philippi). Others say: the Holy Spirit testifies by leading us (Rom. 8:14), thereby testifying in that leading to the factuality of our being children, through the new spiritual life within us, in which we then become conscious of being God's children and have a testimony (Meyer). The true opinion is likely that of Calvin: the testimony of the Spirit of God is, first (Rom. 8:14; Gal. 4:6), that he testifies that we are children of God, and then, in and through that, he leads us (Rom. 8:14) and thereby impels us powerfully to cry "Abba Father" (Rom. 8:15; Gal. 4:6). Through this he awakens new life within us (Rom. 8:10) and powerfully applies to us the promises of the gospel. The ways vary in which that testimony of the Holy Spirit is given to us, but precisely by testifying within us in one of those ways or all of them together, he inspires trust within our own spirit, so that not only he (Gal. 4:6) but also we in him (Rom. 8:15) confidently cry "Abba Father." Heidegger[148] states it correctly: our spirit testifies in that it cries "Abba"; God's Spirit testifies along with ours (or better: goes ahead, with ours depending on his) through his *gifts* (faith, regeneration, etc.) and through his *Word* (in which he comforts us, teaches us, declares that those who believe are blessed, etc.).

But in addition, the Holy Spirit makes us aware of our adoption in that he leads us: "For all who are led by the Spirit of God are sons of God" (Rom. 8:14).[149] The Greek verb ἄγονται (present passive indicative) means regularly, continually working, being led (cf. Gal. 5:18), in distinction from the leading/carrying spoken of in 2 Peter 1:21, where the present passive participle φερόμενοι (from φέρω = "to bear, carry, endure," not φορέω = "to bear for a considerable time, regularly") indicates intermittent, momentary carrying.[150] Those who are led are all "sons of God" and not slaves.[151] That is to say, they are children of God, who possess the Holy Spirit as the determinative, moving principle of their lives. The result is that now, by virtue of that leading,

147. Schneckenburger, *Vergleichende Darstellung*, 1:71–74.
148. Heidegger, *Corpus Theologiae Christianae*, 2:411–12 (locus XXIV, §77).
149. GrO: ὅσοι γὰρ πνεύματι θεοῦ ἄγονται.
150. Ed. note: The point here is that being "carried along by the Holy Spirit" in 2 Pet. 1:21 is ad hoc for the purpose of revelation and inspiration and, therefore, needs to be distinguished from the saving action of the Holy Spirit in believers, which is ongoing.
151. GrO: υἱοὶ θεοῦ εἰσιν; δοῦλοι.

in which they are passive but now themselves becoming active, they put to death the "deeds of the body" (Rom. 8:13)[152] and walk in newness of the Spirit (Rom. 7:6; Gal. 5:25). All virtues are then also fruit of the Spirit (Gal. 5:22–23), the love of God is poured out by the Spirit in our hearts and made to be the content of our consciousness (we know that God loves us, Rom. 5:5). The result of all this is that we have peace, a peace of God (Phil. 4:7, 9; 1 Thess. 5:23), and joy in the Holy Spirit (Rom. 14:17; 15:13; 1 Thess. 1:6).

Assurance and Sealing

But still more needs to be said. The Holy Spirit assures us that we are children of God as a seal and guarantee of our faith. In general, to seal means to stamp a brand somewhere (in ancient times, most often by means of a ring that had a stone with certain letters, a figure, an image, or proverb, which ring was then called a signet ring [Gen. 38:18; Jer. 22:24; Hag. 2:24]). The purposes of the sealing varied:[153]

(a) on letters from rulers and the like, to confirm the content (Esth. 3:12–13; 8:8, 10; 1 Kings 21:8; Neh. 9:38; Jer. 32:10; John 3:33; Rom. 4:11; 1 Cor. 9:2);

(b) on documents, to prevent their content from becoming public (Isa. 8:16; 29:11; Dan. 12:4; Rev. 5:5–6: the book with seven seals; Rev. 20:3; 22:10); and

(c) to preserve an object from being desecrated or stolen (Deut. 32:34; Song of Sol. 4:12; Dan. 6:17; Matt. 27:66, Jesus's tomb).

So, the goal was twofold: either to place something beyond the reach of another (b or c) or to mark something as genuine (a). But a person could also be sealed (Ezek. 9:1–4), such as the faithful in the city who receive a mark from the Lord and escape being slaughtered, just like Cain (Gen. 4:15). Similarly, in Revelation 7:1–4, the servants of God, numbering 144,000, are marked on their foreheads to protect them from the four angels who have been given power to damage earth and sea. This is evidently an extraordinary act of God in the coming great tribulation, to place believers beyond the reach of corruption, though not beyond the reach of suffering—thus,

---

152. GrO: πράξεις τοῦ σώματος.

153. Cf. Staringh, *Bijbelsch zakelijk woordenboek*, 11:163–75, s.v. "*zeegel*"; *De Standaard* 75 (September 5, 1875); H. Zeller, *Bijbelsch woordenboek*, 2:641, s.v. "*verzegelen*"; P. Braun and P. Zeller, *Calwer Bibellexikon*, 872, s.v. "Siegel." Ed. note: *De Standaard* was the daily newspaper founded by Abraham Kuyper in 1872; the Sunday edition to which Bavinck refers here regularly featured Kuyper's meditations on Scripture.

not beyond the tribulation itself but beyond the possibility of apostasy. In other words, in the extraordinary tribulation in which people will seek to seduce even the elect, the elect will receive an extraordinary grace of the Holy Spirit to continue standing firm.[154] In addition, we read of a sealing of Christ (John 6:27b): Jesus had fed five thousand, and those amazed people wanted to make him king (v. 15). Jesus evaded them by crossing the lake during the night. But the multitude came to him the next day and asked, "Rabbi, when did you come here?" (v. 25). Jesus responded: "Truly, truly, I say to you, you are seeking me, not because you saw signs,[155] but because you ate your fill of the loaves" (v. 26). In other words, "You are seeking from me rest, bread without work." Very well, that need not be the case: "Do not work for the food that perishes, but for the food that endures to eternal life, which the Son of Man will *give* to you" (v. 27). Jesus, who *gives* this food, also tells his hearers to *work* because "to work" is "to believe": "This is the work of God, that you believe in him whom he has sent" (v. 29). Why? "For on him God the Father has set his seal" (v. 27).[156]

According to Kuyper,[157] this means that the food lies in Christ, but not for the taking; no, Christ is sealed by the Father. He is a sealed fountain; he begins to flow only for those who have the key—that is, who work, who believe. Kuyper understands by this then "the covering of Jesus's Messianic glory with the form of servanthood and the garment of suffering," so that only the eye of faith could see in him the bread of life. This is entirely mistaken:[158] Christ is an open fountain, not at all sealed; the food is indeed in him for the taking—that is, by one who believes. The intention is simple: the Son of Man will give food, eternal food, because the Father—namely, God—by means of this sign[159] has authenticated him as the Messiah, who is the true bread of life and who can and will give the eternal food. According to Jesus himself, the miracles are thus signs and seals of God, certifying that he is the Messiah who gives the true bread.[160] Just as in John 3:33,[161] whoever accepts

154. See the annotations of the *Statenvertaling*.
155. GrO: σημεῖα.
156. GrO: τοῦτον γὰρ ὁ πατὴρ ἐσφράγισεν ὁ θεός.
157. *De Standaard*, October 3, 1875.
158. DO: *geheel onjuist*.
159. GrO: σημεῖα. Ed. note: We have moved this from a long parenthesis in the main text to a footnote for the sake of clarity: "The miracles, including that of the feeding, were especially σημεῖα; with those miracles God intended that a higher power, strength would be hidden in Jesus; they were indications of something higher, and that is what those who had been fed must understand."
160. See the annotations of the *Statenvertaling* and the commentaries by Godet and Meyer.
161. "Whoever receives his testimony sets his seal to this, that God is true."

God's testimony concerning Christ thereby seals, confirms, factually endorses that God is truthful.

We come now to the ordinary sealing of believers (2 Cor. 1:21–22).[162] Paul had planned to come to the Corinthians (although people in Corinth accused him of not wishing to bother with the church), had firmly planned to do so; his intention was not simultaneously yes and no; he was not a yes-and-no man.[163] To firm up his point, Paul says, "As surely as God is faithful, our word to you (i.e., the promise to come to Corinth) has not been Yes and No" (v. 18). And Paul confirms this by saying, "For the Son of God [i.e., the truthful One], Jesus Christ, whom we proclaimed among you . . . was not Yes and No, but in him it is always Yes" (v. 19).[164] Therefore, the Paul who preached that yes-Christ cannot himself be a yes-and-no man. And that Christ is Yes, for all of God's promises are, in him, yes and amen; that is to say, they are objectively confirmed, fulfilled. That is the objective argument for Paul's truthfulness, but he has also a subjective argument, given in verses 21–22: God is the one "who establishes us with you in Christ [so that we remain faithful to him], and anointed us [namely, with the Holy Spirit to the office of preacher], and who [cannot leave us unestablished, since he] has also put his seal on us [surely by the Holy Spirit] and given us his Spirit in our hearts as a guarantee"—that is, the guarantee that consists in the Holy Spirit.[165] In this text the apostle is not saying that the Holy Spirit is the stamp, the guarantee, the seal for this. But this does appear clearly in 2 Corinthians 5:5. Paul expects a building from God, he desires to be clothed, and then says (v. 5), "He who has prepared us for this very thing [for being clothed so that the mortality of life is swallowed up] is God, who has given us the Spirit as a guarantee."[166] Thus, in that Spirit, Paul has the pledge or surety of God that, at the parousia, that which is mortal in him will be swallowed up by life.[167]

In Ephesians 1:13–14, Paul enumerates many benefits, blessings in Christ: election, salvation through Christ's blood, revelation of the mystery of gather-

162. "And it is God who establishes us with you in Christ, and has anointed us, and *who has also put his seal on us* and given us his Spirit in our hearts as a guarantee." Cf. Resch, "Was versteht Paulus unter der Versiegelung mit dem Heiligen Geist?"; by this he understands baptism. Baptism is called a σφραγίς, "seal" (from Rom. 4:11). The Irvingites make sealing a separate sacrament. Ed. note: The Irvingites were followers of Edward Irving (1792–1834), a revivalist and interpreter of biblical prophecy who inspired the founding of the Irvingite or Holy Catholic Apostolic Church in 1832.
163. Ed. note: Verse 17: "Was I vacillating when I wanted to do this? Do I make my plans according to the flesh, ready to say 'Yes, yes' and 'No, no' at the same time?"
164. GrO: οὐκ ἐγένετο Ναὶ καὶ Οὒ ἀλλὰ Ναὶ ἐν αὐτῷ γέγονεν.
165. GrO: βεβαιῶν; καὶ χρίσας (aorist); σφραγισάμενος; τὸν ἀρραβῶνα τοῦ πνεύματος.
166. GrO: κατεργασάμενος; ὁ δοὺς ἡμῖν τὸν ἀρραβῶνα τοῦ πνεύματος.
167. This approximates the annotations of the *Statenvertaling*, but they add that the Holy Spirit gives us God "in order to assure us (of our glorification)."

ing together all things in Christ. He introduces these in verses 11 and 12: "In him [Christ] we have obtained an inheritance [namely, the messianic glory at the parousia], having been predestined [unto that inheritance] according to the purpose of him who works all things according to the counsel of his will, so that we who were the first to hope in Christ might be to the praise of his glory." Paul continues (v. 13): "In him you also [gentile Christians; Paul begins here to narrow his focus], [after][168] you heard the word of truth, the gospel of your salvation, and believed in him,[169] were sealed with the promised Holy Spirit." The double "in whom" of verse 13 refers to Christ[170] and can then go either with believing or with being sealed. It is even better to read it as follows: "in which (i.e., in the gospel of salvation) you, having believed (i.e., after you have believed), are sealed with the promised Holy Spirit."[171] The sequence is thus as follows: hearing, believing, being baptized, receiving the Spirit (Rom. 6:3–4; Titus 3:5; Gal. 3:2; 4:6; Acts 2:37; 8:12; etc.). After you have believed, you were sealed—that is, established as heirs of the messianic kingdom, established not before others but in your own consciousness (Rom. 8:16)[172]—by means of the Holy Spirit of promise—that is, the promised Holy Spirit. This Holy Spirit (Eph. 1:14) "is the guarantee of our inheritance" in the messianic glory "until we acquire possession of it," until the final redemption of his own, his acquired people in the parousia.[173] These have been acquired[174] (i.e., are being acquired)[175] and are preserved[176] unto "the praise of his glory."

In Ephesians 4:29, Paul admonishes, "Let no corrupting talk come out of your mouths, but only such as is good for building up, as fits the occasion, that it may give grace to those who hear." To this he adds (v. 30), "And do

168. Ed. note: Bavinck has "after" (*nadat*) rather than "when" (ESV, NIV).

169. GrO: ἀκούσαντες; ἐν ᾧ καὶ πιστεύσαντες. Ed. note: Here we are following both the majority text (1550 Stephanus New Testament) and modern critical editions (Tischendorf/Nestle-Aland) with πιστεύσαντες; Bavinck had ἐπιστεύσαντες.

170. In agreement with Luther, Harless, Olshausen, and others. Ed. note: Literally, "in whom . . . having heard the word of truth" (ἐν ᾧ καὶ ὑμεῖς ἀκούσαντες τὸν λόγον τῆς ἀληθείας) and "in whom believing, you were sealed" (ἐν ᾧ καὶ πιστεύσαντες ἐσφραγίσθητε).

171. GrO: ἐσφραγίσθητε τῷ πνεύματι τῆς ἐπαγγελίας ἁγίῳ.

172. Ed. note. "This sealing is the indubitable guarantee of the future Messianic salvation received *in one's own consciousness* (Rom. viii.16) through the Holy Spirit, not the attestation *before others*" (Meyer, *Ephesians*, 331, on Eph. 1:13).

173. GrO: ἀρραβὼν τῆς κληρονομίας ἡμῶν; εἰς ἀπολύτρωσιν τῆς περιποιήσεως.

174. Meyer, *Ephesians*, 332–33.

175. See the annotations of the *Statenvertaling*.

176. Bengel, *Gnomon*, 4:69, on Eph. 1:14: "This future *deliverance* or *redemption*, by the addition of τῆς περιποιήσεως, *of preservation* ('conservationis,' Engl. Vers., *of the purchased possession*), is distinguished from the redemption made by the blood of Christ. So περιποίησις σωτηρίας and ψυχῆς, 1 Thess. v. 9; Heb. x. 39.—περιποίησις is said of that which remains still, when all other things perish: LXX., 2 Chron. xiv.12 (13)."

not grieve the Holy Spirit of God, by whom you were sealed for the day of redemption."[177] This means: do not grieve the Holy Spirit so that you would no longer hear his testimony that you are a child of God (Rom. 8:16), through whom you have received so great a benefit—namely, in/through whom you are sealed (have received assurance of redemption) unto/for the day of salvation at the parousia.

We also have to compare these thoughts with Romans 8:23: not only does the entire creation groan, but we ourselves, believers, do as well, although we already have the firstfruits of the Spirit—that is, the first portion of the Spirit, in contrast to the full possession of that Spirit in the future.[178] Although these firstfruits seal our adoption and inheritance, we look expectantly because we have the Spirit as the initial gift (of the coming state of glory), and therefore the Spirit guarantees us many great gifts to come.[179] We too groan within ourselves as we expect our adoption —that is, the redemption of our body. Others understand the phrase "firstfruits of the Spirit" as a partitive genitive—that is, firstfruits in contrast to subsequent believers.[180] We wonder: Did the first believers receive less of the Holy Spirit than we received after them? (Others understand this to mean the Spirit as firstfruits, an appositive or epexegetical genitive, and this is correct!)

In addition, we take note of 1 Corinthians 2:10–17, especially verse 12.[181] In verses 6–16, Paul wishes to unfold this notion: we show forth wisdom among those who are perfect, not a wisdom that is earthly—that is, for those for whom the cross is foolishness—but a wisdom that is higher, revealed to us by the Holy Spirit and therefore understood only by the person filled with God's Spirit. We read in verse 10 that God has revealed this wisdom (what no eye has seen, etc.) to us by his Spirit, for only the Holy Spirit can do that, because he searches out all things, even the depths of God. For just as our human spirits search out what we are, so too no one knows God other than his Spirit (who is thus the consciousness of God). As verse 12 states: "Now we have received not the spirit of the world, but the Spirit who is from God, that we might understand the things freely given us by God."[182] Said differently, "so that we would know the benefits of the messianic kingdom that have been

177. GrO: ἐν ᾧ ἐσφραγίσθητε εἰς ἡμέραν ἀπολυτρώσεως.
178. GrO: ἀπαρχὴν τοῦ πνεύματος.
179. GrO: υἱοθεσία; κληρονομία. Ed. note: Philippi, *Commentar über den Brief Pauli an die Römer*, 2:98–101, on Rom. 8:23; an additional possible source is Weiss, *Biblical Theology*, 1:447–53 (§83).
180. According to Meyer, *Romans*, 327, on Rom. 8:23.
181. "Now we have received not the spirit of the world, but the Spirit who is from God, that we might understand the things freely given us by God."
182. GrO: ἵνα εἰδῶμεν τὰ ὑπὸ τοῦ θεοῦ χαρισθέντα ἡμῖν.

given to us by God and that we shall one day inherit."[183] In other words, the benefits, the content of wisdom, which formerly was hidden, have now been revealed in the cross, which no eye has seen, and so on (vv. 7–9). In verse 13 Paul continues: "This is what we speak, not in words taught us by human wisdom [dialectics, etc.] but in words taught by the Spirit, explaining spiritual realities with Spirit-taught words" [NIV].[184] "Spiritual realities" refers to the material, the content of wisdom, also spiritual things, taught with spiritual words, and not linked to human wisdom or philosophical discourse. Such a content and form of reasoning is not understood by a "natural person" (v. 14), but "spiritual persons" (v. 15), enlightened by God's Spirit, judge or evaluate everything that happens to them and value it at its true cost; they are able to test everything (1 Thess. 5:21).[185] At the same time, spiritual persons themselves are not understood, judged, by anyone—that is, by those who are not "spiritual persons."[186] Here it is said, however, that the Holy Spirit, not we ourselves, causes us to know the wisdom of God; this belongs to the testimony that the Holy Spirit in us gives to Christ, not to ourselves.[187]

In addition, consider Ephesians 3:16–19: Paul prays for the Ephesians that God may "grant you to be strengthened with power through his Spirit in your inner being, so that Christ may dwell in your hearts through faith—that you, being rooted and grounded in love [i.e., having become established in love], may have strength to comprehend with all the saints what is the breadth and length and height and depth, and to know the love of Christ that surpasses knowledge, that you may be filled with all the fullness of God."[188] See also Ephesians 4:23: "Be renewed in the spirit of your minds"[189] (cf. Rom. 12:2; 2 Cor. 3:18; 4:16; Eph. 2:20; Titus 3:5; 1 John 3:24; 4:13). One more passage: "The God of all grace, who has called us to his eternal glory in Christ Jesus— after you have suffered a little while—will restore you, establish you" (1 Pet. 5:10)[190]—that is, set you in a good place, bring order, restore, liberate from a defect, and then arrange, equip, prepare, finish. In this instance, therefore, it

---

183. Meyer, *Epistles to the Corinthians*, 47, on 1 Cor. 2:6.

184. GrO: πνευματικοῖς; πνευματικά.

185. GrO: ψυχικὸς ἄνθρωπος; πνευματικός; ἀνακρίνω; δοκιμάζω.

186. GrO: ἀνακρίνεται; πνευματικός.

187. Ed. note: See point no. 4, "Testimony and Sealing of the Holy Spirit," in the previous section.

188. GrO: κραταιωθῆναι διὰ τοῦ πνεύματος αὐτοῦ εἰς τὸν ἔσω ἄνθρωπον; ἐν ἀγάπῃ ἐρριζωμένοι καὶ τεθεμελιωμένοι.

189. GrO: ἀνανεοῦσθαι τῷ πνεύματι τοῦ νοὸς ὑμῶν.

190. Ed. note: Translating Bavinck's own version of 1 Pet. 5:10. Bavinck defines the verb καταρτίσει ("to put in order, restore") with two Latin verbs, *restituere* ("to restore") and *constituere* ("to establish").

means "restore in such a way that no defect remains in you." Peter continues with another Greek verb to underscore the point: the same God of all grace "will establish, secure, confirm you"[191]—that is, fortify, encourage; cause to persevere, make steadfast. Similarly, Paul prays for the Thessalonians: "Now may our Lord Jesus Christ himself, and God our Father, who loved us and gave us eternal comfort and good hope through grace, comfort your hearts and *establish them* in every good work and word" (2 Thess. 2:16–17). In other words, may God found you, establish you, and make you secure and steadfast, just as with the house built on the rock (Matt. 7:25; cf. Eph. 3:17; Col. 1:23).

AWARENESS OF ASSURANCE

Let us now summarize our exegesis of Scripture: The Holy Spirit *adopts*, *leads*, and *seals*. Faith is born within us from hearing (through a prior working of the Holy Spirit). Thanks to that faith, we are justified and objectively *adopted* as children. Thereafter we receive (in baptism as a guarantee of the forgiveness to be received) the Holy Spirit as the Spirit of adoption.[192] That Spirit brings to our consciousness the adoption that has already objectively come into existence in faith, because the Spirit himself cries out within us: "Abba! Father!" (Gal. 4:6; cf. Rom. 8:15). In other words, "the Spirit himself bears witness with our spirit" (Rom. 8:16; cf. 1 John 3:24; 4:13). This happens specifically *in* our consciousness. But, in addition, Paul teaches that the Spirit "leads" because he is the principle of the new life that strengthens life (Eph. 3:16; Titus 3:5), produces fruits in us (Gal. 5:22), and pours out God's love in our hearts (Rom. 5:5). This love of God "poured into our hearts" surely refers to the consciousness that God loves us, a consciousness that awakens peace and joy within us (Rom. 14:17; 15:13; 1 Thess. 1:6; etc.). This, too, does not occur *outside* our consciousness. Third, the Holy Spirit seals. God seals all believers, after they have believed (Eph. 1:13), with a view to or for eternal glory (2 Cor. 5:5; Eph. 1:14; 4:30) with the Holy Spirit as a pledge, seal (2 Cor. 1:22; 5:5).

The Holy Spirit is the "guarantee" (Eph. 1:14) and the "firstfruits" (Rom 8:23) of that glory,[193] thereby confirming our faith, so that we persevere in Christ (2 Cor. 1:22); we are thus prepared, established, strengthened, and grounded (1 Pet. 5:10). This also does not occur outside of our consciousness;

---

191. Ed. note: The new Greek verb is στηρίξει ("to set up, establish, confirm, strengthen"); Bavinck attempts to capture all this with two Dutch words, *vaststellen* ("to fix, determine, decide [on], decree") and *bevestigen* ("to fix, secure, confirm, validate").

192. GrO: υἱοθεσία.

193. GrO: ἀρραβών; ἀπαρχή.

what would a strengthening or sealing outside of consciousness even be? The sealing consists precisely in this, that after granting us faith, the Holy Spirit works the consciousness in us (through the Word, through his gifts, through his leading): we are children of God. In this way the Spirit strengthens us, confirms our adoption with a view to the future glory, so that we know assuredly that we will be saved and so that we cling all the more tightly to Christ (2 Cor. 1:22) and confirm our calling and election (2 Pet. 1:10).

In this way, Paul teaches as clearly as possible that we can be conscious of our faith, that such consciousness is infallible because it is worked in us by the Holy Spirit, and that such assurance is related not merely to our present state but also to our future eternal state. The sealing is that act of God whereby he, in the Holy Spirit, whom we have received (also the anxious ones), speaks to our consciousness that we are children of God (through word, life, and gifts in us, leading). We are made to recognize the security, the pledge, and the firstfruits of our future glory, so that we know with certainty that we will be saved. The Holy Spirit is thus a pledge not of us but of the future glory, but for us, to us; and this we know, of this we become aware, because the Holy Spirit testifies within us, leads us, and is the principle of our living, through Word and gifts.

All believers receive the Holy Spirit immediately when they believe, even though their faith be ever so weak, even though they are anxious. That Holy Spirit is and remains a pledge, a seal of the future glory of such believers. Although in an objective sense they are assured and sealed, they are actually assured and sealed only when that Holy Spirit works so powerfully in believers that the believer knows infallibly: I am a child of God, I have the Holy Spirit, and in that Spirit I have the pledge of glory. Sealing and assurance are thus a testimony, in our consciousness through the Holy Spirit, of our glorification. It is thus, on the one hand, not a special, extraordinary revelation (as Rome and many pious people think), for that testimony of the Holy Spirit is mediated by the Word (text), our faith, and the leading of the Spirit (good works).[194]

On the other hand, sealing is not identical with conversion, the infusion of faith, regeneration, but is a moment of development (worked by the Holy Spirit) in the spiritual life distinguished from those other moments. Why that sealing comes much earlier in one person than in another lies in one not possessing purely the three means whereby the Holy Spirit testifies within us about our being children of God—in other words, ignorance of the Word, unbelief, or lack of good works. This testimony of the Spirit regarding our being children of God, and thus regarding our future glorification, is the

194. These are discussed further in nos. 5–7 below.

highest, it is absolute and infallible. It is the only thing about which one
can be absolute. And this is so because in the believer the Holy Spirit, God
himself, comes to dwell and testifies within us; for this reason alone absolute assurance[195] is possible. The other witnesses to be discussed later in this
chapter—the Word, faith, good works—are subordinated to this testimony of
the Spirit. It is through the Spirit that these means bring assurance to us, and
we rely on them to the extent that the Holy Spirit speaks to us through them.[196]

This is also the opinion of the Reformed. Calvin[197] tied this sealing specifically to the assurance of our participation in Christ. The annotations to the
Statenvertaling provide a similar interpretation of "sealed" in 2 Corinthians
1:22: "that is, sealed with the pressing of his seal, namely of our communion
with Christ, and consequently our adoption as children and heirs of God."[198]
The annotation attached to Ephesians 1:13 also teaches that sealing occurs in
faith and upon faith: "The promises of forgiveness of sins, our adoption as
children and our eternal reward are given to us in the Gospel and appropriated
by us in faith. The sealing of the Spirit which is added to these is regeneration or renewal of God's image in us."[199] The Spirit's sealing "impresses [on
our souls], as we believe in Christ, to assure us more and more of the imple-
mentation of his promises."[200] And the annotation on Ephesians 4:30 speaks
of "being assured of future salvation."[201] So too, Heidegger asks, What is
the sealing of the Holy Spirit if believers are not aware of it?[202] "Nor indeed
are [people] inscribed [into the covenant] as irrational sheep who have been
baptized," but as those who are furnished with an internal seal so that they

195. LO: *certitudo*.
196. Thus Calvin; see discussion at the beginning of this chapter.
197. See Calvin, *2 Corinthians, Timothy, Titus, Philemon*, 23, on 2 Cor. 1:21–22; Calvin, *Galatians, Ephesians, Philippians and Colossians*, 131–32, on Eph. 1:13–14; similarly, Calvin, *Institutes*, III.ii.17, 18, 24; II.xxxii–xxxvi; see earlier discussion in this chapter.
198. Ed. note: "no. 47) *verzegeld*, Dat is, als met opdrukking van zijn zegel verzekerd, namelijk van onze gemeenschap met Christus, en vervolgens van onze aanneming tot kinderen en tot erfgenamen Gods; Rom. 8:15, 16; 1 Cor. 2:12."
199. Ed. note: "46) *verzegeld geworden* De beloften van de vergeving onzer zonden, van onze aanneming tot kinderen en onze eeuwige erve, worden ons gedaan door het Evangelie, en worden door het geloof ons toegeëigend. De verzegeling des Geestes, die daarbij gevoegd wordt, is de wedergeboorte of vernieuwing van Gods beeld in ons."
200. Ed. note: "46) *verzegeld geworden* . . . waarmede Hij onze zielen begaaft en daarop drukt, als wij in Christus geloven, om ons meer en meer te verzekeren van de uitvoering van zijne beloften."
201. Ed. note: "57) *verzegeld zijt* Namelijk als door het opgedrukt zegel van Gods evenbeeld van de ongelovigen zijt onderscheiden, en van de toekomende zaligheid wordt verzekerd. Zie Ef. 1:13."
202. LO: *obsignatio Spiritus Sancti*. Heidegger, *Corpus Theologiae Christianae*, 2:411 (locus XXIV, §76).

know that "they are children of God."[203] The Holy Spirit "assures us of our full inheritance";[204] he is the pledge of the future inheritance in its entirety.

The Holy Spirit testifies within us through the Word and his gifts.[205] In a later section[206] Heidegger addresses the objection: But how can we know that such a testimony of our being children of God is from the Holy Spirit? Is it possible that in itself the testimony is sure and infallible, but not with respect to us?[207] Heidegger's answer is no; the testimony is sure and infallible also with respect to us.[208] Our spirit can be just as certain of the testimony of the Holy Spirit within us as it is concerning the truth of Scripture. The same testimony cannot proceed from the Holy Spirit and from the devil; otherwise there would be no difference between the Spirit's testimony—"I am your salvation!" (Ps. 35:3)—and the devil's trickery—"Peace, peace!" (cf. Ezek. 13:10). The devil can never incite a person to call God "Abba, Father." Faith, love, peace, etc. are fruits only of the Spirit.

We find the same conclusion in van Mastricht and Witsius: sealing consists in the deeper imprinting of the divine holiness, goodness, salvation, joy (which we receive in principle in regeneration) whereby believers are assured that they are children of God.[209] D'Outrein says that in regeneration the promises of God are written in our hearts and that the church is the epistle of Christ. However, in addition, a seal is still stamped on this as believers become more assured by the Holy Spirit through the application of the promises to themselves. Assurance is a part, a branch, grown from the sealing.[210] According to Burman, the sealing occurs through the Spirit's operations in the soul, especially through faith itself.[211] For Francken, sealing is a deeper stamping of the image of God whereby believers recognize themselves as children of God.[212]

The sealing of the Holy Spirit consists, then, of a *twofold* act, one objective and the other subjective. Objectively, it is the deeper stamp of the image of God in us which consists of illumination regarding the promises of God in Holy Scripture, confirmation in faith, hope, love, virtues, etc.; in other

203. LO: *non enim ut oves irrationales signantur, sicut baptizati; se esse filios Dei.*

204. LO/GrO: *certos de tota haereditate*; καθ' ἡμᾶς; *secundum nos.*

205. Heidegger, *Corpus Theologiae Christianae*, 2:411–12 (locus XXIV, §§76–77).

206. Heidegger, *Corpus Theologiae Christianae*, 2:413 (locus XXIV, §78).

207. LO: *secundum se*; GrO/LO: καθ' ἡμᾶς; *secundum nos.*

208. Cf. F. Turretin, *Institutes of Elenctic Theology*, 2:622–23 (XV.17.xvii–xviii).

209. Van Mastricht, *Theoretico-Practica Theologia*, I.vi.9, §9 [3:457]; Witsius, *Economy of the Covenants*, 2:73–76 (III.13.xxxiv–xxxvii).

210. D'Outrein, *Proef-stukken*; see *De Standaard* 80 (October 10, 1875).

211. Burman, *Synopsis Theologiae*, VI.x.21.

212. Francken, *Stellige God-geleertheyd*, 2:319–35 (chap. 33: "Van de Bewaaring en Verzegeling" ["Concerning Preservation and Sealing"]).

words, being strengthened in the Word and gifts. Subjectively it is the illumination of our consciousness regarding that image of God in us, so that we
recognize that image as God's image, recognize ourselves as God's children
(at this point it is then identical to assurance). Sealing in its subjective sense
is not an immediate, special act or revelation, but is mediated through the
objective sense. The objective coincides with sanctification, the image of God
being gradually completed in us; in this objective sense, each believer is more
or less sealed. The subjective (recognizing ourselves as children of God) occasionally occurs gradually, at other times more suddenly, but always through
means (mediately); an immediate sealing does not exist. In view of Ephesians
4:30, the Spirit always testifies mediately through Word, faith, and love.[213] The
reason some do not attain subjective sealing can lie in our ignorance about
the major premise (if some of God's promises are not clear to us), sometimes
through ignorance about the minor premise (our own state). Often it happens that a light suddenly rises to shine upon either the major or the minor
premise through various things (a text, a psalm verse, a sermon, a word from
a godly person), and once we have become clear about either the minor or
the major premise (or both), we confidently draw the conclusion: if that is
the case, then I, too, am converted.

MEANS OF ASSURANCE[214]

5. *The Word*.[215] The Holy Spirit, who is the author of the sealing, the
assurance, brings us to that point; first, through the Word by making the
major premise—God's promises are true—clear to us.[216] The Word, with
the sacraments—in a word, the promises of God—are always the objective
foundation of our assurance.[217] Faith must ground its assurance in the Word.
Those grounds are innumerable; think of all those passages that we mentioned in connection with the perseverance of the saints:[218] God, his attributes

---

213. F. Turretin, *Institutes of Elenctic Theology*, 2:622–23 (XV.17.xvii–xviii).

214. Ed. note: Bavinck follows the spiritual writers of the seventeenth century in their use of
the practical syllogism structure. Major premise: the objective truth of God's promises in Christ.
Minor premise: by way of self-examination, a determination of evidence that I am included in
the characteristics of those who are saved. Conclusion: assurance of my own salvation.

215. Ed. note: This continues the seven dimensions of assurance that began with no. 1:
"Definitions."

216. Calvin, *Institutes*, III.ii.21; III.xiv.18–20; Heidegger, *Corpus Theologiae Christianae*,
2:410 (locus XXIV, §73), 413 (locus XXIV, §79); Polanus von Polansdorf, *Syntagma Theologiae
Christianae*, IV.9 (from Heppe, *Reformed Dogmatics*, 130, 423).

217. Heidegger, *Corpus Theologiae Christianae*, 2:411 (locus XXIV, §76), 417 (locus XXIV,
§90); E. Erskine, "Assurance of Faith," 141–87.

218. LO: *perseverantia sanctorum*.

(faithfulness, goodness, love, power, etc.), the permanence of the covenant of grace that is confirmed with sacramental oath, God's delight in conversion; Christ's love, grace, divine and human natures, his person and work, his office and state; likewise, the work of the Holy Spirit, how he remains within us, comforts, etc. Scripture is full of promises upon which believers can base their existence. Now it is true that Holy Scripture speaks in general: whoever believes is saved. It does not say: You, Person A or Person B, are saved. But the particular is included within the general, the universal contains the singular. Nevertheless, no matter how firm and rich those promises may be, our eyes may well be closed to them. Doubt can enter our soul regarding those promises through various causes, including the whisperings of Satan, historical criticism,[219] the misunderstanding and ignorance of Scripture, and through various doubts: Would God, Christ even, desire to have me, such a great sinner? Am I included among those called by God? Preaching from the pulpit and pastoral visitation must counter these doubts regarding the major premise by emphasizing the permanence, richness, extensiveness, omnipotence, etc., of God's promises. This is foundational and must be established. This is then the means whereby the Holy Spirit usually delivers people from those doubts. By means of sermons, home visiting, reading of Scripture, etc., the Holy Spirit occasionally allows new light to fall, so that we suddenly behold the permanence of the promises and are assured.

On occasion the Spirit also does it (often in a preventive fashion!) through laying upon our soul one or another verse of Scripture. People will say, "That verse, that psalm verse, entered my soul"; "I was able to acquiesce to that verse"; "I was convicted by that verse." The Holy Spirit applies the Word of God. This is clear. But we must warn against the incursion of random Bible verses into our consciousness and clinging to them. But *this rule must be fixed*: coming upon a verse as such[220] decides nothing, even though that encounter arouses such passionate feelings (think of Cromwell); this is mysticism. We may apply that verse to ourselves only if we find present within us what is being said in that verse. For example, the statement that the Lord will not withhold good from those who walk uprightly[221] applies to me only if I am walking uprightly. Thus, the encounter as such supplies nothing; and yet it is precisely that encounter that many godly people consider as proof that God's Spirit is doing it. But such encounters on their own prove nothing. Much enters our soul that appears immediately (e.g., brilliant insight, especially

219. Cf. *RD*, 3:36–39, 357.
220. LO: *qua talis*. Ed. note: The expression "this rule must be fixed" is from Buurt, *Beschouwende godgeleerdheid*, 5, §1236.
221. Ed. note: Ps. 84:11.

among artists) because the intermediaries have fallen away from before our consciousness. Nevertheless, these are still mediated and even proceed from our sinful heart. That people take such an encounter as immediate proof of the divine is understandable, but this is to be rejected. In addition, from the fixed rule it follows that what is important in connection with such a randomly encountered verse is not the manner or the form but the material, the content. If we do come upon such a text, then we must first investigate what that verse says; if it appears that our own situation and experience can be subsumed under that which is in the encountered text, only then may we draw the conclusion. A conclusion may be drawn only from two premises, a major premise and a minor premise (correctly subsumed under it). Although Kuyper approves it as a "lovely custom," we must reject "the practice of opening Scripture in an emergency or in desperation in order to ask for a decision from God" (at least if this does not mean consulting, which is a good thing, but simply letting the Bible fall open and then clinging to the first fitting word that strikes our eye).[222] That is what Muslims do with the Qur'an, and it is a fetishistic custom without warranted example in Scripture itself.

6. *Faith*. In the second place, the Holy Spirit works assurance in us by shining light on the minor premise, the state of our soul. In the previous section (5. *The Word*) we described the testimony of the Holy Spirit within us in terms of Scripture, the promises of God, Christ, etc. This is a mediated testimony; the Holy Spirit deposits this testimony within us through faith (regeneration, justification, adoption) and hope. Assurance is an attribute of faith. Now, in this section, we are considering the testimony that the Holy Spirit supplies within us about ourselves. Just as knowing also includes, eventually, the knowing that one knows—that is, the reflexive act of knowing—so too faith also brings with it and includes believing that one believes, the reciprocally inclusive act of faith.[223] In other words, in accord with its own nature, knowing includes consciousness of knowing, a certainty that one knows. The same is true for faith. In its scope, faith is a "direct act," accepting, receiving from Christ, but afterward turns around, knows itself as faith.[224] This is evident from many examples in Scripture: "I believe; help my unbelief!" (Mark 9:24); "We have believed, and have come to know . . ." (John 6:69); "You know that I love you"

---

222. DO: *liefelijk gebruik*; *raadplegen*. Kuyper, *De hedendaagsche Schriftcritiek*, 15. Augustine did the same in *Confessions* VIII.12 and appealed to Rom. 13:13. Also, usually in connection with the Roman people, de la Saussaye, *Manual of the Science of Religion*, 139: "A peculiar way of casting lots consisted in the casual opening of a book. . . . It is certain that Roman poets (sortes virgilianae), and later the Bible, were frequently used for that purpose." Cf. Ritschl, *Geschichte des Pietismus*, 2:16.

223. LO: *actus reflexus*; DO: *weeromsluitende*.

224. LO: *actus directus*.

(John 21:17); "I know whom I have believed" (2 Tim. 1:12).[225] But it appears also from the description of the nature of faith. It must be possible for one to be conscious of one's own faith (cf. Lam. 3:40; Zeph. 2:1; 1 Cor. 11:28); otherwise Paul could not have warned in 2 Corinthians 13:5–6: "Examine yourselves, to see whether you are in the faith. Test yourselves.[226] Or do you not realize[227] this about yourselves, that Jesus Christ is in you?" Aquinas also acknowledges that we can know this, but, as Heiddeger noted, "He adds ineptly: according to the intellect, not the effect." And Bellarmine tries to refute this passage.[228]

Jesus himself promises: "In that day [when I come again to you in the Spirit] you will know[229] that I am in my Father, and you in me, and I in you" (John 14:20). The standard passage is 1 John 5:6–12: the main idea is that Jesus is God's Son, validated by divine testimony.[230] Jesus is the One "who came[231] by water and blood" (v. 6). There are numerous explanations of this.[232] The most likely one says: not through water alone—in other words, in baptism, when Christ was installed into office—but also through blood. The Docetists acknowledged the baptism but denied the blood, thinking that the divine nature of Jesus had receded before his suffering. In verse 6, the apostle adds: "And the [Holy] Spirit [who lives in the church] is the one who testifies [that Jesus is God's Son, John 15:26] because the Spirit is the truth" (that the Spirit bears witness to the Spirit is a foreign idea in the context).[233] Along with the Spirit, John adds two additional "witnesses": "For there are three that testify,

225. GrO: οἶδα ᾧ πεπίστευκα.
226. GrO: δοκιμάζετε.
227. GrO: ἐπιγινώσκετε.
228. Heidegger, *Corpus Theologiae Christianae*, 2:414 (locus XXIV, §81): "Sed ineptè addit: *Secundum intellectum, non* effectum." See discussion at the beginning of this chapter.
229. GrO: γνώσεσθε.
230. LO: *locus classicus.* Cf. R. Erskine, "Believer's Internal Witness," on 1 John 5:10, who views "water" as referring to regeneration and "blood" to justification. Ed. note: The key passage is 1 John 5:7–8: "For there are three that testify: the Spirit and the water and the blood; and these three agree."
231. GrO: ὁ ἐλθών.
232. E.g., the annotations to the *Statenvertaling* take it as water and blood that flowed from Christ, which symbolize the purifying water of the Holy Spirit and the blood of atonement; Augustine, as the two sacraments instituted by Christ; Carpzov, as the baptism of Christ by John the Baptist and Christ's atoning death; Tertullian thought the last most likely.
233. Ed. note: At this point Bavinck introduces 1 John 5:7 from the Textus Receptus: "For there are three that bear record in heaven, the Father, the Word, and the Holy Ghost: and these three are one" (KJV). Nonetheless, it is striking that Bavinck seems puzzled about the reference to the three who testify in heaven. He says: "In the context these words can be but do not have to be present; although it is not clear what they contribute here and in what relationship they stand to the three witness on earth [v. 8 in KJV]; moreover, what is it to bear witness in heaven, how does that benefit us?" Consequently, Bavinck's exegesis does no more with the "three witnesses in heaven" and moves directly to the single, agreeing testimony of "the Spirit, and the

the Spirit and the water and the blood; and these three agree"[234]—that is, they are directed to the one testimony. And this testimony carries great weight, for "if we receive the testimony of men, the testimony of God is greater, for this is the testimony of God that he has borne [through Spirit, water, and blood] concerning his Son" (v. 9). The goal of this objective testimony of God is that we believe Jesus to be God's Son. Therefore, "whoever believes in the Son of God has the testimony in himself"[235] (v. 10). With such people God's objective testimony has become subjective; they feel its power. By contrast, "whoever does not believe God [as witness] has made him a liar, because he has not believed in the testimony that God has borne [in Spirit, water, and blood] concerning his Son" (v. 10). And that subjective power, whereby the objective testimony of God is established for the believer, consists in this: "This is the testimony, that God gave us eternal life, and this life [is one with his Son and] is in his Son" (v. 11). So, "whoever has the Son has life; whoever does not have the Son of God does not have life" (v. 12). Thus, it is being taught here that the objective testimony concerning Jesus's sonship is Spirit, water, and blood; and the subjective testimony corresponds to that, whereby that objective testimony becomes effectual eternal life within us. In addition, it is evident that assurance is a mark of faith because it is called the "substance of things hoped for, the evidence of things not seen" [Heb. 11:1 KJV].[236] Other passages say the same thing about faith: "in whom we have boldness and access with confidence through our faith in [Christ]" (Eph. 3:12); "Let us draw near with a true heart in full assurance of faith" (Heb. 10:22; cf. 11:6; 1 Thess. 1:5).[237] Assurance of faith is also demonstrated by the fruits of the Spirit (fruits of faith), which include boasting in our suffering, peace, and joy (Rom. 5:1–5).[238] Christian hope teaches the same thing:[239] we are saved in hope

---

water, and the blood." We have removed this now-generally-discredited textual reference and reconstructed Bavinck's text to reflect his own argument.

234. GrO: εἰς τὸ ἕν εἰσιν (lit., "are one").

235. GrO: ἔχει τὴν μαρτυρίαν ἐν αὐτῷ.

236. GrO: ἐλπιζονένων ὑπόστασις, πραγμάτων ἔλεγχος οὐ βλεπομένων. Ed. note: The KJV more adequately captures the nuances of the *Statenvertaling*: "a solid ground, of the things that one hopes *and* a proof of the things one does not see" (*een vaste grond der dingen, die men hoopt, en een bewijs der zaken die men niet ziet*). Recent versions such as the NRSV, NIV, and ESV go directly to the key *idea* of the text by translating ὑπόστασις ("substance," "essence") as "assurance."

237. GrO: προσερχώμεθα μετὰ ἀληθινῆς καρδίας ἐν πληροφορίᾳ πίστεως; *Statenvertaling*: "Wij hebben de vrijmoedigheid, en den toegang ment vertrouwen, door geloof aan Hem" ("We have the confidence and the access with trust, through faith in Him").

238. Cf. Heidegger, *Corpus Theologiae Christianae*, 2:413 (locus XXIV, §80); F. Turretin, *Institutes of Elenctic Theology*, 2:626 (XV.17.xxii).

239. Heidegger, *Corpus Theologiae Christianae*, 2:415 (locus XXIV, §84).

(Rom. 8:24); "Hope does not put us to shame" (Rom. 5:5) but leans upon the faithfulness of God (Heb. 10:23). Hope is not simply an opinion but "a living hope" (1 Pet. 1:3), full of "confidence" and "boasting" (Heb. 3:6, 14; 2 Cor. 3:12), with "full assurance and certainty" (Heb. 6:11).[240] It is vain for Bellarmine to oppose the assurance of hope;[241] according to Scripture, hope is an indubitable, certain expectation of future salvation.

Anxiety and the Marks of Faith in the Spiritual Life

This was the view of faith among the Reformed in the early period.[242] According to Olevianus, "the certainty of faith . . . is, as it were its essential attribute."[243] This view of faith as firm, certain trust[244] continued to dominate until about the second quarter of the seventeenth century. At that time, doubt and uncertainty arose; the great majority of believers consisted of anxious believers, stuck in the middle, an intermediate class. And among the practical writers especially, this gradually led to the endless, refined, often subtle marks of the Christian. The question "How does one know that one is elect?" (answer: by faith) was replaced with that other question: "How does one know that one has faith?" That is the most customary path in the Reformed Church for attaining assurance. On the one hand, people said, one must attain assurance; on the other hand, people vigorously resisted enthusiasm: this assurance cannot come through special revelation. The only path that was left was that of testing and self-examination: Do I possess this or that mark to which Holy Scripture connects salvation, grants promises? The marks thus came to have the goal of answering the question: Do I have the right to subsume this minor premise (of my salvation) under that major premise (of God's promise)?

There are a variety of marks; the most important marks identify the nature of grace and seek to answer the question whether we possess grace or not. Additional marks indicate the stage of grace: whether we are infants or mature, a youth or a father, etc.[245] Then there were marks of our state or condition:[246]

240. GrO: ἐλπίδα ζῶσαν; παρρησία; καύχημα; πληροφορία.
241. Heidegger, *Corpus Theologiae Christianae*, 2:415 (locus XXIV, §84).
242. Calvin, *Institutes*, III.ii.14–16.
243. LO: *certitudo fidei essentialis proprietas*, in Heppe, *Reformed Dogmatics*, 586.
244. See also Heidelberg Catechism, Q&A 21: "True faith is not only a sure knowledge by which I hold as true all that God has revealed to us in Scripture; it is also a wholehearted trust, which the Holy Spirit creates in me by the gospel"; *RD*, 4:110–18.
245. GrO: νήπιος; τέλειος. Ed. note: See the discussion in the previous chapter, especially the section including the exposition of 1 John 2:12–14 (§22, "The Growth of the Spiritual Life").
246. Ed. note: Bavinck's term is *gestalten*, which literally means "figure," "shape," or "form."

whether we are good or bad, whether we are spiritually sick or healthy. Lists of marks were also produced for particular virtues and benefits such as faith, hope, love, and the fear of God. Brakel does this, providing marks of election,[247] of faith,[248] of justification,[249] of adoption,[250] of peace,[251] and of joy,[252] and this can be applied and expanded for everything. Finally there were marks of our actions, as to whether they are good or evil.[253]

Here we will speak about the first, most important marks of the nature of grace. Here we need to specify some key features:

a. On the one hand, one must indicate how far unregenerate persons can come in the appearance of a grace-filled life that might provide false assurance:[254] What gifts could unregenerate people receive? What could they experience and yet not have grace? In a word, how far can an "almost Chris-

247. W. à Brakel, *Christian's Reasonable Service*, 1:247–50. Ed. note: À Brakel gives three marks: experience of God's call, faith, and evidence of sanctification.

248. W. à Brakel, *Christian's Reasonable Service*, 2:316–37. Ed. note: À Brakel provides three marks for distinguishing "true believers" from "temporal believers": their sorrow over sin, their exercise of faith, and their practice of holiness.

249. W. à Brakel, *Christian's Reasonable Service*, 2:406–8. Ed. note: According to à Brakel, the "means" by which someone can attain justification "simultaneously serve as proofs and marks which reveal that a person is justified" (406); he suggests three: awareness of and sorrow for one's sin, faith in Christ, and a desire to be sanctified.

250. W. à Brakel, *Christian's Reasonable Service*, 2:428–33. Ed. note: À Brakel first reminds his readers of the marks of justification (428) and then provides three marks of "sonship"— faith, bearing God's image (delighting in the Lord and desiring to do God's will), and "inner motions" (love)—and develops them further by way of analogy with "natural sonship" (wanting to be in God's presence, having a posture of humility, and willing to do God's will).

251. W. à Brakel, *Christian's Reasonable Service*, 2:446–49. Ed. note: À Brakel provides five "infallible marks, in reflection upon which everyone may become manifest to himself . . . that they indeed have true peace with God: being restless when not experiencing peace, being reconciled with God in Christ, inner peace of soul, tenderness of soul that is "readily impaired," and active struggle against sin.

252. W. à Brakel, *Christian's Reasonable Service*, 2:456–61. Ed. note: À Brakel considers "(1) the nature of this joy ('*a delightful motion of the soul, generated by the Holy Spirit in the heart of believers, whereby He convinces them of the felicity of their state, causes them the enjoy the benefits of the covenant of grace, and assures them of their future felicity*'), (2) the opposite of this joy (sorrow), (3) that which resembles this joy (counterfeit joy), and (4) the parameters of this joy (fear of God)" (emphasis in original).

253. Cf. van Aalst, *Geestelijke mengelstoffen*, 1:75.

254. W. à Brakel distinguishes different kinds of unregenerate persons: those who lack knowledge and do not desire it, the indifferent, those who have no earnest concern, those who are externally observant in godliness, those who claim assurance without foundation, and temporal believers (*Christian's Reasonable Service*, 2:310–15). Ed. note: It is important that the reader not become sidetracked from the main concern: assurance of salvation. Bavinck is using the tradition of Puritan piety to provide pastoral guidance for using "marks" of grace to aid Christian self-reflection. His treatment of the "marks" attempts to help us avoid the two extremes of easy and false assurance leading to indifference, on the one hand, and hyperscrupulousness leading to anxiety and doubt, on the other. The message is: do not be fooled by appearances of piety in "almost Christians," and also do not become overwhelmed and discouraged by believing that only heroic faith can save.

tian" come and yet not be a Christian? How near can someone be to the kingdom and still not be in it?[255] It was necessary to call attention to this in order to avoid cultivating false security—for Satan and one's own heart are deceitful (Jer. 17:9)—and in order to unmask hypocrisy (2 Tim. 3:5; 1 Cor. 11:4–5). One finds examples of false security in Scripture as well: King Saul, the rich young man (Matt. 19:16–22), the foolish virgins (Matt. 25:1), Judas, Agrippa (Acts 26:28). Isaiah provides the following description of a people who prayed to God but were nevertheless unacceptable to him:

> Yet they seek me daily
>   and delight to know my ways,
> as if they were a nation that did righteousness
>   and did not forsake the judgment of their God;
> they ask of me righteous judgments;
>   they delight to draw near to God. (Isa. 58:2)

Witsius enumerates the best characteristics of the unregenerate in terms of three features:[256]

First, it is possible for an unregenerate person to act in civic affairs far more honestly and morally than a believer does[257] (Mark 10:21; Phil. 3:6); such people can excel in friendliness, morality, patience, the courage of martyrdom, the power of faith, love for the fatherland, for parents, children, and even for God (an idol). Men like Socrates, Cato, Seneca, Buddha, and Muhammad show a disposition for religion. Scripture testifies to this disposition (Ezek. 33:31–32; Mark 6:20), finding it on one occasion even in wicked King Ahab (1 Kings 21:27–28). It is often found in zeal for religion, for church and Christian interests (2 Kings 10:15–16; Matt. 23:15; Rom. 10:2), so that someone gladly undergoes martyrdom (Augustine).

255. See Perkins, "Hoe verre een verworpene kan gaan in den Christelijken wandel" ("How Far a Reprobate Can Go in the Christian Walk"); Meade, *Almost Christian Discovered*; Witsius, *Geestelyke printen, van een onwedergeboorne op sijn beste en een wedergeboorne op sijn slechtste* (*Spiritual Portraits of the Unregenerate at His Best and the Regenerate at His Worst*). Ed. note: Bavinck took the title of the Perkins pamphlet from the table of contents of *Werken*, 3; the actual title above the text is "Eenige voorstellingen, verklarende hoe verre yemant kan gaan in de belijdenis des euangeliums, en nochtans een godtlooze, en verworpene zijn" ("Several Propositions, Clarifying How Far a Person Can Go in the Confession of the Gospel, and Nonetheless Be Godless and Reprobate"). Matthew Meade (1630–99) was an English Puritan congregationalist minister.

256. Cf. Voetius, "De Simplicitate et Hypocrisi," 2:487. Ed. note: It is important to keep Bavinck's intentions in mind here. He introduces these three characteristics not to praise the virtues of the unregenerate nor to encourage believers to do so but to remind believers that they should not put too much stock in the so-called virtues of the unregenerate.

257. Ed. note: The paragraphs that follow are interpretive elaborations of Bavinck's very cryptic notes.

Second, an unregenerate person can have great intellectual knowledge, can accept God's Word as true (2 Pet. 2:21; Matt. 7:22), and can prophesy in Jesus's name and perform mighty deeds (Acts 8:13, Simon the sorcerer; cf. 1 Cor. 13:1–2). A person can experience a taste for God's Word (Isa. 58:2; Matt. 13:20–21), be enlightened by the Holy Spirit (Heb. 6:4–5) like Balaam was (Num. 24:15–16), and have gifts of the Spirit—for example, of prayer.

And third, in their wills and passions, unregenerate persons can have sadness about and fight against their sins (2 Cor. 7:10, "worldly sorrow"); biblical examples include Pharaoh (Exod. 9:27), King Saul (1 Sam. 24:17; 26:21), Felix (Acts 24:25), and Judas (Matt. 27:4). Such people can have a love for virtue, as Balaam did (Num. 22:18; 24:13); think also of men like Cicero and Seneca. They can have some taste of God's common grace[258] (Heb. 6:4–5; Num. 23:10), and even have a desire for grace (the foolish virgins in Jesus's parable desired oil, Matt. 25:8). If they have a hope for heaven and expect him, they may suffer for Christ (1 Cor. 13:2). They can have the Spirit of God like Balaam (Num. 24:2), prophesy like Saul (1 Sam. 10:11), and, like Judas, cast out devils. Meade enumerates some twenty things that an unregenerate person can have, and Perkins lists about thirty-three.[259]

b. On the other hand, these spiritual writers wanted to indicate the minimum amount of grace needed for someone to be a genuine, upright Christian. The question of "how small an amount still saves" was necessary in order to comfort those weak in faith and anxious.[260] Grace in a genuinely converted person can be very small indeed, not only subjectively but also objectively. There are bruised reeds, faintly burning wicks (Isa. 42:3), newborn infants (1 Pet. 2:2). Witsius discerns this once again in terms of three things:[261]

258. Ed. note: See Bavinck, "Common Grace."

259. Ed. note: Meade, *Almost Christian*, 42–138; providing Meade's list of twenty shows the extent to which Bavinck made use of it; a person *may* have any of the following and be only *almost a Christian*: knowledge; gifts, even spiritual gifts; external profession and conduct; going far in opposing sin; hating sin; strong resolution against sin (vows and promises); internal combat against sin; active church membership; hope of heaven; visible changes in life; great zeal for religion; an active life of prayer; suffering for Christ's sake; being called by God and accepting the call; the Spirit of God (Balaam); faith; love of the saints; obedience of God's commandments; outward sanctification (without real inward renewal); and fulfillment of all duties of worship. Perkins, "Hoe verre een verworpene kan gaan."

260. Perkins, *Het mostaart-zaatjen of de minste mate der genade die 'er is, of wezen kan, krachtig tot de zaligheyt* (original: Perkins, *A Graine of Musterd-Seede: or, The Least Measure of Grace That Is or Can Be Effectuall unto Salvation*, in Perkins, *A Golden Chaine*); Saldenus, *Een Christen vallende en opstande*. Ed. note: Since Saldenus's publication date, 1884, is in the main text of the manuscript and not a marginal note added later, we have here an important clue for when Bavinck composed the manuscript.

261. Ed. note: Bavinck's source here is Witsius, *Geestelyke printen*, chap. 2 of which examines the extent to which unregenerate persons can display good outward behavior (pp. 7–22);

First, Christians can be so weak that they repeatedly fall into sin (Ps. 19:13; James 3:2; Heb. 12:1), even into gross sins, like Noah, Lot, David, and Peter. They can remain in sin for a long time without feeling [remorse], like David (2 Sam. 12:13; cf. Isa. 63:17), and sometimes fall back into the same sin: Peter denied [the Lord] three times,[262] Abraham lied twice (Gen. 12:13; 20:2), Lot [got drunk and sinned with both of his daughters] (Gen. 19:30–38).[263]

Second, a regenerate person can have a very limited knowledge [of] the truth. Some people are like children in their understanding (1 Cor. 14:20), newborn infants (1 Pet. 2:2), inexperienced in the word of righteousness (Heb. 5:13; cf. Acts 19:2, where people know nothing about the Holy Spirit); Peter understood nothing about Jesus's suffering (Matt. 16:22). Thus, many understand very little of the truth, not merely because of limited understanding but also thanks to various prejudices, such as Philip (John 14:9) and the Emmaus travelers (Luke 24:25). It is even possible that doubts arise about the truth of Scripture and of the faith (Asaph in Ps. 73:2).[264]

Third, grace can also be very limited with respect to our wills and affections. Some have no appetite for Holy Scripture, prayer, worship; they live in spiritual desertion (Pss. 77; 119:83), without any feeling for God's grace, being fearful of death.[265]

But Witsius then goes on to indicate why even such regenerated persons at their worst stand far above the most eminent unregenerate person.[266] There is an essential distinction between the grace of the former and that of the latter. Objectively, grace in the regenerate person is the fruit of the regenerating Holy Spirit (John 3:5), as the Spirit of Christ (Rom. 8:9), while in the unregenerate it is only of the Spirit as the Spirit of God.[267] But there is also

---

chap. 3 examines the extent to which unregenerate persons can display gifts and illumination of understanding (pp. 22–30); chap. 4 examines the extent to which unregenerate persons can come in the movement of their wills and emotions (pp. 30–41).

262. See chap. 11, "Pathologies of the Spiritual Life," below; Saldenus, *Een Christen vallende en opstande*.

263. Witsius, *Geestelyke printen*, 27–31 (chap. 6). Ed. note: Bavinck's paragraph restates Witsius's three propositions (*stellingen*) in this chapter.

264. Witsius, *Geestelyke printen*, 31–37 (chap. 7). Ed. note: Bavinck's paragraph restates Witsius's four propositions (*stellingen*) in this chapter.

265. Witsius, *Geestelyke printen*, 37–41 (chap. 8). Ed. note: Bavinck's paragraph restates Witsius's three propositions (*stellingen*) in this chapter.

266. Witsius, *Geestelyke printen*, 41–59 (chaps. 9–11).

267. Ed. note: Bavinck thus indicates an important categorical difference between the general cosmic work of the Holy Spirit in creation and providence (establishing order, giving life, bestowing gifts) and the soteriological or saving, redemptive work of the Spirit post-Pentecost (regeneration, conversion, sanctification, preservation).

a subjective difference. The marks of genuine grace come down especially to these two:[268]

First, the knowledge of the regenerate, no matter how minuscule, is a spiritual knowledge that has as its object not the words but the realities that one knows not from hearing but from one's own experience. It is like the difference between someone who has seen a map of a country and one who has seen the country itself. The knowledge of the regenerate causes Christ to appear as precious and honored (1 Pet. 2:7), it humbles (Matt. 11:29), and it is practical, not speculative (James 3:15–17).

And second, in their wills and inclinations, regenerated persons are no longer slaves of sin (Rom. 6:14) and no longer view sin as their lord, but as their tyrant (Rom. 7:23). They hate sin as sin (Gen. 39:9) and therefore hate not some special sins but all sins, even the smallest (Ps. 119:128). On the other hand, they long for grace, desire to be Christ's property. They will not exchange even the miserable circumstances in which they live for all the good of the world. The desire for Christ within them is upright; they will lay themselves open before God (Ps. 26:2), want to hide nothing.

All these marks can be divided into two kinds:

- *Negative*: spiritual poverty, sorrow for sin, distrust of every creature, withdrawing one's heart from earthly things, and not depending on virtue, money, religion, morality, God's general love, baptism, profession of faith, blessings, chastisement, and the like. In that connection, one must always distinguish between poverty and sorrow that is genuine and spiritual and that which is natural and false.[269]

- *Positive*: faith, conversion, and love for truth, God's people, prayer, reading Holy Scripture, church, fellowship,[270] Christ, God. In that con-

---

268. Witsius, *Geestelyke printen*, 41–59 (chaps. 9–11); Perkins, *Het mostaart-zaatjen*; Taffin, *Marks of God's Children*; E. Erskine, *De verzekering des geloofs*, 73–80. Ed. note: This single monograph in Dutch is essentially a translation of E. Erskine, "Assurance of Faith." But the unnamed Dutch translator has expanded the text and, in the section cited by Bavinck, has significantly reordered and reconstructed it, turning 46 pages of the English text into 102 pages of Dutch text. Consequently, there is a shift in emphasis: the original is primarily concerned with the imperative placed on believers to find assurance, the Dutch more with elaborating the marks. See also R. Erskine, "Believer's Internal Witness"; Heppe, *Geschichte des Pietismus und der Mystik*, 58; Buddeus, *Institutiones Theologiae Moralis*, 295; van Aalst, *Geestelijke mengelstoffen*, 1:71–83; van den Honert, *De mensch in Christus*, 735–36, talks about judging others; W. à Brakel, *Christian's Reasonable Service*, 2:307–40 (§33); Vilmar, *Theologische Moral*, 2/3:65–118. The two paragraphs that follow are Bavinck's summary of Witsius, *Geestelyke printen*, 43–59 (chaps. 10–11).

269. W. à Brakel, *Christian's Reasonable Service*, 2:307–40 (chap. 33).

270. DO: *gezelschap*.

nection one must again distinguish between true and sham believers, between saving faith and historical faith or temporal faith. Genuine faith accepts Christ repeatedly and entirely (also as priest and king, not just as prophet) and him solely (not in part, along with the world), yearns for him, and considers him precious. With a view to those weak in faith, two propositions are defended: (a) lamenting about a lack of grace is itself grace;[271] (b) a desire to believe, to be sure, does not meet the full definition of faith (the nature of faith), but it is faith in terms of God's acceptance; God takes the willing for the deed.[272] Therefore, we go to the greatest length to track down the least, the most minute amount of grace, just as one extends assurance increasingly further. The distance between the first, the smallest grace and the full assurance of faith is made increasingly larger and is filled with various forms of faith, experiences, and kinds of anxieties.

What should we now think of this doctrine of the marks?

- First, self-examination is necessary and profitable. Scripture repeatedly urges that it be done (2 Cor. 13:5–6; Zeph. 2:1). It also involves our state for eternity, our immortal soul. That self-examination—even in the natural realm, self-knowledge is the first lesson—must occur in uprightness, in God's presence, after preparation, and must be repeated again and again. We must warn, however, against repeating it too often. One must not always be constructing the foundation but must build upon it (Heb. 6:1; Rev. 3:2).[273] It is a mistake of Reformed spiritual life always to be peering at oneself, at one's faith, at conversion. Rather, that faith becomes more powerful precisely in love and good works, and one who continues building upon the faith automatically experiences, in this building, a proof of the firmness of the foundation. Self-examination must not be instituted first of all during dark periods but during periods of light and buoyancy. In the dark, we cannot see the tender plant of spiritual life. Neither may we expect that we will always recognize ourselves in every mark that has been established, or that assurance necessarily flows forth from them.
- Second, a benchmark, or marks, is needed for examination.[274] All of these must be derived from Scripture. Establishing those marks is a work

271. Perkins, *Werken*, 3:86.
272. Perkins, *Werken*, 3:84.
273. Cf. van Aalst, *Geestelijke mengelstoffen*, 1:66; van Mastricht, *Theoretico-Practica Theologia*, III.ii.12 ("De Examinatione Sui Ipsius, Eiusque Neglectu").
274. DO: *toetssteen; kentekenen.*

of the most tender sort, requiring knowledge both of Scripture and of one's own heart.[275] In itself there is nothing wrong with looking for the marks in Holy Scripture and identifying them; Scripture is full of marks: whoever believes is saved; whoever is led by the Spirit is a child of God; blessed are the poor, those who mourn, those who hunger, etc. What is meant by these, identifying these, is good; but let this rest upon sound exegesis. The flights of fancy that the doctrine of the marks has taken since ca. 1650, in terms of pulpit, home visiting, etc., have been partially mistaken. The doctrine of the marks originated in the weakened life of faith after the Reformation; they were present in the Reformation itself but undeveloped. In general, that doctrine did not strengthen the life of faith at that time, but weakened it, held it down, and kept it undeveloped.

Therefore, it is our duty to posit only great, clear, transparent, knowable marks that run no risk of eliminating the essential difference between converted and unconverted; all subtlety and personal invention must be avoided most stringently. The marks may never be multiplied endlessly, and they should not be preached from the pulpit constantly and in their totality,[276] as happened especially after Lampe. On the other hand, however, we also have a duty to comfort the anxious by helping them to know the nature of grace in its initial beginnings.[277] Knowledge of the human heart, psychology—both natural and spiritual—is a requirement for the shepherd. The danger of the doctrine of the marks is the same as the danger of homeopathy; homeopaths who are constantly thinking about their own health and sickness usually feel—this is the result— that they are more or less sick, or else they make themselves sick. So too with those who constantly examine themselves in the spiritual realm: they repeatedly see that they are sick, imperfect, and then they continue to stay at that point and lose the objective ground, Christ, from their view. The doctrine of the marks assumes doubt[278] and weakening of the spirit and cultivates that doubt rather than healing persons of it. And even where it brings profit and comfort, it often serves to strengthen the anxious in their doubt and pride and [leads them] to surrender to their delusion of considering themselves to be among the best of believers.

• Third, the doctrine of the marks is also merely a means to assurance. By itself neither the major premise (whoever believes is saved) nor the minor premise (I believe) is able to supply the conclusion; this may be

---

275. Van Aalst, *Geestelijke mengelstoffen*, 1:73.
276. Van Aalst, *Geestelijke mengelstoffen*, 1:77.
277. Ed. note: I.e., that these beginnings may be small.
278. GrO: διάστασις.

possible theoretically, but not practically. But the Holy Spirit wishes nonetheless, by making use of this means, to confirm and establish us. The confidence to draw the conclusion comes from the Holy Spirit;[279] grace and the awareness of that grace comes from him. He leads us to recognize the very image of God in the image of God worked in us by him. The minor premise is certain and fixed when the Holy Spirit speaks to us through it. Thus, we can be infallibly assured of our faith. The accepting of the minor premise (I believe) is an act of faith and not an act of feeling, from which it is different.[280] The act of faith— that is, believing I am saved—is of the same nature as faith in Christ; the former is the reflexive act of the latter.[281] With the same act of faith I embrace Christ and know myself to be the one doing so. The more firmly, the more earnestly, I embrace Christ, the sooner this faith brings about the reflexive act. As long as I know well, then I also know that I know, immediately and automatically. The absence of assurance (al- though this is worked from God's side through the Holy Spirit and is his gift, just as all sanctification is) from our side always has its cause in a less-than-decisive grasping of Christ. And that must be identified and discovered. Often it lurks in a bosom of sin, pride, self-satisfaction, and self-pity and betrays weakness of character. The requirement, the duty of faith, must therefore be preached. And further: when one has properly posited the major and minor premises, then one may confidently draw the conclusion. Nothing prohibits us from doing so. If I dare to say in uprightness, "I believe," then I may confess that and may credit the promises of God to myself. Then I need to wait for nothing else, no special revelation, no confidence-building grace, or the like. Then I appropriate nothing unlawful for myself.

7. *Good Works as Fruit of Faith.* In the third place,[282] the Holy Spirit pro- duces assurance in us by shining light on the minor premise (I believe) from our good works, as the fruit of faith.[283] Good works are fruit, a manifesta- tion of faith (Matt. 21:43; Luke 8:15; 13:9), by which false prophets, etc.,

---

279. Van Aalst, *Geestelijke mengelstoffen*, 1:78.

280. E. Erskine, "Assurance of Faith," 158–60; see no. 7, "Good Works as Fruit of Faith," below.

281. LO: *actus reflexus.*

282. Ed. note: Bavinck's major point in this section is that the Holy Spirit works assurance in the believer in an orderly, threefold manner. He does so, "first, through the Word by making the major premise—God's promises are true—clear to us" (no. 5, p. 672); second, he "works assurance in us by shining light on the minor premise, the state of our soul" (no. 6, p. 674).

283. Schneckenburger, *Vergleichende Darstellung*, 1:38–74 (§3), 265–87 (§14).

are recognized (Matt. 7:16, 20) and the goodness of the tree is known (Matt. 7:17; 12:33). In the Gospel of John, the result of communion with Christ is to be set free from sin (John 8:32, 36), to distance oneself from sin (5:14; 8:11), to bear fruit (15:1–2), to keep the commandments as the expression and proof of love toward him (14:15, 21). And all those commandments of Jesus are concentrated in the great command of brotherly love (13:34–35; 15:12–13, 17). Similarly, we see this in the First Epistle of John: in the love that is born from faith in Jesus, we keep the commandments of God, which is the fruit and proof of our faith, of our being in God (1 John 2:3–6, 29). Whoever does right, is righteous, is born of God (3:6, 9) and is from God, while whoever sins does not know God (3:10). Doing righteousness consists especially of brotherly love (2:7–11; 3:10–11). Love toward God and love toward our brothers and sisters are correlative demonstrations of true love (4:20–21; 5:1–2). The latter is the sign that God abides in us (4:16), a sign that we are born of God (4:7). To have fellowship with God is "to walk in the light" because "God is light, and in him is no darkness at all" (1:5; cf. 1:6). The entailment is clear: "But if we walk in the light, as he is in the light, we have fellowship with one another" (1:7). Paul too is zealous about walking in the Spirit (Rom. 6), emphasizes sanctification, and describes faith as working through love (Gal. 5:6, 22). But he moves from faith to works, unlike John, who ascends from works to faith. James 2, however, says that faith without works is dead.[284]

That is also what the Reformed tradition teaches.[285] But one cannot lean upon good works; absolute assurance cannot be deduced from good works, even though faith and election are manifested in good works.[286]

Good works are indeed imperfect, and thus can never supply an infallible conclusion. But we must remember that an upright attitude can indeed be pure, as Paul says: "For I do not do what I want, but I do the very thing I hate. Now if I do what I do not want, I agree with the law, that it is good" (Rom. 7:15–16). That attitude can comfort us even though our works themselves are imperfect. Furthermore, the Holy Spirit also illumines us about our good works and allows us to see the good in them; he testifies through those good works to our conscience. They are media, instruments of his testimony, for every good work is his fruit, a proof that one is walking in the Spirit.

---

284. As does 2 Pet. 1:10: "Be all the more diligent to confirm your calling and election."
285. Calvin, *Institutes*, III.xiv.18–20; III.xv.8.
286. Calvin, *Institutes*, III.ii.38; Heidelberg Catechism, Q&A 86: "Why should we do good works?" Among other reasons, "so that we may be assured of our faith by its fruits." Cf. Canons of Dort, V.9–13; see Keckermann and others in Heppe, *Reformed Dogmatics*, 176–78.

A distinction must still be made between the assurance of faith and feeling assured.[287] The former is a direct act of faith; the latter is a reflexive act of faith in which faith turns inward and considers itself.[288] The first rests upon God, Christ, and the covenant, upon promises that lie outside us; the second rests upon Christ in us. The first is the cause, the second is the fruit. The first rests upon the promise of God, the second upon the enjoyment of the promise. The first abides even where the second is absent: even Jesus cried out, "*My* God."

Up to this point we have considered, in chapter 7, the nature of the spiritual life (§17), its origin (§18), and its first and basic activity (§19); we have also examined life in the Spirit in the church's history, paying particular attention to mysticism, Pietism, and Methodism (chap. 8, §20). Chapter 9 explored the shape and maturation of the Christian life, specifically its form in the imitation of Christ (§21) and its development and growth (§22). In §23 we have been dealing with assurance in the spiritual life. Assurance is a prominent developmental moment in the spiritual life, a powerful proof of growth. But this assurance does not exclude all doubt; the assurance of faith is indeed shaken by doubt and is not free of all anxiety or worry.[289] Believers always have to fight with their own lack of self-confidence, but nonetheless they never fall away from trusting in the compassion of God.[290] The example of David shows this most clearly; in Psalm 42:5 he says, "Why are you cast down, O my soul, / and why are you in turmoil within me?" But then at the same time he also says: "Hope in God; for I shall again praise him, / my salvation and my God" (similarly Pss. 31:22; 77:8–10). Here faith always comes back to the surface, is strengthened with the promises, with prayer. Doubt arises through the fight against the flesh, through feelings of misery and unworthiness, through fear of death. Faith is still imperfect; we always still suffer from the deadly sorrow that comes from lack of confidence;[291] we are never entirely filled with faith. Faith is indeed assurance, but lack of confidence comes from the flesh.[292]

---

287. See E. Erskine, "Assurance of Faith," 158–60.

288. DO: *inkerende*. Ed. note: This is also a point that Bavinck has taken from Erskine: "I remark, that there is a great difference betwixt the assurance of *faith* . . . , and the assurance of *sense*, which follows upon faith. The assurance of faith is a *direct*, but the assurance of sense is a *reflex* act of the soul. The assurance of faith has its object and foundation from *without*, that that of sense has them *within*. The object of the assurance of faith is a *Christ revealed, promised, and offered in the word*; the object of the assurance of sense is a *Christ formed within us by the Holy Spirit*" (E. Erskine, "Assurance of Faith," 158).

289. LO: *dubitatio*; *sollicitudo*; according to Calvin, *Institutes*, III.ii.17–18.

290. LO: *diffidentia*; *decidere ac desciscere*.

291. LO: *morbus diffidentiae*.

292. LO: *certitudo*; *diffidentia*.

The perfection of faith is never obtained here on earth.[293] Erskine[294] insists that "there is no doubting in faith; for faith and doubting are commonly in scripture directly opposed to each other: but though there be no doubting in faith, yet there is much doubting in the believer, by reason of prevailing unbelief and indwelling sin." According to Erskine, assurance belongs to the nature of faith, as does resting [in God] and trusting God. Though the believer does not always feel assured, "is not always actually staying and resting . . . in the Lord," and "is not always trusting," none of this affects the nature of faith any more than the nature of the eye as an organ for seeing is changed when someone momentarily closes both eyes and cannot see. One needs only to remove the impediments, the unbelief, etc., and immediately assurance of faith returns. It is for precisely that reason that we must maintain that doubt is unbelief and sin and conflicts entirely with the nature of faith. All of us must thus endeavor to come to the full assurance of faith[295] and strive to make our calling and election sure (2 Pet. 1:10), grow in the grace and knowledge of Jesus Christ (2 Pet. 3:18), and become strong in grace (2 Tim. 2:1).

---

293. According to Calvin, *Institutes*, IV.xiv.7–8; similarly, Heidegger, *Corpus Theologiae Christianae*, 2:418–19 (locus XXIV, §94), and Cocceius, *Summa Theologiae*, XLIX.15, in Heppe, *Reformed Dogmatics*, 587–88.

294. E. Erskine, "Assurance of Faith," 155. Ed. note: For clarity we have cited directly and more extensively from Erskine's sermon.

295. E. Erskine, "Assurance of Faith," 177–87.

11

Pathologies of the Christian Life

Like natural organisms, the spiritual life can be afflicted by illnesses that disrupt it. While the spiritual life cannot perish or die, it can be arrested, suppressed, hindered, and thwarted in its growth. These illnesses are manifestations of the old nature, contradict our newness in Christ, and remain with Christians until they die. We are healthy, therefore, to the extent that we imitate Jesus. He is the model for our spiritual life.

There is legitimate diversity in the spiritual life, an inevitable result of our individual identities. These make for a rich human society and are good; variety as such, found also among the apostles, does not imply sinfulness or pathology. Even differences among Christian traditions can be constructive. Our concern is with excessive one-sidedness.

We can identify three major spiritual pathologies: intellectualism in various forms, disorders of the heart (soul), and disorders of the will (action, practice). The first places all the emphasis on the Word, on doctrine and knowledge, and can lead to "orthodoxism," rationalism, and various forms of gnosticism; the second restricts religious life to feelings, to the soul, and leads to mysticism and quietism; the third emphasizes action and practice and comes to expression in Pietism, Methodism, fanaticism or enthusiasm, and moralism. In the fuller life of the church these three spiritual illnesses become manifest in confessionalism, indifferentism, and forms of sectarianism or Donatism. In summary, the three major pathologies of the spiritual life are aridity, which has a confession but no life; morbidity, in the narrow sense of the word: false mysticism and false

415

experiential faith; and lethargy (or excessive zeal, or zeal without understanding),
in which energy for action is lacking.[1]

The causes for these diseases cannot be reduced to the variety of individual
personalities but are rooted in sin, specifically (a) the warfare of flesh against the
Spirit; (b) the struggle against the world; (c) temptations; and (d) spiritual desertion.[2]
The warfare between flesh and spirit as an ongoing reality in the life of God's children
is taught in the Old Testament and in the New Testament writings of Peter, James,
John, and Paul. Though Romans 7 describes a conflict in the life of a believer, the
New Testament clearly teaches that we are not to live "according to the flesh" but
"according to the Spirit." Thus, the struggle in the regenerate is altogether different
and the opposite of that found in the unregenerate. In the former it is a battle between
the new "inner person in Christ" and the sin of the "old person" remaining in us. A
believer is a double person living with conflicting desires. The sins of believers are
"sins of weakness" or, better, "faults or defects" rather than "sins of malice." The
spiritual lives of the regenerate can be weakened but never extinguished.

Biblical words for "tempting" or "testing" point to being put on trial. In that
sense God can test us in order to refine or purify us, but God never tempts us.
Temptation seeks to test someone from distrust or with evil intent. Even God can be
put to such a test in unbelief. Scripture teaches that those in Christ can overcome
temptation and that we ought to count testing, including suffering, as occasions
for joy (James, Peter). God may place us in circumstances of temptation (such as
suffering) in order to test us, but it is the devil and his hosts who wage warfare
against God's people. Regenerated people are the objects of temptation; the goal
is to pull them out of the kingdom of light back into the darkness of the world.
Satan tempts us on one side with riches, power, and honor, which pull us more and
more into the world, and on the other side in circumstances of poverty, disgrace,
contempt, and afflictions, which pull us away from God toward doubt and spiritual
assault.

Spiritual writers also speak of times of spiritual desertion as occasions for
temptation. God may at times withdraw his preserving, restraining grace and allow
a person to fall into sin in order to cure the evil as by venom. Believers who fall into
sin may be forsaken as punishment. Finally, believers may be forsaken in order to be
tested. This last desertion, consisting of desolation and spiritual numbness, is also
referred to as assault; it includes struggle, pangs of conscience, and spiritual despair.
This is mentioned frequently in the Old Testament, notably in the psalms of lament,
but it is absent from the New Testament. Christians do experience God's departure

---

1. Ed. note: See n. 82 on lethargy later in this chapter.
2. Ed. note: Bavinck inserted (b) between the lines later; in the later discussion (a) and (b)
appear to be fused, and Bavinck only treats the three original points in the text. See n. 83 below.

from their lives, but this is a chastisement, not an act of his wrath but of his grace. It often follows upon sin, and the peace and assurance that we are God's children leaves us open to the attacks of Satan. This spiritual desertion is different in kind from melancholy, despair, and being possessed.

§24. DISEASES OF THE SPIRITUAL LIFE AND THEIR ROOTS

The spiritual life, like the natural life, is subject to all kinds of hazards.[3] From our earliest years to the most advanced old age, our natural life can be afflicted by illnesses in all its stages, forms, and manifestations. These can affect plants, animals (think of veterinary science), and the human body, but also human intellectual, moral, and emotional life, domestic, social, and political life, artistic and scholarly life. Everything living is subject not only to birth, growth, and death but also to a host of illnesses during its lifetime. Illness is always a disruption of the living organism, whatever sort of life it has. Health consists in the harmony of the organism. Health and sickness therefore presuppose organic life. In the absence of organic life there can be no question of illness. The genuine, normal condition—that is, the health—of an organism consists in the following: (a) A vital principle animates from its center and controls and regulates everything. (b) No organs, parts, or members of an organism, animated from that center, isolate themselves from each other; rather, they cooperate with each other. This should happen in such a way that each member confines itself to being what it is supposed to be and actually is what it is supposed to be, arrogating nothing to itself (egotistically) but also not withdrawing itself (isolation), such that the hand is the hand and nothing more, the foot is the foot, etc. (c) All members together, through the one vital principle, work toward one goal and consider themselves instruments for achieving the one task of life. When an organism is ill, it means that either the vital principle itself or one or more of the members is impaired and thwarted in its normal operation—in carrying out its task—and the organism is therefore not working as a unit toward the one goal.

That is also the way things are in the spiritual life. But there is a difference. By nature, the spiritual life is a life incapable of sin (1 John 3:9) and therefore unable to perish, become ill, or die; it is eternal life (John 3:16). Therefore, a diseased spiritual life, a morbid form of piety, is in fact a "contradiction in terms."[4] It is possible, however, for the spiritual life, as it unfolds and matures,

3. Vitringa, *Korte schets*, chap. 9.
4. LO: *contradictio in adjecto.* De la Saussaye, "Stellingen over ziekelijke vroomheid," 399.

to be arrested, suppressed, hindered, and thwarted in its growth. By illness of the spiritual life we must therefore understand morbid schools of thought, sicknesses of the mind that arrest a person's spiritual life and overwhelm it. The sickness is not located in the new but in the old nature.[5] The new person manifests itself and operates through the old person; that old self is the shroud, the organ, the garb of the new self. If that old self is not normal—is not in the service of the new self—then the new self cannot manifest itself in purity but only in a one-sided way (e.g., only through reason, not through the heart[6] or the will) or else not at all. With all people the old self is not an adequate organ and never will be; the new self is accompanied by a new, resurrection body. That is why no one has a spiritual life that grows and develops normally, without disruption. All believers are more or less sick and remain so until the day they die.

There are differences, however, in degree of the illness, in its duration, and in its character. The closer the approximation to the ideal, the healthier one is. The ideal—harmony and health—consists in this, that the Word of God, which is the meat and drink of the spiritual life—or, if you will, that Christ himself, who is the bread of life—is received into our consciousness by the mouth of faith, is taken into our heart and there transformed into communion with God through Christ in the Holy Spirit. The final goal is for the Word to manifest itself outwardly in good works and deeds—that is, in love of God and neighbor—throughout all spheres of life, such as family, community, and society. In other words, this Word travels through our consciousness inwardly into our heart, which is the storehouse, the treasure house of our being, and from there, outwardly, through our hands. The Word comes from above, enters through our consciousness (the door to our personhood), into the chambers of our heart, our soul, whence our will takes over those treasures and displays them in words and deeds before the eyes of God and others. They are absorbed by our consciousness, preserved by our soul, and reproduced by our will. We are healthy when the pure food of the Word of God finds its way through our spiritual personhood, encounters no hindrances or disruptions along the way, and engages all our organs—intellect, soul, and will, together with their subordinate faculties, namely, reason, understanding, conscience, feelings and passions, instincts and inclinations.

Only Jesus was perfectly healthy, for in him was full harmony; inspiration and manifestation were one; there was no domination of the mind, of reason, of the will; he did not lack the capacity for reason but knew its proper place

5. Cf. mental illness resulting from concussion.
6. DO: *gemoed*.

and did not succumb to intellectualism;[7] he was not a fanatic or Methodist.[8] He cannot be classified as belonging to any category of person; all classes of people find in him an aspect that they place in the foreground. He is "every-man" in the best sense of the word; to apply to him one of our labels, such as Reformed, Lutheran, or Pietist, would be to disregard his universality and the "dignity" to which Jesus personally lays claim.[9] That would be as foolish as the person who found Jesus rather too "latitudinarian."[10] We are healthy, therefore, to the extent that we imitate Jesus. He is the model for our spiri-tual life.

Legitimate Diversity and One-Sidedness

Every pathology is a deviation from the right path of development (indi-cated above and followed by Jesus), a wrong direction from a sound starting point.[11] Those pathologies, which begin as "one-sidedness,"[12] are to some extent inevitable, based on our individuality and nature. We naturally differ by sex: the woman is a being of feelings, the man of reason; the woman is a creature of emotions (heart), the man of deeds (will). We differ in age: young people are carefree, impetuous, revolutionary; the adult male is political and calculating, and senior citizens more conservative. We differ in character and temperament: one person is sanguine, another choleric, a third is phlegmatic, a fourth is a hypochondriac. We differ in makeup and proportion of faculties: one is more a person of thinking, another of willing, a third of feeling. All these differences, as well as many others, are affected by the spiritual life; to some extent they can be transformed, but they cannot be erased. Whether they exist and remain as such in the spiritual person is difficult to say. It is not evident in Jesus; he was not a man *primarily* of thought or of feeling or of will. He was a male, yet with womanly tenderness; he cannot be classi-fied; in him there was complete harmony. Moreover, we read that in heaven humans do not marry but will be like the angels, so that sex distinctions will

---

7. Ed. note: Bavinck's literal statement is "He did not repudiate the rights of the mind" (*hij miskent niet de rechten van verstand*).

8. Ed. note: Bavinck is not making a judgment about a denomination but simply echoing his critique of mysticism, Pietism, and Methodism earlier in chap. 8 (§20); his concern there and here is with "one-sidedness," a failure to live out the full dimension of the image of God. His concluding sentence in chap. 8 captures this well: "By putting the *will* in the foreground in order to oppose quietism and predestination, Methodism lacks a harmonious anthropology of the whole person."

9. LO: *omnis homo*; DO: *trotsheid* ("pride").

10. DO: *ruim*.

11. De la Saussaye, "Stellingen over ziekelijke vroomheid," 401.

12. DO: *eenzijdigheid*.

be abolished, and that in Christ there is neither male nor female, barbarian nor Scythian, but only a new creature (Gal. 3:28; 6:15; Col. 3:11).

What, therefore, speaks in favor of the cancellation of those differences in the heavenly life is the fact that they are always one-sided, that they do not represent full harmony. What speaks against it, however, is that in heaven, too, people are great and small. These differences are precisely what makes for the richness of life, and abolishing them would make all people the same, whereas everywhere there is variety in unity (e.g., in leaves of the tree), and beauty is based on this variety. Variety as such does not imply sinfulness or pathology; the distinction between men and women existed also before the fall. The apostles, too, exhibit variety in teaching, yet that was not fallible and sinful. Indeed, variety must continue so that humanity may be a single organism in which one member is different from and complements the other. Such variety can even be observed in the character, education, and temperament of the apostles. Paul[13] and Peter are men of thought, thinkers who are set on doctrine (especially in the Pastoral Letters and 2 Peter) and knowledge; yet they also differ in that Paul is a person of faith, Peter of hope. Paul is more a New Testament man, Peter an Old Testament man: Paul sees the New Testament concealed in the Old and draws it out (e.g., the faith of Abraham), whereas Peter sees the Old Testament evident in the New.[14] Accordingly, Paul looks at everything from the perspective of the cross and takes his stand at the cross; Peter stands in the Old Testament and looks forward to the cross. Paul looks at his surroundings, at gentiles, at Israel, taking in past and future; he is the philosopher of the cross, the writer of world history, a prophet of the Old and a seer of the New Covenant. Peter is much more limited in vision; although he looks forward to the cross from the Old Testament, he does not look beyond it to the future and does not draw the consequences from the cross (he has to be deliberately shown that the law has been abolished). Peter is a man of talent, Paul is a philosophical genius. Yet both are thinkers.

By contrast, John is a man of feeling, of the heart. He is the apostle of love and of life. John does not think but ponders; he does not philosophize but contemplates; he does not discourse but delights.[15] He is passionate by nature; therefore, he is called Boanerges, "son of thunder" (Mark 3:17). Indeed, he remains so in his letters: "If anyone comes to you and does not bring this teaching, do not receive him into your house or give him any greeting"

13. For a character sketch of Paul, see Wernle, *Paulus als Heidenmissionar*.
14. LO: *Novum Testamentum in Vetere latet; Vetus Testamentum in Novo patet.*
15. Ed. note: Bavinck wrote in the margin, "What a difference there is between John and Paul on the doctrines of regeneration, justification, and adoption to sonship (υἱοθεσία)."

(2 John 10); "For many deceivers have gone out into the world, those who do not confess the coming of Jesus Christ in the flesh. Such a one is the deceiver and the antichrist" (2 John 7). John is difficult with strangers and off-putting, but that stems from his intimate love of Jesus and the brothers and sisters. He cannot tolerate evil being spoken of Jesus, for he has lain on Jesus's bosom: he knows his love, his goodness. Paul rushes on with his thoughts; his words cannot keep up with his ideas; he cannot write as fast as the ideas come to him.[16] That is why we see Paul breaking off his train of thought and seizing upon another before he has fully finished the first; hence the anacolutha[17] that are so different from the calm writer of the Letter to the Hebrews, who spins out his thoughts without such shifts and sticks to his line of thought despite using the longest parenthetic clauses.[18]

Paul can therefore link the deepest thoughts to simple things, seeing the universal in the particular, as he does in Philippians 2:5: "Have this mind among yourselves, which is yours in Christ Jesus" (cf. 2 Cor. 1:17–20; Gal. 6:6–7). But John wobbles. He revels in the stream of his thoughts; once he has a thought, he does not easily let it go; he will say it again, hence the apparent repetition, the monotony. John does not think logically, does not extrapolate, does not have a train of thought that he pursues, but allows himself to be led, to meander through his meditative contemplation. With Paul, the thoughts are so many, so rich, so deep, that words cannot express them; his sentences literally explode. With John, the words are so sweet and soft that he does not tire of repeating them. Finally, James is the man of the will, of the deed, of practical life. James is not a thinker, nor a mystic, but "the righteous one," a true Israelite. Pure religion before God and the Father is this: to refuse to privilege the rich, to visit widows and orphans, to show your faith by your works, and to be doers of the word. Characteristically, therefore: we have many letters of Paul, the man of thought; from John, we have a Gospel and three epistles, of which the second is addressed to a woman (though she may stand for the congregation); of James we have one letter, filled with ethical

16. "Paul speaks, writes, and acts with full maturity; his eloquence comes from the bitterest grief and the most blissful rapture, tones of the deepest love (1 Cor. 13), paternal admonitions, poignant statements. He has advice for every situation; he is equally at home with doctrine and practice" (Jacobi, "Zur Missionsthätigkeit," 297–99).

17. Ed. note: Plural of *anacolouthon* (ἀνακόλουθον), a sudden grammatical or conceptual shift in a sentence.

18. Ed. note: Bavinck's contrast here is worth noting because it shows he accepted modern critical studies that discount Paul as the author of Hebrews; Bavinck's Bible, the Dutch *Statenvertaling*, explicitly identifies the letter as "the Epistle of Paul to the Hebrews" (*De Zendbrief van den Apostel Paulus an de Hebreën*), and the Belgic Confession (art. 4) does the same. In fact, the entire literary analysis that follows has a distinctly "modern" feel.

lessons, morality. James could not write more: moral lessons always come down to the same thing.

These differences among the apostles did not lead to positions that are mutually exclusive. They were kept from that by the guidance of the Holy Spirit. They complement each other. To elevate Paul at the expense of John and James is to err and to fail to do full justice to Christ. But carry any of the three emphases too far and what you get are symptoms of morbid piety, spiritual disease. These emphases led to a loss of balance[19] already in the Alexandrian school, which strived for "knowledge" or *gnōsis*;[20] in the Asia Minor school, which put John's warmth in the foreground; in the African school, which followed James, the man of practice, and was the first to develop an ecclesiology. There is a one-sided imbalance in the Church of Rome, which is more the church of Peter and the Old Testament; in the Reformed churches, which follow Paul more; and then again among the Lutherans, who tend to take after John and Paul, while the Calvinists tend toward James and Paul (Luther called the Epistle of James a "straw epistle"). More particularly, the following disorders can arise.[21]

The Three Major Pathologies

IN THE DIRECTION OF THE INTELLECT

Here, all emphasis is placed on the Word, doctrine, knowledge, while failing to appreciate the rights of the emotional life and the practical life. This can operate in two directions:[22] people may want to keep the church's teachings pure, or they may wish to change and improve them. This illness is generally called intellectualism—in other words, the school that objectively isolates doctrine from experience and life, subjectively isolates the mental faculty from the life of feeling (the heart) and the will, identifying the mind objectively with doctrine, subjectively with the human being. Among those who wish to preserve the church's teachings, this intellectualism manifests itself as orthodoxism and

19. DO: *eenzijdig* ("one-sided").
20. GrO: γνῶσις.
21. Ed. note: Abraham Kuyper wrote a series of articles in *De Heraut*, nos. 1159–99 (March 11–December 3, 1900), on three spiritual pathologies that threaten the church: intellectualism, mysticism, and pragmatism. These were reprinted as *Drie kleine vossen* ("Three Little Foxes"); see 9–44 for the section on intellectualism. Cf. Kuipers, *Abraham Kuyper*, 331. See also Hugenholtz, *Studiën*, 2:15; Karl Heinrich Sack provides an introduction to spiritual pathologies; see Hagenbach, *Encyklopädie und Methodologie*, 331n8; Rauwenhoff, *Wijsbegeerte van den godsdienst*; Hartmann, *Die Religion des Geistes*; Niemeijer, "Intellectualisme, mysticisme en moralisme." Niemeijer follows Rauwenhoff and Hartmann.
22. Pelt, *Theologische Encyklopädie*, 453–68 (§69, "Übersicht der confessionellen Prinzipienlehre"); de la Saussaye, "Stellingen over ziekelijke vroomheid," 398.

scholasticism. "Orthodoxism" comes from the two Greek words ὀρθός ("correct, right, true") and δόξα ("opinion, judgment"); it is the school that not only holds correctness and purity of thought in high esteem (as orthodoxy does) but considers it the highest and the only criterion.[23] Orthodoxy, in the proper sense of the word, is the school that agrees with the teachings of the church; it is therefore an absolute concept: one is either orthodox or one is not; whoever denies article 36 of the Belgic Confession, for example, is therefore no longer truly orthodox.[24] An orthodoxist (like all who may be identified by terms ending in -ist or -ism) is someone who considers being orthodox the ultimate and decisive criterion of truth and godliness, regards the teachings of the church as immutable (which the orthodox do not do, at least not in theory), and therefore regards them as no longer subject to any scriptural test. We find a good example in the Eastern Church, which, after the great doctrinal controversies, became immersed in orthodoxism, especially under the influence of John of Damascus. The title of the Damascene's dogmatics, *The Exact Exposition of the Orthodox Faith*,[25] illustrates the pride of the Eastern Church in considering itself as *the* orthodox church. This is also the church that, since February 19, 842, annually celebrates the Feast of Orthodoxy.[26]

Although revision of the confession was deemed possible in theory, a similar orthodoxism prevailed especially among the Protestant churches in the seventeenth century. In practice this leads to a doctrinal righteousness, which is worse than a works righteousness; it conceives of saving faith as intellectual assent to the church's doctrine (instead of trusting with the heart in the person of Christ); it turns doctrine into dead formulas, something fossilized and petrified. It is nothing if not Pharisaic: a beautiful confession on the lips but inwardly full of dead men's bones. This is one of the most common and dangerous spiritual sicknesses in Protestantism (far more than in Catholicism). Academically, this doctrine-preserving intellectualism manifests itself in Scholasticism.[27] A "scholastic" is anyone who is connected with schooling, scholars, or researchers, hence educated, erudite, scientific, people "who live in letters"[28]—even if they do this at home. In the medieval period they

---

23. The Scriptures speak of "good doctrine" (τῆς καλῆς διδασκαλίας, 1 Tim. 4:6), "the teaching that accords with godliness" (τῇ κατ' εὐσέβειαν διδασκαλίᾳ, 1 Tim. 6:3), "sound words" (ὑγιαίνοντες λόγοι, 2 Tim. 1:13), "the word of truth" (τὸν λόγον τῆς ἀληθείας, 2 Tim 2:15), and "sound teaching/doctrine" (ὑγιαίνουσα διδασκαλία, 2 Tim. 4:3; Titus 1:9).

24. Cf. the confessionalism that identifies a specific confession with *the* truth and considers it immutable.

25. GrO: Ἔκδοσις ἀκριβὴς τῆς ὀρθοδόξου πίστεως.

26. GrO: ἡ κυριακὴ τῆς ὀρθοδοξίας. Cf. Burger, "Orthodoxie."

27. Cf. F. Nitzsch, "Scholastische Theologie."

28. LO: *qui in literis vivunt.*

distinguished "positive theology," which exposited the teachings of Scripture
and the fathers, from "scholastic theology," which made the various dogmas
into objects of a scientific operation, wishing to give a methodical form to the
content of faith.[29] Thus positive and scholastic theology differed not in content or material but in form and method. The rise of scholastic theology was
inevitable; after all, the church's teaching or doctrine was ready-made, clothed
with divine authority, but her dogmas lay about loose and unconnected.[30]
The human spirit, which seeks unity, needed to see the interconnection of
those dogmas in order to be able to own them, to arrange them according
to a fixed method. In itself, that was not wrong. But what method did they
adopt, which logic and dialectic? Those of Aristotle. And scholastic theology
consisted precisely in the dialectic and systematic reproduction of dogma—
that is, in the endeavor to create a unity of the "separate components" of the
church's doctrine, to bring harmony among the decretals of the councils,
the "teachings" of Scripture and the church fathers.[31] Scholastic theology
also sought further to refine concepts already defined, to provide further
proof for controversial and contested dogmas, and to fill gaps by drawing
implications from church doctrine to matters about which the church had
not yet pronounced. Scholasticism, therefore, is the attempt to absorb into
our consciousness that part of church doctrine that is externally available
to us. In and of itself, that is not wrong.[32] All thoughtful Christians would
do the same; the rational content of the faith must have a point of contact
within our consciousness; otherwise we will never own it (it is impossible to
comprehend $2 \times 2 = 5$). Nor is it wrong to seek connection, unity, and system
in dogmas; everyone does that, including the biblical scholar, who does not
merely discuss the various doctrines haphazardly but follows a certain order
and hence assumes a system, a unity in the dogmas. There are, however, a
number of areas where Scholasticism went wrong, both in the Middle Ages
and in the seventeenth century.[33]

29. LO: *theologia positiva*; *sententiae scripturae et partum*; *theologia scholastica*.

30. Ed. note: Bavinck is not contrasting church doctrine (*de leer der Kerk*) with church
dogmas but pointing out that reflective, scientific work is needed to disclose the inner coherence
and unity of these loosely arranged doctrines/dogmas. For more on Bavinck's reflections on the
unity of doctrine/dogma, see his "Pros and Cons of a Dogmatic System."

31. LO: *disjecta membra*; *sententiae*.

32. There is much that is good in Scholasticism, and clear and insightful. Pope Leo XIII
certainly understood this and commended the study of Thomas Aquinas.

33. Cf. Schweizer, *Die Glaubenslehre*, 1:102; Marckius, *Het merch der christelijke Godts-
geleertheit*, 12 (I.xxvi); de Moor, *Commentarius Perpetuus*, vol. 1; Voetius, "De Theologia
Scholastica"; Alsted, *Praecognitorum Theologicorum, Libri Duo*, 1:135–44 (chap. 18). There
are three periods of Scholasticism:

1. While in theory Scholasticism included Scripture among the sources of theology, calling it the supreme source, in fact it did not draw its material from Scripture but from the councils (and Aristotle?) and the church fathers, and only a few of them and not even the oldest ones.[34]

2. Because it did not consider Scripture the "standard" once the material content was known (even if it was biblical), Scripture was dropped and not regarded as the methodological norm for reflecting on dogmas. In any case, Scripture was no more than a "point of departure."[35]

3. Because it used a method of intellectual reflection based on the rules of Aristotelian logic, it posed every possible question for each doctrine: Why? Where? Whence? When?[36] Consequently, it arrived at the most hairsplitting analysis and came to absurd conclusions (in barbaric language, using unrefined Latin).[37] This resulted in propositions completely detached from real life, disconnected from the church, and of value only for the school (i.e., disputations).

4. Because it sought rationally to prove the self-authenticating doctrines drawn from Scripture and tradition, it elevated faith to knowledge—an impossible task.[38] The beginning, middle, and end of theology is faith; it is the science

---

First Period (*Vetus*), 1000–1220: Lanfranc (professor in Italy, defended transubstantiation against Berengar). The church fathers held in high esteem; the rise of universalism; the study of Roman law, beginning with Irnerius, 1050. The foundation continued to be laid by Anselm, Hugh of St. Victor, Lombard, and Gratian.

Middle Period (*Media*), 1220–1330: Albertus Magnus, Thomas Aquinas, Duns Scotus, William of Occam, Bonaventura, Durandus of Saint-Pourçain. The discovery of Aristotle's philosophy; Aristotle's philosophy was used to defend dogmatic statements. Subtle questions and arguments (*quodlibets*) about what is "real" (*de realitatibus*) and what constitutes the uniqueness or "this-ness" of a particular thing (*de haecceitalibus*).

Later Period (*Nova*), 1330–1517: Pierre d'Ailly, Jean Gerson, Gabriel Biel. Much that had previously been left as an open question is now given a definite answer.

Causes of Scholasticism: ignorance of Greek and Hebrew, of history and antiquity, of philology, of philosophy.

In the Protestant church of the seventeenth century: Alsted (Voetius); Gerhard (Quenstedt). Cf. F. Nitzsch, "Scholastische Theologie"; Voigt, *Fundamentaldogmatik*.

34. Resulting in many false theses about free will, grace, justification, and good works and false opinions on angels, demons, heaven, hell, and creation; see F. Nitzsch, "Scholastische Theologie," 653–54.

35. LO: *norma*; *principium*.

36. LO: *quia, ubi, unde, quando*, etc.

37. DO: *spitsvondigste ontledingen*; *ongerijmdste beweringen*.

38. DO/GO: *in zichzelf begründen*. Very important things were forgotten; e.g., the practice of godliness, prayer, the struggle against temptations, spiritual warfare (*aanvechtingen*); at the same time, there was a desire to determine the most minute matters, making senseless distinctions, and often treating doctrines in the form of questions, not thetically but elenctically, polemically. Ed. note: Here Bavinck adds to his note: "Pierson on Calvin"; he could be referring to one of three works by Allard Pierson: *Studiën over Johannes Kalvijn (1527–1536);*

of faith. Scholasticism began with faith and wanted to end with knowledge. This was a distortion of "faith seeks understanding."[39] Scholasticism attempts to approach and treat dogma rationally; that is its goal. It transplants dogma from the church to the academy.

On the other side rages an intellectualism that seeks to alter the teaching of the faith and will not hold it without changing it. The essence of rationalism in all its forms[40] is that it understands Christianity and its revelation as doctrine, as the divine communication of knowledge. Furthermore, it also conceives human beings as intellects, as understanding or, more correctly, as rational beings. Rationalism is the rupture of humanity from God. Human beings are self-sufficient and require no revelation, no grace, no reconciliation in Christ; each person's own mind, will, and virtue are sufficient.[41] Accordingly, the question became, "What is the relation between doctrine and my understanding?" Whereupon rationalism answered, in principle, that reason not only receives revelation, but produces it; nothing in revelation is truly revealed unless it is rational. And supernaturalism said in principle: revelation is not a product of reason, but neither can revelation be assimilated by it; faith and knowledge are two entirely separate domains; "natural theology" is science; revelation is a matter of faith.[42] Thus rationalism evaporates the whole of revelation, while supernaturalism restricts it as much as possible and shrinks it (like the white population in America eroded the territory of the Native Americans).[43]

Essentially the same is done by gnosticism as in speculative rationalism:[44] paganism had spent itself and no longer had any new ideas; it tendered only

Nieuwe Studiën over Johannes Kalvijn (1536–1541), esp. 228–29; or Studiën over Johannes Kalvijn, derde reeks (1527–1542).

39. LO: fides quaerit intellectum.

40. Including its supernaturalist form, which was present already in the Socinians and Remonstrants and fathered by Descartes, Spinoza, Herman Roëll, Balthasar Bekker, Lodewyk Meyer, Christian Wolff, and the like. Representative of rationalism: Wegscheider, Institutiones Theologiae Christianae Dogmaticae. Representatives of supernaturalism: Reinhard, Vinke, Bouman, Heringa, Van Oort. Ed. note: For more on rationalism, see Bavinck, RD, 1:161–63, 183–89; on the relation between rationalism and supernaturalism, see Bavinck, RD, 1:355–65.

41. Stahl, Wat is de revolutie?, 18.

42. LO: theologia naturalis.

43. Strauss, Old Faith and the New, 1:161.

44. Jacobi, "Gnosis." Ed. note: Bavinck added a comment to this reference which has been reconstructed here for the sake of clarity: "Reason, properly understood, is the organ by which we come to a sound understanding of empirical reality; it is the criterion for true knowledge. In rationalism, reason is not empirical but speculative; the ultimate is not the flat, low-lying reality, but the eternal, moral, spiritual world. Reason reveals to us the ideal by which we measure our capacity for transcendental ideas—good, evil, God—and the impulse within us to test the world within us (thinking, feeling, willing, acting, etc.) and outside us."

eclectic philosophy (Neo-Platonism, Pythagoreanism, etc.). Then Christianity and Judaism came on the scene with a rich store of new ideas. These were now adopted and combined with all kinds of pagan philosophies and theogonies (Platonism, Neo-Platonism, Stoicism; as well as with Sophist and Pythagorean doctrines, Syrian and Phoenician mythologies, Chaldean astrology, Zoroastrian and Manichaean dualism, Egyptian and Buddhist philosophy, and more). Gnosticism is an enormous conception; it combines philosophical problems with the ideas that flow from revelation and conceives of everything as a process that corresponds with a process in the deity. That was its content; it was not clothed in the concepts of Greek philosophy but in mythological images after the manner of the Orient. And the goal was to bring people to salvation by means of speculative knowledge.[45] The essence of Christianity consisted objectively in ideas, subjectively in knowledge, and thus the gnostics said that those who see God are pure of heart. The pagan philosopher considers the standpoint of faith too inferior, deems it a legalistic standpoint, a form of servitude, fit only for the masses.[46] Docetic in Christology, the gnostic is ascetic or antinomian in morality, equating freedom with emancipation from the flesh.[47] A gnostic is one who mixes the ideas of Christianity with pantheism—which is the same as paganism—or with Buddhism, and gnosticism remains a current phenomenon, specifically today in Schelling and Hegel.[48] It is a denial of the uniqueness of Christianity, a linking of heterogeneous (Christian and pagan) ideas and elements. It always leads to absolute idealism[49]—that is, a system which in Christianity separates ideas from facts, discards the facts and lifts out the ideas, isolates them and supposes it can retain them. History becomes allegory: Adam's fall then means the fall of each individual person; the state of rectitude becomes our ideal in the future; the incarnation of Christ becomes our unity with God; atonement becomes our subjective redemption; the Trinity becomes three ideas; this is the method of Kant, Schelling, J. H. Scholten, and others.[50] They want the ideas but not

45. Jacobi, "Gnosis," 207.
46. Jacobi, "Gnosis," 208.
47. Origen, Scotus Eriugena, Abelard.
48. On speculative theology, see J. A. Dorner, "Theologie, spekulative"; Nathusius, *Das Wesen der Wissenschaft*, 265–74, 300, 380; Räbiger, *Theologik*, 150–69. Object and subject are not opposites but identical; both are always in each other. Reason and revelation are not opposites. There is *one* spirit, *one* reason, *one* truth. Reason is the divine within humanity; it seeks to comprehend doctrines, demonstrates their accordance with reason, and sees therein the absolute truth, even though they may be expressed symbolically. Philosophy has the same content as theology, but expresses it in concepts. *Theosophy* is the same in this respect.
49. Subjective idealism in the case of Kant and also Fichte.
50. Karl Daub, Philip Marheinecke, Bruno Baur, Richard Rothe, Christian Hermann Weisse.

the facts of history. The Ethical Theologians, too, are approaching idealism by increasingly separating faith and scientific observation,[51] reducing religion to morality, defined as value judgments.

ON THE SIDE OF THE SOUL (THE HEART)

Here we have mysticism in its many forms. Mysticism in general, such as that which has Pseudo-Dionysius as its originator, restricts the religious life to feelings, to the soul, putting the emphasis on the subject.[52] This is to say, if you want to know God, have communion with him, then you have to give up wanting to know him. When we want to know something, we make it into an object and thereby place it outside ourselves and opposite ourselves. But knowledge can place only finite objects opposite ourselves. God, however, is infinite and therefore cannot, like an object, be placed opposite ourselves and so be known by us. Thus, we share in God only if we step outside ourselves, close the eyes of our soul, and make ourselves completely passive. We must be passive toward the divine since we cannot know it; to know it would be actively to place ourselves opposite it. Instead, we must receive it, allow it to work in us, allow ourselves to sink away into it through our emotions. From this arises contemplation or the vision of God.[53] This is the knowledge of God, the only true knowledge of God. Mysticism therefore seeks a theology of feelings, of the soul, as the fruit of the immediate contemplation of God, born of the affective life. It wants immediate communion with God, not mediated through our consciousness, a communion in which God alone is active and our ego is completely passive.[54] Indeed, our ego vanishes, disappears, and in its place God acts, sees, and hears; the soul becomes a "divine feeling."[55]

Mysticism now appears in various forms. It can completely renounce knowing God through one's consciousness and put exclusive emphasis on living in God, on devotion[56] and contemplation. Or, it might not entirely reject conscious knowledge of God but merely regard it as a lower degree—a preliminary stage[57]—of true, genuine knowledge. Or one might genuinely appreciate speculation but strive to attain it by means other than abstract

51. GrO: πίστις and ἱστορία. Ed. note: "Ethical Theology" refers to a specific school of nineteenth-century Dutch theology associated with Daniel Chantepie de la Saussaye and J. H. Gunning.

52. DO: *het gemoed*; F. Nitzsch, "Scholastische Theologie," 655; see Kuyper, *Drie kleine vosse*, 45–74; for more on mysticism see above, §20.

53. DO: *God aanschouwen*.

54. DO: *ons ik*.

55. GO: *Affektion Gottes*.

56. DO: *andacht*.

57. GO: *Vorstufe*.

concepts, to acquire it immediately, grounding ideas and knowledge on the intuitive grasp of visions and images.[58] Thus mysticism sometimes comes in the form of "illumination" and at other times as "awakening."[59] In other words, at one time it comes more in the form of images and visions, which one sees and contemplates internally and in which God radiates as light, and at other times as an internal hearing in which God speaks to our soul through the internal word.[60] But whatever form mysticism may take, it always rests on the following errors:

1. In its essence mysticism is pantheistic. Human self-consciousness, our thinking—that is, our real selfhood, our *I*—is effaced. All true, authentic mysticism—namely, living in community with a person—presupposes, requires, and affirms human personality, self-consciousness, and self-hood. Love gives itself, but in such a way that it preserves itself; in love, we become one, but in such a way that we also remain ourselves. To be able to give oneself one must *have* oneself. When one no longer *has* a self, it is no longer possible to give oneself. Ethically one, we remain physically and substantially two. But what does mysticism do? It erases the substantial boundaries, it effaces our selfhood, our personality, our self-consciousness, and our self-determination.[61] Mysticism knows nothing of consciousness or the will in human persons. It seeks to efface what is precisely the hallmark of personality, to kill it, to let it sink away into absolute peace and quiet, to deprive it of all activity. That is what it does to the subject. But it also does this to the object, God. God, too, is not the self-conscious, personal, self-revealing God. Instead, he is the one, undifferentiated, abstract *Being* devoid of thinking or willing.[62] He does not allow himself to be known or to be willed, but only to be felt. He does not come to us and into us through our consciousness but (as it were) from the depths, in the center of our being. Stripped of our consciousness and will, going down behind both within ourselves, letting ourselves sink behind ourselves in the darkness of our being, we find, we feel, God.[63] There, God and the self are really one. Indeed,

58. F. Nitzsch, "Scholastische Theologie," 655.
59. GO: *Erleuchtung*; *Erweckung*.
60. See the references in §20, above, to Erbkam, *Geschichte der protestantischen Sekten*.
61. DO: *zelfbepaling*.
62. Cf. Spinoza: God must viewed as essence (*essentia*), as I am who I am.
63. Thus also Gunning, *Jezus Christus*. Ed. note: Gunning was an "Ethical Theologian" who, as his book's subtitle makes clear ("Occasioned by Bavinck's *De theologie van Prof. Dr. Daniel Chantepie de la Saussaye*"), wrote it as a polemical response to Bavinck's work on the "father" of Dutch "Ethical Theology," de la Saussaye.

the separation only occurs through our consciousness and will. This is nothing but the purest pantheism, mixing the substance of God and our substance.

2. Mysticism misunderstands self-consciousness and its correlates, the Word and faith, identifying faith with the Word in one's consciousness. "Christ and revelation are at best still provisional means by which to approach God. But when one is with God, then they are no longer necessary."[64] Mysticism is caught in the error (which also occurs in Fichte and Schleiermacher) that the consciousness can place only finite objects opposite itself and that God, being infinite, cannot be an object of knowledge. It is true that we cannot really make God into an object of knowledge, as we do with nature, for example. However, if we are to know other people, they must give themselves to us to be known; if they close themselves off from us, we will not get to know them. Thus, God himself must actively, freely of his own will, reveal himself. And that is exactly what he does, through his Word, to our consciousness. And mysticism denies this, thinking that this would mean that God is finite, which is incorrect. Mysticism confuses the concepts *infinite* and *endless*. The created world does exist outside of God's being, distinct from his being, even though it exists only through and in God. And so, God still remains infinite, omnipresent. By identifying God and the world, mysticism is forced to drop all means of mediation.[65] Word, sacraments, and consciousness are set aside for the goal of immediate contemplation, feeling God in our inner being, where God and ourselves are still one, before their separation[66] in consciousness and will. Thus, God does not stand outside us, over against us, but resides within us, behind us: the movement is from below to above. God arises from the depth of our being.

3. Mysticism is therefore completely subjective. We ourselves are the source of the knowledge of God, not the external Word. This knowledge ascends from the depths: being at first one with God in our soul, we gradually become one with him in our consciousness and will. God or Christ is then the subject in our being and then also becomes the subject in our consciousness and will. God knows and wills through us and in us. We are nothing; God is everything. God is the subject of all our deeds—our

---

64. Herzog, "Quietismus," 427.

65. GO: *Vermittelungen*.

66. Ed. note: Bavinck coins a Dutch word, *diremptie*, which is likely taken from the Latin *diremptus* ("separation").

knowing, willing, and acting. Thus, all our actions are God's responsibility. In this way mysticism arrives at frightful consequences.

a. What is nothing but a reflex of our own consciousness is passed off as divine, as an example of Christ, etc. Everything objective falls away; everything loses its objective significance. To the mystic, the entire objective world becomes an internal one. The truth in mysticism is this: there is indeed an influence, a communion of God with our soul, behind and beneath our consciousness, a sensory, emotional life, but all awareness or knowledge is mediated by the Word of God. In that case, the criterion is the Word, not our feelings. Ritschl, for example, is wrong to reject all mysticism. Regeneration, sanctification, the influence on us of *habitus* takes place unconsciously, behind our consciousness, our ego, behind our abilities. But knowledge of it comes from the Word alone.

b. Out of a desire to sustain these feelings, this reveling in emotional bliss, this desire to continue such spiritual intoxication,[67] people employ all manner of operations and artifices. These can be negative, such as sinking away in quietism, or positive, such as employing asceticism, meditation, self-torture, etc. Quietism is really absolute rest and passivity of the soul, in which it awaits the influence of God without any mediation of Christ, Word, sacraments, or church and also without any effort on its part, such as prayer, etc.[68] It is a school that originates in Neo-Platonism; it is present in Pseudo-Dionysius, in medieval mystics, in Francis de Sales, bishop of Geneva (1567–1622), in Fénelon, bishop of Cambrai, in Madame de la Motte-Guyon, and in all who regard disinterested love as the highest merit, as justification.[69] Disinterested love has as its object God as he is purely and absolutely good and beautiful in himself, whether or not he is that for us—in other words, God apart from his revelation of love. Fénelon did not draw this quietism from Scripture but from the mystics, even from Socrates, Plato, etc.[70] This mysticism continues to appear later in Tersteegen.[71]

c. All human responsibility is vitiated. Our deeds are God's deeds. And since the Word no longer directs us, what wells up from the depths

---

67. GO: *geistliche Trunkenheit.*
68. Herzog, "Quietismus."
69. FO: *amour désintéressé.* François de Salignac de la Mothe-Fénelon, 1651–1715; Jeanne-Marie Bouvier de la Motte-Guyon, 1648–1717.
70. Herzog, "Quietismus," 447; Heppe, *Geschichte der quietistischen Mystik.*
71. Krafft, "Tersteegen"; Goebel, *Geschichte des christlichen Lebens,* vol. 3.

of the human heart is held to be divine. In this way mysticism leads to antinomianism and to sensualism; spiritual love is confused with carnal love. The spiritual and the sensual lie extremely close in the human heart. Feelings are always distinguished between lower and higher feelings. That which is unrefined and bubbles up from the heart is held to be holy, and what arises from beneath the consciousness, from the darkness, is for that very reason to be loved and praised.

FROM THE SIDE OF THE WILL (ACTION, PRACTICE)

Here we find Pietism, Methodism, and fanaticism in particular.[72] According to Rothe, Pietism presupposes a dead orthodoxy; it wants to extend the Reformation into practice, into life, through the cultivation of piety.[73] It is godliness that is morally empty.[74] Piety alone has value, and piety alone is ever its only concern. Pietists are not indifferent toward the moral element, but are indifferent to morality as such. They are in favor of it, but only inasmuch and insofar as it is religiously commanded and willed by God, inasmuch and insofar as it benefits and supports piety.[75] Thus they do not nurture a moral life, yet wherever it is found they purify it as much as they can and reject the rest that they cannot purify. As a result, they constrict life as much as possible, despising nature, history, art, and science. Pietists withdraw with their families into their homes, away from the world's bustle; they give their children a strict upbringing, withdraw from the big church into the small conventicle; the Pietist is always a separatist. Whatever lies outside is "the world." It follows that such a person has no eye for the whole, for history, not even for the history of Christianity, whose history of dogma the Pietist rejects entirely or fails to appreciate, nor even an eye for the church, whose value the Pietist does not see. Pietism fosters indifferentism toward doctrine, subjectivism toward the church. Next, having no eye for the whole, they set their hope on converting single individuals, through direct contact. Thus, Pietism is not really mysticism (in the sense described above), since mysticism puts all the emphasis on God in us, over against whom we are only passive, effaced. Pietism, by contrast, puts all the emphasis on the subject: *we* have to be active and make ourselves pious by various means. Mysticism does not venture out of the self at all; the objective world becomes entirely subjective.

---

72. Van Andel, "Piëtisme," 153–54; Pierson, *Eene levensbeschouwing,* 1:9–10; Krummacher, *Expectorationen über das Studium der Theologie,* 187; and see above, §20.

73. LO: *praxis pietatis.* Rothe, *Theologische Ethik,* 4:171–80 (§987); Grünberg, *Philipp Jakob Spener,* 1:10.

74. GO: *sittlich leere Frommigkeit.*

75. See Kuyper, *Drie kleine vossen,* 75–152.

But the Pietist tries, through education, missions, philanthropy, to rescue at least a few from the evil world and draw them into one's circle. Mysticism does not want any doctrine or any activity of the mind; Pietism wants Scripture but not the confessions, biblical theology but not dogmatics; the Pietist merely reacts against Scholasticism. Mysticism does not seek understanding; Pietism wants only the sound mind that is simple, clear, sober, and practical. Mysticism kills the will; Pietism incorporates the Word into the will. Pietists are active and want to make themselves and others devout.

Methodism has an affinity with Pietism, but it arose among the English, just as Pietism arose among the Germans, among Reformed and Lutherans alike. Methodism is even more oriented to practice than Pietism, emphasizes a lapsed church, the breaking of covenantal succession, and completely focuses on conversion, conceived as an instantaneous event that occurs with great sorrow and quaking, following the model of Wesley himself. And having been converted myself, I can (must) demonstrate this by converting others. Methodism consequently has an aggressive nature; it seeks not just to win over a few individuals but to gain the masses, the nation, the world, to reconquer it through meetings and penitential sermons. It is filled with an exaggerated zeal for conversions and makes everything subservient to them: Sunday Schools, clubs, tracts, the Bible. It mobilizes every force; it is characterized by flying banners and rolling drums. No wonder the Salvation Army is organized in completely military fashion. Pietism is more inward, Methodism more outward. Pietism wants penitential struggle, a breakthrough followed by sealing,[76] and so recognizes a gradual sequence. Methodism wants instant conversions without any preparation and then leaves the converts alone and puts them to work. Following the conversion, Pietism seeks to foster godliness, while Methodism wants to promote evangelistic zeal. Pietism snatches some from the world and takes them up into the circle of the godly; Methodism takes on the world and enters into it. Pietism establishes conventicles, Methodism establishes mission parishes and missionary societies. Pietism despairs of saving the world and withdraws, forming the silent people in the land with nothing to say, the quietists; Methodism has great faith, marches onward, and threatens to get lost in curiosity or meddlesomeness.[77] Pietism is internally rich, but it does not share; it keeps everything to itself. Methodism is sometimes spiritually poor on the inside, but it gives far more than it has. Pietism is anxious, smug, narrow-minded; Methodism is bold, full of fire, and overzealous.

76. GO: *Bußkampf, Durchbrechung, Versiegelung.*
77. GrO: πολυπραγμοσύνη.

Practice taken to the extreme is fanaticism.[78] The term comes from *fanaticus* ("frenzied"), referring to *fanum* ("temple"), since the oracles at Delphi (the Pythia) were given in an ecstatic state. A fanatic is therefore someone who is divinely inspired. Fanaticism consists of various elements:

a. It eschews intellectual clarity, but incorporates some idea or other in its imagination. If it ends there, the result is *enthusiasm*[79]—that is, surrendering to something higher, to an ideal (not an abstract idea but a concrete ideal), and allowing oneself to be swept along and become obsessed with it—for example, with art, one's country, liberty, with Goethe, Schiller, etc. Now when enthusiasm (which can be very sensual) blurs that ideal through fantasy and emotion, it turns into *fanaticism*, a state of rapture that dwells in a world of fog.[80] It gives birth to a cult that is utterly subjective (like the enthusiasts during the Reformation, i.e., the Anabaptists), one that lives by feelings, by the "inner word," and that uses it to judge the whole external world, paints it as in a novel, and imagines it can turn it around in one stroke, but is therefore doomed to forever remain short-lived and not lasting.

b. The second element in fanaticism is that it turns this idea, that ideal, into an idée fixe. It excludes all other ideas and truths and does not take them into account, does not recognize them in its exclusion. Fanaticism is therefore exclusive, deeming the one ray of truth it possesses to be the whole truth.

c. The third element in fanaticism is that it seeks to attain that one idea with great vehemence. Therefore, it is hostile, abusive, intolerant toward anything or anyone that is not exactly like it. That can lead to a blind rage, deafness to all reason, in pursuit of the single goal, pursued darkly and blindly, with all means at its disposal; fixated on its standpoint, it will not budge.

---

78. C. Beck, "Fanatismus."

79. C. Beck, "Enthusiasmus." Ed. note: Bavinck's entire argument in this paragraph depends on the distinction between two German terms, *Enthusiasmus* and *Schwärmerei*, both of which are often translated into English as "enthusiasm" (we are translating *Schwärmerei* as "fanaticism"). The former is a relatively neutral term indicating an affective response to the good; the latter denotes a morally undesirable fanaticism. *Schwärmerei* was Martin Luther's term for the radical Anabaptists (see Brecht, *Martin Luther*, 137–95). Immanuel Kant regarded *Enthusiasmus* as a positive and essential part of human aesthetic experience but *Schwärmerei* as the delusion of lunatics. In his essay "Maladies of the Head," Kant wrote: "This ambiguous appearance of phantasy [*Phantasterei*] in moral sentiments that are in themselves good is enthusiasm [*Enthusiasmus*], and nothing great in the world has been done without it. Things are altogether different with the fanatic [visionary, *Schwärmer*]. The latter is actually a lunatic with a supposed immediate inspiration and great intimacy with the powers of heaven. Human nature knows no more dangerous delusion" (cited in Toscano, "Raving with Reason"). For more on Kant and "Enthusiasm," see the introduction to Clewis, *Kantian Sublime*, 1–9; I am indebted to Clewis for the reference to Brecht's book on Luther.

80. C. Beck, "Schwärmerei."

Such fanaticism is found in every area: fanaticism for progress, conservatism, reaction, liberty, enlightenment; and in the area of religion, fanaticism for orthodoxy, missions, separatism, etc. Fanaticism seizes upon one (rash and obscure) idea and devotes every force of will to the cause.

Added to all this is *moralism*, which likewise tackles the will.[81] Moralism does in the field of morality what Pietism does in that of piety. Moralism concentrates on morality as such, regarding it as the be-all and end-all, regarding piety as nothing. The main thing is the deed, enacting the moral commandments. This was the tenor of the previous [eighteenth] century. Ethicism goes deeper by focusing not only on behaving morally but also on *being* moral, not just on the quantity but more on the quality. In our time, it is taking on elements of mysticism. The polar opposite of moralism is antinomianism, which, coming from the mysticism that flows out of gnosticism, completely denies morality.

Finally, we must add that on the terrain of the church these spiritual illnesses assume the following forms:

1. The intellectual school, here called *confessionalism*, which swears by the confession and makes it the Palladium and the shibboleth. And this can in turn manifest itself as separatism and "churchism."
2. The emotional school in the church is *indifferentism*, which dismisses the church, considers it useless, and easily assumes an eschatological character.
3. The school of the will rejects the church and wants a different and better church, which leads to *Donatism*.

In the social and political field, the first school is reactionary and conservative; the second is indifferent; the third is sometimes revolutionary, or counter-revolutionary. However, because people are inconsistent and circumstances vary, the characteristics sometimes vary.

Accordingly, we have three major pathologies of the spiritual life: *aridity*, which has a confession but no life; *morbidity*, in the narrow sense of the word: false mysticism and false experiential faith; and *lethargy* (or excessive zeal, or zeal without understanding), in which energy for action is lacking.[82]

---

81. Rothe, *Theologische Ethik*, 4:171–80 (§987).

82. Ed. note: It may seem counterintuitive to link excessive zeal or activism with lethargy or torpor, but the classical treatments of the sin of sloth realized that spiritual sluggishness, faintheartedness, and eventually despair were often accompanied by tendencies to wander, to restlessness. The key point here is that Bavinck is dealing with pathologies of the will that can take the form of excess or lack. On sloth or acedia, see *ST*, IIa IIae q. 35, esp. IIa IIae q. 35 art. 4 ad 2.

Roots of Spiritual Pathologies

But what are the *causes*? These illnesses attach themselves to, but cannot exclusively be explained from, the variety of individual personalities. The apostles each have their own character and temperament, but none of them is pathological. Paul is not arid, John is not morbid, James is no Methodist. So there must be another cause. In general, the cause is sin, and more particularly, (1) the warfare of flesh and blood, (2) the struggle against the world, (3) temptations, and (4) spiritual desertion.[83]

1. THE WARFARE BETWEEN FLESH AND SPIRIT[84]

Sin remains in the believers. We see weaknesses in all believers, Abraham, Jacob, David, Peter, etc. They themselves confess their guilt and sin (Job 9:2, 20). This occurs frequently in the Psalms (Pss. 25; 32:5, 38; 51; 130; 143), where the psalmists pray for holiness of life, for forgiveness, for help from the Lord. Similarly, the prophets: "We have all become like one who is unclean, / and all our righteous deeds are like a polluted garment" (Isa. 64:6); "We have sinned and done wrong and acted wickedly and rebelled, turning aside from your commandments and rules" (Dan. 9:5).

And we find the same in the New Testament. Peter instructs Christians: "As obedient children, do not be conformed to the passions of your former ignorance" (1 Pet. 1:14).[85] He has earlier described that life as "living in sensuality, passions, drunkenness, orgies, drinking parties, and lawless idolatry" (4:3). Believers are urged "to abstain from the passions of the flesh, which wage war against your soul" (2:11).[86] Christians are freed from that by "obedience to the truth" and so are said to have "purified [their] souls" (1:22).[87] Nonetheless, they still have to increasingly realize holiness in their walk (1:14–15) since they are still newborn babes (2:2).[88] Thus, they are told, you must preserve and keep the "good conscience" (3:16) that you received in baptism (3:21), abstain from the "passions[89] of the flesh, which wage war against your soul" (2:11), "conduct yourselves with fear throughout the time of your exile" (1:17), and

---

83. Ed. note: In what follows, (1) and (2) appear to be fused. The second point, "(2) the struggle against the world," was added later by Bavinck between the lines. The original section "(2) temptation," became point 3, and what was supposed to be point 3, "spiritual desertion," became point 4. But in what follows, only the original three points are treated.

84. Vitringa, *Doctrina Christianae Religionis*, 3:413.

85. GrO: μὴ συσχηματιζόμενοι ταῖς πρότερον ἐν τῇ ἀγνοίᾳ ὑμῶν ἐπιθυμίαις.

86. GrO: στρατεύονται κατὰ τῆς ψυχῆς.

87. GrO: ὑπακοῇ τῆς ἀληθείας; τὰς ψυχὰς ὑμῶν ἡγνικότες.

88. GrO: ἁγιότης; ἀρτιγέννητα βρέφη.

89. GrO: ἐπιθυμίαι.

"be self-controlled and sober-minded for the sake of your prayers" (4:7), especially because "the devil prowls around like a roaring lion" (5:8). They are also told to feed on the Word (2:3) and walk "in Christ" (3:16) in patience (2:21–23), because suffering purifies (4:1–2, 12).

In 2 Peter,[90] the knowledge of Christ must add virtue to faith, knowledge to virtue, self-control to knowledge, and so on (1:5), for by such knowledge believers have escaped the "defilements of the world" (2:20) and "the corruption that is in the world because of sinful desire" (1:4).[91] In that virtue those who have thus escaped the world are to make their "calling and election sure" (1:10),[92] "partake of the divine nature" (1:4),[93] live "lives of holiness and godliness," and "be diligent to be found by him without spot or blemish, and at peace" (3:11, 14). Jude warns against libertinism, which misuses grace and liberty (cf. 2 Pet. 2:17–19).

Those born of the word (James 1:18) are required to love God; love for God rules out love of the world, because "friendship with the world is enmity against God" (4:4). The world has a defiling influence, and thus "religion that is pure and undefiled before God the Father is this: to visit widows and orphans in their affliction, and to keep oneself unstained from the world" (1:27).[94] That is why "God has chosen the poor of this world [for whom the temptation is therefore less strong] to be rich in faith" (2:5), while the rich will perish with all their treasures (1:10–11; 5:1–2). One must therefore choose for God and against the world; being "double-minded"[95] (1:8) makes people unstable and their hearts impure (4:8); the devil must be resisted (4:7). And faith, like love, must not be divided between God and the world; doubt must be banned (1:6, 8); this faith must be tested through suffering (1:3). Even though the external world tempts us to sin, God does not tempt us (1:13), but our own desires do so (1:14). Those desires seek to spend what we would receive from God on our passions (4:3; cf. 5:5);[96] thus in James it is especially our sensual desires that wage war in our members (4:1). This longing for pleasure and riches, in turn, fosters dissension (4:1–2) and causes the rich to oppress the poor (2:6). Precisely because those desires reside within us and we constantly stumble in many ways, it is important to rein in the body[97] (3:2), which must be done by the will that opposes those desires. It is especially difficult to bridle the

90. Weiss, *Biblical Theology*, 2:243.
91. GrO: μιάσματα τοῦ κόσμου; ἡ ἐν κόσμῳ ἐν ἐπιθυμίᾳ φθορά.
92. GrO: κλῆσις; ἐκλογή; βέβαιος.
93. GrO: ἵνα διὰ τούτων γένησθε θείας κοινωνοὶ φύσεως.
94. GrO: ἄσπιλον ἑαυτὸν τηρεῖν ἀπὸ τοῦ κόσμου.
95. GrO: διψυχία.
96. GrO: δαπανᾶν ἐν ἡδοναῖς.
97. GrO: χαλιναγωγῆσαι.

tongue (3:5), which is a "restless evil"[98] (3:8), and does great evil, like fire and like poison. James further warns against oaths (5:12), against wanting to be teachers (3:1), and against wrath (1:19) and counsels wisdom (3:17) and meekness (3:13).

Those born of God (1 John 5:1–2), who are already children of God (3:2), now have God's commandments. They show that they abide in Christ (John 8:51) and love him by keeping his commandments (John 14:15, 21; 1 John 2:3–6; 3:22–24); this is also how they show their love for God's children (5:2–3; cf. 3:23). To be sure, the believer has eternal life, does not sin and cannot sin (3:6, 9; 5:18). But, as a matter of fact, believers do sin and are never without sin (1:8, 10; 2:1); they need cleansing and forgiveness (1:7–9), intercession with the Father (2:1–2), and brotherly intercession (5:16); they have to purify themselves (3:3), abide in Christ, in God (2:28), guard against love of the world (2:15) and against temptation (3:7). For the world tempts believers with its seduction (2:26; 3:7; 2 John 7). That world stands in fundamental opposition to them. The world is ruled by the devil (John 12:31; 14:30; 16:11); he is at work in the world (1 John 4:4), and it lies in his power (5:19). True, through Christ—who has overcome the world (John 16:33), who was not of the world (8:23; 17:14, 16), who destroyed the world's works (1 John 3:8)—a church has arisen which also no longer remains under the world's power (John 15:19; 17:14). All the same, the world continues to stand over against the believers (John 14:17–19; 1 John 2:15–17; 3:1, 13; 4:5). It tries to destroy them (John 17:15); it cannot love them (John 15:19) but hates them (1 John 3:13); it deceives them with its enmity but especially with its seduction (1 John 2:26; 3:7; 2 John 7). Therefore, believers have to be warned not to love the world (1 John 2:15), to keep themselves from its idols (5:21), not to love what is in the world—namely, the lust of the eyes and so on (2:16)—to flee false spirits (4:1; 2 John 7) and the deniers of Christ (1 John 2:22). Nevertheless, believers are protected from the world (John 17:15) and have overcome the devil (1 John 2:13–14) and the world (1 John 4:4; 5:4–5).

In Paul,[99] as an advance on their future glory the believers receive the Spirit of sonship/adoption[100] (Gal. 4:6). This becomes the driving force of their lives; they are led by the Spirit of God (Rom. 8:14; Gal. 5:18). That is how they become "spiritual persons"[101] who are governed by the Spirit throughout their whole being (1 Cor. 2:15; 3:21). Whatever they do, they do in the Spirit (Gal. 6:1); they speak (1 Cor. 12:3), pray (Rom. 8:15), and, led by that

---

98. GrO: ἀκατάστατον κακόν.
99. Weiss, *Biblical Theology*, 1:481–89.
100. GrO: υἱοθεσία.
101. GrO: πνευματικοί.

Spirit, walk according to the Spirit and set their mind on the things of the Spirit (Rom. 8:4–5). But although every believer has died with Christ *virtually* (Rom 6:8; Gal. 2:20; Col. 2:12), and the old humanity has been put to death (Rom. 6:6) and is set free from sin (Rom. 6:2, 11, 18, 22), and the new person has been raised with Christ (Rom. 6:4, 8) and now belongs to God (vv. 11, 13), and Christ lives in them (v. 11; Gal. 2:20), nevertheless *actually* or *really* the flesh (the old humanity) continues to exist, to the extent that one is subject to sin.[102] Consequently, a fundamental war arises within the Christian, for the "desires of the flesh are against the Spirit"[103] (Gal. 5:17). In this verse, for several reasons, "Spirit" [πνεῦμα] is likely a reference to the Holy Spirit:[104] (a) In the immediately preceding verse, "walk by the Spirit,"[105] by analogy with Romans 8:4, certainly means "according to the Holy Spirit." (b) In the verse that immediately follows, the phrase "if you are led by the Spirit," followed by "you are not under the law,"[106] is also a clear reference to the Holy Spirit (cf. Rom. 8:14). (c) Once Paul has enumerated the "desires of the flesh" (Gal. 5:19–21), he picks up the "fruit of the Spirit, namely, love, joy, peace, patience," etc., thus again certainly referencing the Holy Spirit. (d) Paul's imagery here involves the conflict between "flesh" and "S/spirit."[107] Their respective "desires"[108] are mutually incompatible and war against each other; they can be said to each have their own wills that oppose each other.

Galatians 5:17 tells us why these are opposed:[109] "These are opposed to each other, to keep you from doing the things you want to do"[110] (according

---

102. LO: *virtualiter*; *actualiter*. Ed. note: It is perhaps important, in a day when "virtual reality" refers to computer-generated simulations of physical reality, to be clear that in this context "virtually" means "with *virtus*, or power; powerfully, effectively" (Muller, *Dictionary*, 327, s.v. "*virtualiter*"). As Bavinck uses the term here, "virtually" is a greater "reality" than the "actual" condition of believers who continue to sin.

103. GrO: ἡ γὰρ σὰρξ ἐπιθυμεῖ κατὰ τοῦ πνεύματος.

104. Contra Calvin, Beza, Gomarus, and the annotations in the *Statenvertaling*, though not very clearly.

105. GrO: πνεύματι περιπατεῖτε.

106. GrO: εἰ δὲ πνεύματι ἄγεσθε, οὐκ ἐστὲ ὑπὸ νόμον.

107. Ed. note: The use of "S/spirit" is appropriate when the Greek word πνεῦμα is ambiguous, potentially referring to the Holy Spirit or to the human spirit. Theologically speaking, the characteristic way the Holy Spirit works in us does blur that line somewhat as in Paul's statement in 1 Cor. 15:10: "But by the grace of God I am what I am, and his grace toward me was not in vain. On the contrary, I worked harder than any of them, though it was not I, but the grace of God that is with me." The "S/spirit" nomenclature is borrowed from Fee, *God's Empowering Presence*.

108. GrO: ἐπιθυμίαι.

109. Ed. note: Here Bavinck inserts a text-critical observation concerning the opening of v. 17: "ταῦτα δέ (according to A, C, D, Tischendorf, Vulgate) or γάρ (according to B, D*, E, F, G, Meyer)."

110. GrO: γὰρ ἀλλήλοις ἀντίκειται, ἵνα μὴ ἃ ἐὰν θέλητε ταῦτα ποιῆτε.

to the tendency of those warring principles that war within the regenerate). Meyer interprets this as follows: the two principles prevent born-again persons from doing what they want to do. "*If he would do what is good, the flesh*, striving against the Spirit, is *opposed to this; if he would do what is evil, the Spirit*, striving against the flesh, *is opposed to that*."[111] Thus the will of the born-again person presumably stands halfway between the flesh and the Spirit: at times, it is governed by the flesh, at other times by the Spirit. That is completely wrong. Romans 7:15–20 clearly teaches that the will desires the good, but the flesh, the sin that lives within me, does what I hate. According to Meyer, Romans 7 refers to the *unregenerate*.[112] In that case, the unregenerate would be better off than the regenerate, who, according to Galatians 5:17, need the Spirit's fight against the flesh "to keep you from doing the things you want to do." In step with Luther, Calvin, and Erasmus[113] we interpret this from one side: "You do not do what you would want"; that is, as a result of, and in keeping with, the tendency of the fundamental war between those two powers within you, you cannot do the good that you want. Romans 7, which ascribes to the will the desire to do the good (that is, the spiritual law), teaches the same thing. Now if the mind, the inner person (Rom. 7:22), in the unregenerate were already oriented toward the good, prevented only by the flesh, then Paul would be a full-blown rationalist. In that case regeneration would not be needed, only some moral improvement and some bridling of the flesh; then it would not be true that "flesh gives birth to flesh" (John 3:6), and Paul would be contradicting himself when he says that "the natural person . . . is not able to understand . . . the things of the Spirit of God" (1 Cor. 2:14; cf. Jude 19).

According to Romans 7 there are two principles warring against each other. The one side is described in a variety of ways: *the flesh* ("I am of the flesh," v. 14), *the act* ("I do not do what I want," v. 15; "the sin that dwells within me," v. 17), *inability to carry out the good* (v. 18), *the evil I do not want is what I keep on doing* (v. 19), "another law in my members" (v. 23).[114] This is in contrast to "knowing":[115] "I know not what I do and want" (vv. 15, 18, 19, 20, 21), the "inner person" (v. 22), "the law of my mind" (v. 22), and "mind" (v. 25).[116] The "inner person" or "inner being" simply means a person's "mind,"

111. Meyer, *Galatians*, 236.
112. Meyer, *Romans*, 288, remark 1.
113. The *Statenvertaling* and its notes take the easy way out and translate ἵνα as "*alzo*" ("thus").
114. GrO: νοῦς; ἔσω ἄνθρωπος; σάρξ; ἡ οἰκοῦσα ἐν ἐμοὶ ἁμαρτία; τὸ δὲ κατεργάζεσθαι τὸ καλὸν οὔ; ἀλλὰ ὃ οὐ θέλω κακὸν τοῦτο πράσσω; ἕτερος νόμος ἐν τοῖς μέλεσίν μου.
115. GrO: γιγνώσκειν.
116. GrO: ὁ ἔσω ἄνθρωπος; νόμος τοῦ νοός μου; νοῦς.

as opposed to one's "body and flesh"—that is, the invisible person as opposed to the visible, bodily person (2 Cor. 4:16; Eph. 3:16).[117] But these two passages [2 Cor. 4:16; Eph. 3:16] teach us that renewal takes place precisely in the sphere of the inner person, and therefore, if the context demands it, the "inner person" can also refer to the new person.[118] And that is what it certainly refers to here—namely, our "self,"[119] our inner person, insofar as we are regenerate. Similarly, the "mind" is the (theoretical and practical) spirit of the human person.[120] Thus, here in Romans 7, the conflict between flesh and spirit[121] is portrayed in a more local sense, as the place and sphere in which the two principles of Galatians 5:17 war against each other. This means that the Spirit resides and works in the inner person, in the mind, in the will, in the depth of our being, but sin lives in the flesh, in our members, in our actions. Thus, in Romans 7 we have the same contrast as in Galatians 5:17, but Romans 7 delineates more closely the two territories dominated by each of the two principles of Galatians 5:17. The born-again person, too, remains "of the flesh, sold under sin" (Rom. 7:14).[122] Nonetheless, believers must not live "according to the flesh"[123] (Rom. 8:12), fulfill the desires of the flesh (Gal. 5:16), sow to their own flesh (Gal. 6:8), or yield their members to sin (Rom. 6:12–13). We find the same contrast between the "new person" (Eph. 2:15) and the "old" (Eph. 4:22; Col. 3:9);[124] for that new person the ideal is the image of God (Eph. 4:10, 24), and one must put on the new person while putting off the old.

Like John, Paul also teaches about the world. The world is in the service of sin, has fallen under the judgment of God (1 Cor. 4:13; 6:2; 11:32; Rom. 3:6, 19), and stands in need of reconciliation (Rom. 11:12, 15; 2 Cor. 5:19). Its spirit is opposed to the Spirit of God (1 Cor. 2:12); its wisdom is foolishness (1 Cor. 1:20, 21, 27–28; 3:19); its grief produces death (2 Cor. 7:10). It is under the rule of Satan (2 Cor. 4:4) and is inspired by him (1 Cor. 2:12; cf. also Col. 2:8, 20; Eph. 2:12; Phil. 2:15).

The Epistle to the Hebrews outlines how members of the New Covenant partake of remission of their sins (8:12; 10:17). But they also receive the Holy Spirit (6:4) and have the law written on their hearts (8:10; 10:16). Hence, they

117. GrO: ὁ ἔσω ἄνθρωπος; νοῦς; σῶμα and σάρξ.
118. GrO: ἔσω ἄνθρωπος; καινός ἄνθρωπος.
119. DO: *ons lk.*
120. GrO: νοῦς.
121. The manuscript is damaged here, resulting in missing text; our reconstruction is an entailment from the following clause.
122. GrO: σαρκικός.
123. GrO: κατὰ σάρκα.
124. GrO: ὁ καινὸς ἄνθρωπος; παλαιός.

strive after holiness (12:14), keep themselves from sin (13:4–5), resist to the point of shedding their blood (12:4); for this God strengthens them (13:9), guides them (13:25), and tests them with chastisement (12:5–10). God himself works in them that which is well-pleasing in his sight (13:21).[125] Let us now consider who experiences this warfare, its nature, and its outcome.

1. The *persons* in whom this warfare is found are only the regenerate.[126] Conflict also occurs within the unregenerate, but it is of a totally different nature. For them the struggle is not spiritual but moral—that is, a struggle between reason (conscience) and the heart, will, and inclinations. By virtue of conscience and reason, people do have some knowledge of God, of good and evil, and this knowledge recoils against their evil deeds and desires.[127] These faculties of reason and conscience hold back the person who wants to sin, lest that person sink utterly; they do not change a person's will, but only bind it. This struggle is common to all people, even in those who have sunk to the lowest level. It resists some sins, not all, often only the abominable public sins, not private sins, which are actually cherished; some sins are not resisted at all. That struggle is waged not against sin as such, or because it displeases God, and thus it is not always and everywhere against every sin but only against some sins, out of fear of punishment, public shame, or public opinion, but not out of love of God. It is not waged perpetually but only now and then, not constantly but occasionally, only under certain circumstances, when sin would cause harm. In this struggle, people can triumph, choose the better part of their nature, listen to their reason,[128] and bridle their will. However, in that case they are nothing more than moral persons, natural persons in whom the best part of nature (but not the Spirit) holds sway; the will or inclination is not changed but merely curtailed, reined in, suppressed. We see this struggle in Balaam, whose reason caused him to desire the fate of the righteous; in Pilate, whose mind would acquit Jesus; in Judas; and in Felix.

The *spiritual* struggle in the regenerate is altogether different and completely the opposite of this.[129] In the regenerate a war is waged to the end; it is a battle of the spirit—the spiritual life-principle, the seed within a person,

125. Cf. Driessen, *Oude en nieuwe mensch*, 106–11 (chap. 7); Ames, *Conscience*, II.11 ("Of the Combat of the Spirit against the Flesh"); Voetius, *De praktijk der godzaligheid*, 446; Buddeus, *Institutiones Theologiae Moralis*, 248; Love, *Combate between the Flesh and Spirit*; Perkins, *Combat of the Flesh and the Spirit*; Harless, *Christian Ethics*, 224–34 (§25); Vilmar, *Theologische Moral*, 2:76–84 (§42).

126. Love, *Combate between the Flesh and Spirit*, 121.

127. Cf. *RD*, 1:301–22, on general revelation.

128. GrO: νοῦς.

129. The struggle within Christ was completely different (Luke 22:44), the struggle to do his Father's will, and a natural (not sinful) desire to live.

the mind, the will, the inner person (ἔσω ἄνθρωπος), the new person—against the flesh and the old person, the sin dwelling in us.[130] These two forces are not really spatially separated in born-again people, as though one part of them were regenerate and another part unregenerate (e.g., the will saying yes and the mind saying no). On the contrary, flesh and spirit are there together, and both are in every faculty of the soul, pervading and overlaying the whole man. The entire will is on the one hand carnal and on the other spiritual; the same is true of the mind, reason, the inclinations, the body, ear, eye, and the rest.[131] Thus a whole person confronts a whole person, a new person is pitted against the old.[132] There are, therefore, two persons in the regenerate; a believer is a double person. This is not in conflict with Romans 7, where the inner person stands over against the flesh.[133] The "inner person" does not refer only to that which is internal, and "flesh" is not something that is external. In Paul, "flesh" refers to the internal person as sinful, and, to be sure, the inner person also becomes publicly manifest through walking according to the Spirit.[134] Nonetheless, the "inner person" may be spoken of as more internal; it manifests itself less clearly than the flesh since our life with Christ is hidden and not seen by the world.

2. The *nature* of this struggle is expressed in *desires* (Gal. 5:17).[135] That is to say, the Spirit tries to arouse in us good thoughts, impulses, inclinations, and desires in our mind, will, and affections, and likewise to suppress the evil. On the other side, the flesh desires what is diametrically opposite. In the mind, for example, there is the struggle between knowledge of God's Word and ignorance, or perversion of it; we all know in part and thus also live between faith and unbelief. At war within the will is the will to do good and the will to do evil. In the inclinations there is a struggle between love and fear. A born-again person is therefore like a person with one good and one bad leg, with the result that the person walks neither entirely incorrectly nor entirely correctly. Mingled in the person, as in lukewarm water, are cold and hot, and light and darkness as at dusk.[136] Paul answers the question of how two contrary qualities can exist in a single subject by saying that this is possible because both qualities are imperfect; perfect love casts out fear; but that is not yet the case here. In one and the same act of the mind, the

---

130. Hoornbeeck, *Theologiae Practicae*, 2:89–106 (VIII.7); Kuyper, "Van de gemeene gratie."
131. Perkins, *Combat of the Flesh and the Spirit.*
132. GrO: καινὸς ἄνθρωπος; παλαιὸς ἄνθρωπος.
133. GrO: ἔσω ἄνθρωπος; σάρξ.
134. GrO: σάρξ; ἔσω ἄνθρωπος; κατὰ πνεῦμα.
135. Perkins, *Combat of the Flesh and the Spirit*, 470.
136. Perkins, *Combat of the Flesh and the Spirit*, 471.

will, and the inclination, both persons (the old and the new) are always more or less bound together. To be sure, there can be differences in degree: one action may exhibit more of the old person, another more of the new. The former asserts itself in the one, the latter in the other; but all actions have something in them of the old and something of the new person. Thus Romans 7:16–17—"The evil that I do not want, that is what I do," etc.— must therefore be taken with a grain of salt.[137] It does not mean that Paul never did any good at all, but that he did not do it as he wanted to according to his new self, and that therefore all his deeds were imperfect. So there is something good in them, but still they are sinful and in need of reconciliation through Christ's blood. Accordingly, we are to guard ourselves against gnosticism, Manichaeism, and antinomianism, which place the old and the new person parallel to each other (e.g., as spirit and matter) and then hold the old person responsible for his deeds. A regenerate person is absolutely not a double person in that sense, with a double series of deeds, not two substances but one, with one self, one will, one consciousness and affect, in whom two qualities are at war with one another.

3. The *outcome* of this struggle is not in doubt, notwithstanding the ups and downs of the Christian life. In a certain sense the Spirit is more powerful, since he is God himself, who enables us.[138] In conversion, our flesh receives a mortal wound, and always remains only a wounded soldier. This Spirit therefore triumphs in the course of a human life, because those who are born of God do not sin (1 John 3:8); the born-again person *walks*—that is, moves, strides forward, walks onward—according to the Spirit (Rom. 8:1); and at the end of life, the believer triumphs completely; faith overcomes the world (1 John 5:5; Rom. 8:37). But that does not take away the fact that the flesh is temporarily and at certain moments more powerful. God could sanctify us all at once by his Spirit, but the spiritual life is an organic life, not mechanical; hence it is (in part and in a certain sense) subject, like the natural life, to birth, growth, and illness. Now and then the flesh triumphs, strengthened by the world and Satan, in gross sins, as in David or Peter; God allows this in order to humble us and to teach us to deny ourselves.[139] However, the question arises whether in the case of sins like that there is a difference between the regenerate and the unregenerate.

The Reformed distinguished between "sins of malice" and "sins of weakness."[140] The former are always committed by the unregenerate, although in

137. LO: *cum grano salis.*
138. Perkins, *Combat of the Flesh and the Spirit,* 472.
139. Perkins, *Combat of the Flesh and the Spirit,* 472.
140. LO: *peccata malitiae; peccata infirmitatis.*

their sins, too, there are gradations; nonetheless, they are all sins of malice. Sins of weakness can only be committed by the regenerate, for an unregenerate person is not weak but dead, lacking all life.[141] (But could there not be sins of weakness among the unregenerate in this sense: not in terms of sin *qua* sin, but could an unregenerate person nevertheless want not to commit some specific sin but yet commit it anyway?) A different question is: Can believers commit only sins of weakness, or also sins of malice?

Perkins says they can also sin against knowledge and conscience from audacity, but he also says that believers never sin wholeheartedly and with their full will like the unregenerate; after falling, they get up again.[142] A sin of weakness is always one in which the spiritual life-principle reacts to a greater or lesser degree, as in Paul (Rom. 7:14–15), yet in which the flesh nevertheless triumphs. This can happen, for example, because of fear or the magnitude of the temptation (Luke 22:31; John 12:42; 19:38),[143] with the result that a person is still weak in knowledge (Heb. 5:12). Examples in Scripture include the disciples not accepting Jesus's coming death (Matt. 16:22–23), the Corinthians' conduct with respect to food offered to idols (1 Cor. 10:18–11:1), and Christians who need to grow more in the faith (Eph. 4:14; 2 Pet. 3:19).[144] However, Perkins does not dare to say that a sin of weakness can only be so designated if one has struggled "with the utmost of one's powers,"[145] because even when people strive to the full extent of their ability and can absolutely do no more, their will is still weak (if taken that strictly, sins of weakness would not exist anymore). Regenerate persons can no longer commit genuine sins of malice;[146] in a broad sense, all sins that the regenerate commit may be called sins of weakness, since those persons' better part always protests against sin "more or less, whether tacitly or explicitly, and whether it is aroused in the act of sinning or soon afterward."[147] But in a stricter sense, when sins are not sins of weakness, they can also fall under the category of "faults or defects,"[148] and these surpass sins of weakness. (Hoornbeeck also poses the questions of

---

141. Perkins, *Combat of the Flesh and the Spirit*, 473; also Buddeus, *Institutiones Theologiae Moralis*, 252–53.

142. Perkins, *Combat of the Flesh and the Spirit*, 473; Hoornbeeck, *Theologiae Practicae*, 2:148–70 (VIII.12).

143. Hoornbeeck, *Theologiae Practicae*, 2:153.

144. Hoornbeeck, *Theologiae Practicae*, 2:150.

145. LO: *ad extremum virium.*

146. Hoornbeeck, *Theologiae Practicae*, 2:154.

147. Hoornbeeck, *Theologiae Practicae*, 2:155. Ed. note: Bavinck writes, "*plus vel minus, magis tacite vel aperte et vel in peccato vel more ad istud,*" but Hoornbeeck has *mox* rather than *more*; our translation incorporates the completion of the clause, which is missing in Bavinck's manuscript: "*ad illud expergefacti.*"

148. LO: *delicta.*

whether regenerate people can sin deliberately and whether they can lapse
into the *same* sin more than once.)[149]

The Reformed had to speak this way, because they denied that the saints
could fall away, and therefore they assumed that the life of the regenerate
could be weakened but never extinguished; therefore, regenerate people must
always react against sin, to a greater or lesser degree. The Lutherans, however,
denied that the sins of the regenerate are all sins of weakness;[150] they said
that faith can be lost entirely, as in the case of David (2 Sam. 12:5; cf. Ezek.
18:24–26; Matt. 13:20–22; Heb. 6:4; 10:26–31; Rom. 8:12–13; 2 Pet. 2:18).
Buddeus reproaches Hoornbeeck for devising a third category of sin, one
that is between malicious sins and sins of weakness, and he also denies that
"grave sins or sins of deliberate choice" can accompany faith.[151]

2. TEMPTATIONS

In Hebrew the terms are as follows:

- בָּחַן means "to watch closely," "to try, or prove" = to assay metals, and
  so it is used of God, who tries or refines us like silver and gold (Job
  23:10; Jer. 9:6; Zech. 13:9; Ps. 66:10). It is also used nonmetaphorically,
  to speak of God as testing hearts and kidneys (Ps. 7:9), the heart (Ps.
  17:3), the kidneys (Jer. 11:20; 17:10). But it is also predicated of persons
  who test God, in parallel with testing, נָסָה (Ps. 95:9), speaking of those
  who put God to the test, to see whether he will open the windows of
  heaven (Mal. 3:10).

- נָסָה, *piel*, means "to prove," "to test," "to put on trial": the queen of
  Sheba comes to Solomon to test him with hard questions (1 Kings 10:1).
  "Test your servants for ten days; let us be given vegetables to eat and
  water to drink" (Dan. 1:12).[152] It is used especially of God, who tests
  people (mostly through suffering). God tries Abraham by demanding
  Isaac (Gen. 22:1). God tests Israel when he provides manna: "Behold,
  I am about to rain bread from heaven for you, and the people shall go
  out and gather a day's portion every day, that I may test them, whether
  they will walk in my law or not" (Exod. 16:4). God leaves some nations

---

149. Hoornbeeck, *Theologiae Practicae*, 2:156.
150. Buddeus, *Institutiones Theologiae Moralis*, 254.
151. LO: *peccata graviora et proairetica.* Ed. note: *Proairetica* is an Aristotelian term, from
προαίρεσις, referring to deliberate choice or premeditation. On the death of the spiritual life,
cf. Löber, *Das innere Leben: Beitrag*, 293–373 (chap. 6).
152. Ed. note: Bavinck's manuscript reads "ten days," which follows the *Statenvertaling*
(and the KJV).

in the land after the conquest: "I will no longer drive out before them any of the nations that Joshua left when he died, in order to test Israel by them, whether they will take care to walk in the way of the LORD as their fathers did, or not" (Judg. 2:21–22). This verb is also often used for times when people put God to the test, doubt his help, distrust him, disbelieve (Exod. 17:2; Deut. 6:16; Ps. 78:18, 41, 56)—for example, Israel in the wilderness.

- צָרַף means "to melt," and thereby purify or purge metals (Jer. 6:29; Isa. 1:25), and then metaphorically, to purify people (e.g., through suffering: Dan. 11:35). In Psalms 17:3 and 26:2 it also means "to prove," "to test."

Accordingly, all three can mean "to test," "to put on trial," and often with God as the subject. The first two can also mean "to tempt," "to doubt," and the like, with people as subject and God as object; but in this sense נִסָּה is used much more often than בָּחַן. The third term also means "to purify."

In the New Testament there are two terms: δοκιμάζω and πειράζω. According to Cremer, δοκιμάζω = "*to try, to examine, to test* in order to approval [*sic*] (literally, *to make approved*)."[153] In the New Testament "the usage of the word . . . corresponds much more with that of profane Greek than with the LXX," and its first meaning is "to examine, to test." "You hypocrites! You know how to interpret the appearance of earth and sky, but why do you not know how to interpret the present time?" (Luke 12:56). "Let a person examine himself, then, and so eat of the bread and drink of the cup" (1 Cor. 11:28). In 1 Corinthians 11:28, δοκιμαζέτω is parallel to ἑαυτοὺς πειράζετε in 2 Corinthians 13:5: "Examine yourselves, to see whether you are in the faith. Test yourselves. Or do you not realize this about yourselves, that Jesus Christ is in you?—unless indeed you fail to meet the test!" Δοκιμάζω is also used with respect to prophecy: "Do not despise prophecies, but test everything; hold fast what is good" (1 Thess. 5:21). God himself tests hearts: "Just as we have been approved by God to be entrusted with the gospel, so we speak, not to please man, but to please God who tests our hearts" (1 Thess. 2:4).

In the second place, δοκιμάζω also means "(by testing) to **recognise, to approve**,"[154] that someone has been proved diligent, has proved himself or herself (2 Cor. 8:22; Rom. 1:28), as in the refining of gold: "So that the tested genuineness of your faith—more precious than gold that perishes though it

153. Cremer, *Biblico-Theological Lexicon*, 699, s.v. "δοκιμάζω." Ed. note: Bavinck explains the parenthetical part of Cremer's definition thus: "actually Δοκιμόν ποιεῖν = to make recognized, accepted, tried."

154. Cremer, *Biblico-Theological Lexicon*, 701, s.v. "δοκιμάζω."

is tested by fire—may be found to result in praise and glory and honor at the revelation of Jesus Christ" (1 Pet. 1:7).

Πειράζω in profane Greek is "to be distinguished from δοκιμάζειν, first of all, in that πειρ[άζω] requires great effort; δοκιμ[άζω], on the contrary, = *to inquire, to prove, to estimate, to approve*, denotes an intellectual act."[155] In other words, δοκιμάζω means "to try or search with the mind" (Rom. 2:18), and πειράζω is "to try or search with the will," with some effort, energy. Furthermore, δοκιμάζω means an investigation that mostly results in a good outcome, hence δοκιμάζω is something like "to appreciate, to recognize, to approve"; πειράζω, on the other hand, is sometimes entirely "middle voice"[156] (2 Cor. 13:5), and usually has the sense of causing one's opponent to fall, and thus mostly indicates a negative result. In the Septuagint, בָּחַן is translated as δοκιμάζω, but נָסָה is rendered as πειράζω. For hostile, biased testing only πειράζω is used. In the New Testament it occurs in two distinct senses:

1. In a good sense, it means "to try" or "to test," "to search." Jesus "tests" his disciples at the feeding miracle: "Seeing that a large crowd was coming toward him, Jesus said to Philip, 'Where are we to buy bread, so that these people may eat?' He said this to test him, for he himself knew what he would do" (John 6:6). Just before receiving his "Macedonian call," Paul and his companions traveled "through the region of Phrygia and Galatia, having been forbidden by the Holy Spirit to speak the word in Asia. And when they had come up to Mysia, they attempted to go into Bithynia, but the Spirit of Jesus did not allow them" (Acts 16:6–7). Clearly they were trying, making an effort, testing. Other examples: "Examine yourselves, to see whether you are in the faith" (2 Cor. 13:5; cf. Heb. 11:17); "You have tested those who call themselves apostles and are not, and found them to be false" (Rev. 2:2).

2. But in the second place πειράζω means "to put someone to the test," from distrust with evil intent—in other words, "to try to tempt someone":

a. It is used of people who tempt God. Peter says to Sapphira, wife of Ananias: "How is it that you have agreed together to test the Spirit of the Lord?"[157] (Acts 5:9). Peter, at the Council of Jerusalem, asks, "Now, therefore, why are you putting God to the test[158] by placing a yoke on the neck of the disciples that neither our fathers nor we have been able to bear?" (Acts 15:10). Paul, warning the Corinthians, says, "We must not put Christ to the test, as some of them did and were destroyed by

---

155. Cremer, *Biblico-Theological Lexicon*, 494, s.v. "πειράζω."
156. LO: *vox media*.
157. GrO: πειράσαι τὸ πνεῦμα κυρίου.
158. GrO: τί πειράζετε τὸν θεόν.

serpents" (1 Cor. 10:9).[159] Our Lord's reply to the devil in the wilderness: "Again it is written, 'You shall not put the Lord your God to the test'" (Matt. 4:7; Luke 4:12).[160]

b. It is used of people, such as the Pharisees, who sought to put Christ to the test (Matt. 16:1; 19:3; 22:18, 35; Mark 8:11; 10:2; 12:15; Luke 11:16; John 8:6, etc.). So this means to try to tempt Jesus and cause him to fall into sin.

c. It is used of all kinds of things—suffering, adversity, the world, Satan—that test believers. Jesus is tempted by the devil, who is called "the tempter"[161] (Matt. 4:3 par., Mark 1:13; Luke 4:2). Paul advises married couples not to be separated too long, "so that Satan may not tempt [them] because of [their] lack of self-control"[162] (1 Cor. 7:5). Paul sends Timothy to the Thessalonians "to learn about [their] faith, for fear that somehow the tempter (ὁ πειράζων) had tempted [them] and [Paul's] labor would be in vain" (1 Thess. 3:5). Christ assures the church in Philadelphia: "Because you have kept my word about patient endurance, I will keep you from the hour of trial that is coming on the whole world, to try those who dwell on the earth" (Rev. 3:10). People are tempted by their own desires, not by God (James 1:13–14). The New Testament does not always specify the temptations: "If anyone is caught in any transgression, you who are spiritual should restore him in a spirit of gentleness. Keep watch on yourself, lest you too be tempted" (Gal. 6:1). Because Christ "himself has suffered when tempted, he is able to help those who are being tempted" (Heb. 2:18; cf. 4:15).[163]

The same is true of the noun πειρασμός = "temptation."[164] Jesus tells his disciples in the garden, "Watch and pray that you may not enter into temptation. The spirit indeed is willing, but the flesh is weak" (Matt. 26:41). Peter warns us not to be surprised by trials, especially the temptations of a sensual nature: "Beloved, do not be surprised at the fiery trial when it comes upon you to test you, as though something strange were happening to you" (1 Pet. 4:12); he also provides comfort for believers from the story of Lot: "and if he rescued righteous Lot, greatly distressed by the sensual conduct of the wicked . . . then the Lord knows how to rescue the godly from trials, and to keep the

159. GrO: ἐκπειράζωμεν; ἐπείρασαν.
160. GrO: οὐκ ἐκπειράσεις κύριον.
161. GrO: ὁ πειράζων.
162. GrO: ἀκρασία.
163. GrO: αὐτὸς πειρασθείς; τοῖς πειραζομένοις.
164. DO: *verzoeking*; *aanvechting*.

unrighteous under punishment until the day of judgment" (2 Pet. 2:9). Various forms of suffering are also spoken of in this way. Jesus, in his parable about the sower, says the seed that fell "on the rock are those who, when they hear the word, receive it with joy. But these have no root; they believe for a while, and in time of testing fall away" (Luke 8:13). Paul, writing to the Galatians, says, "And though my condition was a trial to you, you did not scorn or despise me, but received me as an angel of God, as Christ Jesus" (Gal. 4:14). Paul comforts the Corinthians and us: "No temptation has overtaken you that is not common to man. God is faithful, and he will not let you be tempted beyond your ability, but with the temptation he will also provide the way of escape, that you may be able to endure it" (1 Cor. 10:13).[165] James tells us, "Count it all joy, my brothers, when you meet trials of various kinds" (1:2), and pronounces this benediction: "Blessed is the man who remains steadfast under trial, for when he has stood the test he will receive the crown of life, which God has promised to those who love him" (1:12).[166] Peter sounds a similar note of joy: "In this you rejoice, though now for a little while, if necessary, you have been grieved by various trials" (1 Pet. 1:6).[167] And, once again, our Lord's encouragement to the church in Philadelphia: "Because you have kept my word about patient endurance, I will keep you from the hour of trial that is coming on the whole world, to try those who dwell on the earth" (Rev. 3:10).[168]

In these passages, πειρασμός is not yet something specifically wrong;[169] both James (1:2) and Peter (1 Pet. 1:6) call us to joy, to thankfulness when we encounter trials of various kinds. Yet the transition to the second meaning is already formed here—namely, temptation in the strict sense of the word. New Testament examples abound. Paul warns that "those who desire to be rich fall into temptation, into a snare, into many senseless and harmful desires that plunge people into ruin and destruction" (1 Tim. 6:9).[170] As people are tempted to sin, they put God to the test: "Do not harden your hearts as in the rebellion, / on the day of testing in the wilderness, / where your fathers put me to the test / and saw my works for forty years" (Heb. 3:7b–8). Our Lord taught his disciples to pray: "And lead us not into temptation, / but deliver us from evil" (Matt. 6:13).[171] Does praying "lead us not into temptation"

165. GrO: πειρασμός.
166. GrO: πειρασμοῖς.
167. GrO: ἐν ποικίλοις πειρασμοῖς.
168. GrO: τὸν λόγον τῆς ὑπομονῆς μου; ὥρας τοῦ πειρασμοῦ τῆς μελλούσης ἔρχεσθαι ἐπὶ τῆς οἰκουμένης ὅλης πειράσαι τοὺς κατοικοῦντας ἐπὶ τῆς γῆς.
169. DO: bepaald verkeerds.
170. GrO: ἐμπίπτουσιν εἰς πειρασμόν.
171. GrO: μὴ εἰσενέγκῃς ἡμᾶς εἰς τὸν πειρασμόν. Ed. note: The Greek article τόν does not occur in Matt. 6:13 or Luke 11:4; Bavinck may be citing from memory.

conflict with James 1:13–14? "Let no one," James exhorts, "say when he is tempted, 'I am being tempted by God,' for God cannot be tempted with evil, and he himself tempts no one. But each person is tempted when he is lured and enticed by his own desire." No, God does not tempt, but he does lead us into temptation, which he employs as a trial to test us. When Paul says, "God is faithful, and he will not let you be tempted beyond your ability, but with the temptation he will also provide the way of escape, that you may be able to endure it" (1 Cor. 10:13), he points to God acting. The parallel is with Matthew 26:41: "Watch and pray that you may not enter into temptation." God also keeps us from temptation (Rev. 3:10). However, in the petition of the Lord's Prayer temptation is real and hostile; this is clear from the parallel clause that follows: "Deliver us from the evil one"—that is, from Satan. Scripture speaks explicitly of Satan as the tempter, especially of Jesus (Luke 4:13). When the Gospels speak of Jesus's trials and temptations in general (Luke 22:28), the specific origin is not specified. Satan? The Pharisees? In the case of Jesus, should we speak also of "trials" or only of "temptations"?[172]

Dutch, like German, has three words for this range of concepts: *testing*, *temptation*, and *assault*.[173] Testing[174] is in fact an act of God's grace and is meant to examine and strengthen obedience to God; it does not intend our downfall but our validation. Thus God tested Abraham (Gen. 22:1; Heb. 11:17), and he tested Israel by his laws (Exod. 15:15) and through the manna (Exod. 16:4; Deut. 8:16). Testing is intended, therefore, to bring faith and hope to light from out of the sins still remaining in the flesh (Ps. 7:9–10; 1 Cor. 3:13; 2 Cor. 8:8; 1 Thess. 2:4).[175] Objectively, materially, testing can coincide with *temptation*,[176] because God can test by means of suffering, by the demands of self-denial, etc. Testing is always well meant; it seeks only to bring the truth (what someone is) to light, whereas temptation is intended to make someone worse. Satan, however, employs the same means. Consequently, testing and temptation occur by the same means, but differ in their originator and in their intention. Temptation in a stricter sense is always seduction, an attempt to cause a person to fall, an enticing to sin and away from God toward Satan; to "tempt" is really to persuade (through "seeking";[177] cf. desiring, wishing), to change, to force to comply. Then there is also the third term, *aanvechting*

---

172. Ed. note: Bavinck here plays with the Dutch words *beproevingen* and *verzoekingen*.

173. DO: *beproeving; verzoeking; aanvechting*.

174. GrO: δοκιμασία.

175. Vilmar, *Theologische Moral*, 1:177–78.

176. DO: *verzoeking*.

177. Bavinck here plays on the relationship between the Dutch words *zoeken* ("seeking") and *verzoeken* ("tempting").

(= "attack/assault").[178] This is distinct from temptation in that the latter attaches itself to the sins remaining after regeneration, to arouse them and so cause a person to fall; but *assault* attacks precisely the element of rebirth in us, to cause us to begin to doubt (whether we are forgiven, truly born again; whether it is all a deception, imagination, or hypocrisy; whether we have committed the sin against the Holy Spirit, etc.). Therefore, all *assault* is worry, doubt, anxiety. Temptation tries to push back the element of regeneration in us and to provoke in us evil, sinful lust. *Assault* tries to provoke unease, doubt, anxiety about our condition and state before God. To be sure, temptation often turns into *assault*, because born-again people are still constantly tempted, and when they fall they become anxious and begin to doubt their state before God. Accordingly, *assault* often presupposes temptation, but it can also lead to temptation. This is because *assault* often occurs through suffering (e.g., "If you were a child of God you would not have to suffer so much") and intends thereby to provoke anxiety and doubt about God's grace.[179]

1. *The subject of temptation* [i.e., the one who tempts], according to James 1:13–14, is not God, who is after all the Holy One and can never tempt someone to sin. Nevertheless, people are inclined to blame God. As Goethe put it: "You let the poor become guilty, and then abandon them to pain."[180] And Scripture does seem to give some justification for calling God the subject, the author of temptation. Although it does not directly ascribe temptations to God, God does allow people to be tempted (1 Cor. 10:13).[181] Furthermore, there is the even stronger phrase "to lead into temptation" (Matt. 6:13).[182] Said in other words, this means that God can "so lead and order the conditions and circumstances of our life that they become a temptation for us." Now it should be noted that in this life it is impossible to be free of all temptation; whenever something good coincides with our inclination or something evil coincides with our aversion, it can become a temptation. In Matthew 6:13 we are not praying for an end to all temptation. The sixth petition simply means:

---

178. GO: *Anfechtung*; also *Anfeindung* ("hostility, persecution"). On this type of assault (*aanvechting/Anfechtung*), see Martensen, *Christian Ethics*, 2/1:317–21 (§137). Examples in Scripture include Job (cf. Driessen, *Oude en nieuwe mensch*, 665–76), John the Baptist, and Thomas. Ed. note: We will be using the term "assault" to capture the Dutch *aanvechting* and the German *Anfechtung*; the latter has become a standard technical term (particularly associated with Martin Luther) to describe this phenomenon of spiritual warfare.

179. Vilmar, *Theologische Moral*, 1:160–61; Chr. D. F. Palmer, "Versuchung."

180. GO: "Ihr lasst den Armen schuldig werden, dann überlasst Ihr ihn der Pein." Ed. note: These lines are found in Goethe's ballad "The Minstrel" (*Der Sänger*) in the novel *Wilhelm Meister's Apprenticeship* and are available in *Goethe: Selected Verse*, 85.

181. GrO: πειρασμοί; ἐὰν πειρασθῆναι.

182. GrO: εἰσφερεῖν εἰς πειρασμόν.

do not lead us into a chain of circumstances in which our spiritual strength is not in proportion to—is no match for—the power of a temptation.[183] In this petition we ask not to be spared experiences of testing[184] (for testing is a good thing: Gen. 22:1; Deut. 8:2; Ps. 26:2) but that we not be vanquished by testing, that God give us strength in that testing to stand firm against Satan. Calvin, as well as Augustine, connects Matthew 6:13 to the sixth petition as follows: "In order that we may not be led into temptation, deliver us from evil."[185] And then he says that although it is impossible that in this life we feel no testing (by Satan), since our whole life is a struggle against the flesh, yet "we ask the Lord not to bring us down with temptations, or to let us be overwhelmed."[186] God certainly does lead us into temptation and employs all kinds of means to that end, which Satan also uses; in fact, God uses Satan himself as an instrument for tempting us. Thus one cannot dualistically separate temptations from trials, as if the former are materially, objectively, *concretely*,[187] something wholly other than trials. But they do differ *formally*,[188] according to author, disposition, and intent. Whatever God sends our way as a trial, Satan arranges as a temptation. Satan is the author of temptations (as distinct from trials). He is the tempter of Eve (John 8:44), the tempter of Jesus (Matt. 4; Luke 4:13); he is at work in the children of disobedience (Eph. 2:2), among the gentiles (1 Cor. 8:5; 10:20; Acts 16:16; Rev. 9:20); he still works (although he has been vanquished by Jesus [John 14:30; 12:31; 16:11; Col. 2:15; Heb. 2:14] and the church is no longer under his power [Acts 26:18; 1 John 2:13; 4:4]). Satan attacks believers from the outside, sifts them (Luke 22:31), attempts to gain an advantage over them (2 Cor. 2:11), walks about, roaring like a lion (1 Pet. 5:8), tries to lure them away from the simplicity of the faith (2 Cor. 11:3), spreads false teachings and raises up false teachers (2 Cor. 11:13–14), and with his principalities and powers wages war against the church (Eph. 6:12; 1 Pet. 5:9). Thus, Holy Scripture teaches very clearly that Satan with his demons wages war on the church, prosecutes a guerrilla war, as it were, to inflict harm in all kinds of ways and by all kinds of means, both individually and collectively, assaults them and seeks their downfall. Satan is the author of all temptation. There are not three "causes" or "authors" of temptation (our flesh, the world, and Satan) but only one,

---

183. Calvin, *Institutes*, III.xx.46.
184. LO: *tentationes*.
185. LO: "*Ne in tentatione feramur, nos a malo redime.*" Calvin, *Harmony*, 1:212.
186. LO: *ne tentationibus non subjiciat vel obrui patiatur.* Calvin, *Harmony*, 1:213.
187. LO: *in concreto*.
188. LO: *formaliter*.

Satan, and the other two are not means that are coordinate with Satan but are subordinate to him.[189]

2. *The object of temptation* can only be a creature who has free will and who therefore *can* sin.[190] God cannot actually be an object of temptation: Scripture does repeatedly say that people tempt God, but that means—as a result of unbelief, doubting his power, faithfulness, and love—to dare him, to challenge him, to attempt to make him do something. For example, to curse oneself by saying "God damn me" is to tempt God. But God is unable to sin and therefore cannot be enticed or tempted; he is not tempted by evil (James 1:13).[191] At the other extreme, Satan also cannot be tempted; he no longer needs further persuasion to be tempted to do evil; he does evil of his own accord and with pleasure;[192] he is an author and subject, but in no way an object, of temptation, any more than he can be offended. The object of temptation is therefore the human person, who is neither immutably good like God nor immutably evil like Satan.

But to inquire further: Which human being is the object of temptation? First of all Adam, who was, after all, seduced by Satan and *could* be seduced because he was not yet unchangeably good[193] (the blessed departed are confirmed in the good, and so are no longer susceptible to temptation). Christ too could be tempted (Matt. 4; Heb. 2:18; 4:15; Luke 22:28); although immutably good, he did share in our weaknesses. Then, there are sinners, the unregenerate, but these are not really the object of temptation. Scripture never speaks of them as being tempted for the same reason that there is no spiritual struggle inside them. There is no principle in them that is diametrically opposed to Satan; they follow Satan automatically, according to their own will and desire. They struggle only against certain sins, and wage a moral war only, not a spiritual war; at most, they can be deceived,[194] not tempted. The objects of temptation, therefore, are the regenerated, those who are able to be tempted. On the one hand, the "flesh"[195] is still left behind in them; on the other, the Holy Spirit has implanted within them a principle diametrically opposed to Satan. The purpose of their temptation is to pull those who have been translated into the kingdom of light back

---

189. LO: *causae, auctores.* Vilmar, *Theologische Moral,* 1:162. Ed. note: Bavinck's threefold "our flesh, the world, and Satan" is taken directly from the Heidelberg Catechism's exposition of the sixth petition in Lord's Day 52, Q&A 127, but in reverse order!

190. Cf. C. D. F. Palmer, "Versuchung," 144–46.

191. GrO: ἀπείραστος κακῶν.

192. LO: *sua sponte; lubenter.*

193. LO: *immutabiliter bonus.*

194. Becoming increasingly blinded, 2 Cor. 4:4; 2 Tim. 2:26.

195. GrO: σάρξ.

into the world, into the darkness, to reconquer them, and so to destroy the kingdom of God.

3. *The manner of temptation* can be described to some extent because Scripture recounts the temptations of Eve and Jesus.[196] Temptation is preceded by spiritual desertion, the withdrawal of God's Spirit (2 Chron. 32:31; Pss. 27:9; 38:22; 42; 102:3). This was so in the case of Christ, who was alone in the wilderness with the animals (Mark 1:12–13); not until after the victory do angels come to serve him. He was also alone in Gethsemane, and only later did an angel appear. This loneliness and abandonment is present in every temptation; one feels its depth to the degree that one has lived intimately with God. It is a feeling of being very close to death and hell (see below on spiritual desertion). Satan comes on those occasions and tries, first of all, to provoke doubts within us about God's Word, to rob us of the support, foundation, and certainty of that Word. Thus it was in the case of Eve; in the case of Jesus it had no effect: he says at once, "It is written, man shall not live by bread alone." Satan tries to stifle the good (Matt. 13:19). In the second place, Satan himself employs God's Word, but turns it around ("You shall not surely die") or falsifies it ("If you are the son of God, cast yourself down, for it is written: He shall give his angels charge over you"). In the third place, he awakens the desire to sin ("When you eat of it your eyes will be opened, and you will be like God") or entices one to that desire (Satan shows Jesus all the glories of the world). At first, then, Satan works negatively and tries to detach us from God, to drag us away from God and his Word, and after that he tries to persuade us to do the sinful deed. In other words, he first makes the new person powerless and then awakens in us the old self with its lusts. He takes the true ideal from our eyes, conjures up another one, and tries to get us to reach for it. To be sure, in our case the temptation is much lighter than with Eve and Christ, since we have concupiscence in us (James 1:14–15), since we are forgetful, indifferent to the Word, feel an inner desire for the world, and the like; on the other hand, Satan has been vanquished by Christ, and his power is limited. But the temptation is the same in its character. We can only defeat Satan by applying the Word of God (Matt. 4; Eph. 6:16–17). Satan is no match for that weapon; Christ, the God-man, has defeated him.

4. *The means of temptation.* An important question: Can Satan still tempt us immediately (as he did with Eve and Christ), apart from flesh and the world? People have disagreed about this from the very beginning of the Christian era. Commenting on Matthew 15:19, Jerome says, Satan always tempts in a mediated way through flesh and the world; he is a "helper and an inciter of

---

196. Vilmar, *Theologische Moral*, 1:163.

evil thoughts" but not their author.[197] However, Augustine, in his *Tractates on John* 62, on John 13:26–31, espouses the opposite view and appeals to the case of Judas. Augustine's view was favored in Lutheran and Reformed circles, but opposed in the Dutch Reformed Church by Balthasar Bekker and company. Today it is also opposed by many, including, among others, Friedrich Schleiermacher, who denies that Satan can work within a person.[198] Usually, however, the assumption is that Satan works immediately upon a person, that he turns directly to us and speaks to our consciousness (whether visibly and audibly, or as a hidden and invisible spirit, or directly through other people, the possessed).[199] Besides Eve and Christ, who are exceptional, there is the example of Judas in John 13:2: "During supper, when the devil had already put it into the heart of Judas Iscariot, Simon's son, to betray him . . ."[200] First, Satan puts the evil thought into Judas's heart; later in the chapter John writes: "Then after he had taken the morsel, Satan entered into him" (13:27; cf. Luke 22:3).[201] Yet one must not forget that the lust for money (John 12:6; Matt. 26:15; Mark 14:11; Luke 22:5–6) was definitely a point of opportunity for Satan. One can also refer to 2 Samuel 24:1, where Satan provokes David to hold a census; to Matthew 12:44, where Jesus tells us that when Satan returns to the house he has vacated and finds it empty, swept, and clean, he once again takes up residence there, along with seven other evil spirits. Jesus was certainly speaking of someone enlightened by the gospel (not regenerated), who rejected the gospel and became even worse than before. We can also think of Luke 22:31–32 and Jesus's words to Peter: "Simon, Simon, behold, Satan demanded to have you, that he might sift you like wheat, but I have prayed for you that your faith may not fail." Buddeus, however, correctly observes that this proves that Satan was at work, but not that his work was unmediated.[202]

197. LO: *adjutor et incensor malarum cogitationum*, cited from Buddeus, *Institutiones Theologiae Moralis*, 262. Buddeus incorrectly refers to Matt. 5:19. Jerome writes, "The devil can be a helper and an inciter of evil thoughts, but he cannot be their author. Yet he always lies in wait and kindles small sparks in our thoughts with his own tinder. We should not imagine that he searches the secrets of the heart as well, but from the gestures and demeanor of our body, he guesses what is going on inside of us, for example, if he sees us repeatedly looking at a lovely woman. Then he understands that our heart has been wounded by the dart of love" (*Commentary on Matthew*, 181–82 [PL 26:109]).

198. Schleiermacher, *Christian Faith*, 385–89 (§94).

199. Hoornbeeck, *Theologiae Practicae*, 1:346.

200. GrO: τοῦ διαβόλου ἤδη βεβληκότος εἰς τὴν καρδίαν ἵνα παραδοῖ αὐτὸν Ἰούδας Σίμωνος Ἰσκαριώτου. Ed. note: Bavinck continues with some text-critical and exegetical issues, including Meyer's claim that the phrase βεβληκότος εἰς τὴν καρδίαν refers to Satan. Bavinck calls this nonsense (*onzin*) because "Satan has no heart." He cites as source for his interpretation Godet, *Commentary on John*, 2:245–46.

201. GrO: εἰσῆλθεν εἰς ἐκεῖνον ὁ Σατανᾶς.

202. Buddeus, *Institutiones Theologiae Moralis*, 260.

The possibility that Satan works directly cannot be dismissed, as is shown by those who were possessed in Jesus's day and who are even today; it is possible, in the midst of the holiest transactions, the most earnest prayer, that the most sinful thoughts can suddenly surface, blasphemies arise against our will, and can only be contained with great effort.[203] Thus, Reformed thinkers mostly accepted the possibility of immediate temptations by the devil.[204]

The question was how immediate temptations by Satan could be recognized as coming from Satan.[205] Ames draws up these two rules: if the temptation conflicts with the light of nature and our natural inclinations, and if it arises not slowly but suddenly, with a certain vehemence. Robert Bolton, Christopher Love, and John Arrow-Smith advanced these same two criteria.[206] Ames and Hoornbeeck assert that if we reject and turn aside those "suggestions," we incur no guilt.[207] Still, one must grant, with Buddeus and Bona, that we cannot distinguish absolutely what comes from Satan and what comes out of our own heart.[208] For it is difficult to determine whether something conflicts with the light of reason, nature, and our inclinations (Christopher Love mentions committing suicide); spontaneous thoughts, as such, prove little, for thoughts can suddenly rise up from the dark, secret natural soil of our heart,

---

203. C. D. F. Palmer, *Pastoraal-theologie*, 392, 404–5.

204. Chemnitz, *Dissertatio Theologica*; Buddeus, *Institutiones Theologiae Moralis*, 260, 262; Hoornbeeck, *Theologiae Practicae*, 1:346; Voetius, Τα Ασκητικα, 451–523 (chap. 19); on p. 464 Voetius further distinguishes, among the temptations of the devil, the *external* (when Satan appears visibly or audibly) and the *internal*. The latter are called "instigations, suggestions" (*injectiones*); in the case of madness, etc., "delusional" (*phantasticae*); or they are referred to as "of the mind" (*mentales*): blasphemous thoughts, etc. These suggestions can be thrown directly into the consciousness, apart from the medium of imagination (p. 473). Cf. Ames, *Conscience*, II.xviii; Perkins, *Whole Treatise*, 39–48 (1.10–12); Perkins, *Combat between Christ and the Devil*; Perkins, "Dialogue"; Driessen, *Oude en nieuwe mensch*, 701–17 (chap. 27 §4); Lampe, *Schets der dadelyke Godt-geleertheid*, 545–64 (II.10); van Mastricht, *Theoretico-Practica Theologia*, III. iv.9 [4:813–22]; W. à Brakel, *Christian's Reasonable Service*, 4:235–50 (chap. 95, "The Assaults of Satan"). For modern thinkers, see Vilmar, *Theologische Moral*, 1:169; Martensen, *Christian Ethics*, 2/1:321–24 (§138). Martensen, however, adds that one cannot identify an absolute boundary between mediate and immediate temptation. See also the literature on temptation listed in Voetius, Τα Ασκητικα, 523–24; Köster, *Die biblische Lehre von der Versuchung*; Harless, *System of Christian Ethics*, 248–73 (§28). Ed. note: For an explanation of the format we are using to cite van Mastricht's *Theoretico-Practica Theologia*, see the extended note in the introduction, §1, in the section "Reformed Churches" (pp. 8–9n48). The volume and page numbers come from the 1749–53 Dutch edition used by Bavinck.

205. Buddeus, *Institutiones Theologiae Moralis*, 263; Hoornbeeck, *Theologiae Practicae*, 1:352; Ames, *Conscience*, II.xviii.xlv.

206. Bolton, *Saints Selfe-Enriching Examination*, 206; Love, *Het mergh van de werkige godt-geleerdtheidt*, 6 (Love also wrote an entire treatise on the Christian's struggle with Satan's assaults: *The Christians Combat*); Hoornbeeck, *Theologiae Practicae*, 1:352.

207. LO: *injectiones*. Hoornbeeck, *Theologiae Practicae*, 1:353.

208. Buddeus, *Institutiones Theologiae Moralis*, 263.

in the same way that brilliant thoughts arise there. Only in the case of sinless creatures—Eve, Jesus—did temptation have to come from the outside, from Satan. So, the main issue is not whether the temptation is direct or indirect. For the most part, Satan begins with the sin that is already within us—for example, with Judas in his greed, with Macbeth in his ambition.[209] Surely it is not necessary "to have seen with one's own eyes the devil gnashing his teeth from down below."[210] James ascribes temptation to personal lust (James 1:14–15). We should not be quick to ascribe all temptations to Satan and so make excuses for ourselves (Augustine).[211]

The means through which Satan tempts us are, subjectively, the flesh within us (all sinful desires, thoughts, etc.) and, corresponding with that, objectively, the world with its lusts of the eye and of the flesh, as well as the grandeur of life.[212] Calvin distinguishes two categories of the means of temptation: from the right, riches, power, honor, and the like; and from the left, poverty, disgrace, contempt, and afflictions.[213] The former pull us more toward the world, the latter pull us more away from God, toward doubt and spiritual assaults regarding God.[214]

3. SPIRITUAL DESERTION

In previous eras this topic was seldom treated, at least not separately; it was broached only under the subject of temptations or in commentaries on the Song of Solomon, for example.[215] Practical theologians of the Reformed Church loved to deal with this material, including Perkins, Voetius, Love, Joseph Symonds, Driessen, both à Brakels, and van Mastricht.[216] Despite God's omnipresence, there is a desertion of God, a hiding of his face. In a physical sense, with his substance and essence, he is and remains everywhere, but

209. Martensen, *Christian Ethics*, 2/1:321 (§138); C. D. F. Palmer, "Versuchung," 148.
210. Vilmar, *Die Theologie der Tatsachen*, 41.
211. Hoornbeeck, *Theologiae Practicae*, 1:353.
212. Voetius, Τα Ασκητικα, 486–90; Hoornbeeck, *Theologiae Practicae*, 1:365–75; Buddeus, *Institutiones Theologiae Moralis*, 264; Vilmar, *Theologische Moral*, 1:160–78.
213. Calvin, *Institutes*, III.xx.46.
214. GO: *Anfechtungen*. Ed. note: At this point in the manuscript, Bavinck added "[e.] The purpose of temptation (*Doel der verzoeking*)," but no content follows—only a reference to Vilmar, *Theologische Moral*, 1:171–72.
215. Voetius and Hoornbeeck, *Spiritual Desertion*, 62–78.
216. Perkins, *Declaration of Certaine Spirituall Desertions*, III.415–20; Voetius, Τα Ασκητικα, 524–60 (chap. 20); Voetius and Hoornbeeck, *Spiritual Desertion*; Love, "The With-Drawing of the Spirit," which is the first sermon in *Combate between the Flesh and Spirit*, 1–11; Symonds, *Case and Cure*; Driessen, *Oude en nieuwe mensch*, 633; T. à Brakel, *De trappen*, 25; W. à Brakel, *Christian's Reasonable Service*, 4:171–91; van Mastricht, *Theoretico-Practica Theologia*, III. iv.13 [4:830].

ethically and spiritually he can withdraw. These can very well go together. I can be with someone and yet withhold my favor, affection, and grace, even be angry with that person. Forsaken of God, for example, are the devils, who physically exist only through him, but ethically stand completely outside and opposite him. So also the ungodly, who, though gifted with many benefits (Matt. 5:45), with bodily and spiritual blessings and talents, with external grace and so forth, nevertheless have no peace (Isa. 57:21), and from whom the Spirit of the Lord, though granted for a time for a specific purpose, departs again (1 Sam. 16:14; Heb. 6:4). Prior to their conversion, the elect are forsaken, although already even then they are guarded, prepared, equipped, and saved from blaspheming the Holy Spirit. But after their regeneration such desertion is always only partial (gradual) and temporary (not eternal). To be sure, there are among the elect different ways of being forsaken:

a. Forsaken in sin: when God withholds his preserving, restraining grace. As in the case of David, Hezekiah (2 Chron. 32:31–32), Peter, Noah (in his drunkenness), God allows a person to fall into sin in order to completely cure the evil, as by venom.[217]

b. Forsaken as punishment: so especially in the case of Jesus, who encountered God's wrath, and in the case of many believers when they fall into sin and must do without God's grace and favor (Ps. 51:12).

c. Forsaken in order to be tested: this consists of desolation, spiritual numbness, and is also referred to as *assault*:[218] struggle, pangs of conscience, spiritual despair, etc. These are what we need to discuss here. They consist in the absence of a heartfelt pleasure in God and his service; in the withdrawal of assurance and peace in God, not so much as to its essence, but in terms of experiencing and practicing it; in spiritual deadness and sorrow. Thus Israel in exile (Isa. 54:7) and the disciples when Jesus departed (John 16:20–21). Objectively, according to Scripture, there is indeed a desertion of God. True, his kindness shall never depart from them (Isa. 54:10); he will never leave them nor forsake them (Isa. 49:15; Heb. 13:5; Jer. 1:5; Deut. 4:31); and he preserves in them the faith, the Holy Spirit, the vital principle; but he does withhold his favor and kindness, and takes away their sense of his nearness and grace. Scripture calls this God's going and returning (Hosea 5:15), hiding his face and forgetting them (Ps. 30:1, 7; Mic. 3:4), rejecting and no longer being gracious (Ps. 77:8–10; contrasted with coming, John 14:23), forsaking (Ps. 22:2). And many believers in the Old Testament lament this (Ps. 10:1). Particularly in Psalm 22, where being forsaken consists of two things: God

217. Perkins, *Declaration of Certaine Spirituall Desertions*, III.419.
218. GO: *Anfechtung.*

does not hear the psalmist's prayer, and he does not save him from his distress (vv. 1–2). As a result, he is without peace (v. 2), poured out like water, with a heart as wax, his strength dried up (vv. 14–15), and despised by all as a worm (vv. 6–8). Nevertheless, he holds fast to his God (vv. 1–2), delights in him (v. 8), trusts and praises him (vv. 3, 25), keeps on praying (vv. 2, 4), even urgently with great anguish (vv. 11–18). He pleads to be heard, appealing to the faith of the fathers (vv. 4–5), to the course of his life under God's care (vv. 9–10), and he makes vows (v. 25). At last he is heard, and there is deliverance (v. 24), thanksgiving (vv. 22, 25), and a call to others to praise God (vv. 23, 26). Similarly, in Psalm 38 in its entirety, but especially in verses 21–22: "Do not forsake me, O LORD! / O my God, be not far from me! / Make haste to help me, / O Lord, my salvation!" (cf. Pss. 42; 55; 69; 71:11; 77; 88; Song of Sol. 2:1, 9; Jer. 17:17; 18:17).

Strangely, this desertion does not occur in the New Testament.[219] To be forsaken of God is often not a punishment but chastisement, not an act of God's wrath but of his grace; on the human side, however, it often follows upon sin, since God's forsaking of a person may be caused by sin (2 Chron. 15:2; Ezra 8:22). The Spirit of God, who has been grieved, can turn into an enemy (Isa. 57:17–18, 63; Eph. 4:30), with the result that he stops witnessing in us that we are children of God, stops granting us peace and joy and happiness. This is then often associated with the doubt and unbelief of our own heart, which accuses God (Ps. 73:11–13), with the scorn of the world (Ps. 22:6–8), with the attacks of Satan, like those of Job's friends. We then experience the nearness of hell, death, darkness, and dread, calling for deliverance in our anguish (Ps. 22), sighing and groaning (Job 3:24; 6:5; 7:12, and passim), thirsting after God (Ps. 42). This spiritual desertion is different in kind from melancholy, despair, and being possessed.[220]

---

219. Ed. note: Bavinck provides the following reference: "Cf. Gisbertus Voetius, *Disputaty van geestelicke verlatingen*, 70v." However, such a claim could not be found there or in the ET.
220. Driessen, *Oude en nieuwe mensch*, 634–36.

12

Restoration and Consummation
of the Christian Life

*Having examined the pathologies of the Christian spiritual life in the previous
chapter, we conclude this volume by discussing the spiritual disciplines that provide
remedy to them and help prevent further spiritual disorder. This field is usually called
ascesis by the church's spiritual teachers; this led to monastic asceticism in the early
and medieval church, to a posture of separation from the world and abstaining from
certain activities. The Reformation rejected much of this, including the notion that
ascetic practices were meritorious, but realized the need for spiritual discipline and
developed its own body of writings emphasizing Christian lives characterized by
self-examination, meditation on Scripture, prayer, fasting, and worship, all leading
to self-denial and cross-bearing in imitation of Christ.*

*This chapter considers eight means toward personal renewal: prayer, spiritual
meditation, reading the Word of God* (lectio verbi divina), *hymn singing, solitude,
fasting, vigils, and vows. Prayer takes up most of the attention, with a consideration
of the essence of prayer as a duty and a good work, biblical teaching on prayer,
the subject and object of prayer (human beings and the Triune God), the content
of prayer, the manner of prayer, and answers to prayer. All people, believers and
unbelievers alike, are commanded to pray. Parents should teach their children to
pray and not wait until they see signs of rebirth in them. True prayer is directed to
the Triune God, Father, Son, and Holy Spirit, according to God's will, and in the
name of Jesus. We are to pray for "everything we need, spiritually and physically, as
embraced in the prayer Christ our Lord himself taught us." Our prayers should be
disciplined; prepared and form prayers ought not to be despised. We should pray at*

all times, without ceasing, trusting that God knows what is good for us. Meditation is a spiritual exercise of intense inward communion with God, humbly submitting our wills to God's will, in order to discern godly things, including how to obey him. Regular Bible reading, leading to meditating on God and his law, is an important resource for sanctification, as is singing of hymns (in addition to the Psalms). Self-examination in solitude aids us in becoming aware of our sins and grieving for them, grieving for the suffering of others, longing for grace, and expressing love, joy, and devotion. Fasting is a sign of humility before God; it quiets our passions and desires, helps us resist temptation, and expresses sorrow. Watching and vigil are recommended in Scripture but should not be prescribed. In spite of misuse, the Reformation holds on to the vow as a free act of the believer who wants to dedicate something to God in gratitude for an answer to prayer.

The spiritual life is first made perfect in death and then moves over to eternal life. We must prepare for our own death as an act of humility, to part with the imagination of a long life, and to deprive death of its power over us. Pious people ought never to die fearful and hopeless, without joy.

§25. MEANS OF RESTORATION

What we have to discuss here—many spiritual diseases such as intellectualism (orthodoxism), mysticism, moralism—is usually called "ascesis" and is dealt with in the teachings of asceticism.[1] The Greek word ἀσκεῖν means "to shape or form carefully,[2] to exercise." Later on, this word is especially used for the exercises of athletes. In the New Testament it is found only in Acts 24:16.[3] However, it did not take the Christian church long (e.g., Clement of Alexandria) to call those who lead a withdrawn life and who abstain from many things "ascetics." Subsequently, those who lived withdrawn lives were called ἀσκητής (a monk) and ἀσκήτρια (a nun); a monk's habit was called an ἀσκητικὴ καλύβη (casula monestica), and ἀσκητήριον, along with μοναστήριον (monastery), was used of the place where monks or ἀσκητήριος practiced ascesis.[4] Means to reach that higher step of perfection were necessary as the

---

1. GrO: ἄσκησις. Zöckler, Askese und Mönchtum, 1:3, 24. In general, acceticism can be *communal* or *individual*, *negative* (abstaining from food, marriage, riches) or *positive*. Positive asceticism can be *bodily* (flagellation) or *spiritual* (prayer, contemplation, meditation, reading, staying awake, practicing humility, obedience).

2. But also in a moral sense; Aristotle speaks of "moral exercise" (ἄσκησις ἀρετῆς).

3. Ed. note: "So I always take pains [ἐν τούτῳ καὶ αὐτὸς ἀσκῶ ἀπρόσκοπον] to have a clear conscience toward both God and man."

4. Kögel, "Asketik"; Gass, *Geschichte der christlichen Ethik*, 1:104; Voetius, Τα Ασκητικα, 12–20. Ed. note: Bavinck had ἀσκητήριος as the term for monk, a word not found in LSJ.

church became increasingly worldly and the distinction between precepts and counsels of perfection found acceptance.[5] The following were particularly mentioned among these means: abstaining from food, drink, clothing, wealth, and marriage; retreating from society into a cell or monastery and spending the time there in reading, prayer, fasting, watching, and hard labor. Subsequently, self-castigation and flagellation were added to that. This was also treated scientifically. Ascetic theology—as the science dealing with those means that help orient the will to do good, to strengthen the spiritual life—received its place between ethics (and morality), as the teaching concerning the essence of the good, and casuistry as the application of morality to certain cases in life. We find the preparation for this science already with the church fathers, specifically with Tertullian, Basil, Macarius of Egypt, and Augustine.[6] However, the discipline of ascetic theology was developed especially in the Middle Ages by Hugh and Richard of St. Victor, Jan Ruysbroek, Thomas à Kempis, Johannes Tauler in several devotional tracts, and Bernard of Cluny's *Contempt of the World*.[7] Other works include Bonaventure's *Tractate on the Growth of the Spiritual Life*; Batavus Florentius's *Institutes of the Christian Life*, and so forth.[8] For the most part, these ascetical works describe monk-like exercises.[9]

The Reformation rejected this asceticism. Luther rejected ascetic practices as meritorious[10] and understood them only as necessary for combating the flesh.[11] For Luther the following ascetic practices were especially important: prayer, fasting, watching, and working.[12] However, these should not be held as law or

5. LO: *praecepta*; *consilia*.

6. Walch, *Bibliotheca Theologica Selecta*, 2:1074–78. Ed. note: Walch also mentions Gregory of Nyssa, Ephraim the Syrian, Pseudo-Dionysius the Areopagite, Chrysostom, Ambrose, and Jerome.

7. Walch, *Bibliotheca Theologica Selecta*, 2:1080. Ed. note: Bavinck names the title but not the author. Bernard of Cluny was a Benedictine monk, and his *De Contemptu Mundi* is a satire directed at the failings of society and church in his day (the twelfth century). In the nineteenth century, John Mason Neale translated the initial portion of the poem into English, and it was published as a hymn, "Jerusalem the Golden."

8. Bonaventure, *Tractatus de profectu religiosorum*. Ed. note: Bavinck also mentions another work, *Dieta salutius*, which is listed as "spurious" by the editors of Bonaventure's *Opera Omnia*, 1:xvi; Florentius, Surius, and Poin, *Institutiones Vitae Christianae*; see additional works in Voetius, *De praktijk der godzaligheid*, 19–20; Voetius, *Exercitia*, 496–97; also Walch, *Bibliotheca Theologica Selecta*, 2:1177.

9. DO: *monnikachtige oefeningen*.

10. DO: *verdienend*.

11. DO: *verdienend*. Cf. Luthardt, *Die Ethik Luthers*, 63–66.

12. Think also of Luther's triad of prayer (*oratio*), mediation (*meditatio*), and testing/trial/ temptation (*tentatio*). Ed. note: Luther developed this pattern in his preface to the Wittenberg edition of his German writings (Weimarer Ausgabe 50:657–66; *Luther's Works*, 34:283–88); see Kleinig, "Oratio, Meditatio, Tentatio." Bavinck also took note of the same threefold pattern in William Ames (see §20 above). A possible source was J. J. van Oosterzee, *Sieben Vorträge*. Lecture 5

practiced at certain times but only when necessary, according to one's rank, character, and so on. Everyone is free in this matter. Based on this understanding, ascetic theology was introduced in the Lutheran Church in the seventeenth century. To name a few: Johann Arndt (1565–1621), the author of *True Christianity*, who was more mystical; Stephan Praetorius (1536–1603); Valerius Herberger (1562–1627); Herman Rahtmann (1585–1628); and Johann Valentin Andreä (1586–1654).[13] But a dogmatic scholar like Johann Gerhard in Jena (d. 1637) also dealt with ascetic theology in his *Sacred Meditations, The Teaching of Devotion*, and many others.[14] The Lutherans have benefited greatly in this area from English and Dutch writers, whose works were largely translated into German.[15]

Calvin understands the entire Christian life as one of ongoing self-denial and cross-bearing, in which Christians sacrifice themselves to God.[16] Calvin specifically returns to this theme of cross-bearing again and again. He especially sees in the cross God's fatherly upbringing, through which he tempers our desires[17] and exercises our patience, causing us to find refuge in him. In trials and temptations[18] Christians should find support in the example of Christ, holding to the promises of God, putting on the armor of God (Eph. 6), and especially making use of prayer.[19] Prayer is the best school of humility, patience, and obedience, the constant expression and performance of the Christian life, and teaches us in self-denial.[20]

(pp. 159–92) is titled (in Latin): "*Oratio, meditatio, tentatio.*" A Dutch translation of this lecture, "*Oratie, Meditatie, Tentatie,*" can be found in Oosterzee, *Voor kerk en theologie*, 2:81–106.

13. Ed. note: The identification of Stephan Praetorius is an educated guess; Bavinck's manuscript only has "Praetorius †1610." Stephan Praetorius was a German Lutheran pastor at Neustadt whose dates are 1536–1603. He emphasized purity of life and "was a precursor of J. Arndt and P. Spener, though not Pietist in the narrow sense" (P. Wolff, "Praetorius, Stephan"); cf. Zöckler, *Handbuch der theologischen Wissenschaften*, 2:178). Valerius Herberger was a Lutheran pastor "at Fraustadt (50 m. south-southwest of Posen) where he ministered faithfully under the difficult circumstances of Roman Catholic persecution and pestilence (1613)" (Cohrs, "Herberger"). Herman Rahtman was a Lutheran theologian who was influenced by Caspar Schwenkveld and for whom Scripture was only "an index and a witness to grace. . . . In Rahtmann's theology the testimony of the Holy Spirit becomes an independent, immediate act of the Spirit" (Grützmacher, "Rahtmann"). Bavinck cites Zöckler here as a source for the full list of Lutheran theologians just named. Johann Valentin Andreä was a theologian and satirist who advocated for an end to sectarian strife and for unification of Christian churches (Hölscher, "Andreä").

14. Gerhard, *Meditationes Sacrae*; Gerhard, *Scholae Pietatis*; Walch, *Bibliotheca Theologica Selecta*, 2:1172.

15. Walch, *Bibliotheca Theologica Selecta*, 2:1176n. Cf. also H. G. J. Beck, *Die Erbauungsliteratur*, vol. 1.

16. Calvin, *Institutes*, III.vii–viii; cf. Lobstein, *Die Ethik Calvins*, 79–94.

17. DO: *zinlijkheid*.

18. Calvin, *Institutes*, III.xx.46.

19. Calvin, *Institutes*, III.xx.

20. Calvin discusses fasting in *Institutes*, IV.xii.14–21.

Actual asceticism arose in England through William Whitaker (1548–95), professor in Cambridge, William Perkins (1558–1602) in Cambridge, Lewis Bayly (d. 1631),[21] and many others. The way already prepared by Taffin and Udemans found acceptance in the Netherlands via Willem Teellinck (1579–1629), William Ames (1576–1633), Gisbert Voetius (1589–1676), Johannes Hoornbeeck (1617–66), Ewout Teellinck (1573–1629), and others. It then became less healthy by absorbing mystical and pietistic elements in the works of Johannes Teellinck (d. 1674), Theodorus G. à Brakel (d. 1660), Jodocus van Lodenstein (d. 1677), and so on.[22]

In general, Reformed writers[23] included the following among the ascetic exercises:

For *Lewis Bayly* the entire exercise consisted of meditation and reflecting on (a) "the essence and attributes of God" [28–44], (b) "the misery of people not reconciled to God in Christ" [45–55], and (c) "the state of a Christian reconciled to God in Christ" [56–77]. After this he addresses the exercise of godliness or the glorification of God and first mentions "meditation on the hindrances which keep back a sinner from the practice of piety" [78–93]. Then he describes "how a private man must begin the morning with piety" (reading Scripture and prayer) and provides many practical guides for morning devotions [94–107]. This is followed by "meditations directing a Christian how he may walk all the day with God, like Enoch" [108–18], followed by "meditations for the evening" [119–25]. He then follows a similar pattern for "household piety" with "morning prayer for a family," "the practice of piety at meals" (prayer before and after meals, psalm singing), "and the manner of eating" [126–40]. The next sets of meditations deal with "the true manner of practicing piety on the Sabbath Day" [which includes prayer and "duties in the Holy Assembly," 141–73]. He continues with "of the practice of piety in fasting" [174–82], "holy feasting" [the Lord's Supper, 183–211], "glorifying God in the time of sickness" [212–24, 238–43], death [225–37, 244–50], and martyrdom [256–69].

Gisbert Voetius first deals with devotion and some terminology ("compunction," "excitation," and so on),[24] meditation, and prayer (usage of psalms).

---

21. Ed. note: Lewis Bayly was an Anglican bishop best known for his work *The Practice of Piety*, written originally in 1611. We will be citing the electronic version available at http://www.ccel.org/ccel/bayly/piety.pdf. Page references to this work in the next paragraph will be given in square brackets within the text.

22. See the earlier discussion of pietism in the Reformed churches, §20; Walch, *Bibliotheca Theologica Selecta*, 2:1175.

23. DO: *Gereformeerden*.

24. LO: *compunctio; excitatio*. Ed. note: "Compunction," referring to "the intense effect of conviction upon the affections," is used by Puritan writers such as John Flavel in their discussions of the steps by which some are converted (along with "illumination"); see Boone, *Puritan*

Then he writes more specifically about the practice of conversion (tears), reading, sacraments, Sabbath, fasting, watching, solitude, vows, temptations, spirtual lapses, death, martyrdom. He continues with exercises in relation to others: exhortation, consolation, teaching of others, and so on.[25]

Campegius Vitringa mentions the following as remedies and "help-means": prayer, avoiding sin, reading Holy Scripture, being on guard against all manner of sins (excess, laziness, and so on), singing, public worship, societies, self-examination, solitude, and fasting.[26] However, he rejects the "help-means" of celibacy, poverty, and obedience.

Johann Franz Buddeus lists the following practices: daily penitence, reading and hearing God's Word [310], especially on the Sabbath [313], reading other authors [313], meditation [314], sacraments [315], prayer [319], fasting [337], watchfulness/vigilance [339], imitation of Jesus, and others [340].[27]

We take our starting point here in constant self-examination, in ongoing conversation, in avoiding of sin and causes of it. We will discuss communal practices in the next volume of this work,[28] including the communal practices of morning and evening worship, prayer before and after eating (meals), listening to God's Word in church, use of the sacraments, societies,[29] Sabbath observance, and so on. Here we only discuss the means that can be used for recovery or encouragement of the individual spiritual life, depending on a person's need. These include prayer, meditation[30] (on God and oneself), reading of Holy Scripture, fasting, watching, solitude, hymn singing, and vows.

1. Prayer[31]

We will consider first *what* prayer is, including what the Old and New Testaments teach us about prayer (a and b), about *who* is the *subject* of prayer (c),

---

Evangelism, chaps. 5–6. The term "excitation" is used by critics of any form of intense religious "enthusiasm" or even ecstasy as it appears in the Anabaptist and Pietist traditions; see, e.g., Ritschl, "Prolegomena," in *Three Essays*, 75.

25. Ed. note: This is Bavinck's global summary of the chapter divisions in Voetius, Τα Ασκητικα.

26. DO: *hulpmiddelen; openbare godsdienst; gezelschappen*. Vitringa, *Korte schets*, chaps. 10–14.

27. DO/LO: *dagelijksche poenitentia*; DO: *waakzaamheid*. Buddeus, *Institutiones Theologiae Moralis*, 303–42 (I.v). Ed. note: Page references in this sentence are to Buddeus's work. Cf. T. à Brakel, *Het geestelijke leven*; Rothe, *Theologische Ethik*, 3:464–526 (§§870–86, on ascetics).

28. Ed. note: Bavinck's manuscript refers to Book III, "Humanity after Conversion," which will be the content of our second volume.

29. DO: *gezelschappen*.

30. LO: *oratio; meditatio*.

31. Ed. note: Bavinck wrote a foreword to a book on prayer by F. Kramer, *Het Gebed* (Kampen: Kok, 1905), which begins, "A treatment of prayer like Rev. F. Kramer presents in the following pages deserves a hearty word of commendation in our day." The remainder of the foreword summarizes a number of the key themes Bavinck explores in this chapter.

about *who* is the *object* of prayer (d), about the *content* of prayer (e), about the *manner* of prayer (f), and about the *hearing* of prayer (g).[32]

A. Prayer as a Duty

Prayer is a *duty* and the most important *good work*, according to the regularly repeated divine commands in the Old and New Testament.[33] We do not find any particular prescriptions with regard to prayer in the Pentateuch. Because of this, the Socinians[34] claimed that the law was imperfect and filled in by Christ, including, among other things, the perfect prayer. However, this prayer is not new when we consider the content.[35] This is all the more evident from the examples of prayer heroes in the Pentateuch: Abraham's prayer for Sodom (Gen. 18), Jacob wrestling with God (Gen. 32), Moses praying for Israel's preservation against Amalek (Exod. 17). Similarly, we find examples and prescriptions of prayer in the Psalms and prophets: "Call upon me," and so on. In the New Testament too, Jesus himself prays. Prayer is, as it were, rooted in God's own being, because Jesus prays not only as a human being but as Mediator[36] and teaches his disciples to pray (Matt. 6). Prayer is fitting for us because God is God, because of all his attributes: faithfulness, grace, omnipotence, goodness, and so on. Furthermore, we also depend on him for everything;[37] having nothing from ourselves, we need to receive everything from him. Prayer is therefore deeply grounded in human nature; it is a necessity for its being and exists among all peoples and human beings, even those who curse. Only the Epicureans, Adamites, and Deists consider it redundant, along with people like Willem Deurhoff (1650–1717) and (possibly) Pontiaan van Hattem (1645–1706).[38] Materialist pantheists see an analogy to prayer in

32. De Moor, *Commentarius Perpetuus*, 5:1–120 (XXVI §§1–21).

33. See Ps. 50:15; Matt. 7:7; Rom. 12:12; Eph. 6:18; Phil. 4:6; Col. 4:2; 1 Thess. 5:17; cf. Christ, *Die Lehre vom Gebet*, and the review of Christ's study in *Theologisches Literaturblatt* 7 (1886): 247–48; Kuyper, "Van den Heilige Geest en het gebed" (Kuyper believes that prayer presupposes faith and therefore cannot have regeneration, faith, conversion as its content, only their increase, etc.); M. J. Monrad, "Über das Gebet"; Hettinger, *Apologie des Christenthums*, 1:504–16, 534–49.

34. Ed. note: The Socinians were followers of Fausto Sozzini (Faustus Socinus, 1539–1604), who denied the Trinity, the preexistence of Jesus Christ, and the doctrines of original sin and substitutionary atonement. Much of what was taught by this group is now embedded in Unitarianism. See Zöckler, "Socinus."

35. De Moor, *Commentarius Perpetuus*, 2:712–14.

36. Cf. Löber, *Die Lehre vom Gebet*, chap. 2: "Praying people have their eternal ectype in the Triune God" (GO: *Der betende Mensch hat sein ewiges Urbild in Gott dem Dreieinigen*).

37. Pss. 104:27–30; 145:15–21.

38. DO: *Adamianen*. Ed. note: It is not entirely clear to whom Bavinck is referring here; according to Brackney (*Historical Dictionary*, s.v. "Adamites"), "The name ["Adamites" or "Adamiani in the first five centuries"] applied to various Christian sects that practiced nudity

the crawling, wagging posture of a dog.[39] Prayer is then seen as redundant, because God does not exist or does not care about human affairs. Or, according to pantheism, God already knows everything (cf. Matt. 6:8, 32) since his decree is unchanging and everlasting, and it is in conflict with his majesty to be bothered by us all the time.[40] Prayer is much more a privilege than it is a duty (cf. John 16:26–27). It is a right given by God to man. That is how prayer is always considered in Scripture. This explains why prayer is not included in the law of Moses, in the Ten Commandments. Prayer is not a command but a promise, blessing, benefit.[41]

B. THE ESSENCE OF PRAYER: BIBLICAL TERMINOLOGY

Old Testament Hebrew terms for prayer[42] include the following.

For prayer as a call for intervention, mediation, the following term is used:

- פָּגַע = "to meet, to encounter, to reach"; with בְּ person (Job 21:15; Jer. 7:16) = "encounter with request, to entreat" ("to drop in on someone"); + לְ person (Gen. 23:8) = "to entreat on someone's behalf"; hiph. הִפְגִּיעַ with בְּ person (Isa. 53:12) = "to make entreaty, to interpose"; piel = "to judge"; hithp. = "to intercede."

For prayer as supplication:

---

in self-expression and worship, taking their inspiration from Adam . . . who lived in a state of pure innocence." Aside from the antinomian bent that suggests a lack of any need for divine guidance, there does not seem to be any obvious connection between such practices and eschewing any need for prayer. Willem Deurhoff was a controversial autodidact who raised questions about miracles and considered Christ to be the first act of God's creation (*BLGNP* 4:115, s.v. "Deurhoff, Willem"). Pontiaan van Hattem created significant unrest in the Dutch Reformed Church of the seventeenth century; his Christocentric theology emphasized Christ's death as an example of all-sufficient divine love rather than as the substitutionary atonement for sin and led to a quietist piety (van der Linde, "Hattem"). Bavinck placed a question mark after van Hattem's name.

39. According to Kant, "*Praying*, thought of as an *inner formal* service of God and hence as a means of grace, is a superstitious illusion (a fetish-making); for it is no more than a *stated wish* directed to a Being who needs no such information regarding the inner disposition of the wisher; therefore nothing is accomplished by it" (Kant, *Religion within the Limits of Reason Alone*, 182–83); cf. Willmann, *Geschichte des Idealismus*, 3:492; source taken from Nostitz-Rieneck, "Die 'sociale Decomposition,'" 21; Strauss, *Der alte und der neue Glaube*, 110.

40. De Moor, *Commentarius Perpetuus*, 5:14–15.

41. Goltz, *Das Gebet in der ältesten Christenheit*; see the review by Kunze.

42. De Moor, *Commentarius Perpetuus*, 5:14–15. Ed. note: Bavinck's treatment of each Hebrew term has been reconstructed using Brown, Driver, and Briggs, *Hebrew and English Lexicon*. It is very clear from Bavinck's main points and the specificity of his biblical examples that he used Gesenius's *Lexicon*, and the content of our reconstruction will therefore be practically identical to his original.

- תְּחִנָּה from חָנַן = "to show favor, be gracious"; noun = "favor, grace" (see Josh. 11:20); in the Psalms (6:10; 55:2); this is a prayer from someone who is profoundly humbled (cf. Isa. 37:20; 42:2).

As a cry for deliverance:

- צְעָקָה from צָעַק = "to cry out, to cry for help"; examples: Israel's cry for deliverance from Egypt (Exod. 3:9); from oppressed widows and orphans (Exod. 22:22); from those in misery (Ps. 9:13).
- שַׁוְעָה from שָׁוַע (piel) = "to cry out for help"; Israel's cry in Egypt (Exod. 2:23; Pss. 18:7; 39:13; 102:2).

As prayer for protection:

- תְּפִלָּה from פָּלַל = "to intervene, interpose"; piel = "to arbitrate, judge," and "to intercede, pray"; hithp. = "to put oneself in between" (God and man, 2 Sam. 2:25); prayer toward אֵל. The noun does not include a lament, a cry, but the prayer of someone who is oppressed, who holds the testimony of a good conscience and approaches God with confidence, asking him to intervene and do justice (Ps. 4:2). It is often used in Psalm titles—Psalms 17:1; 86:1; 90:1; 102:1; 142:1—and the prayer of Habakkuk the prophet (Hab. 3:1; cf. Ps. 72:20; the prayers of David come to an end). The rabbis referred to these as φυλακτήρια = safeguard, means of protection (amulets) (cf. Exod. 13:9, 16; טוֹטָפֹת in Deut. 6:8; צִיצַת in Num. 15:38–39).

In addition, from the Chaldean (Dan. 6:8, 14) בְּעוּ; derived from בְּעָה = to search, to pray.

New Testament Greek terms for prayer include the following:[43]

- αἴτημα = a request; derived from αἰτέω = "to desire, pray, claim" (determined by the longing of the will). Αἴτημα should be understood "in a passive sense, that which I have to ask for, from which αἴτησις (not in the N.T.; LXX Judg. 8:24; 1 Kings 2:16, 20; Job 6:8) does not differ."[44] However, "αἴτημα never, like αἴτησις, signifies the act merely of requesting, but always the subject-matter of request." This helps to explain the

43. Ed. note: Bavinck's primary source for the examination of the Greek words that follow, not always explicitly indicated, is Cremer, *Biblico-Theological Lexicon*. Each paragraph, including the formatting of the opening definitions, has been amplified and reconstructed (more in some cases than others) with material taken directly from Cremer's *Lexicon*, with an attempt to reflect the language and ideas of Bavinck's own expression. The notes will specify the exact source; it can be safely assumed that a paragraph's single reference covers all material within quotation marks; multiple sources in a single paragraph will be clearly indicated.

44. Cremer, *Biblico-Theological Lexicon*, 73, s.v. "αἴτημα."

otherwise difficult relation between δέησις and αἴτημα in Philippians
4:6: "Do not be anxious about anything, but in everything by prayer
[τῇ προσευχῇ] and supplication [τῇ δεήσει] with thanksgiving [μετὰ
εὐχαριστίας] let your requests [τὰ αἰτήματα] be made known to God."
"The meaning is not that the αἰτήματα are to be presented as prayer
and request before God in the form of δέησις, but that they are to be
presented μετὰ εὐχαριστίας. As the emphasis lies upon μετὰ εὐχ., δέησ.
and αἴτ. differ respectively as form and subject-matter. Also in Luke
23:24; 1 John 5:15.—LXX Psalms 20:6; 37:4 = מִשְׁאָלָה; 1 Samuel 1:17,
27; Esther 5:7; Psalm 106:16 = שְׁאֵלָה." In sum, "with thanksgiving"
indicates the manner in which the requests are to be offered and belongs
to the verbal phrase "be made known."

- ἐρωτάω = "to ask, beg, pray"; the last is "an application of the word
clearly arising from its employment to render the Hebrew שָׁאַל, which
has made it the most delicate and tenderest expression for prayer or
request."[45] Examples: John 14:16: "And I will ask [ἐρωτήσω] my Father
and He shall give you another Helper, to be with you forever"; John 17:9:
"I am praying [ἐρωτῶ] for them"; cf. verses 15, 20.[46]

- ἐπιθυμέω = "to desire, long after"; this is "to have the affections directed
toward anything"; in passages such as Romans 7:7 and 13:9, "it serves to
denote an immoral and illegitimate longing or coveting."[47] "In classical
Greek, as a *vox media*, **the moral character of the desire** is determined
according to the object named. . . . In the N.T., we might say, it is determined according to the subject, cf. John 8:44, Romans 1:24."[48] The noun
ἐπιθυμία covers the content of our desires, inclinations that flow from
our hearts, our flesh, and our eyes which are, therefore, mostly sinful.

- δέομαι = "to desire, pray"; that is, "*to be deprived of, to need.*"[49] Δεῖ [= it
is necessary, it ought to or must be], the impersonal form of the active
verb "δέω, *to be deprived of, to want, to need,*" leads to the suggestion
that δέομαι is "more correctly to be regarded as middle = *to be in want*

45. Cremer, *Biblico-Theological Lexicon*, 716, s.v. "ἐρωτάω."
46. Ed. note: Bavinck's manuscript contains an additional sentence here: "However rarely
concerning questions to God, 1 Joh. 5:16" [*Overigens zelden van vragen aan God, 1 Joh. 5:16*].
His meaning is not entirely clear. What makes this verse interesting is that the apostle uses two
different words for prayer: αἰτέω for allowable prayers concerning the sins of fellow believers
"not leading to death," and ἐρωτάω for impermissible praying in cases of sins "leading to
death." That the latter word is ordinarily "the most delicate and tenderest expression for prayer
or request" might provide a clue to Bavinck's intention.
47. Cremer, *Biblico-Theological Lexicon*, 287, s.v. "ἐπιθυμέω."
48. Cremer, *Biblico-Theological Lexicon*, 288, s.v. "ἐπιθυμία."
49. Cremer, *Biblico-Theological Lexicon*, 173, s.v. "δέομαι."

of for oneself, to need," than "as passive = *to be reduced to want.*" To need for oneself as a matter of necessity is the beginning point of prayer; to pray from need is a specific kind of praying distinguished from thanksgiving. That is the reason the noun δέησις is sometimes conjoined with προσευχή (= prayer; Eph. 6:18)[50] and sometimes with ἱκετηρία. The latter term comes from ἱκετεύω = to supplicate, to beseech; it is the petitioning of someone who is needy and seeks protection and help. In Hebrews 5:7 ἱκετηρία is used in tandem with δέομαι of the "prayers and supplications" [δεήσεις τε καὶ ἱκετηρίας] offered up by our Lord during his earthly ministry "to him who was able to save him from death." The apostle Paul speaks of the urgency of prayer in 1 Timothy 2:1 and brings together a number of the key terms: "I urge [Παρακαλῶ] that supplications [δεήσεις], prayers [προσευχάς], intercessions [ἐντεύξεις], and thanksgivings [εὐχαριστίας] be made for all people." Δέησις is praying out of need; it is the prayer of the needy person.

- προσευχή = prayer. This word "seemingly does not appear in profane Greek . . . and is a word solely of Hellenistic growth; a characteristic mark of Israel's separation from the gentile world. In the LXX, it is the standard word for תְּפִלָּה."[51] As such it means prayer that is directed toward God and includes some form of homage.

- ἔντευξις = petition, request, prayer; derived from ἐντυγχάνω = to meet, to encounter, to approach. From this, when combined with περί or ὑπέρ τίνος, it is to address someone for the sake of someone as in Hebrews 7:25: "Consequently, he is able to save to the uttermost those who draw near to God through him, since he always lives to make intercession for them" (πάντοτε ζῶν εἰς τὸ ἐντυγχάνειν ὑπὲρ αὐτῶν). In Romans 11:2 it has the meaning of "at the expense of" or "to accuse": "God has not rejected his people whom he foreknew. Do you not know what the Scripture says of Elijah, how he appeals to God against Israel?" (ὡς ἐντυγχάνει τῷ θεῷ κατὰ τοῦ Ἰσραήλ). Ἔντευξις thus points to an intervention, to a third party coming between two others on behalf of one of them. Ἔντευξις is then an encounter, a meeting, that makes a claim; it is intercession and petition, indicating a greater degree of familiarity.

- εὐχαριστία = thankfulness, gratitude, giving honor and praise to God (Eph. 5:4). In 1 Timothy 2:1 we therefore find (?)[52] reference to prayers

50. Cremer, *Biblico-Theological Lexicon*, 720, s.v. "προσεύχομαι."
51. Cremer, *Biblico-Theological Lexicon*, 720, s.v. "προσεύχομαι."
52. Ed. note: The question mark was inserted by Bavinck himself; apparently he was less than fully convinced about the dogmatic categories applied to the terms in 1 Tim. 2:1 by the

for averting evil [δέησις], petitioning for the good [προσευχή], intercession for others [ἔντευξις], and thanksgiving [εὐχαριστία]. Calvin also [53]
judges that this text refers to different kinds of prayers.

In general, *prayer* consists of people who know and sense their dependence
upon the true God—trusting his promises, for Christ's sake (in Christ's name)—
and calling on him for help for physical and spiritual hardship or giving thanks
for received benefits.[54] These can be divided in several ways.[55] According to
form, for example, distinguishing proper, formal prayers from quick prayers.[56]
The latter are expressed without any preparation, suddenly, caused by one or
the other thing, accident, disaster and so on. Some pious people for example
constantly say, "O Lord!" "O my God!" or "Have mercy on me!" These out-
bursts are usually very brief, consisting of one or two phrases or sentences. On
such occasions Roman Catholics may use the Lord's Prayer or only make the
sign of the cross, thereby expressing all the virtues of faith. We can distinguish
mental prayer from spoken prayer.[57] There are different prayers for different
occasions: ordinary times and extraordinary times. Prayers differ according to
content: there are prayers of petition and prayers of thanksgiving. Prayers of
petition can be further divided into those asking for something good to happen
and those that pray for evil to be averted.[58] These prayers apply to spiritual
as well as physical benefits. Finally, the *subject* can be an individual person in
private or public as well as those who pray corporately or communally in the
home or the church. One can pray for oneself by oneself or intercede for others.

c. THE HUMAN SUBJECTS OF PRAYER

Only humans pray; animals do not pray since they cannot know God's
majesty and are unable to know and acknowledge their dependence on him.

---

tradition of Reformed orthodoxy represented here by de Moor, *Commentarius Perpetuus*, 5:23,
according to whom δέησις = *ad malorum* Deprecationem; προσευχή = *bonororum* Petitionem;
ἔντευξις = *pro aliis* Intercessionem; and εὐχαριστία = *denique Gratiarum* Actionem. We have
here solid evidence for Bavinck's cautious sympathy for the tradition of Protestant orthodoxy.
Sympathy, because he does, after all, pass on to his Kampen students orthodoxy's traditional
categories here; at the same time, he shows hesitation that undoubtedly reflected the more
modern biblical scholarship he had encountered at the University of Leiden. His own exegetical
practice is more sophisticated and less dogmatic.
53. Calvin, *Institutes*, III.xx.28.
54. Cf. Calvin, *Institutes*, III.xx.2; Ursinus, *Commentary on the Heidelberg Catechism*,
Lord's Day 45.
55. Voetius, Τα Ασκητικα, 115.
56. DO: *schietgebeden*; LO: *preces ejaculatoriae*. See Voetius, Τα Ασκητικα, 125–34.
57. LO: *orationes mentalis*; *orationes vocales* (*orales*).
58. DO: *toebidden*; *afbidden*.

When Scripture speaks of birds and animals calling out to God (Ps. 147:9; cf. 104:27; Joel 1:18; Jon. 3:7–8), it is speaking figuratively. It is an idle question whether prayer is situated more in the will or in the mind.[59] Just like faith, prayer is an act of the entire human being: it is a longing, desire, sighing, lamenting (situated in the will), but also asking, speaking, knowing. and so on (in the mind).[60] Prayer is an act of our consciousness, lifting up our spirit or mind to God,[61] to which we are driven by an act of the will (we desire something or want to give thanks for something). Furthermore, the subjects of true prayer are regenerated people;[62] they alone possess "a Spirit of grace and pleas for mercy" (Zech. 12:10); they alone can worship "in spirit and truth"[63] (John 4:23). "In spirit" means spiritually, inwardly, not in all kinds of ceremonies and outward appearances bound to place; "in truth" means in accordance with God's being, in accordance with the true God. In fact, even the Christian does not know how to pray properly (Rom. 8:26), neither *what* to pray or *how*,[64] because of weakness and lack. Therefore the "Spirit himself intercedes for us with groanings too deep for words."

The duty to pray, as with all good works, is also required of unbelievers, even if they cannot pray correctly and truthfully.[65] Moreover, the same law that obligates them to pray also enjoins them to pray correctly and well, in spirit and in truth. If they are unable to do this, it is their own fault. It is therefore not correct to say that this limits unbelievers to sinful prayer, to sinning in their prayers, and that it is therefore better simply to let it go. Besides, while unbelievers may lack spiritual awareness, they nevertheless have a rational natural awareness of their own dependence and of God's greatness and goodness.[66] "And it is certainly much better that unrenewed men should pray to God in some manner, with a natural conviction of their wants, and an acknowledgment of the Majesty and goodness of God, than that they should not pray at all. The mere fact of their praying, so far as that is concerned, is not displeasing to God, though the sin which cleaves to it is justly

---

59. The former view is held by Ames, *Marrow of Theology*, 258 (II.ix): "Prayer is a devout presentation of our will before God so that he may be, as it were, affected by it." The latter view is held by Voetius, Τα Ασκητικα, 94.

60. Buddeus, *Institutiones Theologiae Moralis*, 319.

61. LO: *mentis elevatio ad Deum*.

62. De Moor, *Commentarius Perpetuus*, 5:27; Buddeus, *Institutiones Theologiae Moralis*, 321–22.

63. GrO: ἐν πνεύματι καὶ ἀληθείᾳ.

64. GrO: τί; καθὸ δεῖ.

65. Cf. Kuyper, *Work of the Holy Spirit*, 662–68 (III.41, "Prayer of the Unconverted"). Ed. note: Bavinck's original source was *De Heraut*, no. 580, February 3, 1889.

66. Ed. note: Cf. *RD*, 1:241–43, 350.

condemned."[67] This is true even when the way someone prays is wrong, as
we can see in the case of Ahab—whose self-abasement pleased God (1 Kings
21:27–29)—and the Ninevites (Jon. 3:8–10). "To do a good thing in a defective manner is a smaller evil than to omit it altogether."[68] It is therefore "the
duty of parents to instruct and habituate their children, from their earliest
childhood, to prayer, and not to wait till they can discover in them the marks
of regeneration. For who knows at what time, and by what means, the Spirit
will first exert his saving influence? One thing is certain, while believers alone
can pray aright, their faith was bestowed on them for the express purpose
that they may *continue in prayer.*"[69]

Are these prayers of unbelievers answered?[70] Old Testament wisdom provides a negative answer: "If anyone turns a deaf ear to my instruction, / even
their prayers are detestable" (Prov. 28:9). In John 9:31 the man born blind says
to the Jews: "We know that God does not listen to sinners. He listens to the
godly person[71] who does his will." This expression is true in this context—
namely, concerning someone who asks God for a miracle. However, other
passages in Scripture affirm this saying in much more general terms:

If I had cherished iniquity in my heart, / the Lord would not have listened.
(Ps. 66:18)

The LORD is far from the wicked, / but he hears the prayer of the righteous.
(Prov. 15:29)

When you spread out your hands, / I will hide my eyes from you; / even though
you make many prayers, / I will not listen; / your hands are full of blood. (Isa.
1:15)

The prayer of a righteous person has great power as it is working.[72] (James
5:16; cf. 4:3: "You ask and do not receive, because you ask wrongly, to spend
it on your passions.")

67. Witsius, *Sacred Dissertations*, 56 (dissertation no. 2).
68. LO: *minus malum est bonum facere cum defectu quam prorsus omittere.* Witsius, *Sacred Dissertations*, 56; Latin original: Witsius, *Exercitationes in Orationem Dominicam*, II.xx.
69. Witsius, *Sacred Dissertations*, 56; cf. de Moor, *Commentarius Perpetuus*, 5:27.
70. Ed. note: We have broken up Bavinck's very long original paragraph, which might give
the mistaken impression that he is starting an altogether different topic here. The Scripture passages he now goes on to discuss come directly from the beginning of Witsius's dissertation 3,
"On the Preparation of the Mind for Right Prayer" (Witsius, *Sacred Dissertations*, 57). The
content is thus intimately connected with the questions about the prayers of unbelievers that
close dissertation 2 (Witsius, 56).
71. GrO: θεοσεβής ("God-worshiper").
72. GrO: πολὺ ἰσχύει δέησις δικαίου ἐνεργουμένη; Buddeus, *Institutiones Theologiae Moralis*, 321.

The LORD is near to all who call on him, / to all who call on him in truth. / He fulfills the desire of those who fear him; / he also hears their cry and saves them. (Ps. 145:18–19)

How then will they call on him in whom they have not believed? (Rom. 10:14)

But let him ask in faith, with no doubting, for the one who doubts is like a wave of the sea that is driven and tossed by the wind. For that person must not suppose that he will receive anything from the Lord; he is a double-minded man, unstable in all his ways. (James 1:6–8)

God therefore sometimes does grant the wicked what they pray for, but actually he is then not answering their prayer but enforcing his counsel, showing his benevolence.[73] Here is what belongs to a prayer "that truly pleases God and that he listens to":[74] we must truly know our need and misery so that we humble ourselves before the presence of God's majesty; "God opposes the proud / but shows favor to the humble" (1 Pet. 5:5, quoting Prov. 3:34). God does not answer the proud Pharisee (Luke 18:9–14). The wicked do not pray to the true God, or they do not pray about the right things, or they pray feigningly, or simply out of habit, or without trusting God's promises, or apart from Christ the Mediator, or with persistent sin, or with distrust and doubts, without faith.[75]

D. GOD IS THE OBJECT OF PRAYER

"Offer to God a sacrifice of thanksgiving, / and perform your vows to the Most High, / and call upon me in the day of trouble; / I will deliver you, and you shall glorify me" (Ps. 50:14–15). "O you who hear prayer, / to you shall all flesh come. . . . By awesome deeds you answer us with righteousness" (Ps. 65:2, 5). "And it shall come to pass that everyone who calls on the name of the LORD shall be saved" (Joel 2:32). "You shall worship the Lord your God and him only shall you serve" (Matt. 4:10). To God alone is ascribed majesty; he alone is all-knowing (1 Kings 8:39; Matt. 6:8, 32), almighty (Eph. 3:20), and "the overflowing fountain of all good" (James 1:17).[76] Conversely, while blessing those who trust the Lord, Scripture pronounces curses on those who

---

73. Buddeus, *Institutiones Theologiae Moralis*, 322.
74. Heidelberg Catechism, Q&A 117.
75. Ursinus, *Commentary on the Heidelberg Catechism*, Q&A 117 (*Schat-boek*, 2:513).
76. Ed. note: The phrase within quotation marks is not from James 1:17 but rather concludes the first article of the Belgic Confession. Bavinck does not indicate his source here, another indication of how naturally the language of the Reformed confessions enters his discourse. James 1:17 is one of Bavinck's favorite and most cited Scripture verses.

trust in their own strength, as the following parallel from Jeremiah points out: "Cursed is the man who trusts in man and makes flesh his strength, / whose heart turns away from the LORD" (Jer. 15:5). And, on the other hand, "Blessed is the man who trusts in the LORD, / whose trust is the LORD" (Jer. 17:7).

More specifically, the true God, that is to say, the Triune God, Father, Son, and Holy Spirit, is the proper object of our prayer.[77] We pray to the Son as Mediator but not as a human being to the exclusion of angels, other humans, etc. (Matt. 4:10; Deut. 10:20; 6:13). Since there is an economy in the Trinity, in prayer those gifts should be asked for from the Person who is the principal Author of those gifts. For example, anything belonging to the order of creation should be asked of God the Father, and so on. So too, the Son and the Spirit may be asked for certain gifts. Nevertheless, it is more specifically the Father who is addressed in prayer, as our formal prayers do; he is the Fountain of the Godhead,[78] the source of all benefits. We pray to him in the name of Christ the Son, while the Holy Spirit himself prays through and in us. The Belgic Confession (art. 26) speaks very beautifully about praying in the name of Jesus:

> We believe that we have no access to God except through the one and only Mediator and Intercessor, "Jesus Christ the righteous," who therefore was made human, uniting together the divine and human natures, so that we human beings might have access to the divine Majesty.
> Otherwise we would have no access.
> But this Mediator, whom the Father has appointed between himself and us, ought not terrify us by his greatness, so that we have to look for another one, according to our fancy.
> For neither in heaven nor among the creatures on earth is there anyone who loves us more than Jesus Christ does.

Therefore, we do not honor the saints as intercessors but offer prayers solely on the basis of the excellence and dignity of the Lord Jesus Christ. After all, Christ is the way to the Father (John 14:6), also in prayer. "For we do not have a high priest who is unable to sympathize with our weaknesses, but one who in every respect has been tempted as we are, yet without sin. Let us then with confidence draw near to the throne of grace, that we may receive mercy and find grace to help in time of need" (Heb. 4:15–16). The same writer reminds us that "since we have confidence to enter the holy places by

---

77. The answer to question 117 of the Heidelberg Catechism posits this as the hallmark of true prayer: "We must pray from the heart to no other than the one true God."
78. LO: *fons deitatis*.

the blood of Jesus, by the new and living way that he opened for us through the curtain, that is, through his flesh, and since we have a great priest over the house of God," we can approach God "with a true heart in full assurance of faith, with our hearts sprinkled clean from an evil conscience and our bodies washed with pure water" (Heb. 10:19–21). Special mention here needs to made of Jesus's words in the Gospel of John: "Whatever you ask in my name, this I will do, that the Father may be glorified in the Son. If you ask me anything in my name, I will do it" (John 14:13–14). "In that day you will ask nothing of me. Truly, truly, I say to you, whatever you ask of the Father in my name,[79] he will give it to you. Until now you have asked nothing in my name. Ask, and you will receive, that your joy may be full. . . . In that day, you will ask in my name, and I do not say to you that I will ask the Father on your behalf; for the Father himself loves you, because you have loved me and have believed that I came from God" (John 16:23–24, 26). Meyer, Weiss, and others understand "in my name" as "in his mission, in his stead,"[80] but that cannot be. When Jesus says that the Father will give his disciples whatever they "ask of the Father in my name" (16:23), he means "by my order." For similar reasons it cannot mean "according to my will," as in 1 John 5:14. On the analogy of faith it should be understood as "for the sake of my name," resting on my promises and merits.[81] "In Jesus's name" means (a) according to Jesus's command and order and (b) in place of Jesus; that is to say, Jesus has drawn the check[82] of our prayers that we present to the Father, who will accept and honor it. Jesus gives us a blank piece of paper, signed by him, which we fill in and present to the Father. The meaning, therefore, of "in my name" is "on the basis of Christ's merits." It is as if Christ himself in us is making the request of the Father. "In Jesus's name" also means (c) according to his will; this is, therefore, a restriction; it is wrong to use Jesus's name to make requests arising from all sorts of foolish and sinful longings.

When Jesus says, "Until now you have asked nothing in my name," he is not speaking about Old Testament believers, implying that they have been approaching God apart from the promised Messiah. He is speaking about

79. GrO: αἰτήσητε ἐν τῷ ὀνόματί μου.

80. Ed. note: The most likely source is Weiss, *Biblical Theology*, 2:403. Between the lines Bavinck inserted the word *opdracht* ("assignment, order, task"); the German original was *Auftrage* ("commission, charge, order, mission"). The English translator captured the biblical-theological significance of *Auftrage* well by translating it as "mission." The reference to Meyer here is undoubtedly to Meyer, *Kritisch exegetischer Kommentar*. The Gospel of John is examined in vol. 2, which was prepared by Bernhard Weiss after Meyer's death in 1873.

81. Cf. Ebrard, "Gebet im Namen Jesu"; cf. the annotations of the *Statenvertaling*, John 16, no. 43. DO: *verdiensten*.

82. DO: *wissel*.

his disciples, who have thus far, during his time on earth, asked Jesus himself, personally. This relationship will come to an end; after the resurrection they will not ask Jesus anymore, but the Father, albeit in Jesus's name. And they will definitely be answered. Jesus does not need to induce his Father to this, he does not need to ask the Father for them. But rather, because the disciples love Jesus and pray in his name, the Father's heart itself will be inclined to them. Of course this does not exclude Jesus's intercession, nor his mediatorial role,[83] for this is clearly implied in praying in his name. But because the disciples pray in Jesus's name, an additional distinct interession of Christ himself is not needed; it is already included.

E. THE CONTENT OF PRAYER

Question 118 of the Heidelberg Catechism asks: "What did God command us to pray for?" Its answer is comprehensive: "Everything we need, spiritually and physically, as embraced in the prayer Christ our Lord himself taught us." Sometimes people pray for what they do not know, like the mother of the sons of Zebedee (Matt. 20:20–21). Spiritual needs—namely, those benefits without which there is no salvation (forgiveness, faith, sanctification)—may and must be asked of God for ourselves absolutely, without conditions. Do not add qualifications such as "if it is your will and according to your counsel," "if it pleases you and is for your glory," "if it is for our salvation," and the like. In this instance adding conditions expresses doubt and is not prayer made in faith. However, prayers for spiritual blessings, special measures of grace, and so on that are not absolutely necessary for salvation should not have such an absolute character.[84] When it comes to other people, we are permitted to plead conditionally for benefits that are absolutely needed for salvation because we ought not to believe that everyone is chosen unto salvation. Because physical needs are not absolutely necessary for us—apart from the hypothesis of life[85]—they should always be accompanied with conditions. Praying for prolonging of life may only be done conditionally since the petition in the Lord's Prayer is "Give us today our daily bread."[86] Rice Boye, appealing to the absolute character of the petitions in the Lord's Prayer, contended that it was lawful to pray "absolutely for necessary temporal things, without doubting or wavering, and that the saints of God may and ought, as absolutely depend

---

83. According to Weiss, this is the ideal, but in reality we need the intercession: "By this perfect inward fellowship of believers with Christ, there appears to be no need of this promise of His gracious presence and help" (*Biblical Theology*, 2:403n9).

84. Voetius, Τα Ασκητικα, 97.

85. LO: *ex hypothesi vitae*.

86. Voetius, Τα Ασκητικα, 97.

upon God for their daily bread, as they may for the pardon of their sins."[87] Ordinarily, however, without further specification, it is said that we may pray absolutely for spiritual needs and should ask conditionally for physical needs.[88] Intercession for the dead may not take place[89] since there is neither command for it nor precedent in Holy Scripture; Rome appeals to an apocryphal book: 2 Maccabees 12:43–46. A person's fate is decided at the time of death, and therefore prayer cannot effect anything.[90] Nevertheless, intercession for the dead was introduced into the church at quite an early stage and became an occasion for superstition.[91] We may and ought to pray for all the living, especially for the authorities (1 Tim. 2:2), for teachers (Eph. 6:19), and for one another (*Our* Father give *us*, Matt. 6:9; cf. Eph. 6:18; Col. 1:2–3).[92]

F. THE MANNER OF PRAYER[93]

The proper manner of prayer does not involve mystically sinking into passivity, but consists in knowing our needs, praying with our mind (1 Cor. 14:15), reflecting and considering God's majesty in order to increase our reverence and trust, breaking with our sins, and fostering faith in purity and humility of heart. Apart from this general preparation, which needs to be done regularly, a more specific preparation is sometimes required.[94] This preparation includes particularly awakening a feeling of our smallness and insignificance, thinking through the content and form of the prayer, quickening the impression of God's presence by asking for the Spirit of prayer in advance. Such prayers then

---

87. Boye, *Importunate Begger*. Ed. note: The material in quotation marks is taken from the extended title of this work. Cf. Voetius, *Τα Ασκητικα*, 98.

88. Ursinus, *Schat-boek*, 2:515; de Moor, *Commentarius Perpetuus*, 5:34.

89. Stirm, "Darf man für die Verstorbenen beten?" In addition to Stirm himself, the following also favored praying for the dead: Pfaff, *Institutiones Theologia*, 547; Rothe, *Theologische Ethik*, 3:150–56 (§887); Kling, "Fegfeuer," *PRE¹* 4:345; Thiersch, *Vorlesungen über Katholicismus und Protestantismus*, 2:326–44, esp. 339–42 (no. 34). The following was opposed: Thomas Kliefoth. Ed. note: Bavinck's source for all these references is Stirm, "Darf man für die Verstorbenen beten?," 278, 292–93; Stirm provides as his source for Klieforth "Liturgische Abhandlungen, vol. 1," and *Das Begräbnis* ("The Funeral") in a "manuscript prepared for the Dresden Liturgical Conference."

90. Rome teaches the doctrine of purgatory.

91. De Moor, *Commentarius Perpetuus*, 5:30–32. Early church examples include Tertullian and Augustine. Lutherans say "we have received neither command nor instruction," therefore "prayers for [the dead] are not prohibited" (*Apology of the Augsburg Confession*, art. 24; Smalcald Articles, art. 2; Kolb and Wengert, *Book of Concord*, 274.94; 276.96; 303.12).

92. Ed. note: Between the lines Bavinck added "Gerhard VII, p. 94" but provided no title. He took the reference from Stirm, "Darf man für die Verstorbenen beten?," 290.

93. De Moor, *Commentarius Perpetuus*, 5:36; Witsius, *Exercitationes*, III; Witsius, *De practijk des Christendoms*, 202–22.

94. Voetius, *Τα Ασκητικα*, 117.

consist of an introductory address (not too elaborate, not always the same, but corresponding to our request), the prayer itself, which should proceed in an orderly fashion, and a conclusion which briefly restates the petition, followed by the end.[95] "Babbling" and using "many words" characterizes the prayers of the pagans and not the followers of Jesus.[96]

For that reason, *prepared* or *form* prayers are fine.[97] The Independents in the English Church and Jacob Koelman from this country were very much opposed to it.[98] Those who defended the practice appealed to the Aaronic blessing (Num. 6:22–27), the liturgical leadership of the Levites in worship (2 Chron. 29:30), the instructions for worship in psalm titles (e.g., Pss. 92; 102), and the hymn sung by our Lord and his disciples on the night of his betrayal (Matt. 26:30). There were no formulated prayers in the earliest Christian church; the practice was first introduced at the Council of Laodicea (364). Subsequent synods decided that only set prayers were permitted, and Calvin and Voetius both concurred.[99]

There is no prescription for postures during prayer. The Jews observed several:[100] standing (Gen. 18:22), sitting (1 Kings 19:4), kneeling (Dan. 6:11), lying on the ground (Deut. 9:18), with head uncovered for men (1 Cor. 11:4–5),[101] with eyes lifted up or lowered (Ps. 123:1–2; Luke 18:13), with raised hands

95. Voetius, Τα Ασκητικα, 118.

96. GrO: βαττολογία; πολυλογία. De Moor, *Commentarius Perpetuus*, 5:51.

97. DO: *formuliergebeden*. Ed. note: Bavinck follows a reference to *Heraut*, nos. 1038, 1042, with this short paragraph: "True prayer is free prayer, but a proper frame of mind is often missing; public communal prayer can lack intercession, pleading for the needs of others, proper language, and often wanders. Therefore prepared and form prayers are an aid to true prayer, much as we teach children to sing Psalms and pray the Lord's Prayer." The *Heraut* references are to Abraham Kuyper's series *Onze eeredienst* (*Our Worship*), 29–36 (chap. 6, "Liturgical Prayers").

98. Ed. note: The term "Independent" refers to those who advocated local congregational control over the church; they also resisted the standardized liturgy of the Anglican Church. Jacob Koelman (1633–95) was an important Dutch Reformed minister of the Further Reformation.

99. De Moor, *Commentarius Perpetuus*, 5:56. Ed. note: Bavinck does not indicate a source for Calvin's position other than the reference to De Moor, who in turn points to Calvin's October 22, 1548, letter "To the Protector Somerset" (Edward Seymour, regent of England during the minority of Edward VI), in Jules Bonnet, ed., *Letters of John Calvin*, 2:182–98 (no. 229); Voetius, *Politicae Ecclesiasticae, Partis Primae*, 484–90.

100. De Moor, *Commentarius Perpetuus*, 5:41; cf. Pressel, "Gebet."

101. Although covered heads for Jewish men now. Ed. note: Bavinck puts a quotation from Tertullian in parentheses here: "with head uncovered, for we have nothing whereof to be ashamed" (*capito nudo oramus quia non erubescimus*). Tertullian states that Christians are in the habit of praying for their rulers but also making the point that all earthly rule comes from heaven and heaven's King. He then adds: "Thither we lift our eyes, with hands outstretched, because free from sin; with head uncovered, for we have nothing whereof to be ashamed; finally, without a monitor, because it is from the heart we supplicate. Without ceasing, for all our emperors we offer prayer" (*Apology* 30, ANF 3:42).

(Ps. 141:2; 1 Kings 8:22; 1 Tim. 2:8; among the earliest Christians in the form of a cross).[102] We cannot approve the practice in our churches of remaining seated during prayer.[103]

The tabernacle and temple were the place of prayer in the Old Covenant (Isa. 56:7; Ps. 5:8; 1 Kings 8:29–30; John 4:20), the place toward which the Israelites turned their face (1 Kings 8:44, 48; Dan. 6:11), the place of God's footstool (Pss. 99:5; 132:7; Isa. 60:13; 66:13; Acts 7:49). In the New Covenant there is no longer a privileged place for prayer (John 4:19). Prayers should take place in our inner chambers (Matt. 6:6) and publicly in the gatherings of the church (Acts 16:13, 16). Rome leaves churches constantly open and organizes pilgrimages.[104]

The *time* of prayer:[105] The apostle Paul tells us to pray "at all times" (Eph. 6:18), "without ceasing" (1 Thess. 5:17). This must not be understood as the Massilians (Euchites) of the fourth century did or the monks who followed suit.[106] It is our hearts that always need to be fit for prayer, without exception. We should not pray to God only in times of adversity but also during prosperity, at night and in the day.[107] Specifically, we should pray at the beginning of the day and at the end, after work (Ps. 90:14–17), and when eating and drinking (1 Tim. 4:3–5). This was a customary practice early on in the Reformed community and was strongly defended by Reformed leaders, especially by Hofman in his *Food Sanctified by Prayer and Thanksgiving*.[108] Our Lord blessed the loaves and fishes with which he miraculously fed the multitude (Matt. 14:19–20; 15:36–37) and blessed the meal at the Last Supper (Luke 24:30); the apostle Paul practiced (Acts 27:35) and instructed likewise (1 Tim. 4:3–5). In addition, the Jews had set times of prayer (Ps. 55:18; Dan. 6:11). Such set times are good, but the Roman "canonical hours"[109] need to be rejected.

---

102. De Moor, *Commentarius Perpetuus*, 5:47.

103. De Moor, *Commentarius Perpetuus*, 5:48.

104. De Moor, *Commentarius Perpetuus*, 5:59.

105. De Moor, *Commentarius Perpetuus*, 5:63.

106. Ed. note: Bavinck refers to them as Euchites (*Euchieten*). About this group: "Mesopotamia, Syria, and Armenia saw during the 4th and 5th centuries a mystic movement of the Massilians, who sacrificed even self-support to constant prayer, as the means by which the Holy Spirit entered and perfected, giving full knowledge of divine things and of the future. They were known also to the Greeks as Euchites." The name "Massilian" has geographical roots, referring to a group of Western Greek semi-Pelagians who resisted Augustinian anthropology: "From Marseilles (Massilia), the headquarters of these Western leaders, they were often called Massilians, Massalians, or Messalians" (Whitely, "Sects [Christian]," 319, 320).

107. Voetius, Τα Ασκητικα, 95–96; de Moor, *Commentarius Perpetuus*, 5:64.

108. Hofman, *De spys door het gebed*; de Moor, *Commentarius Perpetuus*, 5:66.

109. LO: *horae canonicae*. Ed. note: The canonical hours are officially set times for prayer: prime (first hour of daylight), terce (third hour, 9:00 a.m.), sext (sixth hour, noon), nones (ninth hour, 3:00 p.m.), vespers (evening), compline (end of the [working] day), and lauds (early

G. ANSWERS TO PRAYER

Praying Christians trust and firmly believe that God will answer their prayers (James 1:5–7; Rom. 10:12–14; 1 John 5:14). This is a strong emphasis in Calvin, who finds here the distinction between the prayer of a Christian believer and that of a pagan.[110] According to the Heidelberg Catechism, one of the three elements of prayer that is pleasing to God is to "rest on this unshakable foundation: even though we do not deserve it, God will surely listen to our prayer because of Christ our Lord."[111] This trust rests generally on God's goodness (Matt. 7:11) and power (Eph. 3:20) but more specifically on Christ's merits, by which we are promised answers to our prayers: "Whatever you ask in my name, this I will do, that the Father may be glorified in the Son. If you ask me anything in my name, I will do it" (John 14:13–14). "In that day you will ask nothing of me. Truly, truly, I say to you, whatever you ask of the Father in my name, he will give it to you. Until now you have asked nothing in my name. Ask, and you will receive, that your joy may be full" (John 16:23–24).[112] We should therefore not doubt that our prayers will be answered. In this instance doubt is sin and is the very reason our prayer is not answered (James 1:5–8). Our "Amen" at the end of the prayer gives expression to the very same conviction.[113] So then, are all prayers answered? According to Voetius, they will be if they are according to God's will.[114] Furthermore, a good prayer is a prayer of the Holy Spirit in us and therefore has to be answered. Our prayer does not undo God's decree, nor does it alter it, but is precisely one of the means, included in that decree, by which it is carried out.[115] We therefore do not penetrate into God's counsel with our prayer,[116] but we pray because God himself prompts our prayer. In addition, prayer is[117] the test and thermometer of our spiritual life, its pulse, and the best medication for it (Matt. 26:41; Luke 22:43; Eph. 6:16–18). And the same can be said of our external, physical life.

---

hours). Bavinck provides the following sources: de Moor, *Commentarius Perpetuus*, 5:70–71; Herold, "Brevier."

110. Calvin, *Institutes*, III.xx.12; cf. Lobstein, *Das Ethik Calvins*, 91; Zöckler, *Theologia Naturalis*, 117–18; D. G. Monrad, *Aus der Welt des Gebet*.

111. Q&A 117.

112. Georg Müller in Bristol reported many answers to prayer; *Beweis des Glaubens* 34 (1898): 385ff.; E. F. K. Müller, *Zur christlichen Erkenntnis*, includes an essay on answers to prayer which is very beautiful. See also W. Wolff, "Zur Frage der Gebetserhörung" (especially about Ritschl); Köberle, "Die Motive des Glaubens."

113. "*Amen* means, This is sure to be! It is even more sure that God listens to my prayer, than that I really desire what I pray for" (Heidelberg Catechism, Q&A 129).

114. Voetius, *Τα Ασκητικα*, 129.

115. De Moor, *Commentarius Perpetuus*, 5:39.

116. Contra Kant.

117. C. Beck, "Gebet."

2. Spiritual Meditation[118]

The word "meditation"[119] appears many times in the Psalms:

Give ear to my words, O LORD, consider my meditation. (Ps. 5:1 KJV)

Let the words of my mouth and the / meditation of my heart / be acceptable in your sight, / O LORD, my rock and my redeemer. (Ps. 19:14)

My heart became hot within me. / As I mused, the fire burned; / then I spoke with my tongue. (Ps. 39:3)

My mouth shall speak wisdom; / the meditation of my heart shall be understanding. (Ps. 49:3)

May my meditation be pleasing to him, / for I rejoice in the LORD. (Ps. 104:34)

This meditation is often directed to the law of God: "His delight is in the law of the LORD, / and on his law he meditates day and night" (Ps. 1:2); "I will meditate on your precepts / and fix my eyes on your ways" (119:15); "Meditate upon these things; give thyself wholly to them; that thy profiting may appear to all" (1 Tim. 4:15). In theology this activity is called a number of different names: thinking, consideration or contemplation, mental praying, soliloquy, inner word, devotion, introversion, contemplation.[120] For the mystic this was accompanied by ecstasy, rapture, drunkenness, and the like.[121] Those who wrote about spiritual meditation include Richard of St. Victor, Jean Gerson, Albert the Great, and Thomas Aquinas. Reformed writers in this genre include Joseph Hall, John Downame,[122] and Lewis Bayly. Voetius describes meditation as a religious act or spiritual exercise through which we

---

118. Voetius, Τα Ασκητικα, 42–92.

119. DO: *overdenking* ("consideration, thought, contemplation, reflection").

120. LO: *cogitatio*; *consideratio*; *oratio mentalis*; *soliloquium*; *endologia*; *devotio*; *introversio*; *contemplatio*.

121. LO: *ecstasis*; *raptus*; *ebrietas*.

122. Ed. note: This is Bavinck's first mention of this name, which he spelled "Downam." Since Bavinck did not provide a title, we cannot be sure if he had in mind George Downame (ca. 1563–1634), author of *A Treatise of Justification* and *The Doctrine of Christian Liberty*, or his brother John Downame (d. 1652), author of, inter alia, *The Christian Warfare against Satan* (1609–18), *A Guide to Godliness* (1622), and *The Sum of Sacred Divinity* (1630). Taking a hint from what Bavinck goes on to say about "fighting off the devil" only two sentences later, it would be reasonable to conclude that he has in mind John Downame's *Christian Warfare against Satan*.

discern God and godly things with intense experiential and moving affective knowledge which we apply to ourselves.[123] Spiritual meditation strengthens our communion with God, fights off the devil, and so on.[124] The object of spiritual meditation is God, godly qualities, Christ's person and work, his life, faith and rebirth, death, and so on.[125] This can be distinguished from mental prayer,[126] in which we talk to God, and from self-meditation.[127] It can also be distinguished from the devotion[128] which according to Voetius is more specifically an affect or act of the will, through which we fully surrender ourselves to God. The object of devotion, therefore, is a willigness to obey God (Ps. 57:7; Phil. 2:12). However, Voetius rejects a mystical contemplation in which the contemplative life is separated from an active life.[129] There is no vision of God on earth except through faith.[130] "Reading seeks, meditation finds, prayer asks, contemplation tastes."[131]

3. Reading the Word of God[132]

Reading God's Word is another powerful resource for sanctification.

Seek and read from the book of the LORD: / Not one of these shall be missing; / none shall be without her mate. / For the mouth of the LORD has commanded, / and his Spirit has gathered them. (Isa. 34:16)

"My Spirit that is upon you, and my words that I have put in your mouth, shall not depart out of your mouth, or out of the mouth of your offspring, or out of the mouth of your children's offspring," says the LORD, "from this time forth and forevermore." (Isa. 59:21)

Your words were found, and I ate them, / and your words became to me a joy / and the delight of my heart. (Jer. 15:16)

123. DO/LO: *ingespannend ondervindelijke en aandoenlijke affectuosa kennis.* Voetius, Τα Ασκητικα, 48.
124. Voetius, Τα Ασκητικα, 52.
125. Voetius, Τα Ασκητικα, 51.
126. LO: *oratio mentalis.*
127. DO: *meditatie tot onzelf*; in the margin: "*daad, gezindheid, zachte stille*" ("deed, attitude, quiet stillness").
128. LO: *devotio*, from *de + voveo* ("to vow, promise"). Voetius, Τα Ασκητικα, 20–30.
129. Voetius, Τα Ασκητικα, 68.
130. LO: *visio dei, per fidem.* Voetius, Τα Ασκητικα, 72.
131. LO: *Lectio quaerit, meditatio invenit, oratio postulat, contemplatio degustat*; Hugh of St. Victor, according to Voetius, Τα Ασκητικα, 62.
132. LO: *Lectio Verbi Divini*; Voetius, Τα Ασκητικα, 300–306; Vitringa, *Korte schets*, 242–47 (XII §§11–13).

Jesus tells those who resist him: "You search the Scriptures because you think that in them you have eternal life; and it is they that bear witness about me, yet you refuse to come to me that you may have life" (John 5:39–40). It is said about the Jews in Berea: "Now these Jews were more noble than those in Thessalonica; they received the word with all eagerness, examining the Scriptures daily to see if these things were so" (Acts 17:11). The Word of God is "the sword of the Spirit" (Eph. 6:17), which is "able to make you wise for salvation through faith in Christ Jesus" (2 Tim. 3:15). Peter describes the "prophetic word" as "a lamp shining in a dark place, until the day dawns and the morning star rises in your hearts" (2 Pet. 1:19).

Biblical piety involves meditating on the law of the LORD, as we see in Psalms 1, 19, and 119, because the "words of the LORD are pure words, / like silver refined in a furnace on the ground, purified seven times" (Ps. 12:6). The Word and the law provide sure guidance: "Your word is a lamp to my feet / and a light to my path" (Ps. 119:105); "For the commandment is a lamp and the teaching a light, and the reproofs of discipline are the way of life" (Prov. 6:23). The apostle Paul instructs the Colossians: "Let the word of Christ dwell in you richly, teaching and admonishing one another in all wisdom, singing psalms and hymns and spiritual songs, with thankfulness in your hearts to God" (Col. 3:16). This is a strong Protestant emphasis; from its earliest days reading Scripture in the home became a custom. Schedules were provided to help people read through the Bible in one year. One Lutheran professor is said to have read the whole Bible through eighty times.[133] Calvinists and Lutherans alike were firm in the Bible.[134] In addition, people with pious hearts frequently read the Bible by themselves in solitude for personal edification. "This is the one to whom I will look: he who is humble and contrite in spirit and trembles at my word" (Isa. 66:2); "He may learn to fear the LORD his God by keeping all the words of this law and these statues, to do them" (Deut. 17:19); "All Scripture is breathed out by God and profitable for teaching, for reproof, for correction, and for training in righteousness, that the man of God may be competent, equipped for every good work" (2 Tim. 3:16–17). These Bible readers also read the works of faithful, devout authors.[135]

---

133. Ed. note: Bavinck provides the name "Tholuck" in the margin, likely a reference to Friedrich August Gottreu Tholuck (1799–1877), a beloved scholar, biblical commentator, and evangelical preacher of the nineteenth century. See Schaff, "Tholuck."

134. DO: *Bijbelvast*.

135. Ed. note: Bavinck does not mention specific writers but undoubtedly has in mind the devotional writers of the Further Reformation, those who were affectionately referred to by pious Reformed folk as the "ancient writers" (*oude schrijvers*).

4. Singing[136]

We repeatedly read about this in Holy Scripture; the Psalms constantly spur on believers to sing songs of praise. Here is just a sample:

> Awake, my glory! / Awake, O harp and lyre! / I will awake the dawn! / I will give thanks to you, O Lord, among the peoples; / I will sing praises to you among the nations. (Ps. 57:8–9)

> Sing to him, sing praises to him; / tell of all his wondrous works! (Ps. 105:2)

> Sing to the Lord with thanksgiving; / make melody to our God on the lyre! (Ps. 147:7)

We are told in the Gospel of Matthew that Jesus, in his state of humiliation, sings a song of praise: "And when they had sung a hymn, they went out to the Mount of Olives" (Matt. 26:30). In several places the apostle Paul instructs us to sing: "And do not get drunk with wine, for that is debauchery, but be filled with the Spirit, addressing one another in psalms and hymns and spiritual songs, singing and making melody to the Lord with your heart" (Eph. 5:19).[137] Paul also speaks of singing with understanding: "I will pray with my spirit, but I will pray with my mind also; I will sing praise with my spirit, but I will sing with my mind also" (1 Cor. 14:15).[138] Such singing, based on the Word, instructs and guides: "Let the word of Christ dwell in you richly, teaching and admonishing one another in all wisdom, singing psalms and hymns and spiritual songs, with thankfulness in your hearts to God" (Col. 3:16).[139] Praying and singing cover the whole range of human circumstances and emotions: "Is anyone among you in trouble? Let them pray. Is anyone happy? Let them sing songs of praise" (James 5:13). Our singing does not end when our earthly lives do: "And they sang a new song before the throne and before the four living creatures and the elders. No one could learn the song except the 144,000 who had been redeemed from the earth" (Rev. 14:3). Singing soon became customary in the Christian church.[140] It is not enough to sing only Psalms.[141]

---

136. DO: *gezang*. Vitringa, *Korte schets*, 248–65 (XIII §§1–8); Voetius, *Politicae Ecclesiasticae, Partis Primae*, 520–44.

137. GrO: λαλοῦντες ἑαυτοῖς ψαλμοῖς καὶ ὕμνοις καὶ ᾠδαῖς πνευματικαῖς, ᾄδοντες καὶ ψάλλοντες τῇ καρδίᾳ ὑμῶν τῷ κυρίῳ.

138. GrO: ψαλῶ δὲ καὶ τῷ νοΐ.

139. GrO: διδάσκοντες καὶ νουθετοῦντες ἑαυτούς, ψαλμοῖς ὕμνοις ᾠδαῖς πνευματικαῖς ἐν χάριτι ᾄδοντες ἐν ταῖς καρδίαις ὑμῶν τῷ θεῷ.

140. Lauxmann, "Kirchenlied"; Krüger, "Kirchenmusik"; also Voetius, *Politicae Ecclesiasticae, Partis Primae*, 520–44.

141. Ed. note: Bavinck recommends the songs (*liederen*) of "van Marnix, Lodenstein, Groenewegen, and so on." Philips of Marnix, Lord of Saint-Aldegonde (1540–98), was a Dutch statesman,

5. Solitude[142]

Old Testament wisdom warns against solitude: "Whoever isolates himself seeks his own desire; / he breaks out against all sound judgment" (Prov. 18:1). However, Elijah, Elisha, and John the Baptist lived in the desert, and Jesus regularly sought out solitude: "And rising very early in the morning, while it was still dark, he departed and went out to a desolate place, and there he prayed" (Mark 1:35). "And after he had dismissed the crowds, he went up on the mountain by himself to pray. When evening came, he was there alone" (Matt. 14:23). "But he would withdraw to desolate places and pray" (Luke 5:16; cf. Peter in Acts 10:9). This is in keeping with Jesus's own instruction: "But when you pray, go into your room and shut the door and pray to your Father who is in secret. And your Father who sees in secret will reward you" (Matt. 6:6). Thomas à Kempis said: "Everywhere I have sought peace and not found it, except in a corner with a book."[143] Monologues with God, with oneself, prayers, meditations, self-examinations, and so on can take place in solitude. However, isolation is always temporary and should not last for a person's entire life, as is the case with monastics; we are not called to live alone but to live lives of charity and neighbor-love as long as we are in this flesh (Gen. 2:18; Eccles. 4:10). The monks, including à Kempis and others, highly recommend keeping silence.[144] This is good, in contrast to the people described in James 1:26, and it reflects modesty (Job 40:4–5, following God's questions in chaps. 38 and 39; Lev. 10:3) and patience (Pss. 39:10–12; 62:1;[145] Lam. 3:28). Other than for modestly and patiently waiting upon God, silence is not recommended, and silence for the sake of mystical experience is wrong. Weeping and spiritual tears were also recommended by spiritual writers.[146]

---

poet, and prose writer who prepared a Dutch metrical version of the Psalms as well as a *Book of Holy Scriptural Hymns* (G. Kuiper, "Marnix"). Jodocus Lodenstein (1620–77) was a Dutch Reformed minister and theologian of the Further Reformation who wrote a popular collection of verses (*Uytspanningen*, 1676) (van der Linde, "Lodenstein"). The reference to "Groenewegen" is not as definitive. Mostly likely Bavinck has in mind Jacob Groenewegen (born in 1710), who published two volumes titled *De lofzangen Israels* ("Israel's Songs of Praise") (van der Linde, "Groenewegen").

142. Vitringa, *Korte schets*, 279–86 (XIII §16); Voetius, Τα Ασκητικα, 431.

143. LO: *in omnibus requiem quaesivi et nusquam inveni nisi in angulo cum libro*. Ed. note: The Dutch rhymed saying "a little book in a corner" (*een boekje in een hoekje*) is derived from this quotation, and Bavinck may have had the Dutch saying in his mind because his text has *libello* (dative form of *libellus*, "small book") instead of *libro* ("book"). While the saying is consistently attributed to à Kempis, the exact source is hard to find. Umberto Eco concludes his introduction to *The Name of the Rose* with it.

144. DO: *stilzwijgen*. Voetius, Τα Ασκητικα, 441; cf. Maeterlinck, *De schat des harten*, 1–17.

145. "For God alone my soul waits in silence."

146. DO: *wenen, geestelijke tranen*. Voetius, Τα Ασκητικα, 223–35; Görres, *Die christliche Mystik*.

Now believers do sigh often about the "abominations" of their day (Ezek. 9:4) and because of their suffering (Rom. 8:23, 26; 2 Cor. 5:4–5). They weep because of grief about their sins or because of their joy in God: "Our weapons are prayers and tears."[147] Voetius divides these tears into six categories:[148]

- Tears of grief about our sins: Israel under Joshua (Judg. 2); the woman in Luke 7:36–38; Peter in Luke 22:62; the Corinthian church (2 Cor. 7:9–12). The faithful are admonished to weep over their sins (Isa. 22:12; Joel 2:12–13; James 4:9).
- Tears of suffering: David in Psalms 6, 42, and 102; Hezekiah (Isa. 38:3, 5); Jeremiah (Lam. 2; 3); in compassion for the neighbor, especially when there is disobedience and apostasy among God's people (Pss. 80; 119:136–37; Ezek. 8; Luke 19:41; John 11:35; Acts 8:2; 1 Cor. 5:2; 2 Cor. 12:21).
- Tears of longing for grace and eternal salvation: Psalms 6; 42:1–3; 77:3; Romans 7:24; 2 Corinthians 5:4; Philippians 1:23.
- Tears of love for God or Jesus: Acts 20:19, 31; 2 Corinthians 2:4; Philippians 3:18.
- Tears of joy: Genesis 29:11 (cf. 45:14); Esther 8:17; 9:22; 2 Corinthians 6:10; 1 Corinthians 7:30.
- Tears of devotion: Psalm 6:7; Isaiah 37:2, 5.

All these contrast with the worldy, demonic, hypocritical, superstitious, even hellish (Matt. 8:12) tears found among some Roman Catholics.

6. Fasting[149]

The Old Testament Hebrew word used most often for fasting is צוֹם (Neh. 9:1); a parallel expression used as a synonym for fasting comes from the root עָנָה = "to afflict"; נַפְשׁוֹ עָנָּה = "to afflict one's soul." The LXX uses νηστεία.[150] In the Old Testament fasting is a sign of meekness, of humbling oneself before God.[151] The only fasting required by the law is on the Day of Atonement, from evening to evening of the next day (Lev. 16:29, 31; 23:27, 32;

147. LO: *arma nostra sunt preces et lacrimae.* Voetius, Τα Ασκητικα, 232.
148. Voetius, Τα Ασκητικα, 236–86.
149. Voetius, Τα Ασκητικα, 417; Vitringa, *Korte schets*, 282–84 (XIII §17); de Moor, *Commentarius Perpetuus*, 5:120–21 (§ XXIII); Linsenmayer, *Entwicklung der kirchlichen Fastendisciplin.*
150. Calvin, *Institutes*, IV.xii.14–21; Jacobson, "Fasten."
151. LXX, GrO: ταπεινὸν τῆς ψυχῆς.

Num. 29:7).[152] The Old Testament provides many examples of fasting: Judges 20:26; 1 Samuel 7:6; 31:13; 2 Samuel 1:2; 12:16–23; 2 Chronicles 20:3; Esther 4:3; Ezra 8:21; Daniel 9:3; Joel 1:14; Zechariah 7:3, 5; 8:19. More often than not the prophets consider this fasting as nothing but hypocrisy and call for a spiritual fast—that is, fasting from wickedness (Isa. 58:4; Jer. 14:12; Joel 2:12–13; Zech. 7:5–10; 8:19). The Jews multiplied fasts, especially among the Pharisees, who considered them meritorious works, particularly when done twice a week (Luke 18:13). Luke describes the prophetess Anna as someone who "did not depart from the temple, worshiping with fasting night and day" (Luke 2:37). Jesus himself fasted forty days in the desert (Matt. 4:2); however, although the disciples of John and the Pharisees fasted, Jesus did not impose this on his own disciples (Matt. 9:14–17; Mark 2:18–22; Luke 5:33–39). He does judge fasting to be good; demonic spirits can only be cast out by prayer and fasting (Matt. 17:21; Mark 9:29).[153] When challenged by the disciples of John the Baptist about his disciples' failure to fast, Jesus replied: "Can the wedding guests mourn as long as the bridegroom is with them? The days will come when the bridegroom is taken away from them, and then they will fast" (Matt. 9:15).

We find additional examples of fasting in the New Testament: Cornelius (Acts 10:30)[154] and Paul and Barnabas, with the church in Antioch (Acts 13:2–3) and commissioning elders in all the churches (Acts 14:23). Paul instructs husbands and wives (in 1 Cor. 7:5) to grant their spouses conjugal rights "except perhaps by agreement for a limited time, that you may devote yourselves to prayer (and fasting)."[155] He also says of himself that he was in watchings and in fastings (2 Cor. 6:5; 11:27). In Rome fasting expanded greatly, especially through the monks and because of the creditable nature of it. Especially known are the Quadragesima[156] before Easter, weekly on Wednesday and Friday, the

---

152. Ed. note: The reference to fasting in these verses might be overlooked by readers who are not aware that the translations "to afflict oneself" and "to deny oneself" do refer to fasting, as Bavinck pointed out earlier in this paragraph. Bavinck's next sentence in the manuscript points to Num. 30:11–16 as a passage where fasting is presented as a promise; this is not fully clear.

153. Ed. note: Contemporary translations lack Matt. 17:21 ("But this kind never comes out except by prayer and fasting") as well as the reference to fasting in Mark 9:29 ("This kind cannot be driven out by anything but prayer"). Bavinck's use of these two verses for their reference to fasting is based on the Textus Receptus, used by the translators of the *Statenvertaling* and the KJV.

154. Ed. note: Here too, contemporary translations speak only of Cornelius praying (προσευχόμενος); the Textus Receptus adds "fasting" (νηστεύων).

155. Ed. note: "Fasting" is found in the *Statenvertaling* and the KJV but not in contemporary translations.

156. Ed. note: "Quadragesima," a Latin term meaning "the fortieth," refers to a season of prayer and fasting following the example of Christ (Matt. 4), most characteristically the season of Lent. See Mershman, "Quadragesima."

days Jesus was betrayed and crucified, and four separate weeks during the year (cf. Zech. 8:19) in March, June, September, and December. Then there were also the extraordinary fasts.

The Reformed did not reject fasting, but they did repudiate compulsory fasting and the notion that it was meritorious. After all, the apostle Paul had said, "Food will not commend us to God. We are no worse off if we do not eat, and no better off if we do" (1 Cor. 8:8). He was emphatic: "I know and am persuaded in the Lord Jesus that nothing is unclean in itself, but it is unclean for anyone who thinks it unclean. For the kingdom of God is not a matter of eating and drinking but of righteousness and peace and joy in the Holy Spirit" (Rom. 14:14, 17). Therefore, everything is permissible for eating (1 Cor. 10:25–26) because "everything created by God is good, and nothing is to be rejected if it is received with thanksgiving, for it is made holy by the word of God and prayer" (1 Tim. 4:4 5). In conclusion, "let no one pass judgment on you in questions of food and drink," and since "with Christ you died to the elemental spirits of the world, why, as if you were still alive in the world, do you submit to regulations—'Do not handle, Do not taste, Do not touch' (referring to things that all perish as they are used)—according to human precepts and teachings?" (Col. 2:16, 20–22). Fasting is very good, quieting passions and desires in us, warding off temptations, in times of mourning and sorrow, when the church is declining and deteriorating, in times of plague and war. This was also Calvin's view, which was immediately taken over by the French synod of 1559.[157]

7. Vigils[158]

Vigils are also recommended in Holy Scripture; a negative example is given in the parable of the foolish virgins (Matt. 25). Jesus commends vigils: "Watch therefore, for you know neither the day nor the hour" (Matt. 25:13; cf. Mark 13:13; Luke 21:34). In the garden of Gethsemane, he sorrowfully asks his sleeping disciples, "So, could you not watch with me one hour? Watch and pray that you may not enter into temptation. The spirit indeed is willing, but the flesh is weak" (Matt. 26:40–41).

157. Ed. note: The Reformed churches of France held their first national synod in 1559, at which a church constitution and a confession of faith (the Gallican Confession of Faith) were produced. Bavinck cites the following references: the Gallican Confession, art. 24 (Dennison, *Reformed Confessions*, 2:148–49); the Second Helvetic Confession (1566), art. 24 (Dennison, 2:872–74); and the Bohemian Confession (1535), art. 18 (Dennison, 1:333–34); Jacobson, "Fasten," 509.

158. Voetius, Τα Ασκητικα, 429; de Moor, *Commentarius Perpetuus*, 5:135–36 (§ XXVIII); Neudecker, "Vigilien."

Paul gives similar instruction:

Awake, O sleeper, / and arise from the dead, and Christ will shine on you. (Eph. 5:14)

So then, let us not be like others, who are asleep, but let us be awake and sober. (1 Thess. 5:6)

Be on your guard; stand firm in the faith; be courageous; be strong. (1 Cor. 16:13)

And pray in the Spirit on all occasions with all kinds of prayers and requests. With this in mind, be alert and always keep on praying for all the Lord's people. (Eph. 6:18)

Devote yourselves to prayer, being watchful and thankful. (Col. 4:2)

Similarly, the apostle Peter: "The end of all things is near. Therefore be alert and of sober mind so that you may pray" (1 Pet. 4:7). "Be alert and of sober mind. Your enemy the devil prowls around like a roaring lion looking for someone to devour" (1 Pet. 5:8). Over time the church began to hold particular vigils as preparations for major holy days in the church. The night before was spent in hymn singing, prayer, processions. The important vigils took place prior to Easter, Pentecost, and Christmas; from the twelfth century on there have been vigils for Mary and for Ascension Day, the Holy Day of John the Baptist, All Saints' Day, the Holy Day of Matthias, of Peter, and so on. Here as well the Reformation rejected the compulsory (statutory) nature of these vigils.

8. Vows[159]

A vow is an earnest commitment to dedicate something to God out of gratitude for answered prayer. This is what Jacob did after his dream at Bethel: "Then Jacob made a vow, saying, 'If God will be with me and will watch over me on this journey I am taking and will give me food to eat and clothes to wear so that I return safely to my father's household, then the LORD will be my God and this stone that I have set up as a pillar will be God's house, and of all that you give me I will give you a tenth'" (Gen. 28:20–22 NIV). Vows are regulated by the law (Lev. 27) but are voluntary: "If you make a vow to the LORD your God, do not be slow to pay it, for the

159. Köstlin, "Gelübde."

LORD your God will certainly demand it of you and you will be guilty of sin. But if you refrain from making a vow, you will not be guilty" (Deut. 23:21–22 NIV). "Whatever your lips utter you must be sure to do, because you made your vow freely to the LORD your God with your own mouth" (Deut. 23:23 NIV). In other words, vows made must be kept: "This is what the LORD commands: When a man makes a vow to the LORD or takes an oath to obligate himself by a pledge, he must not break his word but must do everything he said" (Num. 30:1–2 NIV). Scripture warns us against rash vows: "It is a trap to dedicate something rashly / and only later to consider one's vows" (Prov. 20:25 NIV). "Do not be quick with your mouth, / do not be hasty in your heart / to utter anything before God. / God is in heaven / and you are on earth, / so let your words be few. . . . When you make a vow to God, do not delay to fulfill it. He has no pleasure in fools; fulfill your vow. It is better not to make a vow than to make one and not fulfill it. Do not let your mouth lead you into sin" (Eccles. 5:2, 4–6a NIV). In making vows, daughters are subject to their fathers and wives to their husbands (Num. 30:3–14). When one makes vows, it is the attitude that matters (Pss. 66:13–15; 76:12; 116:17–19; Mal. 1:14). Jesus is critical of the Pharisees and scribes of his day for cleverly undermining their own vows by invoking *corban* ("dedicated to God") as a way of avoiding their responsibilities to parents (Matt. 15:3–7; Mark 7:11–13). The New Testament does speak of vows: Paul keeps his own vow (Acts 18:18) and joins others in their vow (Acts 21:23–26). Fasting and the Nazirite vow were important in the Old Testament. There are three important vows in the Roman Catholic Church: celibacy/chastity, poverty, and obedience.[160] There are also vows to go on pilgrimages and the like. Catholicism is able to hold vows lightly because it holds to nonobligatory *counsels of perfection* above required *precepts*.[161] However, according to Protestantism, in all things we are God's;[162] how can we then vow something to him? How can we obligate ourselves to something that is not already an obligation? Furthermore, vows are binding, and how do we know about the circumstances of our lives tomorrow? How can we vow certain future behavior (not to marry, not to drink, etc.)? Nonetheless, the Reformation continued to affirm vows.[163]

160. Vitringa, *Korte schets*, XIV.
161. LO: *praecepta; consilia.* Ed. note: *Consilia,* more fully as *consilia evangelica,* were "a higher obedience not commanded in the law"; those who followed them received merit. The whole notion was "tied directly to the medieval reverence for the monastic life" (Muller, *Dictionary,* 79, s.v. "*consilia evangelica*").
162. Calvin, *Institutes,* IV.xiii.6.
163. Calvin, *Institutes,* IV.xiii.4–5; de Moor, *Commentarius Perpetuus,* 5:144–45.

§26. CONSUMMATION OF THE SPIRITUAL LIFE; MEDITATION ON DEATH[164]

Spiritual life is first made perfect in death and then moves over to eternal life.[165] We need to prepare for death, familiarize ourselves with it, and count our days (Pss. 39:5; 90). With his death Christ has broken the power of death and Satan and set "free those who all their lives were held in slavery by their fear of death" (Heb. 2:14–15). A Christian who hears Christ's word and believes him "has eternal life and will not be judged but has crossed over from death to life" (John 5:24). We must despise this life and meditate on eternal life, though not denying that life is a gift and a blessing.[166] For the faithful "the day of death [is better] than the day of birth" (Eccles. 7:1).[167] Meditating on death is useful for us to humble ourselves (Gen. 18), to help us set aside imagining a long life (Isa. 28:15; Luke 12:13–21), to take away the strength and fear of death, and so on. We are to "face death each day" (1 Cor. 15:31); "after the cross, death is less."[168] Meditating on death is especially needed in times of illness.[169] After that we must die in faith (Gen. 49:18; 2 Chron. 23:2–3; 24:22). Consider Jesus's last words on the cross; he died in obedience. Our death: "For none of us lives for ourselves alone, and none of us dies for ourselves alone. If we live, we live for the Lord; and if we die, we die for the Lord. So, whether we live or die, we belong to the Lord" (Rom. 14:7–8). Why then do many pious people die fearful and hopeless, without joy?[170]

---

164. LO: *meditatio mortis*.

165. Vitringa, *Korte schets*, XVII.

166. Calvin, *Institutes*, III.ix.

167. Perkins, *Salve for a Sick Man*. Ed. note: Bavinck's source is Perkins, *Werken*, 3^2:237–64.

168. LO: *mors post crucem minor est*.

169. Perkins, *Werken*, 3^2:249.

170. Voetius, Τα Ασκητικα, 569–88, on "dying well" (euthanasia). See also Hoornbeeck, *Oratio Funebris*; the wonderful sermon (*schone preek*) by Bourdaloue on "the thought of death." Ed. note: The "wonderful sermon" by the French Jesuit Louis Bourdaloue is "Sermon pour le Mercredi des cendres sur la pensée de la mort." On the reverse of this page (435), Bavinck wrote, "Is duty always absolutely binding? For geniuses, etc.? Could a genius not transgress in exceptional circumstances? Ockins says 'yes' and appeals to Luke 17:14." Most likely, the note was intended to connect this section to the beginning of Book III, §27, where Bavinck starts his discussion on "duties."

Bibliography

BOOKS

Aalst, Gerardus van. *Geestelijke mengel-stoffen.* 2 vols. in 1. Amsterdam: Hendrik Vieroot, 1754.

———. *Proeve des geloofs.* Amsterdam: Hendrik Vieroot, 1755.

Acquoy, Johannes Gerhardus Rijk. *Het klooster te Windesheim en zijn invloed.* 3 vols. Utrecht: Gebr. Van der Post, 1875–80.

Acta Synodi Nationalis, in Nomine Domini Nostri Iesu Christi. Leiden: Isaac Elzevier and Isaac Jansz Canin, 1620.

Alcuin. *De virtutibus et vittis liber ad Widonem Comitem.* In *PL* 101:613–38.

Allestree, Richard. *The Whole Duty of Man.* London: R. Norton for Robert Pawlett, 1673.

Almanak van het studentencorps, "Fides Quaerit Intellectum," voor het jaar 1902. Kampen: Ph. Zalsman, 1902.

Almanak van het studentencorps, "Fides Quaerit Intellectum," voor het jaar 1903. Kampen: Ph. Zalsman, 1903.

Alsted, Johann Heinrich. *Praecognitorum Theologicorum, Libri Duo.* Frankfurt: Hummius, 1614.

———. *Theologia Casuum, Exhibens Anatomen Conscientiae et Scholam Tentationum.* Hanover: Konrad Eifried, 1630.

Alting, Heinrich. *Theologiae Problematica Nova.* Amsterdam: J. Jansson, 1662.

Altmann, Johann Georg. *Delineatio Oratoriae Sacrae Brevibus Praeceptis Exhibita.* Bern: Typographical Society of Bern, 1753.

Ames, William. *Conscience with the Power and Cases Thereof.* Leyden and London: W. Christiaens, E. Griffin, J. Dawson, 1639. Reprint, Amsterdam: Theatrum Orbis Terrarum; Norwood, NJ: Walter J. Johnson, 1975.

———. *De Conscientia et Eius Iure vel Casibus.* 5 books. Amsterdam, 1630.

———. *The Marrow of Theology.* Edited and translated by John Dykstra Eusden. Boston: Pilgrim, 1968. Reprint, Grand Rapids: Baker, 1997.

Ammon, Christoph Friedrich von. *Handbuch der christlichen Sittenlehre.* 3 vols. in 8. Leipzig: Georg Joachim Goschen, 1823–29.

Amyraut, Moses. *La morale chrestienne.* 6 vols. Saumur: Isaac Desbordes, 1652–60.

Andel, J. van. *Jezus' leer.* Heusden: H. Wuijster, 1883.

Anthony of Florence. *Summa Moralis*. 4 vols. Venice: Nicolas Jenson, 1477–90.

Appel, Heinrich. *Die Lehre der Scholastiker von der Synteresis*. Rostock: Universitäts-Buchdruckerei, 1891.

Aquinas, Thomas. *Summa Theologica*. Translated by the Fathers of the English Dominican Province. Allen, TX: Christian Classics, 1981.

Aristotle. *Rhetoric*. Translated by W. Rhys Roberts and Ingram Bywater. New York: Modern Library, 1954. Online at http://rhetoric.eserver.org/aristotle/index.html.

Arnold, Gottfried. *Historie und Beschreibung der mystischen Theologie*. Frankfurt: Thomas Fritschen, 1703.

Augustine. *Against Julian*. Translated by Matthew A. Schumacher. FC 35. Washington, DC: Catholic University of America Press, 1957.

———. *City of God*. NPNF[1] 2:1–511.

———. *City of God*. Translated by John Healey. 2 vols. Edinburgh: John Grant, 1909.

———. *Concerning the Nature of Good, Against the Manichaeans*. NPNF[1] 4:346–65.

———. *The Enchiridion*. NPNF[1] 3:229–76.

———. *On the Holy Trinity*. NPNF[1] 3:1–199.

———. *On the Morals of the Catholic Church*. NPNF[1] 4:37–63.

———. *On the Morals of the Manichaeans*. NPNF[1] 4:65–89.

———. *A Treatise on Rebuke and Grace*. NPNF[1] 5:467–91.

Bahrdt, Carl Friedrich. *Christliches Sittenbuch fürs Gesinde*. Berlin: Vieweg, 1786.

———. *System der moralischen Religion . . . für Zweifler und Denker*. Vols. 1–2. 3rd ed. Berlin: F. Vieweg, 1791. Vol. 3. Riga: Johann Friedrich Hartknoch, 1792.

Bähring, Bernhard. *Thomas von Kempen, der Prediger der Nachfolge Christi*. Berlin: H. Schultze, 1849.

Baier, Johann Wilhelm. *Compendium Theologiae Moralis*. Jena: Bailliard, 1697.

Bain, Alexander. *Mental and Moral Science: A Compendium of Psychology and Ethics*. London: Longmans, Green and Co., 1868.

Balduin, Friedrich. *Tractatus Luculentus Posthumus, . . . Casibus nimirum Conscientiae*. Wittenberg: Paul Helwig, 1628.

Bartholomew of San Concordio. *Summa de Casibus Conscientiae*. Augsburg: Günther Zainer, 1475.

Baumgarten, Siegmund Jakob. *Unterricht von rechtmäßigen Verhalten eines Christen, oder Theologische Moral*. 5th ed. Halle: Johann Andreas Bauer, 1756.

Baur, Ferdinand Christian. *Paul the Apostle of Jesus Christ: His Life and Works, His Epistles and Teachings*. 2 vols. in 1. London: Williams and Norgate, 1873–75.

Bavinck, Herman. *Beginselen der psychologie*. Revised by V. Hepp. 2nd rev. ed. Kampen: Kok, 1923.

———. *De ethiek van Ulrich Zwingli*. Kampen: G. Ph. Zalsman, 1880.

———. *De navolging van Christus en het moderne leven*. Kampen: Kok, n.d. [1918]. Also published in *Kennis en leven*, 115–44. ET: Appendix B in Bolt, *Theological Analysis*, 402–40.

———. *De theologie van Prof. Dr. Daniel Chantepie de la Saussaye: Bijdrage tot de kennis der ethische theologie*. Leiden: D. Donner, 1884. 2nd rev. ed. Leiden: Donner, 1903.

———. *De wetenschap der heilige godgeleerdheid*. Kampen: Zalsman, 1883.

———. *Essays on Religion, Science, and Society*. Edited by John Bolt. Translated by Harry Boonstra and Gerrit Sheeres. Grand Rapids: Baker Academic, 2008.

———. *Gereformeerde Dogmatiek*. Kampen: Bos, 1895–1901. 2nd ed. Kampen: Kok, 1906–11. ET: *Reformed Dogmatics*. Edited by John Bolt. Translated by John

Vriend. Grand Rapids: Baker Academic, 2003–8.

———. "Gereformeerde Ethiek." Bavinck Archives, no. 56. Historical Documentation Centre, Free University, Amsterdam.

———. *Hedendaagsche moraal*. Kampen: Kok, 1902.

———. *Kennis en leven: Opstellen en artikelen uit vroegere jaren*. Kampen: Kok, n.d. [1922].

———. *The Philosophy of Revelation*. Grand Rapids: Eerdmans, 1953.

———. *Saved by Grace: The Holy Spirit's Work in Calling and Regeneration*. Edited by J. Mark Beach. Translated by Nelson D. Kloosterman. Grand Rapids: Reformation Heritage, 2013.

Baxter, Richard. *A Call to the Unconverted to Turn and Live*. London, 1658.

———. *A Christian Directory, or, A Summ of Practical Theology, and Cases of Conscience*. London, 1673. Reprint, 5 vols. London: Richard Edwards, 1825.

———. *The Saints Everlasting Rest: or, A Treatise of the Blessed State of the Saints in Their Enjoyment of God in Glory [. . .]*. London, 1650.

Bayly, Lewis. *The Practice of Piety, Directing a Christian How to Walk That He May Please God*. London: Philip Chetwinde, 1672. Reprint, London: Hamilton, Adams, and Co., 1842. Dutch translation: *De practycke ofte oeffeninge der godsaligheydt*. Edited by Gisbertus Voetius. Utrecht: Esdras Willemsz. Snellaert, 1642. German translation: *Praxis pietatis: Das ist Uebung der Gottseligkeit*. Bern: Daniel Tschiffeli, 1703.

Beard, Charles. *The Reformation of the Sixteenth Century in Its Relation to Modern Thought and Knowledge*. London and Edinburgh: Williams and Norgate, 1883.

Beck, Herman G. J. *Die Erbauungsliteratur der evangelischen Kirche Deutschlands*. Erlangen: Deichert, 1883.

Beck, Jakob Christoph. *Synopsis Institutionum Universae Theologiae Naturalis et Revelatae, Dogmaticae, Polemicae et Practicae*. Basel: J. H. Inhofium, 1765.

Beck, Johann Tobias. *Die christliche Lehr-Wissenschaft nach den biblischen Urkunden*. Stuttgart: C. Belser, 1841.

———. *Outlines of Biblical Psychology*. 3rd rev. ed. Edinburgh: T&T Clark, 1877.

———. *Vorlesungen über christliche Ethik*. 3 vols. Gütersloh: C. Bertelsmann, 1882–83.

Beeke, Joel R. *Assurance of Faith: Calvin, English Puritanism, and the Dutch Second Reformation*. New York: Peter Lang, 1991.

———. *Gisbertus Voetius: Toward a Reformed Marriage of Knowledge and Piety*. Grand Rapids: Reformation Heritage, 1999.

Beeke, Joel R., and Randall J. Pederson. *Meet the Puritans: With a Guide to Modern Reprints*. Grand Rapids: Reformation Heritage, 2006.

Bellarmine, Robert. *Disputationes de Controversiis Christianae Fidei adversus Hujus Temporis Haereticos*. 3 vols. Ingolstadt: David Sartorius, 1581, 1582, 1593. ET: *Controversies of the Christian Faith*, trans. Kenneth Baker. Saddle River, NJ: Keep the Faith, Inc., 2016.

———. *Opera Omnia*. Cambridge, MA: Andover-Harvard Theological Library, 1910.

Belt, Henk van den. *The Authority of Scripture in Reformed Theology: Truth and Trust*. Leiden and Boston: Brill, 2008.

Bengel, John Albert. *Gnomon of the New Testament*. 5 vols. Edited and translated by James Bryce. Philadelphia: Smith, English, and Co.; New York: Sheldon and Co., 1860.

Bernard of Clairvaux. *On Loving God*. PL 182:973–1000.

Bertius, Peter. *Scripta Adversaria Collationis Hagiensis*. Leiden, 1615.

Bestmann, Hugo Johannes. *Geschichte der christlichen Sitte*. 2 vols. Nörlingen: C. H. Beck, 1880–83.

Betz, H. J. *Ervaringswijsbegeerte*. The Hague: Nijhoff, 1881.

Blei, Karel. *The Netherlands Reformed Church, 1571–2005*. Translated by Allan J. Janssen. Grand Rapids: Eerdmans, 2006.

Bolt, John. *A Theological Analysis of Herman Bavinck's Two Essays on the* Imitatio Christi. Lewiston, NY: Edwin Mellen, 2013.

Bolton, Robert. *The Saints Selfe-Enriching Examination*. London: A. Griffin, 1634.

Bonaventure. *Opera Omnia*. 10 vols. Ad Claras Aquas (Quarrachi): College of St. Bonaventure, 1882–1901.

Boone, Clifford B. *Puritan Evangelism: Preaching for Conversion in Late-Sevententh Century English Puritanism*. Crownhill, UK: Paternoster, 2013.

Borst, Jacob. *Geestelicke geness-konst*. Dordrecht: Jacob Braat, 1651.

Bosse, Friedrich. *Prolegomena zu einer Geschichte des Begriffes "Nachfolge Christ."* Berlin: Reimer, 1895.

Boye, Rice. *The Importunate Begger for Things Necessary*. Amsterdam: J. F. Stam, 1635.

Brackney, William H. *Historical Dictionary of Radical Christianity*. Lanham, MD: Scarecrow, 2012.

Brakel, Theodorus Gerardus à. *De trappen des geestelyken levens*. Groningen: L. Groenewout, 1739.

———. *Het geestelijke leven*. Amsterdam: Gijsbert de Groot, 1686.

Brakel, Wilhelmus à. *The Christian's Reasonable Service*. Translated by Bartel Elshout. 4 vols. Vols. 1–3, Pittsburgh: Soli De Gloria, 1992–94. Vol. 4, Grand Rapids: Reformation Heritage, 1995.

Braun, Johannes. *Doctrina Foederum*. Amsterdam: Abraham van Someren, 1691.

Braun, P., and Paul Zeller, eds. *Calwer Bibellexikon: Biblisches Handwörterbuch*. Cologne and Stuttgart: Vereinsbuchhandlung, 1885.

Brecht, Martin. *Martin Luther: Shaping and Defining the Reformation, 1521–1532*. Translated by James Schaaf. Minneapolis: Fortress, 1990.

Brederveld, J. *Hoofdlijnen der paedagogiek van Dr. Herman Bavinck, met critische beschouwing*. Amsterdam: De Standaard, 1927.

Bremmer, R. H. *Herman Bavinck als Dogmaticus*. Kampen: Kok, 1961.

Brown, Francis, S. R. Driver, and Charles A. Briggs. *Hebrew and English Lexicon of the Old Testament Based on the Lexicon of William Gesenius*. London: Oxford University Press, 1907. Reprint, 1968.

Bruch, J. F. *Theorie des Bewußtseins: Ein psychologischer Versuch*. Strasbourg: Treuttel and Wurtz, 1864.

Bruijn, Jan de. *Abraham Kuyper: A Pictorial Biography*. Translated by Dagmare Houniet. Grand Rapids: Eerdmans, 2014.

Buddeus, Johann Franciscus. *Institutiones Theologiae Dogmaticae*. Frankfurt and Leipzig, 1741.

———. *Institutiones Theologiae Moralis*. Leipzig: Thomas Fritsch, 1721.

Burger, Hans. *Being in Christ: A Biblical and Systematic Investigation in a Reformed Perspective*. Eugene, OR: Wipf and Stock, 2009.

Burman, Francis. *Synopsis Theologiae*. Amsterdam, 1699.

Buurt, Adriaan. *Beschouwende godgeleerdheid*. 6 vols. Amsterdam: Jacobus Loveringh & Petrus Schouten, 1763–75.

Cajetan, Thomas de Vio. *Epistolae Pauli et aliorum Apostolorum*. 5th ed. Paris: Iacobus Keruer, 1536.

Calixt, George. *Epitome Theologiae Moralis.* Helmstedt: Henning Müller, 1634.

Calvin, John. *The Epistles of Paul the Apostle to the Galatians, Ephesians, Philippians, and Colossians.* Translated by T. H. L. Parker. Calvin's New Testament Commentaries. Grand Rapids: Eerdmans, 1965.

———. *The Epistles of Paul the Apostle to the Romans and to the Thessalonians.* Translated by Ross MacKenzie. Calvin's New Testament Commentaries. Grand Rapids: Eerdmans, 1960.

———. *The Gospel according to St. John 11–21 and the First Epistle of John.* Translated by T. H. L. Parker. Calvin's New Testament Commentaries. Grand Rapids: Eerdmans, 1959.

———. *A Harmony of the Gospels Matthew, Mark, and Luke.* Translated by A. W. Morrison. 3 vols. Calvin's New Testament Commentaries. Grand Rapids: Eerdmans, 1972.

———. *Institutes of the Christian Religion.* Edited by John T. McNeill. Translated by F. L. Battles. 2 vols. Philadelphia: Westminster, 1960.

———. *Joannis Calvini Opera Quae Supersunt Omnia.* Edited by Edouard Cunitz, Johann-Wilhelm Baum, and Eduard Wilhelm Eugen Reuss. 59 vols. Braunschweig: C. A. Schwetschke, 1863.

———. *Letters of John Calvin, Compiled from the Original Manuscripts and Edited with Historical Notes.* Edited by Jules Bonnet. 2 vols. Philadelphia: Presbyterian Board of Publication, 1858.

———. *The Second Epistle of Paul the Apostle to the Corinthians and the Epistles to Timothy, Titus, and Philemon.* Translated by T. A. Smail. Calvin's New Testament Commentaries. Grand Rapids: Eerdmans, 1964.

———. *Treatise against the Anabaptists and the Libertines.* Translated by Benjamin Wirt Farley. Grand Rapids: Baker, 1982.

Calvin, John, and Jacopo Sadoleto. *A Reformation Debate.* Edited by John C. Olin. New York: Harper and Row, 1966. Reprint, Grand Rapids: Baker, 1976.

Cannegieter, T. *De zedelijkheid: Haar wezen, grondslag en doel.* Groningen: J. B. Wolters, 1879.

Catholic Church. *Canons and Decrees of the Sacred and Oecumenical Council of Trent.* Translated by J. Waterworth. London: Burns and Oates; New York: Catholic Publication Society Company, n.d.

Charles-Edwards, Thomas, and Michael Lapidge, eds. *The Penitential of Theodore and the Iudiccia Theodori.* Cambridge Studies in Anglo-Saxon England 11. Cambridge: Cambridge University Press, 1995.

Chauvin, Pierre. *De Naturali Religione Liber, in Tres Partes Divisus.* Rotterdam: apud P. vander Slaart, sumptibus Samuel Oliver, 1693.

Chemnitz, Christian. *Dissertatio Theologica: De Tentationibus Spiritualibus.* Jena, 1652.

Chesterton, Gilbert K. *St. Francis of Assisi.* 14th ed. Garden City, NY: Image, 1924.

Christ, Paul. *Die Lehre vom Gebet nach dem Neuen Testament.* Leiden: Brill, 1886.

———. *Die sittliche Weltordnung.* Leiden: Brill, 1894.

Cicero, Marcus Tullius. *"De republica," "De legibus."* Translated by Clinton Walker Keyes. London: Heinemann; Cambridge, MA: Harvard University Press, 1928.

———. *De natura deorum.* Translated by Francis Brooks. London: Methuen, 1896.

———. *"De natura deorum" and "Academica."* Translated by H. Rackham. Vol. 19 of *Cicero in 28 Volumes.* LCL. Cambridge, MA: Harvard University Press; London: Heinemann, 1933. Reprint, 1967.

————. *For Milo*. Translated by Charles Duke Yonge. London: George Bell, 1891.

————. *Tusculan Disputations*. Translated by C. D. Yonge. New York: Harper and Brothers, 1888.

————. *Tusculan Disputations*. Translated by J. E. King. London: Heinemann; New York: Putnam's Sons, 1927.

Clement of Alexandria. *The Stromata or Miscellanies*. ANF 2:299–568.

Clewis, Robert R. *The Kantian Sublime and the Revelation of Freedom*. Cambridge and New York: Cambridge University Press, 2009.

Cloppenburg, J. *Disputationes Theologicae XI: De Foedere Dei & Testamento Veteri & Novo*. Hardervici: Nicolai à Wieringen, 1643.

————. *Exercitationes super Locos Communes Theologicos*. Franeker: Idzardus Balck, 1653.

Cocceius, J. *Summa Doctrinae de Foedere et Testamento Dei*. 2nd rev. ed. Leiden: Elsevir, 1654.

————. *Summa Theologiae ex Scripturis Repetita*. Geneva, 1665.

Comrie, Alexander. *The ABC of Faith*. Translated by J. M. Banfield. Ossett, UK: Zoar, 1978.

————. *Stellige en praktikale verklaring van den Heidelbergschen Catechismus volgens de leer en gronden der Reformatie*. Leiden: Johannes Hasebroek; Amsterdam: Nicholas Byl, 1753.

Cooper, John W. *Panentheism: The Other God of the Philosophers; From Plato to the Present*. Grand Rapids: Baker Academic, 2006.

Cramer, J. *Christendom en humaniteit*. Amsterdam: W. H. Kirchener, 1871.

Cremer, Hermann. *Biblico-Theological Lexicon of New Testament Greek*. Translated by D. W. Simon and William Urwick. Edinburgh: T&T Clark; New York: Scribner's Sons, 1895.

Crookshank, William. *The History of the State and Sufferings of the Church of Scotland: From the Restoration to the Revolution*. 2 vols. Edinburgh, 1751.

Crusius, Christian August. *Kurzer Begriff der Moraltheologie*. 2 vols. Leipzig: Ulrich Christian Saalbach, 1772–73.

Culmann, Ph. Theodor. *Die christliche Ethik*. 2 vols. Stuttgart: J. F. Steinkopf, 1864–66.

Daneau, Lambert. *Ethices Christianae*. 3 vols. Geneva: Eustache Vignon, 1579.

Dannhauer, Johann Conrad. *Collegium Exercitationum Ethico-Politicarum*. Marburg: Kaspar Chemlin, 1626.

Dedekenn, Georg. *Trewhertzige Warnung*. Hamburg, 1611.

de Jong, Jelle Michiels. "Gereformeerde ethiek van Profess. Dr. H. Bavinck." Bavinck Archives, no. 197 (HB Diktaten).

Dennison, James T., Jr. *Reformed Confessions of the 16th and 17th Centuries in English Translation*. 4 vols. Grand Rapids: Reformation Heritage, 2008–10.

Doedes, J. I. *De leer van God*. Utrecht: Kemink and Zoon, 1871.

————. *Encyclopedie der christelijke theologie*. Utrecht: Kemink and Zoon, 1876.

————. *Inleiding tot de leer van God*. 2nd ed. Utrecht: Kemink and Zoon, 1880.

d'Outrein, Johannes. *Proef-stukken van heilige sinne-beelden*. 2 vols. Amsterdam: Gerardus Borstius, 1700.

Downame, John. *The Christian Warfare against Satan*. Pelham, AL: Solid Ground Christian Books, 2009.

Driessen, Antonius. *Evangelische zedekunde*. Utrecht: Willem Broedelet, 1716.

————. *Oude en nieuwe mensch gebragt tot een zaamstel der praktikale godgeleertheid*. Groningen: L. Groenewout and H. Spoormaker, 1738.

Drummond, Henry. *The Changed Life*. Philadelphia: H. Altemus, 1898.

———. *Eternal Life*. Philadelphia: H. Altemus, 1896.

———. *The Ideal Life*. New York: Dodd, Mead, 1898.

———. *Natural Law in the Spiritual World*. New York: J. Pott, 1885.

Dürr, Johann Conrad. *Enchiridion Theologiae Moralis*. Altorf: Johannes Göbel, 1662.

Ebrard, Johann Heinrich August. *Christliche Dogmatik*. 2 vols. Königsberg: A. W. Unzer, 1851–52.

Eco, Umberto. *The Name of the Rose*. Translated by Richard Dixon. New York: Houghton Mifflin Harcourt, 2014 (1983).

Eenhoorn, W. van. *Eusooia, ofte: Wel-leven*. 2 vols. Amsterdam: Adriaan Wor, 1746, 1747.

Eglinton, James P. *Trinity and Organism: Towards a New Reading of Herman Bavinck's Organic Motif*. Edinburgh: T&T Clark, 2012.

Elsenhaus, Theodor. *Wesen und Entstehung des Gewissens: Eine Psychologie der Ethik*. Leipzig: Engelmann, 1894.

Endemann, Samuel. *Institutiones Theologiae Moralis*. 2 vols. Frankfurt am Main: Johann Gottlieb Garbe, 1780.

Epiphanius. *The Panarion of Epiphanius of Salamis, Books II and III; De Fide*. Translated by Frank Williams. 2nd rev. ed. Nag Hammadi and Manichaean Studies 79. Edited by Johannes van Oort and Einar Thomassen. Leiden and Boston: Brill, 2013.

Episcopius, Simon. *The Arminian Confession of 1621*. Edited and translated by Mark A. Ellis. Eugene, OR: Pickwick, 2005.

Erasmus, Desiderius. *In Novum Testamentum Annotationes*. Basel: Froben, 1540.

Erbkam, Wilhelm Heinrich. *Geschichte der protestantischen Sekten im Zeitalter der Reformation*. Hamburg: F. and A. Perthes, 1848.

Ernesti, H. Fr. Th. L. *Die Ethik des Apostels Paulus in ihren Grundzügen*. 3rd rev. ed. Göttingen: Vandenhoeck and Ruprecht, 1880.

Erskine, Ebenezer. *De verzekering des geloofs*. Amsterdam: H. Höveker, 1855.

Evangelische Gezangen, om nevens het Boek der Psalmen bij den openbare godsdienst in the Nederlandsche Gemeenten gebruikt to worden. Amsterdam: Johannes Allart, 1802.

Fabius, D. P. D. *De Fransche revolutie: Eene studie*. Amsterdam: Kruyt, 1888.

Fee, Gordon D. *God's Empowering Presence: The Holy Spirit in the Letters of Paul*. Grand Rapids: Baker Academic, 2011.

Fichte, Johann Gottlieb. *System der Sittenlehre*. In *Johann Gottlieb Fichte's Nachgelassene Werke*. Vol. 3. Edited by J. H. Fichte. Bonn: Adolph Marcus, 1835. Also in *Johann Gottlieb Fichte's sämmtliche Werke*. Vol. 4. Edited by J. H. Fichte. Berlin: von Veit and Co., 1845.

Fleck, Ferdinand Florens. *System der christlichen Dogmatiek*. Leipzig: Friedrich Fleischer, 1846.

Florentius, Batavus, Laurentius Surius, and Bartholomew Poin. *Institutiones vitae Christianae*. Cologne: Ionnis Quentel, 1562.

Flottemanville, Samuel Basnage de. *Morale theologique et politique*. 2 vols. Amsterdam: Pierre Mortier, 1703.

Flügel. Otto. *Das Ich und die sittlichen Ideen im Leven der Völker*. 4th ed. Sangensalza: Herman Beyer, 1904.

Forbes, John. *Opera Omnia*. 2 vols. Amsterdam: Henricus Wetstein, 1702–3.

Fox, James J. *Religion and Morality: Their Nature and Mutual Relations, Historically and Doctrinally Considered*. 2 vols. New York: Young, 1899.

Francken, Aegidius. *Stellige Godgeleertheyd*. 6th ed. 2 vols. Rotterdam: P. H. Losel et al., 1757.

Frank, Fr. H. R. *System der christlichen Wahrheit.* 2nd rev. ed. Erlangen: A. Deichert, 1885–86.

Fritzsche, Carl Friedrich August. *Über Mysticismus und Pietismus: Zwei Vorlesungen.* Halle: Gebauer, 1832.

Gass, W. *Die Lehre vom Gewissen: Ein Beitrag zur Ethik.* Berlin: G. Reimer, 1869.

———. *Geschichte der christlichen Ethik.* 2 vols. in 3. Berlin: G. Reimer, 1881–87.

Geesink, Wilhelm. *De ethiek in de gereformeerde theologie: Rede bij de overdracht van het rectoraat der Vrije Universiteit te Amsterdam op 20 october 1897.* Amsterdam: Kirchner, 1897.

———. *Gereformeerde ethiek, voor den druk gereed gemaakt en voorzien van een levensbeschrijving door Prof. Dr. V. Hepp.* 2 vols. Kampen: Kok, 1931.

Gelderen, J. van, and F. Rozemond. *Gegevens betreffende de Theologische Universiteit Kampen, 1854–1994.* Kampen: Kok, 1994.

Gemeenten en predikanten van de Gereformeerde Kerken in Nederland. N.p.: Algemeen secretariaat van de Gereformeerde Kerken in Nederland, 1992.

Gerhard, Johann. *Meditationes Sacrae.* Leiden: Elzivir, 1629. ET: *Sacred Meditations.* Edited by Gaylin R. Schmeling. Translated by Wade R. Johnston. New Delhi: Magdeburg Press, 2008.

———. *Scholae Pietatis.* Jena: Steinmann, 1622–25. ET: *Schola Pietatis.* Edited by Rachel K. Melvin. Translated by Elmer Hohle. 3 vols. Malone, TX: Repristination Press, 2013–15.

Gerstner, Jonathan Neil. *The Thousand Generation Covenant: Dutch Reformed Covenant Theology and Group Identity in Colonial South Africa, 1652–1814.* Leiden: Brill, 1991.

Gesenius, Friedrich Wilhelm. *Hebrew and Chaldee Lexicon to the Old Testament Scriptures.* Translated by Samuel Prideaux Tragelles. London: Samuel Bagster and Sons, 1857.

Gibbon, Edward. *The History of the Decline and Fall of the Roman Empire.* Edited by J. B. Bury. 12 vols. New York: Fred de Fau and Company, 1906.

Glasius, B. *Godgeleerd Nederland: Biographisch woordenboek van Nederlandsche godgeleerden.* 3 vols. 's-Hertogenbosch: Muller, 1851–56.

Gleason, Ronald N. "The Centrality of the *unio mystica* in the Theology of Herman Bavinck." PhD diss., Westminster Theological Seminary, Philadelphia, 2001.

———. *Herman Bavinck: Pastor, Churchman, Statesman, and Theologian.* Phillipsburg, NJ: P&R, 2010.

Gleiss, Otto. *Christliche Sittenlehre.* Bremen: Heinsius, 1892.

Godet, Frédéric Louis. *Commentary on the Gospel of John: With an Historical and Critical Introduction.* Translated by Timothy Dwight. 2 vols. New York: Funk and Wagnalls, 1886.

Goebel, Max. *Geschichte des christlichen Lebens in der rheinisch-westphälischen evangelischen Kirche.* 3 vols. Coblenz: Bädeker, 1860.

Goethe, Johann Wolfgang von. *Goethe's "Hermann and Dorothea."* Translated by Marmaduke J. Teesdale. 2nd ed. London: Frederic Norgate, 1875.

———. *Hermann und Dorothea.* Edited by C. A. and Emma S. Buchheim. Oxford: Clarendon, 1901.

———. *Wilhelm Meister's Apprenticeship.* In *Goethe: Selected Verse,* introduced and edited by David Luke. London and New York: Penguin, 1964.

Goltz, Eduard von der. *Das Gebet in der ältesten Christenheit: Eine geschichtliche Untersuchung.* Leipzig: J. C. Hinrichs, 1901.

Görres, Joseph von. *Die christliche Mystik.* 4 vols. in 5. Regensburg and Landshut: G. J.

Manz, 1836–42. 2nd ed., 5 vols. Regensburg: G. J. Manz, 1879–80.

———. *The Stigmata: A History of Various Cases.* Translated and edited by Rev. H. Austin. London: Thomas Richardson and Son, 1883.

Gorski, Philip S. *The Disciplinary Revolution: Calvinism and the Rise of the State in Modern Europe.* Chicago: University of Chicago Press, 2003.

Gregory the Great. *Morals on the Book of Job.* PL 75:509–1162 (continued in *PL* 76).

Groe, Theodorus van der. *Toetsteen der waare en valsche genade.* 2 vols. Rotterdam: Hendrik Van Pelt and Adrianus Douci, 1752–53.

Groen van Prinsterer, Guillaume. *Ongeloof en Revolutie: Eene reeks van historische voorlezingen.* 2nd ed. Amsterdam: H. Höveker, 1868. ET: *Groen van Prinsterer's Lectures on Unbelief and Revolution.* Translated and edited by Harry Van Dyke. Jordan Station, ON: Wedge, 1989.

———. *Proeve over de middelen waardoor de waarheid wordt gekend en gestaafd.* 2nd ed. Amsterdam: H. Höveker, 1858.

Grotius, Hugo. *Annotationes in Novum Testamentum.* Groningen: Zuidema, 1830.

Grünberg, Paul. *Philipp Jakob Spener.* 3 vols. Göttingen: Vandenhoeck and Ruprecht, 1893.

Gunning, J. H., Jr. *Jezus Christus de middelaar Gods en der menschen; naar aanleiding van Dr. H. Bavinck "De Theologie van Prof. Dr. Daniel Chantepie de la Saussaye."* Amsterdam: Höveker, 1884.

———. *Overlevering en wetenschap met betrekking tot de evangelische geschiedenis: Inzonderheid van de eerste levensdagen des Heeren.* The Hague: W. A. Beschoor, 1879.

———. *Verzameld Werk, Deel 2, 1879–1905.* Prepared by L. Mietus. Zoetermeer: Boekencentrum, 2014.

Guyau, M. *A Sketch of Morality Independent of Obligation or Sanction.*

Translated by Gertrude Kapteyn. London: Watts, 1898.

Hagenbach, K. R., ed. *Encyklopädie und Methodologie der Theologischen Wissenschaften.* Revised by E. Kautzsch. 10th ed. Leipzig: S. Hirzel, 1880.

———. *Lehrbuch der Dogmengeschichte.* 5th ed. Leipzig: S. Hirzel, 1867. ET: *A History of Christian Doctrines.* Translated by E. H. Plumptre. 3 vols. Edinburgh: T&T Clark, 1883–85.

Hahn, August. *Lehrbuch des christlichen Glaubens.* 2nd rev. ed. 2 vols. Leipzig: Friedrich Christian Wilhelm Vogel, 1857–58.

Hall, Joseph. *Gewissens Rath.* Frankfurt an den Oder: Fincelius, 1677.

———. *Resolutions and Decisions of Divers Practical Cases of Conscience.* In vol. 7 of *The Works of the Right Reverend Joseph Hall, D.D.,* revised by Philip Wynter, 268–414. Oxford: Oxford University Press, 1863.

Hammond, Henry. *A Practicall Catechisme.* Oxford, 1645.

Handelingen der een-en-zestigste vergadering van de Curatoren der Theologische School van "De Gereformeerde Kerken in Nederland," gehouden 3–5 juli 1902 te Kampen. Kampen: Kok, 1901.

Handelingen der twee-en-zestigste vergadering van de Curatoren der Theologische School van "De Gereformeerde Kerken in Nederland," gehouden 1–3 juli 1902 te Kampen. Kampen: Kok, 1902.

Harinck, George, and Gerrit Neven, eds. *Ontmoetingen met Bavinck.* Barneveld: De Vuurbank, 2006.

Harinck, George, C. van der Kooi, and J. Vree, eds. *"Als Bavinck nu maar eens kleur bekende": Aantekeningen van H. Bavinck over de zaak-Netelenbos, het Schriftgezag en de situatie van de Gereformeerde Kerken (november 1919).* Amsterdam: VU Uitgeverij, 1994.

Harless, Gottlieb Christoph Adolph von. *Christliche Ethik*. Stuttgart: Sam. Gottl. Liesching, 1842. 6th rev. ed., 1864. ET: *System of Christian Ethics*. Translated by William Findlay. Clark's Foreign Theological Library, 4/19. Edinburgh: T&T Clark, 1868.

Hartmann, Eduard von. *Die Religion des Geistes*. Berlin: Carl Duncker, 1882.

———. *Phänomenologie des sittlichen Bewusstseins: Prolegomena zu jeder künftigen Ethik*. Berlin, 1879.

Hase, Karl August von. *Evangelische Dogmatik*. Leipzig: Breitkopf and Härtel, 1891.

Hausrath, Adolf. *Der Apostel Paulus*. Heidelberg: Bassermann, 1865.

Heidegger, Johann Heinrich (Johannes Henricus). *Corpus Theologiae Christianae*. 2 vols. Zurich: Johann Heinrich Bodmer, 1700.

———. *Ethicae Christianae Prima Elementa*. Edited by Johannes Curicke. Frankfurt and Leipzig, 1711.

———. *Medulla Theologiae Christianae*. Zürich: David Gessner, 1697.

Heideman, Eugene P. *The Relation of Revelation and Reason in E. Brunner and H. Bavinck*. Assen: Van Gorcum, 1959.

Heinze, Reiner. *Bengel und Oetinger as Vorläufer des deutschen Idealismus*. Inaugural Dissertation, Münster, 1969. https://dds .crl.edu/crldelivery/14439.

Heppe, Heinrich. *Christliche Sittenlehre*. Edited by Albert Kuhnert. Elberfeld: R. L. Friederichs, 1882.

———. *Die Dogmatik der evangelisch-reformirten Kirche*. Elberfeld: K. L. Friderichs, 1861.

———. *Geschichte der quietistischen Mystik in der katholischen Kirche*. Berlin: Hertz, 1875.

———. *Geschichte des Pietismus und der Mystik in der reformirten Kirche,* *namentlich der Niederland*. Leiden: Brill, 1879.

———. *Reformed Dogmatics: Set Out and Illustrated from the Sources*. Revised and edited by Ernst Bizer. Translated by G. T. Thomson. London: Allen and Unwin, 1950. Reprint, Grand Rapids: Baker, 1978.

Herbart, Johann Friedrich. *Johann Friedrich Herbart's Sämmtliche Werke in chronologischer Reihenfolge*. Edited by K. Kehrbach and O. Flügel. 19 vols. Langensalza: H. Beyer, 1887–1912.

Hettinger, Franz. *Apologie des Christenthums*. 8th ed. 5 vols. Freiburg im Breisgau: Herder, 1899–1900.

Hielema, Syd. "Herman Bavinck's Eschatological Understanding of Redemption." ThD diss., Wycliffe College, Toronto School of Theology, 1998.

Hilary of Poitiers. *Tractatus super Psalmos I*. Edited by Anthony Zingerle. CSEL 20. Prague and Leipzig: F. Tempsky, 1891.

Hoedemaker, Ph. J. *De verhouding der ethiek tot de dogmatiek en de practijk der godzaligheid*. Amsterdam: Höveker & Zoon, 1881.

Hoekema, Anthony A. "Herman Bavinck's Doctrine of the Covenant." ThD diss., Princeton Theological Seminary, 1953.

Hoekstra, S. *De ontwikkeling van de zedelijke idee in de geschiedenis: Een hoofdstuk uit de zedeleer*. Amsterdam: Van Kampen, 1862.

Hoeven, Abraham des Amorie van der, Jr. *Catalogus der zeer belangrijk Bibliotheken over Theologie en Oostersche Letterkunde*. Amsterdam: Frederick Muller, 1862.

———. *De godsdienst het wezen van den mensch: Brief aan Dr. J. J. van Oosterzee*. Leeuwarden: G. N. T. Suringar, 1848.

Hofman, Johan Martin. *De spys door het gebed en de dankzegging geheiligt*. The Hague, 1765.

Hofmann, Rudolph. *Die Lehre von dem Gewissen.* Leipzig: J. C. Hinrichs, 1866.

———. *Symboliek.* Translated by P. J. de Roode. Abridged by M. A. Adrianni. Utrecht: Kemink and Zoon, 1892.

Hollaz, David. *Examen Theologicum Acroamaticum Universam Theologiam Thetico-Polemicam Complectens.* Leipzig: Breitkopf and Son, 1763.

Honert, Johannes van den. *De mensch in Christus: Soo als hy al en niet bestaat, naar den eisch van den redeliken en evangelischen godsdienst.* Leiden: Samuel Luchtmans and Son, 1749. 3rd ed. Leiden: Samuel and Johannes Luchtmans, 1761.

Honidus, J. *Zwart en wit register van duysent sonden en vertrostingen.* 2 vols. Utrecht, 1724.

Hoornbeeck, Johannes. *Oratio Funebris, in Obitum reverendi et clarissimi viri, D. Jacobi Revii.* Utrecht, 1651.

———. *Summa Controversianum Religionis.* Utrecht: Johannes à Waesberge, 1653.

———. *Theologia Practica.* 2 vols. Utrecht: Henry Versteeg, 1663–66.

———. *Theologiae Practicae.* 2nd ed. 2 vols. Utrecht: van de Water, 1689.

———. *Theologiae Practicae, Pars prior.* Utrecht: Hendrik Versteeg, 1661.

Hottinger, Johann Heinrich. *Typus Vitae Christianae.* Zürich: Conrad Orell and Co., 1748.

Huet, Conrad Busken. *Het land van Rembrand: Studien over de noordnederlandsche beschaving in de zeventiende eeuw.* 2 vols. Haarlem: H. D. Tjeenk Willink, 1882–84.

Hugenholtz, Philip Reinhold. *Studiën op godsdienst- en zedekundig gebied.* 3 vols. Amsterdam: Van Holkema, 1884–89.

Hunter, D. G. *A Comparison between a King and a Monk / Against the Opponents of the Monastic Life: Two Treatises* by John Chrysostom. Studies in the Bible and Early Christianity 13. Lewiston, NY: Edwin Mellen, 1988.

Huther, J. E., and Heinrich A. W. Meyer. *Critical and Exegetical Handbook to the General Epistles James, Peter, John, and Jude.* Translated by Paton J. Gloag and Clarke H. Irwin. New York: Funk and Wagnalls, 1887.

Huttinga, Wolter. *Participation and Communicability: Herman Bavinck and John Milbank on the Relation between God and the World.* Amsterdam: Buijten and Schipperheijn, 2014.

Imbert-Gourbeyre, A. *Les stigmatisées.* 2 vols. 2nd ed. Paris: Palmé, 1873.

Jaarsma, Cornelius J. *The Educational Philosophy of Herman Bavinck.* Grand Rapids: Eerdmans, 1936.

Jäger, C. F. *Die Grundbegriffe der Christlichen Sittenlehre nach dem Grundsatzen der evangelischen Kirche.* Stuttgart: Rudolf Besser, 1856.

Janet, Paul. *La morale.* Paris: C. Delagrave, 1874.

Jansen, Cornelius. *Augustinus, seu sancti Augustini de humanae naturae sanitate, aegritudine, medicina adversos Pelagianos & Massilienses.* 3 vols. Paris: Soly and Guillemot, 1641.

Jelgersma, Gerbrandus. *Het hysterisch stigma: Een psycho-pathologisch onderzoek.* Amsterdam: Scheltema and Holkema, 1903.

Jerome. *Commentary on Matthew.* Translated by Thomas P. Scheck. FC 117. Washington, DC: Catholic University of America Press, 2008.

Jhering, Rudolph von. *Der Zweck im Recht, Zweiter Band.* Leipzig: Breitkopf and Härtel, 1883.

John Chrysostom. *Homilies of S. John Chrysostom, Archbishop of Constantinople on the Gospel of St. Matthew.* London: Oxford, 1843.

————. *Homilies on Genesis, 46–67*. Translated by Robert C. Hill. FC 87. Washington, DC: Catholic University of America Press, 2012.

————. *Homilies on Romans. NPNF¹* 11:329–504.

————. *Homilies on 2 Corinthians. NPNF¹* 12:271–420.

Junius, Franciscus. *Ecclesiastici sive de natura et administrationibus Ecclesiae Dei*. 3 vols. Frankfurt: Andreas Wechel, 1581.

Justin Martyr. *First Apology. ANF* 1:163–86.

Juvenal. *Satires: Juvenal and Persius*. Translated by George Gilbert Ramsay. London: William Heinemann; New York: Putnam's Sons, 1920.

Kähler, Martin. *Das Gewissen: Die Entwickelung seiner Namen und seines Begriffes; Geschichtliche Untersuchung zur Lehre von der Begründung der sittlichen Erkenntniss*. Halle: Julius Fricke, 1878.

Kant, Immanuel. *Religion within the Limits of Reason Alone*. Translated by Theodore M. Greene and Hoyt H. Hudson. New York: Harper and Row, 1960.

Kapp, W. *Religion und Moral im Christenthum Luthers*. Tübingen: Mohr, 1902.

Keckermann, Bartholomaeus. *Systema Ethicae Tribus Libris*. In vol. 2 of *Operum Omnium*, cols. 249–376. Geneva: Pierre Aubert, 1614.

Kempis, Thomas à. *The Imitation of Christ*. Milwaukee: Bruce, 1940.

————. *St. Lydwine of Schiedam, Virgin*. Translated by Dom Vincent Scully. London: Burns and Oates, 1912.

Keulen, Dirk van. *Bijbel en dogmatiek: Scriftbeschouwing en schriftgebruik in het dogmatisch weerk van A. Kuyper, H. Bavinck, en G. C. Berkouwer*. Kampen: Kok, 2003.

Kingdon, Robert M. *Adultery and Divorce in Calvin's Geneva*. Cambridge, MA: Harvard University Press, 1995.

Kist, Ewaldus. *Beöeffeningsleer of de kennis der middelen, om als een waar leerling van Jesus Christus getroost en heilig te leven*. 4 vols. in 2. Dordrecht: A. Blusse & Zoon, 1804–9. ET: *True Practice of Religion*. Translated by V. 2 vols. in 1. New Orleans: John Ball, 1852.

Klinken, L. van. *Bavinck's paedagogische beginselen*. Meppel: Boom, 1937.

Kluit, M. Elisabeth. *Het Protestantse réveil in Nederland en daarbuiten, 1815–1865*. Amsterdam: H. J. Paris, 1970.

Koch, Anton. *A Handbook of Moral Theology*. Vol. 1. Edited by Arthur Preuss. St. Louis and London: B. Herder, 1918.

Kolb, Robert, and Timothy Wengert, eds. *The Book of Concord: The Confessions of the Evangelical Lutheran Church*. Minneapolis: Fortress, 2000.

König, Georg. *Casus Conscientiae*. Nuremburg: Endteri, 1654.

König, Joseph. *Die Theologie der Psalmen*. Freiburg im Breisgau: Herder, 1857.

König, Reinhard. *Collegii Politici Disputatio Duodecima*. Rinteln: Peter Lucius, 1648.

————. *Disputatio, de Bono et Malo Principe*. Rinteln: Peter Lucius, 1651.

————. *Dissertatio Politica de Oeconomia Principis*. Jena: Johann Beithmann, 1618.

Köster, Friedrich. *Die biblische Lehre von der Versuchung*. Gotha: F. A. Perthes, 1859.

Köstlin, Julius. *Luthers Theologie in ihrer geschichtlichen Entwicklung und ihrem inneren Zusammenhange dargestellt*. 2 vols. Stuttgart: J. F. Steinkopf, 1863.

Krummacher, Emil Wilhelm. *Expectorationen über das Studium der Theologie: Vade mecum für meinen Herrmann und für Theologie Studirende überhaupt*. Essen: Bädeker, 1847.

Kuipers, Tjitze. *Abraham Kuyper: An Annotated Bibliography, 1857–2010*. Leiden: Brill, 2011.

Kuyper, Abraham. *Concise Works of the Holy Spirit*. Chattanooga, TN: AMG, 1995, 2001.

———. *De gemeene gratie*. Vol. 2. 3rd ed. Kampen: Kok, 1932.

———. *De hedendaagsche Schriftcritiek in haar bedenkelijke strekking voor de gemeente des levenden Gods*. Amsterdam: J. H. Kruyt, 1881.

———. *De verflauwing der grenzen*. Amsterdam: J. A. Wormser, 1892.

———. *De vleeschwording des Woords*. Amsterdam: J. A. Wormser, 1887.

———. *Drie kleine vossen*. Kampen: Kok, 1901.

———. *Encyclopaedie der heilige godgeleerdheid*. 2nd ed. 3 vols. Kampen: Kok, 1908–9.

———. *E Voto Dordraceno: Toelichting op den Heidelbergsche Catechismus*. 4 vols. Amsterdam: J. A. Wormser, 1892–95.

———. *Lectures on Calvinism*. Grand Rapids: Eerdmans, 1931.

———. *Ons Program*. Amsterdam: J. H. Kruyt, 1879. ET: *Our Program: A Christian Political Manifesto*. Edited and translated by Harry Van Dyke. Bellingham, WA: Lexham, 2015.

———. *Our Worship*. Edited by Harry Boonstra. Translated by Harry Boonstra, Henry Baron, Gerrit Sheeres, and Leonard Sweetman. Grand Rapids: Eerdmans, 2009.

———. *Principles of Sacred Theology*. Translated by J. Hendrik de Vries. Grand Rapids: Eerdmans, 1954.

———. *The Work of the Holy Spirit*. Translated by Henri De Vries. New York and London: Funk and Wagnalls, 1900. Reprint, Grand Rapids: Eerdmans, 1941.

Lactantius. *Divine Institutes*. ANF 7:9–223.

Laertius, Diogenes. *Lives and Opinions of Eminent Philosophers*. Translated by R. D. Hicks. 2 vols. LCL. London: Heinemann; New York: Putnam's Sons, 1835.

———. *Lives and Opinions of Eminent Philosophers*. Translated by C. D. Yonge. London: Henry G. Bohn, 1853.

Laird, Raymond. *Mindset, Moral Choice, and Sin in the Anthropology of John Chrysostom*. Early Christian Studies 15. Strathfield, NSW, Australia: St. Paul's Publications, 2012.

Lamers, G. H. *Godsdienst en zedelijkheid beschouwd in onderling verband*. Amsterdam: W. H. Kirberger, 1882.

Lampe, Frederik Adolph. *Geheimnis des Gnaden-bunds*. 4 vols. Bremen: Philip Gottfr. Saumans, 1716–19. Dutch translation: *De verborgentheit van het genaadeverbondt*. 3rd ed. Amsterdam: Antony Schoonenburg, 1725.

———. *Schets der dadelyke Godt-geleertheid*. Translated by Bernhardus Keppel. Rotterdam: Losel, 1739.

Lange, Johann Peter. *Christliche Dogmatik*. 3 vols. Heidelberg: Karl Winter, 1849–52.

Lapide, Cornelius à. *The Great Commentary of Cornelius à Lapide*. Translated by Thomas W. Mossman. 8 vols. 4th ed. London: John Hodges, 1890.

La Placette, Jean. *The Christian Casuist: or, A Treatise of Conscience*. Translated by B. Kennett. London: A. & J. Churchill and R. Sare, 1705.

———. *La morale chrétienne*. Amsterdam: George Gallet, 1701.

Lasco, John à. *Opera*. Edited by Abraham Kuyper. Amsterdam: F. Muller, 1866.

Laurillard, E. *De zeven hoofdzonden: Zeven voordrachten*. 3rd ed. Amsterdam: Centen, 1881.

Lecky, William Edward Hartpole. *History of European Morals from Augustus to Charlemagne*. 2 vols. 3rd ed. New York: D. Appleton, 1877.

Leeuwarden, N. S. van. *De bevestigde Christen*. Amsterdam: Jacobus Borstius, 1725.

Lichtenfels, Johann. *Lehrbuch zur Einleitung in die Philosophie: Allgemeine Einleitung, Psychologie, Logik.* 5th rev. ed. Vienna: W. Braumüller, 1863.

Liddell, Henry George. *An Intermediate Greek-English Lexicon: Founded upon the Seventh Edition of Liddell and Scott's Greek-English Lexicon.* London: Clarendon, 1888.

Limborch, Philip van. *Theologia Christiana.* 4 vols. Amsterdam: Henricus Wetstenius, 1686.

Lindeboom, C., and W. F. M. Lindeboom. *In uwe voorhoven: Ter herinnering aan het leven en den arbeid van Ds. C. Lindeboom.* Amsterdam: S. J. P. Bakker, 1938.

Lindner, Gustaph Adolph. *Lehrbuch der empirischen Psychologie, als inductiver Wissenschaft.* 8th ed. Vienna: C. Gerold's Sohn, 1885.

Linsenmayer, Anton. *Entwicklung der kirchlichen Fastendisciplin bis zum Konzil von Nicäa.* Munich: Stahl, 1877.

Livy. *The History of Rome.* Translated by D. Spillan. London: Henry G. Bohn, 1853.

Löber, Richard. *Das innere Leben: Ein Beitrag zur theologischen Ethik und zur Verständigung mit der münigen Gemeinde.* Gotha: Gustav Schloessmann, 1867.

———. *Das innere Leben, oder der Verkehr des Christen mit Gott und Menschen.* 3rd ed. Gotha: Schloessmann, 1900.

———. *Die Lehre vom Gebet aus der immanenten und ökonomische Trinität.* 2nd rev. ed. Erlangen: Andreas Deichert, 1860.

Lobstein, Paul. *Die Ethik Calvins in Ihren Grundzügen Entworfen.* Strasbourg: C. F. Schmidt (F. Bull), 1877.

Lodensteyn, Jodocus van. *De weegschaal van de onvolmaaktheden der heyligen.* Utrecht: Henricus Versteegh, 1664.

Love, Christopher. *The Christians Combat: or, His True Spiritual Warfare.* London: Charles Tyus, 1664.

———. *The Combate between the Flesh and Spirit.* London, 1654. Dutch translation: *De Stryd tusschen vleesch en geest.* In *Theologia Practica,* 1–95.

———. *The Sum or Substance of Practical Divinity.* London, 1654. Dutch translation: *Het mergh van de werkige godtgeleerdtheidt,* etc. Translated by Jacobus Coelman. Utrecht: Henricus Versteegh, 1657.

———. *Theologia Practica, dat is: Alle de theologische wercken.* Amsterdam: Jacob Benjamin et al., 1664.

Luthardt, Christoph Ernst. *Die Ethik Luthers in ihren Grundzügen dargestellt.* Leipzig: 1867. 2nd rev. ed. Leipzig: Dörffling and Franke, 1875.

———. *Geschichte der christlichen Ethik.* 3 vols. Leipzig: Dörffling and Franke, 1888–93.

———. *Kompendium der theologischen Ethik.* Leipzig: Dörffling and Franke, 1896.

Luther, Martin. *Lectures on the First Epistle of St. John.* In *Luther's Works,* vol. 30, *The Catholic Epistles.* Edited by Jaroslav Pelikan and Walter A. Hansen. St. Louis: Concordia, 1967.

———. *The Theologia Germanica of Martin Luther.* Edited and translated by Bengt Hoffman. Classics of Western Spirituality. Mahwah, NJ: Paulist Press, 1980.

Maccovius, Johannes. *Casus Conscientiae.* In *Johannes Maccovius Redivivus: Seu manuscripta ejus typis exscripta.* Edited by Nicolaus Arnoldi. Franeker: Idzard Albert, 1654.

Maeterlinck, Maurice. *De schat des harten.* Translated by G. M. v. d. Wissel-Herderschee. Amsterdam: S. L. Van Looy, 1897.

Marckius, Johannes. *Compendium Theologiae Christianae Didactico-Elencticum.* 3rd ed. Amsterdam: R. & G. Westenios, 1722.

———. *Het merch der christelijke Godts-geleertheit*, etc. Amsterdam: Borstius, 1705.

———. *Historia Paradis Illustrata, Libris Quatuor*. Amsterdam: Gerardus Borstius, 1705.

Maresius, Samuel. *Collegium Theologicum: Sive Breve Systema Universae Theologiae*. Groningen: J. Nicholaus, 1649.

———. *Collegium Theologicum*. Geneva: Johann Antonius and Samuel de Tournes, 1662.

———. *Sylloge Disputationum aliquot Selectiorum*. Groningae Frisiorum: Cöllenius, 1660, 1662.

———. *Systema Theologicum*. Groningen: Aemilium Spinneker, 1673.

Marshall, Walter. *The Gospel-Mystery of Sanctification Opened in Sundry Practical Directions . . . to Which Is Added a Sermon of Justification*. London: T. Parkhurst, 1692.

Martensen, Hans Lassen. *Den christelige Ethik*. 3 vols. Copenhagen: Gyldendal, 1871–78. ET: *Christian Ethics*. Translated by C. Spence, William Affleck, and Sophia Taylor. 3 vols. Edinburgh: T&T Clark, 1871–89. German translation of vol. 1: *Die christliche Ethik*. Gotha: R. Besser, 1871; of vol. 2: *Die individuelle Ethik*. Gotha: R. Besser, 1878; of vol. 3: *Die sociale Ethik*. Gotha: R. Besser, 1878.

Martensen, H., and Gottlieb Christoph Adolf von Harless. *Christian Ethics: A System based on Martensen and Harless*. Prepared by Reverend Franklin Weidner. 2nd ed. New York: Fleming H. Revell, 1897.

Mastricht, Petrus van. *Beschouwende en praktikale godgeleerdheit*. 4 vols. Rotterdam: Hendrik van Pelt, et al.; Utrecht: Jan Jacob van Poolsum, 1749–53.

———. *Theoretico-Practica Theologia*. Amsterdam: Boom and Vidua, 1682. 3rd ed. Utrecht: W. van de Water, 1724.

Mattson, Brian G. *Restored to Our Destiny: Eschatology and the Image of God in Herman Bavinck's Reformed Dogmatics*. Leiden: Brill, 2011.

Meade, Matthew. *The Almost Christian Discovered; or, The False Professor Tried and Cast*. New York: Sheldon, Blakeman, and Co., 1856.

Meier, Gebhardt Theodor, and Johann Holste. *Disputationes Theologicae . . . Moralis Exhibentes*. Helmstedt: Heinrich David Müller, 1679.

Melanchthon, Philip. *Enarratio Aliquot Librorum Ethicorum Aristotelis*. Wittenberg, 1529.

———. *Philosophiae Moralis*. Leiden: Sébastien Gryphius, 1538.

Meyer, Heinrich August Wilhelm. *Critical and Exegetical Handbook to the Epistle to the Ephesians*. Translated by Maurice J. Evans. Revised and edited by William P. Dickson. New York: Funk and Wagnalls, 1892.

———. *Critical and Exegetical Handbook to the Epistle to the Galatians*. Translated by G. H. Venables. New York: Funk and Wagnalls, 1884.

———. *Critical and Exegetical Handbook to the Epistle to the Romans*. Edited by William P. Dickson. Translated by John C. Moore and Edwin Johnson. New York: Funk and Wagnalls, 1884.

———. *Critical and Exegetical Handbook to the Epistles to the Corinthians*. Translated by D. Douglas Bannerman. Revised and edited by William P. Dickson. New York: Funk and Wagnalls, 1884.

———. *Kritisch exegetischer Kommentar über das Neue Testament*. 3 vols. Göttingen: Vandenhoeck and Ruprecht, 1886–88.

———. *Kritisch exegetisches Handbuch über die drei Briefe des Johannes*. Göttingen: Vandenhoeck and Ruprecht, 1855.

———. *Romans–Colossians*. Translated by George H. Schodde and Epiphanius

Wilson. Vol. 3 of *A Commentary on the New Testament*. New York: Funk and Wagnalls, 1906.

Michaelis, Daniel. *De Primo Hominis Primi Peccato Exercitatio*. Rostock: Kilius, 1651.

Möhler, Johann Adam. *Symbolik oder Darstellung der dogmatischen Gegensatze der Katholischen und Protestanten nach ihren öffentlichen Bekenntnißschriften.* Mainz: Florian Kupferberg, 1838.

Moll, Willem. *Johannes Brugman en het godsdienstig leven onzer vaderen in de vijftiende eeuw*. 2 vols. in 1. Amsterdam: G. Portielje & Zoon, 1854.

Momma, Wilhelm. *De Varia Conditione et Statu Ecclesiae Dei sub Triplici Oeconomia: Patriarcharum, ac Testamenti Veteris, et Denique Novi*. 2nd ed. Amsterdam: Joannis à Sommeren, 1683.

Monrad, Ditlev Gothard. *Aus der Welt des Gebet*. 10th ed. Gotha: F. A. Perthes, 1890. Dutch translation: *Het Leven des Gebeds*. Translated by A. Michelsen. Amsterdam: Höveker, 1881. ET: *The World of Prayer; or, Prayer in Relation to Personal Religion*. Translated by J. S. Banks. Edinburgh: T&T Clark, 1879.

Moor, Bernardinus de. *Commentarius Perpetuus in Joh. Marckii Compendium Theologiae Christianae Didactico-Elencticum*. 7 vols. Leiden: J. Hasebroek, 1761–71.

Mosheim, Johann Lorenz. *Kern uit de zedeleer der Heilige Schrift*. 2 vols. Utrecht: Gisbert and Timon van Paddenburg, 1865.

———. *Sitten-Lehre der Heiligen Schrift*. 9 vols. Helmstädt: Christian Friedrich Weygand, 1735–70.

———. *Sitten-Lehre der Heiligen Schrift*. 3rd ed. Heimstadt: Christian Friedrich Weygand, 1764.

Müller, E. F. Karl. *Zur christlichen Erkenntnis: Vorträge und Aufsätze für denkende Christen*. Leipzig: Deichert, 1898.

Müller, Julius. *Die christliche Lehre von der Sünde*. 2 vols. 5th ed. Breslau: J. Max, 1867. ET: *The Christian Doctrine of Sin*. Translated by William Pulsford. 2 vols. Clark's Foreign Theological Library 27, 29. Edinburgh: T&T Clark, 1852–53.

Muller, Richard. *Dictionary of Latin and Greek Theological Terms—Drawn Principally from Protestant Scholastic Theology.* Grand Rapids: Baker, 1985.

Murisier, Ernest. *Les maladies du sentiment religieux*. Paris: Alcan, 1901.

Musculus, Wolfgang. *Common Places of Christian Religion*. London: Henry Bynncman, 1578.

Myseras, Lambrecht. *Der vromen ondervinding op den weg naar den hemel*. The Hague: Gerardus Winterswyk, 1725. 9th ed., 1739.

Nathusius, Martin von. *Das Wesen der Wissenschaft und ihre Anwendung auf die Religion: Empirische Grundlegung für die theologische Methodologie*. Leipzig: Hinrichs, 1885.

Neal, Daniel. *History of the Puritans or Protestant Nonconformists from the Reformation in 1517 to the Revolution in 1688*. New York: Harper & Brothers, 1843–44.

Neander, A. *Vorlesungen über geschichte der christlichen ethic*. Prepared by Christian Friedrich David Erdmann. Berlin: Wiegandt and Grieben, 1864.

Neele, Adriaan C. *Petrus van Mastricht (1630–1706)—Reformed Orthodoxy: Method and Piety*. Brill Series in Church History 35. Leiden: Brill, 2009.

Nicholls, Angus. *Goethe's Concept of the Daemonic, after the Ancients*. Rochester, NY: Camden House, 2006.

Nitzsch, Carl Immanuel. *System of Christian Doctrine*. Translated by Robert Montgomery and John Hennen. Edinburgh: T&T Clark, 1849.

Noffke, Suzanne. *Catherine of Sienna: The Dialogue*. Mahwah, NJ: Paulist Press, 1980.

Oehler, Gustav Friedrich. *Theology of the Old Testament*. Translated by George E. Day. 2nd ed. New York: Funk and Wagnalls, 1884.

Olearius, Johannes. *Doctrina Theologiae Moralis*. Leipzig: Johann Christian Wohlfart, 1703.

Oomius, Simon. *Dissertatie van de onderwijsingen in de practycke der godgeleerdheid*. Bolsward: Samuel van Haringhouk, 1672.

———. *Institutiones Theologiae Practicae*. Bolsward: Samuel Harinhouk, 1676.

Oosterzee, Johannes Jacob van. *Christelijke dogmatiek*. 2 vols. Utrecht: Kemink and Zoon, 1876. ET: *Christian Dogmatics: A Text-Book for Academical Instruction and Private Study*. Translated by John W. Watson and Maurice J. Evans. 2 vols. New York: Scribner, Armstrong and Co., 1874.

———. *Practical Theology: A Manual for Theological Students*. Translated and adapted by Maurice J. Evans. London: Hodder and Stoughton, 1878.

———. *Sieben Vorträge: Ein Beitrag zur Charakteristik der gegenwärtigen Bewegungen auf theologischem und kirchlichem Gebiete*. Translated and edited by F. Meyeringh. Gotha: F. A. Perthes, 1875.

———. *Voor kerk en theologie: Mededeelingen en bijdragen*. 2 vols. Utrecht: Kemink and Zoon, 1872–75.

Oppenheim, L. *Das Bewissen*. Basel: B. Schwabe, 1898.

Osiander, Johannes Adam. *Theologia Moralis*. Tübingen: Johann Georg Cotta, 1678.

Ostervald, Jean-Frédéric. *Ethicae Christianae Compendium*. London: William Mears, 1727.

Owen, John. *The Doctrine of Justification by Faith*. Reprint, Grand Rapids: Reformation Heritage, 2006.

Palmer, Christian D. F. *Evangelische Pastoraltheologie*. 2nd rev. ed. Stuttgart: J. F. Steinkopf, 1863.

———. *Pastoraal-theologie*. Freely adapted by J. J. Van Hille. Utrecht: Kemink and Zoon, 1866.

Palmer, Heinrich Julius E. *Der christliche Glaube und das christliche Leben*. Darmstadt: Jonghaus, 1847.

Pareau, L. G. *Initia Institutionis Christianae Moralis*. Groningen: Jan Oomkens, 1842.

Pascal, Blaise. *Pensées*. Translated by W. F. Trotter and Thomas M'Crie. New York: Modern Library, 1941.

Pelt, A. F. L. *Theologische Encyklopädie als System im Zusammenhange mit der Geschichte der theologischen Wissenschaft und ihrer einzelnen Zweige*. Hamburg and Gotha: Perthes, 1843.

Perkins, William. *Alle de Werken van Mr. William Perkins*. 3 vols. Amsterdam: Johannes van Zomeren, 1659–63.

———. *Anatomia Sacrae Humanae Conscientiae*. In *Opera Omnia Theologica, in duos tomos tribute*, 1:1179–268. 2 vols. Geneva: P. & J. Chouet, 1618–24.

———. *Aureae Casuum Conscientiae Decisiones*. Basel: Conrad Walkirch, 1609.

———. *A Case of Conscience, the Greatest That Ever Was*, with *A Brief Discourse, Taken out of the Writings of Hier. Zanchius, wherein the Aforesaid Case of Conscience Is Disputed and Resolved*. Edinburgh: Robert Waldegrave, 1592. Dutch translations: *Eene Verhandeling van de Gevallen der Conscientie*. Amsterdam: J. van Zomeren, 1662. Reprint, *Alle de Werken*, 3:115–265; and *Van de zekerheyt der zaligheyt, uyt H. Zanchius*. Reprint, *Alle de Werken*, 3:273–85.

———. *The Combat between Christ and the Devil*. In *Workes*, 3:371–41. Dutch translation: *Strijdt tusschen Christus, en deb Duyvel*. Reprint, *Alle de Werken*, 3^2:3–44. The superscripted 2 indicates

pages after the page numbering was restarted at 1, after p. 328.

———. *The Combat of the Flesh and Spirit.*
In *Workes,* 1:469–74. Dutch translation:
Van den strijdt tusschen vleesch en Geest.
Reprint, *Alle de Werken,* 3:301–9.

———. *A Declaration of Certaine Spirituall
Desertions, Serving to Terrifie All Drowsie
Protestants, and to Comfort Them Which
Mourne for Their Sinnes.* In *Whole Works,*
vol. 3. Dutch translation: *Een verklaringe
van de Geestelijke verlaatingen.* Reprint,
Alle de Werken, 3^2:165–73. The superscripted 2 indicates pages after the page
numbering was restarted at 1, after p. 328.

———. *A Dialogue Containing the Conflicts betweene Sathan and a Christian.* In
*A Treatise Tending unto a Declaration,
Whether a Man Be in the Estate of Damnation, or in the Estate of Grace,* etc. London: R. Robinson, for T. Gubbin & I. Por-
ter, [1590]. In *The Whole Works of . . .
M. William Perkins,* vol. 1. London: John
Legatt, 1631. Dutch translation: *Strijdt tusschen den Duyvel en een Christen.* Reprint,
Alle de Werken, 3^2:152–58. The superscripted 2 indicates pages after the page
numbering was restarted at 1, after p. 328.

———. *A Golden Chaine: or, The Description of Theologie, Containing the Order
of the Cases of Salvation and Damnation,
according to God's Word.* Cambridge:
John Legat, 1600.

———. *A Graine of Mystard-Seed.* Reprinted in *Workes,* 1:637–46. Dutch translation: *Het mostaart-zaatjen of de minste
mate der genade die 'er is, of wezen kan,
krachtig tot de zaligheyt.* Reprint, *Alle
de Werken,* 3^2:81–92. The superscripted 2
indicates pages after the page numbering
was restarted at 1, after p. 328.

———. *Hoe verre een verworpene kan gaan
in den Christelijken wandel.* Reprint, *Alle
de Werken,* 3^2:93–101. The superscripted 2
indicates pages after the page numbering
was restarted at 1, after p. 328.

———. *A Salve for a Sick Man, or A Treatise . . . the Right Manner of Dying Well.*
London: John Legatt, 1616. In *Workes,*
1:487–516. Dutch translation: *Salve voor
een sieck mensche ('t Rechte middle om
wel te sterven).* Amsterdam: Jan Evertsz.
Cloppenburch, 1604. Reprint, *Alle de
Werken,* 3^2:237–64. The superscripted 2
indicates pages after the page numbering
was restarted at 1, after p. 328.

———. *The Whole Treatise of the Cases
of Conscience, Distinguished into Three
Bookes.* Cambridge: John Legatt, 1606.
Reprinted in *Workes,* 2:1–152.

———. *The Whole Works of . . . M. William
Perkins.* 3 vols. London: John Legatt, 1631.

———. *The Workes of . . . M. William Perkins.* 3 vols. London: John Legatt, 1626–31.

Perty, Maximillian. *Die Anthropologie als
die Wissenschaft von dem körperlichen
und geistigen Wesen des Menschen.* 2 vols.
2nd ed. Leipzig, 1874.

Pfaff, Christoph Matthaeus. *Institutiones
Theologia Dogmaticae et Moralis.* Frankfurt am Main: J. G. Cotta, 1721.

Pfanner, Tobias. *Systema Theologiae Gentilis
Purioris.* Basel: Joh. H. Widerhold, 1679.

Pfleiderer, Otto. *Moral und Religion nach
ihrem gegenseitigen Verhältniss.* Leipzig:
Fues (R. Reisland), 1872.

———. *Paulinism: A Contribution to the
History of Primitive Christian Theology.*
Translated by Edward Peters. 2 vols. Lon-
don: Williams and Norgate, 1877.

Philippi, Friedrich Adolph. *Commentar über
den Brief Pauli an die Römer.* 3 vols. Erlangen: von Heyder and Zimmer, 1848–52.
ET: *Commentary on St. Paul's Epistle to
the Romans.* Translated by J. S. Banks. 2
vols. Clark's Foreign Theological Library,
new series, 60–61. Edinburgh: T&T
Clark, 1878.

———. *Kirchliche Glaubenslehre.* 6 vols.
in 8. 2nd ed. Stuttgart: S. G. Leisching,
1864–82.

Pictet, Bénédict. *De christelyke zedekunst, of schriftuurlyke en natuurkundige grondtregels om godvruchtig le leeven, en zalig te sterven.* Translated by François Halma. 2nd ed. The Hague: Pieter van Thol, 1731.

Pierson, Allard. *Eene Levensbeschouwing.* 2 vols. Haarlem: Kruseman and Tjeenk Willink, 1875.

———. *Nieuwe Studiën over Johannes Kalvijn (1536–1541).* Amsterdam: Van Kampen, 1883.

———. *Studiën over Johannes Kalvijn (1527–1536).* Amsterdam: Van Kampen, 1881.

———. *Studiën over Johannes Kalvijn, derde reeks (1527–1542).* Amsterdam: Van Kampen, 1891.

Plato. *Euthyphro, Crito, Apology, Symposium.* Translated by Benjamin Jowett. Washington, DC: Regnery Gateway, 1953.

———. *Greater Hippias.* Translated by H. N. Fowler. LCL 167. Cambridge, MA: Harvard University Press, 1926.

Polanus von Polansdorf, Amandus. *Syntagma Theologiae Christianae.* Hanover: Johann Aubry, 1615.

Polyander, Johann, et al. *Synopsis Purioris Theologiae: Disputationes Quinquaginta Duabus Comprehensa ac Conscripta per Johannem Polyandrum, Andream Rivetum, Antonium Walaeum, Antonium Thysium.* Leiden: Elzevier, 1625. 6th ed. Edited by Herman Bavinck. Leiden: Brill, 1881. ET: *Synopsis Purioris Theologiae / Synopsis of a Purer Theology: Latin Text and English Translation.* 2 vols. Edited by Willem J. van Asselt et al. Brill Studies in Medieval and Reformation Traditions 187. Leiden: Brill, 2014–16.

Preger, Wilhelm. *Geschichte der deutschen Mystik im Mittelalter nach den Quellen untersucht und dargestellt.* 3 vols. Leipzig: Dörffling and Franke, 1874–93.

———. *Ongeloof en revolutie: Eene reeks van historische voorlezingen.* 2nd ed. Amsterdam: H. Höveker, 1868.

———. *Proeve over de middelen waardoor de waarheid wordt gekend en gestaafd.* 2nd ed. Amsterdam: H. Höveker, 1858.

Proost, Pieter J. *Jodocus van Lodenstein: Eene kerkhistorische studie.* Amsterdam: Brandt, 1880.

Prosper of Aquitaine. *The Call of All Nations.* ACW 14. Edited by Johannes Quasten and Joseph C. Plumpe. Translated by P. De Letter. Westminster, MD: Newman Press; London: Longmans, Green and Co., 1952.

Proudhon, Pierre-Joseph. *No Gods, No Masters: An Anthology of Anarchism.* Edited by Daniel Guerin. Translated by Paul Sharkey. Oakland, CA: AK Press, 2005.

Puerari, Daniel. *Theses Logicae atque Ethicae.* Geneva: Gamonet, 1660.

Qualben, Lars P. *A History of the Christian Church.* Rev. and exp. ed. Eugene, OR: Wipf and Stock, 2008 (1933).

Quasten, Johannes. *Patrologia.* Vol. 3. Allen, TX: Christian Classics, n.d.

Räbiger, Julius Ferdinand. *Theologik oder Encyklopädie der Theologie.* Leipzig: Fues, 1880.

Rauwenhoff, L. W. E. *Wijsbegeerte van den godsdienst.* Leiden: E. J. Brill and S. C. Van Doesburgh, 1887.

Reinhard, Franz Volkmar. *System der Christlichen Moral.* 5 vols. Wittenberg: Samuel Gottfried Zimmermann, 1788–1815.

Reuver, Arie de. *Sweet Communion: Trajectories of Spirituality from the Middle Ages through the Further Reformation.* Translated by James A. De Jong. Grand Rapids: Baker Academic, 2007.

Ridderus (de Ridder), Franciscus. *De mensche Godts: Uyt de geschriften en tractaten van Willem Teellingh.* Hoorn: Gerbrandt and Ian Martensz, 1658. Cf. W. Teellinck, *De mensche Godts,* below.

———. *Het leven van onzen Heere Jesus Christus, tot een voorbeeld van navolging aen allen Christenen voorgesteld.* The Hague: Daniel Langeweg, 1737.

Ritschl, Albrecht. *Die christliche Lehre von der Rechtfertigung und Versöhnung.* 3 vols. Bonn: Adolphus Marcus, 1882–83.

———. *Geschichte des Pietismus.* 3 vols. Bonn: Adolphus Marcus, 1880–86.

———. "'Prolegomena' to *The History of Pietism.*" In *Three Essays*, translated by Philip Hefner, 51–148. Philadelphia: Fortress, 1972. Reprint, Eugene, OR: Wipf and Stock, 2005.

Rivetus, Andreas. *Praelectiones in Caput XX Exodi.* Leiden: Frans de Heger, 1637.

Roessingh, K. H. *De moderne theologie in Nederland: Hare voorbereiding en eerste periode.* Groningen: B. van der Kamp, 1914.

———. *Het modernisme in Nederland.* Haarlem: F. Bohn, 1922.

Rombouts, S. *Prof. Dr. H. Bavinck, gids bij de studie van zijn paedagogische werken.* 's-Hertogenbosch-Antwerpen: Malmberg, 1922.

Roques, Pierre. *Le vray pietisme ou traité.* Basel: Jean Brandmuller, 1731.

Rothe, Richard. *Theologische Ethik.* 3 vols. in 4. Wittenberg: Zimmerman, 1845–48. 2nd rev. ed. 5 vols. Wittenberg: H. Koelling, 1869–71.

Runze, G. *Ethik: Encyklopädische Skizzen und Literaturangaben zur Sittenlehre.* 3 vols. Berlin: Carl Duncker, 1891.

Sabatier, Paul. *Life of St. Francis of Assisi.* Translated by Louise Seymour Houghton. London: Hodder and Stoughton, 1901.

Sack, Karl Heinrich. *Christliche Polemik.* Hamburg: F. Perthes, 1838.

Saldenus, Wilhelmus. *Een Christen vallende en opstande.* Leiden: Donner, 1884.

Sanderson, Robert. *De Obligatione Conscientiae.* London: R. Littlebury, R. Scott, T. Sawbridge, and G. Wells, 1686.

Saurin, Jaques. *Abregé de la théologie et de la morale chrétienne en forme de catechisme.* Amsterdam: Henri du Sauzet, 1722.

Saussaye, Daniel Chantepie de la. *De godsdienstige bewegingen van dezen tijd in haren oorsprong geschetst: Vier voorlezingen.* Rotterdam: E. H. Tassemeijer, 1863.

———. *La crise religieuse en Hollande.* Leiden: De Breuk and Smits, 1860.

———. *Manual of the Science of Religion.* Translated by Beatrice S. Colyer-Fergusson (née Max Müller). London: Longmans, Green, 1891.

Scharling, Carl Henrik. *Christliche Sittenlehre nach evangelisch-lutherischer Auffassung.* Translated by Otto Gleiss. Bremen: M. Heinsius, 1892.

Schenkel, Daniel. *Die christliche Dogmatik vom Standpunkte des Gewissens aus dargestellt.* 2 vols. in 1. Wiesbaden: Kreidel und Niedner, 1858–59.

Scherr, Johannes. *Menschliche Tragikomödie: Gesammelte Studien und Bilder, Erster Band.* Leipzig: Otto Wigand, 1874.

Schleiermacher, Friedrich. *The Christian Faith.* Edited by H. R. Mackintosh and J. S. Stewart. Edinburgh: T&T Clark, 1928. Reprint, London: T&T Clark, 1999.

———. *Die christliche Sitte nach den Grundsätzen der evangelischen Kirche im Zusammenhange dargestellt.* In *Sämmtliche Werke*, 1. Abtheilung zur Theologie, edited by Ludwig Jonas. Berlin: G. Reimer, 1843. ET of selections: *Selections from Friedrich Schleiermacher's "Christian Ethics."* Edited and translated by James M. Brandt. Louisville: Westminster John Knox, 2011.

———. *Entwurf eines Systems der Sittenlehre.* Prepared by Alexander Schweizer. Berlin: Reimer, 1835.

———. *Grundlinien einer Kritik der bisherigen Sittenlehre.* Berlin: Verlag der Realschulbuchhandlung, 1803.

———. *Grundriß der philosophischen Ethik.* Berlin: G. Reimer, 1841.

————. *Lectures on Philosophical Ethics.* Edited by Robert B. Louden. Cambridge: Cambridge University Press, 2002.

————. *Selections from Friedrich Schleiermacher's "Christian Ethics."* Edited and translated by James M. Brandt. Louisville: Westminster John Knox, 2011.

Schmid, Christian Friedrich. *Biblical Theology of the New Testament.* Translated by G. H. Venables. 2nd ed. Edinburgh: T&T Clark, 1877.

————. *Christliche Sittenlehre.* Produced by A. Heller. Stuttgart: S. G. Liesching, 1861.

Schmid, H. F. F. *The Doctrinal Theology of the Evangelical Lutheran Church.* Translated by Charles A. Hay and Henry E. Jacobs. 3rd rev. ed. Minneapolis: Augsburg, 1899.

Schneckenburger, Matthias. *Vergleichende Darstellung des lutherischen und reformirten Lehrbegriffs.* Edited by Eduard Güder. 2 vols. in 1. Stuttgart: J. B. Metzler, 1855.

————. *Vorlesungen über die Lehrbegriffe der kleineren protestantischen Kirchenparteien.* Frankfurt am Main: H. L. Brönner, 1863.

Scholten, Johannes Henricus. *De leer der Hervormde Kerk.* 5 vols. in 1. Leiden: P. Engels, 1848–52. 4th rev. ed., 1861–62.

————. *De vrije wil: Kritisch onderzoek.* Leiden: P. Engels, 1859.

Schopenhauer, A. *Die beiden Grundprobleme der Ethik.* Berlin: Deutsche Buch Gemeinschaft, 1860. 3rd ed. Leipzig: F. A. Brockhaus, 1881.

Schortinghuis, Wilhelmus. *Het innige Christendom.* Groningen: Jurjen Spandaw, 1740.

Schweizer, Alexander. *Die Glaubenslehre der evangelisch-reformirten Kirche.* 2 vols. Zurich: Orell, Füssli, and Co., 1844–47.

————. *Die protestantischen Centraldogmen in ihrer Entwicklung innerhalb der reformirten Kirche.* 2 vols. Zurich: Orell, Füssli, and Co., 1854–56.

Seneca. *Moral Letters to Lucilius.* Translated by Richard Mott Gummere. LCL 75–77. Cambridge, MA: Harvard University Press, 1917–25.

Shedd, William G. T. *Dogmatic Theology.* 3 vols. New York: Charles Scribner's Sons, 1888.

Sibbes, Richard. *The Bruised Reed.* Carlisle, PA: Banner of Truth, 1998 (1630).

Smeding, Hendrik. *Paulinische Gewetensleer.* Utrecht: Kemink and Zoon, 1873.

Sohn, Georg. *Operum Georgii Sohnii Sacrae Theologiae Doctoris.* Herborn: Christoph Rab, 1591.

Souter, Daniel. *Troost-basuyn op alle klaegh-lieden der Christenen in allerley verdriet.* Nimwegen: C. A. Hervelt, 1634. Reprint, 1994.

Spangenberg, August Gottlieb. *Idea Fidei Fratrum oder kürzer Begriff der Christlichen Lehre in den evangelischen Brüdergemeinen.* Barby: Bey C. F. Laux, 1782. ET: *Exposition of Christian Doctrine, as Taught in the Protestant Church of the United Brethren or Unitas Fratrum of the United Brethren.* London: W. and A. Strahan, 1784.

Spiess, G. A. *Physiologie der Nervensystems.* Braunschweig: Vieweg, 1844.

Stahl, Friedrich Julius. *Die lutherische Kirche und die Union: Eine wissenschaftliche Erörterung der Zeitfrage.* Berlin: W. Hertz, 1859.

————. *Fundamente einer christlichen Philosophie.* 2nd ed. Heidelberg: Mohr, 1846.

————. *Wat is de revolutie?* Utrecht: Kemink and Zoon, 1852.

Stapfer, Johann Friedrich. *Sittenlehre.* 6 vols. Zurich: Heidegger, 1757–66. Dutch translation: *De zeden-leer.* 6 vols. The Hague: Pieter van Cleef, 1760–70.

Staringh, J. G. *Bijbelsch zakelijk woordenboek.* 11 vols. Amsterdam: J. De Groot, 1793–97.

Steketee, A. *Babel: Eene bijbellezing over Gen. XI. 1–10.* Kampen: Zalsman, 1883.

Stendel, Adolph. *Kritik der Religion, insbe-sondere der christlichen.* 2 vols. in 1. Stutt-gart: A. Bonz and Co., 1881.

Stoeffler, Fred Ernest. *The Rise of Evangeli-cal Pietism.* Leiden: Brill, 1965.

Strauss, David Friedrich. *Der alte und der neue Glaube: Ein Bekenntniß.* 10th ed. Bonn: E. Strauss, 1879. ET: *The Old Faith and the New: A Confession.* Translated by Mathilde Blind. 2 vols. 2nd ed. London: Asher, 1873.

Suicerus (Schweizer), Johann Casper. *Thesaurus Ecclesiasticus, e Patribus Grae-cis Ordine Alphabetico Exhibens Quae-cunque Phrases, Ritus, Dogmata, Haere-ses, and Hujusmodi Alia Spectan.* 2 vols. Amsterdam: J. H. Wetstein, 1681–82.

Symonds, Joseph. *The Case and Cure of a Deserted Soul,* etc. Edinburgh: R. Bryson, 1642.

Taffin, Jean. *The Amendment of Life.* 4 vols. London: G. Bishop, 1595.

———. *The Marks of God's Children.* Translated by Peter Y. De Jong. Edited by James A. De Jong. Grand Rapids: Baker Academic, 2003.

Taylor, Jeremy. *Ductor Dubitantium, or, the Rule of Conscience in Four Books.* Lon-don: James Flesher, 1660.

———. *The Rule and Exercise of Holy Dying.* London: J. Brown, 1727. Reprint, London, 1901.

———. *The Rule and Exercise of Holy Liv-ing.* London: Francis Ash, 1650. Reprint, New York: Little, Brown & Co., 1864. German translation: *Die Richtschnur und Ubung eines Heiligen Wandels.* Translated by Christian Klein. Frankfurt, 1678.

Teellinck, Ewout (Ewoud). *Christelicke clachte van eenige godsalige luyden over hare onvruchtbaerheydt in het ware christelicke leven.* Middelburgh: Hans vander Hellen, 1618.

——— [Philalethius, Ireneus, pseud.]. *Vyer ende wolck-calomne (Vuur- en wolkkolom).* Amsterdam: Marten Jansz. Brant, 1622.

Teellinck, Willem. *De mensche Godts.* Pre-pared by Franciscus Ridderus. Hoorn, 1658. Cf. Ridderus, *De mensche Godts,* above.

———. *The Path of True Godliness.* Trans-lated by Annemie Godgebeere. Edited by Joel R. Beeke. Grand Rapids: Reformation Heritage, 2006.

Tertullian. *An Answer to the Jews.* ANF 3:151–73.

———. *Apology.* ANF 3:17–55.

———. *Of Patience.* ANF 3:707–14.

———. *On Exhortation to Chastity.* ANF 4:50–58.

———. *On Monogamy.* ANF 4:59–73.

———. *On Prayer.* ANF 3:681–92.

———. *On Repentance.* ANF 3:657–79.

Thiersch, Heinrich W. J. *Vorlesungen über Katholicismus und Protestantismus.* 2 vols. 2nd rev. ed. Erlangen: C. Heyder, 1848.

Tholuck, August (Friedrich August Gottreu). *Ausführliche Auslegung der Bergpredigt Christi nach Matthäus.* 3rd rev. ed. Ham-burg: F. Perthes, 1845.

———. *Die Lehre von der Sünde.* 8th ed. Gotha: F. A. Perthes, 1862.

Trigland, Jacobus. *Antapologia.* Utrecht: P. van den Houte, 1664; also Amsterdam: Joannem Jassonium, 1664.

Turretin, Francis. *Institutio Theologiae Elencticae.* Geneva: Samuel de Tornes, 1682. ET: *Institutes of Elenctic Theology.* Translated by George Musgrave Giger. Edited by James T. Dennison Jr. 3 vols. Phillipsburg, NJ: P&R, 1992–97.

Turretin, Jean-Alphonse. *Dilucidationes Philosophico-Theologico-Dogmatico-Morales.* 3 vols. Leiden: Gottlieb Friedrich Jäger, 1748.

Twesten, August. *Vorlesungen über die Dogmatik.* 2 vols. 2nd ed. Hamburg: F. Perthes, 1829–37.

Udemans, Godefridus. *The Practice of Faith, Hope, and Love*. Translated by Annemie Godgebeere. Edited by Joel R. Beeke. Grand Rapids: Reformation Heritage, 2012.

Ulfers, S. *De loge en de school*. Doetinchem: H. Nijman, 1886.

Ullmann, Carl. *Die Sündlosigkeit Jesu*. 5th ed. Hamburg: F. Perthes, 1846. ET: *The Sinlessness of Jesus: An Evidence for Christianity*. Translated by Sophia Taylor. Edinburgh: T&T Clark, 1882.

Ursinus, Zacharias. *The Commentary of Dr. Zacharias Ursinus on the Heidelberg Catechism*. Translated by G. W. Williard. 3rd ed. Cincinnati: T. P. Bucher, 1861.

———. *Schat-boek der verklaringen over den Nederlandschen Catechismus*. Translated by Festus Hommes. Edited by David Pareus. 2 vols. Gorinchem: Nicolaas Coetzee, 1736.

Van Dyke, Harry. *Groen van Prinsterer's Lectures on Unbelief and Revolution*. Jordan Station, ON: Wedge, 1989.

Vedelius, Nicolas. *De Prudentia Veteris Ecclesiae, Libri Tres: Ex Antiquitate Ecclesiastica Secundum Scripturas Sacras*. Amsterdam: Jan Jansson, 1633.

Veenhof, Jan. *Revelatie en inspiratie: De openbarings- en schriftbeschouwing van Herman Bavinck in vergelijking met die der ethische theologie*. Amsterdam: Buijten en Schipperheijn, 1968.

Vermigli, Peter Martyr. *Loci Communes*. 2nd ed. Zurich: Christophorus Froschouerus, 1580.

Verschuir, Johan. *Waarheit in het binnenste, of bevindelyke godtgeleertheit*. Groningen, 1724.

Vilmar, A. F. C. *Die Theologie der Tatsachen wider die Theologie der Rhetorik: Erkenntnis und Abwehr*. 3rd ed. Marburg, 1857.

———. *Dogmatik: Akademische Vorlesungen, Erster Theil*. Gütersloh, 1874.

———. *Theologische Moral: Akademische Vorlesungen*. Prepared by C. Chr. Israel. 3 vols. in 1. Gütersloh: Bertelsmann, 1871.

Vitringa, Campegius. *Doctrinae Christianae Religionis*. Franeker: Halma, 1702.

———. *Doctrina Christianae Religionis*. 8 vols. 6th ed. Leiden: Joannis le Mair, 1761–86.

———. *Typus Theologiae Practicae*. Franeker, 1716. Dutch translation: *Korte schets van de christelyke zeden-leere, ofte van het geestelyke leven*. Translated by Johannes d'Outrein. Amsterdam: Hendrik Stik, 1717.

Voetius, Gisbert. *Exercitia et Bibliotheca Studiosi Theologiae*. 2nd rev. ed. Utrecht: Johannes à Waesberge, 1651.

———. *Politicae Ecclesiasticae, Partis Primae*. Amsterdam: Johannes à Waesberge, 1663.

———. *Τα Ασκητικα sive Exercitia Pietatis*. Gorinchem: Paul Vink, 1679. Dutch translation: *De praktijk der godzaligheid*. Gorinchem: Paul Vink, 1664. See also the more recent translation of the 1664 edition, with introduction and annotation by Cornelis A. de Niet: *Gisbertus Voetius: De praktijk der godzaligheid*. 2nd rev. ed. Utrecht: De Banier, 2002.

Voetius, Gisbert, and Johannes Hoornbeeck. *Disputaty van geestelicke verlatingen*. 3rd ed. Dordrecht: A. Andriesz, 1659.

———. *Spiritual Desertion*. Translated by John Vriend and Harry Boonstra. Edited by Eugene M. Osterhaven. Grand Rapids: Reformation Heritage, 2012.

Voigt, Heinrich. *Fundamentaldogmatik*. Gotha: Perthes, 1874.

Vos, Arvin. *Aquinas, Calvin, and Contemporary Protestant Thought: A Critique of Protestant Views on the Thought of Thomas Aquinas*. Grand Rapids: Eerdmans, 1985.

Vos Az., Gerrit Jan. *Geschiedenis der vader-landsche kerk, Tweede deel: Van 1651 tot 1842.* Dordrecht, 1882.

Vossius, Gerhard Johann. *Historiae de Controversiis, quae Pelagius eisque reliquiae moverunt.* Amsterdam: L. & D. Elzevir, 1655.

———. *Opera Omnia.* 6 vols. Amsterdam: P. & J. Blaeu, 1695–1701.

Vrijer, M. J. A. de. *Schortinghuis en zijn analogien.* Amsterdam: H. J. Spruyt, 1942.

Wael, Franciscus de. *Revk-offer ofte Practijcke des gebeds.* Rotterdam: I. van Waesberghe, 1637.

Wake, Staniland C. *The Evolution of Morality: Being a History of the Development of Moral Culture.* 2 vols. London: Trübner and Co., 1878.

Walaeus, Antonius. *Compendium ethicae Aristotelicae ad normam veritatis Christianae revocatum.* Leiden: Elhardt, 1625.

Walch, Johann Georg. *Bibliotheca Theologica Selecta.* 4 vols. Jena: Witwe Cröcker, 1757–65.

Ware Beschrijvinghe der Conscientien enz. N.p., 1617.

Warner, Charles Dudley, et al., eds. *The Library of the World's Best Literature, Ancient and Modern.* 31 vols. New York: J. A. Hill and Company, 1896.

Wegscheider, Julius August Ludwig. *Institutiones Theologiae Christiane Dogmaticae.* Halle: Gebauer, 1819. 5th ed. Halle: Gebauer, 1826.

Weingarten, Hermann. *Die Revolutionskirchen Englands: Ein Beitrag zur inneren Geschichte der englischen Kirche und der Reformation.* Leipzig, 1868.

Weiss, Bernhard. *A Commentary on the New Testament.* 4 vols. Translated by George H. Schodde and Epiphanius Wilson. New York and London: Funk and Wagnalls, 1906.

———. *Lehrbuch der biblischen theologie des Neuen Testaments.* 2nd ed. Berlin: W. Hertz, 1873. ET: *Biblical Theology of the New Testament.* 2 vols. Clark's Foreign Theological Library, new ser., 12–13. Translated by David Eaton and James E. Duguid. Edinburgh: T&T Clark, 1882–83.

Wendelin, Marcus Friedrich. *Philosophia Moralis.* Harderwijk: Johannes Toll, 1654.

Wendt, H. H. *Die Begriffe Fleisch und Geist und Geist im biblischen Sprachgebrauch untersucht.* Gotha, 1878.

Werenfels, Peter. *Dissertationis Theologicae de Velamine Iudaeorum Cordibus Impendente, cum Legitur Moses.* 10 vols. Basel: Werenfelsius, 1692–99.

———. *Dissertatio Theologica de Sabbathi Moralitate.* 3 vols. Basel: Werenfels, 1692–93.

Werenfels, Samuel. *Philosophiae Moralis.* Wittenberg: Johann Christoph Tzschiderich, 1745.

Wernle, P. *Paulus als Heidenmissionar: Ein Vortrag.* Freiburg, Leipzig, and Tübingen: Mohr Siebeck, 1899.

Wesley, John. *The Journal of John Wesley.* Edited by Percy Livingstone Parker. Chicago: Moody Press, 1951.

Westerink, Herman. *Melancholie en predestinatie in de vroege moderniteit.* Zoetermeer: Sjibbolet, 2014.

Wette, Wilhelm Martin Leberecht de. *Lehrbuch der christlichen Sittenlehre und der Geschichte derselben.* Berlin: G. Reimer, 1833.

Weygoldt, G. P. *Darwinismus, Religion, Sittlichkeit.* Leiden: Brill, 1878.

Whately, William. *Corte verhandelinge van de voornaemste christelicke oeffeninghen.* Translated by Willem Teellinck. Middelburgh: Adriaen vanden Vivre, 1609.

Whitby, Daniel. *Ethices Compendium.* London: William Innys, 1713.

Wichelhous, Johannes. *Die Lehre der Heiligen Schrift*. Prepared by Theodore Zahn. 3rd rev. ed. Stuttgart: J. F. Steinkopf, 1892.

Wiggers, Gustav Friedrich. *Versuch einer pragmatischen Darstellung des Augustinismus und Pelagianismus*. 2 vols. Hamburg: F. Perthes, 1833.

Willmann, Otto. *Geschichte des Idealismus*. 3 vols. Braunschweig: F. Vieweg, 1894–97.

Winter, F. J. *Die Ethik des Clemens von Alexandrien*. Leipzig, 1882.

Wit, Willem-Jan de. *On the Way to the Loving God*. Amsterdam: VU University Press, 2011.

Witsius, Herman. *De practijk des Christendoms*. Utrecht: Juriän van Poolsum, 1680.

———. *The Economy of the Covenants between God and Man: A Complete Body of Divinity*. Translated by William Crookshank. 2 vols. London: R. Baynes, J. Maitland, T. Lochhead, and T. Nelson, 1822. Reprint, Phillipsburg, NJ: The den Dulk Christian Foundation, 1990. Distributed by P&R.

———. *Exercitationes in Orationem Dominicam*, in *Exercitationes in Symbolum quod Apostolorum dicitur: Et in Orationem Dominicam*. 2nd ed. Franeker: Johannes Gyselaar, 1689. ET: *Sacred Dissertations on the Lord's Prayer*. Translated by William Pringle. Edinburgh: Thomas Clark, 1839. Reprint, Escondido, CA: Den Dulk Foundation, 1994. Distributed by P&R.

———. *Geestelyke printen, van een onwedergeboorne op sijn beste en een wedergeboorne op sijn slechtste*. Utrecht, 1748.

———. *Miscellaneorum Sacrorum*. 2 vols. Herborn: J. N. Andreae, 1712.

———. *Miscellaneorum Sacrorum, Tomus Alter*. Leiden: Conrad Meyer, 1736.

———. *Prakticale godgeleertheid*. 2nd ed. Rotterdam: Henr. Carolinus van Byler, 1732.

———. *Twist des Heeren met zijn wijngaard*. 6th printing. Utrecht: Jacob van Poolsum, 1736.

Wittewrongel, Petrus. *Oeconomia Christiana ofte Christelicke Huys-Houdinghe: Vervat in Twee Boecken; Tot bevoordeeringe van de oeffeninge der ware Godtsaligheydt in de bysondere Huysghesinnen; Naer den Regel van het suyvere Woort Godts te samen-gestelt*. 2 vols. Amsterdam: The widow of Marten Jansz. Brant and Abraham van den Burgh, 1661.

Wolff, Christian. *Vernünftige Gedanken von der Menschen Thun und Lassen zur Beförderung ihrer Glückseligkeit*. Halle: Renger, 1720. Reprint of 4th ed., Hildesheim and New York: Olms, 1976.

Wollebius, Johannes. *Theologiae Epitomen: The Abridgment of Christian Divinitie*. 3rd ed. London: T. Mabb for Joseph Neville, 1660.

Wuest, Kenneth S. *Wuest's Word Studies from the Greek New Testament*. 4 vols. Grand Rapids: Eerdmans, 1966.

Wuttke, Adolf. *Handbuch der Christlichen Sittenlehre*. 2 vols. Berlin: Wiegandt and Grieben, 1861–62.

Wyttenbach, Daniel. *Compendium Theologiae Dogmaticae et Moralis*. Frankfurt am Main: Andreae, 1754.

———. *Tentamen Theologiae Dogmatica Methodo Scientifica Pertractate*. Vol. 1. Frankfurt am Main: Andreae and Hort, 1747.

Ypey, A. *Geschiedenis van de kristelijke kerk in de achtiende eeuw*. 12 vols. Utrecht: W. van IJzerworst, 1797–1815.

Zahn, Detlev. *Die Natürliche Moral christlich beurteilt*. Gotha: G. Schloeszmann, 1861.

———. *Glaubensgewißheit und Theologie: Ein Beitrag zur christlichen Lehre*. Gotha: Schloeßmann, 1883.

Zeller, Eduard. *Über Begriff und Begründung der sittlichen Gesetze*. Berlin: Königl. Akademie der wissenschaften, 1883.

———. *Vorträge und Abhandlungen von Eduard Zeller*. Leipzig: Fues, 1884.

Zeller, H. *Bijbelsch woordenboek voor het Christelijke volk*. 2 vols. Dutch edition prepared by J. A. Schuurman and J. P. G. Westhoff. The Hague: M. J. Visser, 1867, 1872.

Zijthoff, Gerrit J. ten. *Sources of Secession: The Netherlands Hervormde Kerk before the Eve of Dutch Immigration to the Midwest*. Historical Series of the Reformed Church in America 17. Grand Rapids: Eerdmans, 1987.

Zöckler, Otto. *Askese und Mönchtum*. 2 vols. in 1. Frankfurt am Main: Heyder and Zimmer, 1897.

———. *Das Lehrstück von den sieben Hauptsünden*. Munich: Beck, 1893.

———. *Die Lehre vom Urstand des Menschen*. Gütersloh: C. Bertelsmann, 1879.

———. *Handbuch der theologischen Wissenschaften in enzyklopädischer Darstellung*. 3 vols. Nördlingen: C. H. Beck, 1883–84. 3rd rev. ed. 4 vols. Nördlingen: C. H. Beck, 1889–90.

———. *Kritische Geschichte der Askese: Ein Beitrag zur Geschichte christlicher Sitte und Cultur*. Frankfurt am Main: Heyder and Zimmer, 1863.

———. *Theologia Naturalis*. Frankfurt am Main: Erlangen 1860.

Zweep, L. van der. *De paedagogiek van Bavinck*. Kampen: Kok, 1935.

Zwingli, Huldreich. *Commentary on True and False Religion*. Edited by Samuel Macauley and Clarence Nevin Heller. N.p.: American Society of Church History, 1929. Reprint, Durham, NC: Labyrinth, 1981.

ARTICLES

Albers, Petrus Henricus. "St. Lidwina." In *The Catholic Encyclopedia*, 9:233. New York: Robert Appleton Company, 1910.

http://www.newadvent.org/cathen/09233a.htm.

Andel, J. van. "Piëtisme." *De Avondster* 1 (1876).

Bavinck, Herman. "Christianity and Natural Science." In *Essays on Religion, Science, and Society*, edited by John Bolt, translated by Harry Boonstra and Gerrit Sheeres, 81–104. Grand Rapids: Baker Academic, 2008.

———. "Common Grace." Translated by Raymond C. Van Leeuwen. *CTJ* 24 (1989): 25–65.

———. "Conscience." Translated by Nelson D. Kloosterman. *TBR* 6 (2015): 113–26.

———. "De navolging van Christus." *De Vrije Kerk* 11 (1885): 101–13, 203–13; 12 (1886): 321–33. ET: Appendix A in Bolt, *Theological Analysis*, 372–401.

———. "Evolution." In *Essays on Religion, Science, and Society*, edited by John Bolt, 105–18. Grand Rapids: Baker Academic, 2008.

———. "Het geweten." *De Vrije Kerk* 7 (1881): 27–37, 49–58. Also in *Kennis en leven: Opstellen en artikelen uit vroegere jaren*, 13–27. Kampen: Kok, n.d. [1922].

———. "The Pros and Cons of a Dogmatic System." Translated by Nelson D. Kloosterman. *TBR* 5 (2014): 90–103.

———. "Recent Dogmatic Thought in the Netherlands." *Presbyterian and Reformed Review* 3 (1892): 209–28.

———. "Religion and Politics." In *Essays on Religion, Science, and Society*, edited by John Bolt, 261–78. Grand Rapids: Baker Academic, 2008.

———. "The World-Conquering Power of Faith." In *Herman Bavinck on the Christian Life: Following Jesus in Faithful Service*, 235–51. Translated by John Bolt. Wheaton, IL: Crossway, 2015.

Beck, Carl. "Enthusiasmus." *PRE¹* 4:72–75.

———. "Fanatismus." *PRE¹* 4:323–25.

———. "Gebet." *PRE²* 4:762.

———. "Schwärmerei." *PRE¹* 14:41.

Berg, William J. "Émile Zola." In *Encyclopaedia Britannica*. https://www.britannica.com/biography/Emile-Zola.

Boehmer, "Pastor." "Pietismus und Methodismus: Eine kirchengeschichtliche Studie zum Vergleich beider Richtungen in der Gegenwart." *Neue Kirchliche Zeitschrift* 6 (1895): 659–711.

Bolt, John. "Bavinck Speaks English: A Bibliographic Essay." *Mid-America Journal of Theology* 19 (2008): 117–26.

———. "Christ and the Law in the Ethics of Herman Bavinck." *CTJ* 28, no. 1 (1993): 45–73.

Bourdaloue, Louis. "Sermon pour le Mercredi des cendres sur la pensée de la mort." In *Oeuvres de Bourdaloue*, 1:265–89. 6 vols. Paris: Gaume, 1856.

Burger, Karl. "Orthodoxie." *PRE²* 11:117.

Burkhardt, G. "Zinzendorf und die Brüdergemeine." *PRE¹* 18:508–92.

Chapman, John. "Novatian and Novatianism." In *The Catholic Encyclopedia*, 11:138. New York: Robert Appleton Company, 1911. http://www.newadvent.org/cathen/11138a.htm.

Cohrs, Ferdinand. "Herberger, Valerius." *Schaff-Herzog* 5:232–33.

Cremer, Hermann. "Fleisch." *PRE²* 4:573.

———. "Geist des Menschen." *PRE²* 5:8.

Devine, Arthur. "State or Way (Purgative, Illuminative, Unitive)." In *The Catholic Encyclopedia*, 14:254. New York: Robert Appleton Company, 1912. http://www.newadvent.org/cathen/14254a.htm.

Dorner, Isaak A. "Ethik." *PRE¹* 4:185–205.

Dorner, J. A. "Theologie, spekulative." *PRE²* 16:1–13.

Ebrard, Johann Heinrich August. "Gebet im Namen Jesu." *PRE¹* 4:692–94.

Ehrich-Haefeli, Verena. "Die Kreativität de 'Genies' (Goethes 'Wandrer'): Zur psychohistorischen Archäologie der modernen Individualität." In *Von Rousseau zum Hypertext: Subjectivität in Theolorie und Literatur der Moderne*, edited by Paul Geyer and Claudia Jünke, 151–77. Würzburg: Königshausen and Neumann, 2001.

Elsenhaus, Theodor. "Beitrage zur Lehre vom Gewissen." *Studien und Kritiken* 73 (1900): 228–67.

Engelhardt, Johann Georg Veit (Zöckler). "Franz (Franziskus) von Assisi." *PRE²* 4:652–66.

Erskine, Ebenezer. "The Assurance of Faith: Sermon VII on Heb. 10:19–22." In *The Select Writings of the Rev. Ebenezer Erskine*, vol. 1, *Doctrinal Sermons*, edited by the Rev. David Smith, 141–87. Edinburgh: A. Fullarton, 1851.

Erskine, Ralph. "The Believer's Internal Witness; or, The Certain Evidences of True Faith." Sermons cxliii–cxliv on 1 John 5:10. In *The Sermons and Other Practical Works of the Reverend and Learned Ralph Erskine*, 9:191–240. 10 vols. London: R. Baynes, 1821.

Evans, Hubert. "Descartes, René." *Schaff-Herzog* 3:408–10.

Frank, G. "Pufendorf, Samuel, Baron." *Schaff-Herzog* 9:360–61.

Frantzen, Allen J. "The Englishness of Bede, from Then to Now." In *The Cambridge Companion to Bede*, edited by Scott De Gregorio, 239–40. New York: Cambridge University Press, 2010.

Freybe, A. "Die Bedeutung der Sitte in ihre Behandlung bei R. von Jhering in seine Werke *Der Zweck im Recht*." *Neue Kirchliche Zeitschrift* 9 (May 1898): 376–417.

Green, William Brenton, Jr. Review of *Religion and Morality: Their Nature and Mutual Relations, Historically and Doctrinally Considered*, by James J. Fox. *Presbyterian and Reformed Review* 13, no. 49 (1902): 121–26.

Grützmacher, R. H. "Rahtmann, Hermann." *Schaff-Herzog* 9:382–83.

Gutberlet, Constantine. Review of *Ethik: Eine Untersuchung der Thatachen un Gesetze des sittlchen Lebens*, by W. Wundt. *Philosophisches Jahrbuch* 1 (1888): 346–54, 452–63.

Hamberger, J. "Stigmatisation." *PRE¹* 15:118–24 (= *PRE²* 14:728–34).

Harinck, George. "Eén uur lang is het hier brandend en licht geweest." In *Ontmoetingen met Bavinck*, edited by George Harinck and Gerrit Neven, 107–17. Barneveld: De Vuurbaak, 2006.

Haupt, Herman. "David of Dinant or Dinan." *Schaff-Herzog* 3:363.

Healy, Patrick. "Jovinianus." In *The Catholic Encyclopedia*, 8:530. New York: Robert Appleton Company, 1910. http://www.newadvent.org/cathen/08530a.htm.

Heman, Friedr. Carl. "Schleiermachers Idee des höchsten Gutes und der sittlichen Aufgabe." *Jahrbücher für deutsche Theologie* 17 (1872): 442–85.

Herold, M. "Brevier." *PRE²* 2:623–27.

Herzog, J. J. "Geißler." *PRE²* 4:798–802.

———. "Quietismus." *PRE¹* 12:425–55.

Highfield, Roger, Richard Wiseman, and Rob Jenkins. "How Your Looks Betray Your Personality." *New Scientist* 2695 (February 11, 2009).

Hoekstra, S. "Godsdienst en Zedelijkheid: Beoordeeling van de grondstellingen der zoogenaamde Morale Indépendante." *Theologisch tijdschrift* 2 (1868): 117–55.

Hölscher, H. "Andreä, Johann Valentin." *Schaff-Herzog* 1:170–71.

Hoyt, Sarah F. "The Etymology of Religion." *Journal of the American Oriental Society* 32, no. 2 (1912): 126–29.

Irwin, T. H. "Splendid Vices? Augustine for and against Pagan Virtues." *Medieval Philosophy and Theology* 8 (1999): 105–27.

Jacobi, J. L. "Gnosis, Gnostizismus, Gnostiker." *PRE²* 5:204–47.

———. "Zur Missionsthätigkeit der Kirche bis zur Reformationszeit." *Allgemeine Missions-Zeitschrift: Monatshefte für geschichtliche und theoretische Missionskunde* 8 (1881): 289–309.

Jacobson, H. F. "Fasten." *PRE²* 4:505–9.

Kähler, Martin. "Gewissen." *PRE²* 5:150–59.

Kähler, Martin, and Victor Schultze. "Gewissen." *Schaff-Herzog* 3:242–44.

Keulen, Dirk van. "Herman Bavinck and the War Question." In *Christian Faith and Violence*, edited by Dirk van Keulen and Martien E. Brinkman, 1:122–40. Zoetermeer: Meinema, 2005.

———. "Herman Bavinck's Reformed Ethics: Some Remarks about Unpublished Manuscripts in the Libraries of Amsterdam and Kampen." *TBR* 1 (2010): 25–56.

Kim, Alan. "Johann Friedrich Herbart." In *The Stanford Encyclopedia of Philosophy*, edited by Edward N. Zalta. Winter 2015 Edition. https://plato.stanford.edu/archives/win2015/entries/johann-herbart/.

Kleinig, John W. "Oratio, Meditatio, Tentatio: What Makes a Theologian." *Concordia Theological Quarterly* 66, no. 3 (2002): 255–67.

Kling, Chr. Friedr. "Fegfeuer." *PRE²* 4:345.

Köberle, Justus. "Die Motive des Glaubens an die Gebetserhörung im Alten Testament." In *Festschrift seiner Königlichen Hoheit dem Prinzregenten Luitpold von Bayern zum 80 Geburtstage.* Erlangen: Deichtert, 1901.

Kögel, Rudolf. "Asketik." *PRE²* 1:710–11.

Köstlin, Julius. "Gelübde." *PRE²* 5:43–52.

———. "Religion." *PRE¹* 12:641–92.

Krafft, W. "Tersteegen." *PRE¹* 15:537–53.

Kries, Douglas. "Origen, Plato, and Conscience (*Synderesis*) in Jerome's Ezekiel Commentary." *Traditio* 57 (2002): 67–83.

Krüger, C. "Kirchenmusik." *PRE²* 7:783–95.

Kübel, Robert. "Sitte, Sittlichkeit." *PRE²* 14:313.

Kuenen, Abraham. "Ideaalvorming." *Theologisch Tijdschrift* 10 (1876): 316–61.

Kuiper, G. "Marnix." *Christ. Encycl.²* 4:590–92.

Kunze, Johannes. Review of *Das Gebet in der ältesten Christenheit: Eine geschichtliche Untersuchung*, by Eduard von der Goltz. *Theologisches Literaturblatt* 23, no. 33 (August 15, 1902): cols. 389–92.

Kuyper, Abraham. "The Blurring of the Boundaries." In *Abraham Kuyper: A Centennial Reader*, edited by James D. Bratt, 363–402. Grand Rapids: Eerdmans, 1998.

———. "Geldgierigheid is een wortel van alle kwaad." *De Heraut*, no. 289 (July 8, 1883).

———. "God is meerder dan ons hart." *De Heraut*, no. 576 (January 6, 1889).

———. "Mysticisme." *De Heraut*, nos. 1169–73 (May 27–June 24, 1900).

———. "The Natural Knowledge of God." Translated by Harry Van Dyke. *TBR* 6 (2015): 73–112.

———. "Natuurlijke Godskennis." In *Uit het Woord*, 3:165–225. Amsterdam: J. H. Kruyt, 1875. ET: "The Natural Knowledge of God." Translated by Harry Van Dyke. *TBR* 6 (2015): 73–112.

———. "Practicisme." *De Heraut*, nos. 1185–89 (September 16–December 16, 1900).

———. "Van de gemeene Gratie: Deerde Reeks. XLII." *De Heraut*, no. 1057 (March 27, 1889).

———. "Van den Heilige Geest en het gebed, I–V." *De Heraut*, nos. 578–82 (January 20–February 17, 1889). ET in Kuyper, *Work of the Holy Spirit*, 3:39–43.

———. "Van de Wet des Heeren." *De Heraut*, no. 740 (February 28, 1892). Reprint in Kuyper, *E Voto Dordraceno*, 3:501–5 (Lord's Day 34a).

———. "Volmaakt in trappen of in deelen?" In *Uit het Woord*, 3:101–7. 2nd ed. Amsterdam: Höveker and Wormser, [1879] 1896.

Laguna, Gabriel. "The Expression 'Après moi le déluge' and Its Classical Antecedents." *Tradición Clásica*. January 13, 2006. http://tradicionclasica.blogspot.com/2006/01/expression-aprs-moi-le-dluge-and-its.html.

Laistner, M. L. W. "Was Bede the Author of a Penitential?" *Harvard Theological Review* 31, no. 4 (October 1938): 263–74.

Lange, Johann Peter. "Mystik." *PRE¹* 10:152–64.

———. "Selbstsucht." *PRE¹* 14:217–18.

Lauxmann, Richard. "Kirchenlied." *PRE²* 7:767–83.

"The Life of Antonius Geta." In *Historia Augusta*, 2:32–47. Translated by David Magie. LCL 140. Cambridge, MA: Harvard University Press, 1931.

Linde, S. van der. "Groenewegen, Jacob." *Christ. Encycl.²* 3:311.

———. "Hattem, Pontiaan van." *Christ. Encycl.²* 3:378–79.

———. "Lodenstein, Jodocus van." *Christ. Encycl.²* 4:474.

Lobstein, P. Review of *Les maladies du sentiment religieux*. In *Theologische Literaturzeitung* 26 (1901): 648–49.

———. "Zum evangelischen Lebensideal in seiner lutherischen und reformierten Ausprägung." In *Theologische Abhandlungen: Eine Festgabe zum 17. Mai 1902 für Heinrich Julius Holtzmann*, edited by W. Nowack et al., 159–81. Tübingen: Mohr [Paul Siebeck], 1902.

Lucius, E. "Das mönchische Leben des vierten und fünften Jahrhunderts in der Beleuchtung seiner Vertreter und Gönner." In *Theologische Abhandlungen: Eine Festgabe zum 17. Mai 1902 für Heinrich Julius Holtzmann*, edited by W. Nowack et al., 121–56. Tübingen: Mohr, 1902.

Luthardt, Christoph Ernst. "Das 'mystische Element' in der Religion und Theologie." *Theologisches Literaturblatt* 17, no. 45 (1886): 417–21.

———. "Die christliche Ethik." In *Handbuch der theologischen Wissenschaften in encyklopädischer Darstellung*, edited by Otto Zöckler, 5–36. Nördlingen: C. H. Beck, 1883.

Martens, J. G. D. "Israëlietische leerwijze bij Paulus." Review of *Die Begriffe Fleisch und Geist und Geist im biblischen Sprachgebrauch untersucht*, by H. H. Wendt. *Studien: Theologisch Tijdschrift* 4 (1878): 361–419.

Mershman, Francis. "Quadragesima." In *The Catholic Encyclopedia*, 12:589. New York: Robert Appleton Company, 1911. http://www.newadvent.org/cathen/12589a .htm.

Meulen, D. van der. "Ds J. M. de Jong." In *Jaarboek ten dienste van de Gereformeerde Kerken in Nederland*, edited by G. Doekes and J. C. Rullmann, 12:355–57. Goes: Oosterbaan and Le Cointre, 1928.

Monrad, M. J. "Über das Gebet: Ein religionsphilosophisches Fragment; Sendschreiben an Herrn E. Renan in Paris." *Philosophische Monatshefte* 28 (1892): 25–37.

Mulder, H. "Lindeboom, Cornelis." In *Biografisch Lexicon voor de Geschiedenis van het Nederlandse Protestantisme*, edited by Doede Nauta et al., 3:249–50. Kampen: Kok, 1988.

Müller, J. G. "Über Bildung und Gebrauch des Wortes Religio." *Theologische Studien und Kritiken* 8 (1835): 121–48.

Muller, Richard A. Preface to *Systematic Theology*, by Louis Berkhof, v–viii. New combined ed. Grand Rapids: Eerdmans, 1996.

Neudecker, Chr. G. "Vigilien." *PRE¹* 17:194–95.

Niemeijer, C. J. "Intellectualisme, mysticisme en moralisme in den godsdienst."

Bijblad van de Hervorming 8 (August 5, 1893): 113–22.

Nitzsch, Friedrich. Review of *Die Lehre der Scholastiker von der Synderesis*, by Heinrich Appel. *Theologische Literaturzeitung* 16 (1891): 100–101.

———. "Scholastische Theologie." *PRE²* 13:650–75.

———. "Über die Entstehung der scholastischen Lehre von der Synteresis, ein historischer Beitrag zur Lehre vom Gewissen." *Jahrbücher für protestantische Theologie* 5, no. 3 (1879): 492–507.

Nostitz-Rieneck, R. V. "Die 'sociale Decomposition' und die 'culturelle Überlegenheit' des Protestantismus." *Stimmen aus Maria-Laach* 57 (1899): 17–31, 139–49.

Oecumenius. *Commentariorum in Novum Testamentum*. PG 119:635–38.

Oosterzee, Johannes Jacobus van. "Pectoraal-Theologie." In *Voor kerk en theologie: Mededeelingen en bijdragen*, 1:291–321. 2 vols. Utrecht: Kemink and Zoon, 1872–75.

Palmer, Christian D. F. "Das Vorbild Jesu." *Jahrbücher für deutsche Theologie* 4 (1858): 661–713.

———. "Die christliche Lehre vom höchsten Gut und die Stellung der Güterlehre in der theologischen Ethik." *Jahrbücher für deutsche Theologie* 5 (1860): 436–85.

———. "Versuchung." *PRE¹* 17:143–46.

Pierson, Allard. "Kantteekeningen op Prof. Kuenen's 'Ideealvorming.'" *Theologisch Tijdschrift* 10 (1876): 404–68.

Preger, Wilhelm. "Theologie, mystische." *PRE²* 15:487–504.

Pressel, Wilhelm. "Gebet bei den alten und bei den heutigen Hebräern." *PRE¹⁼²* 4:679–86.

Raalte, Theodore G. Van. "Unleavened Morality: Herman Bavinck on Natural Law." In *Five Studies in the Thought of Herman*

Bavinck, edited by John Bolt, 57–99. Lewiston, Queenston, and Lampeter: Edwin Mellen, 2011.

Rabus, Leonhard. "Eine Moralphilosophie aus dem Kreise der neuen Scholastik, I & II." *Theologisches Literaturblatt* 13, no. 20 (1892): 233–37; 13, no. 21 (1892): 241–44.

———. Review of *Die Lehre der Scholastiker von der Synteresis*, by Heinrich Appel. *Theologisches Literaturblatt* 12, no. 1 (1891): 5–6.

Redaction, Die (editorial staff). "Zur Synteresis-Frage (eine bestätigte Konjektur)." *Theologische Literaturzeitung* 21 (1896): col. 637.

Resch, G. "Was versteht Paulus unter der Versiegelung mit dem Heiligen Geist?" *Neue Kirchliche Zeitschrift* 6 (1895): 991–1003.

Riggenbach, Bernhard. "Pietismus." *PRE²* 11:672–85.

Ritschl, Otto. "Religion und Sittlichkeit: Ein Vortrag." *Zeitschrift für Theologie und Kirche* 11, nos. 2/3 (1901): 250–67.

Rüegg, Arnold. "Vinet, Alexandre Rodolfe." *Schaff-Herzog* 12:197–99.

Saussaye, Daniel Chantepie de la. "Stellingen over ziekelijke vroomheid." In *Protestantsche Bijdragen tot bevordering van Christelijk leven en Christelijke wetenschap* 1 (1870): 399–401.

Schaff, D. S. "Tholuck, Friedrich August Gottreu." *Schaff-Herzog* 11:420–21.

Schenkel, Daniel. "Gewissen." *PRE¹* 5:125–42.

Schöll, C. "Methodismus." *PRE¹* 9:450–93; *PRE²* 9:681–719.

Schultz, Hermann. "Religion und Sittlichkeit in ihrem Verhältnis zu einander. Religionsgeschichtlich untersucht." *Theologische Studien und Kritiken* 56, no. 1 (1883): 60–130.

Schulze, L. "Zinzendorf's christliche Weltanschauung." *Theologisches Literaturblatt* 7, no. 20 (1886): 193–96.

———. "Zur Geschichte der christlichen Ethik, I, II." *Theologisches Literaturblatt* 14, no. 23 (June 9, 1893): 263–66; 14, no. 24 (June 16, 1893): 279–81.

Schwarz, E. "Casuistik." *PRE¹* 2:608–19.

Schweizer, Alexander. "Die Entwicklung des Moralsystems in der reformirten Kirche." *Theologische Studien und Kritiken* 23 (1850): 1–78, 288–327, 554–80.

Seeberg, Reinhold. "Melanchthons Stellung in der Geschichte des Dogmas und der Dogmatik." *Neue Kirchliche Zeitschrift* 8 (1897): 126–64.

———. "Occam (Ockham), William of." *Schaff-Herzog* 8:215–20.

Sinnema, Donald. "The Discipline of Ethics in Early Reformed Orthodoxy." *CTJ* 28, no. 1 (April 1993): 10–44.

Stellingwerff, J. "Over de bibliotheek en de boeken van dr. A. Kuyper en over enkele publicaties, die zijn ijdelheid zouden hebben gestreeld of zijn verweer opgeroepen indien ze tijdens zijn leven waren verschene." In *Geboekt in eigen huis: Bevattende een opsomming van de werken van Abraham Kuyper zoals vermeld in de catalogus van de bibliotheek van de Vrije Universiteit*. Amsterdam: VU Uitgeverij, 1987.

Stirm, C. H. "Darf man für die Verstorbenen beten?" *Jahrbücher für deutsche Theologie* 6 (1861): 278–308.

Sullivan, Erin. "Doctrinal Doubleness and the Meaning of Despair in William Perkins's 'Table' and Nathaniel Woodes's *The Conflict of Conscience*." In *Studies in Philology* 110, no. 3 (Summer 2013): 533.

Sytsma, David. "Herman Bavinck's Thomistic Epistemology: The Argument and Sources of his *Principia* of Science." In *Five Studies in the Thought of Herman Bavinck, a Creator of Modern Dutch Theology*, edited by John Bolt, 1–56. Lewiston, NY: Edwin Mellen, 2011.

Thelemann, O. "Lampe, Friedrich Adolf." *PRE²* 8:382–84.

Tholuck, A. "Pietismus." *PRE¹* 11:646–62.

Toscano, Alberto. "Raving with Reason: Immanence and Fanaticism in Kant." www .politics.qmul.ac.uk/news/Alberto%20 Toscano.doc.

Tschackert, Paul. "Ailly, Pierre D'." *Schaff-Herzog* 1:99.

———. "Biel, Gabriel." *Schaff-Herzog* 2:188.

———. "Jansen, Cornelius, Jansenism." *Schaff-Herzog* 6:95–98.

———. "Tradition." *PRE²* 15:727–32.

Veenhof, Jan. "De God van de filosofen en de God van de bijbel: Herman Bavinck en de wijsbegeerte." In *Ontmoetingen met Bavinck*, edited by George Harinck and Gerrit Neven, 219–33. Barneveld: De Vuurbaak, 2006.

———. "Discussie over het zelfonderzoek— Sleutel tot verstaan van het schisma van 1944: Terreinverkenning ten dienst van verder onderzoek." In *Vrij gereformeerd: Verzamelde artikelen*, edited by Dirk van Keulen et al., 183–90. Kampen: Kok, 2005.

———. "A History of Theology and Spirituality in the Dutch Reformed Churches (*Gereformeerde Kerken*), 1892–1992." Translated by Harry Boonstra. *Calvin Theological Journal* 28, no. 2 (1993): 268–71.

———. "Nature and Grace in Bavinck." Translated by A. M. Wolters. *Pro Rege* 34, no. 4 (June 2006): 10–31.

Voetius, Gisbertus. "De Simplicitate et Hypocrisi (14 Propositions)." In *Selectarum Disputationum Theologicarum*, 2:468–95. 4 vols. Utrecht: Johannes à Waesberge, 1648–67.

———. "De Theologia Scholastica." In *Selectarum Disputationum Theologicarum*, 1:12–28. 4 vols. Utrecht: Johannes à Waesberge, 1648–67.

Vogel, Albrecht. "Damianus." *PRE²* 3:466–68.

Wendt, H. H. Review of *Wesen und Entstehung des Gewissens, eine Psychologie der Ethik*, by Theodor Elsenhaus. *Theologische Literaturzeitung* 20, no. 13 (1895): 341–42.

Westhoff, J. P. G. "Francesco Spiera: Een levensbeeld uit den tijd der hervorming in Italië." In *Stemmen voor Waarheid en Vrede* 24 (1887): 453–502.

Whitely, W. T. "Sects (Christian)." In *Encyclopaedia of Religion and Ethics*, edited by James Hastings, 1:315–529. New York: Scribner's Sons; Edinburgh: T&T Clark, 1921.

Wielenga, B. "Ds. C. Lindeboom." In *Jaarboek ten dienste van de Gereformeerde Kerken in Nederland* 23 (1939), edited by F. C. Meijster and K. Schilder, 430–34. Goes: Oosterbaan and Le Cointre, 1939.

Wit, Willem-Jan de. "Beeld van gorilla en chimpansee of beeld van God? De eerste pagina's van Herman Bavincks manuscript 'De mensch, Gods Evenbeeld' (1884). Inleiding, tekst en commentaar." In *Ontmoetingen met Bavinck*, edited by George Harinck and Gerrit Neven, 165–82. Barneveld: De Vuurbaak, 2006.

Wolff, P. "Praetorious, Stephan." *Schaff-Herzog* 9:151.

Wolff, Walther. "Zur Frage der Gebetserhörung." *Studien und Kritiken* 72, no. 4 (1899): 610–18.

Wolman, B. B. "The Historical Role of Johann Friedrich Herbart." In *Historical Roots of Contemporary Psychology*, 29–46. New York: Harper and Row, 1968.

Wood, Allen W. "Fichte: From Nature to Freedom (*System of Ethics* §§9–13)." In *Fichte: System der Sittlichkeit*. Edited by O. Höffe. Klassiker Auslegen. Berlin: Akademie Verlag, 2005. http://philpapers .org/rec/WOOFFN.

Wybrands, W. "Marinus Adriaansz. Booms: Eene bladzijde uit de geschiedenis der spinozisterij in Nederland." *Archief voor de Nederlandsche Kerkgeschiedenis* 1 (1885): 51–128.

Wyck, B. H. C. K. van der. "'Fais ce que voudras': Esquisse d'une morale sans obligation, par M. Guyau; Paris 1885." *De Gids* 49, no. 3 (1885): 1–54.

———. "Twee pleitbezorgers van den godsdienst: Martineau en Rauwenhoff, Tweede stuk." *De Tijdspiegel* 45 (1888): 357–58.

Zöckler, Otto. "Katharina von Siena." *PRE²* 7:626–28.

———. "Louise Lateau, die belgische Stigmatisirte." *Beweis des Glaubens* 11 (1875): 5–16.

———. "Socinus, Faustus, Socinianism." *Schaff-Herzog* 10:486–92.

Zwaanstra, Henry. "Louis Berkhof." In *Reformed Theology in America*, edited by David F. Wells, 153–71. Grand Rapids: Eerdmans, 1985.

Selected Scripture Index

Proverbs

Name Index

Aalst, Gerardus van, 255n78, 256n88, 257n90, 259n103, 262n117, 263n121, 265n131, 265n133, 266nn134–35, 267n137, 376n98, 377n100, 378, 378n160, 404n253, 409n23, 410nn275–76, 411n279
Abelard, Peter, 427n47
Acquoy, Johannes Gerhardus Rijk, 275n5
Adams, Thomas, 292
Ainsworth, Henry, 291
Albers, P. H., 331n69
Albert the Great (Albertus Magnus), 1, 5, 425n33, 483
Alcuin, 5, 5n21
Alexander IV (pope), 330
Alexander of Hales, 5, 177
Alleine, Joseph, 293
Alleine, Richard, 293
Allestree, Richard, 14, 14n107
Alsted, Johannes, 12, 12n81, 424n33, 425n33
Alting, Heinrich, 155n28, 158n59, 217n6, 219n21
Altmann, Johann Georg, 10, 10n66
Amalric of Bena, 287, 287n68
Ambrose, 51, 113, 463n6
Ames, William, 9, 9n50, 12, 12n80, 166, 186, 186nn123–25, 187nn128–29, 188, 188n130, 188nn132–34, 195n174, 196n176, 196nn178–79, 198n193, 200, 200n205, 207, 207n241, 208, 208n245, 209, 209nn248–49, 209n251, 210, 210n257, 211, 211nn258–59, 256, 256n83, 258n98, 265n131, 267n137, 274, 296, 297, 297n120, 373n86, 442n125, 457nn204–5, 463n12, 465, 473n59

Ammon, Christoph Friedrich von, 83, 83n26
Amyraut of Saumur, 9, 9n58
Andel, J. van, 288n72, 432n72
Andreä, Johann Valentin, 464, 464n13
Anselm, 425n33
Anthony of Florence, 179n59, 180n69
Appel, Heinrich, 178nn48–49, 179n53, 179n55
Aquinas, Thomas. See Thomas Aquinas
Aristippus, xxxviii n85
Aristotle, xxxviii, 1, 3, 3n5, 7, 7n27, 10, 157, 229n86, 425, 425n33, 462n2
Arminius, Jacob, 196
Arndt, Johann, 288, 290, 290n80, 464
Arnold, Gottfried, 283, 283n42
Arrow-Smith, John, 457, 457n206
Athanasius, 4
Augustine, 4, 11, 39n30, 51, 69, 69n159, 97, 105n141, 109, 113, 156, 156nn32–35, 157, 177, 178, 232n92, 363, 363nn3–4, 364, 364n6, 367, 386, 400n222, 401n232, 405, 456, 463, 479n91

Bahrdt, Carl Friedrich, 7, 7n37
Bähring, Bernhard, 334n96
Baier, Johann Wilhelm, 7, 7n31
Bain, Alexander, 166, 190, 191n143, 221, 221n36
Baker, Rich, xii
Balduin, Friedrich, 7, 7n32
Ball, John, 292
Bartholomew of San Concordio, 181n72
Basil the Great, 4, 13, 298n127, 463
Basnage, Samuel, 11

541

Subject Index